Britain and tl

Case Studies in British Policy Decision-Making 1939–1968

Also by Andrew Elsby

ETHNOLOGY
The Burghers of Ceylon

MODERN HISTORY
Chamberlain and Appeasement

Britain and the World

Case Studies in British Foreign Policy Decision-Making 1939–1968

Andrew Elsby

_____cHp_____
CentreHouse Press

British Library Cataloguing in Publication Data
A catalogue record for this book is available
from the British Library

ISBN 978-1-902086-26-2

CONTENTS

I am very grateful to Peter Cowlam, my editor, for all his improvements to the work and his support and help, to my brother Jon for his meticulous proofreading and kindness, and to my wife Jackie, for everything.

—Andrew Elsby

List of historical actors

Consequential diplomatic exchanges

Baldwin, Stanley, Prime Minister, June 1935–May 1937.

Bonnet, Georges, French Foreign Minister, 1938–1939.

Cadogan, Alexander, Permanent Under-Secretary at the Foreign Office (PUS), 1938–1946.

Chamberlain, Neville, Chancellor of the Exchequer, November 1931–May 1937, Prime Minister, May 1937–May 1940.

Chatfield, Ernle, Baron, Minister for the Coordination of Defence, February 1939.

Churchill, Winston, Secretary of State for War, January 1919–February 1921, and Secretary of State for Air, January 1919–April 1921, and Chancellor of the Exchequer, 1924–1929.

Collier, Laurence, Head of the Northern Department of the Foreign Office, 1935–1942.

Plunkett-Ernle-Ernle-Drax, Reginald, Head of the British Military Delegation to the Soviet Union, August 1939.

Eden, Anthony, Foreign Secretary, December 1935–February 1938.

Fitzroy Maclean, Northern Department, Foreign Office.

Halifax, Lord, Foreign Secretary, February 1938–December 1940.

Hitler, Adolf, Chancellor of Germany, January 1933–April 1945.

Hoare, Samuel, Home Secretary, May 1937–September 1939, Lord Privy Seal, September 1939–April 1940.

Jebb, Gladwyn, Private Secretary to Cadogan at the Foreign Office, 1939.

Litvinov, Maxim, Soviet Foreign Minister, 1930–3 May 1939.

Maisky, Ivan, Soviet Ambassador to the UK, 1932–1943.

Molotov, Vyacheslav, Soviet Foreign Minister, 4 May 1939–1949.

Morrison, William, Minister of Agriculture, Fisheries and Food, October 1936–January 1939, Chancellor of Duchy of Lancaster, January 1939–April 1940.

Naggiar, Paul-Emile, French Ambassador to the Soviet Union, 1939–1940.

Orme Sargent, Harold, Assistant Under-Secretary at the Foreign Office, 1933–1939.

Ribbentrop, Joachim von, German Minister for Foreign Affairs, 1938–1945.

Schulenberg, Friedrich von der, German Ambassador to the Soviet Union, 1934–1941.

Simon, John, Chancellor of the Exchequer, May 1937–May 1940.

Stanley, Oliver, President of the Board of Trade, May 1937–January 1940, Secretary of State for War, January–May 1940.

Strang, William, Head of the Central Department of the Foreign Office, 1937–1939.

Vansittart, Robert, Permanent Under-Secretary at the Foreign Office, 1930–1938, Chief Diplomatic Adviser to His Majesty's Government, 1938–1941.

Voroshilov, Kliment, Soviet Commissar for Defence, 1925–1940.

Vyshinsky, Andrey, Soviet Deputy Foreign Minister, 1940–1949.

Zinoviev, Grigory, Head of the Communist International in the 1920s.

British foreign policy decision-making towards the Soviet Union during the war

Alanbrooke, Viscount, Chief of the Imperial General Staff, 1939–1945.

Anderson, John, Chancellor of the Exchequer, September 1943–July 1945.

Attlee, Clement, Lord Privy Seal, May 1940–February 1942, Dominions Secretary, February 1942–September 1943, Deputy Prime Minister, 1942–1945, Lord President of the Council, September 1943–May 1945.

Beaverbrook, Baron, Minister of Aircraft Production, May 1940–May 1941, Minister of Supply, June 1941–February 1942, Minister of War Production, February 1942.

Bevin, Ernest, Minister for Labour and National Service, May 1940–May 1945.

Bracken, Brendan, Minister of Information, 1941–1945.

Cadogan, Alexander, Permanent Under-Secretary at the Foreign Office, 1938–1946.

Chamberlain, Neville, British Prime Minister, May 1937–May 1940.

Churchill, Winston, Prime Minister, May 1940–July 1945.

Clark-Kerr, Archibald, UK Ambassador to the Soviet Union, 1942–1946.

Coleville, John, Principal Private Secretary to Winston Churchill, 1940–1945.

Cripps, Stafford, British Ambassador to the Soviet Union, May 1940–1942.

Dew, Armine, Northern Department of the Foreign Office, 1941.

Dixon, Pierson, Principal Private Secretary to the Foreign Secretary, 1943–1948.

Eden, Anthony, Foreign Secretary, December 1940–July 1945.

Halifax, Viscount, British Ambassador to the United States, January 1941–1946.

Harvey, Oliver, Principal Private Secretary to Anthony Eden, 1941–1943.

Hull, Cordell, US Secretary of State, 1933–1944.

Ismay, Hastings, Chief Staff Officer to Churchill, Secretary to the Imperial Defence Chiefs of Staff Committee, 1940–1945.

Jebb, Gladwyn, Head of the Foreign Office Economic and Reconstruction Department, Chairman of the Post-Hostilities Planning Staff to August 1944.

Litvinov, Maxim, Soviet Ambassador to the US, November 1941–August 1943.

Maisky, Ivan, Soviet Ambassador to the UK, 1932–1943.

Molotov, Vyacheslav, Soviet Minister for Foreign Affairs, 1939–1949.

Morgenthau, Henry, US Secretary to the Treasury, January 1934–July 1945.

O'Neil, Con, First Secretary in the German Department of the Foreign Office.

Orme Sargent, Harold, Deputy Under-Secretary at the Foreign Office to Cadogan, 1939–1946.

Portal, Charles, Air-Marshal, Chief of the Air Staff, 1940–1945.

Pound, Dudley, First Sea Lord and Admiral of the Fleet, 1939–1943.

Roosevelt, Franklin, US President, March 1933–April 1945.

Strang, William, Assistant Under-Secretary of State for Europe, 1939–1943, British Representative to the European Advisory Commission from 1943.

Troutbeck, John, German Department, Foreign Office.

Warner, Christopher, Head of the Northern Department of the Foreign Office.

Winant, John, US Ambassador to the UK, 1941–1946.

The Berlin Crisis

Acheson, Dean, US Under-Secretary of State, 1948–1949, Secretary of State, January 1949–1953.

Attlee, Clement, Prime Minister, July 1945–October 1951.

Bevan, Aneurin, Minister of Health, August 1945–January 1951.

Bevin, Ernest, Foreign Secretary, July 1945–March 1951.

Bidault, Georges, French Foreign Minister, 1948.

Bohlen, Charles, Advisor to President Truman, 1947.

Byrnes, James, US Secretary of State, July 1945–January 1947.

Cadogan, Alexander, British Ambassador to the UN, 1946–1950.

Chamberlain, Neville, Prime Minister, May 1937–May 1940.

Churchill, Winston, Prime Minister, May 1940–July 1945.

Clay, Lucius, Military Governor of the US Zone of Germany, 1947–1949.

Cripps, Stafford, Chancellor of the Exchequer, November 1947–October 1950.

Dalton, Hugh, Chancellor of the Exchequer, July 1945–November 1947, Chancellor of the Duchy of Lancaster, May 1948–February 1950.

Dean, Patrick, Head of the German Department of the Foreign Office, 1948.

Draper, William, US Under-Secretary of the Army, July 1947–1948.

Kennan, George, Deputy Chief of US Mission to the Soviet Union, Director of Policy Planning, State Department, 1947–1948.

Jessup, Philip, US Ambassador at Large, March 1949–January 1953.

Kirkpatrick, Ivone, Assistant Under-Secretary at the Foreign Office, 1948, Permanent Under-Secretary at the Foreign Office, 1956.

Lansbury, George, Leader of the Opposition and the Labour Party, October 1932–October 1935.

Malik, Yakov, Soviet Representative to the UN, 1948–1952.

Marshall, George, US Secretary of State, January 1947–January 1949.

Massigli, French Ambassador to the UK, 1948.

Molotov, Vyacheslav, Soviet Foreign Minister, May 1939–March 1949.

Morrison, Herbert, Lord President of the Council, July 1945–March 1951.

Murphy, Robert, US Political Advisor for Germany, 1948.

Orme Sargent, Harold, Permanent Under-Secretary at the Foreign Office, 1946–1949.

Roberts, Frank, Private Secretary to Bevin, 1947–1948.

Robertson, Brian, Military Governor of the British Zone in Germany, 1948.

Sokolovsky, Vasily, Soviet Military Governor, Germany, 1948.

Steel, Christopher, Political Advisor to the Commander-in-Chief in Germany.

Strang, William, Permanent Under-Secretary for the German Department of the Foreign Office, 1947–1949.

Truman, Harry, US President, April 1945–January 1953.

Wedemeyer, Albert, Chief Planning Officer, US Army, 1948.

Eden and Suez

Ben-Gurion, David, Prime Minister of Israel, November 1955–June 1963.

Bridges, Edward, Permanent Secretary to the Treasury, 1946–1956.

Cadogan, Alexander, Permanent Under-Secretary at the Foreign Office, 1938–1948.

Challe, General, French Prime Minister's Personal Staff.

Dean, Patrick, Under-Secretary at the Foreign Office, Chairman of Joint Intelligence Committee.

Dixon, Pierson, British Ambassador to the UN, 1954–1960.

Dulles, John Foster, US Secretary of State, January 1953–April 1959.

Eden, Anthony, Foreign Secretary, December 1935–February 1938, December 1940–July 1945, October 1951–April 1955, Prime Minister, April 1955–January 1957.

Eisenhower, Dwight, US President, January 1953–January 1961.

Gaitskell, Hugh, Leader of the Opposition, December 1955–January 1963.

Gazier, Albert, French Minister of Labour, Acting Foreign Secretary.

Heath, Edward, Parliamentary Secretary to the Treasury, Government Chief Whip, April 1955–June 1959.

Home, Alec Douglas, Commonwealth Secretary, April 1955–July 1960.

Hull, Cordell, US Secretary of State, March 1933–November 1944.

Kilmuir, Lord, Lord Chancellor, October 1954–July 1962.

Lloyd, Selwyn, Minister of Defence, April 1955–December 1955, Foreign Secretary, December 1955–July 1960.

MacMillan, Harold, Foreign Secretary, April 1955–December 1955, Chancellor of the Exchequer, December 1955–January 1957, Prime Minister, January 1957–October 1963.

Monckton, Walter, Minister of Defence.

Morgenthau, Henry, US Secretary of the Treasury, January 1934–July 1945.

Mossadeq, Mohammad, Prime Minister of Iran, July 1952–August 1953.

Nasser, Gamal Abdel, Prime Minister of Egypt, April 1954–September 1962.

Nutting, Anthony, Minister of State at the Foreign Office, 1954–October 1956.

Pineau, Christian, French Foreign Minister, February 1956–May 1958.

Roosevelt, Franklin, US President, March 1933–April 1945.

Salisbury, Lord, Lord President of the Council, November 1952–March 1957.

Shuckburgh, Evelyn, Principal Private Secretary to Eden, 1951–1954, Under-Secretary at the Foreign Office on the Middle East, 1954–June 1956.

Thorneycroft, Peter, President of the Board of Trade, October 1951–January 1957.

Decline and Dependence

Acheson, Dean, US Secretary of State, January 1949–January 1953.

Attlee, Clement, British Prime Minister, July 1945–October 1951.

Benn, Anthony, British Postmaster General, October 1964–July 1966, Minister of Technology, July 1966–June 1970.

Bevan, Aneurin, British Minister of Health, August 1945–January 1951, Minister of Labour and National Service, January 1951–April 1955.

Bevin, Ernest, British Foreign Secretary, July 1945–March 1951.

Bradley, Omar, Chairman of the US Joint Chiefs of Staff, August 1949–August 1953.

Brown, George, British Secretary of State for Economic Affairs, October 1964–August 1966, Foreign Secretary, August 1966–March 1968.

Bruce, David, US Ambassador to the UK, March 1961–March 1969.

Bundy, McGeorge, US National Security Advisor, January 1961–February 1966.

Callaghan, James, British Chancellor of the Exchequer, October 1964–November 1967, Home Secretary, November 1967–June 1970.

Castle, Barbara, British Minister for Overseas Development, October 1964–December 1965, Minister for Transport, December 1965–April 1968, Secretary of State for Employment and Productivity, April 1968–June 1970.

Chamberlain, Neville, British Prime Minister, May 1937–May 1940.

Churchill, Winston, British Prime Minister, October 1951–April 1955.

Cousins, Frank, British Minister of Technology, October 1964–July 1966.

Cripps, Stafford, British Chancellor of the Exchequer, November 1947–October 1950.

Crossman, Richard, British Minister of Housing and Local Government, October 1964–August 1966, Lord President of the Council and Leader of the House of Commons, August 1966–October 1968, and Secretary of State for Social Services, November 1968–June 1970.

Dalton, Hugh, Chancellor of the Duchy of Lancaster, May 1948–February 1950.

Dean, Patrick, British Ambassador to the United States, 1965–1969.

De Gaulle, Charles, President of France, January 1959–April 1969.

Dixon, Pierson, British Deputy Under Secretary of State at the Foreign Office, 1950–1954.

Douglas, Lewis, US Ambassador to the UK, March 1947–November 1960.

Eden, Anthony, British Foreign Secretary, October 1951–April 1955.

Eisenhower, Dwight, US President, January 1953–January 1961.

Franks, Oliver, British Ambassador to the United States, 1948–1952.

Gaitskell, Hugh, British Chancellor of the Exchequer, October 1950–October 1951.

Gordon Walker, Patrick, British Foreign Secretary, October 1964–January 1965.

Gore-Booth, Paul, British Permanent Under-Secretary at the Foreign Office, 1965–1969.

Healey, Denis, British Secretary of State for Defence, October 1964–June 1970.

Heath, Edward, British Prime Minister, June 1970–March 1974.

Jenkins, Roy, British Chancellor of the Exchequer, November 1967–June 1970.

Jessup, Philip, US Ambassador at Large, March 1949–January 1953.

Johnson, Lyndon, US President, November 1963–January 1969.

Kennedy, John, US President, January 1961–November 1963.

Kosygin, Alexei, Premier of the Soviet Union, October 1964–October 1980.

Lord Harlech, British Ambassador to the United States, 1961–1965.

MacArthur, Douglas, US Commander-in-Chief of the United Nations Command in Korea.

Macmillan, Harold, British Prime Minister, January 1957–October 1963.

McNamara, Robert, US Secretary of Defense, January 1961–February 1968.

Morrison, Herbert, British Foreign Secretary, March 1951–October 1951.

Neustadt, Richard, White House Advisor to Kennedy and Johnson.

Nixon, Richard, US Vice President, January 1953–January 1961 and US President, January 1969–August 1974.

Rusk, Dean, US Secretary of State, January 1961–January 1969.

Shinwell, Emanuel, British Minister for Defence, February 1950–October 1951.

Stewart, Michael, British Foreign Secretary, January 1965–August 1966 and March 1968–June 1970.

Strang, William, British Permanent Under-Secretary at the Foreign Office, 1949–1953.

Tedder, Arthur, Chairman, British Joint Services Mission in Washington, January 1950–May 1951.

Thomson, George, British Commonwealth Secretary, August 1967–October 1968.

Truman, Harry, US President, April 1945–January 1953.

Wilson, Harold, British Prime Minister, October 1964–June 1970.

Chapter One

Introduction: British foreign policy between 1939 and 1968

THE MAJOR THEME in British foreign policy between 1939 and 1968 has been the necessity to adjust to a fundamental diminution in Britain's economic, diplomatic and military power, in the first instance relative to that of Nazi Germany and then to that of the US and the Soviet Union during and after the war. Britain's adjustment to such diminished economic, diplomatic and military power has been constrained by the fact that the British political and official establishment remained committed to an ethos of Britain as a world power of the first rank, as the case studies discussed here indicate.

There are five case studies in British foreign policy decision-making presented here. The first is 'Consequential diplomatic exchanges: the failure of the negotiations for an alliance between Britain and the Soviet Union in 1939', which addresses the causes of the British decision to enter into negotiations for an alliance with the Soviet Union to contain Hitler and the ensuing decision, just months later, to abandon the negotiations. The case study compares the influence of anti-communism and anti-Sovietism in the British political and official establishment with the influence of *Realpolitik* considerations associated with a perceived need to contain German power in Europe in the decision to enter into negotiations and with the influence of the experience of Soviet diplomacy in the decision to abandon negotiations. The case study also addresses the effect of the changing dynamic of Cabinet discussions and of the change in Prime Ministerial authority over the issue, especially in the context of the significance of the relationship between Prime Minister and Foreign Secretary for foreign policy formulation, and assesses the manner in which the external context, including Hitler's territorial aspirations in central and eastern Europe and Soviet foreign policy objectives and diplomatic tactics, affected British foreign policy in 1939 through the lens of perception and the attitudinal prism of British policymakers. The case study challenges recent historiographical claims as to responsibility for the failure of the negotiations for an Anglo-Soviet alliance in 1939 and addresses the relative causal influence of ideological or attitudinal orientation and *Realpolitik* considerations predicated upon probable policy consequences in an assessment of the nature of foreign policy decision-making in the British system, the personalities and relationships of individuals within the political and official establishment and the external context in the decisions to enter into negotiations and then to refrain from further concessions.

The next case study, 'British foreign policy decision-making towards the Soviet Union during the war: the Baltics issue and the post-war future of Germany', is related to the previous one as it too concerns policy towards the Soviet Union, albeit in the rather different contexts of a need for the continued resistance of the Red Army in the case of the Baltics issue and of anticipated Soviet power in Europe after the war in the case of the future of Germany. Though there is here less in the way of direct challenge to the existing historiography, there is an attempt to go beyond it in a number of ways. The causes of Prime Ministerial power in Cabinet are addressed, not least the personal dominance derived from there being no alternative premier or senior minister in Cabinet around whom dissent could be mobilised into resistance and the personal attributes and conceptualization of the role of the PM. There is a very detailed consideration of the extent of discussion and diversity of view within the Foreign Office (FO) and of the extent of FO influence on the foreign policy that materialised. And there is in the consideration of the extended debate over the future of Germany between the FO and the Chiefs of Staff (CoS), an indication of the extent of CoS influence on policy. It differs from the approach taken in the previous case study in being based on detailed examination of official documents rather than challenging the validity of the reasoning in the historiography.

The case study on 'The Berlin Crisis of 1948', another instance of British policy towards the Soviet Union in Europe, indicates the influence on the locus of foreign policy decision-making of there being a PM with a less domineering approach to the premiership and to the running of a Cabinet, and the effect of a genuine commonality of view between PM, Foreign Secretary, Cabinet, governing party, and the FO. It indicates too the influence of an extraordinary personality as Foreign Secretary both in Cabinet and on diplomatic audiences such as the US, while also indicating the extent of British dependence on the US in economic and military terms in any Cold War confrontation.

The case study on 'Eden and Suez' is indicative of the influence on foreign policy decision-making of the personal attributes of an interventionist PM with a liberal preparedness to use Prime Ministerial powers and prerogatives. These personal attributes include the Prime Minister's personality and its effect on relationships with other ministers and susceptibility to influence from decisive and confident senior ministers, and the Prime Minister's health and medicinal use. There is a link to the wartime cases in the attempt to trace any continuity of approach to foreign policy in Eden.

The final case study, 'Decline and dependence or choices and consequences – the influences on British foreign policy in the Korean and Vietnam wars in the context of the special relationship between 1950 and 1968', compares the influences on British policy decision-making during the Korean and Vietnam wars, including that of PMs with very different personal attributes, attitudes to power and the premiership, perceptions and objectives, and the influence of the Atlantic relationship under different presidencies in different contexts given Britain's dependence in economic and military terms on the US. It indicates the centrality of the perceptions and objectives of the PM as far as influence on British foreign policy from the US is concerned.

The concentration in these case studies on the influences on the foreign policy decision-making process begins with an identification of those whose positions in the British political and official establishment meant that they were involved in foreign policy decision-making and in a position to exert influence of some kind on the process. In other words the approach is to identify the locus of foreign policy decision-making power and then to assess the resulting influences on the foreign policy that ensued both from the personal attributes of those involved, their including attitudes, objectives, perceptions, personalities and relationships, and from the objective external context that affected foreign policy decision-making through the prism of perceptual and attitudinal factors.

Chapter Two

Consequential diplomatic exchanges: the failure of the negotiations for an alliance between Britain and the Soviet Union in 1939

Introduction and historiography

THE SIGNIFICANCE OF the negotiations for an alliance between Britain and the Soviet Union in 1939, and the British and Soviet experience of them, is clear, in that they represented the first genuine diplomatic contact over the possibility of very much improved relations between Britain and the Soviet Union and the first indication of a British sense of the political and strategic significance of the Soviet Union in European politics. As Keeble notes, 'policy towards the Soviet Union, open or concealed, barely existed between the spring of 1935 and the spring of 1939'.[1]

There was also of course the more specific significance of their representing an attempt to form an alliance that would contain Hitler and so preclude further German territorial expansionism in Europe. Further, the respective experiences of the two sides in the course of the negotiations for an alliance in 1939 were to inform the nature of the relationship in the ensuing periods before, during and after World War II. On the British side the immediate outcome was that British policy towards the Soviet Union became one which was summed up in Cadogan's sense that the Soviet Union did not matter to British policy or interests, in that it would not 'do us any good' or 'much harm',[2] a view predicated on an adverse estimation of Soviet offensive capability and dependability and which was to endure until the German invasion of the Soviet Union in 1941.

The talks themselves ended with the Soviet Union concluding the Ribbentrop-Molotov pact on 23 August 1939, which amazed and outraged many in the British political elite as an act of treachery, indicating as it did that the breakdown of talks with Britain might have resulted from the fact that for some of the time at least the Soviet Union had been pursuing parallel talks with Germany. The resulting pact effectively ceded the Baltics to the Soviet Union and permitted the division of Poland between Germany and the Soviet Union after the German invasion in September 1939.

The experience of the negotiations in the summer of 1939 also affected the British reaction to the Soviet wartime demand that Britain recognise the Soviet takeover of the Baltics. In the Foreign Office (FO), discussions between senior officials over the Baltics took place in November 1941 and again in February 1942, but the opportunism inherent in the Soviet demand was an exemplification of the nature of Soviet diplomacy that was extraordinarily similar to that in 1939. Further, as I shall show, the experience of 1939 served in a more general sense to reinforce and validate British attitudes of aversion and mistrust towards the Soviet Union, which further diplomatic encounters both during and after the war served to confirm as justified. Such British attitudes had not however prevented the initial decision to enter into negotiations for an alliance with the Soviet Union in the summer of 1939, a decision which reflected a *Realpolitik* sense of a need for an alliance with the Soviet Union to deter Hitler from war by facing him with the prospect of war on two fronts.

The immediate context of the negotiations between Britain and the Soviet Union that began in earnest towards the end of May 1939 was Hitler's violation of his undertaking regarding Czechoslovakian territorial integrity, given to Chamberlain at Munich in September 1938, in the German invasion of what was left of Czechoslovakia in March 1939. The issue of a possible British alliance with the Soviet Union is in the historiography inextricably linked to historians' differing views regarding British appeasement of Germany, for during the 1930s Germany was the major focus of British European policy, being seen as the main threat to European peace, and the Soviet

Union became salient to British foreign policy only in the failure of appeasement and the emerging sense of a need to contain Hitler by alliances.

The orthodox view is that Chamberlain and his supporters were guilty of appeasing Germany and of not concluding a system of alliances that could have deterred Hitler from war by the prospect of having to fight on two fronts – Chamberlain is seen as being deluded in his belief that alliances would tend to provoke rather than deter Hitler and as responsible for the failure to abandon a futile appeasement of Germany and achieve an alliance with the Soviet Union which would, it is claimed, have averted World War II.[3]

Revisionists responded to these claims by pointing to the structural constraints that faced Chamberlain, to the reality of British economic and military weakness and the difficulties of imperial overstretch in relation to limited resources.[4] The general argument was that, given such profound constraints, a British policy of appeasing Germany, Italy and Japan in such a way as to permit Britain to protect its vital interests was rational – maintaining European peace was imperative to the defence of existing British interests worldwide. What this meant was that an alliance with the Soviet Union was to be avoided, in that it would alienate Germany and Japan, powers whose expansionist ideas threatened British European and imperial interests and should be conciliated.

More recently counter-revisionists have returned to a more orthodox view, which claims that Chamberlain and the British political elite did have a clear policy choice between appeasement of Germany and the pursuit of alliances to contain Hitler and deter him from war. Alliances, it is claimed, represented a clear alternative even given the realities of British economic and military weakness, and Chamberlain was a decisive influence in their not being chosen. Counter-revisionists see the failure of the talks with the Soviet Union for an alliance in 1939 as part of British failure to confront Hitler with a system of alliances that they claim would have deterred him from war by presenting him with war on two fronts if the Germans attacked Poland.[5]

A work that is germane to the claims regarding Chamberlain's role in the breakdown of the talks yet which is rather outside the extensive historiography referred to above is that of Christopher Hill, who has, in the context of a work that attempts to identify the causes of differing degrees of ministerial involvement in and influence on foreign policy decisions, assessed the nature of the Cabinet discussions that in the end resulted in Britain's entering into negotiations for an alliance with the Soviet Union in 1939. He points to the effectiveness of ministerial contributions in Cabinet in that decision-making process given that the nature of the issue was known and there was sufficient time for the issue to be discussed. He claims that Chamberlain and Halifax, to whom he refers as the 'executive', did not dominate the Cabinet over the issue of whether or not Britain should enter into negotiations for an alliance with the Soviet Union in the way they had over the guarantee to Poland.[6] While he does not assess the influences on the failure of talks to produce an alliance he does point to a situation in which Cabinet ministers were the decisive influence, rather than the previously dominant Chamberlain as PM. This has clear implications for the attributions regarding the breakdown of the negotiations that will be discussed here.

Shaw is firmly located within counter-revisionism. She attributes the breakdown of the negotiations to Chamberlain's exploitation of adverse British attitudes towards the Soviet Union and communism, attitudes which she claims the British political elite could not dismiss. Shaw claims that 'of primary importance was anti-Soviet prejudice, namely ideological hostility and distrust'. She claims that 'what determined the attitudes towards Anglo-Soviet collaboration among all the members of the British political elite, was whether they were willing to put aside the anti-Soviet prejudice they held. Politicians and ministers themselves identified the distinction between *changing* their attitudes and *putting aside* their distrust.'[7] As I shall show below, the existence of anti-Soviet attitudes in the British political elite at the start of the negotiations with the

Soviet Union for an alliance is not at issue. What is at issue is their influence on the breakdown of the talks, and Shaw claims that 'through their unwillingness to overcome their anti-Soviet attitudes, the British Cabinet and Foreign Policy Committee, but especially Neville Chamberlain, caused the Anglo-Soviet-French negotiations to break down and pushed Moscow into Berlin's arms.'[8] Shaw claims that 'Stalin's intention was never ideological' and that, though the British Cabinet was right to suspect that Stalin intended to use a British guarantee of the Baltic states conforming to the Soviet definition of 'indirect aggression' to 'overrun those states on the Soviet border guaranteed by the alliance', the Soviet intention was to obtain security for the Soviet Union rather than to attain any expansionist or ideological objective. She links the idea of the Soviet demand over the Baltics as a test of British sincerity with that of Soviet concerns over security from German attack. Both were, Shaw claims, legitimate and the Soviet definition of 'indirect aggression' should have been accepted by the British delegation at the talks, but 'the issue of reciprocity' 'was simply never appreciated or addressed by the British Cabinet', and British rejection of the Soviet definition of 'indirect aggression' reflected concern regarding Soviet intention to extend communism into eastern Europe, an ideological stance.[9]

Carley, in a slightly earlier but equally counter-revisionist work that draws on PRO records but also French archive material and that part of the Soviet material to which there was access at the time, tends to Shaw's view in claiming that there was minimal British effort expended in the search for an alliance with the Soviet Union in 1939, and that the failure of the negotiations should be attributed to British (and French) aversion for communism and for the Soviet Union, not least that of Chamberlain as PM. Carley claims that 'ideological anti-communism impeded Anglo-French efforts to conclude a war-fighting alliance with the Soviet Union against Nazi Germany' and refers to Soviet mistrust of the British and the French consequent on 'Anglo-French rejection of numerous Soviet initiatives to improve relations during interwar years'.[10] However, even if Carley does have a case for Soviet mistrust of Britain and France from adverse experience of British and French rejection of Soviet overtures in the 1930s (though Soviet mistrust of Britain and France also reflected the Bolshevik attitudinal prism of suspicion of capitalist states and their motives), that does not preclude there being a correspondingly coherent case for British mistrust of the Soviet Union before the start of the negotiations for an alliance in the summer of 1939. And in any event it is the effect on British perceptions of the Soviet Union as a potential ally as a consequence of British experience of the Anglo-Soviet negotiations for an alliance that is relevant to explaining why the talks broke down after having begun despite adverse attitudes on both sides.

There is a clear difference of view between Carley and Shaw, who attribute the breakdown of the negotiations to Chamberlain at least in part, and Hill, who posits genuine ministerial influence – while Hill focuses on the initial decision to enter into negotiations and does not address the causes of the breakdown of the talks he does point to Chamberlain's diminished status in Cabinet in relation to the Soviet issue, which would question Shaw's and Carley's assertion that just months later he retained sufficient prestige to exert influence on ministers (albeit ones, they claim, who had failed to overcome their prejudices).

In a longer view of relations between Britain and the Soviet Union Keeble points to the sequence of British concessions and Soviet escalations of demands that characterised the negotiations. These Soviet demands included considerable latitude for the Soviet Union in the Baltics, obtaining from Britain a very specific military agreement (rather than the British preference for a general understanding) and Britain's arranging Soviet right of passage through eastern European states, including Poland, which both sides knew would not countenance such rights. Keeble indicates that the Soviet Union had options, an alliance with Britain and France, an alliance with Germany that would give it the security buffer in its west that it was trying to extort from Britain and which the latter ultimately resisted, and isolation.[11]

Neilson, in the most recent work to address the negotiations (as part of a longer assessment of relations between Britain and the Soviet Union in the interwar years), avoids the attributions of the guilty men school, to the views of which the counter-revisionist conclusions of Shaw and Carley tend in blaming the attitudes and 'prejudices' of British politicians and diplomats for the failure of the talks with the Soviet Union in 1939. Neilson does not though endorse declinism, a form of revisionism that claims that a sense of British decline informed British foreign policy decisions, which were in that context understandable, in some variants even inevitable. Neilson does not endorse Shaw's attribution of blame for the breakdown of the talks to British anticommunism. Instead he apportions blame for the breakdown to both sides, whose ideological differences resulted in 'mutual incomprehension and suspicion', and sees Soviet policy as influenced by *Realpolitik* and communist ideology.[12] I shall return to these views to discuss them in some detail further below.

My argument focuses on the negotiations themselves and addresses specifically the causes of the stalling of the talks in July 1939 and their breakdown in August 1939. In it I differ from Shaw and Carley, and in conclusion from Neilson's most recent work.

The primary sources referred to in the work are British, from the PRO in the form of FO records and Foreign Policy Committee (FPC) and Cabinet papers and minutes. Apart from such sources I have referred to the existing, especially the most recent, literature. In that my thesis is in part a rebuttal of the claims by Shaw and Carley that adverse British attitudes towards communism and the Soviet Union caused the talks' failure, it does not need reference to foreign archive material. Further, given that I do not claim to have found documents that throw new light on the course of the negotiations and the positions taken in them, the work's contribution to the debate over the reasons for the failure of the negotiations between Britain and the Soviet Union is in its challenging the legitimacy of various interpretations of, and inferences drawn from, known source material.

The context for the Anglo-Soviet negotiations in the summer of 1939

The context of the negotiations in terms of British policy was a British foreign policy in the 1930s that was focussed on Germany as the major threat to European peace and to British European interests. In fact, as Keeble points out, before 1939 there was in effect no unambiguous or developed British policy towards the Soviet Union, which was regarded as a remote and ideologically alien state with a repressive political system.

The context of British foreign policy in the 1930s was the slaughter of World War I that ended in a revulsion for warfare and a peace movement that had a profound hold over British public opinion and public life. Germany had been subject to the punitive terms of the Versailles Treaty, with its imposition of massive reparations, territorial losses and disarmament, which many in the British establishment felt was too harsh and alien to British interests in trade with Germany. In the light of what was seen to be an extinguished German threat radical disarmament and a commitment to world peace maintained by the League of Nations were policies that elicited universal support, even from political figures who later were to advocate rapid rearmament. British military planning was predicated upon the assumption, proposed by Churchill when Secretary of State for War and Secretary of State for Air, that there would be no war for ten years, a rule which began in 1919 and was renewed each year until 1928, when it was made a norm under Churchill as Chancellor of the Exchequer.

The revolution in Russia and the civil war that followed it had resulted in Bolshevik power, which had alarmed and appalled the British political elite and reflected the failure of their material and moral support for the Whites. Yet on 1 February 1924 the Soviet Union was finally accorded diplomatic recognition by the Labour government.

Months later, in August 1924, Baldwin became Prime Minister (PM), and Austen Chamberlain became Foreign Secretary (FS). At that time 'isolationism was a powerful current in British foreign policy', but Austen Chamberlain wanted to 'restore Britain's position as arbiter of the balance of power' in Europe, which meant that 'French security fears had to be assuaged' but 'Germany also had to be conciliated', as 'an isolated Germany might turn to alliance with the Soviet Union'. Despite opposition in Cabinet from isolationists, Locarno was the result, by which Germany accepted the status quo and guaranteed peace in the west of Europe but not in the east.[13] In 1927 British policy towards Europe was complicated by the finding of evidence of subversion by Soviet diplomatic representatives in London and the consequent breaking off of diplomatic relations.

The FO view of European affairs was apparent in the brief Simon, the new Foreign Secretary in the National Government elected in October 1931, received—

> World recovery (the aim of our policy) depends on European recovery; European recovery on German recovery; German recovery on France's consent; and France's consent on security (for all time) against attack.[14]

It is worth noting that in this brief there is no mention of the Soviet Union. At the 1932 Geneva disarmament conference it seemed that the French and German views of acceptable relative armament positions were irreconcilable. The Germans indicated that anything other than equality of armaments would be unacceptable, and the Cabinet had earlier decided that no guarantee could be given to France, which was indicative of a British refusal to underwrite French foreign policy in central Europe. Yet in the context of Hitler's increasing popularity agreement was reached over equality of armaments. Initial reaction to Hitler's accession to power was muted, predicated on the view that Hitler was a passing phenomenon or that he represented legitimate German grievances against the terms of Versailles. The latter explanation had some appeal, for the FO regarded the treaty's terms as 'untenable' and 'indefensible'. In any case, with Britain in military and economic terms unprepared, the general consensus was that there was no alternative but to conciliate Germany in the immediate term. Simon believed that German rearmament was unstoppable, and though his overtures to Hitler were received with evasion he remained opposed to any 'front' that could leave Germany feeling encircled.

Relations with the Soviets had not improved. In March 1933 the arrest of British engineers for espionage, which the FO denied, resulted in the recall of the British Ambassador and the imposition of a trade embargo on the Soviet Union. The influential and outspoken Permanent Under-Secretary (PUS) at the FO, Robert Vansittart, insisted that no concessions should be made to them. And yet that same year saw the beginning of a Soviet policy that was content to defer world revolution in the cause of establishing and consolidating communism in one country, the foreign policy implication of which was the notion of 'collective security' associated with Litvinov. With the Soviet Union at last joining the League of Nations in September 1934 with British and French support, it seemed that Soviet mistrust of Britain as the foremost of the capitalist powers aligned against communism and the Soviet Union as its representative was diminishing. Litvinov noted the improvement in relations,[16] and Vansittart saw that Britain and the Soviet Union had a shared interest in maintaining the balance of power in Europe, in that both were being threatened by Germany and Japan.[17] The trial of British intent was preparedness to engage in an 'eastern Locarno', an idea devised by the French in reaction to a request from the Soviet Union for an alliance. It involved a pact between the Soviet Union, Poland, Czechoslovakia and Germany supported by a French guarantee to the Soviet Union. And yet British reaction was cool, fearing British involvement in war with Germany as a result of French implementation of their treaty with the Soviet Union, which had been concluded on 29 November 1934. A visit by Eden and Simon to Germany and the Soviet Union made it clear that an eastern Locarno was impossible, foundering upon German refusal to provide the guarantees implicit in the idea. The outcome was a sense that Britain and the Soviet Union shared a commitment to the notion of collective security through the auspices of the League of Nations.

Yet the subsequent League of Nations' failure in Ethiopia and Hitler's militarisation of the Rhineland only served to encourage isolationist sentiments in Britain. FO advice was that any alliances with other European nations that hinted at encirclement would make war more likely and that the only alternative was to 'come to terms with Germany in order to remove grievances by friendly arrangement before Germany once again (took) the law into her own hands'.[18] With Baldwin as PM there was no clear initiative from the British as far as relations with the Soviet Union were concerned, and the general tenor of British policy was one of aversion and indifference. Under his successor the aversion was to be more profound.

Chamberlain succeeded Baldwin as premier in 1937, a PM with a profound interest in, and a belief in the worth of his own contribution to, British foreign policy. Under him British foreign policy became orientated exclusively to the containment of Germany (and Italy and Japan) and maintenance of European peace through appeasement. Relations with other countries were relegated to a position of lesser importance, not least that with the Soviet Union, for which he reserved a special antipathy. With a confidence undimmed by inexperience and immune to setbacks, Chamberlain was committed to appeasement of Germany on several grounds.

He felt that Versailles had been harsh to Germany, a sentiment shared by many in British political and official circles at the time. He advocated accepting Germany's legitimate, historical interests in Europe, and Hitler's European aims, which he was convinced were limited and represented no threat to British European interests. And he was committed to avoiding conflict through negotiation and concessions. His policy was informed by a profound loathing and fear of war, a refusal to undertake any policy that might increase the risk of war, and a sense that alliances had caused World War I. 'Not balance of power, but appeasement and the restoration of confidence were the objectives of British policy.'[19] At the time of its initial enunciation it was, given a general climate of revulsion for the horrors of World War I and a public demand for peace, a policy advocated by the FO, agreed by Eden as Foreign Secretary and supported by the British political elite.[20] Yet over accord with Mussolini Eden favoured a harder line than Chamberlain, and he resigned on 20 February 1938, to be succeeded by Halifax, a more reliable appeaser.

Following the Anschluss with Austria, which went unopposed, the next object of Hitler's expansionism was Czechoslovakia, using self-determination for the Sudeten Germans as a pretext. Chamberlain's meeting Hitler to resolve the Czech crisis was supported by Halifax, Hoare and Simon, and by Cadogan at the FO[21] (but not by Vansittart, who had been rewarded for his outspoken Germanophobe views by being removed as PUS to a position that seemed more senior but which in fact removed him from any influence). Yet Chamberlain's proposing to accept Hitler's demand for an immediate cession of the Sudetenland to Germany under threat of German military occupation of the Sudetenland appalled Cadogan,[22] who persuaded Halifax to resist the policy.

Notably this was the first indication of serious opposition to appeasement from the FO or from Halifax. The Munich Agreement of September 1938 included a German guarantee of Czechoslovakia and German occupation of the Sudetenland with a free plebiscite – it seemed to reflect the principle of self-determination but actually the reality that Germany was prepared to go to war, while Britain was not and continued to believe that concessions and reason could prevail.

Soviet exclusion from the Munich Agreement reflected Hitler's insistence and British compliance because for Chamberlain the objective was avoidance of war in Europe through appeasement and negotiation, not because of British prejudices against the Soviet Union and communism, an indication that attitudes towards the Soviet Union did not dictate policy.

The ensuing German violation of Munich in an invasion of what was left of Czechoslovakia on 15

March 1939 was indicative of the consequences of a British foreign policy predicated on appeals to and belief in reason, rather than on power and deterrents, and the consequence of the glaring failure of such diplomacy was a poorly considered guarantee to Poland. A series of exhibitions of weakness followed by an undertaking to resist Hitler indicated dismal disarray in British policy, and did not convince Hitler of British resolution. It was though a consequence of a pragmatic case-by-case approach to British foreign policy, which took no account of the sense in which every concession elicited only another demand, which mistook the real nature of Hitler's intentions and which convinced Hitler that Britain would not ever represent a credible deterrent.

Chamberlain remained immune to criticism and his conceit was such that he derogated dissenters. As early as the time of the German Anschluss, facing the probability of a German threat to Czechoslovakia and demands for a grand alliance from Churchill to deter Hitler from further expansionism, he referred to 'the Russians stealthily and cunningly pulling all the strings behind the scenes to get us involved in war with Germany'.[23] Chamberlain had little confidence in Soviet ability to sustain a credible front in the east and mistrusted their motives. Further, he did not believe that the Soviet Union would ever enter into an alliance with Germany despite warnings to that effect from military advisers (see below) and continued to claim that any formation of an alliance against Germany would be more likely to provoke Hitler to war than to deter him from it.

British policy towards Europe prior to the end of March 1939 was then predicated exclusively on the appeasement of Germany as the major threat to European peace. The Soviet Union was seen as peripheral and remote to British European policy and interests. In fact, as has been seen, 'policy towards the Soviet Union, open or concealed, barely existed between the spring of 1935 and the spring of 1939'.[24] There were adverse assessments of Soviet military effectiveness, and, with the purges of the upper echelons of the Red Army, communist ideology was deemed to have weakened Soviet capability. And beyond such estimations was a fundamental anti-communism, an 'abhorrence of the Soviet system'.[25] There were then a number of reservations in the British political and official elite. There was no conviction in the Soviets' military ability to make war, and there were serious ideological reservations and suspicions regarding the cynicism that pervaded their diplomacy, as was apparent in Butler's assessment of his talks with Litvinov in September 1938.[26] The negotiations for an alliance that ensued were predicated upon a sense of the Soviet Union's deterrent value, which was supposed to be far greater than the actual value of the Red Army.[27]

The sequence of events prior to and during the negotiations

Hitler's violation of the undertaking he had given Chamberlain at Munich regarding Czech sovereignty in the German occupation of Prague on 15 March 1939 had left the British policy of appeasement of Germany discredited. Following adverse reaction in the Commons to a speech by Chamberlain that seemed to indicate no change in policy towards Germany Chamberlain presented his idea of a Four Power Declaration that involved the Soviet Union combining with Britain, France and Poland to 'consult' in the event of further German expansionism to Cabinet on 20 March 1939. The scheme was abandoned on 24 March 1939 in part because of perceived objections from the Poles and in part because of Chamberlain's own mistrust of the Soviet Union. The guarantee to Poland and Romania followed on 30 March 1939, imposed on a passive Cabinet by Chamberlain as PM and Halifax as Foreign Secretary and with terms that permitted negotiation over Poland's frontiers.

On 5 April 1939 Chamberlain told the Cabinet of his 'very considerable distrust of Russia' and his lack of confidence in the Soviets' providing any reliable support.[28] The context was that Chamberlain and Halifax had had the guarantee to Poland (which had been given by Britain and France on 30 March 1939) endorsed by Cabinet on the condition that an approach should be made to the Soviet Union – Stanley and Hoare had been pressing this on Chamberlain and Halifax and it was a condition of their support for the guarantee to Poland. The result was that on 13 April and in spite of his own misgivings, Chamberlain told the Cabinet that he was considering inviting the Soviet Union to 'make a unilateral declaration of support for any state which might be attacked'.[29] This was of course the most minimal step towards involving the Soviet Union in containing Germany and offered the Soviet Union nothing in return. On 17 April Litvinov, the Soviet Foreign Minister, proposed a military alliance with Britain and France which would cover assistance in the event of war not just to each other but also to states in eastern Europe, and included a clause that precluded either state making a separate peace in the event of war.[30]

Chamberlain and Halifax were opposed to any such alliance. When, on 19 April, the FPC met to discuss the Soviet proposal, Halifax did not attend but had registered his endorsement of an FO paper related by Cadogan to the meeting. It referred to British efforts to create a 'Peace Front' and advocated rejection of the Litvinov proposal on the basis that acceptance could 'alienate our friends and reinforce the propaganda of our enemies without bringing in exchange any real material contribution to the strength of our Front'. Chamberlain supported this view and, in a characteristically selective reiteration of that part of CoS advice that lent itself to his case, referred to the uncertain capability of the Red Army[31] (the CoS paper had also referred to the advantage of an alliance with the Soviet Union even if it meant a neutral Poland). The meeting was an exemplification of Chamberlain's manipulative chairmanship of the FPC. While there was some expression of concern from Hoare there was no real opposition to Chamberlain's and Halifax's view that the offer should be rejected on political grounds.

The FPC met again on 25 April to consider the French response to the Litvinov proposals, which had been, unlike the British, positive. Chamberlain and Halifax warned of the adverse effect of acceptance on the 'Peace Front'. As Minister for the Co-ordination of Defence, Lord Chatfield seems to have misrepresented the CoS view, for although the CoS referred to the 'very grave military dangers inherent in the possibility of any agreement between Germany and Russia', Chatfield concluded that the possible value of Soviet assistance had been overestimated in 'certain quarters'.[32] While there were expressions of reservations from ministers on the FPC the sense was clear, that France should be told that a Soviet alliance would impede the formation of a front of eastern European states under German threat.[33]

The FPC had then confirmed the view held by Chamberlain and Halifax, despite the fact that the military advice warned of the possible danger of an alliance between the Soviet Union and Germany. As Halifax put it to Cabinet on 3 May, a pact with the Soviet Union would 'make war inevitable'.[34] Yet just days later Halifax was to change his view radically, following, according to his own implied attribution, a shift in the CoS advice. At the Foreign Policy Committee meeting on 16 May 1939 Chatfield told ministers of the CoS sense of a danger that a British failure to conclude an alliance with the Soviet Union could have as its consequence not just further German expansionism but also a Soviet alliance with Germany.[35] The case for an Anglo-Soviet alliance was then made by the CoS in direct terms, and Chatfield's *volte-face* to favour an alliance represented a decisive shift in the balance of view on the FPC, with five ministers in favour and five against the alliance.[36]

By 24 May 1939 Halifax's *volte-face* was complete. He told the Cabinet that while he 'had never disguised his own views on the subject of close association with the Russian Government' he could not countenance a break with the Soviets, for by this time he had come to the view that war would be more likely should Britain fail to conclude an alliance that could deter Hitler. Chamberlain indicated 'considerable misgiving' for the idea of an alliance with the Soviet Union but said that any breakdown 'would be exploited by the Totalitarian powers' and that he found it 'impossible to stand out against the conclusion of an agreement'.[37]

Cadogan, whose memorandum of 22 May 1939 was circulated to ministers at the Cabinet meeting on 24 May 1939 and set out the case for and against an alliance without making a recommendation,[38] confided to his diary on the matter of the proposed alliance, 'P.M. hates it', and added, 'in his present mood PM says he will resign rather than sign alliance with the Soviet'.[39] Further, even on 23 May Halifax doubted 'whether the PM will agree at Cabinet tomorrow'.[40] Cadogan noted on 24 May itself, 'PM resigned to idea of Soviet alliance, but depressed'[41] and days later Chamberlain confided to his sister Hilda that only Butler had supported his views.[42] He does however seem to have insisted upon reference to the League of Nations, so that it appeared that Britain would be offering the Soviet Union assistance under the charter of the League rather than in the form of a formal alliance.[43] In another of his characteristically frank and self-congratulatory letters to his sisters he told Hilda on 28 May that his idea was 'ingenious' in that it could permit Britain to evade any commitment later on, a typical devious rearguard action on his part that reflected his 'suspicion of Soviet aims and profound doubts as to her military capability even if she honestly desired and intended to help' and his continuing aversion to 'opposing blocs' that would reduce the possibility of 'negotiation' with Germany and Italy.[44]

Such evidence seems to indicate that Chamberlain continued to entertain hopes for a negotiated peace in Europe through conciliation though acknowledging that the Soviet Union was needed to produce a credible threat to Germany in Eastern Europe, an odd combination of lingering hope that appeasement would work and apparent acknowledgment of the reasoning of deterrence.

Even so, and though the evidence of the Cabinet meeting on 24 May is that the only minister to speak before Chamberlain was Halifax, so that there was no general ministerial insistence that could have persuaded Chamberlain that he would have to endorse an agreement at the meeting itself, Chamberlain was by 24 May 1939 confronted by a majority of ministers on the FPC convinced by Hoare and Stanley that an alliance with the Soviet Union was needed, and at the Cabinet meeting itself by Halifax's defection from opposition to the majority view that an alliance with the Soviet Union was needed, a view supported by that of the CoS. The conclusion to such apparently contradictory evidence seems to be that Chamberlain felt so isolated in the Foreign Policy Committee and Cabinet that he felt the alternative was resignation as PM.

On 27 May 1939 the British offer of an alliance to the Soviet Union was made. It provided for 'mutual assistance either in the event of a direct attack, or in the event of a signatory being involved in war as a result of an agreement with or a request from a third country'.[45] The Chamberlain manoeuvre did not work, for the immediate Soviet reaction to the British *volte-face* and the start of negotiations for an alliance was to dispute the reference to the League of Nations included by Cadogan at Chamberlain's request[46] and allege that the terms were not specific enough, as Molotov, who had replaced the urbane and experienced Litvinov on 4 May 1939, made clear to Seeds on 27 May. Molotov told Seeds that Britain and France intended to 'continue conversations indefinitely and not to bind themselves to any concrete engagements'.[47]

On 2 June 1939 Molotov demanded a triple alliance and that guarantees of mutual assistance in the event of attack should cover 'all the states between the Baltic and the Black Sea'.[48] Chamberlain's opposition to any guarantee of the Baltics was clear in the FPC on 5 June, despite Halifax's drawing a comparison between Britain's position in relation to Holland and that of the Soviet Union in relation to the Baltics.[49] Chamberlain was to reiterate his views in an address in the Commons on 7 June, when he said it was 'manifestly impossible to impose a guarantee on states which do not desire it'.[50] Further, he told the FPC on 9 June that the Soviet request over the Baltics indicated a Soviet intention to expand west into Europe.[51]

Molotov's insistence upon guarantees covering the Baltics was a return to a theme he had raised at the end of May with Seeds, when he had referred to the impossibility of Belgium's being permitted by Britain or France to collude with Germany.[52] Halifax responded by saying that Britain did not wish to impose guarantees on the Baltic nations. The British objective was clear enough, to 'prevent our being dragged into war by Russia over a Baltic state without having any voice in the matter'.[53] On 10 June Chamberlain told his sister Ida that he could not decide if 'the Bolshies are double crossing us and trying to make difficulties or whether they are only showing the cunning and suspicion of the peasant. On the whole I incline to the latter view.'[54] In fact, all the way through Chamberlain recorded his reservations regarding the concessions being made to the Soviet Union in response to their escalating demands, both in the FPC and in Cabinet.[55]

On 14 June Strang was despatched to Moscow with revised proposals that required the Baltic nations' acquiescence. Shaw claims that the Soviet Union was insulted that someone of ministerial rank had not been sent, and that this exacerbated Soviet mistrust, yet Strang was sent as he was familiar with the views of the FPC and could represent them, and it is implausible that there was any effect on Soviet policy itself, which Shaw herself claims was driven by *Realpolitik* and opportunism and was in fact reflective of a combination of Bolshevik ideological hostility and paranoia and *Realpolitik*.[56] Bolshevik ideological hostility would have endured even if someone of greater status than Strang had been sent, as would the suspiciousness that accompanied it, and Stalin's *Realpolitik* would have dictated optimisation of returns to the Soviets from the talks in the form of security on their western border and expansionism through extorting whatever advantage seemed possible. Such characteristics were to be the experience of Soviet foreign policy and diplomacy during and after the war, and the fact that Soviet behaviour during the negotiations violated the norms of international diplomacy so often does seem to indicate exclusive attention to results rather than to diplomatic protocol. Though it was the prerogative of Chamberlain as PM even with his diminished authority in Cabinet to choose whom to send it cannot be argued that the choice affected adversely the chances of reaching an alliance. Roberts claims that Halifax was right in feeling that sending any high-ranking individual would be regarded as a sign of weakness,[57] an inference that is consistent with Soviet opportunism and understanding of power.

Though Molotov was offered the triple alliance he had demanded and consultations over the Baltics the British delegation refused to accept the Soviet definition of 'indirect aggression'.[58] Molotov's uncompromising position was that if there was to be no agreement over the Baltics there could be a resort to a triple alliance of mutual assistance in circumstances of a direct attack on the Soviet Union, France and Britain, though that of course would not have elicited Soviet assistance in the event of a German attack on Poland and so would not have rendered the British guarantee of Poland more credible. At the Cabinet meeting on 21 June Halifax informed ministers of Molotov's position and told them that the FPC had decided that Molotov's request for a no separate peace clause would be acceded to if everything else was agreed. Halifax at the time expressed confidence in the negotiations.[59]

There followed some discussion as to the countries to be guaranteed. On 28 June Halifax told ministers that the FPC had found it necessary to agree to the Soviet demand that the states to be covered by guarantees should be enumerated, another concession 'to avoid a possible breakdown of the negotiations'.[60]

By this time Britain had made a number of significant concessions, countenancing withdrawal of any reference to the League of Nations, offering a reciprocal triple alliance, agreement on no separate peace, guaranteeing the Soviet Union against invasion by Poland, and naming guaranteed states. In fact, according to Keeble, when Molotov proposed resort to a triple alliance with no guaranteed states Britain had agreed that the guarantees could cover any country 'the contracting country felt obliged to assist', and when Molotov responded by introducing the idea of 'indirect aggression' that included the abandonment of neutrality or independence by a guaranteed nation and a demand for military talks the only exclusion imposed by British diplomats was anything that could be interpreted as interference in another country's political life, that is, the abandonment of neutrality or independence without the threat of force. Keeble notes that military talks were granted.[61]

The documentary evidence supports Keeble's view, in that Molotov objected to the inclusion of Switzerland, Holland and Luxembourg as guaranteed states, and though he conceded that the list of states guaranteed could be named in an annex to the treaty rather than in the treaty itself, he insisted upon acceptance of 'indirect aggression' defined as 'an internal *coup d'état* or a reversal of policy in the interests of the aggressor'.[62]

On 2 July, in another revealing letter to Hilda, Chamberlain made his own continuing reservations clear. He was 'sceptical of the value of Russian help', was 'more and more suspicious of their good faith', felt that Britain would be little worse off without them, and was reassured that Halifax was at last reacting adversely to the escalating series of Soviet demands.[63]

On 4 July 1939 the latest Soviet demands were considered by the FPC. Halifax presented the committee with a choice between breaking off negotiations and a limited tripartite pact between Britain, France and the Soviet Union, which would have left the British with their unilateral guarantees to Poland and Romania without any Soviet support were the guarantees to be invoked.[64] Stanley pointed out that a limited pact would not protect Poland, reiterating his earlier blunt view, expressed to the FPC on 26 June, that if there was no direct Soviet guarantee to Poland it would be 'no pact at all'.[65] Halifax stressed the difficulties with Molotov over 'indirect aggression' and the feeling that British acquiescence in the Soviet definition of the term would put the Soviet Union in a position to involve Britain in war over the Baltics, which a limited tripartite pact between Britain, France and the Soviet Union would have avoided, involving as it would have undertakings to go to war only if one of the other signatories were attacked directly. Stanley then indicated that Britain could give the required undertaking and then avoid it in the implementation. Simon said that Stanley's proposal could prove embarrassing in the Commons, which prompted an astonishing and revealing outburst from the normally urbane and cautious Halifax.

Halifax had through June seemed sympathetic to and understanding of Soviet concern that the Baltic states might acquiesce in a German takeover, and referred to a need for understanding of Russian paranoia.[66] As late as 26 June he told the FPC that 'the Russians were extremely suspicious and feared that our real object was to trap them into commitments and then leave them in the lurch'.[67] Yet even he, an advocate of an alliance, felt a need to resist a definition of 'indirect aggression' that included a border country abandoning its neutrality without even the threat of force, fearing that the Soviet Union would falsely claim there had been a *coup d'état* in the Baltic states that resulted in a realignment towards Germany or some German interference resulting in a changed political orientation in the Baltics in favour of Germany to involve Britain in war.[68] Normally diplomatic in the extreme, with a tendency to observe the drift of opinion and then side with the emerging majority, his reaction to Simon expressed a radically diminished belief in the worth of any alliance with the Soviet Union in a devastating critique of Soviet diplomacy and foreign policy—

> On the day the Soviet Government would act as it suited them best at the time, and without the slightest regard for any prior undertakings written or otherwise. If, for example, war arose out of the Polish situation, and the Soviet Government thought the moment opportune for the partition of Poland they would partition it with Germany without a qualm. If, on the other hand, they thought it preferable to their own interests to fight Germany then they would support and assist Poland.[69]

Halifax's recommendation was that a tripartite alliance be concluded as it would permit Britain to achieve what he saw as the British objective, which was 'to prevent Russia from engaging herself with Germany', and he noted that he preferred 'a simple Tripartite Pact' to one 'he would be prepared to make with a partner in whom he felt trust and confidence'.[70] Of course a tripartite alliance only committed Britain to declare war if the Soviet Union were attacked, something that would not depend upon Soviet claims alone and that could be verified before a British declaration of war. Further, given Hitler's territorial grievances against Poland, the most plausible beginning to war was a German attack on Poland, and the British had guaranteed Poland against attack on 31 March 1939, so that the British position would not have been altered in the event of a German attack on the Soviet Union through Poland. It was only if the Germans attacked the Soviet Union through the Baltics that the tripartite alliance added anything to British commitments.

There was of course the possibility of the Soviet Union's negotiating a peace treaty with Germany in the event of a German attack on Poland and a British declaration of war despite the terms of the tripartite alliance. British reasoning may have been that the British government had to declare war on Germany if it attacked Poland because of its commitment to defend Poland and that little would have been lost if the Soviet Union refrained from declaring war on Germany under the terms of the tripartite alliance (the presumption here is that its terms would have included declaration of war on any nation that made a declaration of war on a signatory to any tripartite pact and that Germany would have declared war on Britain following the British declaration of war on Germany over Poland) given the Red Army's poor offensive capacity.

The change in Halifax's view as an individual who had set aside his personal reservations to advocate the negotiation of an alliance with the Soviet Union and thereafter to concede over various issues is remarkable and can only be attributed to his intervening experience of the form and content of Soviet diplomacy during the talks. It is worth noting too from the record of this decisive FPC meeting that Hoare, an original advocate of an alliance with the Soviet Union, did not feel that the Soviet definition of 'indirect aggression' should be accepted, and had otherwise by this time fallen silent. And Stanley, the only advocate of acceptance of the Soviet demand over the Baltics, had no intention of honouring any British commitment or of permitting Britain to be dragged into war by Soviet action in the Baltic region. The recommendation of the meeting was that the Soviet Union should be offered the alternatives of Britain's withdrawing Switzerland and Holland in return for a Soviet withdrawal of their definition of 'indirect aggression' or a tripartite pact. The following day Halifax presented two alternatives to Cabinet, that the Soviet Union should drop its definition of 'indirect aggression' with Britain leaving Switzerland and Holland out of the guaranteed states and prepared to consult on 'indirect aggression', and a tripartite alliance. He proposed to present these alternatives to the Soviet Union, and observed that he had 'very little information on the real attitude of Russia to the Treaty', that he did not believe that the Soviet Union would break off negotiations on receipt of the proposed response from Britain, and that if it did that would indicate it had not been serious anyway. Cabinet found the Soviet definition of 'indirect aggression' 'entirely unacceptable' and endorsed the FPC recommendation.[71] The FO then conveyed the British position to Seeds.[72]

Halifax's (and general British) exasperation by this time was clear. He told Phipps on 7 July, 'the Russian business is quite infuriating'.[73] Strang agreed, commenting to Sargent that the negotiations had been a 'humiliating experience. Time after time we have taken up a position and a week later we have abandoned it.'[74] The British position had been weakened by its unilateral guarantee to Poland, which had foreclosed its options, while the Soviets did have the options of isolationism and of alliance with Germany. Sargent told Corbin early in July that the British guarantees to Poland and Romania had been a mistake.[75] And Soviet perceptions of the humiliating sequence of concessions Britain had made to Hitler can only have eroded British credibility as a power that meant what it said. And yet the talks were not abandoned. On 10 July 1939 Seeds sent Halifax a revised Soviet definition of 'indirect aggression', which now was to mean—

Action accepted under threat of force by another power, or without any such threat, involving the use of territory and forces of the state in question for purposes of aggression against that state or against one of the contracting parties, and consequently involving the loss of, by that state, its independence or violation of its neutrality.[76]

This revised definition did nothing to allay Halifax's concerns regarding the possibility of the Soviet Union taking action in the Baltics that would then involve Britain in a war at the behest of the Soviet Union and without any direct attack from Germany. He found it impossible to accept,[77] and the FPC decided to offer military talks in exchange for Soviet movement on 'indirect aggression',[78] which represented yet another British concession. Yet the tone of British diplomacy was altering, reflecting the sense that little more could be given. On 12 July a 'stiff' British note said, 'we are nearing the point where we clearly cannot continue the process of conceding each fresh demand' and warned that the British 'may have to reconsider their whole position'.[79] Chamberlain recorded his pleasure at Halifax's change of view and again expressed his doubts regarding the Soviet Union as an ally. He said he believed the Soviet Union 'would fail us in an extremity' and that he would have taken a different approach all the way through had he had ministerial support.[80]

Any veiled threat had little effect on Molotov, who wasted little time in rejecting the British proposal.[81] On 19 July 1939 Halifax sounded near the end of his tether when he told the FPC that he would prefer a complete breakdown of talks to an acceptance of the Soviet position, and at a Cabinet meeting the same day he told ministers of the Soviet rejection of the British definition of 'indirect aggression', that the Soviet definition permitted them to interfere in other countries and could not be accepted, and that if there was no acceptance of the British definition the alternatives were a 'complete breakdown' or a tripartite pact, adding that a breakdown would not cause him 'very great anxiety' as he did not trust the Soviet Union to meet its obligations if war broke out unless it suited them.[82] Soviet diplomatic tactics had alienated British politicians, and British preparedness to concede seemed to be at an end. Then on 23 July Molotov indicated that the offer of military talks may have resulted in the possibility of some compromise over 'indirect aggression'.[83] The FPC rejected the idea of any further compromises,[84] and the issue was left to be settled while the military mission proceeded.

By this time Strang favoured an 'indeterminate situation' in which the negotiations would be prolonged. Though he must have known that it would have an adverse effect upon the talks, Chamberlain told the Commons on 31 July 1939 that the Soviet insistence on a particular definition of 'indirect aggression' reflected their desire to have a guarantee that permitted them complete freedom to do what they wished in other states. Butler added that Britain was faced with a Soviet demand that they consent to permitting the independence of the Baltic republics to be violated. Such public remarks drew an outraged response from Molotov, who claimed that the Soviet position had been misrepresented. Yet even as late as 11 August 1939 Chamberlain agreed that Strang might make another overture to Molotov so long as Britain were not guaranteeing Soviet interference in the affairs of other states.[85]

Halifax meanwhile seemed to be bewildered by what it all meant. On 2 August he told Drax, who was to run the British military mission, 'it was almost impossible to say whether the Russians really wished to conclude this agreement'.[86] Yet there was also a sense that Molotov would accept the British definition of 'indirect aggression' given the extensiveness of British concessions, having 'gained nothing' by repeated demands. There was 'no danger of an imminent breakdown', so that Britain could afford to take 'a somewhat stiffer line'.[87] What was certainly true by late July was that British politicians and officials had come to the conclusion that nothing more could or should be conceded, even by way of compromise. Chamberlain had been opposed to a military mission, and its having proceeded nevertheless is indicative of his diminished influence on policy.

It might seem that military talks gave the Soviet Union security from a German attack (in that they would deter Hitler from an attack) and indicated British readiness to give effect to the political negotiations. The British military mission had however received instructions to go slow pending the conclusion of a political agreement, which, as has been seen, was stalled over 'indirect aggression'. When talks did commence with Voroshilov the British delegation was treated 'in the manner of a victorious power dictating terms to a beaten enemy'.[88] They also received further demands, for Soviet rights of passage, which both sides knew would be very difficult to impose on Poland, and for very specific military arrangements.

Even so it seems that the French told Voroshilov that Poland would give the Soviet Union such rights when Poland was at war with Germany, and while it rather extended the sense of what the Poles had said the British supported the French indication, having themselves told the Poles that refusal could endanger a British alliance with the Soviet Union that was necessary to give effect to the British guarantee to Poland. It is also true however that this issue of Soviet right of passage through Poland seems less than clear, as Rees, in an account that is based on Soviet material that has been accessible only in recent times, claims that 'when Voroshilov asked directly on 14 August if the Red Army would be permitted to enter Poland to engage the Nazis, the Allied delegation made no reply'.[89] The explanation for the rather different accounts may be that the former account of British and French reassurance is based on Western, British and French sources, while Rees' account is based on Soviet sources.

In any event these further Soviet demands seem in retrospect to have been stalling tactics, for the Soviet Union began to negotiate the terms of a political pact with Germany while the military talks with Britain and France were going on.[90] Though German overtures for political talks had received no positive response from the Soviet Union prior to the beginning of August 1939, Soviet insistence in the talks with Britain and France on the resolution of the rights-of-passage issue does seem to have been a pretext rather than a reason for no progress given that talks with the Germans were going on at the same time and that the Soviet Union knew that Poland was against such a right.

The record would seem to indicate that while economic talks between the Soviet Union and Germany had been continuing before the end of July 1939 German overtures for political talks had received a cool reception before late July, when Molotov expressed greater interest.[91] On 12 August the Soviet Union through Molotov authorised formal political negotiations with Germany, two days before the claimed lack of a British and French response to the right-of-passage issue, so that it does not seem that the latter could have been the cause of the former, and in fact preliminary talks alluding to political issues had been going on since late July between economic representatives of the Soviet Union and Germany, with Ribbentrop involved in indicating German terms and assurances on 25 July and 2 August before a meeting between Molotov and Schulenberg on 3 August 1939.

The passage of time between 3 August and Soviet approval of formal political talks on 12 August seems a possible consequence of Molotov's exploitation of what he perceived was a sense of German urgency and desire for speed.[92] The Soviet experience of German diplomacy was in marked contrast to that of British and French diplomatic tactics. There was a sense of urgency from the German side and of course no concern for German public opinion or for the fate of smaller nations. Ribbentrop indicated that 'the Führer accepts that the eastern part of Poland and Bessarabia as well as Finland, Estonia and Latvia, up to the river Duena, will all fall within the Soviet sphere of influence'.[93] Stalin insisted that the whole of Latvia should be within the Soviet sphere of influence, to which Hitler agreed, and, with ominous German references to the imminence of war against Poland, the Ribbentrop-Molotov pact was concluded on 23 August 1939. On 25 August Seeds was told the talks with the British could not continue.

Alternative explanations

The objective record is not in dispute in the historiography, though different historians select a different mix of the available evidence in support of their cases. What the record represents and how it should be explained do however remain controversial. To start with the record itself, it is one of successive British surrenders to ever escalating Soviet demands, over the withdrawal of reference to the League of Nations, agreeing on no separate peace, guaranteeing the Soviet Union against invasion by Poland, and guaranteeing the Baltics among other states and naming them. There had also been British attempts to conciliate over the definition of 'indirect aggression', which British politicians felt could not be surrendered as it would permit the Soviet Union to decide when and under what circumstances Britain should go to war, first by offering to delete Switzerland, Holland and Luxembourg from the terms of the alliance, then by the offer of military talks, which had seemed for a time to have mollified Molotov. The record is also clearly one of increasing British mystification with, alienation from and mistrust of the Soviet Union.

There have been a number of very different explanations of the nature and end of the negotiations. One question is just what the series of British surrenders actually meant. Are they to be explained by the fact that the British starting point reflected adverse British attitudes towards the Soviet Union and communism, so that to obtain fair terms the Soviet Union was forced into escalating demands? It is true that at first the British had hoped to obtain their objectives, of preventing a Soviet pact with Germany and of concluding an arrangement that did not constitute an alliance with the Soviet Union but which would deter Germany from war in eastern Europe, at minimal cost in terms of British commitment, though this seems to have been less a reflection of adverse British attitudes towards the Soviet Union on political, ideological and racial grounds than of its being optimal as an initial negotiating position given that the first overture had come from the Soviets. There was also a related perception of the value of the Soviet Union as a military ally. For while the British political and official elite abhorred the Soviet Union as a state and communism as an ideology, it also had legitimate reasons for regarding Soviet military capability as poor (especially in offensive terms and so as a deterrent), because of Stalin's purges of the upper echelons of the Red Army in the late 1930s. Such considerations made the British doubt the military value of the Soviets for purposes of a wartime alliance, and the Soviet Union must have seemed more at risk from Germany than Britain because of Hitler's known aspiration for *Lebensraum* in the east, ideological antipathy for Bolshevism and racial derogation of Slavs.

These constitute legitimate reasons for a British starting point of offering little to the Soviets, and ones that do not reflect any British ideological prejudice. It is worth noting in this context that the view expressed so eloquently by Halifax, that the Soviet Union could not be depended upon and that it would pursue its own interests regardless of commitments, would seem to have been a consequence of experience of the negotiations with Soviet diplomats rather than a reflection of previously existing adverse British attitudes towards the Soviets and communism, because while such long-standing adverse British attitudes certainly did exist and would have been part of the prism through which British perceptions would have been formed they had not precluded Halifax and other ministers from recommending or continuing with negotiations with the Soviet Union. The British experience during the negotiations was in fact one of successive British concessions to Soviet demands, of Soviet diplomatic tactics that were indicative of an opportunistic orientation to international diplomacy in a form that violated diplomatic norms, outraged the sensibilities of experienced Western diplomats and precluded trust, and of a final Soviet demand that Britain would not accept because it would have committed Britain to go to war over the Baltics at Soviet instigation, which represented a surrender of control over British foreign policy to a Soviet Union that could not be trusted just from the evidence of the negotiations alone.

From 12 August 1939 (which was admittedly after the impasse over the definition of 'indirect aggression') the Soviet Union was of course running parallel negotiations with Germany to optimise the terms of any pact for the Soviet Union. The idea that previously existing adverse British attitudes were reflected in British diplomacy that caused the breakdown of the talks is then not borne out by the evidence, not least given the series of British concessions, the nature of Soviet diplomacy and of the final Soviet demand over the Baltics and the Soviet negotiations with Germany in August 1939, and though it could be argued that Stalin resorted to political talks with Germany because of British objection to the Soviet definition of 'indirect aggression' and the deliberate slow pace of military conversations the evidence seems to indicate that once the Soviets felt that German talks could be trusted the intention was to compare the terms offered to optimise Soviet security. And in the end the Soviet Union allied itself with a Germany the ideology of which was more antipathetic to communism than Western democratic capitalism was, and the expansionist designs of which in the east for *Lebensraum* were known (not to mention the German view of Russians and Slavs in general as inferior), though of course such antipathetic German ideology was not reflected in a German foreign policy characterised by a preparedness to surrender the Baltics and eastern Poland to the Soviet Union under a non-aggression pact.

The evidence of the extent and nature of British concessions, and of the form and content of Soviet diplomacy itself, seems to establish that it was not previously existing adverse British attitudes towards the Soviet Union and communism that caused the breakdown of the talks, for Soviet opportunism in the form of escalation of demands violated diplomatic norms, which required reciprocity and attempts to establish trust, and the Soviets did from around 12 August have an alternative that did optimise their outcomes, offering them a Soviet sphere of influence in the Baltics and eastern Poland and a virtual guarantee of war in the West rather than the east given that Hitler would have been ceded the western half of Poland under the terms of the proposed pact and that a German invasion of western Poland would have elicited a British declaration of war.

While it is difficult just at an axiomatic level to claim that the attitudinal orientation on either side was not an influence, because each side would have experienced the negotiations through an attitudinal prism that reflected their ideological orientation, the decisive influence on the failure of the talks was the form and content of Soviet diplomacy that seems to have reflected Bolshevik paranoia regarding capitalist intentions and ideologically justified opportunism that disdained reciprocity and so precluded trust, for British attitudes were not directly represented in British diplomacy given the series of concessions to Soviet demands and the parity implicit in the British offer of an alliance in May 1939.

Though it is possible to argue that, had the British trusted the Soviets not to involve Britain in a war of the Soviets' making over the Baltics and the definition of 'indirect aggression' and trusted them also not to violate the Baltic republics' territorial integrity unless such states were actually threatened with German invasion, British resistance over the Baltics would not have occurred, the argument here has been that the British experience of Soviet opportunism and diplomatic practice during the negotiations themselves was the decisive influence on British resistance over Soviet insistence on a certain interpretation of 'indirect aggression' because it elicited mistrust.

For even without adverse attitudes to communism and the Soviet Union the Soviet stipulation that the term should cover any *coup d'état* that resulted in a realignment towards Germany and any German interference that had a similar result could only have indicated to British politicians and diplomats either Soviet mistrust of the Baltics and fear that nationalist Baltic governments would have seen association with Germany as a counterbalance to the Soviet threat to them, that is, an inference of Soviet concern with security on its western border, or that the Soviets regarded the Baltics as part of the Soviet Union and had as a foreign-policy objective in 1939 recovery of lost territories. Assimilation of the Baltic republics would have been seen as relevant to both objectives (it was also the case that the Baltics had only recently become independent states and that the Slovak example had indicated the possibility of a nationalist movement engaging German assistance), and the experience of the negotiations in 1939 would have left the British with the suspicion that the Soviet intention was to find some pretext for an invasion of the Baltics regardless of any German threat either to prevent their possible alignment with Germany or just to restore them to Soviet power.

The British offer on 27 May 1939 provided for a British declaration of war in the event of a German attack on the Baltics if the Baltics requested help. It did not cover the Baltic republics' aligning themselves with Hitler of their own accord and did not offer assistance to the Soviet Union unless the Baltics were attacked and requested Soviet help. That of course did not meet the Soviet demand. It would seem that the British policy that resisted over 'indirect aggression' reflected a British resolve not to be dragged into war by the Soviet Union unless there was German expansionism of the sort it had guaranteed Poland against in March 1939 and certainly not on pretexts designed to justify Soviet invasion and occupation of the Baltics on a pre-emptive basis or for reasons of territorial re-acquisition. Such resistance of course indicated a profound mistrust of the Soviet Union as a party to an alliance.

Another possibility, related to that which argues that Britain started the negotiations in the belief that an alliance with the Soviet Union to deter Hitler from war and prevent the Soviet Union from negotiating a rapprochement with Germany could be obtained cheaply, is that the British concessions which followed were insignificant, while those that would have been significant were refused or subverted. Examples of the latter would in this argument be the Soviet definition of 'indirect aggression' (though that could have left the Soviet Union to expand its and communist influence into eastern Europe and have possibly engaged Britain in war over the Baltic states at Soviet instigation), the British preference for slowness and vagueness in the military conversations in August 1939 (though that did in fact reflect the impasse over 'indirect aggression'), and a claimed British lack of effort in persuading Poland to accept a Soviet right of passage (though this seems to be incorrect).

Such an argument is not made by Shaw and Carley, both of whom claim a more general connection between adverse British attitudes towards communism and the Soviet Union and the breakdown of the talks with no specific, detailed evidence to connect such attitudes and the talks' failure, but is similar to their arguments in that it could be used to attribute blame for the breakdown of the negotiations to such adverse British attitudes. Yet the detailed evidence does not support this hypothesis. For the early British concessions were of real value. The first one, after the attempt to elicit from the Soviet Union a declaration that it would guarantee eastern European states against aggression (which was refused), was the British offer of an alliance with the Soviet Union on 27 May 1939, which guaranteed that Britain would go to war if Germany attacked the Soviet Union or if it attacked any state that requested Soviet assistance, for instance the Baltic republics. This was hardly a small matter, in that the nature and extent of the British undertaking were clear and in that the terms of the proposed alliance were reciprocal.

The offer's inclusion of assistance to any state that requested help from a signatory to the alliance meant that any German attack on the Baltic states would have been included in the British undertaking if such states requested Soviet, French or British help, and of course the Soviet Union was itself guaranteed against any attack through the Baltic republics (Britain had already guaranteed Poland, another route for Germany should Germany attack the Soviet Union), so that legitimate Soviet security concerns were covered. It is worth adding that though Britain had guaranteed Poland's integrity and so was committed to war if Poland were attacked by Germany the Soviet Union was far more an objective of Hitler's expansionist designs than Britain, given his undisguised desire for *Lebensraum* in the east.

The case that Britain was prepared to concede only minor points during the negotiations and wanted an alliance that was unequal in its commitments is not supported by those instances on which the British seemed less enthusiastic, either. For the final Soviet demand was one which would have meant that Britain would have had to undertake to go to war in alliance with the Soviet Union if Soviet action against the Baltic states had taken place without genuine justification and without German aggression through those states, a decision that would present genuine difficulty for liberal democratic politicians with electorates and free presses to consider, regardless of adverse attitudes or 'prejudices', not least given that Soviet designs on the Baltic states were obvious. As to the speed of the military conversations, as has been seen, Halifax instructed Drax to go slow only because the political talks had stalled over 'indirect aggression', and it is worth noting that by this time Halifax's confidence in the talks had diminished radically from an early assurance to the point at which he told Drax that he did not know whether the Soviet Union intended to conclude an alliance, a change that has to be attributed to the experience of Soviet diplomacy during the talks.

Drax in fact left England on 5 August 1939, some time after Halifax's exasperation with and mistrust of Soviet foreign policy and diplomacy as experienced during the course of the negotiations had been expressed on 4 July 1939, and after the talks had stalled over 'indirect aggression', with instructions from Chamberlain and Halifax to drag out the talks to October if he encountered difficulties, as that would make a German invasion of Poland difficult given winter conditions there.[94] The fact that Halifax's experience of the negotiations would have been through a prism of anti-communist and anti-Soviet attitudes does not indicate a decisive role for such attitudes in their breakdown as such attitudes did not preclude his supporting the idea of negotiations in the first place or his continuing with them through a series of British concessions. The argument that Britain had no intention of making any genuine concessions is not supported by the evidence.

This returns one to the events of early August 1939 and to the time at which the Soviet Union indicated to Germany interest in negotiations over a political settlement (talks had been going on for months between the two nations to effect an economic agreement). Though the Soviets did at the time indicate to the Germans that they would conclude an alliance with Britain and France if their terms were met, it is difficult to accept the indication as evidence of the Soviets' genuine intent, for the more plausible inference is that it was a bargaining position for political negotiations with the Germans designed to extort concessions from them.

The most likely explanation, in the light of what is known of Soviet diplomatic tactics in the years that ensued, is that they were undecided and looking for the most optimal outcome for the Soviet Union from both sets of talks. Though the evidence is that it was the German side that pursued the political talks and seemed to have a compelling desire for a quick resolution in the form of a political agreement it is plausible that the caution on the Soviet side reflected a need to be assured that a pact with Germany could be optimal for the Soviet Union in terms of security, not least given the profound public antipathy of national socialism for communism and bolshevism.

Relative Soviet reluctance could have been a Soviet tactic to extort optimal terms from the German apparent need for speed, and it does not follow from the fact that formal political negotiations between the Soviet side and the Germans did not begin before 12 August 1939 that such negotiations began because of the stalling of talks between the Soviet Union and Britain and France, for that is a *post hoc ergo propter hoc* fallacy. It is worth noting that Stalin did not conclude an alliance with Britain and France without exploring the possible terms of a pact with Germany and that he could have intended to compare the terms on offer from both sources all along, for that would be entirely consistent with his calculating nature and with Soviet opportunism and expansionism in foreign policy and international diplomacy just years later and over the same issue, the Baltics, and later on in the war and its immediate aftermath.

Such an explanation would seem to make the British refusal over the definition of 'indirect aggression' less vital in causal terms, not least given the focus in the political talks between the Soviet Union and Germany on the lands between them. For it would indicate that the Soviet Union was optimising its outcomes from parallel sets of talks with the British and French and the Germans. And a pact with Germany offered the Bolsheviks what the British would not concede, territory in the Baltics, Poland and Romania and a guarantee of no war in the east with Germany for which the Red Army was unprepared, a basis of actual territory on the western border of the Soviet Union and of avoidance of war because it would not be in Germany's interests to wage war on two fronts, that is, a pact that did not depend on Soviet trust of the intentions of the British and the French, or the Germans. Such attributes would have been influential given Bolshevik suspiciousness of Western motives. A pact with Germany also offered the appealing prospect of anti-Soviet powers engaged with each other in a war of mutual exhaustion in a period in which the Red Army was becoming more prepared for war.

Though the inference of Soviet optimisation of outcome from parallel sets of talks is entirely consistent with the character of Soviet diplomacy during the discussions between Britain and the Soviet Union in the summer of 1939 it does seem that political talks between the Soviet Union and Germany did not start until there was an impasse between the Soviet Union and the British and the French over the definition of 'indirect aggression', so there remains the possibility that the Soviet Union did intend to conclude an alliance with Britain and France in May, June and even July 1939, and that political talks began with Germany only as a consequence of the impasse over the Baltics.

That returns the discussion to the impasse following the British decision to reject the final Soviet definition of 'indirect aggression' and the British instruction to its military representatives to go slow in the military talks, and the Soviet Union through Molotov having hinted that some form of compromise on 'indirect aggression' would be possible given serious military talks. The reality was that by this time the British had become so profoundly alienated by, and so mistrusted, Soviet diplomacy as practised by Molotov that such offers meant little – after all the previous amended Soviet definition of 'indirect aggression' had been of no reassurance to Halifax, and the FPC had decided on 26 July 1939 that no further compromises should be undertaken. The inference is that Britain had decided by that time that the talks should just be prolonged to preclude a rapprochement between Germany and the Soviet Union and to defer any German invasion until poor weather set in in Poland because of British experience of the nature of Soviet diplomacy in form and content during the negotiations. Even late on though there was no lack of British effort in relation to Soviet rights of passage through Poland, for the evidence is clear that Britain warned Poland that refusal to permit the passage of Soviet troops would bring war nearer and that the result would be that Poland would be attacked.[95]

It is impossible to know if Molotov and Stalin would have agreed to some compromise over the definition of 'indirect aggression' had there not emerged the alternative of a pact with Germany that offered territory to Stalin, for territorial concessions were objective and unlike diplomatic undertakings required no trust, and that guaranteed war in the west rather than the east, for collective security in the form of an alliance with Britain and France would, in the event of the deterrent to Hitler not having had the intended effect, have meant war in the east in Poland and could depending upon the terms have involved the Red Army in war at once. Under the pact with Germany war in the west required no Soviet trust in Germany, merely the avoidance of war on two fronts by Germany as Germany invaded western Poland following the ceding to Germany of western Poland under the pact and elicited declarations of war from Britain and France.

On the British side by early July 1939 the experience of the negotiations was one of having made several British concessions each of which only elicited another Soviet demand and which culminated in a demand that in effect Britain should permit the Soviet Union to decide when and for what reason Britain should go to war. The reaction among British politicians and officials was one of mystification, alienation and outrage, all of which I argue were perfectly reasonable reactions to the form and content, the nature and objectives, of Soviet diplomacy as revealed during the course of the negotiations. They did not necessarily reflect prior adverse British attitudes towards communism and the Soviet Union, though, as I have said, such attitudes would have facilitated the inferences drawn. In fact, any thesis that argues, as Shaw and Carley attempt to, that previously existing adverse British attitudes towards communism and the Soviet Union were alone responsible for the breakdown of the talks has to explain how it was that the British political and official elite overcame such attitudes at the start of the talks and during the series of British concessions that followed and that, after extensive experience of Soviet diplomacy that was profoundly adverse in form and content, those previously existing adverse attitudes were alone responsible for the breakdown of the talks, without any intervening influence from the experience of those talks.

The psychological process envisaged here seems wildly implausible, in its claim that adverse attitudes were overcome by the exigencies of the moment (at the start of negotiations and during a series of British concessions) then reasserted themselves and overwhelmed the influence of such exigencies later (in the breakdown of the negotiations) without any effect from the intervening experience of the negotiations themselves. It is inherently implausible that the intervening experience of the form and content of Soviet diplomacy should have had no effect whatever.

I now turn to a detailed assessment of the nature of the explanations of Shaw and Carley, which are in fact remarkably similar. Shaw claims that Chamberlain, who had been opposed to the idea of negotiating with the Soviet Union at the start and had had to acquiesce in the start of negotiations due to ministerial pressure, succeeded in exploiting ministerial doubts regarding the negotiations to preclude an alliance. Shaw claims that these ministerial doubts should be attributed to British ministers' having failed to overcome their aversion for the Soviet Union and communism. She claims that 'an Anglo-Soviet alliance was not concluded because of the failure of British ministers to put aside their anti-Soviet prejudices'.[96] For Shaw and Carley it was the anti-communist attitudes within the British political elite combined with an aversion for the Soviet regime itself with its purges and general repressiveness that caused the talks' failure, in that these were the attitudes that Chamberlain exploited.

The initial British rejection of Litvinov's proposal for an alliance and proposal that the Soviet Union guarantee eastern European states was, I have claimed, a result more of Chamberlain's and Halifax's perceptions of the effect of Soviet involvement on the cultivation of a 'peace front' in eastern Europe and Chamberlain's view of Soviet military utility than of adverse British attitudes towards communism and the Soviet Union. Beyond the Soviet refusal to comply with this British request there was an extraordinary series of British concessions to Soviet demands. Pownall records as many as six occasions on which British diplomats conceded to their Soviet counterparts.[97] The explanation of such an extraordinary series of concessions has to be a sense of British need for a Soviet alliance on *Realpolitik* grounds, which means that *Realpolitik* considerations overcame any possible inhibiting effect from adverse British attitudes. Given that the matter under discussion here is the extent to which British attitudes resulted in the breakdown of the talks, the record of successive British concessions indicates serious British intent rather than the minimal effort claimed by Carley, and that pragmatic considerations associated with deterring Germany from war mattered more than British adverse attitudes towards communism and the Soviet Union for British policy in the summer of 1939.

The evidence presented by Shaw as to the degree of aversion felt by the British political and official elite for the Soviet Union as a state and for communism is compelling (if far from new).[98] It is also true in general psychological terms that an individual's attitudinal prism would affect that person's preconceptions and so that person's perception and views as to the optimal policy – there is a literature on foreign policy decision-making that points out that the psychological environment in which decisions are made may be different to the actual external environment in situations in which attitudinal orientation affects perception in a profound way, and may intervene to exert influence on policy. It does not however follow that all attitudes serve to distort reality, or that they dominate decisions in all cases, for there may be intervening considerations, such as *Realpolitik*, in this case the sense of a need to deter Hitler by an alliance that meant any war would be on two fronts for Germany.

Further, Shaw does not address the possibility that the attitudes and the brazen, opportunistic diplomatic practices of the Soviet Union were a decisive factor in the eventual breakdown of the negotiations in 1939, that Soviet attitudes towards Britain and the Soviet perception of Britain and its situation were material to the breakdown, and in this sense the entire work has a lopsided quality to it, in that it concerns itself exclusively with the distorting effect of British 'prejudices', though Shaw herself notes that the British concern that the Soviet Union intended to use the Soviet definition of 'indirect aggression' to overrun the Baltic states with British support was justified.[99] Shaw does in fact quote with approval Gorodetsky's claim that Stalin's policy was not ideological but one of opportunism,[100] but does not go on to make the inference that an essentially opportunistic policy was one that was bound to elicit legitimate mistrust in any party to a proposed alliance. Further, it is quite plausible that Soviet means should be opportunistic while Soviet perceptions of the West should reflect an ideological world view that regarded all capitalist powers with mistrust and suspicion (such a view distorted Western motives and objectives). And it is implausible that Soviet foreign policy should have reflected Bolshevik suspicion of Western intentions and desire to export communism and Soviet influence in the 1920s, the 1930s, during the war over the Baltic issue in late 1941 and early 1942 and over the agreement over spheres of influence and the future of Poland, and after the war in the abandonment of the undertaking to free and fair elections in eastern Europe and institution of communist regimes dominated by the Soviet Union, and for there to have been a brief interlude in 1939 when Bolshevik ideology did not influence the objectives of Soviet foreign policy or the Soviet prism of perception of the West. Central attitudes are known to persist and to be resistant to change, and the idea that such attitudes could have been abandoned and then resumed is just psychologically implausible.

Shaw claims that British attitudinal orientation affected British policy in a decisive way, does not acknowledge that Soviet attitudes must have affected Soviet policy, and does not take account of the influence on British policy of Soviet policy itself. It is clearly implausible that attitudinal orientation should affect objectives and perceptions in one group but not in another, and there is no consideration of the possibility that Soviet diplomatic tactics were the cause of British refusal to concede to the final Soviet demand over 'indirect aggression'– there seems to be no consideration of the effect of the British experience of the negotiations on British policy.

The evidence presented above indicates that adverse British attitudes towards the Soviet Union, which were only to some extent apparent in British reservations as to Soviet reliability as an ally prior to the talks (for there were legitimate reasons for concern), had been overcome in the initial decision to enter into negotiations for an alliance. The talks failed because of the final position taken by the Soviet Union over the definition of 'indirect aggression', which Britain refused on the entirely legitimate grounds that the Soviet demand would have committed Britain to support the Soviet Union in a war over the Baltics in the event of the Soviets' claiming there had been a *coup d'état* or German interference that realigned the Baltics with Germany even when in fact there had been no provocation from Germany.

It is worth differentiating the entirely legitimate concern the Soviet Union had over the possibility of a German attack not through Poland, which Britain had guaranteed, but through Baltic states for which there was no such direct British guarantee, from the Soviet insistence on a definition of 'indirect aggression' that would permit Soviet intervention when the Soviet Union decided it was opportune. The inference is not that of a defensive orientation to Soviet policy but one of the sort of opportunism that Shaw acknowledges and then disregards, though there is the argument that a series of buffer states along the western Soviet border would have been seen as a form of protection against attack from the west, for before the German invasion of Poland there was no experience of the devastating speed and power of *Blitzkrieg* or lightning war.

Even so British preparedness to have the alliance cover the Baltics if Baltic governments requested assistance but not on terms that would permit the Soviet Union to involve Britain in a war the Soviet Union had started without open provocation from Germany would seem to have been, even for a government devoid of anti-Soviet and anti-communist attitudes, an appropriate foreign policy, one that protected British interests by declining to involve Britain in a war that the Soviets could have started to acquire the Baltics.

In this context Shaw quotes the suspicions recounted by the notorious Vyshinsky, who indicated in an address to the UN General Assembly on 25 October 1947 that the British did not wish to give guarantees to the Baltic nations even though it was understood that would have permitted Hitler to attack the Soviet Union through these states. Shaw acknowledges that there was no British intent to encourage Germany to attack the Soviet Union through the Baltics, but claims that Vyshinsky's view is indicative of the Soviet concern at the time as to British intentions and that such a view was justified given a lack of British reciprocity of terms offered for an alliance.[101] Yet, as I have indicated, the British were prepared to guarantee the Baltics against German attack if the Baltic governments requested assistance, and to guarantee Soviet territory against attack. As has been seen, there was very adverse experience of Soviet diplomacy during the negotiations, with British concessions eliciting further Soviet demands, and it was a series of British concessions that had culminated in British resistance over the definition of 'indirect aggression' in the Baltics because of the mistrust elicited by Soviet diplomacy in form and content.[102]

The inference is that Soviet diplomatic tactics and extreme demands served to preclude an alliance, in the process bewildering and alienating British politicians. It is worth noting too that Soviet representatives had been in preliminary political talks with Germany during the early part of August 1939, and that their demands included very specific British military undertakings and an insistence that the British should arrange for Soviet right of passage through Poland and Romania on what they claimed were legitimate grounds of having no treaties with them.

There is then only one inference one should draw from a clear British preparedness to negotiate an alliance and to concede to a series of Soviet demands with offers that indicated reciprocity followed by a refusal to concede over a final and very extreme Soviet demand and what seems to have been a wearied indifference to the talks in the end. It is that the final Soviet demand put Britain in a position in which it felt it had to refuse to avoid being implicated in a possible war to further Soviet interests in the Baltics, and that Soviet diplomacy in general, in form and content, caused such British mistrust as to elicit doubts as to the worth of an alliance with the Soviet Union even as a deterrent (the British lack of belief in Soviet military capacity resulted in an orientation to the deterrent possibilities of an alliance rather than its actual effect in the event of war).[103]

Of course any possible deterrent value would have been contingent upon Hitler's perception of the likelihood that the Soviet Union would meet its diplomatic obligations in the event of German action in eastern Europe and on Hitler's perception of Soviet military power. The risk was that an Anglo-Soviet alliance would result in Soviet invasion of the Baltics on some pretext and would be bound to elicit a German reaction that would precipitate war between Germany and the Soviet Union and involve Britain in a war to defend Soviet opportunism and territorial aggrandisement rather than Poland's independence and eastern Europe against German expansionism.

The preceding paragraph covers the British experience of Soviet diplomacy during the negotiations and links the mistrust elicited by Soviet diplomacy in form and content to the final rejection of a Soviet demand of 'indirect aggression' that would have left the British having to trust that the Soviet Union would not take advantage of it to involve Britain in war over the Baltics on a pretext to permit a Soviet takeover there. By July 1939 British mistrust seems to have been general and pervasive, a combination of alienation and indifference as to the outcome of negotiations with a prospective ally seen from experience of the negotiations to be radically untrustworthy.

In strictly rational terms British assessment of the likelihood of Soviet intervention in the Baltics on a pretext should have taken account of the Soviet perception of the likelihood and effectiveness of British military assistance against Germany in the event of war over the Baltics, and of whether or not the Soviet Union believed that an alliance with the British over the Baltics would deter Germany from military intervention in response to a Soviet occupation.

If the British perception was that the Soviet perception was that British assistance and deterrent value would be negligible given the state of British military rearmament and its record of appeasement, and that German intervention in response to a Soviet invasion of the Baltics was certain and would be of decisive power, then the likelihood of Soviet action to invade the Baltics on a pretext should just on grounds of rational optimisation of outcome have been seen by the British as low, which would have meant that an alliance could have been concluded accepting the Soviet definition of 'indirect aggression' without the need for trust in the Soviet Union and in its not using a pretext to involve Britain in war over the Baltic states. For in that event Britain would have been trusting the Soviet Union to do no more than optimise its foreign policy, because given the relative military power of Germany and the Soviet Union at the time, an expectation of no or minimal British help and no deterrent value against Germany should have indicated to the Soviets that invading the Baltics on a pretext would have resulted in the opposite of the Soviet intention in the Baltics, which was to provide a security buffer against western attack. For it would have been seen by the Soviets as producing a German presence in the Baltics. It would have been only if the British government believed that the Soviet government expected British (and French) help sufficient to expel the German army from the Baltics in the event of a German attack, or that the Soviet government expected that a British undertaking would deter Germany from a reaction to a Soviet annexation of the Baltics to avoid a war on two fronts, that a British acceptance of the Soviet definition of 'indirect aggression' should have been seen by the British government as entertaining a risk of the Soviets' involving Britain in war through invading the Baltics on a pretext.

It is of course not unusual for governments to overestimate their diplomatic and military credibility despite evidence to the contrary, in this case the abject record of appeasement and a pace of rearmament that had been restrained by Chamberlain as PM, though the British could with some justification have inferred that the Soviets must have believed in British (and French) diplomatic and military credibility to some extent to have made the overtures they did to engage in negotiations for an alliance in the first place.

In more general terms there remained the possibility of the Soviet Union reneging on any alliance even as a deterrent when another alliance seemed more optimal to its purposes, and Soviet abandonment of the negotiations for an alliance with the British in favour of a pact with Germany does seem to have been a reflection of just that characteristic of Soviet optimisation regardless of diplomatic norms in the summer of 1939. In actuality the experience British representatives had of Soviet diplomacy during the negotiations seems to have been so adverse as to have resulted in a profound mistrust of the Soviet Union and its diplomacy and foreign-policy intentions in general terms, without the sort of specific assessment of actual risk that has been alluded to here.

The general sense seems to have been that Russia could not be trusted to do anything it perceived to be alien to its interests at the time regardless of undertakings and by implication that it could involve Britain in war with Germany over the Baltics having used a pretext to annex the Baltic republics, when in fact there had been no German action against the Baltics. What the Soviet perception was in actuality is not known, though it is plausible that effective British and French assistance to the Soviet Union in the event of a German attack might have been rendered less credible by their abject record of appeasement, and the state of British disarmament would have left the Soviet Union with doubts as to British military capacity to assist in eastern Europe.

Even so it is possible that the Soviet Union believed that an alliance with the British and the French would have a deterrent effect on Hitler because it would present him with the adverse prospect of a war on two fronts, and that an alliance of Britain, France, Poland, Romania and the Soviet Union would provide a credible deterrent even if the deterrent effect of any one or any other combination of those states would have been inadequate as a deterrent to Hitler in eastern Europe. That is a possible explanation for what seemed to be Soviet desire for an Anglo-Soviet alliance.

Of course even if the Soviet Union genuinely believed both in the deterrent value of an Anglo-Soviet alliance (in conjunction with France, Poland and Romania) and in the value of such an alliance in the event of German aggression in eastern Europe, that does not mean that the Soviet Union did not intend throughout the Anglo-Soviet negotiations to compare British and French terms with those offered by Germany or that the terms offered by Germany were not more optimal to Soviet objectives given Soviet mistrust of all capitalist powers and German terms that offered a sphere of Soviet influence in the east of Europe and a virtual guarantee of war in the west rather than the east, which did not involve trusting the Germans. Nor does it mean that the Soviet Union did not intend to use British and French terms as a means of bargaining for better terms with the Germans, for the other explanation of an apparent Soviet desire for an alliance with Britain and France would be that there was a Soviet intention all along to compare terms offered by the British and the French with those offered by the Germans and to that end to extort undertakings from the British and French to use in bargaining with Germany to optimise the terms obtained.

The evidence of the FPC and the Cabinet indicates that there was no such rational consideration of the implications of acceptance of the Soviet definition of 'indirect aggression' in the Baltics. The decisive factor in the British consideration of the Soviet definition of 'indirect aggression' should have been the British perception of the Soviet perception of the relative power and preparedness to use it for or against the Soviet Union of Britain and France, and Germany, or the effectiveness of an alliance of Britain, France, Poland, Romania and the Soviet Union on Germany as a deterrent to German aspirations in eastern Europe, for that would have determined the likelihood of the Soviet Union's using its definition of 'indirect aggression' to invade the Baltics on a pretext and so involve Britain in war with Germany. As it was the adverse experience of the negotiations resulted in a less specific though influential mistrust of the Soviet Union and a sense that it would renege on its undertakings if that proved expedient.

While British aversion for the Soviet Union and for communism was manifest and profound, Shaw is not right to claim that British 'prejudice' (a pejorative term in itself) was the decisive factor in influencing British policy towards the Soviet Union in the late 1930s. The effect of the experience of the negotiations on British policy has been covered. It was true also that British aversion was not without foundation. In fact the nature of communism and Soviet attempts to export revolution to democratic regimes in western Europe represented a clear threat to the British political system – the experience of the Russian revolution itself, the Zinoviev letter of 1924 (that seemed to be an instruction from the Soviet Union to the British Communist Party to enhance the extent of communist agitation in Britain – though that has since been proved to be a forgery that would not have been known at the time), and the very nature of communist rhetoric made Soviet intentions, and contempt for social democracy, clear. Attributing British foreign policy towards the Soviet Union exclusively to an autonomous effect of what Shaw characterises as prejudice in the British political elite would be appropriate only if one could establish not only that British foreign policy objectives and perceptions in general reflected the influence of a British attitudinal ethos, a relationship which one would expect in any nation's foreign policy (in Britain, as has been noted, the dominant ethos was one of maintenance of Britain as a world, European and imperial power rather than one governed by anti-communism), but also that adverse British attitudes served to distort the British perception of the reality of Soviet policy and intentions. For in that case the absence of such British attitudes would have produced a very different set of perceptions and a very different British policy.

If however British perceptions merely reflected the reality of Soviet policy, a characterisation of British attitudes as 'prejudice' would be inaccurate. And in such a case exclusive attribution of blame for the breakdown to British 'prejudice' against the Soviet Union and communism would be inappropriate. As the evidence is that British attitudes towards communism and the Soviet Union did not distort perception of the nature of Soviet aims and trustworthiness one should attribute at least part of the blame for the breakdown of the negotiations to Soviet policy in form and content – there remains the effect of a general British attitudinal ethos on British foreign policy objectives, of course, but its effect was less to do with attitudes towards communism and the Soviet Union than towards Germany and the maintenance of European peace in British interests.

To elaborate upon this further, while it is clear that adverse British attitudes did not distort perception of the nature and purposes of Soviet diplomacy and foreign policy and so were not the exclusive reason for the breakdown of the talks, there was some influence from more general British attitudes, as manifest in the ethos of Britain as a world power with a clear and traditional interest in precluding the domination of the continent of Europe by any one great power. As has been seen above, British European policy in the 1930s was directed towards Germany, and appeasement was the means by which Chamberlain sought to maintain peace without relinquishing British European interests. The British interest in the Soviet Union in 1939 reflected a ministerial sense of a need to form an alliance that would contain Germany when it had become apparent that appeasement had failed. It was then part of Britain's maintaining its place in the world and in Europe as a great power. Yet such a general ethos demanded *Realpolitik* and great power politics, and dictated a policy towards the Soviet Union and towards communism that was pragmatic and optimal to Britain's main concern at the time, control of German expansionism and the maintenance of European peace. Shaw and Carley claim that it was a specific British aversion for the Soviet Union and communism that caused the failure of the talks in 1939.

A major difficulty with Shaw's attribution of blame to British 'prejudice' is that the adverse attitudes towards the Soviet Union and communism she refers to had been overcome in the British decision to pursue negotiations with the Soviet Union for an alliance in the first place. To contend that thereafter the individuals concerned could not overcome their attitudinal aversion is to propose that British politicians and officials attempted to overcome their prejudices and succeeded for some time, in the decision to enter into negotiations and during the course of the negotiations, which involved a series of concessions, but then couldn't dismiss their prejudices, with the result that the negotiations failed. Apart from being implausible, there is something missing in the account, and that is the intervening evidence of Soviet intentions as they materialised in the course of the negotiations, which seems to have exceeded the worst fears of the British political and official elite in their exclusive concern with Soviet security and territorial aggrandisement and a diplomacy characterised by an opportunistic escalation of demands with each British concession, which seemed to be brazen opportunism and which violated diplomatic norms not just in form but also in content, in ending with so extreme a demand that it required the British to be prepared to go to war on the basis of Soviet claims that the Baltics had realigned themselves towards Germany.

Shaw does not assess the influence of adverse British attitudes as a necessary condition (Shaw and Carley claim them to be a sufficient condition) by reference to the likelihood of a nation without such attitudes drawing the same conclusions regarding the implications of the final Soviet demand over the Baltics and the trustworthiness of the Soviet Union in any possible alliance (even given the British objective, which was primarily that the alliance should be one of deterrence).

In the negotiations that failed to secure an alliance with the Soviet Union in 1939, there was so adverse an experience of the actual negotiations themselves, with Soviet demands being escalated each time a previous demand was met, that British FO officials, such as Strang, and even Halifax himself (who had despite serious reservations supported the idea of an alliance), became convinced that any alliance would not be worth anything, that the Soviet Union would only go to war to defend the interests of the Soviet Union rather than to meet any treaty obligations – while there were reservations regarding an alliance with a Soviet Union as representative of an alien ideology and a repressive form of state prior to the experience of the negotiations, the adjective used in regard to Soviet diplomatic practices was 'bewildering', which is clearly indicative of a violation of expectations.

What evidence there is seems to indicate that it was the nature of Soviet diplomatic overtures in form and content that resulted in the failure of the negotiations, which means that one should not attribute their abandonment to British 'prejudice'. To begin with negative British attitudes did not represent 'prejudice' because such attitudes were predicated upon Soviet hostility and ideological antipathy and their existence prior to negotiations does not establish them as a cause of the failure of negotiations – that is *post hoc ergo propter hoc* reasoning. Rather it seems that any prior mistrust, which could have been disconfirmed by British experience of negotiations with the Soviet Union, was instead enhanced by that experience.

The other obvious effect on British policy, apart from attitudinal orientation in the British elite, was *Realpolitik*, that is, a rational reaction to the actual situation that faced Britain in Europe with the German violation of undertakings given at Munich in Hitler's invasion of Bohemia and Moravia in March 1939. The reality of British military weakness and German power (and brinkmanship) had been understood by the British elite, though the optimal policy had been a matter of dispute between appeasers, who felt that German aims in Europe were limited, justified and could be met without endangering British European interests, and those who opposed appeasement and wanted some alliance to deter Hitler from further expansionism.

When the German invasion of Bohemia and Moravia took place in March 1939 it became clear to many ministers (including Chamberlain himself) that Hitler could not be trusted. Some then (but not Chamberlain) made the natural inference that only deterrence of some credible sort would prevent further German expansionism in Europe. But the demands of *Realpolitik* would preclude a British concession that would leave the Soviet Union with such freedom in the Baltics that Britain would have to support a Soviet invasion on some pretext rather than in response to genuine German attack. Further, it would not involve the concluding of an alliance with a nation whose diplomatic tactics were such as to elicit a sense that no undertakings would be honoured unless they accorded with the perception of national interests at the time.

The above represents an explanation, unlike Shaw's, that does have the merit of indicating why negotiations were entered into in the first place and then, with experience of Soviet diplomacy, failed to produce an alliance. Shaw acknowledges the existence of a *Realpolitik* case in May 1939 for an alliance with the Soviet Union, in that she claims that ministers saw the need for an alliance with the Soviet Union to contain Germany in the light of a possibility of an understanding between Germany and the Soviet Union. She also indicates a link between attitudes in the British political elite towards appeasement of Germany and to various means of containing Hitler, one of which was an alliance with the Soviet Union. But such acknowledgement is not reflected in her thesis that it was adverse British attitudes towards the Soviet Union and communism that caused the talks to fail. To the extent that British concern as to the final Soviet demand over the Baltics (and the risk of opportunistic Soviet action there) and as to the Soviet Union as an ally reflected British attitudes of mistrust, it is clear that the nature of Soviet diplomacy during the negotiations had a marked and adverse effect on British diplomats and politicians, albeit possibly facilitated by previously existing adverse attitudes.

It is also worth noting that Shaw, in claiming that Chamberlain exerted the decisive influence on ministers in the final decision to abandon the negotiations, does not refer to a radical decline in Chamberlain's power as PM in relation to his Cabinet following Munich and Prague and the end to appeasement that was imposed by Party and Commons on him and which reflected the diminution of his influence. She refers again to the British political elite's prejudices against the Soviet Union, which she claims caused the British failure to conclude an alliance.

Chamberlain had in fact exerted an extraordinary influence over his Cabinet and British foreign policy since becoming PM in May 1937 as a result of a remarkable combination of personal attributes of tenacity and an immunity to criticism that was sustained by derogation of dissenters and a personal arrogance and assurance that he alone was right while others were mistaken, a form of persuasiveness that involved a selective approach to information and inferences, and the powers consequent upon his position as PM. But by the time the British decided that no further compromise should be undertaken over 'indirect aggression', on 26 July 1939, Chamberlain's reputation was not what it had been, for his policy of appeasement of Germany had been comprehensively discredited by Hitler's invasion of Czechoslovakia in March 1939, signifying as it did a reneging on undertakings given Chamberlain at Munich in September the previous year and establishing that Chamberlain's belief that Hitler's aims were limited and could be accommodated without threat to British European interests was erroneous.

Chamberlain had been forced to accept faster rearmament and had been compelled to accept the start of negotiations with the Soviet Union despite his most serious and expressed reservations. For despite warnings from the CoS as to the possibility of a Soviet alliance with Germany should British attempts to conclude an alliance with the Soviet Union fail, Chamberlain continued to believe that with any alliance Hitler would feel encircled and so be prompted to war rather than deterred from it. Hill dismisses as implausible the reasons Chamberlain himself gave for his *volte-face* over negotiations for the proposed alliance on 24 May 1939 and points to his being compelled by prolonged ministerial disputation and dissent to undertake the commencement of negotiations with the Soviet Union, not least after the defection of Halifax, as ever peculiarly susceptible to the change in the majority view and prepared to endorse it.

Hill argues convincingly that Chamberlain did not change his view of the desirability of an alliance with the Soviet Union. He continued to refuse to believe in the possibility of a German alliance with the Soviet Union (regarding them as ideologically opposed) and to regard a British alliance with the Soviet Union as likely to provoke Hitler to war rather than to deter him, demonstrating yet again an immunity to the views of others he had manifested throughout his premiership, but was simply overwhelmed by ministerial insistence.[104] It is therefore implausible that Chamberlain alone should have exerted decisive influence over British refusal to accept the final Soviet demand over the Baltics. As I have argued, the effect he had on the final breakdown of the talks was as an advocate in Cabinet and the FPC, from his position as PM, of an opposition to concessions and a doubting of the worth of an alliance with the Soviet Union. Such a position became increasingly plausible with British experience of Soviet diplomacy and Chamberlain's influence was thus facilitative rather than decisive.

It is also implausible that a British political elite that had overcome its adverse attitudes in entering into negotiations and making a series of concessions should have refused the final Soviet demand over the Baltics without a mistrust of the Soviet Union that derived in part from the intervening experience of Soviet diplomatic practices. British politicians explained Soviet insistence upon the definition of 'indirect aggression' it chose as reflective of an expansionist desire to acquire the Baltics and to decide when to involve Britain in war, when without the adverse experience of the negotiations the British inference could have been an understanding that nationalist Baltic nations who were not long free from Russian rule and who felt themselves to be under Soviet threat could well align themselves with Germany and so pose a genuine threat to Soviet security. It is of course most probable that both motives, security and expansionism, characterised Soviet diplomacy over the Baltics in 1939.

Shaw does make a specific claim that Chamberlain was instrumental in precluding an Anglo-Soviet treaty at the end of May 1939 by his insistence upon reference to Article 16 of the League Covenant, a stipulation rejected at once by Molotov, who demanded greater specificity to the terms of the proposed alliance. Shaw sees Chamberlain's reference to the League as 'crucial to the failure of the negotiations' as it confirmed Soviet 'suspicion of Western sincerity'. Yet the claim that an alliance would have been concluded at the end of May without Chamberlain's intervention is conjectural and implausible in the context of Soviet diplomacy and foreign policy acknowledged in the Foreword to Shaw's work to have been informed by a combination of ideological objectives and self-interest, for that would in the event of a British offer of a tripartite alliance without reference to the League have expressed itself in precisely what ensued, an optimisation of outcomes by Soviet diplomats in an escalation of demands with each concession and comparison of the terms possible with the UK and France and those offered by Germany in the summer of 1939.[105]

The claim that Soviet demands represented a test of sincerity was to reappear in Eden's argument over the Baltics in late 1941 and early 1942, though that too was to prove mistaken as Soviet policy revealed itself to be opportunistic and expansionist on ideological and *Realpolitik* grounds. Shaw seems to be arguing that there was a need to establish 'sincerity' with the Soviet Union by means of entirely reciprocal terms for an alliance, and that Chamberlain's attempt to 'sabotage' the alliance by reference to the League of Nations resulted in Soviet suspicion of British intentions in the negotiations and their declining to endorse such terms when a tripartite alliance without such reference would have been accepted.[106] Though in the case of Chamberlain's intervention to include reference to the League in the treaty Soviet suspicion would seem to have been justified to some extent, for Chamberlain gloated to his sisters that he had devised a possible means of evading commitment to the Soviet Union by reference to the League, removal of reference to the League was offered thereafter in the form of a triple alliance and produced only a series of Soviet demands. That would of course be consistent with the expectation of Soviet optimisation of outcomes in a foreign policy that was a combination of ideological objectives and suspicion and *Realpolitik*. It is worth noting that Molotov had replaced Litvinov on 4 May 1939, well before Chamberlain's intervention recorded in the Cabinet Conclusions on 24 May 1939, so it was not as if the more hostile and demanding Molotov had been introduced as a consequence of the offer under the auspices of the League.

Chamberlain's previous avoidance of reference to CoS advice that an alliance with the Soviet Union would be advantageous did not exert any influence as the threat of a rapprochement between the Soviet Union and Germany should there be no alliance with the Soviet Union in 1939 resulted in Halifax's *volte-face* and support for an alliance. Shaw does in fact acknowledge that Chamberlain himself told his sister Hilda on 2 July 1939 that he 'had to go warily' because his 'colleagues' were so 'anxious' to conclude an agreement with the Soviet Union and so 'nervous' of the consequences of not doing so, though she does not draw the obvious inference that Chamberlain's authority in Cabinet as PM had been much diminished and his influence on the conduct of the talks reduced.

Shaw also makes reference to the series of British proposals and Soviet rejections and to Chamberlain's comment to the FPC on 26 June 1939 that the Cabinet had made 'concession after concession' and had not refused the Soviet Union on any point that mattered, and though there was the British rejection of the Soviet definition of 'indirect aggression' the statement is indicative of the extent of British concessions to obtain an alliance and of Chamberlain's diminished influence, though Shaw does not comment to that effect. On the contrary, commenting on the end of July, Shaw claims that 'Neville Chamberlain ultimately made the decisions and he now had the support of his Cabinet and Foreign Policy Committee', though she offers no evidence in support of the contention of Chamberlain's influence or any attribution of the reasons for general ministerial disenchantment with the negotiations for an alliance.[107] She does note the annoyance and alienation of Cadogan and Halifax, both of whom had endorsed the negotiations with some reluctance and had countenanced several concessions thereafter.[108] Shaw claims that despite a record of British surrenders to Soviet demands, which she acknowledges meant that by 26 June the British had agreed to the original Soviet proposal for a 'mutual alliance' and 'compromised on a guarantee of the Baltic states', 'the British government continually rejected Soviet proposals', though she provides no evidence of such rejections, it all took too long, and what was needed was more compromise to reassure the Soviet Union of 'London's sincerity' in the form of 'willingness to aid the Soviet Union in the event of war'.[109] Nothing more could of course have been done to assuage what Halifax referred to in the FPC as 'Soviet paranoia' without permitting the Soviet Union to decide when and for what reason Britain should go to war, and Shaw seems to concentrate exclusively on the issue of Soviet mistrust of the West and to avoid addressing that of British mistrust of the Soviet Union enhanced by the experience of the talks.[110]

The obvious inference even from the evidence that Shaw produces is that there was little influence from Chamberlain on the conduct of the talks, that there was a series of British concessions to Soviet demands during the talks, and that it was the Soviet Union that was responsible for the breakdown of the talks in eliciting through undiplomatic behaviour and extreme demands mistrust of Soviet intentions and of any alliance to deter German aspirations in the east of Europe or in war with Germany. Chamberlain's influence if any would have been no more than contextual, for the decisive influence on the changed perceptions of the ministers on the FPC who had insisted upon talks in the first place was their adverse experience of Soviet diplomacy, in that Chamberlain's reservations had made no difference to such ministerial insistence on such talks or the concessions made in them.

Further, Shaw's work is not informed by any explanatory theory that relates attitudes to policy. For cognitive dissonance theory establishes that attitudes influence behaviour most where other influences are minimised. It also indicates that attitudes follow rather than predict behaviour where external factors dictate behaviour different to attitudes held. Cognitive dissonance is an extensively validated theory, and it is worth noting that it would not predict that adverse British attitudes towards the Soviet Union would constrain British policy towards the Soviet Union given the existence of a compelling reason for the dissonance between attitudes and policy, in this case the profound sense of British military weakness and of a need to deter Hitler from war by alliances. In fact, the reality of British economic and military weakness relative to a resurgent and expansionist Germany and the British political and official elite's understanding of Britain's situation make it inherently unlikely that British attitudes should have been a decisive influence on British foreign policy in 1939, in that the pursuit and protection of very widely conceived British European interests and very extensive British global interests (which, in the context of British economic and military weakness, has been referred to as the phenomenon of 'imperial overstretch') required the application of *Realpolitik* to British foreign policy, that is, the concluding of an alliance with the Soviet Union on grounds of necessity. The translation of attitudes into policy was a luxury that Britain could not, in the 1930s, afford given disarmament and the extent of an empire that had to be defended.

Having said that, one should not overdraw the distinction between *Realpolitik* and a policy driven by attitudes, for the latter affect the perception of the purposes of other nations to some extent and so the sense of the optimal policy, though not to the extent of denying the reality of experience of negotiations, as in the case of 1939.

Shaw refers to the British elite's view that Soviet foreign policy was aimed at furthering Soviet interests and remarks that that is so with all nation's foreign policies – that is true, but again the language evades the salient point, which was that Soviet diplomatic tactics and foreign policy during the negotiations left British diplomats, politicians and officials who had been prepared to negotiate for an alliance feeling that Soviet foreign policy would reflect its perception of its needs at the time rather than treaty obligations, which could be disregarded. While all nations pursue foreign policies that reflect their own national interests, diplomatic protocol requires some form of reciprocation in return for a concession (rather than exploitation and escalation of demands) and behaviour that encourages trust so as to facilitate diplomatic understandings. It was not unreasonable for a nation faced with such violations of existing diplomatic protocol and such extreme demands to have reacted as Britain did in 1939.

The record of Cabinet meetings shows less and less enthusiasm for the alliance and the negotiations as time went on. By July there was very little enthusiasm at all in the record of Cabinet meetings, in which Chamberlain's opposition continued to remain firm.[111] To support her inference that it was adverse British attitudes towards communism and the Soviet Union that ended the talks, Shaw quotes the memoir of Samuel Hoare, who had been the most vocal advocate of negotiations with the Soviet Union to effect an alliance to contain Germany.

In his *Nine Troubled Years*, Hoare says that the decision-making process was 'undoubtedly influenced by suspicion of the Soviet', that there were 'solid reasons for distrusting the Soviet', and that 'whilst we fully realised that the prejudices of the past should not affect our later policy, we should not have been human if we had not been influenced by this long record of Russian duplicity and hostility', which he then elaborated upon. What is interesting here is Shaw's line of reasoning. She discounts Hoare's extensive reference to Soviet hostility and agitation in Britain by claiming that, as it was written in the 1950s (during the Cold War), the references to Soviet infiltration are an 'exaggeration'.[112] She does this to discredit the idea that adverse British attitudes towards the Soviet Union had some basis in Soviet policy, which would mean that they could not be described as 'prejudice'. Yet the time of its composition must also have affected the general tenor of the work. Hoare claims that Cabinet ministers were in the late 1930s influenced by adverse attitudes towards the Soviet Union, which at the time of the publication of Hoare's book (1954) were seen as justified by the Western experience of the Soviet Union during the Cold War.

In fact, the relationship between British attitudes and British policy towards the Soviet Union in 1939 was affected by the *Realpolitik* need to effect an alliance, not least in Hoare's own case. It is clear that the inference that Shaw makes lends itself to her thesis, and she does not explore the possibility that the same inference could work against her case also. In fact, the individuals Shaw cites as evidence of adverse attitudes towards communism and the Soviet Union within the British political and official elite are interesting. Hoare himself is a perfect example of the inconsistency in Shaw's work. She makes considerable mention of his acknowledged aversion to communism and the Soviet Union,[113] yet notes that, with MacDonald and Stanley, both of whom shared Hoare's aversion for communism and the Soviet Union but felt that an excluded Soviet Union might seek some rapprochement with Germany, Hoare was one of the first to support the idea of an alliance with the Soviet Union.[114] Hoare and his colleagues were then advocating *Realpolitik* in proposing an alliance with the Soviet Union. What Shaw does not explain is how thereafter Hoare came to express reservations regarding British acceptance of the final Soviet demand over the Baltics and then to fall silent in terms of advocacy of the alliance during July, which Shaw herself notes.[115]

Taking a chronological view of the stances of the other individuals Shaw names as evidence of British aversion for communism and the Soviet Union, one sees similar difficulties for her case that

British politicians failed to overcome their prejudices. She is right in one case only, in fact, which is that of Chamberlain as PM, who was clearly and resolutely opposed to the alliance and to concessions throughout the negotiations. And it is true that his view prevailed in the end, but not because of British prejudice, as Shaw claims, for she presents no evidence of a link between the attitudes of the British political elite and the end of the talks, or of the process by which the elite could have overcome their prejudices and then been overwhelmed by them without any influence from the intervening experience of Soviet diplomacy. Neither does she produce evidence of Chamberlain's influence on the abandonment of the talks, despite Chamberlain's tendency to congratulate himself on anything that could possibly be a cause for self-congratulation and his letters to his sisters that so reflect that attribute in him.

The change in the view of those who had initially, and with varying degrees of enthusiasm, advocated or supported the idea of negotiations was a result of their experience of the negotiations themselves. At the FO Cadogan's initial and reluctant sense of a British need for the alliance was followed by outraged disbelief at the nature of Soviet diplomacy and a wondering if the Soviet Union were even serious in the negotiations for an alliance with Britain and France, and an attitude of indifference at the breakdown of the talks. Finally, the evidence of Halifax is compelling. One of the early and influential advocates of negotiations with the Soviet Union despite personal reservations and a loathing for the Soviet state and communism, Halifax had even as late the middle of June 1939 been confident that an alliance of some sort could be reached,[116] and had expressed some understanding of the Soviet demand that the Baltics should be guaranteed given their fear that the Baltics might choose to accept being taken over by Germany or to ally themselves to Germany (because of the threat of Soviet assimilation).[117] Yet by 4 July 1939, after fairly brief further experience of negotiations with Molotov, his tone had profoundly altered, as had his view of the utility of an alliance with the Soviet Union in terms of their keeping to their commitments. What he told the FPC on that day has been referred to above but is so central to the case being made here that it is worth repeating—

> On the day the Soviet Government would act as it suited them best at the time, and without the slightest regard for any prior undertakings written or otherwise. If, for example, war arose out of the Polish situation, and the Soviet Government thought the moment opportune for the partition of Poland they would partition it with Germany without a qualm. If, on the other hand, they thought it preferable to their own interests to fight Germany then they would support and assist Poland.[118]

So profound a change in Halifax's sense of the worth and nature of any alliance with the Soviet Union within the space of a month must be attributed to his own personal experience of the negotiations and the form and content of Soviet diplomacy during them. As has been seen, he had found them bewildering and infuriating, and had finally drawn the conclusion that an alliance could not be relied upon. Halifax told Lord Linlithgow after the talks' end that he regarded the breakdown as having occurred partly 'because they were double crossing us all the time', and yet also 'because they were genuine in their fear of indirect aggression through the Baltic countries on which we, suspecting motives, were sticky'.[119] Taken in the context of Halifax's earlier advocacy of talks and an alliance with the Soviet Union (even to the extent of opposing Chamberlain's reservations) and his ensuing bewilderment during the negotiations as to what the Soviet Union wanted, the inference is that Halifax's experience of the nature of Soviet diplomacy during the negotiations had been such that the Soviet definition of 'indirect aggression' elicited suspicion at the time (though there may have been an influence from previous attitudes). It is worth noting too that Halifax did not indicate to Linlithgow that the British should have accepted the Soviet definition and so permitted the Soviet Union to decide when Britain should go to war and for what reason, or that Soviet concern with security was not accompanied by an expansionist opportunism (the two are of course not mutually exclusive, as the post-war generation of FO officials and politicians was to discover in the case of the post-war diplomacy of the Soviet Union).

Hoare had been a crucial ministerial voice advocating an alliance with the Soviet Union, and Halifax's conversion left Chamberlain so isolated that even given his powers as PM, and his characteristic confidence in their use, he felt he had to concede to ministerial wishes. At the FO Cadogan was an influential PUS, as had been clear in his effect on Halifax over Munich. Yet these individuals hardly make Shaw's case that British prejudice resulted in the failure of the talks. For while Chamberlain remained opposed all the way through to the alliance and to concessions, so that in his case there was no sense of some hope that could have been disappointed by the experience of Soviet diplomacy, there is a clear relationship between Hoare's, Halifax's and Cadogan's experience of the negotiations and their shift from commitment to the negotiations and an alliance with the Soviet Union to a sense that the final concession over the Baltics should not be made and that the Soviet Union would not be worth having as an ally. It is also worth noting that the resulting view was specific, of the impossibility of trusting the Soviet Union to honour any commitments it might make, rather than the general aversion for communism and the Soviet Union as a state with which British politicians had started.

Shaw's inferences are not supported by the evidence and so remain conjectural (and in fact implausible). As an instance, she expatiates on the views of the anti-appeasers, who were in favour of an alliance with the Soviet Union to contain Hitler, and on those of Morrison and Butler, who supported Chamberlain's opposition to an alliance. Yet by her own admission these individuals (Chamberlain apart) were not influential, so one wonders just what the references to their views add to the claim she is making that the British political and official elite failed to overcome its prejudices and conclude an alliance with the Soviet Union in 1939.[120] All her reference to anti-appeasers does establish is that there was an alternative policy to the conciliation and appeasement pursued by Chamberlain and the Cabinet at the time of the Sudeten crisis in 1938, when the Soviet Union was excluded from the negotiations because of German insistence (this is the time on which she focuses in this chapter). Yet it also shows that the difference of view between the two factions was a function of their differing views on the need to form alliances to deter Germany from war and the possibility that any alliance would serve as a deterrent rather than provoke Hitler to war. Attitudes towards the Soviet Union and communism were common to both groups, and what separated them was their attitude towards Germany and appeasement. In other words, an expansionist Germany was the focus of the debate over British foreign policy, not the Soviet Union. Further, by the time of the start of the negotiations for an alliance with the Soviet Union in 1939 there was no longer a general sense in the British political elite that appeasement was the optimal way of maintaining European peace and containing German expansionism, for the European situation had changed radically with the German occupation of Prague, and Chamberlain was by that time relatively isolated in his continued opposition to negotiations.

Shaw's use of the terms 'attitudes' and 'prejudices' seems to categorise mistrust that is entirely legitimate, in that it is based on extensive evidence, as an attitude or a prejudice, when in fact it is a perception supported by reality. She claims that 'Stalin's motivation was never ideological' because control over the Baltic states was not intended to expand communism but rather to afford the Soviet Union some security on its western frontier.[121]

To begin with, the definition of 'indirect aggression' upon which the Soviet Union insisted was not necessary to the protection of Soviet territorial integrity against German attack, for the guarantee that Britain had offered was sufficient to that end, so the motive would seem to have been opportunist rather than defensive. And Shaw also makes no reference to the continuing difficulty that British politicians and diplomats had even after the war in separating Soviet defensive concerns from opportunistic expansionism, though with diminishing belief in the former. Further, Shaw does not seem to identify the link between Soviet mistrust and suspicion of the West, which were influenced by Bolshevik ideology, and Soviet foreign policy, for that association dictated the consolidation of communism in one country and obtaining as much territory as possible in an opportunistic way in diplomatic encounters (and a preference for war in the west between Nazi Germany and capitalist Britain and France).

Shaw claims that the Baltics represented a Soviet way of assessing British sincerity (which seems an inference drawn from the debate in 1941 and 1942 over the Baltics in the FO), but does not address the possibility that the negotiations themselves might have had an adverse effect on British estimations of Soviet sincerity, as is clear from the changing views of Halifax during the course of the talks. Finally, Shaw says, in the context of a thesis in which she claims that adverse British attitudes towards communism and the Soviet Union caused the breakdown of the talks, that 'realpolitik dominated the international situation by the summer of 1939' – this is what I have argued, but it is the precise opposite of a foreign policy dominated by the 'prejudice' which she claims was so salient to British policy.

Further, Shaw refers to differences of view within the FO as to policy towards the Soviet Union and claims that those who opposed closer relations did so because of 'ideological prejudice' against the Soviet Union.[122] In the case of Collier, of the Northern Department, who argued for better relations with the Soviet Union, Shaw notes that he shared the revulsion for communism and the Soviet Union held by Sargent, Cadogan and Jebb, but though for Shaw Collier would be an instance of an individual setting aside anti-Soviet prejudice, the real difference between those who favoured an alliance and those who did not was one of perception. For Collier felt that the Soviet Union was so weak that its stratagem was to consolidate communism within the Soviet Union rather than seek to export it given the attendant risks of such a policy. He claimed that the resulting foreign policy of the Soviet Union was one concerned with security and, given that he also saw fascism as the major threat to European peace, advocated better relations with the Soviet Union in an attempt to cultivate an alliance that would deter Hitler from war. That is of course the position Halifax took with some reluctance in late May 1939 and that ministers such as Hoare and Stanley took in April 1939 before exerting influence to that effect on ministerial colleagues in the FPC over the ensuing month.

Shaw's use of language in indicating Collier's position is indicative of her general use of pejorative labels such as 'prejudice' to characterise attitudes of mistrust and aversion for the Soviet Union on the part of the British political elite, which were not without justification given previous experience of Soviet diplomacy and what was known of the Soviet regime, for she notes that Collier 'was not as opposed to, or afraid of, collaboration with Moscow' – the use of the term 'afraid' seems to indicate that any legitimate caution predicated upon experience would be derogated as fear.[123]

Her concentration on the case of Collier, and that of the Germanophobe Vansittart, is odd in that neither was in a position to exert any influence on foreign policy, not least as the FO had been marginalised throughout Chamberlain's premiership given the latter's aversion for it and conviction of his own diplomatic prowess and grasp of foreign policy. It seems the point might be to provide examples of members of the establishment who managed to 'overlook their anti-Soviet prejudice', though to establish that adverse British attitudes caused the breakdown in the talks with the Soviet Union for an alliance in the summer of 1939 Shaw would have to explain why Hoare and Halifax, for instance, advocated engagement in talks with some reluctance, and then, during those talks, became indifferent to their outcome without some influence from the experience of negotiating with the Soviets, not least given Chamberlain's diminished influence as PM.[124]

Reference to public opinion, which it seems was in favour of an alliance, is intended to reinforce

Shaw's condemnation of British ministerial failure. Yet in Britain traditionally foreign policy has had a low salience in public opinion, and Chamberlain had manipulated and disregarded public opinion before. Any reference to it is then really an irrelevance, in that foreign policy was generally (and not just in this instance) a matter for the British political and official elite, and Shaw's reference to it is indicative of lack of appreciation of the influence of the locus of foreign policy decision-making power in the British system with its Prime Ministerial prerogatives and powers.

Finally, Shaw concludes that Britain could and should have concluded an alliance with the Soviet Union in 1939, taking a moral tone that is reminiscent of the 'Guilty Men' orthodoxy. Yet the claim that an alliance with the Soviet Union would have averted war and deterred Hitler is conjectural in the extreme, not least given that Germany may not have seen any Soviet threat as a deterrent given Nazi ideological contempt for the Bolshevik regime and communism and the purges of the upper echelons of the Red Army in the late 1930s, though German enthusiasm for a pact with the Soviet Union and for political talks to that end would seem to indicate German aversion for a war on two fronts even with a possible poor view of the Red Army. Further, it is open to question whether Britain and France could have concluded an alliance with the Soviet Union given the attractions for the latter of the terms being offered by the Germans, especially in the lands to the west of the Soviet Union and the virtual guarantee of war in the west rather than the east.

Shaw does not make it explicit, but the thesis that adverse British attitudes towards communism and the Soviet Union caused the breakdown of the talks, given that they foundered over the definition of 'indirect aggression', could be claiming a link between Britain's surrendering to the Soviet Union rights in the Baltics and British attitudes of mistrust of Soviet objectives there, which could be taken to indicate that such adverse British attitudes caused the talks' breakdown. Yet given that any alliance is in effect an exchange of promises, and that that was known before entering into negotiations with the Soviet Union, why was it that the trust Britain was prepared to place in the Soviet Union at the outset was no longer there? In entering into negotiations for an alliance with the Soviet Union Britain was indicating preparedness to 'trust' the Soviet Union as a deterrent to German expansionism and opportunism in eastern Europe or as an ally in war in the expectation of a Soviet declaration of war on Germany should Britain be at war with Germany. And there must have been some worth ascribed to the initial 'trust' that the Soviet Union would honour its obligations and not renege on them if that became expedient to its purposes, for Britain was after all promising to go to war if the Soviet Union was attacked or if any state that asked for Soviet help was attacked, a promise it intended to honour, so there was for the British political establishment a cost to the alliance for which a return would have been expected. It could only have been the British experience of the content and form of the diplomacy of the Soviet Union during the negotiations that could have resulted in resistance over the Soviet definition of 'indirect aggression'. In fact, the very nature of so extreme a Soviet demand might well have in itself elicited suspicion in the British that a Soviet invasion of the Baltic states supported by Britain (and involving Britain in war as a result) was precisely the Soviet intention should any opportunity arise or should there be anything that would be seen to threaten the morbidly suspicious Russians. In addition to this there was the unprecedented British experience of a series of escalating Soviet demands following successive British concessions, which also caused British suspicion as to Soviet intentions. Soviet insistence on a certain interpretation of 'indirect aggression' could in fact only be understood to indicate Soviet expansionist intentions in the Baltics or concern that nationalist Baltic governments would ally themselves with Nazi Germany, because even a tripartite alliance would have committed Britain to declare war if the Soviet Union were attacked by Germany, which means that Soviet territory would have been covered without reference to the Baltics.

Though both Shaw and Carley claim that previously existing British prejudice caused the breakdown of the talks neither produces any direct evidence to that effect. There is however compelling evidence of British dismay at the negotiating tactics of the Soviet Union and their escalating demands, of the inferences drawn regarding the worth of any possible alliance, and of British concern that Britain should be drawn into war over the Baltics by the Soviet Union even without any German aggression in the Baltics.

In the end, then, Shaw claims that British 'prejudice' caused the failure to conclude an alliance with the Soviet Union when that failure can be much more plausibly ascribed to a combination of (1) unreasonable Soviet demands that indicated Soviet expansionist intent (albeit possibly for reasons of security) in the Baltics even without direct German aggression there and which, had they been acceded to, would have permitted the Soviet Union to determine when, and in what circumstances, Britain would go to war, and (2) British mistrust of the Soviets arising from extensive adverse experience of negotiating with them and a resulting sense that any Anglo-Soviet alliance would be worth very little.

Carley also claims that Britain and France failed to put aside their attitudes of aversion and mistrust for the Soviet Union and so failed to conclude an alliance that could have deterred Germany from further expansionism. Using French diplomatic archive material, Carley notes that the French were more prepared to make concessions to the Soviet Union to obtain an alliance they felt was imperative to forestall a pact between Germany and the Soviet Union. The French either did not share the profound British concern regarding being drawn into war over the Baltics by the Soviet Union, or felt that the danger of a Soviet pact with Germany was greater, and seemed prepared to concede the final Soviet demand over the Baltics and to favour a link between the political and the military conversations. Yet, as Carley notes, Bonnet made it clear that the French would defer to the British.[125] It is apparent then both from the French position and from their preparedness to defer to the British view that France cannot be held responsible for the talks' breakdown.

Carley claims that little effort was expended in the course of the negotiations and attributes their failure to Chamberlain and British interwar anti-communism, which he goes on to claim as two major causes of World War II.[126] He uses French and Soviet archives and claims that it was adverse British attitudes towards communism and the Soviet Union that caused the talks' breakdown. Yet establishing that the French may have been more prepared than the British to surrender the Baltics and to agree the Soviet definition of 'indirect aggression', that they ceded the initiative to the British and that the Soviet Union had compelling reason to demand some form of security against attack through the Baltics does not establish that adverse British attitudes towards communism and the Soviet Union caused the talks' failure.

Contrary to Carley's claim, adverse British attitudes towards communism and the Soviet Union from the period prior to the talks do not seem to have been a necessary condition to the talks' failure, for there is no evidence that the British refused the final Soviet demand because of long-term concerns regarding the expansion of communism or Soviet influence into the Baltics or because of general anti-Soviet and anti-communist attitudes in the British political elite. Though Shaw makes the same claim, the record, not least from Halifax's statement to Cabinet on 4 July, is clear that the British were concerned that the Soviet Union would draw Britain into war as a result of a Soviet invasion of the Baltics because of Soviet mistrust of the regimes there, which Shaw claims was justified because on 7 June Estonia and Latvia concluded non-aggression pacts with Germany despite having been warned by the Soviet Union that such actions would violate the existing non-aggression pacts with the Soviet Union, preferences that would have seemed to the Soviet Union to threaten the security of the Soviet state.[127] Though that seems to indicate legitimate Soviet security concerns over the Baltics a tripartite alliance would have guaranteed the Soviet Union against attack by Germany and there remains the possibility of Soviet opportunistic expansionism and optimisation of terms in the Soviet definition of 'indirect aggression'.

Though the differentiation between expansionism and opportunism and security concern in the Soviet demand over the Baltics is problematic both resulted in the same policy, a definition of 'indirect aggression' that would confer on the Soviet Union the right to decide when and on what pretext Britain should go to war.

Shaw and Carley stress the effect of the exclusion of the Soviet Union from the Munich conference, allied as it was to both France and Czechoslovakia at the time.[128] Though Shaw acknowledges that the British perception was that a choice had to be made between appeasing Hitler by excluding the Soviets or antagonising him by insisting upon their inclusion in the settling of the Czech crisis, she claims that 'the British government could have, and should have, at least attempted to deter German aggression over the Sudetenland' and that 'aversion to military alliances, British military and economic weakness and the opposition to Anglo-Soviet collaboration from the Dominion governments and other governments involved in the crisis should have had no bearing on the inclusion of Soviet representatives to settle the Sudeten crisis peacefully'.[129]

This odd reference to what should have been done seems to be predicated upon the supposition that Hitler could have been deterred by a bluff involving British, French and Soviet collaboration over the Sudeten crisis. That is counterfactual and so conjectural. The point is that the exclusion of the Soviet Union was, as has been seen, a consequence of British compliance with German insistence to secure European peace through negotiation, with the conciliation of Germany as the main threat to European peace the objective.

The argument that the Sudeten crisis is evidence that the British political elite did not 'set aside their anti-communist and anti-Soviet prejudices' at that time does not seem to be supported by the evidence of a policy addressed to the containment of Germany through conciliation in the conviction that encircling alliances would provoke Hitler to war rather than deter him, in other words a matter of perception of the optimal means of maintaining European peace. And even were one to accept that the consequence was that the Soviet Union had reason to mistrust Western motives that does not prove that adverse British attitudes towards the Soviet Union and communism, exploited by Chamberlain, resulted in the failure of talks for an alliance, for there was the ensuing evidence that British politicians were prepared to enter into negotiations to effect an alliance and to make several concessions to that end.

When one considers the history of relations between Britain and the Soviet Union, there were other instances of British diplomacy that were conciliatory in nature. Rather than attributing Soviet attitudes and policy to a history of adverse experiences of British diplomacy the more plausible inference is that the attitudinal orientation of Soviet foreign policy and diplomacy, with its suspicion and mistrust of capitalist powers, including Britain, derived from the Bolshevik ideological framework rather than any specific historical or recent experience of any individual western nation. This disposes of the idea that a history of British diplomacy that reflected adverse British attitudes towards communism and the Soviet Union was responsible for Soviet attitudes of mistrust and suspiciousness that in turn resulted in Soviet insistence upon a definition of 'indirect aggression' that would permit them a freedom of action in the Baltics and commit Britain to support any such action. Soviet attitudes and policy were not a passive reflection of some supposed adverse experience of the West.

In more limited terms, to refute Carley's (and Shaw's) specific attribution of the failure of the negotiations to British anti-communism and aversion for the Soviet Union one has only to establish that the diplomatic style and apparent purposes of the Soviet Union were the intervening variable that resulted in British outrage and refusal to concede finally over the Baltics. The reality is that the British were required to make a final concession over 'indirect aggression' that would have conceded to the Soviet Union the right to commit Britain to war over the Baltics without any German attack through them or German interference in the Baltics, and the British inference that an alliance with the Soviet Union would be worth nothing was one that was understandable given the form and content of Soviet diplomacy during the talks, the British experience of which enhanced previously held adverse attitudes towards communism and the Soviet Union. The French preparedness to go further reflected a greater fear of a rapprochement between Germany and the Soviet Union than that which was apparent in the British political elite, in which genuine concern to obtain an alliance as a form of deterrence eventuated in disbelief in its possibility.

Yet as argued above, while it may appear that no previous adverse British attitudes were necessary for such inferences, and that the nature of Soviet diplomacy in form and content was both a necessary and a sufficient condition to the failure of the talks, it is difficult to isolate variables from each other with any final certainty. And while it might seem that to prove that prior British attitudes had no effect all one has to establish is that outrage and refusal to concede the final Soviet demand over the Baltics represented a reasonable British reaction to their experience of Soviet diplomacy in form and content during the negotiations, the fact that a condition was not logically necessary does not of itself mean that it had no influence in the psychological universe of the British political and official elite. For the attitudinal prism through which they experienced the negotiations was informed by a mistrust of and aversion for communism and the Soviet Union. I have confined myself here to what can be established with some certainty, and that is the decisive influence on the talks' breakdown, the British experience of Soviet diplomatic tactics and demands during the negotiations.

Carley claims that Britain was not serious in its pursuit of an alliance with the Soviet Union from the outset, before any experience of Soviet negotiating tactics and purposes, but all the evidence is of reluctant acceptance of the need for an alliance with the Soviet Union to contain Germany. This is the only possible explanation as to why the British, despite their revulsion for the Soviet Union and communism, began the negotiations. Carley does not explain why the negotiations began in the first place and why so many concessions were made to the Soviet Union. The military mission, which Carley claims was a hollow gesture, came after extensive experience of Soviet intentions and diplomacy, with an escalation of demands following each British concession over the Baltics and an impasse over 'indirect aggression', and so is hardly evidence of the influence of British prejudice before the talks. Carley also stresses that Russian distrust of Britain and France was both acute and justified (but see the previous paragraphs), but does not seem to address the validity of British fears of Soviet motives as they emerged during the course of the negotiations for an alliance.

What is missing here is the question of the reasonableness of British attitudes – there were grounds for mistrust of the Soviet Union even before the negotiations, but this did not preclude the talks' starting, and the evidence of the negotiations themselves justifies the resulting British mistrust without any need for reference to prior adverse attitudes towards communism and the Soviet Union.

Carley claims that Britain and France believed Stalin's hope was that Britain, France and Germany would exhaust each other. Such Western suspicion was apparent after the breakdown of the negotiations and an inference drawn from them, but had it been so prior to the negotiations why did Britain enter into them in the first place, and how does one explain the Soviet offer of an alliance? According to Carley the Western powers, especially Britain and the United States, feared that war would result in the bolshevisation of Europe. Yet that was not the motive force behind appeasement, which was much more a function of Chamberlain's adverse attitude to any risk of war, his belief in his own personal diplomacy and in Hitler's essentially limited aims in Europe. He also believed in the power of reason over that of force.

Carley claims that it was Chamberlain's fear of a bolshevised Europe that resulted in his preventing a Russian rapprochement. Yet there seems to be no documentary evidence for this, and given how late it was in Chamberlain's premiership and after the discrediting of his policy of appeasement and decline of authority in Cabinet, as exemplified in his having to acquiesce in the negotiations in the first place, such decisive influence seems implausible. Further, if it is being argued that as PM Chamberlain had the power to block an alliance why did he not refuse to enter into negotiations given his own reservations?

Carley further indicates that Western politicians tended to dismiss Russia's potential military contribution, pointing to a lack of offensive capability and to the deleterious effect of Stalin's purges of the upper echelons of the Red Army, but claims that Western fear of communism was the most influential factor. In fact, it is clear from Shaw's evidence that the reservations regarding the Red Army were counteracted by a sense of the Soviet Union as a deterrent. Carley must offer some explanation, having presented so much in the way of claims regarding British prejudice, as to why negotiations were entered into at all. British reservations regarding Poland's objections to an alliance with the Soviet Union were also justifiable, in that to be effective the Red Army would have to have had permission to enter Polish territory, and negotiations began after the Poles indicated that they did not wish to preclude an alliance.

Carley's claim that adverse British attitudes towards communism and the Soviet Union caused the talks' failure seems contradicted by the very evidence that he himself produces. For he notes, 'Soviet instructions anticipated every weakness of the Anglo-French delegations, and their scornful tone foretold no good result,'[130] and that the Soviet Union was carrying on parallel negotiations with Berlin during June and July, though without any firm commitments or encouragement from the Soviet side. The escalation of Soviet demands is easier to understand in such a context, in that they may have been intended to extort the maximum possible from the British to compare with any German offer. He is also clear regarding the purposes of the Soviet Union in the negotiations, in indicating that, 'the objectives of Soviet policy were state security and the recovery of the tsars' lost territories,' and regarding Stalin's pragmatism, ruthlessness and desire to 'buy time'.[131] This was of course not dissimilar to the combination of security fears and opportunistic expansionism that was to characterise Soviet diplomacy during and after the war, but it does not lend itself to his case that British attitudes were responsible for the talks' failure. Even the more ambiguous attribution that 'the British feared giving the Soviet Union license to threaten Baltic independence or to spread communism' leaves a role not just for British attitudes but Soviet objectives also, and it is worth noting that he presents no evidence of the British concern with the spread of communism over the Baltic issue. Soviet expansionist intent over the Baltic states was such that the only way in which British attitudes could not be blamed for having impeded an alliance would be if they were such that the British were prepared to go to war to promote the interests of the Soviet Union.

Carley goes so far as to claim that appeasement was driven by fear both of Nazi expansionism and of a victory over Nazism that would result in Soviet influence and communism extending west. Yet there is no evidence whatever for the idea that the policy of appeasement reflected adverse attitudes towards communism and the Soviet Union for those involved in British foreign policy, for Germany represented the main threat to European peace and was the object of European policy. In the British government appeasement of Hitler was linked to many other factors, such as, as has been seen, Chamberlain's loathing of war, his belief in his own personal diplomacy and in Hitler's limited aims, and a sense that alliances, which he believed had caused World War I, could antagonise and inflame Hitler.

The object of British European policy during appeasement was European peace through conciliating Hitler and Germany. There was however a link between appeasement and the negotiations for a treaty with the Soviet Union. But it was through Chamberlain's sense that any alliance could be seen as encirclement and so could impel Hitler to war rather than deter him from war, which left him opposed to an alliance with the Soviet Union, and a view held by a number of ministers, not least Hoare and Halifax, by May 1939, that appeasement on its own had failed, as had been dismally clear in Hitler's occupation of what was left of the Czech state, and that an alliance with the Soviet Union was necessary.

Prior to 1939 British European policy was directed at the appeasement of Germany, and, as has been seen, the British sense was that the Soviets could do little to assist or harm British policy or interests, a view which Cadogan, whose endorsement of the negotiations had always been reluctant, was to reiterate some months after the failure of the negotiations, in June 1940.[132] Carley seems here to be attributing to appeasers beliefs that might have since been proved rational (such as concern regarding the westward expansion of communism and the Soviet Union as an influence) but which were not salient to them at the time. Chamberlain's mistrust of the Soviet Union was clear, but it was not a motive force in appeasement.

While it is clear that there was a revulsion for communism in the British political elite, and attitudes of aversion from the Soviet Union, it is also clear that such attitudes were not prohibitive, in that negotiations for an alliance did actually take place. What Carley fails to explain is why, having started, they failed. As I have indicated above, it does seem implausible that the form and content of Soviet diplomacy and British experience of it during the negotiations made no difference whatever to British conviction in Soviet seriousness of intent and the extent to which the British believed that the Soviets would be a trustworthy ally against Hitler as a deterrent or in the event of war.

Carley claims that Soviet demands in the summer of 1939 were not new and had been clear in Litvinov's earlier proposals for collective security as long ago as 1935. In other words Carley denies the notion that there was an escalation of Soviet demands in the negotiations in 1939.[133] Yet even Shaw refers to Molotov's 'shock demand' over 'indirect aggression' on 1 July 1939.[134] Further, the negotiations in 1939 were the first time British politicians and officials had been involved in detailed talks and had heard Soviet demands articulated in the clear way they were in 1939 (and of course British politicians and officials had never prior to 1939 conceded to any such demands). Carley also accuses the British government of 'complacency' at the end of July 1939,[135] an odd term to use given British experience of the negotiations. It is clear that Halifax's main objective at this stage may have been to prolong the military negotiations less in the receding hope that some common ground might be found over 'indirect aggression', over which the FPC had decided not to compromise, than in the assurance that while such military conversations continued 'we should be preventing Soviet Russia from entering the German camp'.[136] But the appropriate inference from this is not that the British were complacent but that they had come to the end of what they felt they could surrender to Soviet demands over the Baltics and had come to a sense that an alliance could not be concluded because of Soviet insistence over 'indirect aggression' and that any alliance that was concluded would be disregarded if Soviet interests dictated it.

Carley and Shaw also point to the lack of reaction late on in the negotiations to military advice of the most direct and compelling kind. On 16 August the deputy CoS, addressing the issue of Soviet right of passage through Poland and Romania, advised that 'the Russians should be given every facility for rendering assistance and putting their maximum weight into the scale on the side of the anti-aggression powers' and that pressure should be brought to bear on both states to endorse such rights of passage given that a treaty with the Soviet Union 'was the best way of preventing a war' and a rapprochement between the Soviet Union and Germany.[137] Shaw claims that 'the Cabinet did not heed their advice' but should have, as if this would have made a difference to the outcome of the talks.[138] But to begin with the British did apply considerable pressure to Poland and did endorse the French assurance that a Soviet right of passage through Poland was agreed (it was not believed), and anyway the issue of 'indirect aggression' had stalled the political talks and the British government had resolved not to compromise over it because it could not countenance surrendering to the Soviets the timing of a British declaration of war over the Baltics without actual German aggression.

Further, by this time the British had lost any confidence in the value of an alliance given their experience of Soviet diplomatic tactics during the talks, and the Soviet Union was engaged in talks with the Germans over a pact, from which it seems that Soviet insistence on rights of passage was, as I have indicated elsewhere, a stalling tactic or a means of exerting pressure on the Germans for concessions. The argument that the CoS should have been listened to is one that judges by hindsight and consequence rather than being a legitimate criticism of British foreign policy in terms of its rationality and influence from attitudinal orientation at the time, because the British concern over the implications and intentions of the Soviet posture over the Baltics was reasoned rather than a reflection of prejudice and the Soviets pursued talks with the Germans to optimise their outcomes and were offered terms the British could not have matched, not least the prospect of a German war in the west rather than the east and parts of Poland and Romania.

In the most recent work to address the negotiations for an alliance between Britain and the Soviet Union in 1939, Neilson argues that while the immediate objectives of Soviet foreign policy might vary, for instance the idea of consolidating communism in the Soviet Union rather than entertaining the risks of exporting it, Soviet perceptions of the objectives of Western powers were driven by ideology and a communist world view rather than by objective evidence.[139]

For Neilson Soviet policy was driven by ideological perceptions that defined ultimate objectives, though it did permit *Realpolitik* means and a choice of short-term objectives.[140] Neilson refutes the claims of Shaw and Carley that the breakdown of the talks should be attributed to adverse British attitudes towards communism and the Soviet Union. He claims that there was communist ideological influence on Soviet policy and points to a fundamental clash of political cultures and interests.[141] He sees Soviet policy as focusing on power (which in fact would be the natural outcome of communist ideology) and on opportunistic hard bargaining, a policy influenced by an ideological suspicion of capitalist powers' motives (which he claims the British implementation of its guarantee to Poland proves was unfounded).

By contrast British policy, Neilson claims, was a reflection of a pluralistic culture, with rearmament, conciliation and negotiation being pursued at different times, with no exclusive or profound orientation to power and with the aim of European peace being pursued through diplomacy.[142] Neilson sees British foreign policy and diplomacy as being informed by standards of morality that included respect for the sovereignty and independence of states and honouring diplomatic promises (Stanley was a possible exception to this standard in his recommendation that the British should assent to the Soviet definition of 'indirect aggression' and then avoid it in practice).

Neilson points out that to conclude the alliance Britain would have had to have forced Soviet guarantees on Poland and the Baltic states (which did not want them), abandon the Baltic states to the Soviet Union and permit the latter to decide when and for what reason Britain should go to war. He also claims that the British believed that acceptance of the Soviet definition of 'indirect aggression' would result either in the Red Army's invading the Baltics and Poland on the grounds that otherwise German control would ensue, or in the Baltics and Poland moving towards Germany, though he presents no direct evidence for these assertions.[143] Ultimately, though, Neilson's own conclusion is unclear. For while he claims that any blame should be apportioned to both sides, he also says, 'the Anglo-Soviet talks collapsed because of Soviet intransigence and a lack of common interests between the two states,' and comments that 'the mental and moral gap between the two states was too wide to be bridged.'[144]

Neilson's work differs from my argument here in that it is a more general assessment of relations between Britain and the Soviet Union between the wars and attempts to identify broad themes and trends in British interwar foreign policy, while my argument focuses on the ways in which various influences exerted themselves during the course and at the end of the negotiations for an alliance between Britain and the Soviet Union in 1939 and considers in some detail the various possible explanations for their failure.

There are also specific points on which I differ from Neilson. I do not accept Neilson's appraisal of British policy as having been informed in any decisive sense by considerations of morality, though it is clear that British politicians and diplomats did have reservations regarding the violation of traditional norms of international diplomacy that was inherent in the surrender of the independence of the Baltic states, and that they were bewildered and appalled by the form and content of Soviet diplomacy, which disregarded such norms. Yet the ultimate British objection to the final Soviet demand over the definition of 'indirect aggression' was that it would cede to the Soviet Union the right to commit Britain to war over the Baltics when it suited Soviet interests in a context of a mistrust of the Soviet Union that was a consequence of Soviet diplomacy during the course of the negotiations, not the issue of colluding in possible Soviet violation of independent states (that in fact seems to indicate Neilson's accepting the public accounts of British politicians over the private evidence of weariness, disgust and aversion among those most intimately involved, such as Cadogan). Permitting the Soviet Union to commit Britain to war over the Baltics without German aggression against the Baltics was seen as antithetical to British foreign policy and interests, and had not been implicit in the previous guarantees Britain had given. Further, the fact that it had been demanded called into question Soviet motives and intentions, and in conjunction with Soviet escalation of demands made British diplomats and politicians doubt the worth of the Soviet Union as an ally against Germany.

When considered in a context in which the British offered very little to begin with (though Britain then did offer the Soviet Union terms that represented reciprocity) and then attempted to prolong the military talks to preclude a rapprochement between the Soviet Union and Germany, one has to conclude that British policy was governed by a realistic appraisal of what best served British interests at the time. It does not of course follow from this that British foreign policy was responsible for the breakdown of the talks, just that the British concessions were made because British ministers and officials had come to the view that Britain needed alliances to deter Hitler from war and that in the end the view was taken that the Soviet Union would not be an ally that could be depended on even as a deterrent.

I also do not see the link Neilson claims between a democratic and liberal nation's pluralistic political system and its foreign policy and diplomacy. It is not clear just what Neilson is claiming here. If he is claiming that in a liberal democratic system public opinion exerts genuine, even decisive, influence on foreign policy he is mistaken in the case of Britain at that time, for there was a low salience of foreign policy to public opinion. In fact, the case of Chamberlain as PM in general is indicative of the irrelevance of public opinion to the actuality of British foreign policy, despite politicians' claims to the contrary, for Chamberlain used public opinion as a pretext for policies upon which he was resolved for other reasons.[145] And so did Halifax. Further, the record of British diplomacy over the negotiations with the Soviet Union in 1939 bears this out, with British preparedness to start negotiations for *Realpolitik* reasons in the sense of a need to contain Hitler through alliances and then not being prepared, despite public expectation of an alliance, to concede over 'indirect aggression', again because of the foreign-policy implications. British foreign policy could not then be described as being a reflection of public demand.

There is a possible influence from a pluralistic political culture that generates genuine diversity of view and debate. In terms of what it means for the negotiations with the Soviet Union in 1939, it is clear that by that time British foreign policy was oriented to the pursuit of alliances to deter Hitler from war, as the series of British concessions to Soviet demands proves. The most plausible conclusion is that within the pluralistic political culture to which Neilson refers it was the change in international circumstances that occurred with the German invasion of Prague that resulted in Party and Commons insistence on replacing appeasement with deterrence in the form of the guarantee to Poland and in ministerial influence in the start of negotiations for an alliance with the

Soviet Union in May 1939. It is worth noting that even in the Soviet Union such changes in the international situation resulted in changes in Soviet policy from isolation to an ostensible commitment to collective security to contain Germany and thence to a pact with Germany that represented an optimisation of security for the Soviet Union.

My argument also differs from Neilson's broader work in that it is far more specific in its assessment of Soviet policy. My sense is that the Soviet foreign policy experienced by British politicians and diplomats during the negotiations represented a combination of factors. Soviet ideological hostility and suspicion produced an inherent Soviet mistrust of British promises and intentions, and a characteristic opportunism and expansionism, which explains the insistence on the final Soviet definition of 'indirect aggression' and their finally choosing a German alliance to acquire a sphere of influence in eastern Europe and war in the west rather than the east – it was hardly that the Soviet Union had found that Germany could be trusted more than the British, and none of the advantages from the pact with Germany depended upon trust. Such Soviet opportunism and expansionism were difficult to distinguish from a Soviet concern with security known to be characteristic of the Stalin regime, for both are possible reasons for the Soviet demand that the Baltics be included in the guaranteed states and even the final Soviet definition of 'indirect aggression'.[146]

Further, these influences did not exist independently of each other. For there was also a link between the communist ideological world view that the Soviet Union held and the opportunism and hard bargaining of their diplomatic tactics, in that the perception of ultimate capitalist hostility to the Bolshevik revolution, the Soviet Union as a state and communism was part of a view of the Soviet Union as a state conspired against by the capitalist West, which meant that any duplicitous diplomacy and opportunism were valid in defence of the revolution.

There is a final difference between my work and that of Neilson. For Neilson claims that 'Chamberlain's conceit, contempt for his advisers and his hatred of war combined to make him keep control of British strategic foreign policy firmly in his own hands. Chamberlain disliked the idea of alliances and felt that an alliance with the Soviet Union put the decision for war or peace into the hands of the Bolsheviks.'[147] Though Neilson refers to earlier differences in the FPC in April 1939, when Chamberlain and Halifax resisted calls from Stanley and Hoare for talks to effect an alliance, he seems not to have drawn the rather obvious inference of very much reduced influence from Chamberlain thereafter when towards the end of May Chamberlain had to give in to ministerial demands for talks with the Soviet Union for an alliance given Halifax's defection from opposition to an alliance. The indication is that without the support of his influential Foreign Secretary Chamberlain's influence on policy towards the Soviet Union was not decisive. Neilson's concentration on the longer term and on mentalities seems to have resulted in no real assessment of the shifting locus of influence on foreign policy within the British political establishment. For he concludes that 'the mental and moral gap between the two states was too wide to be bridged.'[148]

In a very recent assessment of Soviet foreign policy Uldricks refutes the claims of Soviet era Soviet historians that the Soviet Union had been entirely committed to collective security on grounds of national interest and moral principle in the 1930s, and those of a more recent school of Western historians who have argued that there was never any Soviet intention to conclude an alliance with the British and the French in the summer of 1939, that the intention had been to secure terms with which to bargain with Germany, the real objective of Soviet foreign policy, so that the pact with Germany was not an outcome of the fact that collective security proved not to be possible but the intended achievement of Soviet foreign policy in 1939. He points to disconfirming evidence for both points of view in Soviet inconsistences of foreign policy in the 1930s, to Soviet appeasement of Japan, Italy and Germany and Soviet turning to collective security following the rejection of overtures to Germany after which there continued to be contact for a rapprochement between 1935 and 1937.

Uldricks claims that Soviet objectives reflected Bolshevik fears of encirclement by Japan and Germany and of imperialist coalitions and were oriented to the optimisation of security from attack. He claims that the Soviet escalation of demands and insistence upon military conversations and on access for Soviet troops through Poland and Romania during the negotiations for an alliance with Britain and France in the summer of 1939 were a test of Western sincerity indicative of Soviet fear of British and French intention to have the Soviet Union wage war against Germany in the east of Europe without involvement from them. This idea of Soviet policy and its demands and diplomatic tactics being a test of Western sincerity leaves aside entirely the issue of Soviet sincerity for Western diplomats and politicians and does not invalidate the argument that Soviet diplomacy during the course of the negotiations for an alliance in the summer of 1939, were it predicated upon Bolshevik paranoia or rational optimisation of outcomes, was such as to elicit British mistrust in an alliance with the Soviet Union. Nor does it invalidate the idea that Stalin intended to optimise Soviet security by comparing British and French terms with those offered by Germany, for paranoia and concerns regarding Western sincerity would have resulted in just such a policy and in a preference for terms that did not require trust, that is, a sphere of interest in eastern Europe and a guarantee of war in the west not involving the Soviet Union. These were of course precisely the terms offered by Germany, whereas the collective security alternative did involve trust in British and French undertakings. In more general terms a combination of a peasant tradition of hard bargaining, suspicion of Western motives from the Bolshevik ideological perspective and optimisation of outcomes seems to indicate such a policy of comparison of terms.[149] It seems to indicate too a preference for terms that did not require trust.

The difficulty of differentiating Soviet security concerns and Bolshevik paranoia from brazen Soviet opportunism and expansionism was to obtain throughout the early years of the Cold War, though in the end it was understood that either produced the same Soviet policy of expansionism and opportunism and had to be contained by Western resolve. The Baltics were to reappear as an issue in 1941 and 1942, and even in 1939 it would have been consistent with Soviet paranoia for the Soviet Union to invade the Baltics on a pretext to preclude German influence there and to have involved Britain and France in war on that basis as a test of Western sincerity and appreciation of Soviet concerns.

I now turn to other possible attributions. It does not seem that British policy represented a general British failure to understand the situation Chamberlain's guarantee to Poland on 30 March 1939 had placed the country in, for Strang clearly understood that the British guarantee had compromised the British position, while the Soviet Union had options of isolation and a pact with Germany. For the British guarantee to Poland could only be given credibility by presenting Hitler with a genuine threat of war on two fronts, which made a British alliance with the Soviet Union a desideratum if not imperative, not least given the history of British surrender to Hitler's demands under the policy of appeasement, which made any British threat on its own less compelling. There was also no British failure to understand the Soviet view that the British position was weak and could be exploited, as is apparent from Strang's complaint to Orme Sargent that British concessions were expected by the Soviet Union. In fact the British diplomats, politicians and officials involved did come to have an accurate conceptualisation of the Soviet approach to diplomatic exchanges, which was one of hard bargaining and exploitation of any indication of weakness, though with little previous experience of Soviet diplomacy British politicians and diplomats were appalled by its nature. Yet had British understanding of the Soviet approach to diplomacy in terms of content and form been better before the start of the negotiations the overwhelming likelihood is that they would not have started negotiating in the first place.

The case presented here is that the nature of Soviet diplomacy as experienced by the British during the course of the negotiations was such as to confirm previously existing adverse British attitudes of mistrust towards the Soviet Union. While this would seem to make both previously existing British attitudes and Soviet diplomacy necessary conditions to the breakdown of the talks, as has been seen, the final Soviet demand over the Baltics would have left Britain with a commitment to support Soviet occupation of the Baltic republics against the wishes of Baltic governments and to enter the war on that basis even without direct German aggression in those nations, and the inference from experience of Soviet diplomacy during the negotiations was that the Soviet Union should not be trusted – that inference would have obtained even without adverse attitudes towards communism and the Soviet Union in the British establishment prior to the negotiations.

In fact, it was entirely reasonable for Britain to have refused to undertake a final concession that would have committed Britain to war when the Soviet Union felt that it furthered Soviet interests. For, having made a series of concessions to Soviet demands, British negotiators did in the end refuse to countenance a definition of 'indirect aggression' that would have permitted a Soviet invasion even if the country concerned had abandoned its neutrality without threat of force. It does also seem that behind this refusal was a British sense, from the sequence of Soviet demands and British concessions, that the Soviet Union would not meet its commitments if they became inexpedient – there was clear dismay and disgust with the nature of Soviet diplomacy, but that had not precluded an extraordinary series of British concessions (the idea that the British refused to countenance the surrender of the Baltics on moral grounds is unsustainable, as the evidence establishes).

This sense of Soviet untrustworthiness had been presented by Fitzroy Maclean, who was to become the Soviet expert in the Northern Department of the Foreign Office and was at that time an attaché at the embassy, as long ago as 6 March 1939 (in an addendum to a memorandum by Seeds), when he wrote, 'Soviet policy is purely opportunist,' and 'were they to consider that their own interest or those of the Soviet Union required it, the rulers of this country would not hesitate to change horses in mid-stream.'[150] But that had not precluded the entry into negotiations for an alliance or the series of humiliating concessions made by the British during those negotiations. It was, however, the view to which British politicians and diplomats gravitated with experience of the tactics of the Soviet Union during the negotiations. Of course there is a difference between an adverse attitude to the Soviet Union as a state and to communism as an ideology and the much more specific understanding that even the foreign policy and diplomacy of that state were not to be trusted in an alliance, which would not have been understood at the start of negotiations between Britain and the Soviet Union in the summer of 1939.

Further, while Halifax had been confident that the Soviet Union would not abandon the talks over 'indirect aggression', British reaction to the breakdown of the talks was oddly muted, as if very little had in fact been lost. Halifax, a late and reluctant advocate of the talks, seemed to exhibit more indifference than one might have expected from an individual for whom the alliance must have seemed valuable for the talks to start, given his clear reservations over any form of agreement with the Soviet Union. In a diary that is valuable for its frankness, the influential PUS at the FO, Cadogan, having been in favour of an alliance in May 1939 (albeit without much enthusiasm, 'on balance' and to preclude a Soviet pact with Germany),[151] was clearly indifferent to the outcome of the talks with the Soviet Union by 20 June 1939,[152] and when they broke down exhibited no reaction whatever, no surprise, outrage, disappointment, sense of a valuable and missed opportunity or fear for the future of British foreign policy in Europe without an alliance with the Soviet Union to contain Germany.[153] He had also earlier, at the beginning of July, indicated his weariness and alienation in regard to the Soviet Union given the latter's diplomatic tactics.[154] It is possible that Halifax may have been influenced, as he had been over Munich, by Cadogan's changing view, for Halifax gave his scathing account of his perception of Soviet foreign policy to Cabinet on 4 July 1939, which is entirely consistent with the timing of Cadogan's wearied indifference. What is obvious is that, having had a commonality of preference for talks, albeit reluctant in both cases, by 4 July both Cadogan and Halifax had very different estimations of the worth of any alliance with the Soviet Union to contain Germany.

The inference, and in fact the only explanation, is that the sequence of negotiations had resulted in a British sense of the alliance's being worth less than they had expected it would be, as a result of Soviet diplomatic tactics, which had more than confirmed British adverse attitudes by eliciting specific mistrust. There may also have been a British sense that the Soviet Union was not in the end needed in quite the way the French felt it was, as, with a more profound fear of a German alliance with the Soviet Union, it seemed the French were prepared to go further to effect an alliance than the British were. It is worth noting that while pursuing the Soviet Union for an alliance at least in part to preclude an alliance between the Soviet Union and Germany, the British did not know of the talks going on between the Soviet Union and Germany in August 1939. While the existence of adverse British attitudes and initial British misunderstanding of Soviet objectives is not disputed, it seems that they exerted causal influence in an indirect, contextual way, and that it was British experience of Soviet diplomatic exchanges that were opportunistic in nature and governed by Soviet interests regardless of others' and of diplomatic norms that left British politicians and officials feeling with reason that any alliance would not be worth much, and that the final concession over the Baltics was impossible. That makes Soviet demands and diplomatic behaviour during the negotiations the decisive factor in the breakdown of the talks. Without such Soviet diplomacy British attitudes could have remained of little influence on the course of the negotiations (given that they had been overcome in the decision to engage in talks), and an alliance might have been concluded.

Certainly, the ensuing British view of the Soviet Union was that it would meet its treaty and other obligations only if it suited Soviet purposes at the time, and this was a view that endured, assisted by further evidence in its support, during the war (albeit with some apparent aberrations that did not endure long and seem to have been associated with the euphoria of anticipated victory) and after the war (despite an apparent initial conflation of need and possibility). The adverse experience of negotiating with the Soviets of the summer of 1939 intensified previous British attitudes of ideological aversion because of the nature, intentions and tactics of Soviet diplomacy and foreign policy, a Soviet policy seen as driven by a search for security that could not be differentiated from opportunistic expansionism and that was characterised by violations of diplomatic protocols and no concern for norms of reciprocity. The emerging view was that the dominant influence on Soviet foreign policy was a profound Soviet fear of Germany that resulted in opportunistic occupation of territories between them, combined with a Soviet desire to remain uninvolved as capitalist nations exhausted themselves in war with each other.

That does of course indicate a belief in communist ideological objectives as well as *Realpolitik* optimisation of outcomes in security or opportunistic terms. It is worth noting that these attitudes are far more specific than the general attitudinal revulsion for the Soviet Union and communism that had existed prior to the negotiations and can only be a consequence of the British experience of them and of Molotov's impenetrable and obstructive diplomacy.

Given the centrality of a modicum of trust in diplomacy and any formation of an alliance, it is worth considering just how much influence the charmless Molotov exerted on the course of the negotiations. He was certainly loathed by a series of thoroughly exasperated British politicians and officials. Seeds found him 'a man totally ignorant of foreign affairs and to whom the idea of negotiation – as distinct from the will of his party leader – was utterly alien' with 'a rather foolish cunning of the type of the peasant',[155] while Cadogan found him 'almost impossible to deal with',[156] and Halifax found his diplomacy bewildering, noting that he was so 'inarticulate' that it would be difficult for Seeds to find out exactly what was required.[157] And it does seem that he did exert some influence on the outcome of the negotiations, for his diplomacy, characterised as it was by a combination of impenetrability, rudeness and an escalating series of demands, elicited a bewildered mistrust in British politicians and officials and left them feeling that no Soviet undertaking could be relied upon. This was in the event a correct inference, in that he was carrying on a parallel set of negotiations with the Germans (responding favourably to German overtures) from early August 1939. Carley notes that Naggiar, the French ambassador to the Soviet Union, felt that Molotov's rudeness manifested a mistrust of British and French proposals. Naggiar found 'an abruptness that disdained traditional diplomatic usages' that was intentional and inferred that 'the new commissar' 'now intends to obtain more extensive advantages'.[158] Yet it is almost certain that Molotov himself exerted no effect whatever on the content and nature (as opposed to the form) of Soviet foreign policy, for the latter was dictated by Stalin, reflected a combination of perceptions informed by communist ideology and an opportunism of hard bargaining that was a Russian tradition, and was followed to the letter by the obedient Molotov. Yet while British diplomats and politicians alike were revolted and alienated by him Molotov did have a clear sense of the material realities of power and of negotiating postures (if not of diplomatic protocol and manners).

I have established that it was Soviet diplomacy in form and content that was the decisive factor in the breakdown of the talks, which clearly foundered on the definition of 'indirect aggression'. It is also worth noting that it was the Soviet Union rather than Britain which ended the talks in August 1939.

To attempt to trace causal factors further back than the reality of Soviet attitudes as they manifested themselves in Soviet diplomacy during the talks, one could argue that the Soviet experience of British appeasement and its end explains their exploitative attitude, given that they knew that the British had made an unwise guarantee to Poland that could not be given effect to without Soviet help, and that they had reason to feel that the British were weak and would give in to Soviet demands in the same way as they had to Hitler's. While the spectacle of a series of British concessions to Hitler to avoid war cannot have helped British credibility, the ensuing history of Soviet diplomacy during and after World War II tends to indicate that their hard bargaining stance, morbid suspicion and exploitative attitude were the Soviet approach to diplomacy and to power, not least when dealing with western powers whose motives were inherently suspect because they were capitalist.

Another contextual factor may have been rather more compelling in its influence on Soviet diplomacy and so an indirect causal factor in the breakdown of the talks, for from the beginning of August 1939 the Soviet Union had the possible option of a pact with Germany that would give them the Baltics and the possibility of part of Poland, and war in the west rather than the east, while it seemed that Britain needed the Soviet Union to effect a credible deterrent of a war on two fronts for Hitler.

One may use later evidence of Soviet diplomacy as evidence of its reality in 1939, as attitudes and orientations endure for long periods. There was the very similar adverse experience of Soviet diplomacy over the Baltics (again) during the war, between November 1941 and February 1942, when Baggallay advised that Soviet diplomacy should be met with a British tactic of hard bargaining and that unilateral concessions would elicit only suspicion, mistrust and exploitation. The nature of Soviet foreign policy during the negotiations of 1939 did not then reflect a history of mistrust of Britain but rather a Russian tradition of hard bargaining and a communist opportunistic and exploitative attitude that respected only power, and a Soviet prism of attitudes in which the ends (of securing communist government in one state and the creation of a security buffer around the state to that end, which was in itself expansionist) justified any means used (including violation of diplomatic norms and brazen, exploitative opportunism in relation to any perceived weakness, which included any concession) and which included a morbid suspiciousness of capitalist powers and their motives.

One could infer from the fact that the Soviet Union allied itself in the end with Nazi Germany, a state violently antipathetic to communism and the Soviet state (more so than the capitalist powers) and with undisguised designs in the east (for '*Lebensraum*'), that the attitudes of parties with whom they were negotiating were less causally influential in Soviet diplomacy than the optimisation of advantages seen as immediate and material, and so not necessitating Soviet trust, as was so in the Baltics case.

As has been seen, there was an essential asymmetry of need in the talks. It is true that the Soviet Union needed protection against Nazi Germany, an ideological enemy and a great power with a known expansionist intention in the east. Yet the Soviet Union did not have an ally whose independence it had guaranteed in western Europe and for which it needed British military power, whereas Britain had guaranteed Poland's independence in eastern Europe and had no means of giving immediate effect to that guarantee, or in fact of making it credible to Germany, without an alliance with the Soviet Union. The Soviet Union also had a measure of protection afforded them by the British guarantee of Poland, for if Germany attempted to invade the Soviet Union through Poland Britain would go to war to defend Poland, which meant that the Soviet Union would not need an alliance with Britain to elicit British support against Germany in that eventuality. And while there remained the possibility of an attack on the Soviet Union from Germany through the Baltic states, which was the ostensible reason for the Soviet demand that the Baltics be included in the terms of the proposed alliance with the British (for a tripartite alliance would have meant a British declaration of war on Germany in the event of an attack on the Soviet Union by Germany), the Soviet Union did have the options of isolation and a pact with Germany. For, as has been seen, by early August 1939 the Soviet Union had the clear possibility of coming to terms with Germany, though it is not known from what date the Soviet Union knew it could attain its objective of a zone in the Baltics (and eastern Poland) that would serve to distance the Soviet Union from any invasion (there had been no experience of *Blitzkrieg* in 1939).

Soviet diplomacy does then seem to have reflected paranoid perceptions of Western intentions derived from Bolshevik experience, the legitimisation of means by ends and expansionism of communist ideology and a tradition of bargaining and opportunism that may have been enhanced by a sense of relative British weakness, given that the British need may have been perceived to be greater. Further, British appeasement of Germany had demonstrated the extent of British weakness and susceptibility to escalating demands, and there was the fact that the Soviet Union was in a position to collude with Germany and so derive control over the Baltic region (and part of eastern Poland) and guarantee war in the west rather than the east. It is far less likely that Soviet diplomacy reflected a history of British commitment to the Whites during the civil war and of British loathing of communism and the Soviet Union as a state, with concomitant mistrust of British motives, for the record since that time was decidedly mixed, and Britain had endorsed Soviet membership of the League of Nations. The context of the negotiations was one of British need and Soviet options, which does however again argue for an opportunism that was inherent in Soviet policy and diplomacy.

It is not tenable that the British government's ultimate resistance was interpreted by Stalin as evidence that Britain was encouraging Germany to go to war with the Soviet Union, for the sequence of concessions must have made clear British seriousness of intent, and the evidence is that the Soviet Union was attempting to optimise its outcomes in the east of Europe in terms of territorial acquisition and securing war in the west rather than the east. It also seems plausible that Stalin may have realised that war with Germany was inevitable at some time given German ideological antipathy for the Soviet state and communism and aspirations in eastern Europe, and that he concluded the Ribbentrop-Molotov pact in part to permit the Red Army time to prepare for war, for under the terms of the pact both nations undertook to remain neutral in the event of the other going to war and Hitler had security in the east and so would have become involved in a war in the west when he invaded western Poland. In other words the treaty with Germany was the preferred option for the Soviets on entirely pragmatic grounds.

The clear military guarantees the tripartite alliance with Britain and France would have offered seem to preclude attribution of an exclusively defensive orientation to Stalin's policy, though of course securing war in the west between Germany and Britain and France protected the Red Army from war at least for the time being and gave it time to prepare itself for war. Even so it does seem clear that Stalin's diplomacy in 1939 was informed at least in part by a desire to extend Soviet territory westwards and extort every possible advantage. As ever with Soviet diplomacy, whether this apparent expansionism could be described as a concern with security in the desire for the creation of a series of buffer states is problematic, a difficulty that was to endure in assessing the nature of Soviet intentions. In the event, with the talks intended to conclude an alliance between Britain and the Soviet Union stalled, the conclusion of the Nazi-Soviet pact on 23 August 1939 optimised Stalin's outcomes, including cession of the Baltic states except Lithuania to the Soviet Union, the partition of Poland between Germany and the Soviet Union, and virtual certainty of war in the west over Poland.

Part of my argument against Shaw's and Carley's claim that it was prejudice against the Soviet Union and communism within the British political elite that caused the failure of the negotiations and the proposed alliance is that the British political elite were prepared to enter into negotiations with the Soviet Union for an alliance to contain Hitler and to make a series of concessions during the talks, so it must have been their experience of the diplomacy of the Soviet Union that changed their view as to the desirability of an alliance. Having overcome their adverse attitudes, I have argued, it was Soviet diplomatic tactics and demands that alienated the British to the extent that they came to feel that any alliance would be worthless – the final Soviet demand also conferred upon the Soviet Union the right to commit Britain to war over the Baltics when it chose to do so and seemed, in a context of British experience of Soviet opportunism during the negotiations, to bear a likelihood of Britain's being involved in war against Germany in support of Soviet action in the Baltics without any German aggression there.

As has been seen above, however, it could be argued that the adverse attitudes of the British politicians and diplomats involved were apparent in the initial British invitation to the Soviet Union to offer guarantees to eastern European countries, which met British objectives but took no account of Soviet needs and objectives such as security. The course of the negotiations would then have been bound to demonstrate that the Soviet Union was not prepared to undertake such onerous obligations without some return in terms of security. The case would be that British attitudes were reflected in the terms they sought to impose on the Soviet Union and that these were rejected as they were unfair. The ensuing outrage of British politicians and diplomats at the reactions of the Soviet representatives is then explained by reference to the same British 'prejudice' that had informed the terms offered to the Soviet Union.

It has been seen that the initial British position, which invited the Soviet Union to offer promises of support to eastern European states, and the ensuing initial refusal to accept the Soviet offer of an alliance, may have been informed by adverse British attitudes, though it has also been argued that the initial British position may be explained by the fact that it was the Soviet Union that proposed an alliance and seemed to be in greater threat of German invasion. In any event such attitudes and their representation in policy positions were overcome in the ensuing negotiations and the series of concessions that the British made to the Soviet Union. Further, the terms of the proposed alliance provided for mutual assistance in the event of attack by Germany and were evenly balanced in terms of commitment. The Soviet Union may have felt that the British need was greater and that British options were far more limited, but this would indicate an opportunist Soviet policy.

The Soviet Union may also have felt that the likelihood of a German attack in the east was greater, and so have argued that the terms without a British guarantee of the Baltics were unfair. Yet the Soviet Union was guaranteed against German attack by Britain even under a tripartite alliance, and given that the Baltics would also have been covered under the terms of the proposed alliance if their governments requested assistance against German invasion there was no need in defensive terms or on security grounds for the definition of 'indirect aggression' upon which the Soviet Union insisted unless the concern was that the Baltics would seek German protection and so become a threat.

Even so a tripartite alliance would have covered the eventuality of a German attack on the Soviet Union itself. And Soviet diplomacy during the negotiations was such that it was reasonable for a negotiating party to infer that the Soviet Union would not be an ally upon which they could depend. Over the British decision to reject the final Soviet demand over the Baltics the British reaction was also reasonable. British 'prejudice' was not necessary in either case.

One could argue that there was some British incomprehension of the Soviet view of its own position and its possibilities, but had there been no such misunderstanding the likelihood is that the British political and official elite would never have considered negotiations for an alliance in the first place. There was no diplomatic precedent for the series of escalating demands with which British diplomats were faced in the negotiations themselves, and the British had no experience of such diplomatic encounters. Further, the motives of the Soviet Union were to remain a matter of speculation in the West in general, a Western mystification that their diplomatic tactics did nothing to dispel, as the bewilderment of Halifax and after him Eden and Bevin indicates, and as was expressed with characteristic eloquence by Churchill when he referred to the Soviet Union as 'an enigma wrapped inside a riddle'. British incomprehension regarding Soviet tactics and intentions prior to the negotiations and even during them was then comprehensible.

One final possibility that might attribute the breakdown of the talks to adverse British attitudes towards communism and the Soviet Union exists, though it is not one claimed by Shaw or Carley, both of whom point to the influence of such adverse British attitudes without adducing any evidence of any direct effect of such adverse attitudes on British policy at the time. They do not for instance produce any evidence of British concern, at the time of the British refusal over the Soviet definition of 'indirect aggression' (which was after all the ultimate stumbling block), regarding the westwards expansion of communism and Soviet influence, which could be attributed to previously existing adverse British attitudes towards the Soviet Union and communism.

Even so adverse British attitudes towards communism and the Soviet Union may have been reactivated (after having been overcome by *Realpolitik* considerations in the initiation of the negotiations and the series of British concessions that ensued) by the nature of the final Soviet demand, which meant surrendering to the Soviet Union the right to interfere in the Baltics when it chose to do so with British support (in other words, Britain would have ceded to the Soviet Union the right to set the time at which and the circumstances under which Britain would go to war, including the possibility that it would do so to safeguard or optimise perceived Soviet interests). In this explanation British mistrust of the Soviet Union that existed prior to the summer of 1939 would have become salient to British diplomacy again because the final Soviet demand would permit it to commit Britain to war.

The case would be then that such British mistrust of the Soviet Union caused the British refusal. This is persuasive, yet it represents no more than part of a picture at the end of July 1939. To start with, British politicians may have asked themselves why the Soviet Union would have so insisted upon such a definition of the term had they no intention of using it for territorial acquisition. The definition of 'indirect aggression' the Soviet Union insisted upon was not needed for the defence of Soviet territory, as there were British guarantees of (1) the Soviet Union under the terms even of a tripartite alliance, and (2) support for the Baltics in the event of their requesting help against

Germany under the terms of the proposed alliance that included other states. As there was no evidence whatever, at the time of the British refusal, of British concern regarding the spread of communism and Soviet influence, it does seem that the reason for Britain's refusal over the Baltics was fear of being involved in war in support of Soviet expansionism.

It was also not unnatural for Britain to have wished to retain the right to decide when and for what reason it would go to war, a right that Britain's guarantee to Poland had taken care not to remove. And if there was some influence from a general British mistrust of the Soviet Union one should not attribute it solely to previously held adverse British attitudes, given that they had been overcome or set aside (Shaw's own terms) in the initiation of talks and the concessions that followed. For there was also the adverse British experience of the negotiations themselves, in which the diplomacy of the Soviet Union had been bewildering for British politicians unused to an exclusive and brazen concern with power and opportunism and disregard for diplomatic protocol.

There was also a British sense that the British position had moved as far as it should, that the Soviet Union would be an unreliable ally and a sense that no further diplomatic humiliation should be countenanced, all of which were at least in part the result of the British experience of the talks. Experience of the negotiations resulted in British politicians and diplomats abandoning an earlier hope that the Soviet Union might concede over the definition of 'indirect aggression' given so many other British concessions to Soviet demands as a sense of Soviet untrustworthiness diminished the perceived worth of any alliance. Such entirely rational objections to British acceptance of the final Soviet demand over 'indirect aggression' indicate that pre-existing adverse British attitudes towards communism and the Soviet Union (rather than perceptions of Soviet intentions derived from the talks) were not a necessary condition for the British refusal to accept the Soviet definition of 'indirect aggression' which resulted in the talks' breakdown.

Yet one cannot establish with certainty that such prior adverse attitudes towards the Soviet Union and communism had no effect whatever on the mistrust of the Soviet Union that informed the British refusal to accept the final Soviet demand over the Baltics and that left the British political and official elite feeling that any alliance would be worthless. For one would then be attributing the entirety of the British position to the British experience of Soviet diplomacy during the talks, which while plausible, in that the form and content of Soviet diplomacy was no doubt sufficient to seed doubt as to Soviet intent in a government that had no prejudices, the psychological universe of the British political and official elite was pervaded by such attitudes, and the British experience of Soviet diplomacy was through that attitudinal prism. Having said that of course the existence of a factor does not indicate that it was causally significant. What can be said with some certainty is that adverse British attitudes before the talks were not a sufficient condition for the stalling of the talks.

To elaborate upon this distinction, though adverse British attitudes towards communism and the Soviet Union may in logical terms not have been a necessary condition to the final British position in the negotiations, one has to question if it is psychologically plausible that such a context of adverse attitudes, albeit overcome by *Realpolitik* in the sense of a need for an alliance to contain Hitler, should have had no effect whatever on the final British sense of mistrust of the Soviets.

In other words, while it is psychologically implausible that the intervening experience of Soviet diplomacy should have had no effect whatever on British policy and the final British position and feeling, it is also unlikely that previously existing adverse attitudes towards communism and the Soviet Union had no influence at all. This questions what one is discussing when one refers to causal influences and their effect. One may however conclude that such previously existing attitudes did not exert a decisive influence, in that with a different experience of the negotiations they might have exerted no influence whatever.

Further, Shaw's representation of such British attitudes as 'prejudice' is not justified, because 'prejudice' indicates attitudes for which there is no objective justification, and British attitudes of mistrust were confirmed by the content and form of Soviet diplomacy during the negotiations, so much so that even a country without Britain's anti-communist and anti-Soviet attitudes would have declined to accept the Soviet demand over the Baltics because of its expansionist intent and consequence in terms of commitment to war, and would have inferred that the Soviet Union would have been an unreliable ally from the Soviet conduct of the negotiations. Though part of the prism through which the British would have experienced Soviet diplomacy in 1939, previously held British attitudes were not then a necessary condition to the final impasse over 'indirect aggression' and British loss of confidence in the worth of any possible alliance.

It is clear that the British doubt regarding the Soviet Union's military capability was such that the main British purpose in negotiating an alliance was to deter Hitler from war and further expansionism in Europe and to forestall a pact between Germany and the Soviet Union (rather than Britain's expecting that the alliance would have to be implemented as a result of war and expecting Soviet military help).[159] Yet the evidence is clear that such British objectives were genuine and compelling reasons for an alliance as far as the British were concerned. Further, as has been seen, the evidence supports the inference that it was Soviet diplomacy in content and form that was the immediate reason for the talks' failure. It is also clear that since the beginning of August 1939 the Soviet Union was assessing the British terms against those being pursued with the Germans, that is, choosing between their options to secure the most immediate advantage for the Soviet Union. The Soviet escalation of demands following each British concession violated all diplomatic norms of reciprocity and resulted from a combination of communist ideology and a Russian tradition of hard bargaining rather than from a history of adverse British attitudes towards the Soviet Union and communism.

It may have been that there was a British miscalculation as to the preparedness of the Soviet Union to accept the final British position over 'indirect aggression', and it does seem that the British did not know of the beginning of Soviet political talks with Germany at the beginning of August 1939, but such a miscalculation would only be a causal influence on the breakdown of the talks if Britain would have been prepared to concede to the final Soviet demand had they known that the Soviet Union was not prepared to accept the British definition and was pursuing the alternative of a pact with Germany. While the evidence is clear that, without that information, the FPC had decided on 26 July 1939 that no further compromises should be countenanced,[160] it is impossible to assess what effect such knowledge of an imminent pact between the Soviet Union and Germany would have had on British policy.

It was then a Soviet withdrawal from the talks and their concluding a pact with Nazi Germany that ended the negotiations with the British. The reasons behind Soviet diplomacy in its tactics and objectives would seem to be numerous. I have alluded above to the idea that Soviet diplomacy was decisively influenced by a history of adverse British attitudes and policies towards the Soviet Union from the time of the revolution onwards that evidenced a clear British loathing of Bolshevism, communism and the emerging Soviet state. It is certainly true that there had been British involvement to assist the Whites in the Russian civil war that followed the Bolshevik revolution and an uneven and remote relationship during the 1920s. There had also been British refusals to be drawn into any alliance to contain Germany, and the British policy of appeasement of Germany. Yet the latter indicates a foreign policy that was reflective not of anti-Bolshevik loathing but of concern regarding Hitler's aspirations as the major threat to European peace.

The exclusion of the Soviets from the Munich Agreement for instance reflected Hitler's insistence rather than a British and French preference. Further, the record is mixed. There had been and continued to be significant evidence of antipathy for the Bolshevik revolution, communism and the Soviet state in the British political, official and military establishment, but there had also been, in more recent years, British support for the Soviet Union in the latter's joining the League of Nations in 1934, cordial relationships with Litvinov and Maisky, and, in the context of avoiding joining France in an alliance with the Soviet Union in 1935, a clear British commitment to collective security under League of Nations auspices, which one could argue is evidence of a dissonance between British attitudes and British policy pursued for pragmatic reasons.

The more plausible inference is that Soviet experience of British policy and diplomacy towards the Soviet Union and Germany was less compelling as an influence on Soviet foreign policy than a basic mistrust of any capitalist power on ideological grounds, which also resulted in a fear of the Western powers combining against the Soviet Union. It seems more likely that it was a combination of a Russian tradition of opportunistic hard bargaining and an ideology of profound mistrust of capitalist powers that legitimised any means to Soviet ends and that produced a policy in which exploiting British need through an escalation of demands was a natural form of diplomacy in the negotiations. It would also explain why the Soviets felt that an important objective of such negotiations should be obtaining something material rather than undertakings from Britain and France, as in the idea of a series of buffer states to the west of the Soviet Union to protect it from attack.

Soviet experience of British diplomacy prior to the negotiations does not seem to have a necessary condition to Soviet mistrust of British intentions given the major role of ideology in Soviet perceptions of Western motives. The credibility of this explanation is enhanced by the history of Soviet diplomacy during World War II and after, for it seems that the Soviet Union was in 1939 engaging in that form of diplomacy that was to become characteristic of the Soviet approach to international relations. This took the form of impenetrability as to ultimate ends and no attempt to engender trust combined with what seemed to any interacting party to be an exploitative opportunism in which escalation of demands replaced the diplomatic norm of reciprocation, and crude territorial aggrandisement was the undisguised objective.

Further, the history of British policy towards the Soviet Union only reflected a history of adverse British attitudes towards communism and the Soviet Union during periods in which other, more compelling *Realpolitik* considerations did not obtain, which is in fact just what the theoretical literature on the relationship between attitudes and behaviour would indicate. It then seems that the antipathy for, and suspicion of, capitalist powers (including Britain) inherent in Bolshevik ideology and a Russian tradition of opportunistic hard bargaining were in themselves sufficient to produce the type of Soviet diplomacy both in form and objective that British politicians and diplomats experienced in the negotiations for an alliance in 1939 – adverse British attitudes were not a necessary condition to the Soviet attitudes, perceptions, purposes and diplomatic tactics that so bewildered and appalled British politicians and diplomats.

It is also worth noting that from the beginning of August 1939 the Soviet Union was comparing the possibility of an alliance with Britain and France against the advantages of a possible alliance with Germany. That introduces another view of the causation of the breakdown of the talks, for it is plausible to argue that neither adverse British nor Soviet ideological attitudes were necessary conditions, and that Stalin just chose the optimal policy on strict foreign policy grounds in 1939. The collective security option offered by Britain and France was from nations that were steeped in appeasement and whose credibility to Hitler as deterrents was poor, so that Stalin would have had to consider the situation in the event of war rather than the value of a pact as a deterrent. In that event the most plausible initial incident would have been a German attack on Poland as the immediate object of Hitler's latest territorial demand, the Danzig Corridor. That would have meant war in the east and Red Army involvement against German troops to give effect to what had been a British guarantee of Poland (if the alliance dictated defence of eastern European states requesting assistance rather than being a tripartite pact, though even then, if Hitler attacked Poland, there was a likelihood that he would attack the Soviet Union too and so engage the Red Army) and would have left British and French troops less involved than an unprepared Red Army in war in the east.

The alternative for Stalin was a pact with Hitler that gave Hitler what he wanted in western Poland (and a sphere of influence in central and eastern Europe covering Austria, Hungary and Romania that Stalin acknowledged as German, so that German expansion into either of the latter states would not have been a cause of war between the Soviets and Germany) and, with war declared by Britain over the German occupation of western Poland, war between Germany and Britain and France in the west rather than between the Soviet Union and Germany in the east. That of course meant that the Red Army would have had time to prepare for war and the terms of the pact would have meant too that the Soviet Union would have had a perceived buffer against any future German attack through assimilation of most of the Baltics, Bessarabia and Bukovina, and eastern Poland into the Soviet Union because such countries were considered part of the Soviet sphere of influence.

The non-aggression pact with Germany also secured for Stalin avoidance of an alliance between Germany and Japan and of the prospect of war on two fronts, and in fact meant no war on either front. It is worth noting that communist and Bolshevik ideological attitudes need not have been involved in such a rational foreign-policy decision, which disregarded years of anti-Bolshevik and anti-communist German propaganda.

Though British refusal to surrender the Baltic republics to Stalin was ostensibly the cause of the breakdown of the talks, even had the British surrendered the Baltics the German offer would have been better for Stalin because it also gave him most of the Baltics, the eastern half of Poland, Bessarabia and Bukovina as part of the Soviet Union, eastern Finland acknowledged as within the Soviet sphere of influence, and a guarantee of any war being in the west rather than the east following Hitler's invasion of Poland.

Collective security in the form of an Anglo-Soviet alliance was an option that even with British surrender over the Baltic republics could have been seen by Stalin as an ineffective deterrent and as making plausible war in the east through Poland, with Britain and France being less involved in the west (if at all in the Soviet perception, seeing Western capitalist countries as inherently treacherous and antipathetic to the revolution). The German offer was then on any rational grounds just better even had the British surrendered the Baltics.

Such reasoning is of course counterfactual because the influence of rationality existed alongside attitudinal and ideological influences and those of individual personalities. Having said that the influence of rational optimisation and pragmatism in Stalin seems apparent in his finally concluding a non-aggression pact with an even more profound ideological enemy of communism than the Western liberal democracies represented, fascist Nazi Germany, a country that had emitted a stream of anti-Bolshevik and anti-Slav rhetoric during the 1930s. Realism seems to have been more compelling for Stalin in 1939 than adverse ideological or personal attitudes in the choice of a pact with Germany. Such relative importance of *Realpolitik* over ideology was to recur during World War II, when Stalin introduced some liberalisation in the Soviet Union to optimise the war effort through nationalist rather than ideological appeals, and in the alliance with Britain and the US.

Though the preceding paragraph is correct in pointing to Stalinist optimisation of returns to the Soviet Union the political talks with Germany did not begin before the impasse with Britain over the Baltics had been reached, which means that it is possible that if Britain had surrendered over the Baltics an alliance would have been concluded with the Soviet Union on the basis that the British terms would have been the best that were on offer to Stalin at the time. That would only though place responsibility for the breakdown of the talks on British mistrust of the Soviets from their experience of Soviet diplomacy during the negotiations or on previously existing ideological aversion enhanced by such experience of Soviet diplomacy in the summer of 1939, in other words, on Soviet tactics and objectives in the negotiations for an alliance in the summer of 1939.

Further, though the final German agreement to the cession of Finland, Estonia, Latvia, eastern

Poland and Bessarabia to a Soviet sphere of influence was not received by Stalin until 21 August, that date is indicative of previous Soviet demands and of negotiations over such demands in the preceding weeks, as has been seen. The Soviets had been in talks over economic matters with the Germans for months and it seems that the Germans attempted to preclude an alliance between the Soviet Union and the British and the French and the prospect of war on two fronts by the offer of terms for a political settlement that were better than those offered by Britain and France even had the Baltics been surrendered. The Soviets had insisted that an economic agreement with the Germans was a precondition for a political agreement, and there had been reference to the possibility of political discussions well before early August 1939 by the Soviets and the Germans. Hill's view is that by the time Britain decided to negotiate an alliance with the Soviet Union 'developments in German-Soviet relations had already rendered it nugatory', though he provides no evidence to support the assertion, which seems to refer to the Cabinet decision on 24 May 1939. It is possible that he is referring to an implicit Soviet promise of political talks with Germany once the economic talks were complete, though that would not establish that Soviet negotiations with Germany were bound to end in a pact that would be preferred to British and French terms, for though that did in fact happen it could not have been known by the Soviets in May 1939.[161]

The German terms in August 1939 were of course much better for Stalin than the British terms would have been even with the surrender of the Baltics, as has been seen, and the nature of the German offer would have been a decisive influence on the pragmatic and optimising Soviets. It does seem plausible from the above that the timing of the start of the political talks between the Soviets and the Germans just reflected the time taken to conclude an economic agreement and that Stalin intended to optimise outcomes by comparing the German and British and French offers. That would, as has been seen, be entirely consistent with Stalin's pragmatic and opportunistic approach to negotiation. The pact concluded with Germany did in fact leave the Soviet Union with a complete buffer on its western border because Lithuania had at the time no common border with the Soviet Union. Any German attack would have had to come through Poland or Latvia, which were to the east of Lithuania and separated Germany from the Soviet Union. Though it would seem that both a pact with Germany and an alliance with the British and the French depended to some extent upon trust, a significant factor given Bolshevik paranoia that suspected all Western diplomacy, the nature of such 'trust' varied.

In the case of the British and French alliance Stalin would have been trusting those Western powers to come to the aid of the Soviet Union in the event of an attack by Germany. In the case of a pact with Germany Stalin must have been assured that it was in Hitler's interests not to wage war on two fronts (avoidance of having to wage war against Germany and Japan simultaneously would have been an attraction of the pact with Germany for Stalin in 1939), and given that German occupation of western Poland (the most immediate object of Hitler's attention and grievances in the summer of 1939) under the terms of the proposed pact would have elicited British and French declarations of war Stalin was in fact only 'trusting' Hitler to optimise his own outcomes by avoiding war on two fronts by refraining from an attack on the Soviet Union (regardless of ideological imperatives). In the event, when in 1941 Hitler did attack the Soviet Union and violated the principle of avoidance of war on two fronts, in what was seemingly a consequence of the triumph of ideology over rationality, the outcome was decisive and consequential defeat.

Because German aspirations in the east of Europe were known it would then seem that one of the main attractions of the pact with Germany for Stalin, apart from territorial acquisition of buffer states, would have been the virtual guarantee of war in the west rather than in the east, for Hitler's being engaged in a war with the Western capitalist powers would have been optimal for Stalin in seeming to guarantee war in the west between Germany and Britain and France and promise their mutual exhaustion even as it permitted the Red Army time to prepare for any future war. It is worth noting that when Poland was attacked neither Britain nor France did anything in military terms, just declared war on Germany, a diplomatic reaction that did nothing to assist the Poles, and it seems plausible that something similar would have taken place in the event of a German attack on the Soviet Union. It is also worth noting that Stalin initially refused to believe indications of an imminent German attack in 1941, an indication of his conviction that Hitler's war in the west precluded an attack on the Soviet Union for some time at least.

Though Shaw, in what seems to be an attempt to exculpate Stalin from responsibility for the breakdown of negotiations for an alliance with the British and to attribute such responsibility to British rather than Soviet attitudes, claims that Stalin's approach to foreign policy was opportunistic and *Realpolitik* in nature rather than ideological in purpose, Bolshevik paranoia as to Western objectives was very much part of the Soviet prism of perception. It would therefore have informed Soviet objectives and policy choices. It is, of course, possible that both *Realpolitik* and ideology informed Soviet foreign policy in the summer of 1939, with ideology influencing a perception of Western hostility and *Realpolitik* influencing the perception of strategic interests and optimisation of what was possible to achieve in terms of security from attack.[162] Even if Stalin's approach to foreign policy was pragmatic it would not follow that British attitudes of revulsion for communism and the Soviet Union caused the breakdown of talks for an alliance, for it indicates that Stalin intended to compare Anglo-French and German terms to optimise Soviet security and that Stalin would have chosen German over Anglo-French terms even if the latter endorsed the Soviet definition of 'indirect aggression' because the German terms provided for war in the west rather than the east and ceded a buffer zone of states between Germany and the Soviet Union to Stalin. It does not indicate that adverse British attitudes towards communism and the Soviet Union were the cause of there being no alliance, for Soviet behaviour regardless of its source was such as to diminish Soviet credibility as an ally even for a country that had no adverse attitudes towards communism or the Soviet Union as a state.

Conclusion

The preceding paragraphs indicate two conclusions. To begin with the impasse reached by the British with the Soviets over the definition of 'indirect aggression' in the Baltics reflected British experience of an escalation of Soviet demands after each British concession and a British conclusion that the Soviets were not to be trusted to meet any treaty obligation if it did not suit their interests at the time, which of course made any alliance worthless as a deterrent or in the event of war. There was also the fact that the definition of 'indirect aggression' demanded by Molotov could only be interpreted in one way, that is, to facilitate Soviet acquisition of the Baltics with British approval, though possibly to preclude nationalist Baltic regimes affiliating themselves with Germany to counteract the Soviet threat. And there was the implication that the Soviets could obligate Britain to go to war when all that had happened was that the Baltics had resisted Soviet aggression or influence and had turned to Germany for protection, or when nothing had happened in the Baltics at all and the Soviet claims of a realignment towards Germany were false and designed to permit Soviet occupation and assimilation of the Baltics into the Soviet Union.

These are the reasons why the Anglo-Soviet talks stalled and the British military discussions that ensued were instructed to go slow to delay war until the eastern winter. The prospect of an alliance had by this time been abandoned by the British because of the content and form of Soviet diplomacy during the negotiations, which in turn could be attributed to Soviet ideological objectives and suspicion and mistrust of the West, and to a combination of pragmatic security concerns, opportunistic expansionism and rational optimisation of outcomes.

The ultimate cause of the breakdown of the talks was the Ribbentrop-Molotov pact and the fact that even had the British surrendered to the Soviets over the Baltics, the right of passage through

Poland and Romania and over military discussions Stalin's optimisation of outcomes meant that he would have chosen the German offer over any British offer because of the greater territorial acquisitions in the Baltics and from Poland and Romania and because a pact with Germany secured for him a German war in the west rather than in the east with an unprepared Red Army. Though the timing of the start of political talks with the Germans makes it uncertain it seems that Stalin did not intend to conclude a pact with Britain and France without comparing it to any German offer, not least as the Soviets and the Germans had been negotiating an economic agreement prior to political talks during the talks with Britain and France.

That is of course conjecture and it is possible that had the Soviet definition of 'indirect aggression' been accepted in July 1939 there would not have been political talks with the Germans, though that would not be consonant with evidence of Soviet optimisation of outcomes in other circumstances. Though Shaw claims that had Stalin believed that British and French terms would not be worth much he would have made more effort to secure better relations with the Germans, the argument here is that rational optimisation of outcomes for Stalin would have indicated a policy of optimising concessions from the British and French to use as a means of extorting concessions from the Germans when terms were compared and a policy of not seeming too enthusiastic with the Germans to that end.

Arad sees the appointment on 3 May of Molotov in place of the more westernised Litvinov as an indication of a reorientation of Soviet policy from Britain and France to Germany because Litvinov was Jewish and seen by Germany as a barrier to talks with the Soviet Union for a pact, though the continuance of talks with British and French representatives through the summer of 1939 would seem to indicate a desire to compare terms from either alternative and to use talks with the British and French to bargain with the Germans for optimal terms.[163] That would of course be far more consonant with other evidence of Soviet optimisation of outcomes.

Establishing that British and French, and Soviet, attitudes may not have been necessary conditions to the breakdown of talks, that Stalin could have opted for the non-aggression pact with Germany on strictly rational, optimising grounds in a foreign-policy decision unaffected by ideology and attitudinal orientation does not mean that such factors were not influential in actuality. For in the natural experiment that is history there is no possibility of isolation of variables and so no possibility of attributing extent of causal influence to causal factors. Further, all decisions would be informed by perceptions that reflected ideological orientations as well as rational appreciation of the alternatives. Such causal factors would never be isolated from each other or discrete in terms of the experience of those making the judgments and decisions at the time. Instead such factors would be implicit in the way a situation would have been perceived and appraised and alternatives judged, for causal factors interact with each other to produce a Gestalt of personal experience. The argument is that ideological factors were not influential in the British case and that the stalling of the talks reflected experience of Soviet diplomacy in form and content that would have obtained with any country regardless of ideological orientation.

In the case of the Soviet Union a combination of Bolshevik ideological mistrust and rational optimisation seem plausible as causes. It is possible that Stalin regarded Britain and France as having poor credibility as deterrents with Hitler because of their record of appeasement, and that Stalin believed that Hitler would not have been deterred from attacking Poland. It is also possible that Stalin believed that Britain and France would have been content to permit Germany and the Soviet Union to exhaust each other in a war in the east of Europe. But such inferences would not explain why there continued to be Soviet insistence upon a definition of 'indirect aggression' that included any redirection of diplomatic posture in the Baltics towards Germany, for if Stalin believed that any agreement obtained by the Soviet Union with Britain and France would not be honoured in the event of war any agreement reached over the definition of 'indirect aggression' would not have been trusted by Molotov or Stalin. The inference that obtaining such an agreement from the British and the French was intended by the Soviet Union to assist in bargaining with Germany seems possible, though Soviet mistrust of Germany given its ideological antipathy for communism and the Soviet Union would have meant mistrust of the Germans in any pact that required trust.

The terms of the pact with Germany were in the event optimal for the Soviet Union and Germany, precluding a German attack on a Red Army that was unprepared for a war to defend a Soviet Union that could have been convinced that such a war would be observed by Western powers as a means of mutual exhaustion of the totalitarian powers. The inference of no war in the east did not require trust in Germany, just German optimisation of outcomes in avoiding war on two fronts, having been at war in the west after having invaded Poland, the immediate object of Hitler's grievances in 1939. And it would permit the Soviet Union to acquire territory on its western border in the Baltics and Poland that, given Bolshevik suspiciousness, was seen as worth more than any diplomatic undertaking from the West. Such reasoning is of course no more than conjecture, as is so with much of the literature that attempts to discern Soviet intentions from the record of Soviet diplomacy in form and content, and the Soviets would not have known of the German terms before early August 1939. Stalin seems to have attempted to extort the best terms possible from Britain and France and then from Germany in the summer of 1939 to optimise Soviet security and though for a time an alliance with Britain and France seemed to be the best possible German terms then appeared to be much better given the objective of security and Bolshevik mistrust of Western undertakings in alliances.

It follows from the above that Shaw's and Carley's conclusion that British anti-communist and anti-Soviet attitudes were to blame for the breakdown of the talks is indefensible. Such a conclusion does not follow from an inference of rational optimisation of outcome by the Soviet Union. Whether inspired by *Realpolitik* or Bolshevik ideology, Soviet diplomacy in form and content during the talks was such as to engender mistrust in Soviet credibility as an ally in war or as a deterrent to Germany, even for a country without anti-communist and anti-Soviet attitudes. Moreover, Soviet ideological attitudes would have been impossible to dismiss. They provided both the prism through which Western intentions were perceived, and the compelling security objective that seems to have been difficult to distinguish from expansionism and opportunism in Soviet foreign policy.

The form and content of Soviet diplomacy during the negotiations caused the breakdown of the talks. British diplomats and politicians were left with no confidence in the Soviet Union as an ally in 1939 by Soviet violations of established diplomatic protocols that reflected Soviet contempt for and exploitation of perceived weakness, understanding of their having an alternative in the form of a pact with Germany, and attitudes to the West of Bolshevik hostility and mistrust that were reflected in Soviet diplomacy. Even had the talks not stumbled over British reaction to such Soviet diplomacy with its escalation of demands and over British refusal to surrender over the Baltics it does seem that Stalin would have opted for the pact with Germany just on grounds of the advantages it proffered the Soviet Union in terms of security (with territorial acquisition being seen as a buffer and with a virtual guarantee of war in the west between capitalist nations to the ideological and *Realpolitik* benefit of the Soviet Union). Even if the Soviet Union did intend to enter into an alliance with the British and the French in June and July 1939, and the talks with Germany were in fact entered into because of the impasse in the talks with Britain and France, the evidence is that the such talks foundered because of Soviet escalation of demands, the nature of Soviet diplomacy, the nature of the final definition of 'indirect aggression' and the mistrust such diplomatic tactics elicited, not because of adverse British attitudes towards communism and the Soviet Union.

There are then alternative explanations of the cause of the breakdown of negotiations for an Anglo-Soviet alliance in the summer of 1939. One explanation is that the stalling of negotiations over the final Soviet definition of 'indirect aggression' consequent on British rejection of it resulted in Soviet political talks with Germany. That makes the reason for British rejection of the Soviet definition of 'indirect aggression' the cause of the breakdown of the talks and of there being no alliance between the UK and the Soviet Union in the summer of 1939. But as has been indicated here, British rejection of the Soviet definition reflected the very adverse experience of Soviet diplomacy during the course of the negotiations and Soviet escalation of demands with each British concession combined with the extreme nature of the final Soviet demand and its obvious implications, not least given that Soviet diplomacy during the negotiations had been such as to elicit mistrust in any alliance regardless of previously existing adverse attitudes towards the Soviet Union and communism, so that such attitudes were not necessary conditions to the breakdown of the talks.

The other explanation is that Stalin intended all along to compare British and French terms with those offered by the Germans and that the stalling of negotiations for an alliance with the UK made no difference to the outcome, a rational optimisation of Soviet security through the German terms with their Soviet sphere of influence in the east of Europe and guarantee of war in the west rather than the east. The continuance of economic talks with Germany during the period of political negotiations with the UK seems to indicate that Stalin did intend to compare the terms offered from both sets of talks, for it would be odd for him to be concluding an economic agreement with a country that he was attempting to deter from war by encirclement by a political alliance of nations that would be adversaries of Germany should Hitler invade Poland for *Lebensraum* in the east, unless of course the alliance was expected to be an effective deterrent. In this case too the attribution for the breakdown of the talks between the Soviet Union and Britain for an alliance could not be to adverse previously existing British attitudes towards the Soviet Union and communism, but rather to Soviet rational optimisation of foreign policy and security outcomes. The perception of the security threat would have reflected Bolshevik paranoia concerning the motives of capitalist states and so have been ideological to some extent, for the attraction of buffer states to the west and a guarantee of war in the west rather than the east to Stalin was its precluding the possibility of western European nations' conspiring against the Soviet Union and colluding in an attack on it and in the avoidance of a need for trust in undertakings from Germany, as all Stalin was doing was trusting Hitler to pursue his own interests in avoiding having to fight on two fronts.

Notes

[1]Keeble, Curtis, *Britain and the Soviet Union, 1917–89*, Macmillan, London, 1990, page 130.

[2]FO 371/24847, Cadogan minute, 2 June 1940.

[3]For expositions of the orthodox view see 'Cato', *Guilty Men*, Purnell, London, 1940, Middlemas, Keith, *Diplomacy of Illusion: The British Government and Germany, 1937–1939*, Weidenfeld and Nicolson, London, 1972, and Namier, Lewis B., *Diplomatic Prelude, 1938–1939*, Macmillan, London, 1948.

[4]For the revisionist view see Charmley, John, *Chamberlain and the Lost Peace*, Macmillan, London, 1989, and Watt, D. C., 'Appeasement. The Rise of a Revisionist School?', *The Political Quarterly, 36* (1965). For other revisionist texts making similar claims of rationality for appeasement as a policy predicated upon external factors such as British economic and military weakness in relation to responsibilities over a long period and with slightly different emphases see also Kennedy, P., *The Realities Behind Diplomacy. Background Influences on British External Policy, 1865–1980*, London, 1981, Overy, R., and Wheatcroft, A., *The Road to War*, London, 1989, Watt, D. C., *How War Came. The Immediate Origins of the Second World War, 1938–1939*, London, 1989, Robbins, K., *Munich 1938*, London, 1968, and Northedge, F. S., *The Troubled Giant. Britain among the Great Powers, 1916–1939*, London, 1966 – though the latter did not entirely exculpate Chamberlain in his dealings with Hitler, it did stress the difficulties of the British position. See also Gilbert, M., *The Roots of Appeasement*, Weidenfeld and Nicolson, 1966. Some of these

texts were produced before the opening of the official record for the period while others were written with the benefit of the archive material, which they interpreted in a similar way.

[5]For the counter-revisionist argument see Parker, R. A. C., *Chamberlain and Appeasement. British Policy and the Coming of the Second World War*, St. Martin's Press, London, 1993, Aster, S, 'Guilty Men: The Case of Neville Chamberlain', in Boyce, R., and Robertson, E. M., *Paths to War. New Essays on the Origins of the Second World War*, London, 1989. See also, most recently and with specific reference to the British negotiations with the Soviet Union in 1939, Shaw, Louise Grace, *The British Political Elite and the Soviet Union 1937–1939*, Frank Cass, London, 2013, and Carley, Michael, Jabara, 1939, *The Alliance That Never Was And The Coming Of World War II*, Ivan R. Dee, Chicago, 1999.

[6]See Hill, Christopher, *Cabinet Decisions on Foreign Policy: the British experience October 1938–1941*, Cambridge University Press, 1991. Hill's focus is on the dynamics of foreign policy decisions within Cabinet and in the Foreign Policy Committee of the Cabinet, and so excludes any influence from, for instance, the FO. Hill also tends to focus more on the process within Cabinet, that is, the extent of genuine discussion between ministers, than on the content on the actual decision that eventuated as compared with initial positions, which is the area of interest in terms of causation. And while he provides extensive evidence that the question of a possible alliance with the Soviet Union was an instance of genuine ministerial influence he focuses on the effectiveness of ministerial pressure for the opening of negotiations despite Chamberlain's (and Halifax's initial) reservations, and does not cover at all the period of time of the failure of the negotiations. His evidence does however lend itself to the idea that Chamberlain's being the explanation for a British decision to refuse to concede further is implausible.

[7]Shaw, *The British Political Elite and the Soviet Union*, op. cit., page 186.

[8]Ibid., page 142.

[9]Ibid., pages 135–136 and 138.

[10]Carley, 1939 op. cit., page xviii.

[11]See Keeble, *Britain and the Soviet Union*, op. cit. Keeble's account draws on the remarks of FO officials in FO files, and Keeble does not assess the extent to which prejudices or attitudes were behind the expressions of views of individuals whose positions were such that they could exert influence on British foreign policy. Given that he is not assessing the validity of British attitudes, he needs to do no more than take the FO and Cabinet papers at face value.

[12]See Neilson, Keith, *Britain, Soviet Russia and the Collapse of the Versailles Order, 1919–1939*, Cambridge University Press, 2006, pages 40, 316, 323 and 327.

[13]Doerr, Paul W., *British Foreign Policy 1919–1939*, Manchester University Press, Manchester, 1998, page 86.

[14]Dutton, D., *A Political Biography of Sir John Simon*, Aurum, London, 1992, page 154.

[15]See Doerr, *British Foreign Policy 1919–1939*, page 159, for reference to frequent expressions of this view in FO minutes.

[16]Documents on British Foreign Policy (DBFP), 2, 12, no. 121.

[17]DBFP 2, 12, no. 484.

[18]Dilks, D. (ed.), *Retreat From Power: Studies In Britain's Foreign Policy In The Twentieth Century*, Volume 1, Macmillan, London, 1981, page 91.

[19]Fitzsimmons, M. A., *The Foreign Policy of the British Labour Government 1945–1951*, University of Notre Dame Press, Notre Dame, Indiana, 1953, pages 9–10.

[20]Doerr, *British Foreign Policy 1919–1939*, page 213.

[21]Cadogan had succeeded Vansittart as Permanent Under-Secretary at the FO in January 1938. Vansittart was anti-German and felt by Chamberlain to be against his policy, while Cadogan, at least at that time, seemed prepared to support it.

[22]Dilks, David (ed.), *The Diaries of Sir Alexander Cadogan, O. M., 1938–1945*, Putnam, 1972, pages 102–4.

[23]Chamberlain papers, NC 18/1/1042, Chamberlain to Hilda, 20 March 1938.

[24]Keeble, *Britain and the Soviet Union*, op. cit., page 130.

[25]Ibid., page 154.

[26]Ibid., page 138.

[27]See CAB 24/287, CP 124 (39), 'Foreign Office Memorandum on the Anglo-Soviet Negotiations', 22 May 1939 – also in DBFP 3, 5, pages 639–647.

[28]CAB 23/98, CM 18 (39), 5 April 1939.

[29]Hill, *Cabinet Decisions in British Foreign Policy*, page 51.

[30]See DBFP 3, 5, pages 228–229, Seeds to Halifax, 18 April 1939.

[31]CAB 27/624, FP (36), 43rd Meeting, 19 April 1939.

[32]Hill, *Cabinet Decisions in British Foreign Policy*, page 55.

[33]CAB 27/624, FP (36), 44th Meeting, 25 April 1939. For CoS paper see CAB 27/627, FP (36) 82.

[34]CAB 23/99, CM 26 (39), 3 May 1939.

[35]CAB 27/625, FP (36), 47th Meeting, 16 May 1939.

[36]Hill, *Cabinet Decisions in British Foreign Policy*, page 65.

[37]CAB 23/99, CM 30 (39), 24 May 1939.

[38]'Foreign Office Memorandum on the Anglo-Soviet Negotiations', 22 May 1939, CAB 24/287, CP 124 (39) – also in DBFP 3, 5, pages 639–647.

[39]Dilks, *Cadogan Diaries*, pages 181–182, 19 and 20 May 1939.

[40]Harvey, John (ed.), *The Diplomatic Diaries of Oliver Harvey 1937–1940*, Collins, London, 1970, pages 290–291, 23 May 1939.

[41]Dilks, *Cadogan Diaries*, page 184, 24 May 1939.

[42]Chamberlain papers, NC 18/1/1101, 28 May 1939.

[43]CAB 23/99, CM 30 (39), 24 May 1939.

[44]Chamberlain papers, NC 18/1/1101, letter to Hilda, 28 May 1939.

[45]Keeble, *Britain and the Soviet Union*, op. cit., page 148.

[46]Dilks, *Cadogan Diaries*, page 182.

[47]FO 371 23067, Seeds to FO, 28 May 1939.

[48]See Shaw, *The British Political Elite and the Soviet Union*, op. cit., page 118.

[49]FO 371/23067, FPC meeting, 5 June 1939.

[50]348 HC Deb. 7 June 1939, Cols. 400–402.

[51]CAB 27/625, 50th meeting, 9 June 1939.

[52]DBFP 3, V, pages 722–723, Seeds no. 105, 30 May 1939.

[53]DBFP 3, 6, pages 33–41, Instructions for Sir W. Seeds, 12 June 1939.

[54]NC 18/1/1102, letter to Ida, 10 June 1939.

[55]See CAB 27/625, FPC on 9 June 1939, and CAB 23/100, CM 38 (39), 19 July 1939. See also NC 11/1/1108 for Chamberlain's clear view that the talks were not what he would have chosen and would have been discontinued had it not been for ministerial insistence, and see NC 18/1/1107 for Chamberlain's claim that he would have opted for a harder line all the way through, but that it would not have attracted sufficient support.

[56]Shaw, *The British Political Elite and the Soviet Union*, op. cit., page 132.

[57]Roberts, Andrew, *The Holy Fox*, Weidenfield and Nicolson, London, 1991, page 159.

[58]FO 371/23069, Seeds to Halifax, 1 July 1939 and 4 July 1939.

[59]See CAB 23/100, CM 33 (39), 21 June 1939.

[60]See FO 371/23069, FO to Seeds, 27 June 1939, and CAB 23/100, CM 34 (39), 28 June 1939.

[61]Keeble, *Britain and the Soviet Union*, op. cit., pages 148, 149 and 150.

[62]See Shaw, *The British Political Elite*, op. cit., page 119.

[63]NC 18/1/1105, Chamberlain to Hilda, 2 July 1939.

[64]CAB 27/625, FP (36), 56th meeting, 4 July 1939.

[65]CAB 27/625, FP 54th meeting, 26 June 1939.

[66]See CAB 27/625, 49th meeting, 5 June 1939.

[67]FO 371/23069, FPC 26 June 1939.

[68]CAB 27/625, FPC 56th and 57th meetings, 4 and 10 July 1939.

[69]CAB 27/625, FP (36), 56th meeting, 4 July 1939.

[70]CAB 27/625, FP (36), 56th meeting, 4 July 1939.

[71]CAB 23/100, CM 35(39), 5 July 1939.

[72]FO 371/23070, tels. 160, 161, 162, 6 July 1939.

[73]DBFP 3, 7, no. 272. Halifax to HM Ambassador in Paris, 7 July 1939.

[74]DBFP series 3, volume 6, no. 376.

[75]Carley, 1939, op. cit., page 168.

[76]See FO 371/23070, Seeds to Halifax, no. 282, DBFP 3, 6, 10 July 1939.

[77]FO 371/ 23070, Roberts, 'Anglo-Soviet Negotiations', 10 July 1939.

[78]CAB 27/625, FP (36), 57th meeting, 10 July 1939. See also CAB 23/100, CM 37 (39), 12 July 1939 for reference to a British preparedness to have the political and military agreements come into effect at the same time in return for Soviet movement on 'indirect aggression'.

[79]FO 371/23070, FO to Seeds, tel. 167, 12 July 1939. See also CAB 23/100, CM 37 (39), 12 July 1939.

[80]NC 18/1/1107, Chamberlain to Hilda, 15 July 1939. Neilson also cites FO 371/23070/9709/3356/8, Chamberlain's attached note. Without the note it is impossible to tell if it indicates influence from Chamberlain or just represents a record of a discussion. In any case Halifax had expressed no confidence in the Soviet Union as long ago as 4 July 1939 because of experience of the negotiations rather than because of Chamberlain's influence.

[81]FO 371/23070, Seeds to FO, tel. 165, 17 July 1939.

[82]See CAB 27/625, FP (36), 58th meeting, 19 July 1939, and CAB 23/100, CM 38 (39), 19 July 1939.

[83]FO 371/23070, Seeds to FO, tels. 170 and 172, 23 July 1939.

[84]CAB 27/635, FP (36), 59th meeting, 26 July 1939.

[85]FO 371/23072, Cadogan and Chamberlain minutes, 11th and 12th August 1939.

[86]CAB 2/9, 372nd CID meeting, 2 August 1939.

[87]DBFP Series 3, Volume 6, no. 474, Halifax to Seeds, 28 July 1939.

[88]FO 371/23073, Drax to Chatfield, 16–17 August 1939.

[89]Rees, Laurence, *World War Two Behind Closed Doors. Stalin, the Nazis and the West*, BBC Books, 2008, page 15.

[90]See DBFP, Series 3, Volume 7, pages 32–3, for the view of Admiral Drax that the British delegation had been treated to Soviet demands and insistence upon rights of passage and a Soviet threat that they would discontinue the negotiations if such rights were not agreed.

[91]Carley,1939, op. cit., page 179.

[92]Weinberg, Gerhard L., *Germany and the Soviet Union*, Brill Archive, 1972, pages 37–40.

[93]Rees, page 16, quoting the testimony under American interrogation of Andor Hencke, who was Under-Secretary in the German Foreign Office.

[94]Roberts, *The Holy Fox*, page 166.

[95]Neilson, *Britain, Soviet Russia and the Collapse of the Versailles Order*, op. cit., pages 313–314.

[96]See *Diplomacy and Statecraft*, Volume 13 (March 2002), pages 55–74, Shaw, Louise Grace, *Attitudes of the British Political Elite towards the Soviet Union*.

[97]Bond, Brian (ed.), *Chief of Staff. The Diaries of Lieutenant General Sir Henry Pownall*, Volume I, 1933–40, Leo Cooper, London, 1972, page 214.

[98]See Shaw, *The British Political Elite and the Soviet Union*, op. cit., pages 7, 9, 10, 11, 13, 15 and 16 for the anti-communist and anti-Soviet credentials of the Cabinet.

[99]Ibid., pages 135–136.

[100]Ibid., page 131.

[101]Ibid., pages 134–135.

[102]In fact, in general British attitudes towards specific nations have not tended to predict British policy – instead British attitudes towards Britain's world-power status have tended to predict alliances to defend that position against any apparent threat, such as that Germany posed in the late 1930s.

[103]See 'Foreign Office Memorandum on the Anglo-Soviet Negotiations', 22 May 1939, CAB 24/287, CP 124 (39) – also in DBFP 3, 5, pages 639–647.

[104]See Hill, *Cabinet Decisions in British Foreign Policy*, page 59.

[105]See Shaw, *The British Political Elite and the Soviet Union*, op. cit., pages 4 and 189.

[106]Ibid., page 125.

[107]Ibid., page 137.

[108]Ibid., pages 128–130.

[109]Ibid., page 130.

[110]Ibid., page 130.

[111]For evidence of the change in ministerial belief in the possibility of an alliance see CAB 27/625, 49th meeting, 5 June 1939 to 58th meeting, 10 July 1939.

[112]Shaw, *The British Political Elite and the Soviet Union*, page 21.

[113]Ibid., page 19.

[114]For Hoare's advocacy for an alliance with the Soviet Union see CAB 27/625, 47th meeting, 16 May 1939. Yet he had, as Shaw claims, been an advocate for collective action to prevent Germany from war through deterrence and had felt that the Soviet Union should be involved in such a deterrent – see CAB 27/624, 38th meeting, 27th March 1939.

[115]See CAB 27/625, FP (36), 56th meeting, 4 July 1939 for Hoare's concerns regarding the Soviet definition of 'indirect aggression'.

[116]See CAB 23/99, CM 31, 7 June 1939, and CAB 23/100, CM 33 (39), 21 June 1939.

[117]CAB 27/625, 49th meeting, 5 June 1939.

[118]CAB 27/625, FP (36), 56th meeting, 4 July 1939.

[119]FO 800/328/332, 17 October 1939.

[120]See *Diplomacy and Statecraft*, Volume 13 (March 2002), Shaw, Louise Grace, *Attitudes of the British Political Elite towards the Soviet Union*, page 68.

[121]Shaw, *The British Political Elite and the Soviet Union*, op. cit., page 136.

[122]Ibid., page 63.

[123]Ibid., page 66.

[124]Ibid., page 187.

[125]See Carley, 1939, op. cit., page 169, and FO 371/23071, Kirkpatrick minute, 21 July 1939. This French surrender to British policy does of course render much of Carley's evidence as to the French view irrelevant to this thesis, in that their views had no effect on the British position or on the reasons of the breakdown of the talks. Certainly the greater French preparedness to surrender the Baltics and to link political and military talks, both demanded by the Soviet Union, seem to have had no effect on British politicians and officials.

[126]Ibid., page 256.

[127]See Shaw, *The British Political Elite and the Soviet Union*, op. cit., page 138.

[128]France had effected a number of alliances attempting to encircle and isolate Germany in the 1920s, in the form of an alliance with Poland in 1921, one with Czechoslovakia in 1924, others in the second half of the 1920s with Yugoslavia and Romania and one with the Soviet Union in 1935 despite ideological reservations that involved the Soviets in alliance with Czechoslovakia because of the French alliance with that country from the 1920s.

[129]Shaw, *The British Political Elite and the Soviet Union*, op. cit., pages 11–17.

[130]Carley, 1939. op. cit., page 189.

[131]Ibid., page 212.

[132]FO 371/24847, Cadogan minute, 2 June 1940.

[133]Carley, 1939, op. cit., page 211.

[134]See Shaw, *The British Political Elite and the Soviet Union*, op. cit., page 131.

[135]Carley, 1939, op. cit., page 185.

[136]FO 371/23070, FPC, 10 July 1939.

[137]FO 371/23072, CID, Deputy Chiefs of staff subcommittee, 16 August 1939. See also CAB 54/11, 179, 16 August 1939.

[138]Shaw, *The British Political Elite and the Soviet Union*, op. cit., page 139.

[139]See Neilson, Britain, *Soviet Russia and the Collapse of the Versailles Order*, op. cit., pages 320–321.

[140]Ibid., page 321.

[141]Ibid., page 322.

[142]Ibid., pages 323–325.

[143]Ibid., page 315.

[144]Ibid., page 332.

[145]See Dutton, D, *Chamberlain*, Bloomsbury Academic, 2001, pages 183–184, for evidence of Chamberlain's controlling rather than responsive attitude to public opinion.

[146]It is worth noting that this view, which is my own and has been expressed elsewhere in this thesis, negates Shaw's attribution of the breakdown of the talks to adverse British attitudes.

[147]Neilson, *Britain, Soviet Russia and the Collapse of the Versailles Order*, op. cit., page 332.

[148]Ibid., page 332.

[149]See Uldricks, Teddy J., 'Soviet Security Policy in the 1930s', in Gorodetsky, Gabriel, ed., *Soviet Foreign Policy, 1917–1991: A Retrospective*, Routledge, 2014, pages 65–72.

[150]Keeble, *Britain and the Soviet Union*, op. cit., page 140.

[151]Dilks, *Cadogan Diaries*, 16, 18, 19 and 20 May 1939.

[152]FO 371/23069, 30 June 1939, Cadogan minute, cited in Dilks, *Cadogan Diaries*, pages 189–190. Cadogan was prepared to countenance a breakdown in the talks at the end of June 1939, being of the view that continued Soviet insistence over the guarantees to Switzerland and Holland would indicate that they did not intend to have an agreement anyway. It is worth noting that there is little dismay in the tone of the entry, an indication that Cadogan by this time did not value any alliance with the Soviet Union given what he seems to have regarded as their duplicitous diplomacy, in which of course he was proved right by events.

[153]See Dilks, *Cadogan Diaries*, entries for 22nd and 24th August 1939.

[154]Ibid., entries for 3rd and 4th July 1939, page 191.

[155]FO 371/23067, Seeds to FO, 30 May 1939.

[156]Neilson, *Britain, Soviet Russia and the Collapse of the Versailles Order*, op. cit., page 297.

[157]FO 371/23068, FO to Seeds, 22 June 1939.

[158]Carley, 1939, op. cit., page 153.

[159]See Keeble, *Britain and the Soviet Union*, op. cit., page 155.

[160]CAB 27/635, FP (36), 59th meeting, 26 July 1939.

[161]See Hill, *Cabinet Decisions*, op. cit., page 84.

[162]See Shaw, *The British Political Elite and the Soviet Union*, op. cit., page 132.

[163]See Arad, Yitzhak, *The Holocaust in the Soviet Union*, University of Nebraska, 2009, page 37.

Chapter Three

British foreign policy decision-making towards the Soviet Union during the war: the Baltics issue and the post-war future of Germany

Introduction

THERE IS A general consensus among historians that British foreign policy during the war under Churchill as Prime Minister was subordinated to the objective of maintaining the wartime alliance with the US and the Soviet Union to achieve victory over Germany and Italy, and, after December 1941, Japan. Foreign policy was then a reflection of war policy, and Churchill was notoriously uninterested in anything that concerned the post-war disposition unless it was germane to the continuance of the wartime alliance in consequence of being seen to be of concern to Roosevelt or Stalin. The Atlantic Charter insisted upon by the US precluded any post-war settlement prior to the cessation of hostilities, and Churchill tried to defer any contentious issues until after the war to maintain the wartime alliance, not least the Soviet effort in the east given its bearing a disproportionate share of the burden of fighting, suffering and losses of manpower and territory. That though proved difficult given Stalin's surprising insistence, even with the German advance into the Soviet Union threatening the Bolshevik political system and the Soviet state itself, on British acceptance of the Soviet annexations of the Baltic republics. Given Soviet losses of territory and men, the danger of a Soviet peace treaty with Germany and the impossibility of British military assistance except by means of dangerous Arctic convoys, there was a sense that Stalin's request had to be seriously considered. That constitutes the first case study here, from November 1941 through to early 1942. The other was later, beginning in 1943, when the Soviet victory at Stalingrad had indicated that wartime victory over Germany was plausible, and continuing to 1945, and concerned the post-war future of Germany, a case study only ostensibly concerned with policy towards post-war Germany, for policy over post-war Germany was very much a reflection of policy towards the Soviet Union as it emerged as the most likely dominant land power on the continent of Europe. Both the case studies are then in effect concerned with British foreign policy towards the Soviet Union during the war, though also addressing the possible aftermath of the war.

Though Churchill's dominant influence on British foreign policy during the war is not challenged here, this article attempts to assess the differing points of view in the Cabinet, the Foreign Office (FO) and the Chiefs of Staff (CoS) at two different junctures in the war, to indicate the nature of the process of foreign-policy decision-making in the political and official establishment at the time, to assess the extent of possible influence on Churchill as PM, to establish the reasons for his dominance, and to compare the perceptions of the Soviet Union of the different parties within the political and official establishment to assess their accuracy as Soviet intentions revealed themselves late on in the war.

The historiography of British foreign policy in the war is in some cases part of a longer view of British decline relative to the Soviet Union and the US, though there are some more specific assessments of British foreign policy during the war, and appreciations of Churchill in biographical terms and during the war .[1] There does not though seem to be any work that addresses in specific terms the causal influences on British foreign policy during the war or that assesses the relative merits of different views of Soviet purposes and diplomatic tactics and the best manner of dealing with them both when Soviet military power seemed weak and when, later in the war, it seemed a great threat to western Europe and the major land power in Europe.

The Baltic issue (November 1941–March 1942)

The US had dictated through the Atlantic Charter that no agreements on post-war Europe should be made prior to Allied victory. Churchill had agreed. In late 1941 however the German advance into the Soviet Union and the lack of any British military victory in the war left Churchill in an impossible position with Stalin. The maintenance of an eastern front was regarded as a military necessity to draw away German forces from the western theatre, and the Red Army and the Russian people had shown reserves of resistance and endurance that had surprised Western military observers, who had predicted a brief and triumphant German campaign and a Soviet surrender. There was concern that given the enormity of Soviet losses and suffering Stalin might effect a separate peace with Hitler and so put an end to Germany's having to fight on two fronts. Convoys to Archangel and Murmansk were giving Stalin what support the British could afford but did not replace in any way the front in the west that Stalin had demanded to provide relief for the Red Army (in fact the idea was ridiculous given Britain's adverse military position), and British lack of any military success in the war left Britain with low credibility as an ally. Meanwhile it was known that the Red Army and the Russian people were suffering terrible hardships before the German advance and Soviet retreat and there was an understanding that the major sacrifices were being made in the east.

On 8 November 1941 Stalin made his displeasure and demands clear. There was resentment at the absence of a second front, of a 'definite understanding on war aims' and 'plans for the post-war organisation of peace', and of an 'agreement on mutual military assistance against Hitler in Europe',[2] and there was a demand for a British declaration of war on Finland, Hungary and Romania, countries that had joined in Germany's attack on the Soviet Union. This latter demand was pursued by Maisky, the Soviet Ambassador in London, with Eden, as the minimal immediate response. There was a general understanding that, given the adverse Soviet military position and the impossibility of affording them military assistance, something had to be offered, and given US opposition to discussing any post-war territorial settlement, the British made the requested declarations of war on 5 December 1941.

As to Stalin's other demands, Churchill sent Eden to Moscow and indicated to Stalin that he would 'be able to discuss every question relating to the war' and the 'post-war organisation of peace'.[3] Churchill added that the Soviets' communism would not preclude their being involved in a 'plan for our mutual safety and rightful interests',[4] an indication of his vague approach to post-war matters. Eden had at the time of the German invasion counselled 'a cool response', 'as politically Russia was as bad as Germany',[5] but supported Churchill's stance in informing the Commons and assuring Maisky, the Soviet Ambassador, of British support. As Foreign Secretary Eden was surprised by the FO's anti-communist and anti-Soviet attitudes and, with no such leanings himself (unlike the majority of the British political class), wanted to build bridges with the Soviets. 'Soviet hypocrisy sometimes appalled him,'[6] but Eden's disgust related to experience of Soviet diplomacy – it was concerned with Soviet violations of diplomatic protocol and brazen pragmatism in foreign policy rather than ideological. In October 1941 he advocated acceding to the Soviet request for declarations of war on Finland, Hungary and Romania so as not to 'arouse their latent suspicions as to our motives'.[7] And on practical grounds he attempted to resist being sent to Stalin empty-handed. Eden records the Cabinet prior to his departure as 'all maintaining that I needed nothing, and ignoring that Stalin had been told I was bringing armies!'.[8] Dutton notes that Eden was constrained by the fact that 'Churchill's latent anti-Bolshevism began to reassert itself.'[9]

By this time, in late November 1941, it was clear that the Soviets were not going to collapse in the manner predicted by British military experts. The British position was then to offer something less than a treaty but enough to keep the Soviets in the war against Germany, an indication of the extent of ideological and diplomatic aversion in the British political and official establishment for the Soviet Union but also of a profound British misunderstanding of what Stalin would accept. This conflict between profoundly held adverse attitudes towards communist and Bolshevik ideology and towards the repressive Soviet regime (and previous adverse experience of Soviet diplomacy in the Anglo-Soviet discussions for an alliance that eventuated in the Ribbentrop-Molotov pact) and the imperatives of wartime collaboration in the cause of optimising the war effort against Germany is an enduring theme in the assessment of influences on British policy towards the Soviets over Germany in the war period.

The view taken by senior FO officials in a series of critical meetings held between 14 and 18 November 1941 to consider British policy towards the Soviet Union and the British response to Stalin's communiqué of 8 November in particular, including the brief for Eden's visit to Stalin in December, was that some form of vague statement of principles in a 'Volga Charter' would suffice given Stalin's parlous military situation.[10] It would also permit time to assess Soviet intentions in the context of their already considerable demands. The FO and Cabinet brief for Eden on political matters then defined the British position, which was one of avoiding commitments as to the Soviet Union's 1941 western frontiers (which were a function of the Soviet pact with Germany) and doing just enough to keep the Soviets in the war by an Anglo-Soviet declaration as to continued collaboration after the war. Sargent counselled against any discussion of the post-war future of Germany, for instance the possibility of partition, 'for I take it that the idea is one we do not want to encourage in any way'. Cadogan, Permanent Under-Secretary at the Foreign Office, remarked, 'we should all like to see Germany broken up but that is a process which, to be lasting and genuine, must come from within.'[11] Eden did express reservations regarding seeing Stalin with nothing to offer him, yet acknowledged in his submission to the War Cabinet on 29 November 1941 that over the Baltics 'we shall have to decline for the present to go beyond the first and second clauses of the Atlantic Charter' and that there would have to be consultation with the United States which would involve 'the extent to which the United States Government will be prepared to discuss the peace settlement in advance with the Soviet Government'. Reference was made to the need to allay Soviet suspicions over their exclusion from the peace settlement, but Eden seems to have accepted the general view that a declaration to work with the Soviet Union during and after the war would have to suffice.[12]

Britain was in fact already economically exhausted by the period prior to the Lend-Lease agreement under which Britain was able to obtain war goods on credit from the United States. The latter had been supplying Britain with goods on credit and Britain was 'committed to vast purchasing programmes in the United States which still had to be paid for'.[13] The legislation was signed on 11 March 1941, and has been seen by Barnett as the end of Britain's independence in pursuit of a continuation of world-power status, achievable only by dependence on the United States.[14] The consequences for British policy were considerable, for the terms of the Atlantic Charter, concluded between Britain and America in August 1941, required self-determination for occupied peoples after the war, which precluded any territorial settlements in its duration.[15]

Eden's arrival on 15 December 1941 coincided with US entry into the war consequent on the Japanese attack on Pearl Harbour and with Soviet success in halting the German advance outside Moscow, which were not without influence. For it meant that the United States was now in the war as a belligerent and that Britain was at war with Japan in the Far East. Stalin had a Neutrality Pact with Japan and had a clear interest in avoiding war on two fronts, and told Eden that he was as unable to declare war on Japan as the British were to open a second front in northern France. And on the day of Eden's final meeting with Stalin 'the British Chiefs of Staff and their American counterparts, the Joint Chiefs, agreed, as a result of considerable persuasion by Pound, Portal and Brooke, and to Churchill's enormous relief, that the Atlantic-European theatre was the decisive one, that Germany is still the key to victory as it had been described during the American-British Staff Conversations in February 1941, and that the defeat of Germany should precede the defeat of Japan.'[16] For Churchill this was vital, yet in the immediate term it did not reduce the need for Soviet resistance in the east.

Stalin told Eden he wanted a formal military alliance for the duration of the war, but also some accord on post-war boundaries and reconstruction. This would involve the ceding to the Soviets of the territory annexed in the period of the Nazi-Soviet Pact, and the dismemberment of Germany. Poland should be given East Prussia (Stalin saw this as 'the only guarantee which will ensure that Germany would be permanently weakened', part of his concern regarding post-war security). And Austria, the Rhineland and possibly Bavaria should be separated from Germany. Additionally reparations were to be paid to the Soviet Union by Germany. Stalin wanted a secret protocol on the post-war future of Europe, but in the immediate term 'the restoration of the position in 1941, prior to the German attack, in respect of the Baltic states, Finland and Bessarabia' and insisted on British acceptance of these Soviet annexations.[17] Directed by Churchill to make no undertakings Eden was given the 'Stalin treatment'. In a pattern that was to become characteristic, charm on the first day was followed by bitter recriminations, hostility, insinuations, insults and demands on the second, and reconciliation on the last day. These demands, and Soviet refusal to sign a joint declaration if they were not met, were reported by Attlee to the War Cabinet on 19 December. Eden needed instruction on how to proceed. The Cabinet view (endorsed by Churchill in transit to the US) was that Soviet claims might not be resisted at a peace conference, but no undertakings could be given because of the Atlantic Charter and the understanding with the Americans that there should be no territorial settlements during the war.[18]

Eden found his experience of Soviet diplomacy 'deplorable',[19] yet in his broadcast on 4 January 1942 said 'that closer political collaboration between us can and will be realised'. Eden saw 'a legacy of suspicion on both sides' and 'a contrast in forms of government' yet went on 'what matters in foreign affairs is not the form of internal government of any nation but its international behaviour', and stressed commonality of purpose, as 'the Soviet Union is determined upon the utter defeat of Germany; so are we'.[20]

Eden then told Churchill that British acquiescence in the Soviet annexation of the Baltics was indispensable to wartime collaboration with the Soviets and an 'acid test of our sincerity'. He characterised his position as 'stark realism', for 'if Russians are victorious they will be able to establish these frontiers and we shall certainly not turn them out.' He pointed to the 'essential need at the present time for really close and intimate collaboration and consultation with U.S.S.R., which, if we do not meet them on this, will be, I feel sure, limited to matters on which they require our help and that of the United States of America', a reference to wartime imperatives, and added, 'this may make all the difference after the war as well as now'. Eden acknowledged 'that great difficulty with United States Government' would ensue because of the apparent conflict with the Atlantic Charter but suggested a plebiscite in the Baltics to give the impression of a democratic vote for inclusion in the Soviet Union, which he felt that the Soviets might accept as they would 'foresee no obstacle, when time came, in arranging for necessary vote in their favour'.[21]

Eden's argument that concessions were indispensable to relations with the Soviets mirrored that of Cripps and Beaverbrook. Eden understood that nothing would be lost in *Realpolitik* acquiescence in the Soviets' acquisition of the Baltics,[22] as they would be overrun by the Red Army in any German defeat anyway and so were a way of securing Soviet trust and assistance that actually would cost Britain nothing. This was before any discussion with his FO officials apart from Sargent,[23] who was to favour reciprocal, not unilateral concessions.

Churchill's reply on 8 January 1942 was emphatic in its dissent. He referred to Soviet acquisition of the Baltics 'by acts of shameful collusion with Hitler' and to the Soviet Union's 'fighting for self-preservation', having 'entered the war only when attacked by Germany, having previously shown themselves to be utterly indifferent to our fate'. He said 'there can be no question of settling frontiers until the Peace Conference,'[24] and denied that the Soviets would be in an unassailable position in Europe after the war, remarking that the British Empire and the United States would be the most powerful force in the world.

And, having told Eden that Soviet claims might not be resisted at a peace conference, Churchill now proclaimed that 'any government that he, Churchill, headed, would stand by the principles of freedom and democracy in the Atlantic Charter'.[25] Charmley imputes to Churchill a primary concern with Anglo-American relations. He claims that the line 'America would not like it if Britain granted Stalin's demands'[26] served as an effective prohibition, and that Churchill's policy was 'to allow FDR to determine the foreign policy of the British Empire'.[27] Yet Churchill saw that the war could not be won without American assistance, and it was to maintain the 'special relationship' that Churchill so often deferred to Roosevelt and declined to proceed without his support.

Eden was concerned that the Soviets might effect a separate peace as their forces advanced westwards if alienated from the British. His other concern was that of alienating a power which, if the war were won, would be dominant on the continent of Europe and could only, in Eden's view, be constrained by the cultivation of better relations then, in early 1942.[28]

Eden's view combined pragmatism and an assumption of Soviet sensitivity to British diplomacy. Others wondered if Soviet demands were mere opportunism. Attlee was convinced that acquiescence in one demand would result in others, and Bevin wanted confirmation that Stalin's demands over the Baltics were the end rather than the beginning of a process of demands. These doubts as to Soviet intentions were to endure in these Labour politicians during and after the war. There are also interesting analogies here with appeasement. Taking the issue on its own pragmatism dictated British acquiescence in the Soviet annexation given that the nations concerned would be lost anyway to the Soviet advance westwards in the event of allied victory. This was Eden's case. Yet such a policy of conceding to Soviet demands could elicit further demands, the logic of opposition to appeasement.

There was also the recent history of negotiations with the Soviet Union to effect an alliance to contain Hitler in 1939, in which the British had experienced just such an escalation of demands with each British concession and had been appalled by Soviet diplomacy. To deliberations regarding British policy the British perception of Soviet policy, its intentions and practices, was central, with Eden and Cripps claiming that trust would be established by the surrender of the Baltics and Churchill and Cadogan, and Attlee and Bevin, concerned that any concessions would be exploited, having been seen as weakness by the Soviets.

On 6 February 1942 the Cabinet was split. Beaverbrook endorsed Eden's view of a sensitive Soviet Union and advocated recognition of its 1941 frontiers, asserting that 'these frontiers were necessary for Russia's security',[29] though he accepted that acquiescence would have to be subject to the American view. Morrison too felt that self-determination could interfere with good Anglo-Soviet relations. Eden spoke in favour of recognition if US approval were obtained, and said that 'such reconciliation was by no means out of the question'.[30] But Churchill, supported by Attlee, who threatened to resign if Soviet annexations in the Baltics were recognised, and by the rest of the Cabinet, rejected the notion that concessions to the Soviets were necessary to their continued military resistance, and proposed a 'balanced presentation' of the case to the US. Beaverbrook resigned on 9 February as a result. Roosevelt then claimed he could resolve the matter with Stalin. Though other ministers had doubts, Churchill told the Cabinet that there was 'more likelihood of an agreement being reached if the negotiations were so handled'.[31] The military context was adverse. There had been no British victory in the war, and Singapore fell on 15 February,[32] a military disaster which, in bitter contrast to Soviet resistance, dismayed Churchill, who cannot have been oblivious to its effect on Soviet views of the joint war effort.

Yet Roosevelt continued to resist any territorial settlements in wartime, and on 7 March 1942 Churchill told him that as the Soviets were already in the Baltics at the time of the Atlantic Charter 'this issue should not stand in the way of making a treaty with them'.[33] On 9 March he told Stalin that he had 'sent a message to President Roosevelt urging him to approve our signing the agreement with you about the frontiers of Russia at the end of the war'.[34]

Churchill was then in March 1942 prepared to acquiesce in the Soviet Union's 1941 frontiers. Yet Roosevelt's implicit undertaking of continued support had to be safeguarded before any change of policy was made, and there followed intensive diplomatic activity, both direct, from Churchill to Roosevelt, and through Eden, Halifax in Washington and Winant in London to persuade Roosevelt that Britain had to consider the possibility of Stalin's withdrawing from the wartime alliance then or when the Soviet Union's 1941 frontiers had been recovered by military advances. In the meantime Roosevelt's discussion with Litvinov elicited the tersest of acknowledgements from the Soviets.

On 25 March 1942 the War Cabinet noted Eden's report of the Soviet rebuff to Roosevelt. It agreed with Eden's recommendation that he should 'explain our difficulties to the United States Government', though efforts had been continuing to this end for some time. Halifax in Washington should indicate that 'in present circumstances we felt bound to go ahead with treaty negotiations with the Soviet Government on the basis of their frontier claims. But, before doing so, should like an assurance that whatever his views on the proposed treaty, the President was satisfied that we had taken all possible steps to consult the United States Government in the matter.'[35] Further, 'even if the President felt unable to agree definitely to the course proposed, we hoped that he would not take any step which indicated a marked divergence of view.'[36] Finally, Halifax was advised, 'stress may be laid on the military situation. The fact that we could do little by way of military aid to Russia made the conclusion of a Treaty all the more necessary.'[37] The importance of squaring the Americans and of giving something to the Soviets in view of the adverse military situation facing them is clear.

Roosevelt then indicated that permitting emigration from the Baltics would assist him with US public opinion, and Eden accordingly included this in his draft of the treaty. Roosevelt 'could not indicate approval' but would avoid public criticism of British policy.[38]

On 8 April 1942 the War Cabinet 'authorised the Secretary of State for Foreign Affairs to proceed'.[39] Eden then told Maisky that negotiations could proceed on Stalin's terms. Yet Woodward observes that the negotiations that resulted in the Anglo-Soviet treaty showed that 'a surrender to Russian demands was followed – as in 1939 – not by concessions on the part of the Russians but by more demands.'[40] There was no agreement on the British requirements for some reference to the United Nations and for some provision for the possible emigration of people who wished to leave territories becoming part of the Soviet Union. There was also an implicit Soviet demand 'for tacit British withdrawal of its public non-recognition of the 1941 Soviet-Polish frontier'.[41] There was no accord either on the FO idea of a confederation of small states in eastern Europe, and a new Soviet demand for Soviet bases in Finland and Romania. Eden then took up Cadogan's proposal for a twenty-year pact of mutual assistance and a promise of post-war co-operation and concern to safeguard Soviet security, which, as Rothwell puts it, 'in the first of many astounding political somersaults'[42] Molotov accepted. The treaty was devoid of clauses covering frontiers, but Molotov had apparently been convinced by Winant, the US Ambassador to Britain, of US objections over the Baltics and may have been concerned not to prejudice the likelihood of a second front being promised by Roosevelt. Ross notes, 'a talk with Winant had apparently convinced him (Molotov) of the importance of calming American susceptibilities before arriving in Washington,'[43] yet 'Stalin's motives were and must remain conjectural.'[44]

Eden's recommendation was then for a *Realpolitik* acknowledgement that if the war was lost recognition of Stalin's right to the Baltics would be an irrelevance given a decisive German victory in the east and that if the war was won the Baltics would be overrun by the Red Army and lost to the West because of the disposition of forces on the ground, an argument predicated upon relative power. The logic of Eden's case was then that Britain would in fact be guaranteeing continued Soviet sacrifice in the war and preservation of an eastern front in return for British recognition of the Baltics as Soviet when the Red Army would overrun the Baltics if the war were won in any event. Churchill was initially aghast at such a violation of the Atlantic Charter, yet just months later recommended to Roosevelt that such recognition should be offered given that the Red Army was doing so much of the fighting. It is worth noting that both Eden's advocating rearmament and resistance to Hitler based on British military power and deterrence in the appeasement era and his endorsing Stalin's right to the Baltics on the basis of lack of British military influence in the east of Europe reflected Eden's understanding of *Realpolitik* considerations in foreign policy, the idea that diplomatic negotiations had to be backed by credible military power and the intention to use it and that assuming foreign policy positions without the power needed to give effect to them did not aid credibility. It is possible that Eden kept the Baltic issue alive and exerted some discreet influence on Churchill in the early months of 1942, after Churchill's initial moral outrage.

There is however no documentary record of such influence, and it is possible that Churchill came to the conclusion that Britain should recognise the Soviet right to the Baltics on his own given the continuing lack of British military success, not least the calamitous and humiliating loss of Singapore on 15 February 1942, the extent of Red Army sacrifice and resistance to the German advance and the limited relief proffered by the convoys of ships on the northern route, and the perceived risk that Stalin might effect a separate peace with Hitler. Even with such compelling objective arguments it may have been the case that having an advocate in Cabinet kept them salient. What is certainly the case is that Eden formed a foreign policy view on his own over the Baltics and persevered with it even against opposition from Churchill and members of the FO, and that the policy he had advocated would have become British policy had Molotov not effected a *volte-face* on the issue.

Churchill's initial disapproval and Cabinet rejection of Eden's proposal that Britain should accept the Soviet annexations of the Baltics do seem to reflect Churchill's enduring concern not to alienate the Americans by violating the principles of the Atlantic Charter to which they were so attached rather than some principle that rejected the sacrifice of small states. Churchill's ensuing acceptance of the Soviet annexations of the Baltics once Roosevelt had been consulted indicates the extent to which Churchill subordinated his own attitudes to his primary objective of winning the war, to which the Soviets and the US were vital. Eden concurred as to the need to maintain the Soviets in the war and as to the utility, necessity and rationality of concessions, but regarded the form of diplomacy as influential, and was concerned also to obtain post-war advantages by concessions. Yet Eden also understood the need for US support, had reservations over the Soviets' enduring 'crust of suspicion',[45] and took care not to take his case for concessions too far with Churchill (he prided himself on discretion and deplored clumsy diplomacy).[46]

Barker sees Churchill and Eden changing roles, and the latter sometimes being impetuous and subject to Churchill's restraint. Addressing the notion of Churchillian dominance Barker points to Eden's creativity in dissenting over 'Churchill's more aggressive impulses or higher flights of fancy'[47] while trying to 'avoid direct confrontations',[48] change the manner of execution of a policy, delay it or make it conditional on circumstances.[49] On the Baltic issue, Barker claims Eden persuaded Churchill to send the communiqué of 7 March 1942 asking for Roosevelt's approval of British acquiescence in the Soviet annexation of the Baltics.[50] There is no documentary evidence to support her claim. With Eden's type of influence, involving tact and restraint in private conversations, evidence may be in its very nature hard to find, but its absence does leave any supposition as to influence conjectural. While Churchill's view seems to have prevailed over Eden's in Cabinet where there was open disagreement such interaction in Cabinet does not of course preclude instances of private influence on Churchill from Eden.

Eden's relations with his senior FO advisers have also attracted controversy, and the direction of influence between Eden and the FO, in particular with Cadogan and Sargent, has been characterised in varied ways. Folly sees the relationship as being driven by Eden over formulation of policy towards the Soviets and the Baltic issue. He claims that 'there was a greater and more notable shift in FO attitudes led from the top by Eden',[51] who had 'a personal sense that policy towards the USSR was drifting aimlessly',[52] and continues, 'Eden put forward his argument for concessions to secure long-term political cooperation before there was much debate in the FO on what method was best,'[53] yet adds 'in the FO debate he appears at times to belong to both sides, for the reservations in his attitude had also by no means disappeared.'[54] Rothwell concurs that Eden 'set the tone for the streak of pro-Sovietism which existed in the Foreign Office in the 1940s',[55] while Kitchen sees Eden as a man 'who usually followed Cadogan's advice'[56] and, referring to the FO, 'not the man to put up too much of a fight in the face of such strong opposition'.[57]

A fundamental question here is the extent of influence of FO views on Eden, Churchill and the Cabinet over policy towards the Soviets over the Baltic issue. Yet it also involves investigating the extent to which there was one FO policy, and, in terms of causal influences, the effect of FO attitudes towards the Soviet Union and communism, as opposed to an FO sense of what was necessary to win the war by sustaining wartime alliances, on the recommended FO policy. FO perceptions of the Soviets had changed only when their resistance made them valuable to the British war effort.[58] Further, the complexion of FO advice as to policy towards the Soviet Union changed again, between November 1941 and May 1942, and I shall deal with the two distinct phases of intense discussion in the FO – one between 14 and 19 November 1941, and then again in February 1942 – separately for purposes of clarity.

The first phase was initiated by the need to respond to Stalin's demands on 8 November 1941. On 14 November Eden, Cadogan, Warner and Sargent decided that Eden should visit Stalin to discuss his demands and reach some form of understanding. Minutes by Dew on 15 November and Warner on 17 November indicate a sense of a need to deal with Soviet suspicions.[59] On 18 November a meeting between Cadogan, Sargent, Strang, Harvey, Ronald, Law, and Warner elaborated upon the detail of the FO view. The presumption was that 'Stalin's desire to secure a definite understanding on war aims and on plans for the post-war organisation of peace arises out of a suspicion that it is the desire of H.M. Government to see Russia weakened by the struggle with Germany and at the conclusion of the War to make an Anglo-American peace from which Russia will be largely excluded'.[60]

Remarkably, it was also felt that Stalin feared that the Soviet Union would be weak relative to Britain after the war and so would prefer an agreement prior to its end. Dew's minute observed, 'it was no doubt Stalin's hope to see Germany and Great Britain fight each other to a standstill with the result that Russia would play a predominant role in the peace.'[61] This was an enunciation of the 'mutual exhaustion' theory. Soviet frontier demands 'might, however, be revised if an efficient scheme for disarmament and an international police force can be devised'. The FO sense was, even after experience of negotiations with the Soviet Union in 1939 (in which legitimate Soviet security concerns were accompanied by brazen Soviet opportunism and expansionism), that the major objective of Soviet foreign policy was security and if the threat to the Soviet Union 'from any European or Asiatic Power' could be removed 'by some international scheme, then Russia would not necessarily have to adopt the policy which led to the partition of Poland, the absorption of the Baltic States and the establishment of Russian bases in Finland'.[62] Not a great deal had, it seems, been learned of the nature of Soviet diplomacy from the experience of negotiations in 1939, not least regarding their seeing minimal concessions for what they were, a radical mistrust of Western motives that derived from communist ideology and that made territorial acquisition and military assistance more appealing than promises, and their orientation to power and exploitation of opportunities (even in so adverse a situation as that facing them in late 1941 and early 1942).

All of these had been all too apparent in 1939, and many of those addressing themselves to the issue of policy towards the Soviet Union late in 1941 had been involved at that time, not least Cadogan, Sargent and Strang, all of whom had been aghast at their experience of the nature of Soviet diplomacy and profoundly alienated by it. While it is possible that there was a sense that the Soviet Union would be prepared to accept such a scheme given the appalling Soviet military situation, it had been made clear to British FO officials just how little such undertakings meant to the Soviet Union. Nor it seems had much been learned from the abject failure of the League of Nations in terms of the effectiveness of international organisations aimed at securing international peace or their credibility to pragmatic states such as the Soviet Union. The Dew minute pointed out that both the FO and the Soviets were unclear as to their respective positions in terms of post-war affairs and expressed the hope that 'it may be possible to confine any agreement with the Russians to some declaration reaffirming the intention of Great Britain and the Soviet Union to continue the war until the defeat of Germany and stating that the two countries are resolved to co-operate in making the peace settlement and to co-operate thereafter in maintaining that settlement.'[63] This was vital, for the FO felt constrained by the agreement with the 'Americans not to undertake during the war commitments which would bind us at the peace and after'.[64] On 23 November Warner reiterated that the visit should be exploratory in nature. These views were very apparent in the resulting Cabinet Paper dated 29 November 1941.[65]

This complex of perceptions and views is so explicit that there is a clear consensus in the historiography.[66] Yet thereafter historiographical differences do emerge, for according to Kitchen, despite the Atlantic Charter, the FO had heard from Harriman that the United States favoured an accord with the Soviets as to the post-war period,[67] which would have removed the United States as an obstacle. For Kitchen the FO wanted to resolve Soviet suspicions by discussing post-war arrangements but was overruled by Churchill, who forbade all territorial negotiations in the war and opposed concessions.[68]

Rothwell infers that the FO understood that Stalin would insist on the territorial acquisitions made prior to the German invasion in June 1941, which would include the Baltics. He claims that, by December 1941, the FO view was that the Baltics should be surrendered to convey a desire for genuine collaboration to the Soviets. He concludes that, by the end of 1941, 'officials were concocting almost a doctrine that small states in vulnerable strategic locations had no right to exist.'[69] That such a view existed within the FO at the start of December 1941 is apparent in Dew's personal, *Realpolitik* view – 'I do not feel that the independence of the Baltic states is a European necessity.'[70] That such views did not translate themselves into policy recommendations would then seem to be attributable to the known constraints of the Atlantic Charter and Churchill's view (but see below for the diversity of view within the FO and the final, much tougher consensus in February 1942 as to how Britain should deal with the Soviet Union).

Folly notes that the FO favoured a 'vague statement of principles' in a 'Volga Charter' which would allude to post-war British collaboration with the Soviet Union but avoid commitment over territorial questions. This, he claims, was predicated upon the view that the Soviets would be content with less territory than they started with (after the Ribbentrop-Molotov pact). He regards it as indicative of a 'vestigial unwillingness to consider seriously Soviet points of view',[71] which was of course consistent with anti-Soviet and anti-communist attitudes in British military and diplomatic circles. In this he differs from Rothwell.

However, Folly also claims the meetings represent the start of a change in the FO view to one of possible collaboration based on a perception of Soviet sensitivity to diplomatic treatment, Soviet suspiciousness of British intentions, limited Soviet aims associated with security considerations and a policy of socialism in one country, and a realistic approach to foreign policy.[72] By mid-October 1941, he sees the FO as having been 'driven' by Eden,[73] who felt better relations with the Soviets were possible if Soviet suspicions could be allayed, into a sense that their analysis of Soviet imperviousness to external influence might have been mistaken, a sense that British actions could arouse or dampen Soviet suspicions. The FO was then inclined to reconsider their rejection of Cripps' notion of Soviet sensitivity and suspicion that the intention behind Western policy was the mutual exhaustion of the Soviet Union and Germany. Eden and Beaverbrook favoured political overtures in place of unavailable military assistance to assist Soviet morale, and Cripps' appeals for the Soviets to be treated with some diplomatic courtesy began to resonate in the FO.

The FO was unclear as to what might be wanted by the British and the Soviet Union in terms of the detail of post-war arrangements, but there was an FO perception that the Soviets were suspicious and had concerns over security. It seems that some officials in the FO perceived a need to offer something to the Soviets, but were constrained by political commitments and Churchill to confine themselves to some form of guarantee of security rather than territorial concessions. However, as I shall show below, such views were far from unanimous, for Cadogan, the influential Permanent Under-Secretary at the FO, opposed concessions all the way through the deliberations over the optimal way of dealing with the Soviet Union and over the debate regarding Stalin's demand for British recognition of the Soviet annexation of the Baltic states.

The resulting FO paper referred to a Soviet desire for approval of 'their annexation of the Baltic states and Eastern Poland' but went on, 'it will be difficult to give the Soviet Government much satisfaction on these points, and presumably we shall have to decline for the present to go beyond the first and second clauses of the Atlantic Charter.'[74] This view does seem to have reflected the presence of Cadogan at the meeting on 18 November 1941, for he supported Churchill's view that concessions were unnecessary and inappropriate. There was, then, notwithstanding the opinions of individuals within the FO, an acceptance by Eden, the Cabinet and the most senior FO echelon that Eden should offer Stalin assurance regarding Soviet involvement in the post-war settlement but no commitment as to frontiers. It seems that Churchill's opposition to concessions and the diplomatic constraint of the Atlantic Charter were decisive at this point.

The second phase of intense FO discussion of policy towards the Soviet Union took place in February 1942, after Eden's conversations with Stalin in December 1941. Folly claims that 'the FO had come to the conclusion that Stalin was interested in cooperation in November 1941.'[75] Yet he also claims that Eden and Sargent developed the idea of 'concessions to secure long-term cooperation'[76] in advance of FO consideration of what the notion might mean in policy terms, and that Eden presented the issue to the War Cabinet in January 1942 while FO discussions were proceeding.[77] The latter does appear to be the case, an indication of timing and sequence which is vital for any analysis of causation.

Folly sees this as the start of FO belief in the possibility of collaboration with the Soviets. Yet Soviet concern with security and sensitivity to diplomatic treatment did not preclude Soviet opportunism and expansion, as had been apparent in the Anglo-Soviet negotiations preceding the Nazi-Soviet pact, during which Soviet diplomacy had combined concern with security and expansionist opportunism. Even so there was in the FO, early in 1942, a desire to exert influence on the Soviets through diplomatic treatment, given that Britain was unable to help militarily or to acquiesce in Soviet post-war territorial demands, which does imply some perceived sensitivity. There was also a sense of the Soviets' being suspicious of British intentions and concerned over security. Yet neither interpretation is inconsistent with an attribution to the Soviets of pragmatism and realism, nor of opportunism and expansionism. Further, documentary evidence of an FO sense of Soviet desire to co-operate is absent in November 1941. A major influence on British policy was the British perception of Soviet military capability, and it may have been that the FO had some confidence in a Soviet desire to collaborate given the latter's military situation. There was though a clear difference of view between those who felt that the Soviet Union was sensitive to diplomatic treatment and those who felt, as Eden did, that unilateral concessions were necessary to secure the trust and collaboration of the Soviet Union. Meanwhile Churchill and Cadogan conceived of Anglo-Soviet relations in military rather than political terms, opposed unilateral or other concessions, felt that a British exhibition of military power was necessary (there had been no wartime British victory at that time), and believed that the Soviet Union respected power rather than concessions or promises.

The idea that the Soviets considered British policy over the Baltics an 'acid test of our sincerity'[78] came from Eden rather than the FO. Sargent shared Eden's view that 'Stalin was testing British attitudes with his frontier demands,'[79] but while Eden, Cripps and Beaverbrook proposed unilateral concessions Sargent argued for hard bargaining and reciprocity. On 5 February 1942, addressing the risk of Stalin's negotiating a separate peace with Germany once the Soviets' 1941 frontiers had been recovered and the alternative scenario of Soviet forces overrunning and communising Germany, Sargent recommended 'improving relations with the Soviet Govt.'. Yet he counselled against attempts to 'propitiate Stalin by one-sided sacrifices and surrenders'.[80] To achieve a 'Treaty of Alliance to cover not only the war but the peacemaking and the post-war reconstruction of Europe' Britain would 'have to make concessions not only on the Baltic issue but probably on other matters', but concessions 'should be balanced by corresponding concessions on the part of Stalin',[81] a pragmatic approach to Anglo-Soviet relations.

Cadogan worried that if Soviet forces recovered the Soviets' 1941 frontier Britain could be 'double-crossed by Stalin'. He continued, 'one ought to hope for continued pressure by the Soviet, with erosion of further manpower and material and not too great a geographical advance!'[82] Even Eden's remarks didn't resonate with confidence – doubting the likelihood of Soviet advances he admitted the difficulties a victory for Stalin would bring and added, 'we must do all in our power to lessen grievances and come to terms with him for the future. This may not prevent him from double-crossing us, but it will at least lessen pretexts.'[83] British mystification regarding Soviet motives then continued even after the experience of the nature of Soviet foreign policy and diplomacy of the Anglo-Soviet negotiations in 1939, and was reflected in the diversity of view within the British political and official elite.

There followed during February 1942 a debate in the FO as to the best means of handling the Soviets given their military utility and incessant demands. The sequence was started by the British Chargé d'Affaires in the Soviet Union, Baggallay. His views are important because of their persuasiveness to the FO, which is attributable to the dearth of alternative sources of reliable information as to Soviet policy and to their consonance with emerging FO views. He claimed that the 'Soviet Government are only interested in us as allies to the extent to which they think our activities will assist:

(a) their own victory in the war
(b) their own security after the war.'[84]

Baggallay regarded Soviet policy as pragmatic. The Soviets respected above all power, as manifested in 'results alone', and were 'not interested in the reasons or motives' (that much might have been inferred from Leninism, with its notion of counter-revolution not by intent but by results, and was an inherent part of Soviet reasoning). The Soviets' view of British military utility was low (unsurprisingly), and British assent to Soviet territorial demands seen as necessary to Soviet post-war security was a test of British good will. Though he saw the Soviets as 'suspicious to unbelievable degree'[85] he claimed that non-acceptance would not necessarily make the Soviets 'more difficult to deal with perhaps the contrary'. Baggallay then supported the notions of Soviet suspiciousness and susceptibility to British policy but not unilateral concessions. Summarising, his view was that

> 'the Soviet Government are supremely self-centred and so long as they get all they want or all we can give (I do not mean only "give" material things but collaboration in every field) will give not more than they have to in return.'[86]

He agreed that 'it is imperative that the eastern front should hold and that we should make every effort in our power to help it hold' but pointed out that if the Soviets received all they wanted without conditions 'they will not trouble to fulfil their obligations to ourselves even in small matters'.[87]

Pointing to British attempts to meet all Soviet requests Baggallay also remarked on the adverse effect of applauding Soviet military feats. The British press and public were 'free to criticise any failure, apparent or real, to support Soviet Government'.[88] This he felt gave the Soviets little incentive to meet even minimal obligations.

On 20 February Baggallay said he would not expect British acquiescence over the Baltics to elicit from the Soviets 'any noticeable increase in their readiness to meet our requests meanwhile, especially as they would have one incentive the less for meeting them' and that non-acceptance could make the Soviets wonder 'how they had displeased us with a view to remedying the matter or at any rate to decide that as we appear to be hostile on at least one issue they must try to conciliate us as long as there is a chance of our being useful to them'.[89] Baggallay concluded that policy should be made without consideration of the effect on the Soviets being 'more or less "difficult" for the moment'.[90]

Warner, looking for an 'agreed doctrine' regarding policy towards the Soviets, concurred with Baggallay's views. In particular 'we should moderate our adulation of the Russian effort, not offer them assistance they have not asked for, examine any requests for assistance and give a straight answer based on reasonable and fully explained grounds; and occasionally, when we have reason to feel that we are not getting a satisfactory deal from them, show our displeasure not by complaint or threats or (I think Mr. Baggallay would add) attempts to drive bargains, but merely by not responding to some Russian desideratum.' Treatment of the Soviets should take account of the knowledge that 'the Russians resent being singled out for special methods of treatment as if they were something peculiar (Eden remarked here, "I agree"). They would wish to be treated in a normal way and not cajoled nor treated to fine complimentary phrases, but taken into our full confidence, and told what we can do and what we cannot do on a reasonable and collaborative basis of examination,' despite 'the fact that they are peculiar.' As a 'corollary' Warner said the Soviets should be consulted on all matters affecting the war and peace to the extent that this was possible, a proviso indicative of mistrust of the Soviets – he minuted, 'in practice consultation with the Russians on many of these wider matters would be difficult, if not impossible,' which drew from Cadogan the comment, 'it is they who make it so.'[91] Warner's covering comment on 17 February is telling in admitting that 'it may be said that the enclosed minute aims at the impossible.'[92] Warner then acknowledged Soviet sensitivity to Western treatment, but proposed a policy of limited Soviet inclusion with no concessions. Folly has characterised this policy as one of firmness and frankness.[93]

These views were endorsed by Lockhart with the added advice that Soviet demands should be met then, in February 1942, to avoid having to acquiesce later,[94] a policy therefore differentiated from Warner's. His 'therapeutic trust' notion argued for decent treatment of the Soviets on the basis that the Soviets would then reciprocate, though Soviet diplomatic behaviour had in the negotiations for an alliance with Britain in 1939 been exploitative of any concessions. It is worth noting that Lockhart's view was accompanied by the aversion that seems to have characterised all British dealings with the Soviets at this time—

> 'treat them like civilised beings and decent people and they will try to behave like civilised beings.'[95]

Strang, who had been involved in the negotiations with the Soviet Union in 1939, and who had been appalled by the experience, agreed—

> It is essential to treat the Russians as though we thought they were reasonable human beings. But as they are not, in fact, reasonable human beings, but dominated by an almost insane suspicion we have to combine this treatment with infinite patience.[96]

He counselled against any 'indication that we distrust them', 'threats' and 'flattery, adulation and the sentimental approach' and commented, 'they are pursuing their interests and they expect us to pursue ours. The more successful we are in our part of the war, the more they will respect us.' Suspicions as to British will to fight and public adulation of the Soviet effort had 'aroused in them something akin to contempt'.[97] Eden annotated, 'I agree. This is good sense,' a remarkable comment given Strang's focus on the importance of demonstrations of military power and hard bargaining rather than the sort of unilateral concession Eden had been advocating over the Baltics. Though Eden's seeming to agree with views apparently antithetical to his own or seeming to endorse opposing positions seems to have been characteristic of him, it is possible that he did not view appreciation of the utility of military victories, hard bargaining and *Realpolitik* concessions over the Baltics as being incompatible with one another. The latter two at least do seem entirely inconsistent. The diversity of view within the FO under Eden seems indicative of a lack of consensus and of any firm indication from Eden, though it is also possible that the FO was in a formative period in the development of policy towards the Soviet Union as a wartime ally and that Soviet diplomacy was so erratic and 'undiplomatic' as to elicit very different views. Having said that the experience of negotiations for an alliance in 1939 should have been instructive for the FO.

Stalin's Order of the Day on 23 February interrupted these FO discussions. It referred to the 'liberation of Russian territory rather than a struggle against Nazism'.[98] Was this a sign of intent to pursue a separate peace with Germany once the Soviet Union's 1941 frontiers had been recovered? Baggallay tended to discount such doubts, referring to the Soviets' desire for 'security against second attack' and to Stalin's interest in pursuing any Soviet advantage to accomplish the 'annihilation of German military power'.[99] Dew saw the communiqué as an attempt to divide German opinion and to nullify the effects of anti-Bolshevist propaganda, but also as indicative of Stalin's feeling that 'Russia was fighting the war on her own and without sufficient assistance from the Allies and that consequently she will follow her own policy. As regards an agreement between Russia and Germany, Mr. Baggallay shows, and I entirely agree, that this is possible though not probable.'[100] Warner concurred.[101] The issue demonstrates the continuing centrality to British policy of keeping the Soviets in the war but different views of what was necessary to that end. The 'theme was central to the discussions of frontier recognition in early 1942',[102] and for Churchill it was a major factor in his final decision over the Baltics, overcoming FO recommendations for reciprocal concessions.

Sargent was unmoved, remarking that the notion that 'if we have nothing tangible to offer the

Soviet Government we can make up for the deficiency by frequent administrations of flattery and congratulations' was 'a minor form of appeasement and is open to the same objections and dangers which are the inevitable consequences of appeasement, whatever form it may take'.[103]

Churchill may have concurred with some of Strang's and Sargent's sentiments, though not with Sargent's advocacy of reciprocal concessions over the Baltics, for in February 1942 he remained opposed to any concessions. And Cadogan pointed to repeated and unavailing attempts to treat the Soviets as 'normal allies'[104] in reminding his subordinates of the necessity of military success in negotiations with the Soviets, a perspective that focused on Soviet respect for power rather than the form of diplomatic encounters.

Eden again appended 'I agree', presumably with Cadogan, as he continued, 'I should find my task easier if we could occasionally have a military success, but this is to ask too much – in the next few months.'[105] Yet he had only days earlier agreed that the Soviets did not want special treatment, an indication that he believed the form of diplomatic activity made a difference. This apparent confusion of views in Eden was to continue, yet it also points to a general difficulty in differentiating individuals' views on policy towards the Soviet Union. The conclusion to this exchange of views within the FO is Warner's undated and handwritten minute, 'it was later decided not to proceed with this'.[106]

The FO was then, in February 1942, to some extent divided over the Baltics. Sargent regarded their surrender as unavoidable but wanted reciprocal concessions. Warner felt 'the British Government might have to go it alone',[107] without US approval but seems to have disapproved of unilateral concessions. Cadogan remained opposed to acquiescence in the Soviet annexation. Yet there was an emerging FO view as to how best to deal with the Soviet Union in general, and a consensus on no unilateral concessions and a tough, hard bargaining stance, supported by British military power if possible. Meanwhile the Foreign Secretary remained in favour of just such a unilateral concession over the Baltics. On 24 February Cadogan deplored Eden's 'amoral, realpolitik line', which 'was never his', approved of American principles and was confident of Churchill's position.[108] By 25 March however he noted Eden was 'determined to give in to Stalin. P.M has now been brought round, so I have no doubt Cabinet will agree.'[109]

Rothwell concludes that 'the consensus seemed to be that there was no magic key to achieving results in dealings with the Russians',[110] and Folly attributes the final absence of an FO policy to the intervention of political decision, recording that Churchill in the end decided that a concession should be made over the Baltics given the Soviets' adverse military situation, with their offensive stopped and a German offensive imminent.[111] On 25 March 1942 the Cabinet decided to acquiesce in the Soviets' annexation of the Baltics, but only for reasons associated with the prosecution of the war, that is, to sustain the Soviet war effort.

FO involvement over the Baltics then separates into two distinct phases. When Eden met Stalin in December 1941 there was an official though not unanimous FO view that no undertakings on post-war frontiers should be made, which was congruent with the views of the Cabinet and Churchill and consonant with the Atlantic Charter. Pleas from Eden and the views of some FO officials that concessions should be made were disregarded. Then, in March 1942, the finalisation of an FO view was pre-empted by a Cabinet decision at variance with all the expressed FO views around that time. Despite their respective relationships with Eden and Churchill, Sargent and Cadogan were in the end disregarded in decisions made at the political level. For Churchill the reasons were military, a need to keep the Soviets in the war given their adverse position, while for Eden the concession seemed rational and was related also to post-war co-operation in Europe.

In assessing Eden's relationship to the FO one has to differentiate between November and December 1941, and February, March and April 1942. In November and December 1941 Eden did favour concessions to the Soviets to allay suspicions (as did some in the FO). Yet Eden did see

Stalin without anything to give, an ultimate acquiescence in the wishes of Churchill, the Cabinet and senior FO officials. On his return he was clear that concessions were necessary. Early in 1942 Eden's position seemed unaffected by the debate in the FO, though he did seem to concur with various (incompatible) FO positions in a customary avoidance of open dispute. In the end an emerging FO view favouring reciprocal concessions and hard bargaining was overtaken by a Cabinet decision to concede over the Baltics without any Soviet concessions. Eden's case for unilateral concessions prevailed in the end, not for the reasons Eden presented but rather military ones.

The Baltic issue was then one in which the Cabinet, and Churchill in particular, represented the locus of decision-making power, with policy not influenced by FO views despite their extensive discussions of the options for dealing with the Soviet Union. It was then the personalities and the dynamics of the War Cabinet that mattered, and in particular the pivotal characters of Churchill and Eden and Churchill's perception of wartime military necessity, possibly influenced by Eden's views.

Churchill's position as wartime PM was dominant in relation to Eden and the Cabinet, and Charmley sees Churchill's resistance to concessions to the Soviets and any discussion of post-war territorial arrangements between November 1941 and March 1942 as deferring to the wishes of the United States. Charmley claims that 'it was a measure of American influence on Churchill, as well as of Churchill's influence on British foreign policy, that Eden's Soviet policy was defeated,'[112] that Churchill ran British foreign policy in the war and that 'running through Churchill's attitude like a leitmotif was the theme of America'.[113] Charmley links 'Churchill's obsession with defeating Germany and his need for American aid in this task'.[114] He refers to 'Eden's inability to challenge Churchill successfully'[115] and concludes that 'Eden wanted Britain to have a foreign policy of her own, and he would have liked to have run it himself; in neither endeavour was he successful; instead Churchill's Atlanticist preferences won the day.'[116]

As to the Soviet annexation of the Baltics Charmley, noting that 'it was Churchill who vetoed the idea of granting Stalin his 1941 frontiers',[117] indicates that 'Churchill's rejection of Stalin's territorial ambitions owed more to his fear that acceptance of them would upset the Americans than it did to anything else.'[118] Yet there was also Churchill's abiding anti-communism and his opposition in principle to unilateral concessions. And Charmley does not mention the *volte-face* by Churchill in March 1942 on grounds of needing to sustain the Soviet war effort, albeit after protracted efforts to secure from Roosevelt understanding and acquiescence.

Eden was then in an awkward position between the FO and Churchill, especially given the mistrust and disdain that the FO and Churchill felt for each other. For Churchill the FO was tainted by its support of appeasement, while the FO detested Churchill's interference but also deplored his lack of interest in post-war matters. Over the Baltic issue it does seem that Eden had clear views in advance of a formulated FO policy, and that the FO was overruled in March 1942 by decisions taken by Churchill under the influence of the perceived necessities of the war situation rather than Eden's case for acceptance of the Soviet annexations to keep the Soviet Union in the war, to elicit a sense of trust, to take account of Soviet sensitivity to diplomatic treatment and to secure post-war collaboration. Eden's reintroducing the issue into Cabinet discussions may have made some difference, though it was also the case that the issue forced itself through Stalin's insistence onto the agenda of Anglo-Soviet relations. Eden's influence on Churchill is alluded to by Harvey in his diary, in his reference to Eden's private conversations with Churchill, which are evidenced in terms of their having taken place but not in terms of their content. On 6 March 1942 he notes, 'P.M. dined with A. E. last night. Now at last P. M. has come round about Russia. He says he agrees that we should accept Stalin's demand for recognition of 1941 frontiers and that Roosevelt must be pressed to agree or let us agree.'[119] There is however no clear attribution of decisive influence to Eden here, for while the implication is that Churchill had at last seen reason, the possibility of his having done so at least in part for reasons beyond Eden's advocacy is not excluded.

Other Cabinet ministers influential in foreign policy were the Labour politicians Attlee and Bevin, both of whom shared Churchill's anti-communism. Attlee was concerned that acquiescence in one demand would result only in further demands, and even threatened resignation if Soviet annexation of the Baltics was accepted, yet in the event accepted Churchill's decision. Bevin also wanted confirmation that Stalin's demand over the Baltics was his last. Yet neither presented Churchill with the realistic possibility of Cabinet division and were thus not a constraint on his final decision. Harvey's view of the influence of the Cabinet was clear. Referring to the question of Soviet frontiers he commented, 'A. E. will have a lone fight as no one else in the cabinet will speak up to the P.M.'[120]

In conclusion it does seem that the Cabinet rather that the FO was the major locus of decision-making power over the Baltics issue, and that within it the influence of Churchill as Prime Minister was dominant for a number of reasons. These included public confidence, his background as an anti-appeaser, the relative isolation of Eden and the subservience of the rest of the Cabinet, and, beyond all this, the complexities of Churchill's formidable personal attributes and relationships with Eden and other Cabinet ministers. Eden's influence was also constrained by a sense of Churchill as wartime Prime Minister with all the prerogatives and responsibilities of that office in time of war and by a clear sense of how far it was wise to pursue any issue. Yet amidst such considerable differences of view as to the means necessary to maximise the war effort and so avoid defeat, there was also within the Cabinet a broad commonality of view as to ends, an ethos of the survival and victory of the British Empire, and as to attitudes, in terms of antipathy for communism and aversion for the Soviet regime and for Soviet diplomatic practice.

Further, part of Churchill's enormous power as PM derived, as has been seen, from the absence of an alternative war premier. The lack of consensus as to policy over the Baltic issue makes clear the effect of Churchill's domination of the Cabinet and disregard of the FO. Yet there was a shared understanding that the Soviets and the Americans were needed for British national survival and ultimate victory (a factor in Churchill's *volte-face* was that there had not been a single British military victory at that time), and differences were confined to how to achieve a balance between their competing demands and how much in the way of British concessions was needed to keep both nations in the war against Germany – Eden may have been something of an exception to this exclusive orientation to the war effort in his concern with better post-war relations with the Soviet Union and his lack of profound aversion to communism, but the resolution of the issue revolved around what was necessary to prevent a Soviet exit from the war without alienating the US. I shall now turn to the influences on decision-making as a consequence of Churchill's domination.

As has been shown, allaying Soviet suspicion of British motives by a policy of concessions became an option favoured by Eden on his return from Moscow in December 1941, supported by Beaverbrook, Cripps and to an extent by Sargent (who however insisted that concessions should be reciprocal rather than unilateral), but resisted by Cadogan and Churchill, who continued to insist on Soviet realism in foreign policy rather than sensitivity to diplomacy and who wanted no concessions on principle. Churchill took the view that Anglo-Soviet relations were military rather than political and believed the Soviets took that view too. Concessions, he felt, have no effect on realists and would elicit further demands in an opportunistic way but have no effect on the military situation whatever. Within the FO Cadogan wondered if concessions were necessary given a renewal of the German offensive, though there was also a sense that 'the Soviets often manufactured such grievances in an attempt to win concessions',[121] which indicates a British perception of Soviet opportunism. With Attlee supporting Churchill the Cabinet was split, but not evenly, with Eden in the minority. Folly sees Sargent, Jebb, Warner, Lockhart and Eden as clear in their view of the Soviets as sensitive to British diplomacy, concerned with security yet realistic and so limited in aims, but in fact both Sargent and Warner entertained grave suspicions regarding Soviet diplomacy and advocated firmness and frankness rather than unilateral concessions that would be interpreted as weakness. The conclusion is that there were in the FO different interpretations and views as to the optimal policy for dealing with the Soviets but that the emergence of an FO view was pre-empted by the Cabinet decision to acquiesce in the Soviet annexation of the Baltics.

The evidence of FO papers and Cabinet minutes is clearer in its outlines of policy options and situations than on processes of decision-making, relationships and individual influence on policy, which necessitates consideration of other available forms of evidence. Churchill's version of events, understandings, intentions, roles and influences was for some considerable time the only source. It is informing but also a selective, cultivated impression of the relationship with Eden, and there is the possibility of either deliberate or inadvertent bias, in selection and omission, but also in explanation – Churchill for instance does not give an account of his indecision over the Baltic states but rather a clear basis for his change of view, yet it seems he has one eye on the future and his place in history, and the other on the past. It is also noteworthy that he departed in writing his history from an initial focus on his own minutes.[122] There are other tendencies peculiar to autobiographical accounts – one is the tendency to misremember the past in self-enhancing ways. Other accounts do have their own bias, of course, as for instance the diaries of Eden's Private Secretary and personal friend, Oliver Harvey.

Eden seems to have been cautious, indecisive and discreet, especially in terms of expressing a clear personal view and defending it, though the Baltics issue does seem to be an exception. Eden's memoirs are curiously unrevealing, pervaded by a sense of restraint apart from a clear personal fondness[123] and admiration for Churchill, an indication of the influence of differences in personality, expressive style, sense of propriety and purpose. What was conveyed in private conversations between Churchill and Eden seems to be beyond both the documentary record and Eden's personal account.

Churchill's power and influence over foreign policy were derived from a number of different sources. To begin with there were the prerogatives of the Prime Minister in the British political system, which include powers of appointment and dismissal of ministers, control of the Cabinet agenda and of the issue to be decided upon. Eden owed his return to the front rank of political life to Churchill, and it is notable that Churchill appointed in Eden someone unlikely to resist him over foreign policy. In fact Eden acknowledged that foreign-policy decisions were ultimately a matter for the PM. Added to this was Churchill's enormous stature in the country and as a war premier, the history of his role in the Battle of Britain and the emotional effect on political circles and the nation as a whole of the stirring eloquence in his great war speeches, which left a sense of Britain's having a historic duty to perform – his oratory seemed to embrace adversity in conviction of the triumph of British valour to come.[124] Kennedy remarks that unlike Chamberlain, whose 'mutual dislike' for the Labour movement was clear, 'Churchill was a genuinely popular leader of a national coalition' who had 'no real rivals'.[125] And Charmley refers to Eden's 'isolation in Cabinet', which 'enabled Churchill to get his way in foreign policy'. I now turn to the influence of Churchill's and Eden's personal attributes.

Churchill has been described as 'emotional and impulsive',[126] 'combative' and possessed of 'great vitality, confidence and determination' yet also of 'pessimism and a depressive streak'.[127] On occasion he could be 'insensitive, tactless and inconsiderate', yet also exhibit 'generosity of spirit, magnanimity, humour and at times an unexpected streak of humility'.[128] Addison refers to Churchill's 'great ruthlessness' and 'enormous egotism', but also his ability to woo, cajole and flatter where necessary.[129] Charmley observes that 'Churchill's views on Soviet policy fluctuated as much as did his views on strategy, and in both areas he was capable of being simultaneously optimistic and pessimistic'.[130]

Other factors were also not without influence. Apart from his profound swings of mood, Churchill was already sixty-seven by the time of the Baltic issue, and on 26 December 1941 he suffered a heart attack, which was kept secret even from him.[131] Yet these factors did not preclude his resisting Commons pressure for Cabinet changes (not least Churchill's ceasing to be both Prime Minister and Minister of Defence) in a context of British military failures early in 1942. In the event Churchill prevailed, testament to his personal resilience and there being no alternative to him as wartime Prime Minister, but Charmley, noting Churchill's dismay at British military fortunes in a context of Soviet resistance, remarks that 'Churchill's doctor wondered whether it was a loss of the 'old crusading fire' which made Churchill more willing to contemplate making concessions to the Russians than he had been in December and January'.[132] Jefferys notes that 'the Prime Minister was, at least initially, downcast by this turn of events. On 21 January 1942 he told Anthony Eden that the majority of the Conservative Party hated him; he would, he claimed, gladly relinquish his burdens to make way for a younger man. But this mood was quickly overtaken by a determination to hit back at the critics.'[133] The latter does throw doubt on any specific effect of Churchill's difficulties with the Commons on his *volte-face* regarding the Baltic issue,[134] but it also brings one to Churchill's extraordinary personal qualities, which made him so resilient under fire and meant that his working relations were not uni-dimensional, which may in part explain why the exasperation that his erratic behaviour caused did not translate into any enduring rebellion. Ismay, Churchill's Chief of Staff, excused Churchill's continual interference by saying 'Churchill could not be judged by ordinary standards,' for 'he was indispensable and completely irreplaceable,' and 'his courage, enthusiasm and industry were boundless, and his loyalty absolute.'[135]

Churchill also expressed genuine appreciation of Eden, and their relationship was one of trust, affection and common purpose.[136] And there was, added to the anti-appeasement credentials which had brought Churchill to office and the sense in which he represented the nation at war, a general admiration for Churchill's personal qualities, which included an astonishing work rate for a man of his age and health, a resolution that outlasted his swings of mood and what Harvey, not an ardent fan of Churchill's policies towards the Soviet Union, referred to as the 'energy and gallantry of the old gentleman'.[137] Maddening though his interventions could be, there was no doubt as to Churchill's physical bravery, his tirelessness and self-sacrifice.[138] And instances of irrepressible and idiosyncratic, very human behaviour also serve 'to explain the hold which Churchill was able to establish over his intimates'.[139] Eden did have good pragmatic reasons (associated with his political future and his abhorrence of indiscretion) to fear and so to support Churchill, but the picture is more complex than sheer self-interest or the force of Churchill's personality, for he was regarded as a figure for whom there was no substitute and who was held in considerable esteem and affection, despite periods in which his policies and roles were challenged. Though written in 1965 Attlee's obituary essay is, for a man not given to sentimentality, noteworthy. For Attlee Churchill was 'brave, gifted, inexhaustible and indomitable', possessed of 'energy and poetry'.[140]

Eden's personality was clearly complex. Suave, sophisticated, charming of manner, a skilled negotiator, ambitious and confident in some instances though indecisive and uncertain in others, he was plagued with indifferent health, and was touchy, irascible and sensitive as to the prerogatives of his own position as Foreign Secretary. Having said that he acknowledged the prerogatives and powers of the Prime Minister in regard to foreign policy and seems to have disliked open confrontation. As Foreign Secretary under Churchill the evidence is that Eden was more diplomat than policy-maker, adept at following a clear brief but averse to taking policy positions and defending them. Having said that the evidence of the Baltic issue itself is of Eden's discreet perseverance despite Churchill's and Cabinet disapproval at the outset and for some time thereafter.

Charmley points to Eden's understanding of Churchill's limited capacity for change. Churchill would not 'work with a War Cabinet', for he liked 'to move all the pieces himself'. Eden observed that there was 'no day to day direction of the war except by the Chiefs of Staff and Winston', but recognised that, 'Winston is probably constitutionally incapable of working any other way'.[141] Having been encouraged to take on Churchill and demand reforms in the way the war was being managed Eden was, according to Charmley, 'not the man for such a fight', 'as he himself recognised'. And Charmley concludes that 'doubts about his own capacity, loyalty to Churchill, and self-interest all combined to make Eden a loyal (if complaining) lieutenant.'[142]

Dutton points to a relationship 'characterised by mutual affection and an inherent loyalty on Eden's side'[143] but one in which 'as Foreign Secretary in wartime Eden had to work within parameters set by Churchill,'[144] a situation Eden accepted, for 'in wartime, Eden later wrote, diplomacy is strategy's twin, and the figure of the premier was the dominant one in both,'[145] and 'in the last resort Eden had to accept that there would be moments when Churchill would continue to take the lead in whichever aspect of British foreign policy attracted the attention of his fertile, but not always predictable, brain. Having accepted that the Prime Minister was essential in embodying the national will to continue the struggle against Hitler, Eden knew that this was a price he had to pay.'[146] Yet Dutton also refers to Eden's 'tenacity and patience', a preparedness to take Churchill on. Eden was 'no yes-man and serious disagreements did occur', and 'it often fell to Eden to represent his department's longer-term view against Churchill's short-term military objectives.' He does however mention Eden's inclination to use 'charm' rather than 'bluster'. Dutton also notes the limited parameters to any discord, commenting that 'in terms of the underlying goals of Britain's diplomacy Eden and Churchill were fundamentally at one.'[147] In the immediate context of the Baltic issue in late 1941, Dutton mentions that Harvey noted, 'after his first enthusiasm the premier was getting bitter as the Russians become a liability – no-one stands up to him but A. E.'[148] Harvey also remarks that Bevin's foreign policy was 'much what Anthony's would have been if he had ever been allowed to have one'[149] and that 'he could never have stood another Government as No. 2 to Winston'.[150] While Churchill and Eden did share overall objectives in terms of wartime victory and Britain's place in the world they did disagree on the means by which those aims should best be achieved on occasion as they had different perceptions of for instance the effect of concessions to the Soviets, over which Eden was proved wrong as it elicited further Soviet demands rather than inspiring trust or confidence in British intentions.

Eden's role and influence in Cabinet and in relation to Churchill do then continue to invite controversy. This cannot be explained entirely by reference to a confusion of form and content, with Eden averse to open confrontation but not to diplomatic persistence over an issue such as the Baltics, and it seems that Eden did accept that Churchill's dominance in Cabinet was inevitable and also his own limitations in terms of preparedness to confront him and the possibilities of constraining him.[151] Eden's influence seems then to be limited to persevering with the issue and continuing to make the case until circumstances became propitious for a change of policy.

Folly's interpretation of Eden's proposal is that it is evidence of a belief in Soviet sensitivity to diplomatic treatment and is linked to perceived Soviet concerns regarding security, a view that is seen to be an alternative to attributions of realism and pragmatism by Churchill and Cadogan. This seems to be part of a rather different view of Eden to that held elsewhere, for Folly sees the FO as having been run by Eden, who was the first to identify the need for a policy towards the Soviet Union, and who recommended acceptance of the Soviet annexations of the Baltics to the Cabinet prior to the FO's forming a view on the Soviet Union's 1941 frontiers. This idea that Eden introduced a new slant into British foreign policy that represented a departure from the traditional pragmatism and from Churchill's exclusive focus on military matters and winning the war has however been challenged by Charmley, who points out that Eden's endorsement of Soviet claims to the Baltics and Eastern Poland could be seen to have a pragmatic basis, in that 'if the Soviets lost the war, the question would be largely irrelevant. However, if they won it, their armies would be so far west that they would already have occupied the territories which they were asking for.'[152]

It is worth noting that this was in fact Eden's argument, and that not long after this time Eden remarked, in the context of the British Military Mission's policy of toughness with the Soviets, that 'it is pointless to bargain with the Soviets, particularly from a position of weakness',[153] a *Realpolitik* stance. The differences in the British official and political establishment can then it seems be overdrawn, but in any event, while it is true that Eden did keep the Baltic issue live by repeatedly introducing it into Cabinet discussions it is also the case that the issue was never going to go away just because of Stalin's continued insistence upon it.

In fact the evidence tends to support not the influence of a new attitudinal disposition towards the Soviet Union but rather the pre-existing pragmatic interpretation. There had clearly been no abandonment of a profound British anti-communism or mistrust for Soviet diplomacy, and any apparent change was based on commonality of interest against a new adversary in Germany, with the alteration merely from a British policy of detachment and reserve to association on pragmatic grounds only and with reservations.

The only change was then circumstantial, firstly in the reality of the German attack upon the Soviet Union, which reoriented the focus of Soviet diplomatic activity from Germany to Britain, and secondly in the unexpected character of Soviet resistance and endurance. British policy was then pragmatic (as was Soviet policy), disregarding the Soviets when the assessment was that they could do nothing to assist the war effort and taking advantage of Soviet resistance when it materialised and when the Soviets' position rendered them amenable to Western overtures. In other words it was only the reality of Soviet resistance that changed the optimal policy, in that assessments of Soviet capability were revised. The decisive changes were then in circumstance and so in perception of the best means to pursue national interests at the time. The documentary record indicates continuing British reservations set against a need to retain the Soviets as wartime allies – though some, such as Eden, looked further, to post-war European security. Finally the issue may turn on semantics and the meaning of words such as pragmatism and realism. It does seem that it was pragmatic and entirely rational to disregard the Soviets during the time of the Nazi-Soviet pact and equally so to alter the policy, albeit with reservations as to Soviet trustworthiness, when the Soviets became allies in the war against Germany and had displayed some utility to the British war effort through their resistance. In terms of the question of Soviet immunity and susceptibility to British influence, one has a rational British perception of Soviet immunity during the period of the Ribbentrop-Molotov pact, in which Stalin's motives were perceived to be an opportunistic search for security through annexation of parts of Poland and of the Baltic republics, and one equally so of susceptibility in the period of wartime necessity of alliance with Britain. It is then difficult to concur with Folly that the pragmatic version of British policy is incorrect and that the late 1941 period represented a radical departure in British policy towards the Soviets in terms of attitude or actual policy, the entirety of which seems to have been oriented to winning the war.

Keeble differentiates a developing 'respect and sympathy for the scale of the Soviet war effort and the depth of suffering of the Soviet people' from the political and diplomatic in saying 'the day to day conduct of relations was rarely free from friction', and 'there was no point at which it could be said that a genuine mutual understanding had been arrived at'. He continues with references to Churchill's 'innate dislike' for the Soviets, and concludes that 'mistrust was never wholly eradicated' and that 'the bond between Britain and the Soviet Union, in so far as it existed, depended upon the common enemy and dissolved with his defeat,'[154] a clear attribution of pragmatism and maintenance of the wartime alliance to optimise the war effort.

Some of the confusion in the debate may be attributable to a conflation of meaning of terms that seems to beset discussion of the perception of Soviet intentions in general. For instance, a perception of there having been an overriding security motivation behind Soviet foreign policy does not predict any specific Soviet foreign policy, in that expansionist and opportunistic polices can also be represented as being driven by security concerns, and the two motivations are not mutually exclusive, as the British found in regard to Soviet diplomacy in 1939. And there is a corresponding uncertainty as to what constitutes pragmatism, for the term may be attributed to both Churchill's position of opposition to concessions in principle and to Eden's advocacy of recognition of the Soviet annexation of the Baltics. The term *Realpolitik* meanwhile could be used to describe Eden's recommendation that the Soviet annexation of the Baltics should be recognised, Churchill's sense that military power was all that would ever be respected by the Soviets, and Attlee's and Bevin's concern that each British concession would only elicit another Soviet demand.

Folly's analysis assumes that there was some departure from the previous policy of reserve.[155] Yet the notions of Soviet immunity to British influence when part of a pact with Germany in 1939 and 1940 and susceptibility to such influence thereafter, when at war with the latter, are entirely consistent inferences. And Soviet demands to be treated as an equal and to have its security concerns considered may well have been associated with opportunism and expansionism in a state pervaded by paranoia in its political establishment yet also at the same time quite capable of cynically misrepresenting opportunism as a concern with security.

Folly warns against permitting post-war experience and attitudes to influence one's view of British attitudes towards the Soviet Union in the war, but then seems to infer from a slender interlude of apparent collaboration between Britain and the Soviet Union later in the war, informed by the success of the wartime alliance and the projected opening of a second front in northern France, that in the discussions between 14 and 19 November 1941 there took place some initial indication of a change in British attitude, a revision of the previous policy of reserve to one of belief in the possibility of genuine collaboration. In fact such hopes, to the extent that they ever existed, came in a brief interval in 1944 and were accompanied by a sense of need for continued wartime collaboration and the desirability of good relations with the Soviet Union after the war given that Soviet power in post-war Europe was by 1944 expected to be overwhelming and was accompanied by fears regarding a return to US isolationism. They were also however accompanied by serious reservations and expressions of mistrust.

My own view is that there was no departure from a pragmatic policy, and that the FO and Eden attempted to find some means of improving the relationship with the Soviets to keep the latter in the war because of the paucity of possible British military assistance to the Soviet Union at that time. The assumption in the Northern Department of Soviet sensitivity seems one driven by necessity, in that between November 1941 and February 1942 there was no possibility of assisting the Soviets or keeping them fighting by means of the direct military assistance Stalin periodically requested (for twenty-five to thirty divisions to be sent to the eastern front) or the opening of a second front in northern France. British policy was then left to search for means of ensuring continued Soviet resistance. There was then it seems a conflation of necessity and desirability with probability and plausibility, with some FO clinging to a notion of influence over the Soviets by means of diplomatic overtures that committed Britain to nothing, such as the 'Volga Charter' and attempts to postpone territorial changes. Yet even here the ultimate aim of the policy was military, and there were significant differences as to recommendations for policy. Some favoured unilateral concessions, as was the case with Eden's advocacy of acceptance of the Soviet Union's 1941 frontiers, though even here the policy is not inconsistent with pragmatism, as has been made clear. Others, such as Orme Sargent, stipulated that concessions should be made only if reciprocal concessions were made by the Soviet Union, which is also consistent with the notion of pragmatism in British policy. The distinction Folly is drawing is worth elaborating upon, between Churchill and his conviction of

Soviet realism and respect for power, as in displays of military prowess, and the assumption of Soviet sensitivity to diplomatic treatment and desire for collaboration. For Folly differentiates his view, which is of a belief in Soviet sensitivity (rather than immunity) to British overtures and concessions and desire to collaborate, from what he represents as the prevailing wisdom, which is that British policy was pragmatic, was never predicated on a co-operative Soviet Union, and was driven by the need to win the war against Germany with Soviet military assistance (and, later, to police Germany after the war).

Taken together the evidence does not lend itself to Folly's attribution of genuine conviction in the British political and official establishment as to the possibilities of continued collaboration between Britain and the Soviets or of an understanding that was mutual and realistic. Keeble refers to a particular instance over the arctic convoys and the restrictions placed upon, and general treatment of, British personnel. Churchill made it clear he did not regard the convoys as a 'contract or bargain'. There followed the tersest of exchanges between Stalin and Churchill, in the course of which the former was so insulting that the matter had to be smoothed over by Eden, with Stalin and Molotov, in October. Keeble observes that

> 'intergovernmental exchanges illustrated only too clearly the classic problems of British-Soviet cooperation and the deep difference of approach. As with the controversy over the opening of the second front, the Soviet Union made it a matter of national pride to regard British help as a contractual obligation and having done so, left the British government to regret having embodied a goodwill gesture in a formal document. Even at a time when the two countries were allied in a common struggle for survival and the British individuals concerned were suffering in the common cause, the rigidity of Soviet bureaucracy could not be eased, nor could normal considerations of humanity be made to prevail without the personal intervention of the Prime Minister.'[156]

And even Harvey, a supporter of Eden and the notion of Soviet sensitivity, seems to endorse Keeble's view: 'I fear the truth is that there is so deep a gulf between British and Russian mentality that we never have and never will have confidence and understanding.'[157]

This evidence does confirm the supposition of the Soviets as morbidly suspicious but also as opportunistic and antipathetic to the West, and very much endorses the view that after the war became a commonplace in Cold War rhetoric but is mentioned above as existing within the FO at this time, of the Soviet Union as an 'abnormal state' with which normal diplomatic relations were not possible.

There was no attitude change at a fundamental level, for pre-existing anti-communist and anti-Soviet attitudes endured throughout the war despite developments in the Soviet Union that were approved of, for instance the temporary muting of ideology and reasserting imperial history and nation as motivating forces. Such persistence of central attitudes is precisely what one would expect from the literature on attitude change. My case is that in any event British attitudes, whether based on pre-existing prejudices or wartime experience, exerted little influence on wartime policy, which was pragmatic in the sense of optimising the war effort by keeping all allies content enough to maintain the support without which the war could not be optimally prosecuted. This meant a focus on military activity while the war lasted, with political arrangements to be resolved at the peace. Churchill certainly took this view. In terms of the locus of decision-making it does seem that the Baltic issue and the period from November 1941 to May 1942 as far as policy towards the Soviet Union was concerned were instances of diversity of view within the FO and of no influence on policy, the changes in which emanated from the Cabinet and from the Prime Minister as its dominant figure – though Eden's role in keeping the Baltic issue salient should not be diminished, the final decision was Churchill's and was taken for reasons of maximising the effectiveness of Britain's wartime alliances and keeping the Soviet armies in the field against the Germans.

Folly does, as has been mentioned above, seem to conflate Soviet sensitivity with a desire for collaboration, yet the former may be seen to be compatible with pragmatism, realism and opportunism, and collaboration is not a natural associate of sensitivity. And Folly notes that as late as the autumn of 1943 Dew shared the views of many in the FO that Soviet policy was being evolved, that their actions 'could still bear two interpretations, cooperation or unilateralism'.[158] The notion of pragmatism as the central orientation of British foreign policy does not preclude a desire for co-operation in the war or the ensuing peace with the Soviet Union. As will be seen below, there is subsequent evidence indicating a perceived desirability for co-operation in the post-war settlement in Europe within the FO, though seeing the desirability of harmonious Anglo-Soviet relations does not mean that British policymakers were sanguine regarding their prospects. The overwhelming impression is one of perceived desirability and some doubt as to plausibility.

Rothwell clearly takes the view that Anglo-Soviet accord was entirely contingent upon the existence of a common enemy in Germany. His view is that it was an alliance governed by expediency temporarily overcoming deep-seated aversions as to having to deal with Soviet officials and mistrusting them as communists, that is to say, British policy was always pragmatic and believed in the minimum necessary for common pursuit of war aims. As Rothwell says, '1941 ended with the British-Soviet alliance as it was to remain throughout, one based solely on having a common enemy, whose existence still failed to transcend the differences of mentality between the British and Soviet ruling elites. The traditional animosity between the two had left an abiding legacy.'[159] William Strang observed in November 1941, at a time at which FO policy towards the Soviets had, according to some versions, radically changed, that, 'ideologically we are as far removed from the Soviet as from the Nazi regime: they are both hideous tyrannies' but went on to add that the national interests of Britain and Russia had brought them together, a clear indication of a policy towards the Soviets predicated upon a common enemy and nothing else, an entirely pragmatic approach even as late as the period in which Britain was allied with the Soviets against Germany. Yet Rothwell also mentions that some officials, including the later hawkish Christopher Warner, then head of the Northern Department that dealt with the Soviet Union, felt that genuine collaboration was possible. As has been seen above, however, Warner himself expressed the most serious reservations and doubts as to the possibility of better relations with the Soviet Union, as did Cadogan (and both were to continue to do so even when the reality of Soviet power in Europe after the war became clear, in 1944 – see below). The diversity of view within the FO was not over the necessity for decent relations with the Soviets but rather regarding their possibility and the means by which they might be attained. Throughout British policy represented a pragmatic pursuit of British interests, and the evidence does not support the notion that at any predispositional level there was any change of sentiment towards the Soviet Union. To return to the case of Warner, his hope seems to have been of diplomatic understanding of respective interests between the two nations rather than any ideological rapprochement, which would have been inconceivable. This is evidenced by his concern, in November 1941, that 'an alliance might oblige us, if things went wrong in Russia, to restore a certain form of regime in that country'.[160]

It does then seem that neither Soviet nor British policy changed in any fundamental sense, with both pursuing what was optimal and ideologically hostile to each other. All that had changed between the policy of detachment and reserve in 1940 and that of attempting to influence the Soviets in the months after June 1941 was the Soviet need for Western assistance and an altered British view of Soviet military utility in the war. My case is that British policy changed only to the extent that Soviet policy did and for similar reasons, a common enemy. At an underlying level nothing had changed apart from the perceived utility of the Soviets militarily in the war, with a complete absence of attitudinal commonality at any level other than war aims.

The general case here is that the state of war with Germany informed relations with the Soviets in late 1941 and early 1942, after an interlude in which the Soviet Union had been regarded as a remote and irrelevant power with an abominated political system and poor military capability, immune to external influence of any kind and with a diplomacy driven by ideological suspicion and that regarded any overtures or concessions as signs of weakness. Once the Germans had invaded the Soviet Union, however, the Soviet Union was seen as an ally on entirely pragmatic grounds, though there was no British belief in its capacity for prolonged resistance, an analysis based partly on an adverse perception of the effect of the Soviet system on the will to resist. And finally, in the light of continued and unexpected Soviet resistance, the Soviet Union was seen as an ally. This was a radical change in the British perception of the Soviet Union, but fundamental attitudes towards the Soviet Union remained unchanged, while policy was driven by the need to maintain the military wartime alliance against Germany.

The influences on British foreign policy towards the Soviet Union over the Baltics in late 1941 and early 1942 are then clear. In fact, despite the extended digression above into the various views (especially that of Folly) regarding the relationship between British attitudes, British perceptions of Soviet policy and British foreign policy, one has to start with the locus of foreign policy decision-making power in the British system. For despite exhaustive deliberations within the confines of the FO as to the optimal policy towards the Soviet Union it is clear that the FO was ignored by Churchill. This was possible because of the fact that in the British political system the power to make foreign policy is with the Cabinet, and that within the Cabinet the PM exerts genuine influence not because of the extent of his defined powers but precisely because powers are not defined as they would be in a written constitution (which the British system does not have).

The PM has informal powers of appointment and dismissal of Cabinet ministers and enormous influence over political careers, and his majority in the Commons is assured by the first-past-the-post system and the discipline imposed by government whips on the governing party. The personality, interests, attitudes and confidence of the PM are then very influential. With a PM not interested in foreign policy, as was so with Baldwin, and a Foreign Secretary of no firm views, as was so with Simon, it is possible that the Cabinet or the FO should exert genuine influence on policy. With Churchill however there was phenomenal confidence in the use of his powers as PM and in his contribution to foreign policy. There was also the force of his personality and the loyalty it commanded even from those infuriated by his continual interference. Finally, he was a wartime premier to whom there was known to be no alternative. Churchill dominated the Cabinet and the discreet Eden, and disregarded the FO. It was then his judgment that dictated British foreign policy, and though Churchill's adverse attitudes towards the Soviet Union and its opportunistic diplomacy (and towards legitimising a Soviet annexation of the Baltics that had been achieved through duplicitous Soviet diplomacy while negotiating with Britain for an alliance in 1939, which had resulted in a pact that left Hitler free to attack in the west in the assurance of having no front in the east) did not alter, he assented to the Soviet annexation to maintain the Soviet war effort at a time when a further German attack was imminent. The imperative to sustain the war effort was then the major influence on British policy at this time (rather than British attitudes), part of which was ensuring that US support would not be affected.

Other factors exerted no influence. There was within the FO an array of preferred policies but not different attitudes, which were long-held and never abandoned. There was sentimental attachment to the Russians among the public, who did not it seems differentiate between the nature of the regime and its foreign policy and the resistance and resilience displayed by the Red Army and the Russian people, and who wanted greater assistance to be provided to the Soviets (apparently not understanding that in opportunity cost terms there would be a deleterious effect elsewhere). There was press coverage that reflected the popular mood.

The Commons showed signs of rebellion over the Baltics and the acceptance by Britain of the Soviet annexation of the region. Yet none of these factors seems to have had any decisive influence on policy outcome. Within the 'central column' of foreign policy decision-making in the British establishment there were prevalent attitudes that were profoundly antipathetic not just to communism but to the Soviet Union and its various representatives – diplomatic, political and military. And the recent experience of the Soviets' opportunistic rejection of alliance with Britain in favour of the Ribbentrop-Molotov pact was adverse. Yet it does seem that all these views and prejudices were subordinated to the solitary aim, expressed early on by Churchill, of defeating Hitler as speedily as possible. And to that end the maintenance of harmonious international relations with Britain's allies (which equated to any country at war with Germany regardless of the circumstances or history of that nation's relations with Britain or Germany) was fundamental.

There was a difference of orientation between Churchill, who regarded the Anglo-American relationship as absolutely vital to the winning of the war, and Eden, who regarded the Americans with some impatience at times and saw Anglo-Soviet relations as critical (though Eden did of course understand that any British foreign policy would have to be agreed with the US). At this juncture the relative roles and personalities become important, for Churchill dominated the Cabinet, in which Eden was relatively isolated, and also dominated Eden as Prime Minister and personally. Though he was to re-introduce the issue of the Baltics time and again, in a policy that seemed one not of confrontation but attrition, Eden did not directly oppose Churchill's wishes.

Any possible influence from Eden would then have been contextual, in his maintaining the salience of the issue (though Stalin himself did this) and in his offering a rationale for British acquiescence in the Soviet request, that is, that if the war were won the Baltics would be lost to the Soviet Union anyway. Eden's other rationale, that British recognition of the Soviet annexations of the Baltics would create trust, was rejected by Churchill's pragmatic sensibilities, and Eden's argument that such recognition would enhance post-war collaboration would have been of no interest to Churchill as he was focused exclusively on wartime victory.

The Cabinet, though far from content and with Beaverbrook resigning over non-recognition and Attlee threatening to if the decision was made to recognise the Soviet annexations, acquiesced in Churchill's desire to leave it to Roosevelt.

The FO view was divided. Cadogan supported Churchill's resistance to concessions generally and to recognition in particular, and agreed with Churchill's insistence on US support. Sargent supported Eden's *Realpolitik* view that little would have been surrendered that would not be lost in any case, though he added that some reciprocity should be exacted and that unilateral concessions would not accomplish the goal of decent relations. Eden, 'who usually followed Cadogan's advice'[161] and was unwilling to stand up to Churchill, endorsed with some reluctance and private petulance the need for US support. Warner did not concur, and sensed that it might be necessary for Britain to disregard the US view. In the event the sequence of British positions reflected Churchill's own views and no one else's.

There was an initial refusal to be rushed by Eden into a policy regarding which he had serious reservations on principle, on pragmatic grounds of efficacy and on grounds of the need to maintain the US alliance. And then there was the *volte-face* in which Churchill indicated willingness to accede to the Soviet request provided he were assured of US support or acquiescence. He then argued the case for recognition with Roosevelt. A characterisation that portrays Churchill as attempting to balance US and Soviet demands to accomplish the preservation of the wartime alliance against Germany without any diminution of effort in any quarter may be the most accurate attainable from the available evidence.

Though Churchill remained anti-communist and anti-Soviet and averse to concessions in general and the surrender of the Baltics in particular, the decisive locus seems to have been in relations between the USA and the USSR (in the sense that Molotov became convinced that Soviet insistence upon territorial questions might affect Roosevelt's support for a second front). For it was this that resulted in Soviet acceptance of Eden's (Cadogan's) suggestion of a twenty-year pact of mutual assistance. The resulting Anglo-Soviet treaty committed both powers to refrain from making independent overtures to Germany to make peace and to providing assistance to each other during and after the war but made no mention of frontier issues.

The Soviet change of view permitted Eden to negotiate a treaty with the Soviets, and at the same time avoid alienating the US and Parliamentary resistance. In terms of causation the intervention of the US-Soviet connection and understanding meant that Britain's preparedness to acquiesce in the Soviet annexation of the Baltics was in the end irrelevant. It is however instructive as to the locus of decision-making within Britain, in terms of the (relative lack of) influence of the FO view (to the extent that one had been formulated) and the dominance of the PM over the Cabinet and Foreign Secretary. For the FO view, albeit incipient, seemed to be tending towards resistance to concessions without return, that is, towards a stance that was in opposition to the policy Churchill endorsed after his change of view. This change in policy by Churchill was as has been seen attributable to the military situation rather than his being persuaded by Eden's case for concessions, though Eden did maintain the issue's salience.

When Eden went to visit Stalin in December 1941, the emerging view in the FO was one of uncertainty over British and Soviet policy as to the post-war period and a sense of being bound by the terms of the Atlantic Charter, though there was some diversity as to the importance of the territorial integrity of small states. Eden's line in his discussions with Stalin was then in accord with the general tenor of Britain's commitments and Churchill's views, but also those of the senior officials in the FO. The situation in February and March 1942 was different, with the FO either antipathetic to any form of concessions or at least to concessions without return, and the political establishment precluding the formation of a definite FO policy by political decisions that were taken above the official level and which were completely out of step with the developing FO view.

Eden's emollient expressive style was then over the Baltic issue in contrast with his maintaining his argument for recognition of the Soviet annexations of the Baltic states despite Churchill's emphatic Prime Ministerial opposition and despite there being few Cabinet colleagues or FO officials prepared to endorse his view, a trait of perseverance that was seen in the period prior to his resignation from the Chamberlain Cabinet. Over the Baltic issue Eden did on his return from the Soviet Union manifest an autonomy of view despite opposition from Churchill, from the majority of the Cabinet, and from the influential Cadogan and Sargent at the FO and persevered with a policy that was eventually accepted by Churchill as necessary to keep the Red Army in the war and to maintain an eastern front.

Though the policy which did emerge over the Baltics, that of recognition of the Soviet annexation of the Baltic states, concurred with Eden's recommendation, Churchill's reason for agreeing to Soviet annexation of the Baltics was to keep the Red Army in the war, not post-war considerations. And Eden's *Realpolitik* was in fact limited in understanding, for it emerged that the Soviets were less sensitive to diplomatic treatment, a sensitivity which Eden had believed in, than to military power and the intention to use it. Soviet diplomacy was in fact as it had shown itself to be in the Anglo-Soviet negotiations for an alliance in 1939, opportunistic and expansionist and exploitative of concessions as indicating weakness.

While taken as an issue on its own Eden's logic seemed to make sense, Eden does seem to have been mistaken in his recommended policy, as the British concession over the Baltics served to elicit more demands from Molotov and was then abandoned in favour of an Anglo-Soviet treaty that made no reference to frontiers, indicating that the demanded British recognition of the Soviet annexations of the Baltics was not needed to maintain the Soviet effort in the war. In fact the positions of Churchill, Cadogan, Baggallay and Sargent, all of whom opposed unilateral concessions, were proved correct, as were the reservations of Attlee and Bevin, who wanted assurance that a concession over the Baltics would not result in a series of Soviet demands. And Eden's belief that conceding over the Baltic issue could result in improved understanding between the two countries after the war was proved by Soviet behaviour later in the war and after it to be nothing less than naïve.

The future of Germany after the war

The issue of German dismemberment was central to Anglo-Soviet relations. For the Soviets it was associated with security concerns over Germany, the question of reparations, the future of Poland and the western frontier of the Soviet Union. For the British it was central to maintaining good relations with the Soviets but also reflected concerns over communist influence in Germany and Europe.

After the Anglo-Soviet treaty in May 1942 the timing of the opening of a second front became central, for it moved from September 1942 to 1943, with a British and American campaign in the North African desert, and thence to June 1944. Anglo-Soviet relations were also exacerbated by the halting of Arctic convoys because of the appalling casualty rate to the PQ 17 convoy in July 1942. The Soviet military situation was desperate, with the Germans advancing beyond Rostov towards Stalingrad, but their exclusive preoccupation with the Soviet position was accompanied by a tone that took no care to avoid insult. Yet the overwhelming reality of Soviet military sacrifice and peril dominated the British response. In August 1942 Churchill visited Stalin to explain the reasoning behind the delay of the second front and the choice of a North African campaign.

The visit typified Soviet negotiations in their combination of hard bargaining and demands with aspersions and insults that served only to alienate and to confirm the gap not just in ideological terms, which had not diminished, but also in diplomatic ones.[162] There was though eventual understanding of the military and strategic merit of the North African campaign as the primary focus for 1943. And by the end of 1942 even the cautious and pragmatic Cadogan seemed optimistic regarding Anglo-Soviet relations. Yet FO overtures to the Soviets in the belief that concluding an agreement on post-war matters would improve relations were stopped by Churchill in early 1943, opposed as ever to such discussion and no longer having to make concessions in the context of Soviet reverses.[163] It is however worth locating such evidence in the context of the first FO paper on the post-war future of Germany, which is discussed below and which did see the Soviet Union as a major threat to western Europe. Hope seems to have existed alongside genuine concern and reservation in British foreign policy towards the Soviet Union in 1943.

On 9 February 1943 Churchill indicated to Stalin that the British-American invasion was planned for August or September. Yet by May it was apparent that preparations would not be ready in 1943. An invasion of Italy was seen as the best military option. Another decision had been taken without Soviet participation, but again it seems that the military necessity of the alliance meant discord was contained for the time being.

Yet there were reports of Soviet overtures to the Germans after Stalingrad at the end of January 1943. According to Dew Soviet policy could be seen as implying collaboration with the allies on a separate peace, though Sargent did not believe that Stalin would accept any relationship with Germany apart from Soviet domination.[164] Rothwell observes that though British reaction was muted, 'Churchill and the Foreign Office were therefore right to suspect Russia's fidelity as an ally'.[165]

There were then genuinely intractable questions that made Anglo-Soviet relations difficult. These included the long-delayed second front, lack of understanding regarding the difficulties in maintaining supplies, and Soviet insistence on discussing the post-war settlement after repeated explanations of why this was impossible. Soviet violations of diplomatic protocol exacerbated matters, for Stalin's demands disregarded the British position, and Soviet diplomacy was opportunistic, with any concession eliciting a further demand, and was characterised by accusations, insults and a bewildering inconsistency as to form and content.[166]

Even so, early in 1943 British policy towards the Soviets over Germany took on a new dimension, with initial FO consideration of the post-war treatment of Germany and an FO desire to be responsive to the issue's importance to the Soviets. For with the victories at El Alamein and Stalingrad defeat had receded as a possibility.

In his conversations with Eden in December 1941 Stalin had proposed separation from Germany of Austria, Bavaria, Alsace-Lorraine and the Czech Sudetenland, with what remained of Germany being divided into three states. Eden, constrained by the Atlantic Charter and by an FO and Cabinet brief to avoid discussion of the post-war treatment of Germany, exceeded his brief by saying that he had 'no objection in principle' to partitioning Germany, the sort of cryptic remark that was to characterise Eden on the issue of dismemberment. At that time wartime exigencies dominated, and the issue was not resolved but was to became salient again when the imminence of victory made it so.[167]

Formal British consideration of policy towards post-war Germany started with the FO paper to the War Cabinet of 8 March 1943. Referred to as a 'preliminary study'[168] it drew on earlier work by the Foreign Research and Press Service at Oxford,[169] in which the possibility of ideological conflict with the Soviets and the need for Germany on the western side was made explicit. It expressed hope that democratic central government would be possible for Germany, and then differentiated the various options for Germany's post-war future. There was 'truncation', 'frontier rectification', 'decentralisation' in the form of 'voluntary' or 'compulsory' 'federalism', and 'dismemberment'. The dismemberment option was rejected because of 'the strength of centripetal forces in Germany' and the need for enforcement and political will over time. Even the envisioned three large German states would require continuing alliance control to prevent reunification, and this would be exacerbated by the creation of smaller states. Eden and the FO concluded that 'voluntary federation' 'would be the best long-term solution',[170] and could be facilitated by the encouragement of separatist movements, restoration of national boundaries for Austria and Czechoslovakia, the return of Alsace-Lorraine to France, and acquisition by Poland of East Prussia. The paper made clear one of the main purposes behind British policy towards Germany—

> 'To forestall any orientation of German policy towards the U.S.S.R., and the conclusion of a Russo-German alliance directed against the West, one of our tasks will be to convince the German people that their best long-term interest lies in the integration of their national life with that of Europe as a whole and of western Europe in particular.'[171]

This is an early indication of an FO sense of Soviet threat after the war and of an FO policy of German unity or at least German acceptance of any scheme for the future of Germany, a stance against imposition and for a voluntary arrangement. Yet later that month Eden visited Roosevelt and found that 'the President appeared to favour the dismemberment of Germany as the only wholly satisfactory solution',[172] though Hull was undecided. Eden told Churchill that 'I said that we had also been studying the question' and that 'on the whole I favoured the idea of dismemberment as you had often spoken to me in favour of it,' which implies that Eden's view was contingent upon that of Churchill. Harrison at the FO noted the attraction of dismemberment for many in Britain, the USA and USSR yet noted also 'what exact connotation they attach to the word "dismemberment" is unknown',[173] a confusion that was to become a feature of diplomatic discussions on it. On 13 April, Strang minuted that Eden had not communicated the contents of the FO paper to Roosevelt because, while Roosevelt 'spoke in favour of the "dismemberment" of Germany, our paper emphasises the difficulties of a policy of "dismemberment"'.[174] Strang went on to resist the case for amending the FO view to accord with Roosevelt's, an indication of FO autonomy but also of possible influence on Eden from Churchill or the US.

In August 1943 a Cabinet Committee was set up under Attlee to consider the post-war settlement, and in October what was to become the German department was created under Troutbeck, assisted by O'Neill. The FO regarded Churchill as a 'menace'[175] in his interference in foreign policy. Churchill's idea of a Danubian federation included part of southern Germany, but the FO remained opposed to dismemberment of Germany on the grounds that the Germans would never reconcile themselves to it, that Germany was an economic unit and that separate units would be individually unsustainable, and that diplomatic difficulties in enforcing partition would be bound to ensue over time.[176] Churchill was so reluctant to consult the FO that he was attempting to circumvent it by involving the SOE in encouragement of separatist tendencies. Yet given that Churchill's proposal was exceeded by Roosevelt's, which advocated a radical dismemberment of Germany and which Stalin was seen to favour, the FO was bound not to rule dismemberment out overtly.

In preparation for the forthcoming Foreign Ministers' Conference in Moscow in October 1943 the War Cabinet met on 5 October. Eden's paper of 27 September 1943 on German dismemberment was discussed. It proposed the surrender of East Prussia to Poland, and also part of Silesia, but said that 'the only policy holding out any real hope for the future is one which, while taking all necessary safeguards, aims ultimately at the re-admittance of a reformed Germany into the life of Europe.'[177] This echoed the non-punitive sentiments of the March 1943 paper, yet Eden also said of dismemberment that 'I myself am not opposed to such a course'[178] and asked for Cabinet authority to tell the Soviets that no decision had been reached over Germany's political future but that Britain favoured encouraging separatist movements. Eden's refusal to endorse either the retention of Germany as a post-war economic and political unit or German dismemberment, and his distancing himself somewhat from his own FO paper's recommendation, was typical Eden.

One attribution would be indecision and difficulty in forming a view on vital long-term issues. Another would be the diplomat's disinclination to assuming a foreign-policy posture without being entirely cognizant of the consequences in diplomatic terms. Rothwell sees Eden as taking the view that European economic prosperity needed a thriving Germany, which meant no genuinely punitive economic treatment of Germany. He also however notes Eden's wish for a good relationship with Stalin to control post-war Germany and that Eden had deplored Churchill's reference to using Germany against the Soviet Union after the war.[179] Churchill attempted to defer discussion on Germany's future. He 'deprecated, in particular, any attempt to reach binding conclusions on these questions',[180] and expected the conference to be the means of 'ascertaining the views of the Russians',[181] an indication of his orientation to the views of allies. The Cabinet favoured German dismemberment by means of developing separatist tendencies but doubted 'the feasibility of forcing a solution on these lines on an unwilling Germany'.[182] Yet a difficulty for causation is that there is no indication of the relative influence of the various views expressed, and even attribution remains undisclosed in some cases, as with the significant remark that 'one view advanced in discussion was that the increasing power of Russia might make it inexpedient to carry too far a policy of breaking up the unity of Germany'.[183]

In the event Molotov was able only to indicate a Soviet preference for forced dismemberment. Then, despite knowing that Hull's view was that federation might lessen the threat from a Germany also denied east Prussia or with Prussian influence diminished, Eden said that Britain favoured the division of Germany into smaller states and wished to encourage separatism in Germany, though he added that Britain was 'unable as yet to assess the prospects of imposing separation by force'.[184] This was however an accurate representation of the Cabinet's view. Hull then told Eden that the United States was less enthusiastic than it had been regarding dismemberment.

By the time of the Teheran Conference, held between 28 November and 1 December 1943, German forces were retreating along the entire eastern front, where the Soviet armies were planning retaking the Baltic states and Poland, and in the western theatre German armies had been expelled from north Africa and were being attacked in Italy by British and American forces. Military strategy was being co-ordinated in a comprehensive sense for the first time in the war, and there was something of the euphoria of anticipated victory and an obvious commonality of purpose and of accord on the means of winning the war. Most significantly the Soviets obtained an undertaking on the date of the opening of a second front in northern France, May or June 1944, which Stalin took as indicating that the West had abandoned eastern Europe to the Soviets.

Roosevelt and Stalin had remained in favour of the radical dismemberment of Germany during 1943. Churchill was cautious, concerned that Germany should be a viable state but denied Prussia, which he regarded as the centre of German militarism.

On 1 December 1943 Roosevelt proposed partitioning Germany into five smaller states. Stalin supported the proposal, and both rejected Churchill's Danubian federation. Churchill argued that states too small to be viable on their own would have an imperative to join together to create a viable nation. Stalin agreed that German states 'would want to unite', but would have to be neutralised by various economic measures, and 'by force if necessary'. Churchill then said the discussion 'was only a preliminary survey of a vast historical problem',[185] a policy of postponement to which Churchill 'was able to secure the agreement of the other two',[186] for Teheran was dominated by the need to maintain the wartime alliance. The resolution of Germany's future was delegated to the European Advisory Commission (EAC).

The FO wanted some elucidation of the British position. Yet Churchill refused to take account of FO views as to Germany's future, and continued to refer to the future partition of Germany without elucidating the meaning of the term, as late as October 1944. And in January 1944 Eden expressed himself in characteristically circumlocutory terms yet similarly without elucidation – 'Personally I am far from convinced against dismemberment.'[187]

As the months went on both Hull and Eden were to wonder if partition were practicable. FO plans continued, at the beginning of February 1944, to be 'based on a unified Germany'.[188] This is indicative of the diffuse nature of the foreign-policy formulation process (but not the decision-making system) under Churchill, with erratic Prime Ministerial interference and general disregard of Eden's views and FO papers that proposed different policies to those of the PM. Yet uncertainty as to what to do with work done in the FO was clear—

> Should we circulate documents although some of these are against dismemberment? Should the Secretary of State and the Prime Minister talk it over first?[189]

There followed a campaign to convince Churchill of the FO case. Yet it seems that Eden was realistic in his belief that no matter how powerful the FO case Churchill would not accept it.[190] In October 1944 Churchill told Stalin that Germany should be divided into a northern and a southern state, with the Ruhr and the Saar as a third state. Eden's idea that international control over the Ruhr and the Saar could be a substitute for dismemberment was disregarded.

Eden had meantime indicated to Attlee and his Armistice and Post-War Committee that he would like to see dismemberment come from within, through the encouragement of separatist tendencies rather than being imposed by force,[191] which is consistent with his earlier aversion to imposition of dismemberment and with the FO sense of practical enforcement difficulties.

In the ensuing period two sequences of papers were being developed side by side. There were papers on German dismemberment, and there was another series on probable Soviet policy and British policy towards the Soviet Union. If the FO paper of March 1943 was the first to address the treatment of Germany after the war, then that of 29 April 1944 was the first attempt to address probable post-war Soviet policy. The two issues were inextricably linked. For the duration of the war policy towards the Soviet Union would continue to reflect its position as a needed ally in Britain's war with Germany. Yet, as victory became certain, policy towards post-war Germany reflected policy towards the Soviet Union. For Kitchen the FO paper of 29 April 1944 saw 'the fixed point of Soviet policy' as being 'the search for security' and that 'the key to exorcising Soviet suspicions therefore seemed to lie in the treatment accorded to Germany and Japan'.[192] There was an understanding that 'any friction there is between us and Russia will not arise so much out of ideological disagreement but chiefly, if not solely, because we and the Russians may take different views as to the post-war treatment of Germany,'[193] and that 'Stalin is an advocate of the complete dismemberment of Germany.'[194]

The FO favoured 'voluntary federation' for Germany but wanted good relations with the Soviets, yet reconciled the dissonance with the complacent view that if the Soviets could 'achieve a satisfactory co-operation with the other three in ordering the post-war system, this would give her a better assurance than any other of freedom from external preoccupations',[195] a view which disregarded Soviet perceptions of Western intentions. For while it is possible that such a scheme would have been best for the Soviet Union in terms of security, what is astonishing is the British belief that the Soviet Union would accept such assurances given the recent experience of a similar attempt in late 1941 to offer the Soviet Union guarantees of security instead of actual concessions and Stalin's insistence on punitive dismemberment. Part of the view was that the FO felt that 'Russia will be pre-occupied with her post-war rehabilitation and will constitute no menace to British interests.'[196] The expectation was that the Soviet need for United States and British assistance to recover from the war would offer an interlude of Western influence. The FO felt that Soviet foreign policy was unlikely to be expansionist. Policy towards Germany was then central to the maintenance of good relations with the Soviets, who were presumed not to want even a communised Germany, as they themselves, so it appeared to the experts in the FO, were gradually abandoning communism[197] and becoming a nationalist power with understandable security concerns – an astounding view and one which was not to endure long.[198] Kitchen concludes that 'the FO felt that the preservation of the Anglo-Soviet Alliance in the post-war world should be one of the main aims of British policy.'[199] Warner noted that 'the most important point in securing Russian collaboration after the war will be to convince Russia of our determination to go with her in holding Germany down.'[200]

The Post-Hostilities Planning Sub-Committee (PHPS), which was 'dominated by the military',[201] was then tasked by the Cabinet with assessing the likely effects of Soviet policy on British strategic interests. Its paper of 6 June 1944 agreed with the FO that the Soviet Union would attend to economic recovery and liberalisation rather 'than to follow a policy of external aggrandisement'.[202] Yet the Committee also noted Soviet power in post-war Europe, and was uncertain as to Soviet measures 'to neutralise Germany'.[203] It recommended that Britain attempt continued co-operation but maintain sufficient forces to deter Soviet opportunism. Ensuing PHPS papers assumed that the Soviet Union would be able to achieve post-war reconstruction and enhance her military capability. The FO was appalled that the Soviet Union was seen as a possible enemy, and more so when in August the PHPS favoured German dismemberment 'into three or more independent States, without any central Government or federal organisation' as it 'would reduce the likelihood of the whole of Germany combining with the U.S.S.R. against us, and that, as an insurance against a hostile U.S.S.R., it would be to our long-term strategic advantage'.[204]

A long and acrimonious debate ensued between the FO and the Chiefs of Staff (CoS) as to the desirability of German dismemberment from a security point of view, which involved estimations of Soviet intentions, the possibility of continued collaboration with the Soviets, and the nature of the Soviet regime. This had been initiated by an FO request of 7 June 1944 for the CoS view as to the effects of dismemberment should the latter reflect the occupation zones.

The FO view was that defeat of Germany was the aim of foreign policy, that Germany would remain the major threat to European peace, and that nothing should be done to imperil the 'continuance of the closest possible degree of co-operation with the Soviet Government'. British policy should include an avoidance of weakness towards Germany. As to 'Russian draconian ideas about the post-war treatment of Germany', compromise and convincing explanation were advocated.[205] The FO and the CoS were agreed as to US unreliability, but the FO inference was that it made good relations with the Soviet Union more vital.

The CoS had an exclusive security brief, regarded the Soviets as the main threat, and drew from its perception of US isolationism and unreliability the need for a west European alliance against Soviet incursion. In this Germany would be vital, as 'there might well come a time when we should have to rely on her assistance against a hostile Russia'.[206] Alanbrooke, Chief of the Imperial General Staff, noted that 'Germany is no longer the dominating power in Europe – Russia is,' and that the Soviet Union 'cannot fail to become the main threat in fifteen years from now. Therefore, foster Germany, gradually build her up, and bring her into a Federation of Western Europe.'[207] The CoS's response to the FO on 9 September reflected the views expressed in the PHP paper of 25 August (as the FO had anticipated)[208] in its claim that dismemberment would preclude any German revival but also provide 'an insurance against a hostile U.S.S.R.'.[209] Dismemberment would give Britain the possibility of German help against the Soviets and 'prevent Germany from combining with the Soviet Union against us'.[210]

Eden was beginning to doubt the wisdom of dismemberment even by separatism rather than enforcement. Yet it is unclear whether this was as a result of being persuaded by FO argumentation, of the Soviet request for time on the EAC and the Americans' finding the notion less appealing than earlier,[211] or of reservations regarding Soviet dominance of Europe without a viable Germany. The memorandum to the Armistice and Post-War Committee on 20 September 1944 was the FO response to the CoS view. It claimed that a united Germany and polices to persuade the Soviets of British good intentions could produce good Anglo-Soviet relations, and repeated that any imposition of dismemberment would be unworkable. Eden characteristically confined himself to remarking that he found 'it hard to resist the conclusion of this paper that dismemberment would fail to advance the main object', which for Eden was 'security from the German menace',[212] though, balancing himself elegantly on the fence, he added that he might abandon unity were he convinced 'that dismemberment would be in the interest of security'.[213] And Eden referred again to the federal option first raised in March 1943, which meant that any German central government would have little power. The FO case, tentatively endorsed by Eden, remained that Germans would resist dismemberment and that it would have to be imposed and maintained by joint action by the victorious powers over time, with adverse effects on British public opinion and strain between the wartime allies. To Eden the idea that a forcibly dismembered Germany would assist the West against the Soviets and eastern Germany was 'little less than fantastic'.[214]

He noted the difficulty of assessing Soviet desires on dismemberment given their absence of a view on the EAC and Stalin's endorsement of Roosevelt's dismemberment proposal at Teheran, but feared that a policy of dismemberment to contain the Soviets could endanger post-war collaboration with them and hoped that German unity might 'prove a factor of the first importance in holding the Soviet Union and ourselves together'.[215] He added that US policy was unlikely to favour dismemberment if it were to involve 'active policing measures on their part'.[216]

The CoS denied anti-Soviet bias and pointed out that their role was to examine the possibilities of danger from all quarters.[217]

Sargent's note for Eden in preparation for his meeting on 4 October with the CoS expressed concern over any reference to 'war with the Soviet Union',[218] yet in the March 1943 FO paper a Russo-German alliance had been openly considered. He said the FO concurred with the CoS 'that the Soviet Union is a possible enemy', but did not see a likelihood of war for 'a number of years'.[219]

As to FO policy rather than perception Cadogan had earlier commented that 'there is no doubt that our policy must be directed to cooperation: if it fails, it must not be through our fault.' Eden had added, 'this is so. It is all very difficult, but at least we are convinced that we are trying to operate the right policy. The Russians may make it impossible. If we fail it should not be through our fault, not through an undue display of weakness on our part towards Russia.'[220]

The difference between the FO and the CoS was then not over views of possible adverse Soviet intentions, especially over time, but rather regarding the most desirable policy as a consequence. FO officials did not want to exclude the possibility of good relations, for

> We cannot quarrel with Russia in present circumstances.... Such a quarrel might well endanger the security of this country...either by driving the Soviet Union back into isolation or, worse still, forcing her into collaboration with Germany as soon as occasion offers.[221]

These statements, that there should be no weakness towards and yet also no quarrel with the Soviet Union, are indicative of Eden's and of FO uncertainty regarding just how to deal with the Soviet Union, with a sense of need for good relations and it seems an old feeling that any weakness would be exploited. It is odd however that it should have been Eden who enunciated the need to avoid indications of weakness given his recommendation for a unilateral concession over the Baltic issue. Such concerns seem in fact far more reminiscent of the FO view formed in February 1942, that unilateral concessions should be avoided and that reciprocal concessions and hard bargaining were the optimal means of dealing with Soviet diplomatic tactics, a view that was disregarded by Churchill in the end and by Eden. On 4 October the CoS reiterated 'that in the worst case we might find ourselves faced with a unitary Germany, dominated or in collaboration with Russia'.[222] Eden accepted the possibility of differences with the Soviets over time, but regarded Germany as the main threat and was concerned that CoS views might reach the Soviets and so produce the CoS scenario, a hostile Soviet Union. The meeting agreed that any reference to 'the hypothesis of a hostile Russia' should be 'restricted'.[223]

Churchill was apprised of the differences of view between the FO and the CoS in advance of the Moscow conference by Ismay, who said that Eden felt 'it would pay us not to dismember Germany, whereas the Chiefs of Staff felt that the military arguments for dismemberment were very strong; the problem was being given further study.'[224] Churchill said that Roosevelt and Stalin favoured rather more radical dismemberment than he did, another indication of his orientation to his own views and to diplomatic audiences rather than to expert advice. 'He proposed to talk it over with the Foreign Secretary,'[225] yet a file note indicates that 'the S/S says that he and PM did not have this talk',[226] which is indicative of Churchill's view of the issue's importance. In his ensuing conversation on 17 October 1944 with Stalin Churchill favoured isolation of Prussia and the creation of two German states, one comprising Bavaria and Austria, the other Wurttemberg and Baden, with the industrial areas of the Rhine under international control. Stalin concurred.[227] Eden said the Cabinet had not decided on German dismemberment but referred to various possible options – dismemberment with or without using existing German states as a basis, and permanent international control over the Rhine, the Ruhr, the Saar and Westphalia and asked for some acceleration in Soviet participation on the EAC.[228] Churchill's sense of Prime Ministerial powers and his ease in their use is apparent in the fact that he introduced his own scheme to Stalin without any prior reference to the FO or, it seems, to Eden. It is also an indication of his sense that the disposition of influence in an entire continent could be settled by the interactions between great men, of whom he believed himself to be one.

On 27 November 1944 an FO paper to the Armistice and Post-war Committee (APW) on the future of Germany reiterated the FO view that 'no system will work in the long run unless it is broadly acceptable to the German people,' and pointed to Germans' desire for unity. Any attempt to impose separation (apart from Prussia) could cause friction between the wartime allies and problems with public opinion. Federation would have the security advantages of dismemberment, that is, to 'weaken Germany', without the adverse features of imposition, for 'dismemberment would have to be imposed by force'.[229] Eden continued to avoid taking a definite view. He said, 'I agree with much of it but not with all,' without specifying what he did concur with, and then, 'I am rather embarrassed by these A.P.W. papers. It rarely happens that I am in full agreement with their views on the future of Germany, and this is surely natural enough given that they are in the nature of studies. Can they not go forward in the name of their authors, but blessed by me as a contribution to thought on the subject without my having to commit myself to every line?' And he added, 'I should particularly like P.M. to see this.'[230]

The expected companion to this paper, one on dismemberment, never appeared, but on 5 December 1944 a report from the Post-Hostilities Planning Committee to the CoS advocated dismemberment of Germany on the basis that, though it might 'accelerate the inevitable tendency for Eastern Germany to fall within the Soviet sphere of influence',[231] it would deny German assistance to the Soviets. The reasoning was not new, that a north-western and a southern German state might support the West, while a unitary Germany would be dominated by the Soviets. The FO drafted a memorandum for Eden reiterating the FO view that 'dismemberment would raise grave political as well as practical issues to which an answer would have to be found before we could support such a policy,'[232] and a paper dismissing the benefits of dismemberment as 'illusory'. Eden refused to send it, and 'came to Yalta sceptical but not yet committed to outright opposition'.[233] By this time Eden had been sitting on the fence over German unity or dismemberment for a considerable period of time, and it seemed almost as if he felt that taking a position on German dismemberment would be an indiscretion, an indelicate violation of diplomacy. Yet he had resigned from Chamberlain's Cabinet over Prime Ministerial insistence on appeasing Italy, and was to prove all too decisive and resolute over Suez as PM.

One inference is that it was his sense of his position as Foreign Secretary under Churchill as a wartime PM to whom there was no alternative that rendered him so reluctant to take a view and defend it – as has been seen, Eden accepted that in the end Churchill would have to have his way over foreign policy, and that that was bound to be so in wartime. Yet there was also Eden's personal relationship with Churchill and the force of Churchill's personality, which made him difficult to resist not just to Eden but also to others in whose work Churchill interfered. It is also possible that he was genuinely undecided over what was a complex issue in which the merits of the case would in the end be dictated by the nature of the foreign policy of the Soviet Union. Set against such an interpretation, Eden did avoid confrontation and had a tendency to agree with his interlocutor, or at least give that impression, which would indicate that he was averse to defending a view. In any event he seems to have exerted no influence on the debate over German dismemberment in 1943 and 1944.

Further promised papers on dismemberment failed to materialise prior to Yalta. According to Woodward, 'since the European Advisory Commission continued to postpone their discussion of dismemberment there was at the beginning of 1945 no agreed policy among the Allies whether or not to dismember Germany.'[234]

The positions of Eden and Churchill on the future of Germany were apparent in their reception of O'Neill's paper 'German Reaction To Defeat',[235] which included a recommendation against imposition of harsh territorial terms. Eden distanced himself from the conclusion 'that Germany will necessarily turn to the East rather than the West', 'though this danger admittedly exists',[236] and Churchill's response was, 'I will read it when I can.'[237]

By the time Churchill, Stalin and Roosevelt met at Yalta between 4 and 12 February 1945 Churchill and Eden had had the adverse experience of the Quebec Conference in September 1944. There, despite an uncharacteristic display of independence from Eden in Roosevelt's presence, in his rejecting the Morgenthau plan for the pastoralisation of Germany, Churchill insisted that Britain was forced to choose between acceptance of the plan and the possibility of a much-needed American loan to Britain and rejection that would protect Germany at Britain's expense.[238] The aftermath to acceptance of the Morgenthau proposal was one of regret on both sides and no further discussion of the treatment of Germany until Yalta. Churchill was convinced that understandings in wartime would reflect public desire for retribution and should not be made. Sainsbury notes an absence of clarity in Anglo-American policy on Germany prior to Yalta.[239] He continues, 'historians have found it difficult to agree on what was actually decided on this matter at Yalta,'[240] an echo of the 'shambles' of Teheran and a portent of things to come at Potsdam, not least in its separation of discussion of Germany into short-term, zonal issues, and final peace terms, a characteristic putting-off of what seemed difficult or intractable to the future for fear that frankness should imperil the wartime alliance.

The context of the discussions on German dismemberment at Yalta was one of overwhelming Soviet power in Europe following Red Army advances, and of British doubts as to the desirability of punitive treatment of Germany in light of incipient fears as to Soviet intentions. The EAC had failed to devise a scheme for German dismemberment because of the Soviet delegate's not having a brief, which raised the suspicion that for the Soviets it was preferable that the Red Army should resolve issues on the ground. EAC representatives did however concur that 'each zonal commander should have supreme authority within his zone while broad policy was to be made by unanimous agreement in an Allied Control Council (ACC)'.[241] The other factor was Roosevelt's indication that he expected the withdrawal of US troops from Europe within two years, which seems to indicate an extraordinary naivety on his part in that it left the Red Army in undisputed control of the east of Europe.

For Sainsbury Yalta resolved nothing over the partition of Germany. In his view, while Stalin's demand for German dismemberment was reiterated, Churchill was responsive to Eden's pressure for a 'decentralised, federal Germany',[242] and Roosevelt wanted 'to postpone a decision'.[243] Woodward concurs that Stalin demanded dismemberment and that Churchill refused to be drawn into any undertaking on dismemberment, but also records that 'the President himself was in favour of decentralisation, and therefore of dismemberment, whether into five or seven, or more or fewer States.'[244]

Smyser even disputes Stalin's demand for dismemberment, claiming that 'Stalin opposed dismemberment openly,'[245] while Rothwell notes 'Stalin's demand for a commitment to the dismemberment of Germany'.[246] Rothwell sees the Yalta Conference as having 'pronounced favourably on the dismemberment of Germany and stopped short only of saying that Germany had to be dismembered',[247] and Churchill as refusing to listen to FO advice.

The documentary record indicates that Stalin introduced the question of dismemberment. On 5 February he told Roosevelt and Churchill that 'he understood that all of them favoured dismemberment, but the exact form of dismemberment had still to be decided'.[248] Churchill remarked that 'in principle they were all agreed on the dismemberment of Germany'[249] but that extensive work was needed to establish 'how Germany should best be divided to secure future peace',[250] adding that 'he would feel free, after detailed examination, to change any tentative view he might express.'[251] Roosevelt did favour dismemberment into 'five states or seven, or more or less', but also wanted agreement 'in principle' 'but not in detail' at Yalta. Stalin was 'prepared to accept the President's compromise' but wanted 'a general statement to the effect that Germany would be dismembered' added to the terms of surrender.[252] Churchill said he could not commit the British government beyond agreement in principle. The matter was then referred to the Foreign Ministers. Molotov echoed Stalin's demand for a statement indicating that dismemberment was considered imperative, but Eden resisted commitment to the necessity of dismemberment until its 'practicability' had been considered.[253] After a protracted discussion and reference to Churchill the matter was referred to a committee to be comprised of Eden and the US and Soviet foreign ministers without any movement in the British position. Eden then communicated the decision to the FO, including the need for planning for some form of dismemberment.[254]

Churchill did then refuse to acquiesce in the radical form of German dismemberment proposed by Stalin and Roosevelt. Yet there was no real departure from his policy of maintaining the wartime alliance, for Roosevelt also favoured delay, which was the expedient Churchill used to avoid outright refusal.

On 7 March 1945 the Dismemberment Committee, chaired by Eden, discussed the very necessity of dismemberment as the only effective means to securing European peace .[255] Eden's subsequent memorandum to the Armistice and Post-War Committee on 19 March 1945 also reflected the Foreign Office's reluctance in planning for dismemberment – Germany would need a central government in the immediate post-war situation, for refugees and labour redistribution would require central direction, and the desire of small states to unite would be difficult to prevent. It defined dismemberment as the complete political and economic separation of Germany into a number of small states and reiterated the associated administrative onus. It also wondered if, with the removal of 'both a large part of Old Prussia and the whole of the Rhine-Ruhr industrial area, the effect on her size and potential strength would be so great that it might prove unnecessary to partition her further'. The paper's apparent preference was for a three-state arrangement, with a western state, a southern state and an eastern state, rather than a multiplicity of small states.[256] This could be construed as minimal conformity to German dismemberment, which was also linked to reparations.

Anderson, the Chancellor of the Exchequer, had told the War Cabinet that 'we can have either a reparations policy or a dismemberment policy, but certainly not both.' He repeated that 'a practicable reparations policy must be one which leaves to the Germans some prospects of a minimum subsistence.'[257] This linked dismemberment, reparations, German territorial losses to Poland, and the standard of living in and the taxation burden of the British zone. He pointed to the prospect of US withdrawal, the need for US support in Germany, and, assuming the Soviet zone would 'develop into a governmental or administrative system which is amenable to Russian policy', suggested that a 'unified western Germany which can be fitted into the general economy of the Western European countries'[258] should be considered, a new variation on the theme of German unity/dismemberment. Eden felt the idea that 'an extension of Russian control in Eastern Germany might have to be matched by a unified Western Germany linked with other Western European Countries' was a 'dangerous policy',[259] and wanted to maintain allied unity over Germany, the long-held FO policy.

When the War Cabinet met on 22 March 1945[260] Churchill repeated that Stalin had insisted on dismemberment at Yalta, his own view that dismemberment required study and could not be hurried, and his preference for isolation of Prussia and a south German state. Then, on 26 March 1945, the Soviets told the Foreign Office that their interpretation of the Yalta accord was that dismemberment of Germany was not 'an obligatory plan' but rather a means of 'exerting pressure on Germany with the object of rendering her harmless in the event of other means proving inadequate'.[261]

There had then been the most alarming misunderstanding. This, despite experience of previous and equally blasé about-turns in Soviet policy, was received with some amazement by Churchill, Eden and Cadogan[262]. The issue disappeared from view and seems not to have been mentioned again.

Churchill's attitude to post-war issues in general was notorious. He disapproved of their discussion while the war continued, and seemed indifferent to them[263] except when they were discussed without him. The FO favoured reconciliation on post-war issues with Stalin in early 1943, but Churchill's continuing dominance was apparent in March 1943, when, shown FO correspondence on renewed discussions with the Soviets as to the post-war settlement, he 'ordained that the whole subject of post-war matters should be dropped'.[264] Charmley continues, 'Churchill's outburst reflected not just the state of his health, but also that of his relationship with the Foreign Office. The Foreign Office was the one major department of state of which Churchill had not been the head, and his opinion of it, based partly upon its propagation of "appeasement", was not high.'[265] Dutton refers to Churchill's confidence regarding diplomacy and his disinclination to defer 'to the supposed professionals of the Foreign Office'. And Morton, one of Churchill's aides, told O'Neill in the German Department at the FO that as late as November 1944 Churchill knew he needed information regarding Germany but was unwilling to seek it from the FO.[266] In August of that year Dixon noted Churchill's inconsistency in his criticism of the FO, alleging that 'the FO were always wanting to do something' yet also accusing the FO of having difficulty in reaching any conclusion, claiming that their papers were so balanced in their opinions as to preclude any conclusion.[267] Dutton remarks, 'this could be exasperating for Eden. Against Churchill's plea in September 1943 that he should "try to have a little confidence in my insight into Europe", Eden wrote, "he might have a little in mine!"[268] In the last resort, however, it was something Eden had to accept.'[269].

In 1943 the FO found it impossible to obtain a view from Churchill on the future structure of Germany (apart from his Danubian federation idea, viewed with 'disdain'[270] in the FO). Efforts to convince him of the case for German unity and the disadvantages of dismemberment were unavailing. FO experience of attempting to obtain a view from Churchill is indicated by the absence of any reaction to an FO minute dated 25 January 1944 on the Soviet Union's western frontiers. Warner remarks on 18 July 1944, 'I have seen no sign of any reply from the Prime Minister on this proposal.'[271] And on 8 May 1944 Eden told Churchill that 'my Department have recently prepared two excellent papers on Soviet Foreign Policy,' and continues 'I enclose copies, which you may not feel it necessary read,' a clear understanding that Churchill was inaccessible on such matters at that time.[272] Yet at Teheran Churchill opposed the draconian dismemberment scheme proposed by Roosevelt and endorsed by Stalin, with the result that the matter was referred to the EAC, a safe place for an issue on which a decision was not wanted, and at Yalta he prevaricated over German dismemberment.[273] Churchill then came late to the issue but was circumspect in his dealing with it, employing the tactic of postponement after his Danubian federation was rejected by Roosevelt and Stalin – that it was deplored by the FO did not seem to have any effect.

As an indication of just when Churchill began to see a viable German state at the centre of Europe as essential to resisting Soviet domination Harvey noted in his diary on 6 October 1943 that Churchill had said, 'we mustn't weaken Germany too much – we may need her against Russia,'[274] to a 'horrified'[275] reaction from the Cabinet and anger from Eden. And part of Churchill's purpose in postponement at Yalta may be inferred from his remark to Colville that he 'hardly liked to consider dismembering Germany until his doubts about Russia's intentions had been cleared away'.[276]

Eden's position is harder to characterise. Since November 1942 he had been overwhelmed by his dual role as Foreign Secretary and Leader of the House of Commons. Dutton notes Cadogan's frustration at being unable to secure Eden's attention to FO issues, including 'longer-term planning' and Harvey's concurrence that Eden could not give foreign policy 'first attention or adequate reflection'.[277] As has been seen, Eden's expressive style, diplomatic, discreet, even circumlocutory use of language, and avoidance of confrontation make identification of his real views, to the extent that he had definite views, problematic. For his stance seems to differ with context. The initial FO paper of 8 March 1943 favoured voluntary federation, which Eden seems, in a rare expression of personal view, to have endorsed, if with qualifications indicating that his rejection of dismemberment was because it seemed impracticable rather than because of 'scruples as to its harshness' and the remark that he 'had not at this time come to a fixed decision about Germany's future'.[278] Yet Eden did not oppose dismemberment on his visit to Roosevelt the same month. Sainsbury observes that Eden 'appears to have simultaneously given Roosevelt (who had come to favour partition) and Hull (who was dubious about the idea) the impression that he agreed with each of them'.[279]

Thereafter he seems to have drifted between diplomatic expressions favouring dismemberment but private leanings against it, and to have refused to commit himself even in December 1944. Yet the difficulty was not semantic – dismemberment was used in various contexts with different meanings, but the FO was clear that it meant 'the destruction of Germany as a political entity by splitting it into pieces'.[280] It then seems that imprecise use of the term was instrumental in avoiding discord with different audiences. Eden did however remain averse to forcible dismemberment, which was consistent with FO concerns as to practicalities of enforcement.

The evidence indicates that Eden was unwilling to take any firm policy stance as to German dismemberment, possibly because it would then involve defending it against resistance from Churchill, the FO or Cabinet colleagues. Instead he manifested traits associated with the FO tradition of pragmatism, avoiding committing himself, seeking compromise, and treating each case on its merits. Yet the FO was unanimous in its rejection of German dismemberment. It is possible that Eden's balancing himself on the fence and avoiding a definite policy is attributable also to the diplomatic value of avoidance of discord with wartime allies who favoured dismemberment and to Churchill's exclusive orientation to that audience. Eden's commitment to avoiding a view over German dismemberment extended to Yalta, at which he was content to pursue Churchill's policy of postponement – only after it is there evidence of some antipathy to dismemberment in Eden, associated with concern regarding Soviet power and behaviour in eastern Europe.

The documentary evidence supports Kitchen's observation that Eden was not a person to carry through a policy preference.[281] In fact it seems that he had difficulty in knowing what that preference might be. There is little of Eden in the FO files, with initials or comments that express no view as to their contents, such as the ubiquitous 'I agree' and 'a remarkable paper'.[282] In fact the only instances of extended commentary from Eden are when it seemed a policy position was being attributed to him. One was when German dismemberment demanded some commitment to a position in view of the discord between the CoS and the FO, when Eden refused to send to Cabinet an FO paper outlining the case against dismemberment that stressed the practical difficulties. In an indication of how well he knew Eden, Harvey had noted, 'provided the Secretary of State is not committed to the views expressed, I hope he will agree to circulate this paper.' Yet Eden's reaction was remarkable. He appended, 'No, sir! But we had better discuss it. This is not a study, it is an election address.' And continuing, even after Cadogan's favourable comment on the paper, Eden remarked

> This paper shows little sign of any approach to this question with an open mind. It is merely the case against, which I admit is very strong. So strong indeed that I should have thought it unnecessary to invoke so much special pleading.

I certainly could not forward this paper as it stands to my colleagues, nor do I think Dept would be wise even from their own point of view to urge me to do so.[283]

This extraordinary outburst and refusal even to send an FO paper to Cabinet if he himself were dissociated from its recommendations is indicative of Eden's desire to keep his options open and to avoid being committed to any position on German dismemberment even at the end of 1944. It would seem that Eden was also concerned that the Soviets would see the dismemberment option as a means of containing Soviet influence and excluding it from western Europe. Such continuing uncertainty in Eden does make any influence on Churchill prior to Yalta most improbable, and indicates Eden's concern for audiences, not least Churchill himself, and his considering it a virtue not to take a position or cause division. Any contribution to British policy over the future of Germany that Eden may have made may then be difficult to trace, and be in the nature of smoothing differences over and so facilitating apparent accord where none existed rather than persevering with a position regardless of opposition. It seems Eden was concerned as to the effect of any firm view on the diplomatic and political audiences he faced, and that he deplored the FO paper's clarity of advocacy, which he may have regarded as confrontational.

Eden's continuing doubts as to the advisability of German dismemberment and Soviet intentions are apparent in his remarks on a discussion he and Churchill had with Stalin over Germany's future on 17 October 1944 – 'as he went on to oppose any grouping of states in central Europe, I became more wary of the advantages the Soviets might seek in a weak and divided continent.'[284] Eden noted prior to Yalta that Stalin had let the independent Poles be slaughtered by the Germans by withholding his assistance, and told Churchill on 28 January 1945 that Stalin's not 'fulfilling his promise' of 'a free and independent Poland' would affect 'our future co-operation with him'.[285] As to discussions at Yalta, 'I was ready to consider the dismemberment of Germany in the context of future European security, but not to commit myself in advance to decisions for which Molotov was showing increasing eagerness in order to aggrandise Soviet power.'[286]

Eden did then have views on individual matters but avoided irreversible stances on policy. His memoirs are unrevealing, lacking clarity of expression, which leaves one with others' impressions of him. Alanbrooke's view was that, 'delightful as he is in my opinion he always seems to just miss the point',[287] yet one wonders whether that was Eden's approach, to avoid addressing the point and so confrontation in an attempt to smooth over discord, and Alanbrooke would have been referring to Eden's grasp of military strategy. In diplomatic encounters Eden was it seems at his best, even if his means were avoidance of conflict at the expense of clarity. Ismay, remarking on the occasion of Eden's meeting with Stalin in Moscow in October 1943, regretted having seen Eden as 'one of fortune's darlings' and referred to his 'masterly' managing of a meeting with Stalin.[288]

Churchill's domination of the Cabinet and of Eden is well evidenced, though there have been dissenting voices.[289] And though Eden's non-confrontational tactics, which involved persuasion and perseverance, may have been influential with Churchill, evidence is absent in documents and personal accounts. And while it may be in the nature of such influence that it should remain beyond the documentary record, it also means it cannot be substantiated from the evidence available and remains conjectural. By 1943 and 1944 Eden was under some strain, because of his dual role and because of working with a Prime Minister as dominant, erratic and interfering as Churchill. At the beginning of 1944 Churchill expressed confidence in Soviet advances and changes in the Soviet regime, which inspired 'new confidence' in Stalin.[290] Yet on 30 October 1944 Churchill's doctor, Moran, noted 'he cannot decide whether to make one last attempt to enlist Roosevelt's sympathy for a firmer line with Stalin' or 'to make peace with Stalin and save what he can from the wreck of Allied hopes,' and observes, 'all this havering, these conflicting and contradictory policies, are, I am sure, due to Winston's exhaustion.'[291]

Direct evidence of Eden's influence on Churchill is then absent. Charmley mentions Eden's reproaching Churchill for his indifference to post-war planning, as it meant that 'America makes a policy and we follow.'[292] Yet it had no effect on Churchill's attachment to the Americans or his aversion to post-war issues. And when Eden tried to minimise a rude communiqué from Stalin Churchill said acidly, 'there is no need for you to attempt to smooth it over in the Foreign Office manner,'[293] a lapse of manners indicative of Churchill's view of Eden as conciliator and the FO balancing itself on the fence over issues. This was unfair to the FO, for they did have a policy, and one that Churchill would not even consider, but it is evidence of Churchill's prejudice against the FO. Yet, as Ross notes, Eden contributed to Churchill's isolation from the issue, for it seems he considered referring the debate between the FO and the CoS to Churchill but decided not to do so.[294]

There were reasons for Eden's lack of influence on Churchill during the war. There was Eden's genuine admiration and affection for him and understanding of the need for Churchill's premiership for wartime victory because of a lack of alternative wartime premiers. There was the fact that Eden was Churchill's chosen successor, and amidst constant Prime Ministerial interference, there were interludes of warmth and appreciation. And, commenting on attempts to reduce Churchill's powers, Charmley remarks that 'Eden was not the man for such a fight,' an indication of Eden's aversion for confrontation.

By Yalta the strain on Eden was apparent. Charmley notes that Churchill's interventions in foreign affairs were 'a series of romantic improvisations', and though he might 'adore' Churchill Eden was 'harassed by his interference'.[295] Cadogan's diary entry for 8 January 1945 says of Eden that 'he strides about the room, gabbling, and I, at least, can't hear what he says.'[296] And Colville's diary entry of 9 January 1945 notes the effect of a minute from Cherwell contradicting Eden, who 'told me he would resign if inexpert, academic opinions were sought on subjects to which he had given so much thought. I put him through to the P.M., to whom he ranted in a way in which neither the P.M. nor I (who was listening in) had ever heard him before.'[297] This alludes to a characteristic that infuriated those involved in foreign policy, Churchill's proclivity for taking informal advice rather than that of the FO or Eden – Lord Cherwell was Lindemann, Churchill's scientific adviser. On this occasion Churchill displayed another of his facets, the ability to placate and draw people to him, but also adding that he was entitled to consult Cherwell.[298] And Eden's own comment at the time of the loss of the 1945 general election is quietly eloquent as to the difficulties of his working relationship with Churchill – 'fond as I am of W, I do not feel I have the strength to undertake life or work with him again, it is too much strain and struggle.'[299] Dutton claims that, as the war in Europe drew to an end, Eden and Churchill concurred over the possible threat of Soviet power and intentions in Europe. Eden may have joined Churchill in the latter's view that Germany should perform its historic role in Europe as a countervailing force to Russian power – or he may have wanted a unitary Germany as a focus of British and Soviet collaboration, the old FO position, yet more in hope than from experience.

Either was in a way an odd conclusion, as similar fears had resulted in the opposite policy's being recommended by the CoS on the basis that the east of Germany would be lost anyway. Yet Eden's relations with Churchill also became more difficult, for 'as the purely military problems simplify themselves the old boy's tireless energy leads to ever closer attention to foreign affairs.'[300]

The War Cabinet continued to exert minimal influence on policy. This is apparent from the absence of dissent from the views of Churchill, yet Cabinet minutes give no indication of the relative influence of Cabinet ministers and in some cases, as with the phrase, 'the view was expressed that', no indication of its author. The evidence of Eden's influence from the documentary evidence and from his uninformative memoir is that in Cabinet he did not advocate any policy with any vehemence.

Eden himself has said that there was a clear sense of how far one could go, a sense that he prided himself on prudence and caution. Eden says Cabinet was 'enlivened by the sweep and dive of the Prime Minister's discourse'.[301] One infers that the rest of the Cabinet had little to say. Alanbrooke, Chief of the Imperial General Staff, refers to Eden and Attlee as 'Yes' men prepared to support Churchill in discussion 'irrespective of the degree of lunacy connected with some of Winston's proposals'.[302] He also notes of Churchill that 'his personality was such, and the power he acquired adequate, to place him in a position where parliament and Cabinet were only minor inconveniencies to be humoured occasionally, but which he held in the palm of his hand, able to swing both at his pleasure.'[303] Policy was then often a matter of debate between Churchill and his harassed generals and the Chiefs of Staff.

Mackintosh claims that 'Cabinet colleagues were content for him to conduct the war by himself' and refers to Bevin's statement that he 'knew nothing about the war and neither did the others: Churchill should get on with it, or get out.'[304]

Other evidence draws similar conclusions as to the function of the Cabinet. Hankey noted of the Churchill administration: 'it is a complete dictatorship. The War Cabinet and the War Committee on military matters consist of a long monologue by one man. The others are just "yes men". The Chiefs of Staff, worn out by incessant late night meetings of the Defence Committee, are reduced almost to the position of "Joint Planners",'[305] an assessment with which Menzies, the Australian Prime Minister, would have concurred.[306] And of Eden's own view of the Cabinet Charmley comments that he 'could not deny that Churchill neither had, nor wanted to have, an effective Cabinet.'[307] On the specific issue of German dismemberment Sainsbury observes that as late as 8 February 1945 a Cabinet member remarked that 'German partition' 'had not so far been discussed by the war cabinet', and that another minister queried the term's meaning, remarkable indications of absence of Cabinet discussion of the issue, though Sainsbury attributes this less to Churchill's dominance than to the other preoccupations of ministers.[308]

Churchill was then the dominant force in foreign-policy decision-making over the issue of German dismemberment. For much of the period during which the issue was under discussion at the FO and with the CoS Churchill's exclusive focus on victory in the war meant that his involvement was confined to exchanges at diplomatic encounters such as Teheran and Yalta, at which his views bore no relation to the FO case, to which he had declined to listen.

Eden's view, apart from a consistent aversion to imposition of dismemberment, seemed to depend on his audience and there is no evidence of his influencing Churchill – he was resolved to refrain from committing himself to either side of the debate. The Cabinet was dominated by Churchill and made no autonomous contribution to causation of policy on Germany's future. It is however worth noting that while Eden remained undecided over a long period of time he was not alone, as Churchill continued to decline to consider FO papers on the future of Germany and to attempt to maintain the wartime alliance by deferring the issue, Roosevelt endorsed and then abandoned the radical Morgenthau Plan for the pastoralisation of Germany and even Stalin dispensed with an initial insistence upon German dismemberment at the end of the war (on both the Baltics issue and that of German dismemberment Stalin effected about-turns without any apparent sense of needing to explain them).

I have outlined the FO and CoS views on German dismemberment and their connection to perceptions of probable Soviet policy, and the views of Churchill, Eden and the War Cabinet. When policy over post-war Germany was considered with some seriousness rather than deferred to maintain the wartime alliance, it came to be seen partly as a means of containing possible Soviet expansionism, as a consequence of Soviet behaviour in the east of Europe following the Red Army advance into Germany in late 1944 and 1945. There remained divergence of view as to how best that should be achieved. There was a preference in some quarters for the existence of a viable

German state at the centre of Europe – this emerged as Churchill's view, and one to which Eden seems to have gravitated as his suspicions as to Soviet intentions in post-war Europe grew. The CoS saw a dismembered Germany as the safest means to securing western Europe from Soviet expansionism. And the FO view, which had received Eden's tentative but not unreserved support but which was predicated on a positive view of Soviet intentions he found difficult to sustain in the period up to, during and after Yalta,[309] was that a Germany constituted in a voluntary federation scheme could enhance Anglo-Soviet relations. The FO perception was that continued collaboration with the Soviets was possible – there was also a sense of an enduring German menace in the FO.

The centrality of Churchill to any foreign policy decision-making (as opposed to planning) in the wartime administration[310] means that the sources of his power are causal influences and that factors that influenced his perceptions and so his decisions are of causal significance.

To begin with there was no alternative to him as PM given his stature in the country and the sense in which he embodied the will of the nation to resist. There were the formidable powers and prerogatives of the PM in the British political system and Churchill's liberal interpretation of them. Churchill dominated the Cabinet and Eden because of such powers, the absence of an alternative as wartime premier, and his extraordinary personality, which drew people to him and resulted in acceptance of his continual interference. His ease and confidence in the use of power exploited the enormous possibilities of Prime Ministerial power, and his dominance was accepted as inevitable and proper in time of war by Eden. Yet another factor in Churchill's grasp of and dominance of foreign policy was Attlee's management of all other issues, which permitted Churchill time and freedom for foreign policy and diplomacy.[311] And Churchill's period of tenure as wartime premier and his various exhibitions of personal resilience and defiance of critics, as well as the transformed fortunes of the British military effort, enhanced his association with the national war effort and victory and silenced opposition – after the tribulations of 1941–42, Churchill 'knew he was the undisputed master'.[312]

There were also Churchill's personal qualities, which, while they may have infuriated, also endeared him to his colleagues and subordinates.[313] And though accounts of Churchill do necessarily reflect the character of the relationship and the author, the remarkable extent of corroboration from very different sources lends such accounts a credibility any one would not have alone. Churchill's own account has not been used much here, given that it was written for posterity and some time after the events, with natural tendencies to rationalisation.

Churchill's dominance over policy had consequences for the pattern of influences on British policy on German dismemberment as on all other foreign-policy issues. The first was that for some considerable time there was, given Churchill's absence of interest in post-war issues and exclusive attention to winning the war, no policy on German dismemberment apart from the Danubian federation idea devised by Churchill himself (derided by the FO) and rejected by Roosevelt and Stalin at Teheran. In this context the lengthy FO-CoS debate represented planning that had no influence on Churchill and his policy as, to begin with, he had no interest in German dismemberment.[314] Second, when the issue did become salient to him, he declined not only to seek FO views but to attend to them when offered – it cannot therefore be argued that the FO and CoS papers served to establish the 'social context for debate'.[315] In fact Churchill's antipathy for the FO and refusal to consult it is a causal factor in policy on German dismemberment – the FO was remarkably consistent in its opposition to German dismemberment and its favouring of 'voluntary federation', so lack of FO unanimity cannot be the reason for its utter lack of influence on policy. And Eden was hardly an enthusiastic advocate for FO policy given his own doubts, orientation to diplomatic audiences, resolute avoidance of a definite view, and detachment from FO planning resulting from overwork with his dual role as Foreign Secretary and Leader of the House of Commons.[316] As a result any FO influence on Churchill is unlikely and, if it existed, impossible to establish by evidence. It seems that FO influence required not only a unanimity of FO view but also a Foreign Secretary and a PM amenable to it. The worst situation for FO influence would seem to be diversity of FO view, a weak Foreign Secretary and a PM possessed of a profound antipathy for the FO, which obtained over the Baltic issue, but the evidence of the issue of German dismemberment is that FO unanimity alone does not rectify the situation.

A similar situation existed in Churchill's relations with the Cabinet over German dismemberment, for a remarkable consequence of Churchill's dominance was the total absence of Cabinet discussion of the issue and ignorance even of the meaning of the term 'dismemberment' as late as February 1945[317] – an extreme instance of the PM's availing himself of his ability to control the agenda. It was also the case that the Cabinet was dependent for information regarding diplomatic encounters on reports from Churchill and Eden. Policy then seems to have been evolved by Churchill alone and oriented to the diplomatic arena unaffected by the FO case against and the CoS case for German dismemberment and by any Cabinet discussion whatever.

Churchill's orientation derived partly then from his colossal confidence as PM and his sense of having a perfect right to disattend to Eden and the FO (and to keep the issue off the Cabinet agenda) and to pursue his own exclusive preoccupation with winning the war, which meant that his attention was directed towards Britain's alliances with the US and the Soviets to maximise the war effort. Policy on German dismemberment then meant some accommodation with the desire for radical dismemberment proposed by Roosevelt and endorsed by Stalin at Teheran. What resulted was a series of evasions, by both Churchill and Eden, using various expedients, of agreeing in principle, vague use of the term dismemberment and postponing the issue, while the war continued.

The issue was, from its early stages of policy formulation in the FO, one of long duration, but actual policy is apparent only in these diplomatic exchanges, and even this was presentational in nature given that German dismemberment was not decided but rather postponed. And even when German dismemberment became salient to Churchill for reasons other than maintaining the wartime alliance and avoiding alienating either ally, his policy was constrained by the need for alliances for victory, and the policy of postponement continued at Yalta. There Roosevelt's indication of US troop withdrawal from Europe oddly makes Churchill's resisting making any commitment on dismemberment more remarkable, in that good post-war relations with the Soviets might then have seemed imperative, yet also more comprehensible, in that the need for a viable German state to offset Soviet power in Europe may have seemed yet more pressing. The constraint of maintaining the wartime alliance is clear in the policy of postponement as a means of avoidance of open discord. But by this time, after a long period in which he experienced alternations of confidence in Stalin and doubts regarding Soviet power and intentions and the spread of communism in Europe, Churchill had come to the view that Soviet domination of post-war Europe should be resisted by the retention of a viable German state at the centre of Europe. I now turn to identifying the influences on Churchill at this time.

I have mentioned above Eden's lack of influence on Churchill in the long period of Churchill's aversion to discussion of German dismemberment and all other post-war issues. Yet did Eden have a role in altering Churchill's view of the advisability of German dismemberment just prior to Yalta, when the issue became salient again and any policy seemed likely to be implemented soon? Did Eden exert some influence on Churchill by changing 'the social context of debate'[318] in private conversations and the unending stream of FO papers to Cabinet? Folly sees this context as 'difficult to trace except in a fragmentary way, though it was a factor in the spreading of assumptions within what was a fairly small and socially cohesive elite'.[319] Two observations may serve to settle this question. The first is that Churchill's view did not change much between Teheran and Yalta in terms of actual policy, which was postponement on both occasions. And the second is that Eden did not, even just prior to Yalta, have a settled view of his own.

Sainsbury infers that Churchill's concern to maintain a viable German state in Europe derived from a sense of a need for 'a bulwark against an over-powerful Russia',[320] which is supported by Kitchen's reference to Churchill as being, in the summer of 1943, in a 'belligerently anti-Soviet mood'[321] and considering a viable post-war Germany as a necessary balance to Soviet power, and by Harvey's observation on 6 October 1943 that Churchill had told the Cabinet that Germany should not be weakened too much as 'we may need her against Russia'.[322] That such serious doubts regarding Soviet power and intentions alternated with periodic bursts of confidence in Stalin that continued to and beyond Yalta[323] does not alter the fact that policy was predicated on Churchill's reservations. And though such doubts were not too far from a concern regarding a Germany facing east expressed by the FO paper of 8 March 1943, in the intervening period FO policy had been predicated upon the cultivation of the Soviets and continued collaboration in the post-war period.

It does then seem that Churchill's emerging concern regarding post-war Europe and attachment to the notion of limited dismemberment seems to have owed less to the diplomatic practicalities and administrative onus that concerned the FO than to the desire to have a viable Germany play its historic role at the centre of Europe to act as a counterbalance to Soviet power. Some historians have pointed to a tendency in Churchill to be influenced by other, official (as in the War Cabinet) and unofficial quarters. These included an interest in decoded messages from Bletchley and in the views of particular individuals with no official position in foreign policy but with whom he had an affinity or history, such as Lindemann (whose influence on Churchill prompted Eden's outburst noted above),[324] Bracken, who became Minister for Information, and Morton, an old associate. Yet Charmley observes that Churchill 'preferred to work with the Whitehall machine',[325] though he does point to Churchill's unpredictability and interference.

Few in the FO would have concurred that Churchill was responsive to civil-service advice.[326] In fact it seems that over foreign policy Churchill was more susceptible to a form of impressionistic influence from international events such as the actuality of, and Soviet reaction to, the Katyn Forest massacre, and Soviet behaviour over the Warsaw uprising, over Poland in general, and in eastern Europe occupied by the Red Army, and that Churchill's caution over German dismemberment at Yalta is attributable to changed perceptions of Soviet power and intentions in Europe predicated on such events – any possible influence on Churchill from Eden seems unlikely in view of Eden's remarkable record of uncertainty over the issue even as late as the end of 1944 and Churchill's clear aversion to considering any post-war issue up to the time of Yalta. Whether any other Foreign Secretary would have exerted more influence on Churchill is conjectural, but it seems a remote possibility – in the first place Churchill may not have appointed such an individual, and in any case it seems he would not have tolerated resistance from any individual in the role of Foreign Secretary.

Eden's position, to the extent that he had one, seems to have been somewhere between Churchill's, on the basis of diplomatic expediency in wartime, and the FO's, on grounds of practicality and avoidance of an adverse diplomatic outcome with the Soviets. For Eden seems not to have been involved in the formation of FO policy on Germany's future in the context of probable Soviet policy as presented in the many FO papers. This may be inferred from Cadogan's and Harvey's complaints that Eden was not enough involved in planning after his assumption of his dual role,[327] added to which was his tendency not to contradict the FO that Kitchen notes. In his memorandum to the Armistice and Post-War Committee on 20 September 1944 (APW (44) 90) his detachment is evident – he found it 'hard to resist the conclusion of this paper'[328] but indicated a preparedness to alter his position 'if I believed it would be in the interest of security'.[329] Roberts did not regard Eden as 'an originator of policy' but rather a protagonist of FO views.[330] The first does seem true, but the second is not borne out by the evidence. For the only expression of vehemence from Eden over German dismemberment came in his insistence on not being committed to any definite position. In fact Eden seems to have reflected the most proximate influence at the time, as his performances in Washington in March 1943 evidence. Yet it seems Eden did gravitate, if with characteristic qualifications and reservations, towards the FO view that voluntary federation was desirable to avoid the diplomatic and practical disadvantages of dismemberment. Part of the attraction may have been that opposition to forced and radical dismemberment chimed with Churchill's and his own developing reservations regarding Soviet influence in a Europe without a viable German state at its centre. By Yalta both Eden and Churchill were opposed to radical dismemberment schemes and wanted to postpone or amend them.

For some considerable time, and possibly for reasons associated with the avoidance of diplomatic discord, the term dismemberment, while defined and understood in the FO, was used to cover a broad spectrum of options, though by Yalta, with some imminence of translation of policy into action, the need for precision as to meaning and consequence was clear in Churchill's response. As late as 8 February 1945 the War Cabinet felt 'it was by no means clear what precisely was involved in "dismemberment"',[331] and noted that 'it was desirable to avoid any commitment until the matter as a whole could be reviewed by the Cabinet',[332] a caution similar to the way in which Churchill's intermittent doubts over Soviet intentions had developed into reservations over German dismemberment as the war drew to its close in Europe in a context of Red Army occupation of eastern Europe and colossal Soviet reparations demands. On 12 February the War Cabinet draft communiqué on Yalta recorded that 'the principle of dismemberment had been accepted, but there remained ample room for discussion.'[333]

There was then a clear relationship between attitude to German dismemberment and fears and uncertainty regarding Stalin's intentions (and Soviet power) in Europe for Churchill, who when he addressed the issue regarded a viable Germany as necessary to counteract Soviet power, and possibly also for Eden. The CoS meanwhile favoured dismemberment to contain the Soviets in Europe by safeguarding the western part of Germany, which reflected a brief that required them to assess and avert the danger of possible future adversaries and to address worst-case scenarios. The FO meanwhile felt a need for collaboration with the Soviets that resulted in a policy that refused to countenance the possibility of a collaborative policy's failing, and regarded voluntary federation for Germany as a means of securing post-war collaboration with the Soviets in Europe.

There were identifiable continuities amid the confusion of differing views. One was the opposition of the FO and Eden to enforced dismemberment, for reasons of practicality and enforceability, and Eden's preference for voluntary rather than imposed arrangements. There was also Eden's sense, as he expressed it to Roosevelt in March 1943, that even if it were 'Stalin's aim to overrun and communise the Continent', 'we should make the position no worse by trying to work with Russia',[334] a rationale that was to inform the FO view in its long debate with the CoS, though it is also true that Eden was dismayed by Soviet brazenness in the period after Yalta, with reduced conviction in the possibility of collaboration. Another continuity was, once he became interested in the issue of the future of Germany beyond what was required to maintain the wartime alliance, Churchill's aversion to any dismemberment scheme that would leave no viable German state in Europe.

The avoidance of open discord over German dismemberment, and its abandonment once the Soviets indicated no further interest in it, do point to the constraining influence of Soviet wishes on British policy over post-war Germany. FO planning for German dismemberment (under political direction) after Yalta, despite FO resistance and Churchill's and Eden's reservations, reinforces this view of Soviet influence on British policy. Rothwell concludes that the consequence of confirmation of German unity 'owed most to calculations within the Kremlin over which no one in the office of Foreign Secretary in 1945 could have any influence'.[335] Yet the evidence also indicates American influence in terms of constraint on policy, for by this time the general sense from various diplomatic contacts was that enthusiasm within the Roosevelt administration for

German dismemberment had waned and that it was no longer the favoured option – Churchill's reaction in Quebec to the Morgenthau proposals indicates the extent to which British policy was susceptible to American pressure, and the abandonment of the dismemberment option reflects an absence of such pressure for the option. Preparedness to continue to plan for dismemberment reflected Churchill's orientation to the maintenance of the wartime alliance for the duration of the war. Yet Churchill did find some British room for manoeuvre, as in the tactic of postponement at Teheran and Yalta, and the resulting paper[336] maintained British opposition to a multiplicity of small German states, proposing instead three states, one in the east, one in the south and one in the north, which would leave a viable Germany in Europe, as Churchill wanted. This is a remarkable example of indirect British influence on allied policy beyond its own power, for Roosevelt by this time wanted to discuss policy with Stalin without Churchill's agenda being there. And by Yalta Roosevelt was ailing, needed Stalin's support in the continuing war against Japan, and indicated that US troops would leave Europe within two years of the end of the war. This left the British constrained by their 'gullible Americans partners' and so 'powerless to foil the machinations of the Soviets'.[337] In this context, given also Britain's weak position and Churchill's, Roosevelt's and Stalin's understanding of it, Churchill's ability to resist Stalin and Roosevelt at Yalta over German dismemberment, albeit by the expedient of postponement, was remarkable.

Yet absence of enthusiasm for even this measure of accommodation to allies' wishes, and the latter's influence, is also apparent, in the immediate abandonment of dismemberment once it became clear that the Soviets (and the Americans) did not favour it any longer. What would have happened if the Soviets or the Americans had continued to demand dismemberment is an imponderable. But it does seem that Soviet and American demands would have constrained British policy, for the wartime alliance with them was seen as imperative by Churchill, the Cabinet, Eden and the FO, and post-war accord with the Soviets desirable with expected US withdrawal from Europe. And of course continued good relations with the Americans were seen as imperative to British foreign policy.

Sainsbury sees Churchill as having 'fought a long delaying action against the extreme courses on which Roosevelt and Stalin seemed to be agreed: until, in fact, the march of events and pressures within his own administration led Roosevelt to conclude that it would be best not to impose any drastic solution without careful and prolonged consideration.'[338] He might have added something similar in regard to the Soviets.

There remains the question of the influence of attitude and perception on policy. Folly's is the latest historiography on British policy towards the Soviet Union and a rare attempt to explain its causes, in this case in terms of what he sees as altered attitudes. It does also highlight the semantic problems consequent on use of terms without clear definition or distinction, and the difficulties of generalising as to British policy, which indicate an inevitable particularity in historical causation.

Folly does see FO influence on policy towards the Soviet Union, which would include policy on German dismemberment. Folly observes a change in the FO view of the Soviets from reserve to a perception of Soviet sensitivity to diplomatic treatment and concern for security, and then the notion of a co-operative Soviet Union. He thus disputes Churchill's claim that British policy towards the Soviet Union was pragmatic, did not involve belief in genuine accord and maintained the wartime alliance only to achieve victory. As has been seen, for Folly British views of Soviet foreign policy, and British attitudes and policy towards the Soviet Union, were derived ultimately from perceived changes within the Soviet Union that included 'Stalin's sagacious realism, Soviet fear of Germany and concern to prevent post-war German resurgence, the centrality of the security motivation, Soviet suspiciousness and Soviet reconstruction needs'[339] – the effect of a radical reassessment of Soviet military capability on British policy and evidence that the FO perceived the Soviets to be concerned over security and sensitive to diplomatic treatment (as in exclusion from Anglo-American discussions) have been covered above.

Folly claims that Churchill came to embrace the FO view of possible collaboration with the Soviets, albeit on the basis of personal contact with Stalin. Though he remarks that 'for Churchill himself, his geopolitical outlook meant that the rapid advances of the Red Army caused him to revise somewhat his preference to avoid contentious issues,'[340] and notes also that 'Churchill's attitude appears to veer from one extreme to the other,'[341] he refers to 'the aims of Churchill and the FO, in terms of securing, if possible, Soviet friendship'.[342] Yet he characterises the hypothesis of pragmatism as one of hoping for but not being assured of Soviet collaboration.[343] This is in contradistinction to his own collaborative hypothesis. The alternatives are then not defined as mutually exclusive, and it would seem that Churchill's aims as described were 'pragmatic'. Such semantic issues seem to plague discussion of historiographical differences as to Soviet intentions and the character of British policy. For without clear definitions as to the meaning of terms and the means by which they may be proved or disproved discourse can only remain confused. For instance, pragmatism in the ordinary sense may be seen to be a superordinate term under which collaboration with the Soviets on certain terms but not on others could be subsumed.

The change in FO perceptions of the Soviet Union during 1943 and 1944 may be inferred from the remarkable confidence of the FO paper of 29 April 1944 in future relations between Britain and the Soviet Union. Such confidence was however not universal and existed in a context of adverse experience of Soviet diplomacy and enduring anti-communism and anti-Sovietism. Rothwell has noted the pragmatic function of the Anglo-Soviet alliance for both partners, Keeble observes that 'intergovernmental exchanges illustrated only too clearly the classic problems of British-Soviet cooperation and the deep difference of approach',[344] and even Harvey remarked 'there is so deep a gulf between British and Russian mentality that we never have and never will have confidence and understanding.'[345]

Clark-Kerr indicates that the difference in conceptual universe was so profound that it had linguistic implications, for 'cooperation' meant to the Soviets an acceptance of 'the division of the world into spheres of interest', and 'democracy'[346] did not preclude the imposition of Communist regimes. Clark-Kerr's case is that Soviet cynicism and opportunism were such that they were regarded as natural, and that the Soviets were mystified at any intrusion of principle into *Realpolitik* considerations. Yet more likely is that Stalin understood the difference and exploited it, deriding Western conceptualisations as susceptible to manipulation. Dew shared the views of many in the FO that Soviet policy 'could still bear two interpretations, cooperation or unilateralism'.[347]

These views do indicate an absence of unanimity of assurance that co-operation with the Soviets was possible. In this context the FO paper of 29 April 1944 seems anomalous. There was certainly no repetition of such confidence in ensuing papers, but rather an insistence that the possibility of collaboration should not be surrendered by regarding the Soviets as the main threat to European peace and British interests, which represents a subordination of attitude to *Realpolitik*.

And if there was a brief change of perception, did it extend beyond the confines of the FO? For there was a considerable period in which there was little relation between FO and CoS deliberations on German dismemberment and probable Soviet policy and Eden's and Churchill's orientation to maintaining the wartime alliance by avoiding confrontation with Roosevelt and Stalin. Churchill's own erratic and oscillating views, so salient to foreign-policy decision-making given his domination of his wartime administration, have been evidenced. Keeble refers to Churchill's 'innate dislike' for the Soviets, and concludes that 'mistrust was never wholly eradicated' and that 'the bond between Britain and the Soviet Union, in so far as it existed, depended upon the common enemy and dissolved with his defeat,'[348] a clear attribution of pragmatism and maintenance of the wartime alliance to optimise the war effort. Folly's own acknowledgement of Churchill's oscillations of sentiment towards the Soviets, from confidence after meetings with Stalin to doubts over Soviet intentions, has also been mentioned. There was no

FO influence on Churchill over policy, and no evidence that he was ever anything but pragmatic in his trying to keep the Red Army fighting as part of optimising the war effort.

Folly differentiates a belief in the possibility of genuine collaboration from the pragmatic thesis he sees as the received wisdom. Yet as a generalisation it seems that the diversity of view that obtained within the FO is better described as pragmatic in dealing with the Soviets, cautious and attempting to cultivate accord even with reservations as to its possibility over time. The issue is difficult to resolve by reference to policy, in that both a pragmatic orientation to optimising the war effort and an attitudinal shift towards belief in the possibility of genuine collaboration with the Soviets would have eventuated in identical policies, that is, attempts to conciliate and to establish a relationship with them. At best then the inference of new perceptions and attitudes' influencing even FO policy is conjectural. And the evidence is in any event of the co-existence of some altered briefly held perceptions and confidence with long-held aversion and mistrust, especially in Churchill himself, and of policy being decided in the realm of diplomacy between the wartime alliance partners rather than through influence from the FO, though as Folly says indirect influence is difficult to prove or disprove.

In fact the evidence tends to support the pragmatic interpretation. There had clearly been no abandonment of anti-communism or of doubts as to Soviet intentions, expressions of which continued even within the FO. Any altered perceptions of the Soviet Union existed with such pre-existing attitudes, and the major effect on policy was commonality of interest with another adversary of Germany. The change was then from a policy of detachment to association on pragmatic grounds only and with reservations. Previous Soviet policy had not been immune to external influence. The Nazi-Soviet pact and the Soviets' appeasing Hitler indicate that security concerns and opportunistic expansionism had informed Soviet policy throughout. The only changes were then the German attack upon the Soviet Union, which reoriented Soviet diplomacy from Germany to Britain, and Soviet resistance. British policy was then pragmatic (as was the Soviets'), disregarding the Soviets until they could assist the war effort. The evidence of actual policy does not differentiate pragmatism from conviction, for as has been noted both would have produced the same policy. Yet the documentary record does indicate continuing British reservations towards, and a focus on retaining, the Soviets as wartime allies – though some, such as Eden and the FO, looked to collaboration in the post-war period, if with diminishing confidence as the war approached its end.

Folly's case does then seem not to be borne out by the evidence even within the FO. The extrapolation to influence on Churchill or an indication of changed attitudes in Churchill is even less evidenced. And it is impossible to find any effect on policy, with the locus of decision-making power with Churchill and orientation to American and Soviet wishes to sustain the war effort while not surrendering central Europe to the Soviets. Far from believing in the possibility of genuine collaboration, Churchill postponed any decision on German dismemberment at Teheran and at Yalta from a clear concern as to Soviet domination of Europe without a viable Germany at its centre.

In terms of the locus of decision-making power and the influences on policy that followed the PM's conceptualisation of his role is vital, for his powers are immense in the British system. Churchill had confidence in his right and ability to take decisions, even if they were uninformed or based on poor advice from the wrong quarters. An indication of Churchill's sense of his right to ignore or take advice as he pleased, to the infuriation of Eden and the FO, may be found in Alanbrooke's record of Churchill's having 'asked whether he was not entitled to consult whoever he wished!'.[349] And, as has been seen, Eden had complained in outraged terms over Churchill's consulting other advisors as to foreign policy.

Over German dismemberment the powers of the Prime Minister are vividly apparent, rendered so by the preparedness of Churchill to use them to attend to his own priorities, to intervene and overrule, to disregard FO advice and that of his Foreign Secretary, and to control the agenda in Cabinet. And while the constraints on British foreign policy are also apparent in the need to maintain alliances, and for a stratagem of postponement when accord was impossible, these very policies reflected Churchill's exclusive attention to optimising the war effort and achieving victory, which was defined as unconditional surrender, as soon as possible. Balancing the demands of allies was part of achieving the objectives of British policy, and while the need to maintain the wartime alliance obtained regardless of the character of the PM the continuing significance of allies reflected Churchill's insistence upon unconditional surrender. There is here an interaction between structural and attitudinal factors in causation, an example of the difficulty in differentiating causal factors from each other in terms of contribution. And there were Churchill's personal qualities, which have been elaborated upon above in the Baltics case study and which enhanced his use of the powers of the PM and his stature with Roosevelt and Stalin. Over the future of Germany Churchill does not seem to have been influenced by FO papers, as he does not appear to have read them, or by Eden, who remained uncertain over policy regarding the future of Germany between 1943 and 1945. It seems rather that Churchill gravitated on his own to wanting a viable Germany in Europe to counteract the possibility of Soviet incursion, a view predicated not on FO or Eden's influence but on his unaltered anti-communism and anti-Sovietism, reinforced by the emerging situation of Soviet power in central Europe and Soviet actions in eastern Europe, not least in Poland.[350]

Churchill did not have a *volte-face* regarding his view of the Soviets but rather a continuing series of alternations of view that reflected both his enduring anti-communism and revulsion for the Soviet system and an uncertainty exacerbated by Stalin's personal warmth at meetings that itself alternated with insistent demands and the most insulting accusations – after the conclusion of such meetings Churchill's conviction in Stalin's good intentions would dissipate.[351] Yet Churchill did tend to differentiate Stalin from the Soviet system, and he did have a belief in personal diplomacy as an effective means of foreign policy, which may have been part of his susceptibility to impressionistic data and his volatility. As an indication of Churchill's difficulty at the time of Yalta and beyond, Colville's diary entry for 23 February 1945 records Churchill as being 'rather depressed', considering 'the possibilities of Russia one day turning against us' and saying that 'Chamberlain had trusted Hitler as he was now trusting Stalin.'[352] But all this did not result in any difference in policy, for, with Churchill's perception of the forces he saw Stalin as trying to control in the Soviet Union caution and avoidance of controversial issues seemed the policy most likely to maximise the war effort during the war given the need for the Red Army in the east, as the policy of deferring a decision on German dismemberment indicates. By Yalta though Churchill was concerned as to 'the changing power relationships in Europe' and to use Germany to counter 'Soviet expansionism'.[353]

To appreciate the extent of Churchill's personal influence on British policy towards German dismemberment it is worth noting that Churchill could have agreed to the radical dismemberment of Germany at Teheran or Yalta, given Roosevelt's and Stalin's approach to the issue at those times, an instance of Churchill's resisting even those upon whom he depended for wartime victory, his own primary objective. One does however wonder whether any such undertaking would have survived the casual and insolent Soviet *volte-face* in March 1945, such was their influence regarding the future of Europe at that time, in a context of the focus of the United States on the war against Japan and the desirability of Soviet assistance in it and Roosevelt's ailing health combined with his indication of a US withdrawal from Europe two years after the end of the war.

Policy seems to have proceeded in parallel lines over German unity or dismemberment. There was Churchill's remoteness, his aversion to discussing post-war issues and then pursuing his own scheme, his orientation to diplomatic encounters on the world stage with Roosevelt and Stalin, and his attempts to maintain the wartime alliance by means of postponement in a context of gathering doubts as to Soviet intentions and over the need for a viable Germany in Europe.[354] The FO had meanwhile continued to plan for German unity without any influence on policy. And Eden in the middle teetered between one policy and another, dependent it seems on audience, and unwilling to express any clear preference. By Yalta Eden and Churchill were of the same view, that decisions on dismemberment should be postponed and considered in detail and not in haste, yet to some extent for different reasons. Eden was against the imposition of dismemberment on Germany, and may have favoured postponement on the basis that a decision averted was desirable in itself, while Churchill was concerned to maintain the alliance but also to leave a viable Germany to counteract Soviet power in Europe. Eden did however by this time share Churchill's concern over Soviet power and intentions in post-war Europe.

Eden's lack of influence on policy over the future of Germany after the war seems then to reflect the dominance of Churchill as PM and as a personality and Eden's own character with his valuing of diplomacy, his uncertainty as to the optimal policy and deference to Churchill as PM in wartime. Had another individual been PM during Eden's tenure as wartime Foreign Secretary Eden's influence on foreign policy could have been far greater, and Eden does seem to have been unfortunate in serving as Foreign Secretary under two domineering PMs in Chamberlain and Churchill, both of whom took a liberal view of Prime Ministerial prerogatives in general and over foreign policy in particular and dominated their Foreign Secretaries, not least because both of them had an interest in and confidence in their personal contribution to foreign policy.

Eden seems over the post-war future of Germany to have shown genuine autonomy in relation to the views of his Foreign Office, not least the FO attempt to commit him to a definite view (!), for Eden seems to have been averse to having a definite view on the future of Germany attributed to him, possibly because he understood that Churchill did not wish to consider the matter during the war, though the more plausible inference is that Eden was genuinely uncertain as to the optimal future of Germany after the war. Having said that his diplomat's desire to explore all possible hope for post-war collaboration with the Soviet Union over Germany seems to have given way over time and with experience of Stalin's policy over Poland to reservations as to Soviet intentions in Europe after the war, a concern to which Churchill also gravitated.

I should add a final word on the possibility of Commons influence. Though there had been other, earlier Commons debates as to the general treatment of Germany after the war they had been regarding issues such as the removal of German capacity for war and reparations rather than dismemberment. The first debate in which there is specific reference to German dismemberment is on 27 February 1945, when Churchill reported to the Commons on the 'Crimea Conference', and then Beveridge seems to have been a lone voice in expressing the hope that 'we will not attempt to partition or dismember Germany',[355] but not on the basis of Germany's providing a countervailing force in Europe to that of Soviet power – this dimension seems quite absent from the entire discussion, which is unsurprising given the favourable representation of the Soviets as performing military heroics in the east and the FO's preoccupation with secrecy regarding any suspicion as to Soviet motives. The government won the ensuing vote by 396 to 25, another indication of absence of Commons influence on policy, for a victory of such magnitude must have been anticipated and so had no anticipatory effect on policy. Again, the reasons for the Commons' lack of influence are to be traced to the British political system and to Churchill's personal ascendancy in the Cabinet, Commons and country – Addison observes that though he had a troubled period in the Commons in 1941–42, Churchill knew he was 'the undisputed master thereafter'.[356]

Conclusion

From the two case studies assessed here it does seem that Churchill's Prime Ministerial dominance over British foreign policy during the war was such that the CoS, the FO and Eden as Foreign Secretary, and the Cabinet itself, exerted little if any influence on the foreign policy pursued, oriented as it was to the maintenance of the wartime alliance and wartime victory. Churchill was the dominant influence throughout both by virtue of his position as PM and as a consequence of his extraordinary personality, sense of entitlement as PM, stature as a PM for whom there was no possible replacement, and personal qualities that despite his maddening interference endeared him to those with whom he interacted over British foreign policy during the war.

The FO, never respected by Churchill, was marginalised, the CoS view was disregarded, and Eden was dominated by Churchill both as a consequence of what Eden saw as Prime Ministerial prerogatives and as a result of his own close personal relationship with Churchill that seems so to have disarmed him even when grievously offended. It does seem that Eden, periodic tantrums apart, was deferential to Churchill as PM. Eden does seem to have defied the FO view as it emerged from discussions in late 1941 and early 1942 despite earlier diversity of view as to how best to deal with the Soviet Union and seems to have defied Churchill in continuing to advocate acceptance of the Soviet demand over the Baltics in 1941 and early 1942, though in the end the decision to accept the Soviet demand reflected Churchill's concern to keep the Red Army fighting in the east and his having obtained the approval of Roosevelt for an exception to the terms of the Atlantic Charter rather than Eden's argument that the Soviet demand was a test of sincerity and could enhance the prospects both of the alliance in the war and of a continuance of the wartime alliance with the Soviet Union in the event of victory over Nazi Germany at no cost given that in that event the Soviet Union would take over the Baltic states.

Over the optimal form of post-war Germany, Eden seems to have been genuinely uncertain, as were Churchill, who came to have doubts as to Stalin's intentions and to advocate the need for a robust Germany at the centre of Europe as a consequence, and Roosevelt and Stalin, who favoured radical dismemberment and then abandoned it. There is no evidence of influence from Eden over post-war Germany, though there is evidence of his resistance to FO papers on Germany after the war.

The FO view of Soviet foreign policy objectives, and of the optimal means of dealing with Soviet diplomatic tactics, varied between different FO officials and over time, though that taken by Baggallay in 1942 was not too dissimilar to that received from Frank Roberts in 1946. And Roberts' advice was so influential in the FO and with Bevin as Foreign Secretary precisely because it was consonant with the apprehensions as to Soviet objectives and tactics that the FO and Bevin were gravitating to in the immediate post-war period as evidence of Soviet rule in the communist east and of Soviet purposes in Germany resulted in understanding of Soviet foreign policy as expansionist and opportunistic and ideological in purpose. Before that time British foreign policy during the war was to maintain the wartime alliance and to optimise the prospects of continuing the alliance with the Soviet Union as the major European land power after the end of the war.

Of the various views of Soviet objectives and intentions, the CoS view that Germany should be dismembered seems to have been more validated by events than the others, though it is possible that the CoS view reflected its brief to plan for the worst, unlike the FO brief, which was to exhaust all the possibilities to optimise outcomes. Churchill and Eden, and the FO, seem to have come late to an accurate understanding of the nature of Soviet foreign policy and its objectives and in fact seem to have arrived at such an understanding only as a consequence of Soviet violations of undertakings in eastern Europe, not least over Poland. For there the disdain for diplomatic undertakings became difficult to disregard, and Soviet intentions were seen to be aimed at both security and opportunistic expansionism.

Though the case has been made that Churchill was the dominant influence in British foreign policy during the war as a consequence of a combination of circumstantial factors and personal attributes, the extent of external influence should not be underestimated, in that any wartime PM would, given British economic and military weakness even at the start of the war, have had to cultivate the alliance with the Soviet Union and the US just to sustain the war effort and avoid military defeat by Germany. Having said that, the policy of unconditional surrender seems to have been insisted upon by Churchill and so represents a personal influence on the conduct of the war and British foreign policy towards Germany, not least as it seems to have prolonged the war, and Churchill's avoidance of any perceived risk to the wartime alliance and prioritisation of its maintenance as the objective of foreign policy would appear to be another Churchillian influence in that another PM could have taken a very different view of the risk of Soviet or US withdrawal from the wartime alliance and had a greater sense of freedom as to foreign policy, over both the Baltics and the future of Germany.

What may be inferred from just two case studies is open to challenge, though both were selected at random apart from their being major foreign-policy issues during the war and their being instances of British foreign policy towards the Soviet Union with a wealth of evidence regarding the nature of decision-making in the British political and official establishment during the war. There is then no inherent bias in them and no reason to suppose that they are not representative of the locus of foreign policy decision-making power in the British political and official establishment during the war or of British foreign policy towards the Soviet Union during the war, or that the diversity of view in the FO and Cabinet, and the view of the CoS is unrepresentative.

Notes

[1]For works that do have such a longer view see Barnett, Corelli, *The Collapse of British Power*, Stroud: Alan Sutton, 1972, Charmley, John, *Churchill's Grand Alliance, The Anglo-American Special Relationship 1940–57*, Hodder and Stoughton, London,1995, and Kennedy, P., *The Realities behind Diplomacy: Background Influences on British External Policy, 1865–1980*, Allen and Unwin, London, 1981. For work with more specific reference to British foreign policy during the war see Rothwell, V., *Britain and the Cold War 1941–1947*, Jonathan Cape, London, Kitchen, M., *British Policy Towards the Soviet Union During the Second World War*, London: Macmillan, 1986, Sainsbury, Keith, *Churchill and Roosevelt at War*, Macmillan, London, 1994, Barker, E., *Churchill and Eden at War*, Macmillan, London, 1978, Jefferys, Kevin, *The Churchill coalition and wartime politics, 1940–1945*, Manchester University Press, Manchester, 1991, Dewey, Peter, *War and Progress: Britain 1914–1945*, Routledge, 2014, and Ross, Graham, *The Foreign Office and the Kremlin*, Cambridge: Cambridge University Press, 1984. For British policy towards the Soviet Union see Keeble, Curtis, *Britain and the Soviet Union, 1917–89*, Macmillan, 1990 and Folly, M. H., *Churchill, Whitehall and the Soviet Union, 1940–45*, London: Macmillan, 2000. And for works on Churchill see Charmley, John, *Churchill: The End of Glory*, Hodder and Stoughton, 1993, Gilbert, Martin, *Churchill: A Life*, Heinemann, London, 1991, and Best, Geoffrey, *Churchill: A Study in Greatness*, A & C Black, 2001.
[2]Keeble, *Britain and the Soviet Union*, op. cit., page 172.
[3]FO 371/29469, Churchill to Stalin, 21 November 1941.
[4]Ibid.
[5]Rothwell, Victor, *Anthony Eden: A Political Biography, 1931–1957*, Manchester University Press, 1992, page 60.
[6]Dutton, David, *Anthony Eden, A Life and Reputation*, Arnold, London, 1997, page 183.
[7]Ibid., page 185.
[8]See Mawdsley, Evan, *December 1941: Twelve Days that Began a World War*, Yale University Press, 2011, page 305, for Eden's diary reference to Stalin's having been told Eden was bringing armies – the

reference is to the Birmingham University Library, Lord Avon Papers, AP 2/1/21, Eden Personal Diary, 4 Dec. See also Lord Avon, *The Reckoning*, Cassell, London, 1965, page 282 for reference to Churchill's reluctance to consider anything relating to after the war, and page 283 for Eden's not being keen on going to see Stalin in December 1941. Yet Eden's memoirs seem oddly muted, formal in their treatment of Churchill, and to have a sanitised quality of extreme discretion, as if intended for an audience or part of a diplomatic encounter.

[9]Dutton, *Eden*, op. cit., page 185.

[10]Folly, *Churchill, Whitehall and the Soviet Union*, op. cit., page 36. See also Harvey, J. (ed.), *The War Diaries of Oliver Harvey, Collins*, London, 1978, diary for 14 November 1941.

[11]FO 371/29469, Sargent and Cadogan, 3 December 1941, initialled without comment by Eden on 4 December 1941.

[12]FO 371/29469, W.P. (41) 288 (Revise), 29 November 1941.

[13]Barnett, *The Collapse of British Power*, op. cit., page 591.

[14]See ibid, page 589 for a detailed exposition of this view.

[15]See Dewey, *War and Progress: Britain 1914–1945*, op. cit., for reference to controversy as to just how critical Lend Lease was for the British war effort, for as a percentage of GNP it was relatively small.

[16]Gilbert, *Churchill: A Life*, op. cit., page 713.

[17]FO371/32874, W.P. (42) 8, Eden's Visit to Moscow, 5 January 1942.

[18]CAB 65/25 WM (41)131C.A., 19 December 1941, cited in Barker, *Churchill and Eden at War*, op. cit., page 235.

[19]Kitchen, *British Policy Towards the Soviet Union*, op. cit., page 113, and CAB 65/24, Eden to FO 18 December 1941.

[20]FO 371/32874, Eden broadcast on 4 January 1942.

[21]FO 371/32874, Eden to Churchill, 5 January 1942.

[22]See Avon, *The Reckoning*, op. cit., pages 319–20 and 323–24 for an indication of Eden's pragmatic reasoning that the Soviets would occupy the Baltics in the event of Allied victory anyway and of his disdain for American diplomacy over the matter yet understanding that the alliance with them was vital.

[23]Folly, *Churchill, Whitehall and the Soviet Union*, op. cit., page 105.

[24]FO 371/32874, Telegram from Churchill to Eden, 8 January 1942.

[25]Barker, *Churchill and Eden at War*, op. cit., page 236.

[26]Charmley, *Churchill's Grand Alliance*, op. cit., page 48.

[27]Ibid., page 49.

[28]PREM 3, 395–12, Eden to Halifax, 10 February 1942.

[29]CAB 65/29, W.M. (42) 17th Conclusions, Minute 5, 6 February 1942.

[30]Ibid.

[31]CAB 65/29, W.M. (42) 24th Conclusions, minute 2, Confidential Annex, 25 February 1942.

[32]Gilbert, Martin, *Second World War*, Phoenix Press, London, 2000, page 300.

[33]Kitchen, *British Policy Towards the Soviet Union*, op. cit., page 120.

[34]FO 371/32877, Churchill to Stalin, 9 March 1942.

[35]CAB 65/29, W.M. (42) 37th Conclusions, Confidential Annex, 25 March 1942.

[36]Ibid.

[37]Ibid.

[38]Woodward, Llewellyn, *British Foreign Policy In The Second World War, Volume II*, HMSO, London, 1971, page 243.

[39]CAB 65/29, W.M. (42) 44th Conclusions, Minute 4, 8 April 1942.

[40]Woodward, op. cit., page 245.

[41]Barker, *Churchill and Eden at War*, op. cit., page 241.

[42]Rothwell, *Cold War*, op. cit., page 97.

[43]Ross, *The Foreign Office and the Kremlin*, op. cit., page 23.

[44]Rothwell, *Cold War*, op. cit., page 97.

[45] FO 371/32884, minute by Eden, 11 November 1942.

[46] See Harvey, *War Diaries*, op. cit., entry for 10 February 1942, page 93 on the subject of the Baltics – 'A.E. feels he can do no more with the P.M. for the moment and it would be tactless anyway.'

[47] Barker, *Churchill and Eden At War*, op. cit., page 16.

[48] Ibid., page 16.

[49] Interestingly, such a way of dealing with someone of greater power is seen as common in social psychology. They are known as 'weak power tactics', and include timing, tact, diplomacy, clever use of language, manipulation and persuasion. For an example of the literature see Sabini, John, *Social Psychology*, W. W. Norton and Company, New York, 1995, pages 513 and 514.

[50] Barker, *Churchill and Eden at War*, op. cit., page 238.

[51] Folly, *Churchill, Whitehall and the Soviet Union*, op. cit., page 32.

[52] Ibid., page 34.

[53] Ibid., page 105.

[54] Folly, *Churchill, Whitehall and the Soviet Union*, op. cit., page 32.

[55] Rothwell, *Eden*, op. cit., page 61.

[56] Kitchen, *British Policy Towards the Soviet Union*, op. cit., page 120.

[57] Ibid., page 47.

[58] Folly, *Churchill, Whitehall and the Soviet Union*, op. cit., pages 25 and 32.

[59] FO 371/29470, Dew minute, 15 November 1941, and Warner minute, 17 November 1941, cited in Ross, G. (ed.), *The Foreign Office and the Kremlin, British Documents on Anglo-Soviet Relations 1941–45*, Cambridge University Press, Cambridge, 1984, pages 16 and 17.

[60] FO 371/29469, Dew minute, 21 November 1941.

[61] Ibid.

[62] Ibid.

[63] Ibid.

[64] FO 371/29469, Dew minute, 21 November 1941.

[65] FO 371/29469, W.P. (41) 288 (Revise).

[66] See Rothwell, Cold War, op. cit., page 84, Kitchen, op. cit., page 108, and Folly, op. cit., pages 35–37.

[67] Kitchen, *British Policy Towards the Soviet Union*, op. cit., page 108.

[68] Ibid.

[69] Rothwell, Cold War, op. cit., page 84.

[70] FO 371/29269, Dew minute, 1 December 1941, cited in Rothwell, *Cold War*, op. cit., page 85.

[71] Folly, *Churchill, Whitehall and the Soviet Union*, op. cit., pages 36–37.

[72] See Folly, *Churchill, Whitehall and the Soviet Union*, op. cit., pages 3–6 for this thesis, which attempts to establish a link between changes within the Soviet Union and altered FO attitudes.

[73] Kitchen sees Eden as influenced by the FO rather than an influence on it.

[74] FO 371/29469, W.P. (41) 288. (Revise), 29 November 1941.

[75] Folly, *Churchill, Whitehall and the Soviet Union*, op. cit., page 105.

[76] Ibid., page 105.

[77] Ibid., page 105 and WM (42) 48, 28 January 1942, FO 371/32874, Dew minute 22 February 1942, and FO 371/32876, Warner minute, 2 March 1942.

[78] FO 371/32874, Eden to Churchill, 5 January 1942.

[79] Folly, *Churchill, Whitehall and the Soviet Union*, op. cit., page 105.

[80] FO 371/32905, Sargent memorandum 5 February 1942.

[81] Ibid.

[82] Ibid., Cadogan remarks.

[83] Ibid., Eden's remarks.

[84] FO 371/ 32876, Baggallay's telegram to FO of 11 February 1942, No. 186.

[85] Ibid.

[86]Ibid.

[87]FO 371/32876, Baggallay to FO, 11 February 1942, No. 187.

[88]FO 371/ 32876, Baggallay's telegram to FO of 11 February 1942, No. 187.

[89]FO 371/32876, Baggallay to FO, 20 February 1942.

[90]Ibid.

[91]FO 371/32876, Warner minute of 16 February 1942.

[92]Ibid., Warner minute of 17 February 1942.

[93]Folly, *Churchill, Whitehall and the Soviet Union*, op. cit., page 106, Rothwell, *Cold War*, op. cit., pages 92 and 93.

[94]FO 371/ 32876, Lockhart minute 20 February 1942.

[95]Folly, *Churchill, Whitehall and the Soviet Union*, op. cit., page 107.

[96]FO 371/32876, Strang minute of 20 February 1942.

[97]Ibid.

[98]Kitchen, *British Policy Towards the Soviet Union*, op. cit., page 118.

[99]FO 371/32876, Baggallay minute, 28 February 1942.

[100]FO 371/32876, Dew minute, 3 March 1942.

[101]Ibid., Warner minute, 3 March 1942.

[102]Folly, *Churchill, Whitehall and the Soviet Union*, op. cit., page 101.

[103]FO 371/32876, Sargent minute, 28 February 1942.

[104]Ibid., Cadogan minute, 28 February 1942.

[105]Ibid., Eden minute, 1 March 1942.

[106]Ibid., Warner minute March 1942.

[107]Kitchen, British Policy Towards the Soviet Union, op. cit., page 120.

[108]Dilks, D. (ed.), *The Diaries of Sir Alexander Cadogan O.M. 1938–1945*, Putnam, 1972, page 437.

[109]Ibid., page 443.

[110]Rothwell, *Cold War*, op. cit., page 93.

[111]Folly, Churchill, Whitehall and the Soviet Union, op. cit., page 108, and CAB 65/29, WM (42) 37th 25 March 1942, FO to Halifax 26 March 1942.

[112]Charmley, *Churchill's Grand Alliance*, op. cit., page 33.

[113]Ibid., page 48.

[114]Ibid., page 23.

[115]Ibid., page 30.

[116]Ibid., page 48.

[117]Ibid., page 48.

[118]Ibid., page 28.

[119]Harvey, *War Diaries*, op. cit., entry for 6 March 1942, page 105.

[120]Ibid. entry for 8 January 1942, page 86.

[121]See FO 371/ 32905, Cadogan minute 7 February 1942, and Cadogan diary 24 February 1942. See also Folly, *Churchill, Whitehall and the Soviet Union*, op. cit., page 93.

[122]Barker, *Churchill and Eden at War*, op. cit., page 16.

[123]See Rothwell, *Eden*, op. cit., page 59 – 'Eden was capable of real tenderness towards Churchill'. It is worth noting again that Eden did take a firm stand on the necessity for British rearmament as a precondition to negotiation with Hitler before the war and persevered with it despite relative isolation in Cabinet. He also radically opposed Chamberlain over conciliation of Mussolini. It may then be that some of Eden's wartime behaviour and experience is to be attributed to the personal nature of his relationship with Churchill as wartime PM.

[124]For a résumé of Churchill's eloquence and his visits to bombed areas see Best, Geoffrey, *Churchill: A Study in Greatness*, A & C Black, 2001, pages 185–190.

[125]Kennedy, P., *The Realities behind Diplomacy: Background Influences on British External Policy, 1865–1980*, Allen and Unwin, London, 1981, page 345.

[126]Charmley, *Churchill's Grand Alliance*, op. cit., page 22.

[127]Sainsbury, *Churchill and Roosevelt at War*, op. cit., page 4.

[128]Ibid., page 7. For corroborative evidence on Churchill's volatile character, his remarkable work rate, personal courage and commitment to winning the war, his erratic interference, the stoical endurance of loyal and admiring subordinates, his stature in the country and remarkable oratory see Best, op. cit., pages 195–212. On these characteristics there is a broad consensus in the historiography and biographical literature.

[129]See Addison, P., 'Winston Churchill', in Mackintosh, J. P., *British Prime Ministers In The Twentieth Century, Volume II – Churchill to Callaghan*, Weidenfeld and Nicolson, London, 1978, page 8.

[130]Charmley, *Churchill: The End of Glory*, op. cit., page 556.

[131]Moran, Lord, *Winston Churchill, The struggle for survival, 1940–1965*, Constable, London, 1966, page 17.

[132]Charmley, *Churchill: The End of Glory*, op. cit., page 492. See also Moran, *Churchill*, op. cit., page 32, for comment on the difference between Churchill's initial outrage over Eden's suggestion as to acquiescence over the Baltics and his relenting in March 1942.

[133]Jefferys, *The Churchill coalition and wartime politics*, op. cit., page 89. See also Harvey, *War Diaries*, op. cit., entry for 3 March 1942, page 105, which records Churchill as having said, 'anyone can have my job. Anything can happen to me at any time now.'

[134]See below for Churchill's defiant performance in the Commons and refusal to change.

[135]See Addison, Paul, *Churchill: The Unexpected Hero*, OUP, 2005, page 182.

[136]See Avon, *The Reckoning*, op. cit., Foreword, for Eden's reference to Churchill as a man he 'grew to love throughout our general agreement and occasional difference', the latter remark a not unypical example of Eden's gift for understatement. And see Barker, *Churchill and Eden at War*, op. cit., page 20 for Eden's claiming that Churchill was 'indulgent' towards him.

[137]Harvey, *War Diaries*, op. cit., entry for 30 July 1942, page 145.

[138]See Best, op. cit., page 191 for MacArthur's appreciation of Churchill's 'inspiring gallantry and valour'.

[139]Charmley, *Churchill: The End of Glory*, op. cit., pages 504–5.

[140]Best, op. cit., page 334.

[141]Charmley, *Churchill: The End of Glory*, page 491.

[142]Ibid., page 492.

[143]Dutton, *Eden*, op. cit., page 145.

[144]Ibid., page 144.

[145]Ibid., page 144.

[146]Ibid., page 185.

[147]Ibid., page 145.

[148]Ibid., page 185.

[149]Charmley, *Churchill's Grand Alliance*, op. cit., page 184, and Harvey to Emrys Evans, 26 August 1945, British Library.

[150]Harvey, *War Diaries*, op. cit., entry for 28 July 1945, page 385.

[151]See Harvey, *War Diaries*, op. cit., entry for 10 February 1942, page 93 on the subject of the Baltics – 'A.E. feels he can do no more with the P.M. for the moment and it would be tactless anyway.'

[152]Charmley, *Churchill's Grand Alliance*, op. cit., page 29.

[153]Ibid., page 59.

[154]Keeble, op. cit., page 168.

[155]Folly also seems to assume that Soviet sensitivity in its mistrust of Western intent and suspicion regarding being left out of diplomatic encounters between Britain and the US, and Soviet realism as manifest in regard for military power and prowess, hard bargaining and results in an exploitative and opportunistic form of diplomacy, are mutually exclusive, when they are not, as Baggallay had stressed. In fact Soviet diplomacy was characterised by all these features.

[156]Ibid., page 182.

[157]Harvey, *War Diaries*, op. cit., entry for 31 October 1942.

[158]Ibid., page 96.

[159]Rothwell, *Cold War*, op. cit., pages 89–90.

[160]Rothwell, *Cold War*, op. cit., page 80.

[161]Ibid., page 120.

[162]See Kitchen, *British Policy Towards the Soviet Union*, op. cit., page 135.

[163]Ibid., page 150 and FO 800, 301, Warner to Clark Kerr, 16 March 1943.

[164]FO 371/37031/6851, Dew, Sargent and Cadogan 15–20 October 1943.

[165]Rothwell, Cold War, op. cit., page 103.

[166]For the nature of Soviet diplomacy see Barker, *Churchill and Eden at War*, op. cit., pages 221–232 and 235, Rothwell, *Cold War*, op. cit., pages 4 and 88–89, and Kitchen, *British Policy Towards the Soviet Union*, op. cit., pages 73–74, 112–113 and 122–123 among many other references.

[167]See also FO 371/31083, 21 April 1942, for FO consideration of the possibility of 'separate states in south Germany'. And FO 371/30928, for indication that with the adverse military situation 'it would be premature to discuss with the United States and Russia the division of Germany'.

[168]CAB 66/34, W.P. (43) 96, FO paper, 'The Future of Germany', 8 March 1943.

[169]FO 371/34456, 'Federalism for Germany?' Foreign research and Press Service, Balliol College, Oxford, 16 February 1943.

[170]Ibid.

[171]Ibid.

[172]FO 371/34457, Eden to Churchill, 16 March 1943.

[173]FO 371/34457, Harrison minute, 23 March 1943.

[174]FO 371/34458, Strang minute, 13 April 1943. See also FO 371/34458, Jebb minute, 1 May 1943, for a view favouring German unity if there were a break with Russia.

[175]Rothwell, *Cold War*, op. cit., page 31.

[176]CAB 66/34, W.P. (43) 96, FO paper, 'The Future of Germany', 8 March 1943.

[177]CAB 66/41, W.P. (43) 421, 27 September 1943.

[178]Ibid.

[179]Rothwell, *Eden*, op. cit., page 78.

[180]CAB 65/40, W.M. (43) 135th Conclusions, Minute 4, 5 October 1943.

[181]Ibid.

[182]Ibid.

[183]Ibid. See also FO 371/34460/11296, Eden memorandum of 27 September 1943, and FO case against dismemberment – FO 371/ 34457/3667 – April 1943.

[184]Woodward Volume V, op. cit., page 77.

[185]WP (44) 8

[186]Sainsbury, *Churchill and Roosevelt*, op. cit., page 148.

[187]FO 39079/1866, Eden minute, January 1944.

[188]FO 371/39122, agenda for Cadogan meeting, 2 February 1944.

[189]Ibid.

[190]Rothwell, *Cold War*, op. cit., page 43, *Eden*, 31 December 1944, FO 46871/387 and *The Reckoning*, page 505.

[191]APW (44) 11th meeting, 27 July 1944.

[192]Kitchen, *British Policy Towards the Soviet Union*, op. cit., page 194.

[193]FO 371/43335, FO paper on 'Probable Post-War Tendencies In Soviet Foreign Policy As Affecting British Interests', 29 April 1944.

[194]Ibid.

[195]Ibid.

[196]Ibid.

[197]Ibid.

[198]In fact the change was entirely rhetorical and intended to maximise the resistance of the Soviet armies and people to the German occupation. The centrality of communist and Bolshevik ideology remained, and as the Red Army advanced westwards the ideological imperative in Soviet foreign policy became clear in their attitude to the free and fair elections in eastern Europe they had promised and in their attempts to protect their own zone in Germany and turn it communist while subverting democracy in the western zones through communist propaganda. It was an amazing confusion in British understanding.

[199]Kitchen, *British Policy Towards the Soviet Union*, op. cit., page 198.

[200]FO371/40741A, Warner minute, 17 July 1944.

[201]Rothwell, *Cold War*, op. cit., page 119.

[202]CAB 81/45, PHP(44)13(0)(F), 'Effect of Soviet Policy on British Strategic Interests', 6 June 1944.

[203]CAB 81/45, PHP(44)13(0)(F), 6 June 1944.

[204]FO 371/39080, PHP(44)15(O) (Final), 'The Dismemberment of Germany', 25 August 1944.

[205]CAB 66/53, W.P. (44) 436, 'Soviet Policy In Europe', 9 August 1944.

[206]CoS (44), 248 meeting, Minute 14, 26 July 1944.

[207]Alanbrooke, Lord, *War Diaries 1939–1945*, Weidenfeld and Nicolson, London, 2001, entry for 27 July 1944, cited in Dockrill, Michael and McKercher, Brian J. C., *Diplomacy and World Power: Studies in British Foreign Policy, 1890–1951*, CUP, 2002, page 230.

[208]FO 371/39080, Ward minute, 25 August 1944.

[209]FO 371/39080, C.O.S. (44) 822 (0), 9 September 1944.

[210]Ibid.

[211]See FO 371/39080, Halifax to FO, 7 September 1944, in which he says that Harry (Hopkins) had indicated that 'the drift of opinion here is against partition'.

[212]FO371/39080, FO paper to Armistice and Post-War Committee (44) 90, 20 September 1944.

[213]Ibid.

[214]Ibid.

[215]Ibid.

[216]Ibid.

[217]See Rothwell, V., Review of M. Kitchen, 'British Policy towards the Soviet Union during the Second World War', in *Soviet Studies 39* (1987), pages 680–1, for the remark, 'Kitchen confirms that…the military planners came close to taking Soviet malevolence for granted whereas the politicians and the Foreign Office were more optimistic,' which is not an accurate representation of either position. See also Ovendale, Ritchie, reviewing the same book in *History*, Vol. 73, 1988, page 553, for a similar oversimplification of the nature of and contrast between the views of the CoS and the FO rather than an appreciation of the nature of the CoS' brief, which was to consider any possible threat, and their consequent attention to the reality of Soviet power in Europe after the war.

[218]FO 371/39080, Sargent minute, 4 October 1944.

[219]Ibid.

[220]FO 371/43143, Warner, Cadogan and Eden comments, 2–6 July 1944.

[221]Sargent minute 1 April 1944 FO 371/43304/N1908, Sargent minute 2 September 1944, FO 371/39410/C11277. See Folly, *Churchill, Whitehall and the Soviet Union*, op. cit., page 131.

[222]FO 43336/6177, Minutes of Eden's meeting with the CoS, 4 October 1944.

[223]Ibid.

[224]FO 371/39080, CoS (44) 330th meeting (0), 6 October 1944.

[225]Ibid.

[226]Ibid., handwritten note dated 17 November.

[227]FO 371/39080, PM to President, 22 October 1944.

[228]Print 'Anglo-Soviet Political Conversations in Moscow', 9–17 October 1944, Premier 3/434/4.

[229]Ibid.

[230]FO 371/39080, Eden minute, 18 November 1944.

[231]FO 371/39080, P.H.P. (44) 15 (O) (Revised Final), 15 November 1944.
[232]FO 371/46871, Draft memorandum covering FO paper, 'The Dismemberment of Germany', undated(?).
[233]Ross, op. cit., page 55.
[234]Ibid., page 244.
[235]FO 371/39226, 'German Reaction To Defeat', 2 January 1945.
[236]FO 371/39226, Eden to Prime Minister, 3 January 1945.
[237]FO371/39226, Prime Minister to Eden, 8 January 1945.
[238]Sainsbury, *Churchill and Roosevelt*, op. cit., page 152.
[239]Ibid., page 154.
[240]Ibid., page 155.
[241]Smyser, W. R., *From Yalta to Berlin*, Macmillan, London, 1999, page 11.
[242]Sainsbury, *Churchill and Roosevelt*, op. cit., page 156.
[243]Ibid., page 156.
[244]Woodward Volume V, op. cit., page 274.
[245]Smyser, *From Yalta to Berlin*, op. cit., page 14.
[246]Rothwell, *Cold War*, op. cit., page 139.
[247]Ibid., page 43.
[248]CAB 66/63 and FO 371/46871, 1st Plenary Meeting (Political), 5 February 1945.
[249]Ibid.
[250]Ibid.
[251]Ibid.
[252]Ibid.
[253]CAB 66/63, F.S.M. 4th Meeting, 6 February 1945.
[254]FO 371/46871, Eden to FO, 7 February 1945.
[255]FO 371/46871, Informal Meeting of Dismemberment Committee, 7 March 1945.
[256]FO 371/46871, APW (45) 40, Dismemberment of Germany, 19 March 1945.
[257]CAB 66/53, W.P.(45)146, Reparations and Dismemberment, Memorandum By The Chancellor Of The Exchequer, 7 March 1945.
[258]Ibid.
[259]Foschepoth, Josef, 'British Interest in the Division of Germany after the Second World War', *Journal of Contemporary History*, Vol. 21 (1986), page 394.
[260]CAB 65/51, W.M. (45) 35the Conclusions, Minute 3, Confidential Annex, 22 March 1945.
[261]Woodward Volume V, op. cit., page 335 and C1354/292/18.
[262]Rothwell, *Cold War*, op, cit., page 44.
[263]Avon, *The Reckoning*, op. cit., pages 441–2.
[264]Charmley, *Churchill: The End of Glory*, op. cit., page 528 and Kitchen, *British Policy Towards the Soviet Union*, op. cit., page 150.
[265]Charmley, *Churchill: The End of Glory*, op. cit., page 528.
[266]Rothwell, *Cold War*, op. cit., page 41.
[267]Pierson Dixon diary, page 98, entry for 11 August 1944, cited in Gilbert, M., *Winston S. Churchill, Volume VII, Road to Victory 1941–1945*, Heinemann, London, 1986, page 888.
[268]FO 954/1, Churchill to Eden 7 September 1943.
[269]Dutton, *Eden*, op. cit., page 144.
[270]Rothwell, *Cold War*, op. cit., page 32.
[271]FO371/43335, Warner minute, 18 July 1944.
[272]FO 371/43335, Eden to Churchill, 8 May 1944.
[273]See Gilbert, *Road to Victory*, op. cit., page 1179.
[274]Harvey, *War Diaries*, op. cit., entry for 6 October 1943, page 304.
[275]Ibid.

[276]Gilbert, Martin, *Churchill: A life*, op. cit., page 832.

[277]Dutton, *Eden*, op. cit., page 198.

[278]Avon, *The Reckoning*, op. cit., pages 370 and 371.

[279]Sainsbury, *Churchill and Roosevelt*, op. cit., page 140.

[280]CAB 66/34, W.P. (43) 96, 'The Future of Germany', 8 March 1943.

[281]Kitchen, *British Policy Towards the Soviet Union*, op. cit., page 47.

[282]FO 371/43335, FO paper on 'Probable Post-War Tendencies In Soviet Foreign Policy As Affecting British Interests', 29 April 1944.

[283]FO 371/46871, Eden minute on undated Draft FO paper on dismemberment, 31 December 1944.

[284]Avon, *The Reckoning*, op. cit., page 488.

[285]Ibid., page 508.

[286]Ibid., page 516.

[287]Alanbrooke, Field Marshall Lord, *War Diaries*, University of California Press, 2003, page 709, entry for 23 July 1945.

[288]See Eden, Anthony, and Eisenhower, Dwight D., *Eden-Eisenhower Correspondence, 1955–1957*, University of North Carolina Press, 2006, page 20 for reference to Ismay's admiration of Eden. See also Rhodes, James, *Anthony Eden*, Papermac, 1987, page 277.

[289]The historiography is not unanimous as to the domination of Eden by Churchill – see Barker, *Churchill and Eden at War*, op. cit., page 28 for the view that Churchill was constrained not just by Eden but also by the FO, the War Cabinet and the CoS, the latter on military rather than political matters such as foreign policy.

[290]Prem 3/399/6 – Churchill to Eden, 16 January 1944.

[291]Moran, Lord, *Winston Churchill, The struggle for survival, 1940–1965*, Constable, London, 1966, entry for 30 October 1944, page 206.

[292]Charmley, *Churchill: The End of Glory*, op. cit., page 530.

[293]Ibid., page 549.

[294]Ross, *Foreign Office Attitudes*, op. cit., page 266.

[295]Lockhart diary 6 January 1945.

[296]Dilks op., cit., entry for 8 January 1945, page 693.

[297]Jenkins, op. cit., page 774, Colville diary entry for 9 January 1945.

[298]Gilbert, *Road to Victory*, op. cit., pages 1145–46.

[299]Charmley, *Churchill: The End of Glory*, op. cit., page 647, and Eden diary 27 July 1945, page 551.

[300]Harvey, *War Diaries*, op. cit., entry for 11 November 1944, page 365.

[301]Avon, *The Reckoning*, op. cit., page 497.

[302]Alanbrooke, op. cit., page 529, entry for 6 March 1944.

[303]Ibid., page 170.

[304]See Addison, *Winston Churchill*, op. cit., page 20.

[305]Charmley, *Churchill: The End of Glory*, op. cit., page 446.

[306]Ibid., page 444. See also Addison, *Winston Churchill*, op. cit., page 21 for the view that 'there was also a broad consensus between Churchill and his advisers', though the necessity of this to Churchill's dominance of the agenda and decisions is difficult to assess.

[307]Ibid., page 470.

[308]Sainsbury, Keith, 'British policy and German unity at the end of the Second World War', in *English Historical Review (Great Britain)*, 94 (373), October 1979, page 789.

[309]See Avon, *The Reckoning*, op. cit., pages 488, 508 and 516 quoted above.

[310]Only decisions constitute policy – planning may or may not influence it.

[311]See Addison, *Winston Churchill*, op. cit., page 24 for Churchill's appreciation of Attlee's control over the 'home front' by means of committees.

[312]Addison, *Winston Churchill*, op. cit., page 25.

[313]See Barker, *Churchill and Eden at War*, op. cit., page 22, for the effect of Churchill's personal warmth and humour on Eden.

[314]See Kitchen, *British Policy Towards the Soviet Union*, op. cit., page 219, for reference to Sargent's feeling in the autumn of 1944 that Churchill's involvement in the FO-CoS debate over German dismemberment and Soviet policy was imperative but unlikely, and Jebb's complaint regarding Churchill's lack of interest in the post-war situation. See also Kitchen, M., 'Winston Churchill and the Soviet Union During the Second World War', *Historical Journal*, XXX-2 (1987), page 430 for Churchill's leaving 'the British government without a coherent policy' on German dismemberment.

[315]Folly, *Churchill, Whitehall and the Soviet Union*, op. cit., page 5.

[316]Not only was Eden's influence on the sequence of FO papers minimal (if it existed), but his reaction was as if they came from another department for his view, a remarkable detachment.

[317]Sainsbury, *British policy and German unity*, op. cit., page 789.

[318]Folly, *Churchill, Whitehall and the Soviet Union*, op. cit., page 5.

[319]Ibid., page 5.

[320]Sainsbury, *Churchill and Roosevelt*, op. cit., page 147.

[321]Kitchen, *Winston Churchill*, op. cit., page 427. See also Kimball, W. F., *Forged in War, Churchill, Roosevelt and the Second World War*, HarperCollins, London, 1997, page 253, for FO favouring 'Russian collaboration' to contain Germany but Churchill's wondering 'if Stalin planned for all Europe to be made up of small, weak states' – this was at the end of May 1943.

[322]Harvey, *War Diaries*, op. cit., entry for 6 October 1943, page 304. See also Gilbert, *Road to Victory*, op. cit., page 518, for the observation that the minutes of the meeting do not mention any such remark and that Harvey must have learned of it from Eden – in fact the minutes do contain the remark but the view is unattributed. See also page 1070 for Churchill's reference to a western bloc aimed at containing not Germany but Russia.

[323]See Rose, N., *Churchill, An Unruly Life*, Simon and Schuster, London, 1994, page 313.

[324]See Harrod, R. F., *The Prof, A Personal Memoir of Lord Cherwell*, Macmillan, London, 1959, page 226, for an indication that Lindemann had been offered a ministerial post by Churchill on his accession to power.

[325]Charmley, *Churchill: The End of Glory*, op. cit., page 425.

[326]See Rothwell, *Eden*, op. cit., page 59, for an indication of FO dismay at Churchill's tendency to consult anyone but the FO.

[327]Dutton, *Eden*, op. cit., page 191.

[328]FO 371/39080, A.P.W. (44) 90, 'The Dismemberment of Germany', 20 September 1944.

[329]Ibid.

[330]Barker, *Churchill and Eden at War*, op. cit., page 25.

[331]FO 371/46871, W.M. (45) 16th Conclusions, 8 February 1945.

[332]Ibid.

[333]Ibid., page 298, and WM (45) 18.3.C.A.

[334]Avon, *The reckoning*, op. cit., page 373.

[335]Rothwell, *Eden*, op. cit., page 80.

[336]FO 371/46871, APW (45) 40, 'Dismemberment of Germany', 19 March 1945.

[337]Rose, op. cit., page 313.

[338]Sainsbury, *Churchill and Roosevelt*, op. cit. page 159.

[339]Folly, *Churchill, Whitehall and the Soviet Union*, op. cit., page 6.

[340]Ibid., page 134.

[341]Ibid., page 138.

[342]Ibid., page 139.

[343]Ibid., page 3.

[344]Keeble, op. cit., page 182.

[345]Harvey, *War Diaries*, op. cit., entry for 31October 1942.

[346]Charmley, *Churchill's Grand Alliance*, op. cit., page 152.

[347]Folly, *Churchill, Whitehall and the Soviet Union*, op. cit., page 96.

[348]Keeble, op. cit., page 168.

[349]Alanbrooke, op. cit., page 336, entry for 29 October 1942.

[350]Churchill's aversion for communism has been noted. See Colville diary, entry for 30 April 1944, cited in Gilbert, *Road to Victory*, op. cit., page 753 for reference to Churchill's 'gloomy forebodings about the future tendencies of Russia', and page 768 for Churchill's fears of the spread of communism as expressed to the Dominion Prime Ministers on 5 May 1944. Yet see also his optimism as to the changes in the Soviet system in a speech to the Commons on 24 May 1944, an interesting parallel with the remarkable FO paper of 29 April 1944 in its expression of a confidence that was not to last. And see page 890 for Churchill's concerns regarding communism in Yugoslavia, page 919 for similar concerns regarding Greece, and pages 994 and 999 for the percentages accord with Stalin in October 1944, which may be seen as an early attempt at containment. The latter also illustrates Churchill's extraordinary belief in personal diplomacy and his ability to reach understandings with Stalin, and his confidence in Stalin. See also page 1234 for reference to Churchill's Commons speech on 27 February 1945, in which he expressed confidence that Stalin would live up to his undertakings and page 1027 for differentiation of him from the Soviet system and its tendencies – in October 1944 he warned Attlee that 'behind the horseman sits dull care', though this was a confidence that waned and was replaced by suspicion once he was away from Stalin.

[351]See Rose, op. cit., page 312. See also Kitchen, *Winston Churchill*, op. cit., for reference to Churchill's enduring uncertainty and his superordinate objective of military victory, to which his loathing of communism and the Soviet system were subordinated – an interpretation that imputes to Churchill a pragmatic policy towards the Soviet Union.

[352]Heyward, Samantha, *Churchill*, Routledge, 2003, page 104, referring to Colville's diary entry for 23 February 1945.

[353]Kimball, op. cit., page 312.

[354]See Addison, *Winston Churchill*, op. cit., page 26 for the view that Churchill permitted the FO to plan while believing that 'power would follow in the wake of the forces he was directing'.

[355]House of Commons, 27 February 1945, Hansard Volume 408, page 1313.

[356]Addison, *Winston Churchill*, op. cit., page 25.

Chapter Four

The Berlin Crisis of 1948

THE BERLIN BLOCKADE represented the first direct expression of British policy towards the Soviets over Germany after the formative interlude of British understanding of Soviet intentions after the war. It lasted between 1 April 1948 and 11 May 1949, an endurance test of Western resolve in response to Soviet attempts to reopen the issue of Germany's political future or to remove the West from Berlin by exerting pressure on the Western presence in the city. In so long a crisis some selection is required, and I shall focus on the times at which major decisions were made over Berlin. These include March 1948, when the Western decision to stay in Berlin was made in advance of any actual Soviet interference, though there was expected Soviet pressure over Berlin, and earlier causal factors, for the Berlin blockade represented a Soviet response to Bevin's 'western union'.[1] And in June 1948 there was the critical initial British reaction to the interference with traffic to the western sectors of Berlin, which committed Britain to staying in Berlin and on which all further policy was predicated. I shall also mention the major policy landmarks in the crisis to assess the relative influences on policy.

The early historiography on the Berlin blockade suffered from lack of access to Foreign Office (FO) and Cabinet records and was reliant on press coverage and the accounts of individuals involved.[2] They can then only provide a narrative of events but no sense of the various influences on British policy. More recent accounts have benefited from access to FO and Cabinet records, and have followed the historiography of the Cold War in being separable into traditional, revisionist accounts, and post-revisionist theses. Traditional accounts portray the Berlin blockade as another instance of Soviet brinkmanship, a means of ideological expansionism which was met with Western resolution. Revisionists see Western violations of Potsdam and its four-power accord over Germany at the London Conference as having forced the Soviets into retaliation – the Soviet Union is seen as a normal state with understandable security interests.[3] And post-revisionist accounts consider in detail the sequence of events without an ideological slant and accord a role to nations other than the US and the Soviet Union, including Britain. It is on this latter literature that I shall focus, though it is quite limited. Tusa's work on the Berlin Crisis is in the nature of a historical narrative rather than an exhaustive assessment of the causal influences on British policy. In a major analysis of the Berlin Crisis Shlaim claims that it was Bevin's dynamism and speed of response that set the context of the Western response.[4]

My own argument endorses Shlaim's interpretation of the extent of Bevin's influence on Western policy over the Berlin Crisis and assesses the extent of and reasons for Bevin's autonomy in Cabinet over British foreign policy towards Germany and the Cold War in 1948 and the extent to which he influenced or had to concede to the Americans over policy on Berlin and why. What follows is intended to assess all the possible influences on British policy over the Berlin Crisis, including those that preceded it in British policy towards the Soviet Union and Germany and the defence of western Europe against communism and Soviet influence.

I shall begin with the context of attitudes and foreign-policy objectives in the British political and official establishment and of British policies towards the Soviet Union and Germany prior to and at the beginning of 1948, then outline the sequence of events in the Berlin Crisis itself before assessing the influence on British policy over Berlin of Bevin and the Foreign Office (FO), Attlee and the Cabinet, and external influences in the form of Soviet policy over Germany and Berlin and that of the Americans and the French.

The Background

There are two aspects to the background to the Berlin Crisis of 1948. There is the emerging nature of Britain's relationship with the Soviet Union during the immediate post-war period and especially over Germany as the country was ostensibly under Four Power control and with an ostensible intention to agree on a unified Germany. For in that immediate post-war period there was experience of Soviet ideological hostility to the UK and to social democracy as an alternative to communism, and of Soviet expansionism and opportunism both in eastern Europe, where Stalin's undertaking to hold free and fair elections was reneged upon in an imposition of communist governments under Soviet influence, and over Germany, where Soviet diplomatic tactics precluded economic unity and demanded reparations the West was not prepared to concede. Such experience resulted in a conviction in the post-war Labour government that a continuance of the wartime collaboration with the Soviet Union would be impossible, and that Soviet intentions were ideological and expansionist in western Europe and elsewhere, in Iran and Greece, for instance, and had to be resisted. There was an understanding too that the relative economic and military weakness of the UK meant that the US would have to be persuaded of the threat of Soviet foreign policy to capitalist democratic nations to the end of securing US economic, military and diplomatic support to contain Soviet influence and communism, not least over Germany at the centre of Europe, which was seen as vital to the security of the UK.

The other context to the Berlin Crisis was the emerging dynamic within the post-war Labour government with its personalities and their relationships, the most important for foreign policy being that between Attlee, given his powers and prerogatives as PM, and Bevin as Foreign Secretary. By the time of the Berlin Crisis in 1948 both sets of contextual influences were established. Unlike his predecessors in the premiership Attlee, though interested in foreign policy, did not see it as his role to dominate the foreign-policy decision-making process or his Foreign Secretary, and his choice of the influential personality of Bevin seems to have been predicated upon more general decisions regarding appointments to ministerial roles of the 'big guns' of the Labour Party and on an attitudinal commonality between Attlee and Bevin that translated itself into a common understanding over foreign policy, not least given their shared aversion to the Soviet state, to the extension of Soviet influence in Europe, seen as a threat to the security of the UK, and to the spread of communism. There was between Attlee and Bevin a common understanding too as to the need to obtain US economic, military and diplomatic support against the Soviet Union in the post-war world. The autonomy that Attlee permitted Bevin was then a reflection of Attlee's conceptualisation of the premiership and their shared understanding as to the optimal foreign policy for the UK given the threat of Soviet incursion in Europe and elsewhere, imperial overstretch and the economic and military relative decline of the UK. That autonomy was enhanced by Bevin's standing in the Labour Party and Labour movement and by Bevin's robust certainty, grasp of foreign policy and personality, and meant that Bevin was the decisive influence on policy over Germany and Berlin.

By the time of the first Soviet interference with western traffic, on 31 March/1 April 1948, a combination of continued adverse American experience of Soviet foreign policy and Bevin's personal standing and persuasiveness with the Americans had convinced the Truman administration that Soviet foreign policy was ideological, expansionist, opportunist and a threat to the security of the free world if not contained. US commitment to the defence of western Europe began with Byrnes's offer in Paris to fuse the US zone with any other and continued with his announcement on 6 September 1946 that US troops would remain in Germany for an indefinite period. Thereafter Bizonia, the joining of the British and US zones in Germany, was instituted on 1 January 1947. It was followed by the Truman Doctrine, the Western policy that became known as 'containment', which was enunciated on 12 March 1947, and by the Marshall Plan for European economic recovery, which was announced on 5 June 1947.

US experience of Soviet diplomatic behaviour and Bevin's expatiation on its expansionist and opportunistic tendencies resulted in a US foreign policy that drifted in the early months of 1946 towards Kennan's view that 'Soviet hostility towards the capitalist world was inevitable and immutable.' For 'instead of trying to accommodate the Soviet regime, Kennan recommended that the United States concentrate on containing the expansion of Soviet power.'[5] This was very much the view that Bevin had been enunciating to the Americans and was endorsed by the Truman administration and elaborated into the Truman Doctrine's strategy of containment, which involved confining communism to the places in which it had already taken hold, that is, to eastern Europe.[6] Its timing was influenced by Britain's economic difficulty in sustaining its European commitments, for in February 1947 the British told the Americans that they could no longer afford to keep troops in Greece. The American reaction was summed up by Acheson, then Under-Secretary of State, 'the British are pulling out everywhere and if we don't go in the Russians will.'[7] The Truman Doctrine relinquished eastern Europe to the Soviets but stipulated that no further communist advances should be countenanced. As a statement of general intent the policy was welcome. Over Germany however the policy had relatively little effect on FO concerns over US resolve and over their reliance on Clay, the Military Governor of the US zone in Germany, whose behaviour was unpredictable and it seemed autonomous of Washington.

At the ensuing Council of Foreign Ministers (CFM) meeting in Moscow in March and April 1947 a familiar pantomime was enacted, with Bevin rejecting Soviet demands for reparations out of current production and for international control over the Ruhr, insisting upon economic unity as a precondition. Though there was for some time a risk of a different outcome, 'the Moscow Council was the most positive proof for Whitehall that the Americans would follow a policy in line with that enunciated by Byrnes in September 1946 and did not intend to withdraw from Germany at the earliest opportunity, or do a deal with the Soviet Union.'[8]

The Marshall Plan followed in the summer of 1947, ostensibly 'directed not against any country or doctrine, but against hunger, poverty, desperation and chaos'[9] and designed to accomplish the economic revival of Europe, including the Soviet Union. Bevin welcomed it as evidence of US commitment to Europe in view of Britain's and western Europe's desperate economic condition but did not want the Soviets included. At the Paris CFM, held between 27 June and 3 July 1947, Bevin's purpose was to 'secure Soviet exclusion from Marshall's offer if their diplomats would not agree to Western conditions, and to do this without actually ejecting the Soviets from the discussions. This was entirely consistent with the Whitehall strategy for dealing with the Soviet Union at the Council of Foreign Ministers. Negotiation was never seriously considered'.[10]

Molotov's insistence on national sovereignty reflected Soviet concern that the Marshall Plan sought to bolster up western Europe against Soviet infiltration and ideology through elimination of the poverty and deprivation on which communism thrived and so represented an attempt to enforce the Truman Doctrine, not least in Germany as part of a western bloc. Molotov was also concerned that the Marshall Plan was a means of Western penetration into the Soviet zone of eastern Europe, and demanded reparations and participation in the Ruhr as preconditional to Soviet participation. This was rejected, and Molotov withdrew from the conference. Bevin's reaction to the plan had been governed by the economic necessity for continued aid, but he had also seen the strategic value and necessity of accepting to keep the US committed to western Europe. Relations with the Soviets deteriorated, and by December 1947, after the London CFM, at which Molotov had demanded 'four-power control over the Ruhr, the end of the Bizone, and half the total of $20 billion of reparations',[11] the CFM system of arriving at treaties was abandoned.

The failure of the London CFM in December 1947 was accompanied by agreement between the British and the Americans to integrate their zones into a western Europe to be reconstructed to combat the Soviet threat in Europe, to develop the Ruhr without Russia, and to institute a federal structure for western Germany. The European Recovery Programme was then applied to the western zones as a precursor to their unification, and Bevin was able to speak publicly for the first time of a 'western union' that would constitute a 'defensive system in Western Europe'[12] that would have 'the backing of America and the Dominions'.[13]

Referring to Bevin's reaction to the failed London CFM, Greenwood notes that 'the breakdown of the CFM and the progress of the ERP (the European Recovery Programme) had banished his long-standing caution over appearing to build a bloc against the Russians and had opened the way for an attempt to secure a greater measure of co-operation among the countries of Western Europe.'[14]

At the beginning of 1948 a series of papers submitted by Bevin to Cabinet on policy over Germany and towards the Soviet Union indicated his abandonment of all hope for any accommodation with the Soviets over Germany following the breakdown of the London CFM and his sense of the need to take measures to preclude further Soviet expansionism and infiltration into central and western Europe.

On 4 January 1948 Bevin noted that physical barriers and economic progress would not be adequate to stopping the 'further encroachment of the Soviet tide',[15] and pointed to a need for a 'Western democratic system comprising Scandinavia, the Low Countries, France, Portugal, Italy and Greece'[16] (with Germany and Spain joining later) which would 'organise and consolidate the ethical and spiritual forces inherent in this Western civilisation'.[17] There was an understanding that any such alliance would be regarded by the Soviets as 'an offensive alliance directed against the Soviet Union'[18] and would have to be underwritten by US power, but the anticipation was that Britain would pull together social democratic forces in western Europe to offer an alternative to communism. In an accompanying paper Bevin advocated 'foreign policy publicity designed to oppose the inroads of Communism' by propagating the 'vital ideas of British Social Democracy and Western Civilisation'.[19]

The following day, in a major paper on Soviet policy, Bevin provided a résumé of their ruthless control of eastern Europe in violation of diplomatic undertakings to hold free elections and their attempts at penetration of political parties and propaganda in Germany. The understanding that East-West relations were now a fundamental struggle run on ideological lines is clear, as is disgust with a Soviet diplomacy characterised by intransigence towards reasonable proposals and 'unwarranted accusations and insults'.[20]

There was another Cabinet paper dated 5 January 1948, one specifically on 'Policy in Germany', and it is worth quoting from it at some length given the clarity of exposition of Bevin's sense of Soviet intentions in Germany, the impasse reached with the Soviet Union over Germany, and the need to counteract Soviet intentions. While making ritual observances regarding the desirability of German unity and saying, 'we should avoid taking any irrecoverable step which would make final agreement between the Four Powers on a unified Germany impossible,' Bevin noted that the 'guiding principle' in British policy over Germany was the avoidance of a 'Communist-controlled Germany'.

To that end British policy was the inauguration of a democratic Germany in the Western sense of democracy in the event of Four Power Control being impossible to achieve. Bevin referred to economic integration of the western zones and to the need for economic recovery in western Germany. He noted that 'the failure of the Council of Foreign Ministers to reach agreement on any outstanding issues is a milestone in our German policy' and that 'the conflict is between the Soviet desire to dominate Europe politically and economically and the desire of the three Western Powers to put Europe on its feet again with American backing.' Bevin noted the economic and political Sovietisation of the Eastern Zone and its assimilation into the 'Soviet system in Eastern Europe', which was 'totally contrary' to the Western objective in Germany, and observed that the Soviet purpose was to 'extend their political and economic power into the Western Zones with the object of winning Germany over to communism' through committing the Western powers to the idea of a united Germany and through securing the Eastern Zone against any penetration. Bevin noted that there had been no change in the Soviet attitude at the CFM over Germany and that 'the division between East and West in Germany, which itself is part and parcel of the same division throughout the world, will continue and is likely to be sharper.'[21]

These three papers from Bevin, on western union, on Soviet policy and on Germany, were considered by ministers in Cabinet on 8 January 1948. Cabinet 'approved the policy, set out in C.P. (48) 5', the paper on Germany, without objection, 'took note' of the paper on Soviet policy, and 'endorsed the policy outlined in C.P. (48) 6', the paper on western union with the proviso that there should not be too much emphasis on the 'anti-Soviet aspect', though Bevin had made it clear that the purpose of western European union was 'to resist the increasing penetration of Soviet influence'.[22]

Bevin's 'western union' speech to the House of Commons on 22 January 1948 made public these ideas, blaming Soviet behaviour for the breakdown of Potsdam and of the possibility of four-power control of Germany. Bevin was careful not to disclose the implications, not precluding for instance German unification while leaving open the possibility of west Germany joining a western system of defence.

The sequence of events over Berlin

Berlin had been divided between the victorious powers in the same manner as the rest of Germany, and its western zones represented islands of British, French and American presence surrounded by the Soviet zone of Germany and the eastern, Soviet sector of Berlin. Routes into west Berlin were officially by means of air corridors, with land routes being reliant on Soviet acquiescence. Yet almost all basic supplies came by land and so were dependent on the Soviets. The effect of the failure of the London CFM on the Western powers' presence in Berlin was felt. According to Northedge, after the failure of hopes for a central German government at the end of 1947, 'when Russia followed the West in shaping its own zone into a separate state, it was of great moral importance to the future East German Republic to capture Berlin.'[23] Robertson, the Military Governor of the British Zone in Germany, regarded the Western presence in Berlin as being seen by the Soviets as an impediment to 'the final absorption of the Eastern zone into the Soviet orbit'[24] and anticipated attempts to disrupt communications in an effort to expel the Western powers, though neither he nor Strang believed the Soviets would risk war over Berlin.[25] Bevin had expected Berlin to be the scene of likely conflict between the Soviets and the Western powers even at the start of 1948.

In his major Cabinet Paper on 'Policy in Germany' dated 5 January 1948 referred to above Bevin had anticipated that the Russians would be 'most anxious to get the three Western powers out of the city' because they regarded the Western presence in Berlin as precluding the accomplishment of Soviet plans 'for the political assimilation of the Eastern zone'. Yet he shared Robertson's views as to the likelihood of the Soviets' risking war, feeling rather that the Soviets would 'avoid pushing things to extremes at present' and instead attempt 'to make our position in Berlin as uncomfortable as possible, and ultimately to convince us that we should lose more face by staying on in the city than by evacuating it'.[26]

In an accompanying Cabinet paper Bevin told ministers 'it seems unlikely that the Soviet Union is making plans to start a war with Great Britain or the United States' because it could attain its ends by other means and because its estimate of the likelihood of victory in a war was low, and Attlee did not express any difference of view at the ensuing Cabinet meeting on 8 January 1948.[27] Attlee's concurrence with Bevin's view was more explicitly articulated in his telling the CoS at the Defence

Committee at the end of July 1948 that 'though there was, of course, a risk that the Berlin situation would lead to war, he did not consider that risk to be essentially different from those in Trieste or Italy' and indicating to them that though their advice was appreciated it was for ministers to make the decision as to policy over Berlin and Germany after taking account of the political implications of alternative policies.[28] Previously, on 9 July, Attlee, Bevin and Alexander, who was Minister for Defence, had been asked by the CoS 'whether the risk of war should be run over Berlin' and had told them that it would be 'prudent to plan on the assumption that there might be a war', for 'we could not withdraw from Berlin without the most strenuous effort to stay there.'[29]

The indication is that CoS desire to halt the westward spread of Soviet influence and communism in Europe, which it shared with Attlee, Bevin, the Cabinet and the FO, did not result in CoS confidence in a stand being made in Berlin, a position similar to that of the US military, though it is possible that such CoS concern reflected its brief to plan for the worst case. In fact Montgomery, at the time Chief of the Imperial General Staff, regarded Berlin as being of 'no military value' and a 'first class military liability' that 'would have to be written off once the shooting started', and was concerned that concentration on Berlin would divert attention from the more feasible and vital defence of western Germany.[30]

As to the Americans, Bevin remarked, 'on many matters I expect them to be truculent with the Russians, particularly if the latter try and force the Western Allies out of Berlin'.[31] There was also a sense shared by the British and American governments that the Soviets would use Berlin as a means of stopping the formation of a west German government. Tusa and Tusa comment, 'nearly everyone had reached the conclusion that if the western Powers were to leave Berlin, it would be a grave blow to their prestige in Europe and would almost undoubtedly result in the whole of Germany coming under the control of the Soviet Union.'[32]

On 23 February 1948, despite Soviet protests at their exclusion and warnings that the Western powers were violating the terms of Potsdam, talks in London between Britain, the United States, France, Belgium, the Netherlands and Luxembourg over Germany began. On 25 February a communist coup in Czechoslovakia gave additional impetus to the proceedings. On 8 March an 'initial communiqué' from the London Conference referred to the need, given the failure of the CFM system to decide Germany's future, to achieve 'the economic reconstruction of western Europe including Germany'. There was also reference to the necessity of 'establishing a basis for the participation of a democratic Germany in the community of free peoples', though 'ultimate Four Power agreement is in no way precluded'.[33]

Western Union was accomplished on 17 March in the form of the Brussels Treaty between Britain, France and the Benelux nations. On 12 March Marshall had ended fears of American isolationism with an offer of talks over an Atlantic Pact, which began, with Canadian participation, on 22 March. This was the result of repeated requests from Bevin and Marshall's own insistence that the initiative should come from the Europeans, and after a demonstration of European unity. The Soviet reaction to their exclusion from the London talks was to end the meetings of the Allied Control Council on 20 March 1948. In the western zones measures taken to develop free-market economics and democratic institutions eventuated in plans for a western Deutschmark, an open acknowledgement that the Potsdam requirement of economic unity was being abandoned.

Bevin was resolved that the West should stay in Berlin, and on 24 March the FO conveyed Bevin's instruction to Robertson, 'we must stay in Berlin – he did not want withdrawal contemplated in any quarter'.[34]

As early as 22 January 1948 his Commons speech had referred to the need for resistance to Soviet attempts to achieve their ends through intimidation, subversion and revolution, and he remained opposed to any concessions to the Soviets over Germany, warning that conciliation would only serve to discourage the western European powers from collaboration and the development of western Europe.[35] He was however not oblivious to the possibility that, in a war of nerves, the Soviets 'may miscalculate and involve themselves in a situation from which they feel they cannot retreat', despite not intending to do more than to wreck the European Recovery Programme and maximise political embarrassment by means that avoided war. Bevin told Cabinet on 8 April of Soviet interference with passenger traffic in the form of stopping passenger trains to inspect documentation, though there were no restrictions on road, freight train or canal traffic between the western and the Soviet zones.

In an indication of the extent to which Bevin's resolve to remain in Berlin was moderated by caution Bevin told his ministerial colleagues, 'it would be inexpedient to allow this minor inconvenience to be made the occasion for a serious breach with the Soviet authorities'.[36] Bevin's advocacy of toughness and prudence was to continue to be characteristic of his approach to the Berlin Crisis,[37] for while on 4 May he told the Commons, 'we are in Berlin as of right and it is our intention to stay there,'[38] he told Attlee the following day that silence and avoidance of provocation while continuing to be firm over staying in Berlin was the best policy.[39]

The domestic setting of British foreign policy was entirely different to that in early 1946 by the time of the Berlin Crisis, for by the beginning of 1948 almost the entirety of the British Labour Movement had 'step by step, abandoned its sentimental attitude towards the Soviet Union and ranged itself behind Bevin'. This was 'due not only to disillusionment with the Soviet Union, especially after Prague, but to a more positive view of the USA in the light of the Marshall Plan'.[40]

In the international context Bevin's perennial reservations regarding American reliability and commitment to the defence of Europe against communist encroachment had been comprehensively dealt with following the hardening of American opinion in 1946 and 1947, eventuating in the Truman Doctrine and the Marshall Plan. But there were continuing reservations as to US reliability over Berlin, associated partly with the imminence of an American presidential election that Truman was not expected to win (but did) and partly with US military concern that remaining in Berlin would not be militarily feasible, and with US military consideration of a pre-emptive withdrawal to a more defensible frontier further west.

There were also concerns over the resolve of the French in view of a Cabinet crisis there. Bevin and the British government were then the only major stable force in the Western world at the time, and Bevin's certainty and resolve, so apparent in his initiatives over western union and defence, characterised his response to the news of the blockade of Berlin and do seem to have been an influence not just on British policy over Berlin but also on that of the US in setting a public context of resolution not to be intimidated out of Berlin by Soviet interference with western access to Berlin and the final barrier to land access imposed by the Soviet Union.

The pressure from the Soviets rose gradually, through bureaucratic requirements relating to access to Berlin from the west that culminated in new regulations issued on 30 March. These involved individual inspection and a need for permits for freight traffic, which represented very restrictive controls on western use of land routes to Berlin. The intent was clear, to convey to the West that west Berlin was unsustainable without Soviet acceptance, and that this had been withdrawn. Robertson regarded it as a serious escalation of attempts to drive the West out of Berlin but reacted calmly, prepared to discuss matters but resisting unilateral interference with traffic.[41] And in April there was a Soviet cutting-off of military trains and the Nord Express.

At a meeting with Strang, Kirkpatrick, Steel, Hankey, Johnston and Dean on 23 April Robertson said that 'he expected the position in Berlin to get considerably worse owing to increased Soviet pressure. He thought that the line we should take should be to decide to stay in Berlin in spite of inconveniences however serious' and that 'we should say nothing and simply stay put.' The minutes indicate that 'the meeting agreed with this view' and that 'the present would be the worst moment to evacuate Berlin for prestige reasons both in Berlin and the rest of Germany.'[42] Yet Strang's subsequent note to Bevin makes clear that 'the purpose of this meeting was not to lay down, or even to suggest, any new policy, since you have decided, and it is clearly understood on all hands, that it is our intention to stay in Berlin.'[43] Such evidence establishes that the FO was not the instigator of the policy to remain in Berlin and confirms that, as has been seen above in the reference to Bevin's instruction to Robertson on 24 March, the decision to remain in Berlin came from Bevin. Yet the difficulty of assessing causation from apparent commonality of view is a question to which I shall return, for on 18 March there had been a memorandum from Strang to Bevin (in response to a request from Bevin) indicating the FO view that Britain should stay in Berlin come what may, a view with which Bevin appended his agreement in the margin.

On the minute of 23 April Bevin's appended remark, 'PM should see', represents Bevin's continuing concern for Attlee's knowledge and support. This, a typically enigmatic annotation, indicates nothing on its own but in context is not inconsistent with there having been a commonality of view between the PM and the Foreign Secretary.

On 28 April Strang and Robertson had a meeting with Douglas, the US Ambassador, and Clay. Clay felt that the Soviets would ratchet up the pressure on Berlin and wanted to know if Britain was prepared to go to war to remain in Berlin. Robertson and Strang said they had 'contemplated the possibility that, while we would stay in Berlin as long as we could, we might have to withdraw under pressure or deteriorating conditions in the end'.[44] They could not give an official answer, but felt that Bevin would approve an indication of British rights in Berlin but not threat of war to maintain them. This minute was seen by Bevin, Sargent and Kirkpatrick, and by Pakenham, who told Bevin he was convinced Britain should stay in Berlin as a result of a 'moral right' and a 'moral obligation' and to maintain British 'diplomatic prestige'. He referred Bevin to the history of appeasement and his understanding that 'you were determined to stay in Berlin come what may'.[45] It received only Bevin's normal response of scrawled initials, yet there does seem to be some deference to Bevin as Foreign Secretary and the person with whom the decision rested. There is in such evidence an indication that Bevin and the FO concurred that policy over Berlin should be one of resolve but also restraint and avoidance of provocation.

There followed an American proposal to send a note to Stalin indicating Western rights in Berlin and intention to stay. Bevin was against notes that could result in an escalation of tension 'without making sure that we had the necessary force with which to back it up'.[46] His general approach was to avoid communication that could be interpreted as weakness or as provocation and rather to indicate by resolute action without rhetoric a policy of firmness and endurance. The US overture failed, amid a characteristic hail of accusations from Molotov. Parcel post became the subject of restrictive controls on 4–5 May, another twist in the pressure on the West in Berlin.

In accordance with a policy of refusing to be intimidated by Soviet policy over Berlin into making concessions elsewhere in Germany, moves continued in the west to create a federal state (which was not inconsistent with the notion of German unity) through a decision on 6 June to combine the three western zones into a single economic unit with a new currency, a western mark, to be introduced on 20 June. It was now June 1948, and the economy of the western sectors of Berlin was frozen by the measures taken by the Soviets to interfere with traffic from the west to the western sectors. Bevin told Attlee that Soviet reaction was unpredictable.[47] On 18 June the Military Governors of the western sectors advised Marshall Sokolovsky, the Soviet Military Governor, of the nature of the currency reform to be introduced in the western sectors. Soviet reaction was not long in coming. That evening all traffic from west Germany to Berlin was stopped and then subjected to new, harsher regulations. There would be no passenger trains, and freight traffic would be subject to inspection. Cars with west German passes would not be permitted to traverse east German territory. The electricity supply, almost all of which came from the Soviet zone, began to fail, and Sokolovsky claimed that no Western currency could be used in Berlin as the latter was located in the Soviet zone.

On 23 June the situation deteriorated as the Soviets were told that the Western mark was being circulated in the western sectors, for on 24 June all land traffic from the western zones of Germany to the western sectors of Berlin was stopped and electricity to the western sectors of Berlin was cut off. That day the Soviets issued the Warsaw Declaration, which denounced the London Conference for its exclusion of the Soviet Union and demanded a return to Four Power control of Germany, including the Ruhr, the setting up of a German government and a peace treaty with it, the restarting of reparations and withdrawal of all occupation forces.

Both the Americans and the British regarded this as an attempt to go back to discussion over the entirety of Germany's future and to reintroduce the possibility of communist control of Germany. An aerial supply campaign was now the only option, the population of the western zones of Berlin being entirely dependent on it.

On 24 June 1948 the Cabinet was told in Bevin's absence on holiday that there had been no progress on a single currency, that there had been a Soviet announcement that the new currency for the Soviet zone would be extended to the whole of Berlin, that the Military Governors of the western zone had announced in reaction that the new currency of the western zones would be introduced in the western sectors of Berlin, and that the Soviets had stopped all traffic between the western zones and the western sectors of Berlin and had stopped electricity from east to west Berlin.

The Cabinet concluded that 'it was not yet clear whether these restrictions were designed as a tactical reply to the action taken by the Western Powers on the currency question or whether they were the first move in a major offensive to force the Western Powers to withdraw from Berlin.' It 'recognised that a very serious situation might develop in Berlin; and it was important that the Western Powers should take their stand on a position which they were confident of being able to sustain.' Though Attlee was present, that cautious conclusion left open the possibility of withdrawal from Berlin to a more defensible frontier to the west. It was agreed that Bevin would be apprised of the developments on his return from holiday by McNeil, who had attended the Cabinet meeting as the Minister of State at the Foreign Office, and that when the report of the Military Governor was received the Minister of State, Attlee and Bevin would consider 'whether the British Military Governor of Berlin should be recalled for consultation with ministers'.[48]

That Cabinet meeting took place at ten a.m. on 24 June 1948. Bevin's initial reaction to the Soviet blockade seems to have come on his return from holiday at a meeting with 'senior colleagues' later that day, when he represented the Berlin Crisis as an 'issue of will. If we now showed signs of weakness, we were in danger of being forced out of Europe.' Bevin added that he believed that if there were a display of resolution 'the Russians would in the end come to terms'.[49]

The following day, when General Brownjohn, the British Deputy Military Governor in Germany, apprised the Cabinet of the impossibility of road and rail supply to west Berlin and expressed doubts as to the possibility of supplying the civil population of the western sectors by air, Bevin seemed rather more restrained, confining himself to indicating that he was considering the basis of a joint approach with the US and France in reaction to what he termed the 'latest Soviet move to force the Western Powers out of Berlin' and to proposing a group of ministers to keep apprised of 'developments in Berlin'.[50] Harrington attributes Bevin's reticence to his uncertainty as to the views of his fellow ministers, even that of Attlee, though that does seem implausible, for by the time of the Berlin Crisis there was an understanding even on the Labour left regarding Soviet hostility to British social democracy and the danger of Soviet opportunism and expansionism in Europe, and Bevin took great care to consult Attlee in private to elicit Attlee's support and was a domineering and combative presence in Cabinet .[51] Ensuing Cabinet minutes indicate no ministerial opposition to Bevin's conduct of the Berlin Crisis, and Harrington presents no evidence for his claim that Bevin was reticent in Cabinet on 25 June because he was unsure of the views of fellow ministers.

What followed was an indication of Bevin's extraordinary dynamism and decisiveness and his influence on the Western response to the Berlin Crisis. As has been seen from his reaction on 24 June, Bevin regarded an exhibition of Western resolve as imperative. On 25 June, he proposed to Douglas the setting up of some liaison in London between him (Bevin) and 'a United States representative invested with the necessary authority, who might well be himself'.[52] Bevin also proposed that the Chiefs of Staff and the Joint Chiefs of Staff should discuss the military situation over Berlin,[53] and that the Military Governors should assess the need for Western assistance in the city. On 26 June Bevin told Douglas that the consequence of withdrawal 'would be disastrous. We should not be able to hold western Germany if we quitted Berlin,'[54] which represented the clearest possible linkage of resistance over Berlin to the future of the western zones of Germany. Bevin refused to listen to talk of difficulties in supplying the western sectors of Berlin from Brownjohn, liaised with the Americans and the French to effect supplies, and issued a communiqué on 26 June to the effect that, 'the statement that we intend to stay in Berlin holds good'.[55]

The Western context to the Soviet challenge to the Western presence in Berlin on 24 June was unpropitious, with Truman facing an imminent US presidential election that he was expected to lose and France in the middle of a Cabinet crisis that resulted in a new government, so Britain was the only major Western power with a stable government. On 27 June Marshall concurred with Bevin's suggestions, and on 28 June Douglas confirmed to Bevin that 'the United States Government had made up their mind quite definitely to continue to take a firm but unprovocative attitude regarding Berlin.'[56]

The same day Bevin exhorted Douglas, Under-Secretary of the Army Draper and General Wedemeyer to enhance the capacity of the airlift to Berlin, pointing not just to the material but also the psychological effect of a demonstration of Western ability to sustain Berlin. The Americans promised to do what they could even though this was in advance of a formal US decision.[57] According to Tusa, Bevin employed his entire repertoire of 'low cunning' in this encounter, 'flattery', 'cajolery', 'pathos' and 'nostalgia' to convince the generals to do what they could, a remarkable example of the effectiveness of his inimitable style of personal diplomacy.[58]

Also on 28 June Bevin told Cabinet ministers that 'the Foreign Office had issued a statement over the weekend confirming the Government's intention to maintain their position in Berlin and the US government were being asked to make a similar statement. There could be no question of yielding to Soviet pressure.' Bevin rejected what he said could be a Soviet attempt to secure Four Power control over the Ruhr in return for the restoration of links to the western sectors of Berlin.[59] The declaration of intent to remain in Berlin seems to have been a decision taken by Bevin and the FO without prior consultation with or approval from Cabinet, though it is not known if Attlee was consulted in private before the announcement. There seems to have been no adverse reaction from ministers.

Formal American support for Britain's stance over Berlin came, after an interlude in which only Britain had reacted, with Marshall's statement on 30 June and its confirmation as official policy from Truman, yet only however after Bevin's having impressed upon Douglas the need for a US statement.[60]

Bevin opposed any talking prior to the withdrawal of the blockade, telling Attlee on 30 June that 'there must first be a return to work, after which one could talk',[61] a clear indication that his approach was one that he might have taken in a trades union dispute. The same day Bevin issued a warning that 'a grave situation might arise' in a long speech to the Commons that explained the origins of the crisis, though he was clear that there was no alternative to his policy but surrender, 'and none of us can accept surrender'.[62] Bevin also referred to the resistance of the authorities in the western zones of Berlin to the imposition of a Soviet currency despite intimidation and threats. This was vital, for it meant that the West did have a constituency in Berlin, a cause to be defended.

The committee to handle the crisis recommended by Bevin was the Cabinet Committee on Germany or the Berlin Committee, which comprised Attlee, Bevin, Morrison as Lord President of the Council, Alexander as Minister for Defence, and the Chiefs of Staff and was 'dominated by Bevin'.[63] One of its first acts was to authorise Bevin to accept the US offer of B-29 bombers on British soil, an issue that was not presented to Cabinet for approval prior to the decision and that was notified to the Defence Committee as late as 10 September.[64]

The perennial FO concern over the diffuse nature of the American political system and the uncertainty as to when decisions were reached had been borne out by the American failure to make a formal decision over Berlin for many days. The Joint Chiefs of Staff felt that Berlin could not be defended and that withdrawal would be inevitable and have to be followed, if the West were resolved to stay in Berlin, by war, which they took to be inconceivable. They then advocated standing firm for the time being but reserving the US position as to the future.[65] This was politically hopeless, for it involved a demonstration of defiance that could be followed by a humiliating withdrawal and an example to the Soviets of the limited nature of Western resolve to resist Soviet diplomatic tactics and Soviet and communist expansionism, opportunism and brinkmanship.

Shlaim sees Truman's decision to stay as an example of 'the assertion of Presidential leadership in crisis'[66] in its apparent immunity to the advice of the bureaucracy below him. Truman's reaction was supported by Clay, who had always advocated standing firm in Berlin – in fact his reaction to early Soviet interference with western traffic had been to propose a land convoy to challenge it. 'He believed that the Russians were bluffing, that their bluff should be called, and the sooner the better, since time was not working to the advantage of the West, and the only way to do this was by a show of force.'[67] Further, it seems that Clay in inaugurating the airlift without any consultation with Washington was intent upon pre-empting any other decision on political or military grounds by establishing that breaking the blockade was possible.

Robertson offered calmer and wiser counsel to the British from Berlin, a policy with which Bevin concurred, in that he favoured no provocation but firmness, a refusal to make any concessions, and letting time elapse, a policy of perseverance. Yet there had not been complete accord between the two, for Robertson had wanted, even as late as May 1948, just weeks prior to the start of the blockade, to invite the Soviets to talks over the entire future of Germany. Bevin rejected the idea[68] given the history of Soviet diplomacy and the sense that responding to such Soviet tactics by any sort of concession would only invite such tactics to obtain Soviet objectives in future, an old concern with concessions to the Soviets that Attlee and Bevin had had at the time of the Baltic issue in late 1941 and early 1942.

The next immediate issue was the American desire to send a note to Stalin. Bevin was not against such a note in principle but insisted that any 'talks should be restricted at the present stage to the Berlin issue', as he expressed it to Attlee on 30 June, for, 'it was essential that there should be no impression created of a weakening in the Western attitude' and Bevin 'was most anxious to avoid a situation developing out of the note in such a way that the Russians might hold up all progress on Western Union'. He was also concerned regarding the possibility of resumed four-power negotiation over Germany, and preferred to delay the sending of the note – very much Bevin's natural approach. Attlee agreed with Bevin.[69] The minute of this meeting is indicative of Bevin's general orientation to the Berlin situation, for, having been joined by Douglas and Strang, he said he did not favour 'the proposals to refer the matter to either the Council of Foreign Ministers or to U.N.O.'.[70] 'The Secretary of State summed up his argument in the phrase that there must first be a return to work after which one could talk,'[71] an indication of his belief that the Soviets responded to exhibitions of resolve and power and would take advantage of any perceived weakness.

That the FO and Bevin were very much of one view at this time (as was so earlier) is indicated by Strang's telling Bevin that he objected to the proposed American note as it gave the Soviets just what they had wanted, the chance to re-open the question of Germany in the CFM system, in return for the restoration of western rights of access to Berlin 'which we enjoyed a few weeks ago'.[72] Strang's minute of Bevin's conversation with Attlee on 2 July 1948 indicates that Bevin had wanted time to permit Sokolovsky to 'restore communications' before sending the note.[73]

In the event the note to Stalin was sent on 6 July 1948 at US insistence. It referred to being in Berlin as a 'matter of established right', insisted that access should be 'restored', resisted 'duress' yet also referred to the possibility of four-power negotiation over Berlin if the blockade were lifted first, though there was, as Bevin wanted, no reference to the CFM system in the note .[74] Soviet confidence was undimmed. On 14 July, insisting that the West had violated the Potsdam principle of treating Germany as a whole and of four-power control of Germany by its measures to institute political institutions and a western currency in the western zones, their position was that the West had by such action forfeited their right to be in Berlin. The Soviets also insisted there should be no preconditions to negotiations. Bevin remained clear that in such circumstances talking was of little use, especially if it could be taken as indicative of a willingness to make concessions, and promoted the airlift as the first objective, though he wanted any action to counteract the Soviet threat to be taken in concert with the French and the Americans. It was obvious, with western Europe failing to exhibit any real decisiveness on the issue and anyway too weak to exert much influence, that nothing could be achieved by way of resistance or of winning any resulting war without the Americans in terms of money and military power. As a consequence every step of policy had to be co-ordinated with them lest they should feel they were being dragged into a war by British policy. Bevin's other reaction was to arrange for the stationing of B-29 bombers in the UK.

In the United States, with the military doubting the possibility of holding on in Berlin and developing plans for nuclear attack, Truman favoured an oral personal overture to Stalin to resolve the crisis. Bevin preferred a note to Molotov to a personal approach to Stalin, and on 22 July he told Douglas that personal overtures lent Stalin influence and legitimacy and were 'a weak way of doing things'. Even so, on 26 July 1948, at a meeting with Strang, Bohlen, Smith, Douglas and Massigli, Bevin assented with some misgivings to a personal approach to Stalin because of American insistence. In a reference to proposed US threats to Stalin, Bevin told Bohlen, 'I know all you Americans want a war, but I'm not going to let you 'ave it.' Bevin's policy over Berlin though seems to have remained unchanged, for the same day Bevin told Douglas, 'if we left Berlin the Slavs would settle on the Rhine, and that would be the end of western Europe. We must therefore hang on to Berlin at all costs.'[75] Bevin's resistance to the US proposal for a direct approach to Stalin involving threats was seen by the Americans as 'redolent with appeasement' and a 'definite weakening' of Bevin's previous position on Berlin.[76] For the Americans the nature of Bevin's proposed note represented a faltering of willpower to see the crisis through – and it is an indication of Bevin's effect on those with whom he worked in close proximity that Douglas was so quick to defend him. 'As to Bevin's intentions, purposes and determination, there can be no question whatsoever,' Douglas told Washington, and quoted Bevin as having said, 'the abandonment of Berlin would mean the loss of Western Europe.'[77]

Bevin's assessment of the Berlin situation on 28 July 1948, written in clear understanding of the impossibility of holding Berlin in a military sense, had no trace of any logic of concessions, over Berlin, the rest of Germany or the Ruhr. It anticipated severe conditions in Berlin as a result of the continued blockade, and said that there was no alternative to continued Western resistance. As ever his policy was perseverance, steadiness and refraining from giving any indication of any weakening of resolve, which was the reason for his reluctance to indicate a desire to talk to Stalin.[78]

Though Bevin had in the end to agree to talks with Stalin, to avoid any indication of British weakening he directed Frank Roberts, his private secretary and envoy at the British Embassy in the Soviet Union to resist any compromise and to maintain the Western position, which was that all traffic restrictions were to be removed prior to talks, and that the Soviet currency should not be used in the western sectors of Berlin.[79] Thereafter he subjected Roberts to a stream of communiqués of encouragement, support and instruction while attempting to enhance the airlift. Roberts appreciated Bevin's constancy and 'being able to rely absolutely upon Bevin's resolution and judgement'.[80]

Stalin seemed to want the abolition of the western mark, and even seemed prepared to waive his earlier condition that the London proposals should be delayed pending the outcome of a four-power conference on all aspects of the German situation, but ensuing talks with Molotov revealed that the intention was to preclude the formation of a German government as had been planned in London in February, to attain possession of Berlin by denying the western right to a presence in the city, and to preclude the use of Western currency in it.

The talks were now thoroughly bogged down, with the suspicion that the Soviets were confident that the coming winter would resolve the situation in Berlin in their favour. Bevin, while not wanting to break off the talks (as part of his policy of not backing an adversary into a corner by hostile postures), pointed to the need to avoid a position in which the West might permit 'the Soviet Government to achieve by means of their hold on the currency of Berlin that which they have not been able to achieve by their blockade'.[81]

Bevin insisted that lifting the blockade was the only conceivable reason for the talks, overcoming American objections that the Soviets should be told of western rights. For Bevin the crisis remained a matter of the exhibition of power rather than some insistence upon notional rights that could be argued over indefinitely and cloud the central issue, a very basic difference of approach. Bevin also wanted to avoid referral to the UN for similar reasons. In this instance, in early September 1948, Bevin prevailed, an indication of the sense of American need for allies on diplomatic grounds rather than American conviction that Bevin was right.[82]

At these critical junctures the role of Douglas and the warmth and understanding of his relationship with Bevin were central in explaining to the Americans the nature of and reasons for British policy. He referred to British concern at a foreign policy run by another power and a British feeling that their diplomatic capability was superior in experience and expertise and that there was little appreciation in Washington of the difficulties of European politics. Douglas then concluded with what was a typical defence of Britain's and Bevin's policies, remarking that Britain 'has faced its many difficulties, both at home and abroad, with a good deal of courage, determination and ingenuity' and counselled 'against jumping to the conclusion that there is something wrong simply because the British disagree with us'.[83]

Though Bevin reassured the Commons as to the adequacy of supplies to Berlin in the coming winter,[84] it became obvious that more planes were needed. It was clear too that the addition of civilian planes was not likely to be enough. On 22 October Truman authorised sixty-six C-54s for use in flights to Berlin, securing the supplies for the winter. Despite the fact that west Berlin had little electricity in conditions of bitter cold and severe rationing, west Berliners preferred blockade conditions to communist rule.

Meanwhile Bevin, despite his reservations regarding referral of the Berlin Crisis to the UN, had to acquiesce in the US demand that it should be referred there. The Berlin Crisis was then referred to the UN on 26 September 1948. Bevin was concerned that there would be a tendency to compromise and encouragement to the Soviets to obtain concessions, and did not believe that the UN could achieve anything positive. The FO concurred, remarking that 'it is very unlikely that reference to the United Nations would result in any positive action being taken to resolve the present situation',[85] a view endorsed by Cadogan as British Ambassador to the UN, who was keen to 'disabuse' the FO of any belief in the UN's utility in any case in which the antagonists could not agree among themselves.[86] Yet the alternative of another CFM to discuss the entirety of Germany was unacceptable unless the blockade had been removed prior to it and without commitment.[87]

As has been seen, Bevin was not prepared to countenance any concessions or compromise, and was resolved that withdrawal from Berlin should not be discussed. He told Schuman, the French Foreign Minister, that nothing should be done that might give the Russians an indication that Western resolve to continue to support the western sectors of Berlin was weakening, for 'any sign of weakness would encourage the Russians'.[88] Tusa and Tusa comment that 'Bevin hated forcing issues,' while Marshall believed a diplomatic settlement was possible.[89] Bevin and the FO were proved right. The Soviets refused to take part in any discussions and the UN's deliberations stumbled on without hope of any accord's being reached.

Matters were in the end overtaken by events in Berlin, where elections to a City Assembly were boycotted by the communists, who effected what amounted to a coup in their own sector on 30 November 1948 and left the democratic, elected government in control of the western sectors only. Yet even then the western mark was not the only currency in the western sectors, for having submitted the question to the UN the West had to await the result of its deliberations, which were, in their proposal for a Soviet mark, utterly unacceptable.

Yet Bevin, who had opposed the referral to the UN, insisted that the decision had to be respected and exhibited a mixture of concern over timing, a need to reconsider the options and the links between policies, and a desire to let time pass, quite unlike the vigour and certainty of his policy over the blockade and implacable opposition to any weakening over the right to remain in Berlin and to any concessions to Soviet intimidation. He wondered to Robertson on 24 January 1949 if the Soviets were soon to end the blockade and was concerned that the currency issue should imperil the effect of resistance to the blockade by provoking the Soviets and making it impossible for them to back down.[90] Another interpretation is of course that Bevin continued to pursue an entirely consistent policy of support to the western sectors of Berlin to indicate to the Soviets that unilateral action would not work while not pushing them too hard, a policy of firmness without provocation that was characteristic of Bevin and does seem like the disciplined pursuit of a trade union dispute. Yet any uncertainty was over almost as soon as it had begun, for he told the British Cabinet on 7 February that a western mark would be used in the western sectors from 10 March 1949, which makes his fleeting interlude of indecision seem a momentary crisis of confidence.

In America Truman had against all odds been elected for a second term and so had a new mandate, a North Atlantic Treaty been drafted by 24 December 1948, the Ruhr was to be subject to an international authority that excluded the Soviets and used for western recovery, and a Basic Law that represented a form of constitution for west Germany was being developed. Then on 31 January 1949 Stalin told an American journalist that he would consider raising the blockade if the Western powers postponed the creation of a west German state and held a CFM on Germany. There was no mention of the currency to be used in Berlin. Bevin's view was that it was an attempt to unravel the unity of the west and to preclude the formation of a west German government rather than a change in Soviet policy.[91] He told Washington that the currency issue was outstanding, that he did not anticipate the lifting of the blockade soon, and that the western mark should be introduced to west Berlin.

There followed an odd sequence of a cautious and noncommittal reply through the press by Acheson and a series of exploratory meetings between Jessup, the deputy American representative at the UN, and Malik, the Soviet representative at the UN. Bevin worried that if the West were to accede to a Soviet request for a CFM out of a desire to have the blockade lifted there could be a return to the old wrangle over Soviet participation in the Ruhr and over west Germany as a state, a reopening of old questions over the future of Germany, and was concerned over possible interference with the ratification of the North Atlantic Treaty.[92] This was another instance of his perennial concern with timing but also an example of his overriding caution and that ability to see the possible linkages between different issues.

Acheson was confident that everything was falling neatly into place, and wanted the blockade lifted as soon as possible. And after a hiatus between the parties in western Germany over the Basic Law was resolved by the delayed issue of a message indicating some freedom of manoeuvre for the Parliamentary Council, the Jessup-Malik talks resumed. On 4 April 1949 the North Atlantic Treaty was signed in Washington. And on 4 May Malik approved Jessup's demand that the blockade be lifted on 12 May and the CFM be held afterwards, on 23 May. On 9 May the Parliamentary Council approved the Basic Law and provided the mandate to set up a Federal Republic. And despite some typical foot-dragging from the Soviets in Berlin over the withdrawal of the blockade the crisis was over.

The west German nation was created four months after the end of the Berlin airlift, based on a Western perception that part of the Soviets' motivation in the blockade had been to delay the creation of a west German nation allied to the West. An east German state was set up in response under Soviet auspices months later. The Berlin Crisis had introduced a military component to considerations over Germany, and the experience of the Berlin blockade and the division of Berlin confirmed that Germany would remain in the front line in the Cold War. In May 1949 the Russia Committee's assessment was that though the Soviets had been persuaded by Western resolution over Berlin that 'toughness' was not going to secure their ends, their ultimate aim remained 'a united Germany inside the Soviet sphere of influence'.[93]

The Berlin Crisis could then be regarded as the first expression of Western resolve to give effect to the policy of containment of the Soviets in Europe. In particular the British approach over Berlin in 1948 can be seen as establishing the lengths to which Britain was prepared to go to defend even such isolated territory and provide a demonstration of resistance to Soviet expansionism and the spread of communism.

The influence of Bevin as Foreign Secretary, of Attlee as PM, and of the Cabinet
Given the powers and prerogatives of the PM in terms of appointment and dismissal of ministers, control over the Cabinet agenda, over the way in which an issue is presented to Cabinet and over summing up of Cabinet meetings, and Prime Ministerial entitlement to initiate personal diplomatic overtures, the attributes of the PM exert influence on British foreign policy as a result of the nature of the political system. That influence may be direct, in the nature of domination of foreign policy, as was so under Chamberlain before appeasement was publicly humiliated and under Churchill, both of whom were domineering personalities with an interest in foreign policy and a sense of Prime Ministerial entitlement to intervene combined with confidence in their own prowess in relation to foreign policy decision-making, or indirect, in the form of Prime Ministerial refraining from intervention in foreign policy, as was so under Baldwin, whose interest was in domestic policy.

In the case of Attlee as PM a number of factors obtained. Attlee did have very developed views as to what British foreign policy objectives should be and as to the optimal foreign policy, but he also conceived of the role of PM as that of a chairman and developed a system of Cabinet committees to get through the immense amount of government business that the Attlee administration attempted in an uncertain post-war world and as an administration committed to major social reforms. That system of Cabinet committees may have diminished the extent to which ministers had to account to the entire Cabinet. Attlee was personally unlike his predecessors in having no aspiration to dominate his Cabinet and in being self-effacing, unlike the conceited Chamberlain with his disdain for his ministerial colleagues and anyone who took a different view, and Churchill with his sense of entitlement to govern as PM regardless of the views of his Foreign Secretary or Cabinet.

In addition to Attlee's sense of the role of premier as chairman there was his relationship with Bevin, which was one of genuine warmth and closeness and of reciprocated loyalty (seen by Attlee to be the paramount political virtue) and trust .[94] Bevin had demonstrated loyalty to Attlee in 1945, when Morrison attempted to challenge him just before and after the Labour election victory, and continued to be loyal to Attlee, though it would not be legitimate to infer that Attlee permitted Bevin autonomy in regard to foreign policy because he was dependent upon him to remain in power, for Attlee seems to have been indifferent to remaining as PM and perfectly prepared to be replaced by another minister if it was generally felt that he had lost the confidence of Cabinet or Party. He was most certainly averse to being threatened by fear of loss of post. On the contrary, Bevin's freedom regarding policy over Berlin was attributable to an anti-communism and anti-Sovietism, an understanding of Soviet objectives in Germany and Europe, and a sense of the need for British resolution over Soviet expansionism that Attlee and Bevin shared, and that the Cabinet shared by the start of 1948. Burridge says of Attlee that in the early part of 1948 'the anti-Soviet tone of his speeches markedly increased',[95] and on 1 May 1948 Attlee referred to the Soviet Union as 'the land of fear and suppression' and 'the supreme example of imperialism', remarking that 'its imperialism is ideological'.[96] It seems clear that there were unrecorded private conversations between Attlee and Bevin, in which Bevin obtained Attlee's view, but possible influence from them cannot be evidenced.

The attitudinal commonality and resulting shared foreign policy objectives regarding policy towards the Soviet Union and communism in Europe and elsewhere and the closeness and mutual affection and trust that existed between Attlee and Bevin did not preclude differences over foreign policy that did not involve Soviet expansionism, for Attlee did differ from Bevin over Indian independence and imposed his policy preference over Bevin's objections in that instance, though he acquiesced in Bevin's preferred policy over the Middle East. It could not then be inferred that Attlee permitted Bevin autonomy over foreign policy in relation to Berlin in 1948 and 1949 because of a need for Bevin's support against challenges to his premiership from other ministers, quite apart from Attlee's indifference to losing the premiership (in which he seems to have been unlike any other PM). The inference that the attitudinal commonality over the Soviet Union and communism was genuine rather than reflective of Bevin's influence is supported by the fact that Attlee and Bevin had in the wartime coalition opposed concessions to Stalin over the Baltics in 1941 and early 1942 because both had been convinced that concessions would only elicit further Soviet demands.

The other indirect influence Attlee exerted on British foreign policy over Berlin in 1948 and 1949 was in his having appointed Bevin as Foreign Secretary in the first place, despite Bevin's preference for the Exchequer. In fact Attlee had initially planned for Dalton to be Foreign Secretary and appointed Bevin instead at the last minute.

Dalton was seen by one observer as the 'most left-wing member of the Big Five' (the others being Attlee, Bevin, Morrison and Cripps) and so could be expected to have pursued a rather different policy over the Soviet blockade of Berlin.[97] For as Chancellor of the Exchequer Dalton regarded spending overseas as the area where cuts in expenditure could and should be made, rather than in the radical domestic welfare programme, which may be seen to be an indication of Dalton's ideological priorities, for had it been just his role as Chancellor of the Exchequer with an obligation to control government expenditure the cuts would have been more random and less concentrated on the foreign expenditure that Bevin regarded as necessary to maintain British world, European and imperial power status and remain an influence in the post-war world and especially on the Americans upon whom Britain so depended for economic support to remain a world power and for diplomatic and military support against Soviet expansionism.

The inference from the evidence set in context is that British policy over Berlin in 1948 and 1949 would have been different had Attlee appointed Dalton as Foreign Secretary, for even if Dalton had shared Attlee's and Bevin's sense of a need to show resistance to Soviet expansionism and opportunism over Germany and Berlin in 1948 it would not follow necessarily that he would have proposed remaining in Berlin rather than retreat to a more militarily defensible location further to the west to protect the western zones of Germany against Soviet expansionism, as seems to have been the CoS preference.

For Bevin's dynamism, certainty and resolution in response to the news of the Soviet blockade of the western sectors of Berlin do seem to reflect attributes that differentiated Bevin from his contemporaries in the Cabinet, not least his confidence that the Soviet Union would not risk war over Berlin and his corresponding confidence in American support for remaining in Berlin, his sense that a stand had to be made in the first challenge to Western resolve to implement the Truman Doctrine of containment to deter the Soviet Union from other instances of opportunism and brinkmanship, his conviction that without resolve over Berlin the entirety of Germany and of western Europe was threatened, and his cautious, unprovocative approach of persevering without inflammatory rhetoric that would preclude a settlement, very like his conduct of a trades union dispute.

Another indirect causal influence was Bevin's brutal destruction of Lansbury at the Labour Party conference in 1935 that opened the way for Attlee to obtain the leadership of the Labour Party and so be an influence on policy over Berlin as PM, not least in his support of Bevin. In terms of attitude to the responsibility of government, both Attlee and Bevin had had extensive experience of government in the wartime coalition, when Bevin was Minister for Labour, with enormous wartime powers and responsibilities, and Attlee as Deputy Prime Minister was responsible for domestic policy in general.

What the relationship and attitudinal commonality with Attlee meant was that Bevin was the major influence on British foreign policy over Europe, Germany and Berlin in 1948 and 1949 and that Bevin's attributes, his personality, his attitudes, his approach to foreign policy and to crises, and his effect on other politicians and officials in the UK and elsewhere, are central to any assessment of the causation of British foreign policy over Berlin in 1948 and 1949. Here I shall point to Bevin's vision and ability to link issues in foreign policy and his dynamism in the crisis, and assess the extent to which his policy reflected Cabinet influence.

Though the Cabinet in 1948 included Labour's big guns in the form of the personalities of Dalton, Cripps, Morrison and Bevan, Cabinet records indicate no ministerial resistance to or dissent regarding Bevin's stance over western union or over Berlin in a foreign policy that seems to have been dominated by Bevin's dynamism and certainty and to have reflected a general ministerial endorsement of Bevin's approach to the Berlin Crisis. Even the left wingers Bevan and Cripps were supportive of resistance to Soviet expansionism in Europe, for Bevan 'proposed dispatching an armed land convoy' to break the Soviet blockade of the western sectors of Berlin, and Cripps expatiated to the Commons on 11 November 1948 on Soviet methods, indicating Soviet attempts to cause strikes and the economic disintegration of the west.[98] Though the evidence does seem to indicate a genuine commonality of understanding over the need to resist Soviet and communist expansionism and opportunism in Germany and western Europe by 1948 within the Cabinet the support of Bevin by Attlee as PM does seem a plausible influence on foreign policy over Berlin given the powers and prerogatives of the PM in the British political system and the centrality of the axis between the PM and Foreign Secretary in terms of the locus of control over foreign policy, as the very different cases of Chamberlain and Eden and Halifax, and Churchill and Eden, indicate.

By the start of 1948 Bevin saw his foreign policy in terms of a metaphor of a table with four legs. These were the European Recovery Programme (ERP) and the European Organisation for European Economic Co-operation (OEEC), the Treaty of Brussels and Western Union, American military commitment to western Europe and the organisation of west Germany. Bevin felt that any Western weakening over Berlin either by withdrawal or concessions over Germany to sustain the

Western position in Berlin would result in a loss of confidence in Germans in the West's preparedness to defend them. The policy was dependent on all legs,[99] the simultaneous pursuit of which was Bevin's major preoccupation in the early months of 1948. Implicit in this was abandonment of the Soviet zone to the Soviets and a policy of containment of any communist expansion westwards through developing western Europe's economic and military power.

Bevin told the Labour Party Conference that communist polices in eastern Europe could not be altered, but that 'we are not prepared to sit idly by and see a similar process of communization carried on over a weakened, distracted and disunited Europe'.[100]

Bevin's tendency had been to deliberate upon questions for some time and to decline to be rushed into decisions. Yet his reaction in June 1948 was decisive and resolute, convinced that the Western allies should stay in Berlin and that no concessions should be made over Germany to resolve the crisis. In fact his immediacy of reaction meant that it was the British Cabinet that first decided on the Berlin airlift (in fact Bevin told ministers on 28 June 1948 that the FO had indicated Britain's resolve to stay in Berlin, just days after the Soviet interference with traffic to the western sectors of Berlin that precipitated the crisis and without prior Cabinet approval of such an announcement) and resolved not to make any concessions. As Bullock puts it,

'Bevin saw the Berlin dispute as a trial of strength and thought it would be won by the side which had the stronger nerves and did not encourage the other side by pressing too hard to find a solution.'[101]

And Barker sums up Bevin's conceptualisation of his task as to

'stand firm in Berlin; next, to de-fuse the situation through diplomatic negotiations (or at least the appearance of negotiations); at the same time to restrain any American tendency towards "blustering" or war-like gestures or action, while also putting heart into the French.'[102]

Yet, as has been seen, FO papers indicate that Bevin's reaction was not an instinctive one to an unexpected crisis but the implementation of a policy agreed by the FO in March 1948 (though the Cabinet was not told at that time) of standing firm despite Soviet pressure on Berlin. This moves the initial decision point from June 1948 to March 1948, though the nature of the blockade may not have been foreseen.

There are in fact a number of distinct but related phases to Bevin's influence on British policy over Berlin. For without Bevin's policy of 'western union' there might have never been a Berlin Crisis, for Soviet pressure on Berlin was in direct response to what they saw as the violation of Potsdam in their exclusion from the London Conference. Thereafter there was the initial decision-making process between Bevin and his FO officials in March 1948, prior to the Soviet pressure on Berlin that precipitated the crisis. Only then was there Bevin's reaction to the crisis itself, with its remarkable certainty and influence on the Western response, and his steadiness under pressure and refusal to be deflected from a policy of perseverance and firmness but no provocation.

Part of this derived from Bevin's having come to an understanding that the Soviets understood above all power, but it was also a policy similar to that he might have pursued in a trades-union dispute, in which nothing provocative should be done to imperil a resolution but no hint of any ground being given should be apparent, a policy of perseverance and indication of intention to endure. This had been apparent in the interlude prior to the crisis itself, when Clay had called for a note to the Soviets indicating Western intention to go to war over Berlin if necessary.

Bevin approved an indication of Western right to remain in Berlin, but not the provocative addition that they were prepared to go to war. Bevin's policy was one of a combination of caution, avoidance of unnecessary provocation, and firmness.[103] Strang's view of the utility of Bevin's trades-union background indicates its connection with diplomacy. Strang remarked, 'the art of diplomacy is the art of negotiation, exercised in a special sphere,' and in trades-union disputes, 'as in foreign relations, the objective is not so much victory as a tolerable settlement.'[104] The only exception to this analogy is that for Bevin the matter was not negotiable, for he was utterly opposed to any concessions over Berlin or Germany which could weaken his 'western union'. That Bevin's approach to the Berlin Crisis reflected his trades-union background is reinforced by his difficulty in conceptualising problems and his tending to resort to his own experience.[105]

The minimal influence of Cabinet on policy may be seen from the extensive series of Cabinet minutes that record implicit or explicit Cabinet approval of Bevin's policy over Germany as pursued at the London Conference and his policy over the developing situation in Berlin. Cabinet approval of Bevin's policy positioning papers on the Soviet Union, Germany and western Europe in early January 1948 has been covered above, but references to Germany and Berlin in Cabinet meetings continued during the spring of 1948. In each case the Cabinet 'took note', 'endorsed' or 'endorsed with approval' Bevin's position.[106]

Cabinet meetings at which Bevin's stance on the future of Germany was endorsed without apparent reservation by the Cabinet continued into the summer and the drift into the crisis itself .[107] On 24 June, with the start of the blockade, the Cabinet noted 'that a very serious situation might develop in Berlin' and that 'the Western Powers should take their stand on a position which they were confident of being able to sustain.'[108] The implications of the situation were at the time uncertain, and this minute and the fact that the Cabinet 'took note' the following day that Bevin would 'concert a common policy in this matter with the Governments of the United States and France'[109] are unremarkable, for they committed the Cabinet to nothing by way of policy. Yet what is remarkable is that on 28 June, just days later, Bevin informed the Cabinet that 'the Foreign Office had issued a statement over the weekend confirming the Government's intention to maintain their position in Berlin and the United States Government was being asked to make a similar statement. There could be no question of yielding to Soviet pressure' for, 'if the Western Allies were forced out of Berlin, the project of Western Union would be weakened.'[110] This was an indication of Bevin's agenda over Berlin but also a clear imposition of a policy position on the Cabinet, yet it was received without dissent. The pattern continued.

On 1 July 1948, with the blockade in force, the Cabinet 'took note' of Bevin's statement regarding a note to the Soviet Government,[111] and on 22 July 1948 Bevin reported that he had resisted referral of the Berlin Crisis to the United Nations, again without adverse Cabinet reaction,[112] a remarkable compliance. On 26 July 1948 Bevin reiterated his stance on Berlin without dissent from Cabinet colleagues.[113] By 10 September 1948 Bevin was yet more resolute, informing Cabinet that he told Molotov 'conversations could not be held under duress',[114] which meant an end to the blockade was a precondition to discussion. The Cabinet 'took note' of this and of Soviet intimidation in Berlin. And on 22 September 1948 Bevin told the Cabinet that talks between the Military Governors had come to nothing, and that there was a suspicion that the Soviets were intending to use the winter to oust the Western allies from Berlin. He said that a note was being sent to Stalin asking whether he was 'prepared to remove the blockade measures', and that, though there would be no indication to Stalin, the matter would, failing a satisfactory response, be referred to the United Nations. This was not in any expectation of a settlement, only as a means of focusing world opinion. The Cabinet 'endorsed' the policy.[115]

There is in fact no instance of Cabinet opposition to Bevin over Germany or Berlin in this long and critical period. Blackwell has observed that Attlee had indicated that ministers should refrain from requesting that their dissenting views should be specially recorded in Cabinet minutes,[116] yet the absence of any indication of collective or individual dissent seems conclusive evidence of

Cabinet approval or compliance. For whether this was because Bevin dominated the Cabinet by force of personality, because of Attlee's Prime Ministerial support, or because the climate of opinion had by this time changed so utterly in the period since 1946, is difficult to evidence directly. Yet by this time not only was antipathy for the communists and the Soviets widespread even in the Labour Party, but so also was a resolution to cease futile and exploited attempts at conciliation, and some commonality of view between Bevin, Attlee and the Cabinet seems a plausible explanation for the extraordinary absence of any Cabinet dissent. Such general commonality of view and ultimate purpose does not though explain why every tactic that Bevin presented to Cabinet throughout the Berlin Crisis was endorsed without dissent, for that tends to indicate a combination of a sense that Bevin knew best, that it was his business as Foreign Secretary, that it could be unwise to dissent given Bevin's robust personality and expressive style, and that Bevin was supported by Attlee as PM.

The relationship between and relative influence of Bevin and the Foreign Office

Given Bevin's autonomy in Cabinet a natural question is the extent to which Bevin was influenced by the mandarins in the FO. The relationship between Bevin and his FO officials seems to have been complex and influence reciprocal, to have included personal affection, admiration and trust, and to have been informed by a profound sense of attitudinal commonality and common purpose. Assessing relative causal influence is not assisted by Bevin's oral mode of working with his FO officials, nor by meetings the minutes of which do not reveal the exchange of views between identified individuals. Bevin made few annotations to FO papers and even Bevin's Cabinet papers seem to have been written by his FO officials, though that would not be unusual and does not of itself preclude their representing Bevin's ideas.

There has been an active debate between the traditionalist view that Bevin was the originator of British foreign policy in the immediate post-war period and the revisionist view that he was very much influenced by the mandarins in the FO. There has also been the view that there was from the outset a commonality of attitude and objective between Bevin and his FO officials because Bevin's political orientation was traditionalist and right wing rather than socialist, so that there was little need for influence either way, a criticism levelled at Bevin from historians on the left.[117] There has for instance been the comment that Bevin's foreign-policy orientation and objectives represented continuity with those of his Conservative predecessor as Foreign Secretary, Eden, which seems to be corroborated by primary evidence of an exchange in the Commons between Bevin and Eden in which the commonality of foreign policy approach between the two Foreign Secretaries was explicitly acknowledged, and Oliver Harvey, Eden's Personal Private Secretary, believed that Bevin's foreign policy represented what Eden would have pursued as a foreign policy had he been allowed to have one under the domineering Churchill as PM with his periodic susceptibility to Stalin's influence.

Central to this claimed commonality of attitudinal and foreign-policy orientation was Bevin's anti-communism and detestation of the Soviet Union and suspicion as to its ideological foreign-policy objectives in Europe and elsewhere, and Bevin's attachment to the traditional ethos of Britain as a world power. Though Bevin did regard Soviet foreign policy as expansionist and opportunistic there was extensive evidence to support the supposition, not least over Germany. The maintenance of Britain's world-power status was regarded by Bevin and other members of the British establishment as a primary desideratum. Though Cadogan's reference to Bevin as 'the heavyweight of the Cabinet' who would 'get his way with them' 'if he can be put on the right line', and his view that Bevin had 'sound ideas – which we must encourage' could be interpreted as class prejudice and upper-middle-class mandarin arrogance rather than evidence of influence, the evidence is of the time of Bevin's arrival at the FO, not of his time there, and does seem to indicate that Cadogan regarded Bevin's views as similar to those of the FO before any FO influence.[118]

The documentary evidence prior to early 1948 does seem to establish that Bevin did share a broad commonality of view with his FO officials on arrival at the FO, especially in the attachment he had to Britain as a world power and his revulsion for communism and the Soviet Union as a state. There was also a shared sense that Soviet expansionism and opportunism had to be resisted on a case-by-case basis, though it does seem that the FO came to the view that no rapprochement even on the basis of Soviet experience of British firmness would be possible because of Soviet expansionist objectives, opportunism and open hostility to social democracy earlier than Bevin, who seems to have become persuaded to the FO view through a combination of characteristic private rumination, discussion with FO officials and continued adverse experience of Soviet diplomacy rather than as a consequence of FO influence alone.

By the time of western union in January 1948 there was then a commonality of view between Bevin and the FO not just on attitudinal orientation but on actual policy towards the Soviet Union over Europe and elsewhere. Such commonality of attitude, objective and general policy does not though mean that there would have been commonality too over remaining in Berlin, for withdrawal to a more defensible frontier to protect western Germany would have been just as consonant with anti-communism and resolve to resist Soviet expansionism and opportunism in Europe and Germany, and with the maintenance of world and European power status. Strang's minute to Bevin on 18 March 1948 is indicative of FO policy recommendations, of Bevin's consonant views, and demonstrates that policy over Berlin had been agreed between Bevin and the FO before the first Soviet interference with traffic on 30 March and long before the crisis erupted on 24 June 1948, for, as has been seen above, pressure on Berlin in response to 'western union' was expected. Responding to a request from Bevin this document outlined the policy options. Withdrawal and remaining in Berlin but being prepared to evacuate the city later were rejected because of their likely effect on German, world, US and French opinion. The favoured option was 'to demonstrate by action, rather than by words, our determination to remain in Berlin, despite Soviet pressure, even if this becomes severe'.[119] By this Bevin scrawled, 'we must stay'.[120]

This indicates a common policy over Berlin but not the direction of any influence. Yet from the unusually definite and emphatic nature of Bevin's annotation on the document itself and Bevin's other scribbled commentary, which for him was extensive, and from contextual information regarding Bevin's understanding that pressure on Berlin to prevent western union was probable, it does seem that the FO view endorsed rather than influenced Bevin's own.

Yet it is worth noting that the FO minute of 18 March 1948 was part of a process, in that it records Bevin's way of working, which had not changed in its inviting dissent and views from his FO officials. In fact the reference in the minute to 'our counter-proposal' makes it seem as if the idea of remaining resolved to stay in Berlin regardless of pressure and in silence came from the FO, not Bevin.

Having said that Kirkpatrick's minute to Robertson of 24 March 1948 refers to a meeting in which Bevin had made it clear that Britain should stay in Berlin and remarked that 'you will probably like to know of his firm attitude on this point', from which one could infer that Robertson had not known of Bevin's specific resolve to stay in Berlin prior to this – Bevin had earlier indicated that he concurred with Robertson's conviction that the Soviets would not go to war over Berlin, but resolution to resist in western Germany was very different from a specific resolve to remain in Berlin regardless of pressure.

Such evidence dated 24 March does not of course preclude FO influence on Bevin on 18 March, and beyond the immediate impression of a more dominant Bevin in 1948 it seems that the Foreign Secretary's relationship with the FO had remained unchanged since 1946 and was one of reciprocation of influence in a process of verbal discussion and disputation within a context of very extensive commonality of attitude and policy preference at the outset and more so over time between 1946 and 1948.[121] The most plausible inference is that such commonality between Bevin and the FO extended to agreement without influence from either side over policy in regard to Berlin should the Western presence there be threatened. Another strand of evidence that would seem to indicate that Bevin was not persuaded by the FO against his better judgment over Berlin is that he and Attlee had been concerned as to concessions to Soviet demands as long ago as 1941 and 1942 over Stalin's demand for British acceptance of a Soviet takeover in the Baltics and had been concerned that surrender could result in more demands, an indication of an understanding of the need for resolve as a form of deterrence when dealing with the Soviet Union over Europe, and there was in both Attlee and Bevin a long-standing aversion to the Soviet Union and to communism from their previous experience, in Bevin's case from his trades-union experience.

Having said that there is a difference between commitment to contain Soviet influence and communism in Europe and to avoid concessions that could elicit more Soviet demands in general terms and a specific resolve to remain in Berlin despite a Soviet blockade of the western sectors, though Bevin's reaction to Strang's memorandum of 18 March 1948 seems to indicate a commonality of view rather than extensive persuasion by the FO.

It has been observed above that by the start of 1948 Bevin had abandoned all hope of accord with the Soviets predicated upon displays of British resolve. There is no direct evidence of the reasons for the change, but a combination of working with FO officials who had long regarded Soviet intentions as hostile on ideological grounds and so immune to Western overtures, continued adverse diplomatic experience of Soviet foreign policy and Bevin's own private ruminations seems most probable as an explanation of Bevin's altered view that Soviet intentions were such that accord would not be possible even given a British policy of firmness on a case-by-case basis to indicate that Soviet expansionism and opportunism would be resisted. Such an inference is consistent with Bevin's own autonomous personality, his confidence in his own judgment and the nature of the relationship he had with his FO officials, as well as his reactions to Soviet diplomacy at intervening CFMs and his policy initiatives. Bevin's notion of 'western union' resulted. It is worth noting however that this altered view of Soviet intentions may not have been necessary to the policy Bevin followed over Berlin, in that the latter was quite consistent with his firm case-by-case approach that he had formed as early as February 1946 – as may be observed from Bevin's language, he saw Berlin as just another case of Soviet opportunism.

The nature of the Bevin-FO relationship in regard to policy towards the Soviets over Germany had then evolved in the period since the first half of 1946. As mentioned, the FO had come earlier than Bevin to the conclusion that the Soviet Union was hostile to Britain on ideological grounds and had as a result as long ago as early 1946 abandoned any hope of long-term accommodation with the Soviets. Yet there had from the outset been broad attitudinal commonalities. With his trades-union background and commitment to social democracy Bevin shared the FO's (and the CoS's) anti-communist and anti-Soviet sensibilities, and had even in late 1945 and early 1946 agreed with the FO that Soviet policy was expansionist and opportunistic and should be resisted by a British policy of firmness on a case-by-case basis, a policy which he impressed upon the US as being imperative. Yet Bevin had at that time continued to hope that exhibitions of British (and US) resolve and diplomatic firmness might persuade the Soviets of the desirability of an accord on the basis of mutual acceptance of each other's vital interests. It is worth noting that this gap between Bevin and the FO was not over attitudinal orientation or ultimate purposes, and not even over the actuality of policy, but in the realm of aspiration as to that policy's possible consequences. By the start of 1948 however that small gap between Bevin and the FO had disappeared.

As an indication of an emerging commonality of view between Bevin and the FO not just over firmness as a policy but also as to Soviet intentions and the possibility of accord, FO pressure for more vigorous propaganda tactics against the communists, which had to some extent been resisted by Bevin in 1946, was sanctioned by Bevin at the start of 1948 by the creation of an Information Research Department within the FO. The FO position reflected their understanding of Soviet intentions and the notion of Britain as the social democratic alternative to communism[122] was then propagated. The FO also advocated a 'western association' to avoid being '"outclassed" by Russia, dependent on the United States and with Britain and Western Europe reduced to "pigmies between two giants"'.[123] Bevin's 'western union' did then receive support from the FO, for its purpose was consistent with the FO view that Britain should stand up to the Soviets in Europe on the basis that diplomacy was manipulated by them and accord was impossible, though it seems the vision itself came from Bevin, as those present at the time have indicated. And it was this 'western union' initiative that elicited the Soviet reaction of the Berlin blockade.

The CoS did however have doubts regarding the worth of the French military contribution. They also argued against any commitment to Europe without sufficient military power to meet any undertakings given. Yet Bevin needed the French for his 'western union', and they had insisted on military support. It was clear to Bevin and the FO that the only means of offering security to the west Europeans was the obtaining of American support, for any resistance to Soviet expansionism in Europe was impossible without US support. That need for US support had been clear even in the first half of 1946, when Soviet intransigence and intentions over Germany and overwhelming power in Europe became an obvious threat in a context of British and western European economic and military weakness.

In April, with the first sign of Soviet pressure, there was some uncertainty in the FO and the military not over the desirability of remaining in Berlin but as to the feasibility of remaining there, with withdrawal seen as a possibility by Robertson and Strang. As has been seen, Pakenham was violently opposed to withdrawal, but there is no documentary evidence of Bevin's reaction. Yet an absence of written response was characteristic of Bevin, and does not indicate any wavering of resolution to stay in Berlin. In fact other evidence at the time indicates a policy of continuing firmness over staying in Berlin but no provocation.[124] Bevin disregarded FO and military doubts, as his dynamic response to the crisis indicates, and FO officials seem relieved to have had the decisions made at the political level. Policy during the crisis exhibits other commonalities of view between Bevin and the FO, over the undesirability of involving the UN and over avoidance of any concessions elsewhere in Germany to resolve the crisis.

FO admiration for Bevin's advice and steadfastness is also clear. In April 1948 Sargent was 'rather shocked' at the French Ambassador's opinion that 'we ought to be preparing for our departure from Berlin' as it would be humiliating to be expelled by Soviet pressure (as if ceding Berlin to the Soviets without any pressure would not be!).[125] Sargent pointed to the adverse consequences of a Western surrender over Berlin for the confidence of Germans in Western resolve to resist communism. Kirkpatrick annotated that Massigli had been propagating his views 'in a more than defeatist manner' and that the French attitude was 'reminiscent of 1938, 39, and 40',[126] references to the salience within the FO of appeasement. And Patrick Dean was dismayed to note that the US ambassador to the Soviet Union would not admit that 'if we give up Berlin we shall lose western Germany and probably in due course western Europe as well'. Dean did note though that it might be possible to withdraw from Berlin in some months' time, and Hankey of the Northern Department, though agreeing that 'we must not give way now', claimed that once western Germany was organised he could not see 'what further function we can fulfil in Berlin', an indication of FO resolution not to be pushed out of Berlin as a consequence of Soviet intimidation and brinkmanship though of concern as to the Western presence in Berlin so far in the Soviet zone.[127]

There was then a consensus between Bevin and the FO as to policy over Berlin and its links to the defence of western Germany and western Europe against Soviet expansionism. In terms of derivation the evidence indicates that the consensus reflected a commonality of approach, as, for instance, Sargent had long been implacably opposed to appeasement of any sort, and Bevin's policy may be seen as a continuation of his firmness case by case of early 1946. It seems that the relationship between Bevin and the FO continued to be characterised by mutual trust and admiration, reciprocal influence and a commonality of purpose and understanding. As to Bevin's remarkable dynamism at the start of the crisis, one has to attribute this assurance to prior understandings with the FO and the US over Berlin. It does also appear that the actuality of an immediate crisis threw into relief the understood demarcations as to role and function between Bevin and the FO.

Bevin's remarkable reaction at the inception of the crisis does seem to have been accepted as leadership. On 25 June 1948, a minute of a meeting with Kirkpatrick, Strang, Roberts, Henderson, Dean and Brownjohn is noteworthy for its recording of Bevin's views almost exclusively, with little or no comment from the others (this is in marked contrast to 1946, when the opposite tended to occur, with Bevin silent and non-committal on policy), for Bevin's clarity as to the need 'to remain firm', for his understanding of the need for an American response 'backing the agreed policy', and for his dynamism in organising the Western response, including political and military liaison with the Americans.[128]

Bevin's sense of the relative roles of the Foreign Secretary and the FO had always been clear – his as minister was to assess arguments, make decisions and secure Prime Ministerial and Cabinet assent, and theirs as officials was to apprise him of all the information and 'alternative courses of action'.[129] His confidence and ascendancy were apparent again over the possibility of a note's being sent to the Soviets. On 25 June 1948 Kirkpatrick had suggested that a note similar to the US communication in April should be sent to them. Though such an overture might 'reopen negotiations on Germany', he argued that 'this risk should be run'.[130] This was seen by Bevin without apparent comment. Yet on 28 June Kirkpatrick indicated to Robertson that 'the Secretary of State's present view is that we should in any case not approach the Russians until our impressive air lift has been organised.'.[131] He also made Bevin's position clear—

'Retreat would be disastrous. The abandonment of the many Germans who have stood by us in Berlin would cause such a lack of confidence in the Western Zone that we should find it almost impossible to maintain our position there. With the loss of Western Germany we should face not only the collapse of our whole Western system, but the complete domination of Europe by Russia reinforced by a Communist controlled Germany.'[132]

And during the long period of the crisis Bevin's steadiness of purpose was endorsed and supported by his FO officials, as was his policy of no concessions or hint of weakness, of not going to the UN unless unavoidable and of no provocation over Berlin. It is though true that this was based not just on Bevin's ascendancy but also on a broad commonality of view between Bevin and the FO as to Soviet intentions, the need to resist them in Europe and the vital role of 'western union' in that endeavour, and the relevance of Berlin to the credibility of 'western union'. Yet in moments of faltering resolve not as to the desirability but rather the feasibility of remaining in Berlin it was Bevin who was clear that no withdrawal or intimidation should be countenanced.

Strang's view of Bevin and his officials at work indicates a remarkable commonality of view over Berlin (as in the minute of 18 March) and reciprocity of influence in Bevin's relations with his FO officials in a process of discussion, disputation and consideration of alternative views,[133] but also a sense that by this time the initiative, decisions and timing of any resultant action rested with Bevin.[134] This does not preclude FO influence or even the notion that FO agreement was preconditional, but rather that the overall vision and the linkages between the different components of policy were ultimately Bevin's, even if they were shared and endorsed by the FO. For, as Strang remarks, Bevin had 'that sense of international relationship which is the first word and the last in diplomatic wisdom'.[135]

By the end of March 1948 then the basic outline of British policy over Berlin was clear and shared between Bevin and the FO, as were the linkages to 'western union' and to the Truman Doctrine that expressed Bevin's sense of the need for exemplary resistance to Soviet encroachment case by case that made resolution over Berlin so vital, in a genuine commonality of view rather than one masking an underlying dominance from one over the other. Subsequent to this the FO's deferring to Bevin as Foreign Secretary is apparent from what followed a meeting on 23 April in which Robertson told Strang, Kirkpatrick, Steel, Hankey, Johnston and Dean that 'he expected the position in Berlin to get considerably worse owing to increased Soviet pressure' but that Britain should 'stay in Berlin in spite of inconveniences however serious' and 'should say nothing and simply stay put', a reflection of Bevin's and the FO's agreed policy. The minutes go on to record that the 'meeting agreed with this view', but add that 'the present would be the worst moment to evacuate Berlin for prestige reasons both in Berlin and the rest of Germany'.[136] In sending this to Bevin Strang's note is clearly concerned to make it clear that 'the purpose of this meeting was not to lay down, or even to suggest, any new policy, since you have decided, and it is clearly understood on all hands, that it is our intention to stay in Berlin'.[137] This indicates that while the FO view had been clear that Britain should stay in Berlin regardless of pressure on 18 March 1948 there was also an understanding that Bevin insisted that there should be no withdrawing from that position – this minute is further evidence that there was very significant commonality of view between Bevin and the FO, but also that the FO accepted that Bevin would not permit his resolute policy over Berlin to be altered.

There is also a sense that Bevin and the FO concurred that policy should be one of resolve but also restraint and avoidance of provocation. It is clear that Bevin understood that the Soviets 'may miscalculate and involve themselves in a situation from which they feel they cannot retreat',[138] and he told Attlee that silence and avoidance of provocation while continuing to be firm over staying in Berlin was the best policy.[139] If there is a difference between Bevin and the FO at this time it is in Bevin's refusal to consider the ultimate possibility of being compelled to withdraw from Berlin. On 4 May he told the Commons, 'we are in Berlin as of right and it is our intention to stay there.'[140]

CoS concerns regarding the feasibility of defending the western sectors of Berlin in a war against the Soviet Union seem to have exerted no influence on Bevin's initial decision to remain in Berlin in defiance of Soviet pressure to withdraw or on his ensuing conduct of the Berlin Crisis, and as has been seen Attlee reminded the CoS that foreign policy was a decision to be taken by ministers and predicated upon political considerations, an indication of the lack of influence on policy over Berlin from the CoS.

External influences – the Soviet Union, the United States and France

Here I shall discuss the influence on British policy over Berlin in 1948 of international diplomatic pressures, which include US policy preferences, the US political system and Soviet understandings and reactions, but also wavering French resolve.

A critical factor in British policy over Berlin was the international setting in 1948, with by then a considerable and very adverse history of expansionism and opportunism in Soviet diplomacy and ideological hostility apparent in Soviet propaganda aimed at social democracy. There had also been the Truman Doctrine of containment of Soviet influence and communism to eastern Europe already under Soviet control. Britain had since the end of the war needed US support against the Soviets in any stand-off, given Britain's post-war economic and military weakness, but by 1948

American tendencies towards isolationism in the immediate post-war period had been replaced by an understanding of the indispensability of American power in Europe, which had been made clear initially with Byrnes' speech in Stuttgart in September 1946 and had been confirmed by the Truman Doctrine of containment of Soviet influence to eastern Europe. There followed the Marshall Plan in the summer of 1947 and the shared experience of the CFM in London in December 1947, and the conclusive offer of talks regarding an Atlantic Pact on 12 March 1948. Yet it was also by this time clear that the British economic recovery from the effects of war anticipated in 1946 was not going to occur, and that Britain's post-war decline in relation to the superpowers was not a fleeting interlude.

To what extent was there genuine autonomy in British policy formulation over the question of remaining in Berlin regardless of pressure to withdraw from the Soviets? The evidence indicates that Bevin's policy of resistance over Berlin was predicated upon an understanding that the US would support it. For even as early as1946 almost every Cabinet paper regarding the future of Germany had carried the qualification that it could not become British foreign policy without US support. In the first clear indication of a British policy to stay in Berlin, Strang's minute to Bevin dated 18 March 1948, to which Bevin appended 'we must stay', there was reference to an assurance that it was clear that 'the U.S. authorities are prepared to make a fundamental issue of the maintenance of the status quo', and the observation that 'we shall have to concert our actions with the U.S. and French Governments in the face of any serious Soviet threat' was part of an argument against early withdrawal and referred to the prospect of an adverse American reaction to any withdrawal.[141] It seems then that the FO and Bevin, who expressed no dissent, felt at that time assured of US support over remaining in Berlin. Yet the evidence is mixed in regard to Bevin's assurance of American support. For in a conversation with Bidault on 17 April 1948 Bevin referred to a need to know 'what the U.S. Government were ready to do if things went wrong' and referred also to getting the 'Americans to face up to their responsibilities in regard to supporting the Brussels Treaty',[142] an indication that Bevin remained unsure as to the specific nature of US policy over Germany and Berlin. Bevin and Bidault agreed that representations should not be made to the Soviets without first being clear as to US policy. This characteristic note of caution may have been part of Bevin's sympathetic diplomacy with the doubting French, but on 29 April 1948 Bevin told Douglas that he needed to be assured of US support for the Brussels Treaty before sending notes to the Soviets of protest and insistence on notional rights over Berlin[143] (over which it seems Bevin did acquiesce, at American insistence, despite his own feeling that it was better policy to remain silent but resolute).

From the documentary evidence it would seem that Bevin's response in the crisis period starting on 24 June preceded any specific undertaking from the Americans as to remaining in Berlin regardless of pressure to withdraw, though Tusa and Tusa claim it was in fact predicated upon private assurances from Douglas as to American resolution.[144] Yet even as late as 25 June 1948 Bevin wanted to be sure of US support over Berlin with 'no chance of their wavering'.[145] Bevin's view was that 'if the Russians failed to get us out of Berlin by the end of August they might give up their efforts',[146] but Berlin's enduring even to that time was contingent, as in 1946, on US support. It would then be remarkable if the cautious Bevin had permitted the period between 17 April and 25 June to elapse without securing some indication of US support, and it is possible that he received such assurance from Douglas though not in the form of an official decision, which would indicate that Bevin's continuing concern is attributable to a characteristic caution regarding US resolve even after private assurances.

Though there followed an attempt to secure formal, public US support, a British policy that seems to have been autonomous in its initial phase does then seem to have been a reflection of understandings as to US support without which resistance to the Soviet blockade could not have been contemplated. There had also for some time been British understanding as to the views of the Americans over western Europe and Germany after the Czech coup, if not in any specific way Berlin. And it does seem that persuasion of the Americans as to the British case for remaining in Berlin was seen by the British to be less difficult in 1948, at a time at which the world had divided into two ideological camps.

It is also true that beyond the initial phase Bevin's acquiescence in US policy over the sending of a note to Stalin and over referral to the UN was only after a long and tortuous process of attempted compromise, and US agreement that any referral would focus on Berlin rather than Germany as a whole and with the note delayed until 6 July, both of which were at Bevin's insistence.[147] Around the time of the Berlin Crisis there was then a sense of real British confidence in the relationship with the US and an understanding that Britain and the US had decided to resist the Soviets over Germany and the security of western Europe. Even so there seems to have been no initial certainty of US support for remaining in Berlin regardless of Soviet pressure, which was the position Bevin took in June 1948.

In fact British policy seems to have been less a function of that of the Americans than one might presume given the obvious asymmetry in power between the two nations. By this time the world was clearly divided between the US and the Soviet Union in terms of power, yet Shlaim points to US independence being 'circumscribed' in the Berlin Crisis by the fact that Britain and France were also occupying powers in Berlin,[148] and contrasts the influence of Britain and France – 'unlike Britain, however, France played a relatively passive role, exercising virtually no influence over American policy and providing little support for it'.[149] Bevin's position with the Americans was not one of influence as a result of British economic or military power, though there was the diplomatic utility of an ally in Europe that was profoundly anti-communist in nature. Yet Bevin himself may have exerted influence over the direction of Western policy by the immediacy and clarity of his reaction, the coherence of his diplomacy, and the force of his personality in dealing with US military personnel and politicians. This is evidenced by his effect on Draper and Wedemeyer prior to the formal US response over Berlin. And during the Berlin Crisis his relationship with Douglas was such that the latter, rather than being an advocate for American policy to Britain, became an apologist for British policy and for Bevin as an individual to Washington. Douglas' series of communiqués to Washington served to explain British reservation at difficult moments and provide assurance as to Bevin's absolute reliability.

The result was that policy and its timing were matters discussed between Bevin and Douglas (with obvious reference to their respective governments), with Bevin's displaying remarkable initiative, dynamism and clarity of expression of reservation while also being prepared to compromise to sustain the relationship and US support. Bullock says of Bevin, 'as the American documents make clear, he was the one man in office in Europe on whom the State Department felt they could rely'. But Bevin was no 'Yes-man'.[150] This meant that Bevin was able to influence American policy, and that British policy did not mirror an autonomous US policy over Berlin. Attlee's view was that Bevin's greatest achievement was 'standing up to the Americans',[151] and Bullock adds that no other political figure in western Europe did. Yet part of his ability was to do this without alienating them but rather commanding their respect and affection, and the record above indicates that Bevin sometimes prevailed and at others was forced to acquiesce in US desires, as in the futile referral of the Berlin Crisis to the UN and the sending of notes to Stalin.

Of Bevin's role at the start of the Berlin Crisis Shlaim notes—

'London moved with greater speed and decisiveness in making its basic choice to stay in Berlin, in announcing this decision and in asking the American Government to make a similar statement. Led by its forceful and staunchly anti-communist Foreign Secretary, Ernest Bevin, the British Cabinet quickly resolved to do everything possible to supply Berlin by air and to concert a common policy in this matter with the governments of the United States and France.'[152]

Though the evidence is that Bevin did exhibit remarkable dynamism in setting the context for the American and the French responses and in arranging concerted military and diplomatic liaison at the outset of the crisis, Shlaim indicates that Truman made his decision to remain in Berlin autonomously and in accordance with his own 'basic world-view' that there should be 'no surrender to a nation which flouted all the conventions of civilised international behaviour'. Harrington claims that Truman only ruled out 'immediate withdrawal' and left reconsideration of that decision in the light of ensuing events open, and that Marshall's statement of the US right and intention to remain in Berlin lacked Bevin's robust emphasis and did not preclude reconsideration of related issues or over remaining in Berlin.[153] Whatever is true of Truman's decision, the indication of US intent was enough for Bevin at the time. And in fact the context had been set by Bevin's public intention to resist Soviet brinkmanship over Berlin and would have been an influence on Truman's decision because to decline to follow Bevin's announcement that the British intended to remain in Berlin the US administration would have had to announce in public that the US was not prepared to support the US sector of Berlin even though Britain was to remain in Berlin, and would have had to have been prepared to be seen to abandon west Berliners who wanted to resist the Soviet Union and communism. And of course US abandonment of west Berlin would have violated the Truman Doctrine of containment, the deterrent value of which would have been negated.[154]

The disparities between the US and British political systems in decision-making processes and in experience of and confidence regarding European politics were apparent in the speed and certainty of response in the British case and the delay and diversity of policy preference apparent in the formulation of US policy. The decision to remain in Berlin was in the end Truman's, for the American military doubted the wisdom of enunciating a policy of remaining in Berlin at all costs, in that they doubted Berlin's defensibility if it came to war – this was of course their brief, and reflected a caution that was to continue.

There was a clear commonality between Britain and the US on the nature of Soviet intentions, the need to defend western Europe from communism and acceptance of the US role in 'western union'. Yet while the Berlin Crisis may not have occurred without these factors they did not on their own mean that Berlin would be defended. There was the alternative of abandoning a Berlin deemed to be indefensible and making a credible stand, one that could be sustained, over western Germany. The link that made defence of Berlin necessary was that Western resolve and trustworthiness were being challenged in Berlin, and that for Bevin and the FO if Berlin were to be abandoned 'western union' would be imperilled due to loss of confidence on the part of western Europeans in British and US resolve to stand firm. It is this perceptual link that was vital for Bevin and his resolution over Berlin. Yet the role of the Americans was seen to be indispensable.

Beyond all these predisposing factors are then Bevin's role, personality, perceptions, attitudes, relationships and influence in diplomatic, political and official circles. Bevin and his FO officials were agreed that it was very desirable that the West should stay in Berlin, but, unlike FO officials, who did consider the possibility of withdrawal[155] and the attractions of negotiation,[156] Bevin was clear throughout that remaining in Berlin was imperative to British credibility in Germany and our 'whole Western system' and should continue regardless of the pressure and risks – he also indicated his preference for silence and action rather than overtures and negotiation,[157] which he saw as undesirable as they would reopen the issue of Germany's future and convey weakness. And he displayed from the very outset a remarkable assurance as to what should be done regarding the blockade itself and an equally remarkable personal dynamism in inspiring confidence and getting things done. Bevin's insistence on an exhibition of Western power and capability and a disdaining of any policy that involved concessions elsewhere in Germany to resolve the Berlin Crisis reflected his sense that the Soviets understood above all power rather than the weakness implicit in endless negotiation, and Bevin's unhesitating response provided a moral and political context for all others and the standard against which all others would be compared.

Whether or not this was Bevin's purpose in enunciating the British intention prior to a public American indication of intent is a matter for conjecture. But it does seem that Bevin's insistence on rights and entitlements, his political will and resolve, and dynamism as to the means by which Berlin might be supplied, were vital in securing a firm Western policy over Berlin, for his commitment to remain in Berlin meant that Truman would have had to abandon Britain and Berliners in the US sector of west Berlin if he chose another policy. One does not know what US policy might have been without Bevin, but it seems that Bevin exerted some influence on Washington, and was effective in restricting, by making clear his opposition to communiqués as conveying weakness, overtures to Stalin to the minimum and to the Berlin Crisis, avoiding the wider issue of Germany.

Thereafter Bevin remained steady and persevering, giving no enduring indication of any weakening of resolve and every indication that no concessions would be made over Berlin or Germany as a whole, yet also avoiding any provocation that could escalate the crisis or preclude Soviet understanding that relenting over Berlin was possible without loss of face. As has been indicated, Bevin had come to accept that the Soviets responded well to power rather than expressions of rights and legalities, which they were prepared to abandon when inexpedient without shame. Bevin's policy over Berlin reflected his background in the trades-union movement and his tendency to relate diplomatic crises to his own experience rather than to conceptual frameworks.[158] British policy over the Berlin blockade reflected both Bevin's understanding of Soviet intentions and foreign policy and his older tendencies to permit time to elapse, to avoid open confrontation that might become irretrievable yet to display firmness on a case-by-case basis. It also reflected his understanding of the way in which different issues were related both in terms of the simultaneous pursuit of different policies, as in this case a west German state, US involvement in Europe and west European recovery, and the sense in which any weakness would result only in further brinkmanship as a matter of policy on the part of the Soviets in Europe. Bevin was then pivotal to policy over Berlin, not just in his reaction to the Soviets but also in his dealing with the Americans at the start of and during the crisis, the latter a remarkable achievement given Britain's relative weakness. US support was decisive, yet British diplomacy made a difference to Western policy over Berlin.

British policy in Europe had even in 1946 been predicated on US support against Soviet expansionism and diplomatic pressure. And since that time Soviet diplomacy had continued to alienate the Western allies, not least in attempts to forestall any western union or division of Germany. As has been seen, in 1947 the Truman Doctrine and the Marshall Plan confirmed much needed US diplomatic, military and economic support for western Europe. In an indication of British understanding of the reality of dependence upon the US, on 4 February 1948 Bevin told the CoS of the need for an immediate US response to any Soviet attack on western Europe, and on 27 July told the Defence Committee of the need to recognise the primacy of the US effort against the Soviet Union in any war.[159] These comments are indicative of Bevin's understanding of the need to persuade the US as to policy over Berlin and to compromise at times during the crisis, not least because Bevin understood that the decision to remain in Berlin did bear the risk of war, and of course the maintenance of what was needed for life in the western sectors of Berlin required US power.

There was also the causal contribution of the enduring legacy of Potsdam, which had left the four powers in a zoned Berlin. As Shlaim observes, the 'design for Germany, which presupposed trust and harmony on the part of the allies, was doomed to failure from the very beginning' in that it required 'unanimous agreement' to any decision on the part of allies in what had been, in the war, 'an alliance of necessity par excellence'.[160] For without Potsdam's unrealistic arrangements over Germany and over Berlin itself east-west conflict might have taken place somewhere else in the world. Potsdam made Germany and Berlin the central battleground in the emerging Cold War, and though Germany's position and history in Europe did make it vital to both sides Potsdam's four-power division of a Berlin that was an island in the Soviet zone made it a natural focal point of Soviet pressure on the West over Germany.

Conclusion

I have established that Bevin was unconstrained in the formulation of policy over 'western union' and Berlin by the Cabinet and by Attlee as PM. I have argued that this is attributable to a broad consensus as to Soviet expansionism, opportunism and ideological hostility to British social democracy and the need for Western resolution to resist them in Europe and elsewhere between Bevin and both Attlee as PM and the Cabinet by this time rather than to Bevin's imposing a policy over Berlin on ministerial colleagues who did not agree with its general orientation or purpose. For by 1948 events had made the sense of a need to resist the Soviets in Europe a common one throughout the political and official establishment, including even the once dissenting voices on the Labour backbenches in the Commons. It is possible though that there was some ministerial reservation and restraint as to its expression over tactics in the Berlin Crisis that should be attributed to Attlee's support for Bevin or to Bevin's personality and role as Foreign Secretary.

There was also a commonality of purpose and policy between Bevin and the FO over Berlin and its links to 'western union' in a relationship that seems to have been one of reciprocal influence, for both Bevin and the FO saw resistance over Berlin as essential to the preservation of 'western union'. Though it does seem that the FO came earlier than Bevin to the view that there could be no rapprochement reached with the Soviet Union because of Soviet ideological hostility Bevin even at that time was committed to a case-by-case firmness, and by the start of 1948 he had abandoned all hope of understanding predicated upon firmness and had developed western union to combat Soviet influence and communism in western Europe.

Over the course of the Berlin Crisis itself there are instances of FO difference of view from Bevin that indicate Bevin's dominance over foreign policy over Berlin and FO acceptance of it as entirely proper. Given the support of Cabinet ministers and Attlee as PM Bevin seems to have experienced something approaching autonomy over British policy in the Berlin Crisis. That of course meant that Bevin's personality and trades-union experience were major influences on British policy over Berlin and the respect and admiration the Americans had for him meant that he was an influence not just on British policy over Berlin but also in setting the context for US policy in the initial Western response to the crisis and in the relationship that ensued. As to factors that were preconditional to the Berlin Crisis, it was 'western union' that resulted in it, and 'western union' itself was a result of Bevin's abandoning hope of accord with the Soviets, which was attributable to continued adverse experience of Soviet diplomacy in form and content that represented evidence of Soviet ideological hostility and expansionism.

There are also questions as to less obvious causal influences, which, being indirect, are more difficult to evidence. FO influence on Bevin in its setting what Folly has referred to as 'the social context of debate' seems possible particularly at the time of Bevin's alteration of view as to the possibility of ultimate accord with the Soviet Union. That change of perception was what resulted in Bevin's sense of Soviet intentions in Europe being such that a western union was imperative to resist them and was what caused the Berlin Crisis as the Soviet reaction to exclusion from decisions made regarding the security of western Europe and western Germany. And there is also Attlee's possible influence in his private and unrecorded conversations with Bevin. Such influence cannot be established by direct documentary evidence, yet this does not mean that it did not obtain, which means that conclusions regarding causation of policy are in a crucial sense incomplete in being predicated on *available* evidence, with more speculative inferences relegated to the status of conjecture.

The nature of any conclusions is then tentative. Yet a judgement as to their relative influence compared to other causal factors has to be made. In the cases of possible indirect influence on Bevin from the FO and Attlee other factors militate against the notion of any decisive influence on Bevin. One was his broad commonality of view with both Attlee and the FO, which by 1948 had obtained for some time. Another is Bevin's tendency to arrive at his own conclusions in private ruminations and the wealth of personal accounts that evidence Bevin's not being susceptible to manipulation, his remarkable and continuing autonomy of view, and his confidence in his own deliberations and policy.

Further, if anything the time dimension points to an increasing ascendancy of Bevin over FO officials as his diplomatic experience became more extensive, as is apparent in the tenor of Strang's and Kirkpatrick's minutes, which clearly acknowledge that decisions were Bevin's province, a demarcation of roles and responsibilities Bevin insisted upon – Bevin pursued a policy of no withdrawal and no overtures throughout, despite Strang's and Kirkpatrick's wondering if Berlin could be held. Such dominance from Bevin over the FO during the course of the Berlin Crisis does not of course preclude FO influence on Bevin before 1948, in the abandonment of any hope of accord with the Soviet Union over Europe or Germany. Attlee seems between 1946 and 1948 to have receded yet further from foreign policy, and the agreement between Attlee and Bevin seems attributable to common conclusions as to Soviet intentions rather than to Attlee's discretion or restraint.

The Berlin Crisis demonstrates the influence of the individual in a context of structural factors of seemingly overwhelming power. For it should have been a matter of American power against Soviet encroachment in Europe. The fact that Britain exerted any influence at all was attributable to British diplomatic experience, US uncertainty and the reality of four-power control of Berlin, but also to Bevin's extraordinary personality and interrelationships. For it was British policy, which represented a consensus between Bevin and the FO, that provided the initial public indication of intention to remain in Berlin and Bevin who thereafter remained unaffected in his resolve not to withdraw or make any concessions over Berlin or elsewhere in Germany or Europe.

For the Berlin Crisis for Bevin had implications for Western credibility, for the rest of Germany and western Europe, and the involvement in Europe of the US. These connections were made by Bevin and informed his policy over Berlin. And there was, given Bevin's tendency to relate issues to his own experience rather than to conceptual frameworks, a clear analogy between his prosecution of the Berlin Crisis and the conduct of a trades-union dispute, which makes his trades-union background of causal significance to policy over Berlin. Yet many background factors existed in the British political and official establishment in 1948 as necessary conditions for British policy as it transpired over Berlin.

There was an antipathy towards communism and Soviet diplomacy, an ethos of Britain as a major European power and a sense that accord with the Soviets was not going to be possible given Soviet ideological hostility, expansionism and opportunism. This combination of factors resulted in Bevin's 'western union', which sought to develop and defend western Europe against communism and which was the cause of the Berlin Crisis. And given Britain's economic and military weakness the congruence between British and US policy in terms of resisting communism and the Soviets in

Europe was also necessary to British policy as it evolved – in fact a western European association seems to have been a precondition stipulated by Marshall for US support, and US support in the policy formulation period and in the crisis itself was seen as indispensable.

The Berlin Crisis does illustrate the difficulties of assessing causation in conditions in which there is so much commonality of view not just regarding general orientation but also specific policy regarding western Europe. This commonality obtained between the FO, Bevin, Attlee, the Cabinet and even the Commons by the start of 1948 and continued during the crisis itself. And it does seem that the commonality over the defence of the western zones of Germany and Berlin was genuine and does not reflect the working of discreet influence.

A similar commonality of view and of purpose existed between Britain and the US over Germany, western Europe and Berlin. Between both Bevin and the FO, and Britain and the US, differences of view were regarding possibilities and tactics rather than desiderata and aims. Yet there were a sufficient number of occasions on which Bevin differed with the FO (over Strang's considering ultimate withdrawal and the negotiation advocated by Kirkpatrick) and the US (over the sending of notes to Stalin and reference to the CFMs and the UN) to demonstrate Bevin's ultimate ascendancy over the FO and his reliance yet also his influence on the US – Bevin's influence on the US is apparent in the search for compromise over the note to Stalin in early July 1948, its confining itself to the Berlin issue and its delay, and in Bevin's prevailing over US wishes later on, in his opposition to insistence on notional rights and focus on removal of Soviet interference with western traffic to and from Berlin. And of course Soviet policy not just over Berlin but also over Germany since the war was a decisive influence, without which the crisis would not have occurred, for their diplomatic practices had resulted in the British loss of hope of accord and resorting to 'western union', and it was their policy of using Berlin to reopen the issue of Germany that resulted in the crisis itself. The latter in turn, as it was based on interpretations of Western intent in Europe and Germany, reflected the Soviet perceptual lens and Western actions in Europe in 1948.

'Western union' was then a cause of the Soviet blockade. Yet beyond it exist others that continued to be necessary background conditions but were alone insufficient to explain British policy formulation and implementation over the Berlin Crisis. These factors served an objective function in causation, for without them no crisis might have occurred in the first place, as was the case with 'western union' itself. But they also had a subjective function, as part of an emerging lens through which Soviet pressure on Berlin was anticipated, a policy of resistance to leaving Berlin and to any concessions was devised, and the escalating crisis was seen.

The attitudinal lens was critical. Britain's right to a major role in Europe (as a world power) was an accepted premise in British official and political circles, as was the anti-communism and anti-Sovietism that had endured during the wartime alliance but had been subordinated to pragmatic considerations concerned with optimising the war effort. The FO had since 1946 gone further and abandoned hope for accord with the Soviets based on their ideological hostility to social democracy, and by the start of 1948 this had been accepted by Bevin, Attlee and the Cabinet. These factors were then preconditional to Bevin's idea of a 'western union', which proposed to link western Europe in political and economic development to resist the spread westwards of communism and involve the Americans in Europe's defence. This meant the open abandonment of the charade of observance of Potsdam and resulted in a direct way in Soviet pressure on Berlin. Thereafter Berlin became seen by Bevin as a trial of Western resolve and credibility indispensable to 'western union'.

Another way of conceptualising the causation of British policy over the Berlin Crisis of 1948–49 is to differentiate contextual causal factors from more immediate causal influences and to differentiate objective from subjective causal influences. Contextually there was of course the post-war emergence of undisguised Soviet hostility to British social democracy and Soviet expansionism, opportunism and diplomatic intransigence over the future of Germany, Europe in general and elsewhere. And there was British economic and military weakness relative to Soviet and American power in the post-war world and the accompanying reality of imperial overstretch, the difficulty of defending the empire as a result of lack of economic and military power.

The British reaction to these objective conditions was to begin with to opt for reliance on a renewed US loan to sustain domestic spending and that on the defence of the empire, a policy that reflected an ethos in that part of the British political and official establishment involved in foreign policy formulation as a consequence of their roles in the Cabinet, FO or CoS, of Britain as a world, European and imperial power whose existing interests were to be defended. Though some Labour MPs on the left of the Party advocated a policy of withdrawal from empire (on ideological rather than economic grounds), the voting arithmetic of the Commons and its being outside the locus of foreign policy decision-making meant that it exerted no influence on British foreign policy under the Labour government of 1945.

The ethos of Britain as a world, imperial and European power was one part of the attitudinal prism of the Labour government that defined its foreign-policy objectives. Another part of that attitudinal prism was a commitment to the defence of social democracy against Soviet and communist hostility and expansionism in Germany and western Europe that reflected both commitment to the preservation of British social democracy against threats to its security and the pervasive anti-communism and anti-Sovietism of the British Cabinet, not least that of Attlee as PM and Bevin as Foreign Secretary, of the FO and of the CoS, all of whom also believed by 1948 that western Europe had to be defended against Soviet communist influence to maintain the security of the British Isles. The mismatch between such an ethos and such ideological objectives in British foreign policy and much diminished relative British economic and military power was resolved by the Atlantic alliance, under which the US provided economic, diplomatic and military support for Britain against Soviet expansionism in Europe in a US foreign policy that became the Truman Doctrine of containment of communism.

Even with such a combination of objective, attitudinal and perceptual factors as a context it did not follow that Britain and the US would be prepared to stand firm against Soviet pressure to withdraw from Berlin or to reopen discussions regarding the future of Germany to be permitted to remain in Berlin in 1948, an objective consideration for Western policymakers in early 1948. As has been seen, objective factors were influential on policy because of their interaction with the attitudes and objectives of those in positions of influence on foreign policy. As has been noted, these were in particular Attlee as PM, Bevin as Foreign Secretary, the Cabinet, the FO and the CoS. The dominant influence on British foreign policy within this locus of foreign policy decision-making derived from the respective personalities, relationships and conceptualisations of role.

Bevin was the dominant influence on British foreign policy towards the Soviet Union following diplomatic experience of Soviet expansionism and ideological hostility towards British social democracy after the war and on British policy over Berlin in 1948. One explanation for Bevin's apparent dominance over foreign policy was Attlee's conceptualisation of the role of premier as chairman. That was of course very unlike that of his interventionist predecessors, who wished to dominate foreign policy and felt entitled to do so. Such Prime Ministerial restraint was combined with Bevin's frequent references to Attlee to ensure his agreement and support and their commonality of view over policy towards the Soviet Union and communism and the need to show resolution and avoid concessions or appeasement to contain Soviet expansionism. In foreign policy decision-making in the British system the relationship between the PM, with all the powers and prerogatives of that office, and the Foreign Secretary, whose job it ostensibly is to formulate and implement foreign policy, is a major influence on the extent of influence of both the PM and the

Foreign Secretary on foreign policy, as the contrast between Chamberlain and Eden or Halifax, and Churchill and Eden, both cases of Prime Ministerial dominance over foreign policy (if in Chamberlain's case only for a period), and Attlee and Bevin, indicates.

In addition to Attlee's conceptualisation of the role of premier there was the personal warmth, trust and loyalty that existed between Attlee and Bevin, demonstrated in Bevin's support for Attlee when there were challenges to his leadership of the Labour Party and premiership and commented upon by Attlee when remembering the post-war Labour government. The commonality of attitude and objective between Attlee and Bevin was by 1948 shared by the Cabinet and the FO in a common understanding that Soviet influence and expansionism represented a threat that had to be resisted. Bevin's personal ascendancy over foreign policy over Berlin in 1948 could also have reflected to some extent the control over information the Foreign Secretary has, with other Cabinet ministers being briefed by the Foreign Secretary, and Bevin's robust and direct personality, his grasp of his brief, his stature in the Labour movement and Party (not least the support Bevin had from his union power base), and the fact that other ministers were engaged in a radical welfare programme.

The consequence was that it was Bevin's attributes and experience that dictated British policy over Berlin. Bevin's western union was the consequence of his perception of a need for western Europe to combat Soviet influence and his policy over Berlin followed from his sense that it had to be an exemplification of Western resolve to protect western union and to enhance Western prestige amongst Germans, that the Soviet Union would not wish to go to war over Berlin, that their behaviour was intended to expel the Western powers by means short of war, and that US support for a stand of remaining in Berlin was assured.

As to tactics, Bevin seems to have referred to his trades-union background for his conduct of the crisis by means of avoidance of any indication of weakness through an apparent need for communication and of any provocation that would make a Soviet withdrawal from a policy of isolating west Berlin difficult in terms of propaganda in the Cold War, another very individual causal factor. And Bevin's influence on the Americans before and over the Berlin Crisis reflected Bevin's resolute and coherent approach to Soviet influence and communism, its expansionism and opportunism, and its ideological objective, Bevin's grasp of foreign policy and straightforwardness, all of which made him admired and trusted by US politicians and diplomats.

The preceding paragraphs indicate an assessment of the causation of foreign policy that begins with the locus of foreign-policy decision-making power that defines who is involved in or influential on foreign policy formulation. That locus is of course a function of the institutional framework of government and its modes of decision-making in regard to foreign policy – the difference between British Cabinet government and the more diffuse American system is indicative of the effect of political system on the identification of those involved in foreign-policy decision-making.

The extent of influence on foreign policy of such identified individuals is affected by their respective roles and by their personal attributes, including their conceptualisation of role and prerogatives, extent of interest in and sense of personal competence in regard to foreign policy, their personalities and their relationships with others within and outside the locus of foreign-policy decision-making. That establishes who exerted influence on foreign policy and explains why such individuals had such influence. The nature of the influence such individuals bring to bear on foreign policy reflects personal attitudes that define foreign-policy objectives and influence perceptions regarding the intentions of other nations and the most plausible outcomes of alternative foreign policies. External factors such as the Soviet Union and the US, and British economic and military weakness, became influences on British foreign policy over Berlin through the prisms of the attitudes, preconceptions and perceptions of those involved in foreign policy as a result of their role in government.

The Berlin Crisis was the final outcome of a long process of adjustment of British foreign policy to the reality of British economic and military decline relative initially to Germany and thereafter to the US and the Soviet Union in a context of a continuing ethos of Britain as a world, European and imperial power of the first rank and of commitment to defend its traditional European interest in the avoidance of the domination of the continent of Europe by any major power on security grounds. Initially, before the war, the variant of appeasement pursued by Chamberlain sustained the delusion that negotiation with Hitler and a rapprochement consistent with Britain's traditional European interests were possible despite Britain's relative economic and military weakness and despite too Chamberlain's having advertised his desire for the avoidance of a European war through concessions to German aspirations. That delusional interlude was of course brief and resulted in a guarantee of Poland's independence when Hitler violated the undertakings he had given Chamberlain at Munich in invading what was left of Czechoslovakia in March 1939.

The guarantee to Poland represented a form of deterrence that was not a credible threat given British economic and military weakness and the record of Chamberlain's appeasement. It was an undertaking to the Poles that could not be met and was not met when Hitler disregarded the British threat of war and invaded Poland. Chamberlain could have compensated for British economic and military weakness with cultivation of alliances. He did not because of his conviction that alliances would serve to provoke rather than deter Hitler. He could also have accelerated rearmament and concentrated less on rearmament that was entirely defensive in nature, for defensive rearmament hardly enhanced the notion of credible threat.

There followed the wartime period in which the wartime alliance and the resistance and then victories of the Red Army on the eastern front were vital to the defeat of Nazi Germany, an interlude of British understanding of the need for and extent of Soviet power during the war and its being the major land power in Europe after the war. Soviet hostility on ideological grounds to Britain and British social democracy and expansionism and opportunism were combined in the immediate post-war period with British need for a US loan to pursue the welfare state and to defend the empire and then understanding of the need for US diplomatic and military support against Soviet communism and its expansionism and opportunistic tactics.

The future of Germany represented the central theatre of the emerging Cold War, and the Berlin Crisis was an exemplification of British need for the US in any defiance of Soviet expansionism in Europe. The extent of such dependence on American power meant that British foreign policy was thereafter to have to defer to that of the US for approval and support and was constrained by US demands, as was so over Korea just a few years after the Berlin Crisis.

The Berlin Crisis indicated that the British interest in the defence of western Europe could not be pursued without US commitment to the defence of western Europe in NATO and so meant that British foreign policy was compelled to follow that of the US where the US insisted upon it and threatened withdrawal of support for sterling or from NATO. Though foreign policy decisions reflect the attitudinal prism and lens of perception of those whose positions in the political and official establishment involve them in foreign policy decisions, especially the PM, the Foreign Secretary and the Cabinet and FO, and so may be delusional or mistaken and not reflective of the external circumstances and their dictates in any direct way, such policy errors do not endure over long periods of time as such errors are punished, as was so with Chamberlain's foreign policy.

Thereafter the war and the post-war period in the late 1940s necessitated the cultivation of alliances to win the war and to permit Britain to remain a world power after the war and to ensure its security from Soviet expansionism and opportunism and from communism. The need for US military support in the Berlin Crisis in 1948 and 1949 confirmed British dependence for security and world-power status on the US, and the need for the US in any foreign-policy initiative aimed at resisting Soviet expansionism and opportunism. In another sense too the Berlin Crisis was part of the drift into the Cold War, for there was a genuine difference between notional or diplomatic US support for the defence of western Europe in the form of the Truman Doctrine of 1947, intended as a deterrent to Soviet expansionism and opportunism anywhere in the world, and even the Marshall Plan of the same year, and defiance of the Soviet blockade of west Berlin in practice. For Western resolve to remain in Berlin was a matter of judgment and had attendant risks that were difficult to assess with any confidence because of the ambiguities of Soviet diplomacy and Western experience of them, and there was the enormous cost of the Berlin Airlift given its continuance over a long period of time.

The Berlin Crisis really was an exhibition of Western resolve to contain communism and Soviet expansionism and opportunism even when the risks and costs were obvious. British doubts regarding the worth of the relationship with the US and the extent to which the US could be depended upon when not actually directly threatened or at war, exacerbated by Roosevelt's stated intention to withdraw US troops from Europe after the war, must then have been dispelled by the US commitment over Berlin in 1948 and 1949. And of course Berlin represents the last instance of British influence on US policy because after that commitment to the containment of Soviet influence and communism became the informing principle of US foreign policy, US inexperience of European politics had been replaced by experience, and there was no one of Bevin's stature and personality to influence the US.

Notes

[1] A focus on British reaction to Soviet interference with western traffic to west Berlin at the start of April 1948 or after 24 June 1948, when the blockade became complete, disregards the fact that the perceptions on which policy was predicated had a history of their own. For pressure on Berlin consequent on Bevin's plans for western Europe at the London Conference was expected, and the decision to stay in Berlin made much earlier, in March 1948.

[2] Examples are Morris, E., *Blockade, Berlin and the Cold war*, Hamish Hamilton, London, 1973, and Davison, W. Phillips, *The Berlin Blockade, A Study in Cold War Politics*, Princeton University Press, Princeton, 1958.

[3] For a revisionist account and the triumph of the Riga over the Yalta axioms see Yergin, D., *Shattered Peace, The Origins of the Cold War and the National Security State*, Andre Deutsch, London, 1977, pages 370–75 and 383–85. See also Kolko, J. and G., *The Limits of Power, The World and United States Foreign Policy, 1945–1954*, Harper and Row, New York, 1972, pages 488–97 for reference to US intention to 'rebuild a capitalist Germany'. Neither of these works accords Britain a real role in the crisis, presuming lack of influence from economic weakness but also pointing to Bevin's desire to avoid war while not mentioning his policy over Berlin.

[4] See Shlaim, A., *The United States and the Berlin Blockade, 1948–1949: A Study in Crisis Decision-making*, University of California Press, London, 1983.

[5] Powaski, Ronald E., *The Cold War: The United States and the Soviet Union, 1917–1991*, OUP, 1997, page 70.

[6] Though Bevin and Kennan and his 'Long Telegram' of 22 February 1946 seem to have influenced US policy and Frank Roberts of the British Embassy in the Soviet Union seems to have influenced Bevin and British policy, both Kennan and Roberts seem influential because their views were very much consonant with those in Washington and London respectively at the time.

[7] Boettcher, William A., *Presidential Risk Behavior In Foreign Policy. Prudence Or Peril*, Palgrave Macmillan, 2005, page 74. The reference to 'everywhere' seems to be to other British withdrawals, from India, Burma, Egypt and Palestine, and the quotation seems to have been in a context of Acheson's belief that each country that fell to communism would result in another country becoming communist. Such comments from Acheson seem to be an early example of what became known as domino theory.

[8] Deighton, Anne, *The Impossible Peace: Britain, the Division of Germany and the Origins of the Cold War*, Clarendon Press, 1990, page 162.

[9]Sirimarco, Elizabeth, *The Cold War*, Marshall Cavendish, 2005, page 15, quoting Marshall's speech at Harvard on 5 June 1947.

[10]Deighton, Anne, *The Impossible Peace*, page 188.

[11]Tusa, A. and Tusa, J., *The Berlin Airlift*, Atheneum, 1988, page 87.

[12]Gladwyn, Lord, *The Memoirs of Lord Gladwyn*, London: Weidenfeld and Nicolson, 1972, page 208.

[13]Ibid., page 209.

[14]Greenwood, S., *Britain and the Cold War, 1945–91*, Palgrave Macmillan, 1999, pages 53–54.

[15]CAB 129/23, C.P. (48) 6, The First Aim of British Policy, 4 January 1948.

[16]Ibid.

[17]Ibid.

[18]Ibid.

[19]CAB 123/23, C.P. (48) 8, Future Foreign Policy Publicity, 4 January 1948.

[20]CAB 129/23, C.P. (48) 7, Review of Soviet Policy, 5 January 1948.

[21]CAB 129/23, C.P. (48) 5, Policy in Germany, 5 January 1948.

[22]CAB 128/12, CM 2 (48), 8 January 1948.

[23]Northedge, F. S., *Descent From Power, British Foreign policy, 1945–1973*, Allen and Unwin, 1974, page 87.

[24]FO 371/70489, Berlin Prospects, undated memorandum by Robertson.

[25]FO 371/70489, Strang to Bevin, The Future of Berlin, 24 February 1948.

[26]CAB 129/23, C.P. (48) 5, Policy in Germany, 5 January 1948.

[27]See CAB 129/23, C.P. (48) 7, 5 January 1948.

[28]See Hennessy, Peter, *The Prime Minister: The Office and Its Holders Since 1945*, Palgrave Macmillan, 2001, pages 166 and 167.

[29]DEFE 4/14, CoS Committee (48), 96th Meeting, 9 July 1948.

[30]See Cornish, Paul, *British Military Planning for the Defence of Germany, 1945–1950*, Springer, 1995, pages 121 and 122, and Grogin, Robert R., *Natural Enemies: The United States and the Soviet Union in the Cold War*, Lexington Books, 2001, page 151.

[31]CAB 129/23, C.P. (48) 5, Policy in Germany, 5 January 1948.

[32]Tusa and Tusa, *The Berlin Airlift*, op. cit., page 88.

[33]See Shlaim, *The United States and the Berlin Blockade*, op. cit., page 34.

[34]FO 371/70490, Kirkpatrick to Robertson, 24 March 1948.

[35]Hansard, 1947–1948, No. 446, 5th Series, HMSO, 'Foreign Affairs', pages 348–409.

[36]CAB 128/12, CM 27 (48), 8 April 1948.

[37]See for instance FO 371/71670, Bevin to Inverchapel, Ambassador to the US, 29 April 1948. See also FRUS, 1948, Volume IV, Eastern Europe. The Soviet Union, Document 561, 30 April 1948, Inverchapel to Secretary of State.

[38]HC, 4 May 1948.

[39]FO 800/467/GER/48/17, Bevin to Attlee, 5 May 1948.

[40]Bullock, Alan, *Ernest Bevin, Foreign Secretary, 1945–1951*, Heinemann, 1983, page 549.

[41]FO 371/70490, Robertson to Foreign Office, 31 March 1948.

[42]FO 371/70492, Meeting in Sir W. Strang's room, 23 April 1948.

[43]FO 371/70492, Strang to Bevin, 24 April 1948.

[44]FO 371/70492, Strang minute on 'Situation in Berlin', 28 April 1948.

[45]FO 371/70492, Pakenham to Secretary of State, 28 April 1948.

[46]FO 371/70492, Bevin to Inverchapel, 29 April 1948.

[47]FO 800/467, Bevin to Attlee, 16 June 1948.

[48]See CAB 128/13, CM 42 (48), 24 June 1948.

[49]See CAB 130/38, GEN 24/1st Meeting, cited in Becker, Josef, and Knipping, Franz, *Great Britain, France, Italy and Germany in a Postwar World, 1945–50*, Walter de Gruyter, 1986, page 29.

[50]See CAB 128/13, CM 43 (48), 25 June 1948.

[51]See Harrington, Daniel F., *Berlin on the Brink: The Blockade, the Airlift, and the Early Cold War*, University Press of Kentucky, 2012, page 79.

[52]FO 371/70497, Bevin to Franks, 25 June 1948.

[53]Ibid.

[54]FO 371/70497, Bevin to Franks, 26 June 1948.

[55]Bullock, Bevin, op. cit., page 576.

[56]FO 371/70497, Bevin to Franks, 28 June 1948.

[57]FO 371/70499/, Minute by Roberts, 29 June 1948.

[58]Tusa and Tusa, *The Berlin Airlift*, op. cit., page 155.

[59]See CAB 128/13, CM 44 (48), 28 June 1948.

[60]FO 371/70497, Bevin to Franks, 28 June 1948.

[61]FO 371/ 70498, conversation between Bevin and Attlee, 30 June 1948.

[62]HC, 30 June 1948.

[63]See Hennessy, *The Prime Minister*, op. cit., page 109 and Hennessy, Peter, *Never Again: Britain, 1945–1950*, Penguin UK, 2006, page cccxxxii, for reference to GEN 241, the Cabinet Committee on Germany that met to control the British response to the Soviet blockade between June and September 1948. And see FO 371/70498 for its meeting on 28 June 1948.

[64]Barker, Elisabeth, *The British between the Superpowers, 1945–50*, Springer, 1983, page 122.

[65]See Shlaim, *The United States and the Berlin Blockade*, op. cit., pages 223, 224 and 226.

[66]Shlaim, *The United States and the Berlin Blockade*, op. cit., page 209.

[67]Ibid., page 193.

[68]FO 371/70501(?), memorandum by Robertson, 25 May 1948, and Bevin's response, 9 June 1948.

[69]FO 371/70499, Roberts minute of a conversation between Attlee and Bevin, 30 June 1948.

[70]Ibid.

[71]Ibid.

[72]FO 371/ 70500, Strang to Bevin, 30 June 1948.

[73]FO 371/70499, Strang minute of Bevin's meeting with Attlee on 2 July 1948.

[74]See Shlaim, *The United States and the Berlin Blockade*, op. cit., page 231.

[75]See FO 371/70503, Bevin to Franks on conversation with Douglas, 22 July 1948, and FO 371/70505/C6250, minute of meeting on 26 July 1948. See FO 371/70504, Bevin to Franks, 26 July 1948, for what Bevin told Bohlen and for Bevin's insistence on remaining in Berlin regardless of circumstances, cited in Harrington, *Berlin on the Brink*, op. cit., page 149. And see Grob-Fitzgibbon, Benjamin, *Continental Drift*, Cambridge University Press, 2016, pages 89, 90, and 495 for reference to Documents on British Policy Overseas, Series 3, Volume VI, Document Number 80, Record of Conversation between Bevin and Douglas, 22 July 1948, and Document Number 82 for the Record of a Conversation between Bevin and Douglas on 26 July 1948.

[76]See Marshall, George Catlett, and Stevens, Sharon Ritenour, *The Papers of George Catlett Marshall: The Whole World hangs in the Balance*, JHU Press, 1981, page 509.

[77]See Foreign Relations of the United States (FRUS), 1948, V II, Germany and Austria, Document 587, Douglas to Secretary of State, 24 July 1948.

[78]See Bullock, *Ernest Bevin*, op. cit., page 589, and Bullock, *Ernest Bevin, Foreign Secretary, 1945–1951*, 1985 edition for reference on pages 589 and 590 to the quotation's being from FO 800/502/SU/48/8, Bevin to Attlee, 28 July 1948.

[79]FO 371/70505, Bevin to Moscow, 3 and 4/8/48, and Roberts to Strang.

[80]See Ovendale, Ritchie, *The Foreign Policy of the British Labour Governments, 1945–1951*, Leicester: Leicester University Press, 1984, page 30.

[81]FO 371/70508, Bevin to Moscow, 18/8/48.

[82]See Shlaim, *The United States and the Berlin Blockade*, op. cit., pages 339 and 342.

[83]Bullock, Bevin, op. cit., page 603.

[84]*The Times*, 23 September 1948.

[85]FO 371/70509, FO minute dated 11 August 1948.

[86]See FO 371/70509, Cadogan to Strang, 16 August 1948, for his scathing view of the UN and the Soviets.

[87]Ibid., meeting of Bevin and Marshall, 4 October 1948.

[88]Bullock, Bevin, op. cit., page 608, and FO 800/502/SU/48/44.

[89]Tusa and Tusa, *The Berlin Airlift*, op. cit., page 287.

[90]Ibid., page 302, and FO 371/76541, Bevin to Berlin, 24 January 1949.

[91]Ibid., page 329, and CAB 130/38, 241/4, Memorandum for the Committee on Germany, 4 February 1949.

[92]FO 371/76577, Bevin to Strang, 1 April 1949.

[93]Barker, Elisabeth, *The British Between The Superpowers, 1945–50*, Macmillan, London, 1983, page 176.

[94]See Field, Frank (ed.), *Attlee's Great Contemporaries: The Politics of Character*, Bloomsbury Publishing, 2009, pages lii, liii and 117, for Attlee's reference to his reciprocated fondness for Bevin and for repeated references to Bevin's loyalty, not least in 1948, when in response to a suggestion from members of the government that Attlee should resign Attlee recalled that Bevin had said he would go if Attlee resigned and that he should remain as PM.

[95]Burridge, Trevor, *Clement Attlee: A Political Biography*, London: Jonathan Cape, 1985, page 233.

[96]Harris, Kenneth, *Attlee*, London: Weidenfeld and Nicolson, 1982, page 313.

[97]See Phythian, Mark, *The Labour Party, War and International Relations, 1945–2006*, Routledge, 2007, page 24 for that reference to Dalton's left wing credentials.

[98]See Gordon, Michael R., *Conflict and Consensus in Labour's Foreign Policy, 1914–1965*, Stanford University Press, 1969, page 124.

[99]FO 800/EUR/48/26, Bevin's talk with Attlee, 19 June 1948.

[100]Bullock, Bevin, op. cit., page 555.

[101]Ibid., page 390.

[102]Barker, op. cit., page 121.

[103]FO 371/70492/C3579 – Strang to Secretary of State, 28 April 1948, and Shlaim, *The United States and the Berlin Blockade*, op. cit., pages 140–1.

[104]Strang, op. cit., page 288.

[105]Bullock, Bevin, op. cit., page 83.

[106]For examples see CAB 128/12, C.M. 21 (48), 11 March 1948, and C.M. 27 (48), 8 April 1948.

[107]See CAB 128/13, C.M. 34 (48), 31 May 1948, C.M. 36 (48), 7 June 1948, and 37 (48), 8 June 1948.

[108]CAB 128/13, C.M. 42 (48), 24 June 1948.

[109]CAB 128/13, C.M. 43 (48), 25 June 1948.

[110]CAB 128/13, C.M 44 (48), 28 June 1948.

[111]CAB 128/13, C.M. 46 (48), 1 July 1948.

[112]CAB 128/13, C.M. 53 (48), 22 July 1948.

[113]CAB 128/13, C.M. 54 (48), 26 July 1948.

[114]CAB 128/13, C.M. 59 (48), 10 September 1948.

[115]CAB 128/13, C.M. 61 (48), 22 September 1948.

[116]Blackwell, Michael, *Clinging to Grandeur*, Westport: Greenwood Press, 1993, page 14.

[117]See Saville, John, *The Politics of Continuity*, Verso, 1993, for the general argument that Bevin's policies represented continuity with those of his Conservative predecessor and that he had no idea of what a socialist foreign policy should be, and see page 6 for Harvey's comment on 11 November 1941 that the Labour leaders who were in the Cabinet were more anti-Soviet than Eden himself was, a reference it seems to Attlee and Bevin. See page 93 for reference to Eden's support for Bevin's foreign policy and comment that there had never been an occasion of difference between them in the wartime Cabinet over foreign policy in the Commons on 20 August 1945.

[118]See Becker and Knipping, *Great Britain*, op. cit., page 11. The comments from Cadogan seem to have

been made on 10 August 1945, before any time for FO influence. The Labour victory in the General Election had been as recent as 26 July 1945.

[119]FO 371/ 70490, Strang to Bevin, 18 March 1948.

[120]Ibid.

[121]In fact many of the personal accounts that support the inference of there having been a relationship of reciprocal influence between Bevin and the FO are concerned with this period rather than earlier. This is true of Roberts, Kirkpatrick, Franks, and Barclay.

[122]CAB 128/11, CM(48)2, CAB 129/23, CP (48) 8, 8 January 1948.

[123]Greenwood, *Britain and the Cold War*, op. cit., page 53.

[124]FO 800/467/GER/48/17, Bevin to Attlee, 5 May 1948.

[125]FO 371/70491, Minute by Sargent, 13 April 1948.

[126]Ibid.

[127]Barker, op. cit., page 123.

[128]FO 371/70497, minute of 25 June 1948.

[129]See Bullock, *Bevin*, op. cit., page 100.

[130]FO 371/70497, Kirkpatrick minute, 25 June 1948.

[131]FO 371/70498, Kirkpatrick to Harvey, 28 June 1948.

[132]Ibid.

[133]See Bullock, *Bevin*, op. cit., page 100.

[134]Strang, Baron William, *Home and Abroad*, Deutsch, 1956, pages 288, 292–93.

[135]Ibid., page 288.

[136]FO 371/70492, meeting in Sir W. Strang's room, 23 April 1948.

[137]FO 371/70492, Strang to Bevin, 24 April 1948.

[138]FO 371/70492, Record of lunch at the Foreign Office between Bevin, Strang, Robertson, Douglas and Clay, 28 April 1948, cited in Tusa and Tusa, *The Berlin Airlift*, op. cit., page 119.

[139]FO 800/467/GER/48/17, Bevin to Attlee, 5 May 1948. The context is interesting, for in April Churchill had advocated the use of the West's atomic advantage to expel the Soviets from Berlin and eastern Germany, claiming they understood only force. Bevin may have concurred with the latter, but his sense was of a judicious use of power by demonstration of resolution, of resistance and no concessions, without provocation over Berlin rather than overt threat.

[140]HC, 4 May 1948.

[141]FO 371/70490, Strang to Bevin, 18 March 1948.

[142]FO 371/70491, minute of a conversation between Bevin and Bidault, 17 April 1948.

[143]FO 371/ 70492, Bevin to Inverchapel, 29 April 1948.

[144]See Tusa and Tusa, *The Berlin Airlift*, op. cit., page 155 for the view that the British perception was that US support was assured. Yet see Shlaim, *The United States and the Berlin Blockade*, op. cit., pages 111–12, who claims that 'the nature of the U.S. commitment to remain in Berlin emerged during the crisis itself and emerged very slowly.' There would seem to be a difference here between the actual and perceptual situation faced by Bevin, in that US policy had not been decided but Bevin had had private assurances from Douglas as to US support over Berlin.

[145]FO 371/70497, Bevin meeting, 25 June 1948.

[146]Ibid.

[147]See FO 371/70499, Bevin to Franks, 2 July 1948 – No. 950, and FO 371/70500, Bevin to Franks, 2 July 1948 – No. 964, FO 371/70500, minute of meeting between Strang, Massigli and Douglas, 3 July 1948, and FO 371/70500, Bevin to Franks, 3 July 1948, No. 965.

[148]Shlaim, *The United States and the Berlin Blockade*, op. cit., page 37.

[149]Ibid., page 198.

[150]Bullock, *Bevin*, op. cit., page 437.

[151]Ibid., page 416.

[152]Shlaim, *The United States and the Berlin Blockade*, op. cit., page 198, and C.M. (48) 43rd Conclusions,

Minute 3, 25 June 1948, and C.M. (48) 44th Conclusions, Minute 4, 28 June 1948.

[153]See Harrington, *Berlin on the Brink*, op. cit., pages 89 and 92.

[154]See Shlaim, *The United States and the Berlin Blockade*, op. cit., page 222 for the inference that Truman's decision to remain in Berlin reflected Truman's own predisposition regarding international behaviour rather than military advice.

[155]FO 371/70492, Strang minute on 'Situation in Berlin', 28 April 1948.

[156]FO 371/70497, Kirkpatrick minute, 25 June 1948.

[157]FO 371/70498, Kirkpatrick to Harvey, 28 June 1948.

[158]Bullock, *Bevin*, op. cit., page 83.

[159]See DEFE 4/10, CoS (48), 18th Meeting, 4 February 1948, and CAB 131/5, Cabinet Defence Committee, DO (48), 13th Meeting, 27 July 1948.

[160]Shlaim, *The United States and the Berlin Blockade*, op. cit., page 15.

Chapter Five

Eden and Suez

Introduction

THERE IS A very considerable literature on the Suez Crisis of 1956 from various viewpoints, its antecedents, its significance in twentieth-century British foreign policy and British post-war decline and its consequences for the British role in the world, the nature of the relationship with the US, and British international credibility and prestige.[1] There is also a smaller historiography on British foreign policy decision-making during the Suez Crisis.[2] That is the object of interest here, especially the role of Eden as PM in a context of his previous involvement in British foreign policy in the appeasement period, during the war, and after its end.

There does seem to be a historiographical consensus regarding Eden, his intentions, attitudes, competence as diplomat rather than statesman, volatile personality and relationships, alternations of mood, uncertainty, indecision and susceptibility to audiences. Such attributes make it possible to find evidence that seems to indicate that Eden was in favour of a policy and of its opposite within the same period, for instance – though one explanation is that for an individual whose aptitude is for diplomatic negotiation and who is by nature indecisive and cautious evidence of contrary policies are not necessarily mutually exclusive but represent Eden's pursuing all possible avenues to attain his ends, not least those of diplomacy, rather than engaging in a policy from which there is no return without due consideration of consequence. Such characteristic caution does seem to have been true of Eden before and throughout the Suez Crisis before late October 1956 though not thereafter.

Eden has been criticised for lack of vision in foreign policy (in contrast to the visionary qualities of his post-war successor – and in fact predecessor – at the Foreign Office, Ernest Bevin), being seen more as an astute diplomat. He has been seen to have been lacking in any firm political convictions, engaging in *Realpolitik* (which refers to a pragmatic orientation to policy and diplomacy that reflects understanding of the realities of power rather than any attachment to ideals or principles), and being dominated by Churchill as Prime Minister (PM) for a significant part of his political life. And there has been a consensus as to Eden's lack of emotional stability in the appeasement period, as Foreign Secretary under Chamberlain, in the World War II under Churchill as PM, in the 1951 Conservative administration, again as Foreign Secretary under Churchill, and during the Suez Crisis as PM, when his poor Prime Ministerial judgement has been blamed for a calamity for post-war British foreign policy. It is the Suez Crisis which has come to define Eden as politician, diplomat and statesman, though in fact, as I shall show, there were circumstances that set it apart from other parts of Eden's long political career.

Eden's volatile personality and propensity for taking personal offence are well documented in the views of his contemporaries, including other British politicians, foreign political figures and officials in British government.[3] Before his premiership, in his terms as Foreign Secretary, Eden seems to have had periodic rages when he believed that his prerogatives as Foreign Secretary were being usurped, and with Chamberlain and Churchill both interfering and domineering premiers as far as foreign policy was concerned, there were genuine provocations. Even so there was a difference between Eden's emotional reactivity and his successor Halifax's more urbane and calm acceptance of Chamberlain's unorthodox treatment of Foreign Secretaries. Eden and Chamberlain had a public row over talks with Mussolini in front of Grandi, the Italian Ambassador to London, an extraordinary violation of diplomatic protocol. And Eden had a difference of view with Churchill at the Quebec Conference in 1944 over the Morgenthau plan for the pastoralisation of Germany, which Eden rejected despite its being approved by Roosevelt at the time and over which Churchill had to tell Eden that US preferences had to be considered to obtain US economic support after the war. One wonders then to what extent Eden's periodic displays of pique are to be attributed to genuine policy differences and to what extent to perceived violations of his prerogatives as Foreign Secretary. It is possible that Eden expected to be treated with respect as Foreign Secretary and had a sense of the proper protocol and of the prerogatives of the role of Foreign Secretary from his time under the very different premiership of Baldwin, whose interest in foreign policy was minimal and who did not interfere with his Foreign Secretary.[4] When protocol was violated Eden's volatile nature resulted in what have been referred to as 'tantrums'.[5] As has been noted in a previous case study above, Cadogan's diary entry for 8 January 1945 says of Eden that 'he strides about the room, gabbling, and I, at least, can't hear what he says,'[6] and Colville's diary entry of 9 January 1945 notes the effect of a minute from Lord Cherwell (chief scientific adviser to Churchill) contradicting Eden, who 'told me he would resign if inexpert, academic opinions were sought on subjects to which he had given so much thought. I put him through to the P.M., to whom he ranted in a way in which neither the P.M. nor I (who was listening in) had ever heard him before.'[7] Hamilton refers to the diary of Evelyn Shuckburgh, who was Eden's Principal Private Secretary during Eden's tenure as Foreign Secretary between 1951 and 1954 and then Under-Secretary at the Foreign Office specialising in the Middle East between 1954 and 20 June 1956, and so had extensive immediate experience of Eden in the earlier period (though not a source on Eden's conduct of the Suez Crisis itself). Shuckburgh confided to his diary that Eden was 'terribly vain and egocentric', given to petulance, acting like a 'child', aspiring and very sensitive to the impression he was making on audiences and to criticism. Between outbursts Eden's concern for audiences meant that he could be so emollient as to seem to have been in favour of and against German dismemberment on a visit to the US in 1943. As has been noted, Sainsbury observes that Eden 'appears to have simultaneously given Roosevelt (who had come to favour partition) and Hull (who was dubious about the idea) the impression that he agreed with each of them'.[8] A diplomat's concern for diplomatic harmony and use of ambiguous language to that end could explain such inconsistencies.

Beyond such an odd combination of emotional volatility and diplomatic urbanity and ambiguity Eden's approach to foreign policy prior to Suez seems to have been cautious, indecisive, and governed by prudence that dictated avoidance of foreclosure of the possibility of diplomatic resolutions to issues. Another characteristic of Eden's foreign policy was that it advocated avoiding assuming diplomatic positions not supported by military power or alliances, as in his advocating rearmament and cultivating good relations with the Soviet Union, the US and central European nations when he was Foreign Secretary under Chamberlain, and in his recommendation to an outraged Churchill in early 1942 that the Soviet annexations of the Baltic republics should be accepted by Britain. For as has been noted despite his anti-appeasement credentials Eden advocated acceptance of Stalin's demand for British recognition of the Soviet annexation of the Baltic states, a policy that seemed to be one of appeasement, even when Attlee and Bevin expressed concern that concessions would result in further demands, and Churchill and Cadogan opposed concessions on principle. Eden's reasoning was that Britain would not in the event of an allied victory have any military power in the Baltic states and so could not reverse Soviet annexations of the Baltic states, a *Realpolitik* position consistent with his sense of the need for military power through rearmament and alliances to support any diplomatic position in the appeasement period. What Eden does not seem to have understood was the opportunistic and expansionist nature of Soviet diplomatic tactics, despite the then recent adverse British experience of negotiations for an alliance with the Soviets in 1939, in which Soviet diplomatic tactics had precisely such qualities, for he hoped to elicit Soviet trust after the war by the concession over the Baltics in 1942.

Eden was then by the time of the Suez Crisis known for his emotional volatility and for having resisted Chamberlain over appeasement of Mussolini even to the point of resignation as Foreign Secretary. He had been placated by Churchill during the war over the latter's consulting Lord Cherwell over foreign policy in preference to Eden, and had persevered over the Baltic issue despite vigorous opposition from Churchill and much of the FO. There is also evidence of Eden's indifferent health during the war, including a duodenal problem and migraine,[9] both possible reactions to the strain of working under the domineering Churchill and of Eden's volatility of temperament. In what follows I shall outline the context of and sequence of events during the Suez Crisis, identify the influences on Eden's policy over Suez, and address the extent to which Eden's conduct of the Suez Crisis was at variance with his previous *Realpolitik* approach to foreign policy and his characteristic caution over assuming diplomatic positions that could not be supported by credible threat. I shall also attempt to establish why the Suez Crisis represented a partial departure from Eden's previous approach to foreign policy.

Postwar opposition and the 1951 – 1955 Conservative Government as the context for Eden over Suez

After the war Eden became a long-suffering Foreign Secretary again under the domineering premiership of Churchill in the 1951 Conservative government, finally becoming Prime Minister on 6 April 1955, and then architect of the misguided British policy over the Suez Crisis, which signalled to the British establishment and the world that British foreign policy would, to have any credibility in the future, require the specific prior approval and diplomatic and military support of the Americans. Suez has been described as a disaster for British foreign policy and prestige, as of course it was, even if it was only indicative of the reality of Britain's economic, military and diplomatic decline relative to the US and the Soviets, the dominant countries in world politics in the Cold War of the 1950s.

The dominance of the Americans in relation to British foreign policy became more profound once their diplomatic uncertainty in the post-war world and lack of experience of European politics had ended in US commitment to the defence of western Europe against communism and Soviet influence in the Truman Doctrine of containment. Bevin, Foreign Secretary in the Attlee Labour government of 1945, had been influential in the development of the Truman Doctrine, in that he had facilitated US understanding that Soviet policy was ideological in its hostility to capitalism and democracy, was opportunistic and expansionist in objective, and could only be contained by Western firmness in diplomatic and if necessary military terms on a case-by-case basis. Anything less would, Bevin argued, elicit Soviet exploitation of perceived Western weakness or lack of resolve to contain Soviet and communist expansionism. And as has been seen in the previous case study it was Bevin who understood the need for a policy of enduring Western firmness without provocation (very much the stance a trade union would take in a dispute) over Berlin in 1948 and who by his early public indication of intent to stay in Berlin put an end to the vacillation of US military chiefs as to whether or not there should be a retreat from Berlin to a more defensible frontier further west.

Eden shared Bevin's views on British foreign policy, so the bipartisan approach of the immediate post-war period was less one of tradition than of shared genuine belief, though in diplomatic style they were different, with Bevin's style direct and informed by his experience of trade-union negotiations (an experience which seems to have assisted him in diplomatic encounters with the Soviets) and Eden urbane, the practised diplomat whose manner was so accommodating that it seemed at times as if the diplomatic encounter itself mattered more than the foreign-policy outcome, as if harmony was itself the overriding value. In fact of course such diplomatic behaviour reflected also Eden's prudence and calculation of consequence, and seems to have been a tactic of keeping diplomatic options open rather than closing them off before the consequences were understood, which for a Britain of declining power relative to the US and the Soviet Union was understandably seen as a means of achieving initial post-war objectives such as the maintenance of the wartime alliance, though that was to prove impossible because of Soviet ideological hostility and expansionism. It also reflected Eden's understanding of *Realpolitik* and of the implications of Britain's declining relative military power, which precluded some diplomatic postures. Though they were different in expressive style Bevin and Eden shared a policy of prudence and caution in what was a *Realpolitik* approach to foreign policy, so by the time of the Suez Crisis the context of the Cold War and of British policy oriented to joint action with the US to resist Soviet and communist expansionism and opportunism was established. Thorpe claims, referring apparently to Eden's term as Foreign Secretary in Churchill's 1951 administration, that 'the central theme of Eden's Foreign Secretaryship was that of maintaining Britain as a front-rank power in the face of superpower competition and economic difficulty.'[10] What may have separated Bevin and Eden somewhat was the difference between Bevin's pragmatic acceptance of the need for American economic, diplomatic and military support and Eden's understanding of but resentment of American predominance and British dependence on the US.[11]

The Suez Crisis that so ruined Eden's political reputation was then set in such an actual and experiential context for Eden as he became PM. At last having attained the premiership as expected and winning an election on 26 May 1955 with an increased majority of sixty seats (from a previous majority of seventeen seats) Eden nevertheless made an uncertain start, not making the Cabinet changes many felt were necessary or deciding on his Cabinet until December 1955, and moving Macmillan from the Foreign Office (FO) after a matter of months to the Treasury in place of Butler, who became Leader of the Commons, a move he regarded as a demotion, to resume control over the FO by the appointment of Lloyd as Foreign Secretary. And despite his own personal experience as Foreign Secretary under Chamberlain and Churchill, both PMs who interfered with ministers and their briefs and who had dominated foreign policy in their premierships, Eden interfered in a similar way, calling ministers to account over trivial matters at all hours and alienating them, as Butler noted. Press criticism regarding Eden's 'dithering' had a very adverse effect on the sensitive Eden, whose delicate health had deteriorated following botched operations in 1953 that had left him dependent upon medicine, and 'he became obsessive about not appearing to dither'.

Over the Middle East Eden was concerned regarding Soviet intentions in a region needed to secure supplies of Middle Eastern oil for the British economy, and supported the Baghdad Pact to resist Soviet incursion from the north, efforts to negotiate a Middle Eastern settlement between Israel and Egypt (as the most influential Arab nation), and attempts to secure Nasser's ideological allegiance in the Cold War through involvement in financing the Aswan High Dam.[12] Even in 1955 though Eden, in an indication of the unpredictability and volatility he had exhibited periodically before and during the war and was to show during the Suez Crisis itself, alternated between a rational, prudent and cautious diplomacy towards Nasser, regarding whom he entertained suspicions, and an irascibility at Nasser's ambiguity and rhetoric and an impulsive desire to be rid of him.

It was in such a context that by June 1955, infuriated by Egyptian press coverage, Eden had taken against Nasser, referred to the 'gross impertinence' of Egyptian accounts of British 'aggression' against Saudi Arabia and, wanting to punish Nasser by denial of aid, had to be counselled by Macmillan that Nasser was needed for any Middle East defence system.[13] Even so, and despite abhorring Nasser and regarding him as another Mussolini, Eden then reacted to news of Nasser's purchase of Soviet arms and the possibility of Soviet offers of arms to other Arab nations with some calmness, advocating in a Cabinet meeting on 4 October an overture to the Soviets warning of the delicate balance in the Middle East and of the prospect that conflict between Israel and Egypt could result in a 'threat to world peace', recommending avoidance of any punitive action against Egypt through withholding sterling balances or threat to the Aswan High Dam, and arguing for reinforcing the 'Northern Tier countries' to keep them out of the Soviet orbit by inducing them not to accept Soviet arms. Though Eden noted that US association with the Northern Tier would help, he argued that the Middle East was a sphere of greater interest to Britain than to the US because of British dependence on Middle Eastern oil, and indicated that British policy should be formed without reference to the US, with the Americans being asked to support it to the extent they felt they could.[14]

Eden's position over Suez was complicated by the fact that it had been Eden himself who, as Foreign Secretary, had negotiated the Suez Canal Base Agreement of 19 October 1954, under which British troops were to be withdrawn from Port Said by 18 June 1956, for it was a policy that was very controversial in the Conservative Party, and Eden had felt compelled to justify it in a speech in December 1955 and to the Conservative Foreign Affairs Committee on 6 March 1956 by reference to the adverse effects of remaining in Suez on relations with the Arab world and to possible conflict with the Soviet Union in the Middle East.[15] The withdrawal of British troops from Suez was in fact complete by 13 June 1956, and it was just over a month later that Nasser announced his intention to nationalise the Suez Canal, which made the withdrawal seem to some in the Party injudicious and an error of judgement by Eden.

Another part of the context for British foreign policy over Suez was the Abadan crisis, which took place between 1951, when Mossadeq nationalised the Anglo-Iranian Oil Company, regarded as the UK's major foreign asset, and 1953, when the UK and the US in the form of the CIA effected a *coup d'état* that removed Mossadeq from power, though the restored Anglo-Iranian Oil Company was divided between the UK, with a forty percent share, and the US, also with a forty percent share, and there were concessions over the profits to the Iranians and the Saudis. Whereas Eden seems to have been more influenced over Suez by the experience of Abyssinia and Munich Macmillan's view seems to have been influenced by the experience over Abadan, seen as an instance of a British climbdown. Convinced that British authority in the Middle East was vital to the securing of oil supplies and to British great power status, Macmillan saw a link between the Abadan crisis and Suez and referred to the Abadan experience when advocating the removal of Nasser or decisive military intervention over Suez.[16]

In January 1956 Eden and Lloyd met Eisenhower and Dulles in Washington for a summit meeting at which Eden expressed his reservations regarding Nasser. The American reaction was to wait and see with Nasser. Then, on 1 March 1956, Glubb, the British commander of the Arab Legion in Jordan, was dismissed and ordered to leave the country. Eden blamed the dismissal on Nasser's Arab nationalist rhetoric, and on 5 March told Eisenhower of his conviction that the Soviets intended to destroy the Baghdad Pact and that Nasser was complicit in that purpose, of his disenchantment with what he referred to as a policy of 'appeasement' of Nasser, and of his belief that US membership of the Baghdad Pact would enhance its effect.[17] In an indication of Eden's volatility some time before Nasser's nationalisation of the Suez Canal, Anthony Nutting, Minister for Foreign Affairs, notes in his memoir that Eden had shouted on the telephone on 12 March 1956, 'what's all this nonsense about isolating Nasser or 'neutralising' him, as you call it? I want him destroyed, can't you understand? I want him removed, and if you and the Foreign Office don't agree, then you'd better come to the Cabinet and explain why'.[18] The odd aspect of such behaviour in Eden was that it was just the sort of disdain for the judgement of the experts in the FO that he had himself as Foreign Secretary so resented, and seems to have been representative of Eden's treatment of the FO and of political associates when his temper was aroused.

There followed a diplomatic sequence in which Britain and the US withdrew financial support from Nasser for the Aswan Dam after Nasser's recognition of communist China. Nasser in retaliation announced on 26 July 1956 his intention that the Suez Canal should be nationalised. British and French forces invaded using the pretext of an Israeli invasion of Sinai starting on 29 October 1956. The Eisenhower administration was faced with a public relations difficulty in criticising the Soviet crushing of the Hungarian revolution of 1956 while possibly being seen to endorse the British and French invasion of Egypt, and Eisenhower was outraged by information that indicated that the British knew of the Israeli invasion. There was also the matter of an impending US Presidential election on 6 November 1956 and Soviet threat of rocket attacks on London, Paris and Tel Aviv in what seemed to be a threat of a more general war. The US used the UN Security Council and then the UN General Assembly to force a ceasefire and threatened economic sanctions should Britain not withdraw, including selling British Government bonds, which would have resulted in the devaluation of sterling and could not have been withstood given Britain's low foreign exchange reserves. In weeks of such US action Britain would not have had the means to pay for necessary imports of food and energy and the Saudi oil embargo exacerbated matters as the US refused to assist prior to British withdrawal from Suez. This is the bare outline of the crisis, its genesis, duration and outcome. The interesting questions for this essay are however those relating to the locus of decision-making power within the British establishment in the Suez Crisis, the extent of Eden's personal dominance as PM in developing and implementing British policy over Suez, the causation of the final outcome, the extent to which Eden over Suez manifested the approach to foreign policy apparent in Eden's previous career, and the extent to which Eden's policy was justified or at least rational despite the obviously adverse outcome.

The historiography on Eden and Suez

Smith refers to Eden's 'splenetic stewardship' and to the British government's being 'fixated on Egypt' and on Nasser. Smith claims that 'the British premier's apocalyptic visions of the consequences of letting Nasser "get away with it" unbalanced his judgement and hardened his predisposition neither to seek nor to listen to contradictory counsel,' and refers to Eden's 'tendency to rely on the advice of those in Whitehall or Westminster who were in fundamental sympathy with his attitude', citing Home, Lennox-Boyd and Macmillan as hawks who shared Eden's perception of what was at stake over Suez and the need for a decisive and punitive response to Nasser.[19] Smith makes no reference to what seems to have been a vital and influential conversation between an initially indecisive Eden and a more certain and hawkish Macmillan on the morning of 27 July 1956 on how to proceed, and his claim of Eden's decisive influence seems to be a general one rather than one that takes account of the sequence of events in the British government response over Suez.

Kyle seems to endorse Smith's attribution of decisive influence on British policy over Suez to Eden, for he too does not refer to the meeting between Eden and Macmillan on the morning of 27 July and concentrates instead on accounts that claim that 'Eden dominated the meeting' in Downing Street on the evening of 26 July and insisted 'Nasser could not be allowed to get away with it.' He also cites an account that claims that Eden had gone 'bananas' and could insist upon an immediate military response, though Kyle notes that such a response was discounted because it could not be sustained.[20] Of course insisting that Nasser should not be allowed to nationalise the Suez Canal with impunity did not commit Eden to any specific course of action, and the reference to Eden's outrage and possible insistence upon a military reaction to what Eden regarded as Nasser's temerity in repossessing the Suez Canal is no more than another indication of Eden's volatility, and is not incompatible with an ensuing combination of uncertainty, caution, and susceptibility to influence from the more certain and decisive Macmillan. Kyle's claim that British policy over Suez was one of military intervention from the start and initiated by Eden is not supported by the evidence of Eden's continuing to exhaust all diplomatic means of resolving the crisis consistent with the British interest in the restoration of the Suez Canal as an international waterway and with the maintenance of British prestige in the Middle East that had been challenged by Nasser. And of course any diplomatic resolution that restored the Suez Canal to international control would have been a humiliation for Nasser and so consonant with the objectives of both Eden and Eisenhower without resort to use of force.

Pearson, assessing the existing historiography on the Suez crisis, argues that there has been a mistaken attribution of British policy to Eden's having decided upon military intervention from the start of the crisis or at least from the end of July 1956 that he sees as derived from the account of William Clark, who was press secretary to Eden during the Suez crisis, though as Pearson points out Clark's own diary, a more immediate source, contradicts his memoir. Pearson attributes the mistake in part to Eden's own explanation of the invasion as the consequence of 'the approved plan' of 'Anglo-French military staff' who 'had been studying the problem since the end of July', which Pearson claims reflects Eden's having been 'keen to conceal the results of the meetings at Sèvres, and collusion', and Eden's desire to refute allegations of 'irresolution' over his handling of the crisis because of an enhanced 'sensitivity' to such 'accusations' resulting from 'his illness and the prescribed medication' he was taking. It is worth noting that even Lucas's reference to Clark's record of Eden's claimed certainty as to the necessity for military action over Suez and conviction that Nasser had to be deposed from the outset refers to Clark's diary for '26–27 July 1956', that is, an entry that appears to cover the following morning, when Eden consulted Macmillan and received the latter's hawkish advice.[21] And though, as has been seen above, on 31 July 1956 Murphy, the US Defence Secretary, reported to Dulles that Eden and Macmillan had both indicated to him their decision to use force over Suez, he noted that Macmillan had been the more hawkish, and the date does not rule out the possibility of Macmillan's having influenced Eden in the preceding days.

Pearson claims that Eden's strategy was to produce a credible threat of invasion of Suez to elicit US pressure on Nasser to make concessions to keep the peace, which turned out to be a miscalculation as to the US reaction. Referring to Eden's deteriorating health and his hospitalisation in early October, Pearson claims that Eden's final decision to intervene militarily was taken 'simply because Eden was not the same man in October that he had been in July 1956, and, under increased pressure, agreed to use force to resolve the crisis', differing from the historiography in arguing that 'Eden believed throughout August, September and early October 1956 that international pressure brought to bear upon Nasser would preclude the need for more drastic action' and pointing to confusion in the British decision-making process rather than some decided long term plan.

Though such uncertainty does seem to be borne out by the evidence both of Eden's personality and history of decision making in government and of Eden's diplomatic initiatives to resolve the crisis, it could be argued that the diplomatic initiatives were undertaken to appease the US and retain Eisenhower's support for military intervention rather than in the conviction that they would resolve the crisis. Having said that, though the evidence does not establish that Eden was at any time entirely convinced that diplomacy would resolve the Suez crisis, it does not conclusively establish that Eden was resolved all along on military intervention and engaged in diplomatic activity over Suez only while British forces were preparing for military intervention either. Pearson's claim that Eden did in fact believe in a diplomatic resolution between July and early October 1956 does not though seem consonant with Pearson's claim of confusion over Suez. Macmillan's diary entry for 1 August 1956, following his meeting with Dulles, supports Pearson's claim that the optimisation of US diplomatic pressure on Nasser was the British objective at the time. For Macmillan, who was so influential with Eden in this early stage of the Suez crisis, confided to his diary that he had told Dulles—

'It was not a question of honour but of survival. We must get Nasser out by diplomacy or by force'.

He continued—

'We must keep the Americans really frightened. Then they will help us get what we want without the necessity of force. But we must have a) international control of the Canal b) humiliation and collapse of Nasser'.[22]

Though Wilby has made pejorative reference to the reliability of Macmillan's diaries it is difficult to know just what the objection is, for they are contemporaneous with the events being referred to and even in his later memoir Macmillan admitted his having been in error over his expectation of US support over Suez.[23] The Macmillan diary evidence presented here does seem to indicate a misplaced confidence in threatened British military intervention being influential with the Eisenhower administration on the part of Macmillan and, given his influence on Eden at the time, of Eden too, a belief in the possibility of restoring international control to the Suez Canal and of reaffirming British prestige in the Middle East through the public humiliation and downfall of Nasser, without resort to force, though with a preparedness to resort to force should diplomatic pressure not accomplish British objectives.

Pearson claims that Eden's memoirs have been dismissed and should be treated as evidence of his intentions over Suez, though he does not indicate why they should not be treated as self-serving or self-justifying in the manner that so many memoirs are. In a review of Pearson Williamson points to another difficulty with Pearson's argument, that is that Eden could at any time have explained to Eisenhower and Dulles that his policy was to produce a credible threat of military action over Suez to Nasser, and did not do so. The counterargument is of course that if Eden's intention was to induce the US administration to believe in a British threat of war to secure US pressure on Nasser to avoid war he would hardly have notified the US that the references to military preparations were intended to have the US believe in an actual threat of war. Williamson also wonders why Eden permitted Macmillan to represent the UK government's views to the US administration, when as Chancellor of the Exchequer it was hardly his brief, though if Eden intended to convince the US administration of the danger of war and need for the US to pressure Nasser to make concessions he could have used Macmillan's wartime association with Eisenhower to that end.[24]

Rhodes James, the first biographer of Eden to use Eden's private papers, concludes that 'Eden saw the seriousness of Nasser's actions immediately, and at once took charge. He led, rather than followed, Cabinet and Party feeling.'[25] It is worth noting that Rhodes James makes no reference to the role of Macmillan in these early days of the Suez Crisis in making this general statement and that Thorpe notes of Rhodes James' biography that 'some critics felt that Rhodes James had paid too heavily for the help afforded him by the widow, the dilemma faced by many "authorised" biographers.'[26]

Harold Wilson claims that 'Eden was at first a reluctant warrior' and Macmillan was the minister who advocated a tough British stance. Wilson also records the effect of Macmillan's toughness on the Americans, seeming to claim that when the news of Nasser's intended nationalisation of the Suez Canal came through on 26 July 1956 Macmillan 'and Lord Salisbury were entertaining Robert Murphy, the US Defence Secretary'. Wilson claims that 'Macmillan took an extremely tough line about Nasser's action, which, he later explained, was designed to stiffen the American administration. Murphy was left to draw the conclusion that Britain would certainly go to war to secure the Canal and ensure free passage for the world's ships'. Wilson also notes that 'American leaders, from President Eisenhower downwards, took Macmillan's comments as representing a decision of the British Cabinet' (he points out too that this tough stance over Suez and its effect on the Americans is a curious omission from Macmillan's memoirs, an accusation that is in fact untrue, as Macmillan was entirely open as to his having been mistaken regarding the US reaction to a *fait accompli* of British intervention in Suez).[27]

Gaitskell, who was with Eden when the news of Nasser's intended nationalisation of the Suez Canal came through, also notes Eden's initial uncertainty as to how to respond. Gaitskell claims that Eden wondered if the matter should be taken to the Security Council, and it was according to Gaitskell Selwyn Lloyd rather than Eden who answered the question of what should be done should Nasser disregard world opinion. Gaitskell says that Selwyn Lloyd referred to the possible necessity of an ultimatum, while Eden, one presumes, refrained from committing himself.[28] Though Macmillan was not present at the ensuing initial meeting at Downing Street on the evening the news of Nasser's intention was received, and though the outcome of that meeting on the evening of 26 July 1956 was an intention to prevent Nasser's nationalisation of the Suez Canal, it does seem plausible from the evidence that Eden could have been decided upon the ends, the preservation of the Suez Canal as an international trade route, though not nearly so certain as to the means, between the exhaustion of all diplomatic possibilities, including reference to the UN and obtaining US endorsement, and resort to military action. And it seems plausible that there was influence from Macmillan's confident and eloquent hawkishness on Eden to the extent that Eden was lacking in certainty in an early morning call the following day, 27 July, made by Eden to Macmillan, and in an ensuing meeting with Macmillan to decide upon a statement to the Commons.[29]

Verbeek, in an analysis of the nature of the decision-making process in the British establishment over Suez, claims that in the crisis conditions that Suez represented there was a characteristic centralisation of foreign-policy decision-making that isolated an 'inner circle' of senior ministers around Eden as PM from influence from other quarters, such as departmental expertise, more junior Cabinet ministers and backbench MPs. Verbeek claims that the 'inner circle' tended to meet prior to Cabinet meetings and those of the Egypt Committee created by Cabinet to run the Suez dispute and was composed of Eden himself, Butler, Home, Kilmuir, Macmillan, Monckton, Salisbury and Lloyd. Verbeek claims that within that small group of senior ministers the emotional stress of the Suez Crisis resulted in 'directive leadership' and 'Groupthink' and resort to core cognitive beliefs reflective of the view of the world of Eden, Macmillan, Salisbury and Lloyd, resulting in rationalisation of evidence against government policy over Suez. These core beliefs included US acknowledgement of British pre-eminence in the Middle East and US defence of British interests there 'as long as British diplomacy persisted in its efforts to convince Washington' in a Cold War context of common desire to exclude Soviet influence. As to Eden, Verbeek sees the dominant influences on his behaviour over Suez as being a worldview that included observance of international protocol and respect for 'legitimate security interests' that in the case of the UK meant continuing influence in the Middle East to maintain the defence of the empire and British prestige in the world, with the UN no longer seen as effective given Soviet use of the veto.

Verbeek claims that in the initial reaction to Nasser's nationalisation of the Suez Canal Eden manifested 'directive leadership' in indicating his worldview to Cabinet on 27 July 1956 that the UK had to 'safeguard our interests' over Suez, though he did not impose military intervention on ministers, instead asking for their view on military action if the US and French did not offer assistance, though Verbeek observes that the inference was that there would be US 'tacit support'.[30] Verbeek does acknowledge unanimous Cabinet approval of resort to force should diplomacy not succeed in resolving the crisis, though he makes no reference to Eden's initial uncertainty or to Macmillan's hawkish influence on Eden even when noting Eden's talk with Macmillan on the morning of 27 July and their agreeing on the note to Eisenhower.

Even from the evidence Verbeek produces Eden does not seem to have been as influential during the initial phase of the crisis as Verbeek indicates, though Eden did rule out reference to the UN Security Council both in Cabinet on 27 July and in the Egypt Committee on 30 July because of the Soviet veto. Verbeek claims that in the initial phase of the crisis 'British policy-makers went to great lengths to ensure that their interpretation of messages from Dulles and Eisenhower fitted their own assumptions regarding the American attitude,' citing as evidence Dulles' having elucidated Eisenhower's intention in his message to Eden on 1 August 1956 by indicating that the UK should make a 'genuine and sincere effort to settle the problem and avoid the use of force' and that 'if the attempt were made to use force alone, he saw great difficulties.' Verbeek makes no reference to the fact that even in these quotations from Dulles there is no ruling-out use of force at any time. Having said that Verbeek notes that Lloyd told ministers on 1 August that Dulles had told him he would 'deprecate' 'any premature use of force', from which Verbeek rightly infers no 'fundamental opposition to use of force'. I shall return to the evidence of 1 August 1956 regarding American policy over Suez below. Later in August Verbeek notes that though Eden told the Egypt Committee that the US could not join the UK and France in any military action over Suez Dulles had told Eden that he had informed the Soviet Union that the US would provide material support for the UK and France in the event of military action in Suez, an indication of indirect US support. Verbeek does not then establish his case that the small group of British ministers of the 'inner circle' took care to misinterpret Eisenhower's and Dulles' communications to justify military action in Suez, for the US messages were indicative of no more than exhortation to pursue all diplomatic avenues first.[31] What does seem justified is Verbeek's claim that Eden and a small group of senior ministers dominated decision-making in the Suez Crisis, meeting prior to Cabinet meetings to discuss the presentation of policy to ministers to limit dissent and to facilitate approval in Cabinet. What is not established by the documentary evidence is the claim by Verbeek of Eden's dominant influence, not least given his indecisive initial reaction and his dithering at various points during the crisis and the greater certainty of Macmillan, Salisbury and Kilmuir, for instance.

In more general terms Verbeek analyses the Suez Crisis in terms of a number of concepts, such as 'directive leadership', worldview and Groupthink, and does not take account of Eden's personality with its uncertainty and susceptibility to influence, not least from the more certain and outspoken Macmillan, or explain his departure from a characteristic caution, prudence and indecisiveness to certainty and confidence in October 1956. As has been seen, though Verbeek does acknowledge the ambiguity of Eisenhower's and Dulles' communications with Eden he claims that the small group of senior ministers around Eden and Eden himself distorted the meaning of such messages to make them accord with their preference for military intervention. The inference of selective interpretation by Eden and his coterie of senior ministers is of course no more than that, an inference, and it is not possible to attribute any extent of causal influence on British policy over Suez to it, common though it is in human judgement.

There seems to be no direct conclusive evidence as to Eden's intentions in regard to the means of restoring the Suez Canal's status as an international waterway, though it is very clear that such restoration was his objective over Suez both for economic and strategic reasons and to maintain British prestige in the world and the Middle East. What I shall argue here is that the most plausible inference from the documentary evidence and Eden's personality and behaviour throughout the crisis is that his immediate reaction was one of outrage and desire to retaliate accompanied by a characteristic caution and indecision as to the best means of doing so, that thereafter he attempted to resolve the crisis by diplomatic means and to secure US approval of or at least acquiescence in a British intervention in Suez should that become necessary following the exhaustion of all diplomatic means, through compliance with US requests for continued diplomatic engagement, and that even following the failure of the UN Security Council to resolve the crisis on 13 October Eden sent a cable to Lloyd the following day indicating preparedness to continue to exhaust diplomatic possibilities in more talks with the Egyptians.

In other words the argument here is that Eden remained uncertain as to how to resolve the Suez Crisis at the outset and for most of the crisis, and that it was not long before 24 October, when the Sèvres Protocol was agreed, that his perception of or attitude to risk changed as a consequence of the cumulative effect of the medicines he was taking to combat his health problems. That indicates that the discontinuity between the Eden of the period prior to the Suez Crisis and for most of the conduct of the crisis and the Eden of its latter stages is to be attributed to his poor health and to medicines, in contrast to claims that Eden dominated policy over Suez from the outset and intended to intervene with troops from the beginning of the crisis.

The lack of reference by Smith, Kyle and Rhodes James to the early views of Macmillan, acknowledged as he has been to have been very influential during the Suez Crisis, is difficult to account for, not least as primary accounts indicate Eden's initial uncertainty as to how to respond and as Wilson claims that it was Macmillan who displayed initial certainty as to the need for toughness over Suez. Though Wilson's account may be inaccurate in seeming to claim that Macmillan and Salisbury were dining with Murphy when the news of the nationalisation of the Suez Canal came through on 26 July 1956, when in fact Murphy was sent to London only on 28 July 1956, and Kyle claims that Salisbury was in Downing Street on the evening of 26 July 1956, there seems to be little doubt as to Macmillan's hawkishness from the start. According to Kyle Murphy was briefed by Eden, Macmillan and Lloyd and 'left in no doubt that the British government believed that Suez was a test that could be met only by the use of force', which he reported to Washington on 31 July 1956.[32] The American documentary record of Murphy's report to Dulles on these meetings is long and specific, referring to separate conversations with Eden and Macmillan, both of whom were according to Murphy calm and reasoned and who both told Murphy of their conviction that military intervention was necessary, that the intention was 'to drive Nasser out of Egypt', that they 'hoped US would be with them in their determination, but if we could not they would understand and our friendship would be unimpaired', that 'they are flexible on procedures leading up to a showdown' but 'at the end are determined to use force'.[33] Of the two, it is apparent that Murphy found Macmillan the more hawkish. What is worth noting in the reference to British understanding should the US not join British intervention over Suez is Eden's and Macmillan's implicit confidence that the US would not do more than refrain from military involvement over Suez. The idea that the US could refuse Britain diplomatic or economic support seems to be quite absent.

According to Lucas the CoS were ready to resign rather than have British forces committed to an immediate operation in Suez given the general state of military unpreparedness, though Eden is claimed to have been undeterred in his intention to resolve the Suez Crisis by military intervention early on.[34]

The minutes of the Cabinet meeting after the statement to the Commons on 27 July indicate that the Cabinet agreed that international control over the Suez Canal had to be restored for Western economic life and prestige and that economic pressure alone would not be effective. Cabinet understood the need for 'maximum political pressure' on Nasser, and did not rule out, 'in the last resort', 'the use of force'. In fact the Cabinet minutes, which are often unclear, are as clear as they could be in this case. Eden himself was very specific both as to the decision that had to be made and to the role of the Cabinet in deciding policy. Eden said 'the fundamental question before Cabinet' was 'whether they were prepared in the last resort to pursue their objective by the threat or even the use of force, and whether they were ready, in default of assistance from the United States and France, to take military action alone'. The minutes continue, 'the Cabinet agreed that our essential interests must, if necessary, be safeguarded by military action' and 'even if we had to act alone, we could not stop short of using force to protect our position if all other methods of protecting it proved unavailing.'[35] While ignorance of context and significance could be attributed to Cabinet ministers it is then clear that the Cabinet was consulted and informed of the nature of the issue and what was at stake, and that it agreed with Eden's stance.

The general reaction in Britain amongst the press and public at this time seems to have been one of outrage at Nasser's action over Suez. It is worth noting that Eden did not propose military action over Suez even if the US was opposed to such intervention or in defiance of the US but rather confined himself to a decision as to action without US assistance. The policy approved by Cabinet on 27 July 1956 became known as the 'dual-track policy'. It involved pursuing diplomatic means of resolving the dispute while preparing for military intervention in case diplomacy did not produce a resolution that restored the Suez Canal to international control, for only that would guarantee the supply of Middle Eastern oil to the UK and reassert British prestige in the Middle East at Nasser's expense.

As has been alluded to above, Pearson claims that Eden's policy in July 1956 and thereafter, until October, was to engage in military preparations for an invasion of Suez as a credible threat to Nasser to induce him and the US to respond positively to the other strand of Eden's policy over Suez, which was to pursue obtaining the support of the US for diplomatic overtures to restore the Suez Canal to international control, which would of course have had the desirable consequence of discrediting Nasser before the Arab world.[36] As to Macmillan's influence on Eden and policy over Suez between July 1956 and the middle of October, when he was a reassuring influence on Eden over Eden's colluding with the French and the Israelis, it seems that Macmillan was instrumental in devising the 'dual-track policy' of engaging in diplomatic activity and undertaking military preparations for an invasion of Suez. Both Eden and Macmillan understood the need to secure US diplomatic support to exert diplomatic pressure on Nasser and to obtain US understanding for any military intervention in Suez.

In Eden's letter to Eisenhower on 27 July 1956, the same day as the first Cabinet meeting on the Suez Crisis, Eden notes, 'we are unlikely to attain our objective by economic pressures alone,' and continues, 'my colleagues and I are convinced that we are must be ready, in the last resort to use force to bring Nasser to his senses. For our part we are prepared to do so. I have this morning instructed our Chiefs of Staff to prepare military plans accordingly.' Eden concluded however with his customary emollient tone, 'the first step must be for you and us and the French to exchange views, align our policies and concert together how we can best bring maximum pressure to bear on the Egyptian Government.'[37]

Eisenhower's response of 31 July 1956 was delivered to Eden on 1 August by Dulles, whom Eisenhower sent to London to confer with Eden over the Suez Crisis. Eisenhower referred to Murphy's information that Eden and Macmillan had indicated 'your decision to employ force without delay or attempting any intermediate and less drastic steps' and told Eden, 'we recognize the transcendent worth of the Canal to the free world and the possibility that eventually use of force might become necessary to protect international rights,' before proposing a conference to exert pressure on the Egyptian government and to provide justification for any ensuing military action to US and world opinion. Even though Eisenhower did refer to 'the unwisdom even of contemplating the use of military force at this moment', he did acknowledge that military action could come 'to seem the only recourse', and went on to apprise Eden of the processes in the US system necessary to the commitment of US military force, which Eden had not asked for, before concluding by indicating the worth of being seen to have exhausted all diplomatic means of resolving the crisis should force become necessary to protect western shipping through the canal. Dulles added a covering note to Eisenhower's letter to Eden to the effect that a conference should not be regarded as 'going through the motions' before military action and that it should be a 'genuine and sincere effort to settle the problem and avoid the use of force'.

What does seem clear is that Eisenhower did not rule out US approval of military force should all diplomatic avenues be exhausted. In fact Eisenhower refers to the adverse effect on public opinion of invasion without exhausting diplomatic means, and recommends a conference as a good way to advertise the efforts being made to resolve the crisis by diplomatic means. There is also explicit recognition of the possible need for military action by the West in Eisenhower's sentence, 'we recognize the transcendent worth of the Canal to the free world and the possibility that eventually the use of force might become necessary in order to protect international rights.'[38] Dulles' note does no more than exhort Eden to exhaust diplomatic attempts in a genuine manner before use of force should that become necessary. And though there is Dulles' account of his warning Eden, in a context of reference to British and French military intervention that 'United States public opinion was not ready to back', 'that for the British and the French to undertake such an operation without at least the moral support of the United States would be a great disaster', the rest of the document indicates that Dulles is advocating that diplomatic means should be exhausted first and that US support could not be given for a British and French military intervention in Suez before such diplomatic efforts had mobilised world opinion to support such action.[39]

It would not have been irrational for Eden to infer that Eisenhower was not ruling out US approval of the use of force over Suez after diplomatic means had been exhausted or for him to have inferred from Eisenhower's words implicit US approval of British military action over Suez once diplomatic avenues had been exhausted, not least as that would have been the desired inference for Eden. And in fact it seems from Eden's own account that Eden interpreted the Eisenhower letter as indicating that 'the President did not rule out the use of force'.[40] Further, it seems clear from the conversation between Dulles and Eisenhower on 12 August 1956 that Dulles felt that Britain and France should be given 'moral and economic support' should Nasser decline to accept a reasoned policy and it was felt by Britain and France that there was no alternative to the use of force 'to protect their interests'.[41]

Kyle notes Eisenhower's 'high regard' for Dulles' expertise in foreign affairs and the manner in which Dulles presented his case to Eisenhower to deal with Eisenhower's concerns, and Gorst claims that Eisenhower's warning against use of force was reinforced by Dulles in London on 1 August 1956. The American record of Eden's conversation with Dulles on 1 August indicates Eden's requesting American economic and moral rather than military support for the 'prompt forcible action' he believed was necessary over Suez (and diplomatic support with the Soviet Union to permit Britain and France to resolve the Suez Crisis) and Dulles' agreement that Nasser should not be permitted to 'get away with it', that he should be made to 'disgorge'. Though the record indicates that Dulles told Eden that US public opinion was not ready to support a 'military venture', warned Eden against proceeding without 'at least the moral support of the United States', and exhorted Eden to pursue diplomatic means of resolving the crisis and to avoid any immediate resort to the use of force, there was no threat of US economic sanctions for any British military intervention in Suez and no actual ban on military action in any circumstance.[42]

Dulles had another meeting the same day, with Lloyd and Caccia, the British Ambassador to the United States designate. The record by Murphy indicates that Dulles told Lloyd that Nasser had to be made to 'disgorge', though 'force is the last method to be tried. We do not exclude it if all other means fail, but if it is used it must be backed by world opinion,' another indication of Dulles' not indicating US resistance to use of force under any circumstances and of Dulles' giving no indication of the sort of US reaction that in the end occurred.[43] The consequence was British agreement to the US request for a conference of all interested parties on the Suez Crisis.

As to Eden's intentions at this time, though Lucas claims that Eden was committed to military action and to diplomatic activity only during the period of needed military preparation for military intervention in Suez, citing in support of his contention Eden's indications to Pineau on 31 July and the Egypt Committee a day earlier, the actual quotation he refers to is as follows (the reference to a Conference is to US advocacy of an international conference of all interested countries on Suez)—

> 'action against Egypt if it were necessary would...in any case take some time to prepare. If
> the Conference could achieve this end without prejudicing the military action that might be
> necessary, it might be admirable.'[44]

Here Eden has referred twice to the possible necessity of military action, not its certainty, and
such evidence does not establish that Eden was from the outset committed to military action or to
anything more than the restoration of international control to the Suez Canal and the ensuing public
humiliation of Nasser. The conclusion by Lucas that Eden intended to 'use the Conference for
diplomatic cover' does not then seem justified even by the evidence he produces.[45] As to the
evidence of the American records referred to above that appear to indicate Eden's having been
decided on use of force as early as 1 August 1956, that is only an indication of an American
perception, and Eden did, as shall be demonstrated, continue to pursue exhaustive diplomatic
overtures to exert pressure on Nasser. The far more plausible inference is that, as had been so in
Eden's previous foreign policy and diplomatic experience as Foreign Secretary and as PM at the
beginning of the Suez Crisis, Eden remained uncertain as to how best to proceed, cautious and
indecisive, and possibly receptive to the most proximate or intense audience at the time, another
trait seen in the wartime period.

At the Cabinet meeting on 1 August 1956 Lloyd told ministers that Dulles had indicated support
for the UK over Suez, and had said that Nasser would have to relinquish Suez, but that the US
would 'deprecate any premature use of force' and advocated an international conference that
would have to include the Soviet Union to resolve the Suez Crisis. The conference involving the
principal users of the Suez Canal took place in London between 16 and 23 August 1956, though
Greece and Egypt declined to attend, leaving twenty-two principal users. On the 14th Eden
introduced a sense of urgency in Cabinet in a statement that UK forces 'could not be maintained in
a state of readiness for a protracted period', and ensuing Cabinet meetings on the 21st and 23rd
indicated a desire for a US decision on enforcement on decisions made by the conference.[47] The
result of the conference was that India, Ceylon, Indonesia and the Soviet Union declined to endorse
the resolution and that Menzies was sent to Nasser to represent the demand of the remaining
eighteen principal users that the Suez Canal should remain under international control. The
demand was rejected by Nasser.

At the Cabinet meeting on 28 August there was reference to the involvement of the UN Security
Council to resolve the crisis as the US response to Egyptian rejection of international control, to
which ministers seem not to have objected. Eden as PM seems to have regarded reference to the
UN as advantageous as Soviet rejection would mean isolation for them and he was confident of the
support of the majority in the UN Security Council. In what seems to have been a more extensive
ministerial discussion on Suez Macmillan noted the need for oil through the canal for the UK
economy, Monckton as Minister of Defence agreed that force should be used if there proved to be
no alternative but stressed the disadvantages of use of force and the need to exhaust all diplomatic
possibilities, Salisbury as Lord President of the Council alluded to the need to use force with the
maximum international support and approved of reference to the UN, Kilmuir as Lord Chancellor
approved of force if there were no other means of securing the canal and of reference to the UN,
and Butler as Lord Privy Seal recommended no resort to force before exhaustion of all diplomatic
possibilities. Eden, summing up, noted the ministerial view that use of force had been agreed as a
last resort and provided there were no other means of securing the canal, and that such means
needed to be exhausted for domestic and international audiences. There seems to have been no
dissent from outside the circle of senior ministers around Eden during Cabinet meetings in July and

August 1956, though of course at that stage diplomatic channels were being pursued and no decision to commit troops was before ministers.[48]

Rothwell claims that messages from Eisenhower to Eden in the first week of September ruled out use of force 'utterly'.[49] This would appear to represent a radical change in the US position in warning that force should not be used at all rather than that it should not be used until all diplomatic means were exhausted. In fact Eisenhower told Eden on 3 September that American public opinion was against the use of force, 'particularly when it does not seem that every possible peaceful means of protecting our vital interests has been exhausted without result'.[50] The inference from this latter qualification was that use of force could be approved once all diplomatic means had been exhausted.

On 6 September Eden told Cabinet of a message from Eisenhower expressing 'disquiet' over the possibility of British and French military action before all the possibilities of a diplomatic settlement had been exhausted and that reference to the UN Security Council had been approved.[51] The same day Eden wrote to Eisenhower to apprise him of the implications of Nasser's succeeding over the Suez Canal, arguing that the West could be expelled from the Middle East by Egypt in association with the Soviet Union, and referring to the context of appeasement, when Hitler's aspirations were not anticipated and reacted to before it was too late, and of the Berlin Crisis, when the British and Americans resisted Soviet pressure to expel them from west Berlin as a means of expelling them from Germany.[52]

Despite such overtures, the US warning seems to have been reiterated when on 8 September Eisenhower told Eden of his 'misgivings' regarding British preparations for military intervention. British 'use of military force' could cause 'serious misunderstanding' between the US and Britain, Eisenhower said, because 'there is yet no opinion in this country which is prepared to support such a move'. Here again Eisenhower, rather than issue an explicit disapproval of the use of force under any circumstances, uses the term 'yet' to indicate that military action would not be approved before US public opinion was convinced to support such intervention, and indicates a public expectation that the UN should resolve such issues before going on to recommend further exploration of diplomatic means of resolving the crisis. And Eisenhower even explicitly acknowledges the possibility of a necessity for military action in telling Eden, 'I assure you that we are not blind to the fact that eventually there may be no escape from the use of force.'[53] It is hardly surprising that Eden, with significant wartime experience of the Anglo-American alliance and a warm and friendly relationship with Eisenhower, should, in the context of the Cold War and a willingness to pursue diplomatic avenues while preparing for invasion, have assumed that at bare minimum the US would remain neutral over Suez. There is no threat of US sanctions for military intervention in Suez in the message.

The situation over Macmillan is rather different. In his official biography of Macmillan, Horne notes that Macmillan received from the Treasury several explicit warnings, on 8 August and 7 and 21 September 1956, of the need to secure US support for any military action over Suez to avoid adverse economic consequences for Britain, including the possibility of devaluation. On 8 August Bridges, Permanent Secretary at the Treasury, warned Macmillan 'of the costs of "going it alone", without American support' and advised of a possible need for 'measures to support sterling' even without involvement in hostilities over Suez. Despite Bridges' reference to a threat to the balance of payments, Macmillan's indifferent reaction is apparent in his note on 12 August, when he observed, 'we are pretty well armed for Suez'[54]

Macmillan's indifference to Bridges' warning of adverse economic consequences was apparent again at the ensuing Cabinet meeting on 28 August (referred to above), when Macmillan seems to have confined himself to the costs of 'precautionary military measures' for the Suez Crisis and possible additions to the defence budget. Remaining hawkish over Suez Macmillan told ministers that the 'national economy depended upon supplies of oil from the Middle East' and that Nasser threatened such supplies and Britain's relations with the oil producers in the Middle East. The Treasury paper, 'The Egypt Crisis and the British Economy', supported Macmillan's advocacy, indicating the adverse effects on the British economy of closure of the Suez Canal in the form of interference with oil pipelines and diminished dollar reserves should Britain have to obtain its oil from the western hemisphere, and informed ministers that without oil from the Persian Gulf the British economy could not be sustained. Macmillan told ministers that it was Nasser who threatened the free and efficient running of the Suez Canal and that he had to be challenged. Macmillan's influence on Cabinet remained one that advocated use of force. Though there was 'general agreement' on 'reference to the Security Council' provided Britain could be assured of the support of the US, Macmillan seems not to have alluded to Bridges' warning of the possible adverse economic consequences of British military action without US support at all.[55]

On 7 September Macmillan received another warning from Bridges of possible devaluation of sterling if there were no US support and of 'the vital necessity from the point of view of our currency and our economy of ensuring that we do not go it alone, and that we have the maximum United States support'. Horne observes that the passage was 'sidelined' by Macmillan, who added the note, 'Yes: this is just the trouble. US are being very difficult,' an indication of Macmillan's understanding of the US position. Horne then asks, 'but had he, "hawk" that he was, made the Treasury warnings sufficiently clear to the Egypt Committee? And had Eden heard them? Certainly they did not diminish Macmillan's enthusiasm for action.'[56]

Hennessy notes that Macmillan's diary entry for 10 September 1956 indicates appreciation of Bridges' reference to the need to secure US support and Macmillan's understanding of the significance of the impending US election. Hennessy quotes Macmillan—

'What will make the Americans willing to give us the maximum economic and financial aid? Will it be by conforming to their wishes or by "going it alone"?' And 'How I wish the Presidential election were safely over!'[57]

It is apparent that Macmillan, though appreciating the need for US economic aid, rationalised the advice from Bridges to make it consistent with his preference for military intervention in Suez, despite Bridges' explicit exhortation to refrain from 'going it alone', by introducing the possibility that US economic support would be optimised by just such unilateral action over Suez. Kyle finds further evidence in Macmillan's diary of his rationalising Bridges' advice—

'The more we can persuade (the Americans) of our determination to risk everything in order to beat Nasser, the more help we shall get from them.'[58]

Despite Bridges' unambiguous and repeated warnings, then, Macmillan seems to have managed to convince himself that a military solution could elicit US support and that an aggressive military posture would help to elicit such support.

Macmillan's public reaction in the ensuing Cabinet meeting on 11 September was 'hawkish', telling ministers that it was 'unlikely that effective international control over the Canal could be secured without the use of force' and that he regarded the proposal from Dulles and Eisenhower for a Suez Canal Users Association (SCUA) 'as a step towards the ultimate use of force', noting that from the point of view of the 'national economy', a quick and effective resolution would mean that 'confidence in sterling should be restored', whereas 'uncertainty would undermine our financial position'.[59] Johnman comments that Macmillan's representation to Cabinet constituted an 'intriguing reformulation' of Bridges' advice.[60] According to Gorst and Johnman Macmillan did not 'formally' tell the Egypt committee or the Cabinet of the warnings of dire economic consequences from adverse US reaction to British military action over Suez he had received until 6 November, after the invasion of Suez.[61]

If as seems plausible Macmillan also neglected to tell Eden privately of such warnings and if Eden did not receive such information from any other source Macmillan would have exerted a decisive influence on British foreign policy over Suez through manipulating Eden by withholding vital information from him until the imminence of US action forced him to do so, which was after British troops had invaded Suez. Though Horne claims that Macmillan believed that the US would never resort to sanctions against Britain or France in the context of the Cold War, that does not diminish Macmillan's role in the causality of the policy that emerged over Suez through his influence on Eden or his culpability over the Suez debacle. Warner notes that Macmillan acknowledged his error of judgement in his memoir in his reference to the use of force over Suez as follows—

'I felt that the American Government, while publicly deploring our action, would be privately sympathetic, and thus content themselves with formal protests. We had learnt from many of our American friends that they were anxious to see the end of Nasser.'

The authenticity of Macmillan's account of his conviction at the time that the US would not impose sanctions on Britain over British military intervention in Suez seems enhanced by the fact that it is hardly the most expedient admission, in that it indicates poor judgement on Macmillan's part during the Suez Crisis. The inference to be drawn is that Macmillan did genuinely believe in US implicit endorsement in the form of nothing more than an adverse diplomatic response, though Warner notes that Dulles had asked Macmillan to ensure that Eden refrained from action over Suez prior to the US Presidential election on 6 November 1956 and that Macmillan knew of the possible adverse consequences for sterling and the economy of military action alone if the US did not support sterling. Warner concludes, 'in these circumstances, Macmillan's optimism regarding the American attitude is almost incredible'.[62] What might explain Macmillan's confidence is some combination of the diplomatic ambiguity of Dulles, the closeness of Macmillan's relationship with Eisenhower from the war period and Eisenhower's diplomatic expressive style, the context of the Cold War, the human tendency to believe that what is desired or needed is in fact possible or even most plausible (the initial post-war Foreign Office belief in the possibility of a continuation of the wartime collaboration with the Soviet Union is an instance of the conflation of desire or need and perceived possibility regardless of evidence to the contrary), and Macmillan's personality.

It does seem that if Eden had been apprised of the economic risks of military action without US approval he would have referred to them in Cabinet. One factor could have been Eden's lack of understanding of the economy, for Eden's 'abysmal ignorance of economic matters' was well known and Macmillan could have exploited it by refraining from detailed explanation of the economic implications of British military action in Suez without American approval.[63]

At the Cabinet meeting on 11 September referred to above there was general approval for the SCUA because of its direct involvement of the US, and approval too of a preliminary notification to the Security Council. As has been seen, Macmillan supported the SCUA 'as a step towards the ultimate use of force'. Monckton hoped that the SCUA would not be just a prelude to force and pointed to the adverse consequences of 'premature recourse to force, especially without the support and approval of the United States', though without reference to adverse economic consequences, and Kilmuir, Salisbury and Butler felt force was justified if the SCUA and the Security Council did not succeed. Eden summed up by saying that Cabinet had approved use of force once all diplomatic means had been exhausted .[64]

There followed another conference in London between 19 and 21 September, to relaunch Dulles' SCUA. Eden and Lloyd felt that the original conceptualisation was diminished and that the plan for execution was poor. Matters were exacerbated by comments made by Dulles to a press conference on 2 October, when he indicated that the SCUA had not had its 'teeth' pulled because there had never been any 'teeth' in it in the sense of 'use of force'. On 23 September, with disappointment at the evident lack of US pressure on Nasser through the SCUA, Eden referred the Suez Crisis to the UN Security Council, much against Dulles' preference and with no positive outcome as the Soviet Union voted against a resolution insisting that Egypt conform to the Six Principles. The Security Council debate started as late as 5 October. All these represented continued diplomatic efforts to resolve the Suez Crisis and involved the US. The UN outcome was a Cold War one, for on 15 September the Soviet Union indicated that 'the USSR, as a Great Power, cannot stand aloof from the Suez question' and that Soviet interests were involved in the Middle East.[65]

There are indications that reference to the UN represented Britain's going through the motions rather than a genuine attempt at a diplomatic resolution of the Suez Crisis. Kyle notes that on 23 August 1956 a meeting between Macmillan, Salisbury, Butler, Heath (as Chief Whip) and Sir Pierson Dixon continued 'the discussion which had started that morning in the Egypt committee, on how it might be possible to dress up British and French military action for the sake of world opinion', which one assumes meant the US.[66] There seems to have been concern over the existence of significant support for the UN in the Conservative Party, with the hawkish Salisbury feeling on 2 August that reference to the UN would be necessary, which differentiates him from the even more hawkish influence of Macmillan, who was at the time in favour of military collaboration with Israel and who presented to the Egypt committee on 7 August a plan for a military intervention to remove Nasser rather than just to occupy the Suez Canal as an international waterway.

The plan was rejected in favour of the CoS plan for occupation of the Suez Canal. Macmillan's ardour for military intervention seems to have been undiminished, however, for at an ensuing Egypt committee meeting on 24 August 1956 he provoked an 'outburst' from Monckton, the Minister for Defence, which did not however result in his resigning. Such evidence indicates that it was Macmillan who exerted influence in favour of military intervention on Eden both then and earlier in the crisis, when it started on 26 July 1956. Salisbury was to tell Eden again, on 24 August, that the Suez Crisis should be referred to the UN, and that Britain should leave the UN if it failed to resolve the crisis, a more hawkish stance than the earlier one.[67]

It does then seem that British involvement in the London Conference, the proposal to Nasser, and British and French referral of the Suez Crisis to the UN, were predicated upon an expectation by the British political establishment of a refusal from Nasser and no positive outcome at the UN and the hope that such experience would result in greater US diplomatic pressure on Nasser or US understanding of the need to use force over Suez. Macmillan's diary provides more evidence of his continuing hawkishness despite warnings from the Treasury as to the economic consequences of no US support over Suez, for entries on 13, 15 and 16 September 1956 indicate that Macmillan had found it necessary to provide support for Eden against Commons opposition to the use of force in Suez, though he notes on 15 September that securing US support was needed to avoid 'financial ruin'. As with his memoir, publication of these diary entries indicates their credibility, as they are evidence of Macmillan's exhorting Eden to persevere with the policy of military intervention in Suez, a policy that was to result in a great calamity for British diplomacy and credibility. It is unfortunate that Macmillan's diary for 1956 ends on 4 October, though the latest entries seem to indicate that Macmillan was not involved in the negotiations with the French to devise a pretext for an Anglo-French invasion of Suez and that he was in fact immersed in Treasury concerns. By that time though Macmillan's influence had seen Eden through a number of interludes of doubt as to the wisdom of military intervention in Suez and had been an antidote to Eden's characteristic uncertainty and a caution he then seems to have abandoned.

Selwyn Lloyd's view was that Eisenhower and Dulles should be told that reference to the UN was only a means of securing 'the best possible posture internationally over the action which we propose to take', a view which the Egypt committee endorsed to avoid 'consequences of the greatest gravity', one assumes in the mistaken belief that the US would support Britain if Britain went through all the diplomatic possibilities before resorting to military action. At this time Dulles noted that Macmillan and Salisbury were resolute in their views while Eden was 'somewhat vacillating', which is consistent with Macmillan's claims in his diary for the middle of September that he felt he had to support Eden over opposition to the use of force over Suez. Macmillan remained the foremost advocate of the *casus belli*, with Brendan Bracken feeling that Macmillan's 'bellicosity was beyond all description', 'wanting to tear Nasser's scalp off with his own fingernails'.[68]

On 26 September Eden told Cabinet of his impending visit to Paris with Lloyd for discussions with the French. He anticipated agreement to an international system of control over the Suez Canal, though he expected to be pressed by the French for an undertaking that 'if the proceedings of the Security Council were inconclusive, immediate recourse would be had to force'. The French had in fact been negotiating with the Israelis in the apparent conviction that any Franco-Israeli action would involve Britain over Suez. Cabinet agreed that Eden could say that if the UN proved to be 'powerless to enforce respect for international obligations' 'in the last resort it might become our duty to take whatever steps were necessary, including force, to ensure that such obligations would be respected'.[69]

Eden and Lloyd then went to France for talks on the Suez Crisis, and the Americans received a report to the effect that the British were 'restraining' the French (who wanted an invasion and regarded diplomatic channels as a distraction) during the talks.[70] On 3 October Eden reported to Cabinet on his meetings with the French, alluding to French resentment at the attitude of the US and fear that Nasser could conclude a mutual assistance pact with the Soviet Union and so complicate the Suez issue. Eden is also said to have told a 'trustworthy minister' the same day, albeit somewhat cryptically, 'the Jews have come up with an offer'.[71]

By this time Dulles had made the unfortunate comment referred to above to the press to the effect that the SCUA had 'no teeth', a development that convinced Eden that no US support for military intervention regardless of Egyptian provocation would be forthcoming. Pearson notes the predicament Eden found himself in, trying to maintain a balance between the demands for restraint of the Americans and the demands for action of the French, who were needed to impose a settlement on Nasser, and the Conservative right wing, not least Macmillan, for Eden 'continued to receive bellicose advice and pressure from Macmillan'.[72]

By the beginning of October Eden was unwell, and on 5 October he was hospitalised for three days. Pearson claims that on his return he continued to hope for a resolution to the Suez Crisis through the UN. The deliberations of the UN Security Council finally ended on 13 October, with a Soviet veto precluding any resolution of the Suez Crisis through the UN. Though Eden continued to communicate with Eisenhower regarding Anglo-American relations in more general terms, without reference to Suez, on 14 October at Chequers French representatives presented Eden with a French proposal for collusion with the Israelis to contrive a pretext for invasion of Suez. Lucas supports Pearson's claim that Eden continued to be prepared to pursue diplomacy by citing evidence from 14 October, following Lloyd's report from New York of the Soviet veto of the eighteen-power plan, that Eden proposed continued talks with the Egyptians with a view to having them seen as defying a UN resolution so as to isolate them. For Lucas the evidence of Eden on 14 October 1956 indicates that Eden's 'resolve for an assault had disappeared'.[73]

There is some controversy regarding the significance of the Chequers meeting as evidence of Eden's changing approach to the crisis, for Shlaim claims that Eden received the French proposal with 'glee' and ordered Lloyd to return from New York, though Shlaim does note that Eden was concerned to avoid any perception of British instigation of an Israeli attack on Egypt, itself an indication of Eden's continuing concern for diplomatic consequences and audiences, not least it would seem that of the US administration. Shlaim does rely on evidence from Nutting, who was present at the meeting, long after the event, though Gorst and Johnman agree that Eden recalled Lloyd after the Challe proposal for an Israeli invasion as a pretext for an Anglo-French intervention in Suez, and claim that Eden was committed to the French plan (they too rely on Nutting's evidence as the only record of the Chequers meeting).[74] The timing here is of course indicative, and it does seem that Lloyd's report from New York was received on the morning of 14 October and was presumably responded to that morning with Eden's authorisation of continuing negotiation, before Eden's meeting with Gazier and Challe on the afternoon of 14 October. The evidence indicates that Eden was even as late as 14 October prepared for further talks with the Egyptians, if only to secure their diplomatic isolation and to appease the US as Eden's primary diplomatic audience, and that on that day he was impulsively drawn to the Challe plan for an Israeli pretext for an Anglo-French invasion of Suez. That is in itself an indication of Eden's altered approach to foreign policy and his unpredictability by the middle of October 1956.

Pearson's claim that Eden continued to hope for a resolution of the Suez Crisis at the UN even as late as early October does seem consistent with the evidence of Macmillan's diary entries for 13, 16 and 18 September, when Macmillan noted that he had to comfort, reassure and exhort Eden to disregard Commons opposition to the use of force because Eden had begun to 'waver'.[75] That susceptibility to political opposition from within his own party is though distinct from conviction that the UN would impose a resolution of the Suez Crisis on Egypt that Britain could accept. Boyle refers to Thomas Risse-Kappen's conclusion that Eden and Lloyd 'convinced themselves that Dulles' ambiguous remarks throughout the crisis 'supported' the 'assessment' that the US would in the event support the use of force over Suez, though Boyle does not note the ambiguity of Eisenhower's communications with Eden and his refraining from direct opposition to the use of force under any circumstances. On the contrary, Boyle quotes Eisenhower's own attribution of Eden's silence in October 1956, 'it was undoubtedly because of his knowledge of our bitter opposition to using force that when he finally decided to undertake the plan he just went completely silent'.[76] What Boyle does not mention is that though Eden, Lloyd and Macmillan do seem to have been convinced of American ultimate acquiescence in intervention in Suez by the UK and France there had, by the time of the decision to collude with the French and the Israelis to devise a pretext, been significant diplomatic efforts to resolve the Suez Crisis on the part of the Eden government to appease Eisenhower and Dulles, and there had been no unambiguous indication from Eisenhower or Dulles to Eden of the threat of US economic sanctions that would make military intervention impossible to sustain. In fact, as has been seen, Eisenhower explicitly indicated on 8 September that he understood that it was possible that force would in the end have to be used over Suez. The belief in the UK government that the US would acquiesce in the event of an invasion of Suez was then not entirely irrational. It was even so a departure from the greater caution of the preceding period of diplomatic activity over Suez. As has been noted above, the evidence seems to indicate a continuing uncertainty in Eden over the alternatives of continued diplomacy and resort to use of force that started at the beginning of the Suez Crisis and had been characteristic of him as Foreign Secretary.

At the Cabinet meeting on 28 August referred to above Eden had told ministers that a UN resolution endorsing the principles of the London Conference would enhance the case against Egypt and there had been 'general agreement that the balance of advantage lay on the side of making some appropriate reference to the Security Council, before military operations were undertaken, if we could be assured in advance of the full support of the United States and other friendly powers', for

Eden told ministers that 'a Russian veto' would demonstrate 'the obstructive nature of Communist tactics', an indication that reference to the UN was regarded by the Cabinet as no more than a prelude to eliciting greater US pressure on Nasser or US approval of military intervention over Suez. And at an ensuing Cabinet meeting on 3 October Eden told ministers that Egyptian intransigence at the UN would persuade 'world opinion' that military intervention could not be avoided.[77]

The influences on the decision by Eden to engage in secret talks with the French and to proceed with such talks, both without consultation with the US, seem critical for any evaluation of Eden's responsibility for the Suez debacle in refraining from informing the Americans of the secret plan with the French to engage in military intervention in Suez on a pretext provided by an Israeli invasion of Sinai. Assessment of such influences is also relevant for an estimation of Eden's autonomy from ministerial colleagues, not least the influential and hawkish Macmillan, whose influence on the Suez outcome was in part derived from his refraining from notifying ministers, it seems including Eden, of the warnings of economic sanctions from the US and their very adverse effects on the economy. There was also his general hawkishness, and it seems that it was Macmillan who first proposed urging the Israelis to attack Egypt, though not it seems as a pretext for military intervention over Suez, for as early as 3 August he had said that the Israelis should be 'encouraged to attack Egypt' to a 'very shocked' Eden.[78] The influence of Macmillan on Eden and his policy throughout the Suez Crisis does then seem to have been profound, starting on the morning of 27 July 1956 and continuing through advocacy of immediate military intervention in Suez and withholding of information regarding the threat of US economic sanctions and their effect on the economy despite repeated Treasury warnings over military action in Suez Macmillan received.

Rothwell draws a distinction between the earlier phase of the crisis, from late July to late September, when Eden did what any other British PM would have done, and a later phase, in October and November, when a departure from the norms of British foreign policy was apparent.[79] That differentiates the cautious, uncertain, prudent Eden of the appeasement and wartime periods and of the earlier phase of the Suez Crisis, when Eden pursued the diplomatic means of resolving the crisis indicated by Eisenhower, a policy consonant with Eden's long-standing conviction that diplomatic postures should be supported by military and diplomatic power, from the later phase of Suez, when Eden excluded the US from the secret talks with the French to facilitate an Israeli invasion of Sinai as a pretext to justify British and French military action to establish control over the Suez Canal zone. That does seem far more persuasive and supported by the evidence of Eden in the earlier and later stages of the Suez Crisis than claims that Eden became entirely different in approach to foreign policy and to decision-making in general once he became premier, which is of course psychologically implausible though indicative of Eden's desire to appear statesmanlike and not to be seen to be dithering and indecisive having assumed the premiership.

The influences on Eden at the time of his engaging in secret talks with the French would have included the Cold War context and what seemed to Eden (and to Macmillan) the inconceivable prospect of US abandonment of Britain and France, the two major nations of the free world outside the US, and American imposition of threatened sanctions for an invasion of Suez to secure an international waterway against an Arab leader who was supported by the Soviet Union and who was detested in the US. There was also the hawkish advice and exhortation of the influential Macmillan, and possible conflation of an understood need for US acceptance if not approval and conviction that such US acquiescence was plausible. There was the insistence from the French that military action should be undertaken, and there was Eden's possible susceptibility to the most proximate audience combined with the effects of the medicine he was taking at the time, which could have resulted in misplaced confidence in the Franco-Israeli plan and US tacit approval of a *fait accompli* over Suez.

Thorpe claims that the Suez papers, released in 1987, indicate that 'Cabinet members discussed, at various times, the Challe scenario of initiating an Israeli attack with the object of making Anglo-French intervention possible', with 'varying degrees of reluctance' among Cabinet ministers in endorsing British action as peacemaker in the Cabinet meetings on 18, 23 and 25 October.[80] The record of the Cabinet meetings mentioned does not bear such a claim out, for on 18 October Eden told the Cabinet that while Britain would continue to work towards a diplomatic resolution of the Suez Crisis in accordance with the Security Council resolution, 'it is possible that the issue might be brought to a head more rapidly as a result of military action by Israel against Egypt', which did not of course refer to British instigation of such an Israeli attack. According to Verbeek, Eden proposed that the Israelis should be told that the UK would not defend Egypt, and when ministers were asked for agreement that there was no obligation to defend Egypt against an Israeli attack ministerial reaction was one of 'no adverse comment'. On the 23rd Eden told Cabinet an Israeli attack seemed less likely and that as a result Britain was faced with a choice between prolonged negotiations over Suez and military action, and on 24 October Eden indicated that British forces could not be maintained 'in their present state of readiness', which was no more than an oblique indication that an Israeli attack would be opportune. Eden noted that there would not be a better 'pretext' for disposing of Nasser than the nationalisation of the Suez Canal.[81]

On 25 October 1956, just four days before British military action commenced, Eden's statement to Cabinet continued the fiction that Britain was reacting to international events rather than to a pretext he had secretly arranged with France of an Israeli invasion to justify a British and French invasion of Suez—

'It now appeared, however, that the Israelis were, after all, advancing their military preparations with a view to making an attack upon Egypt. They evidently felt that the ambitions of Colonel Nasser's Government threatened their continued existence as an independent State and that they could not afford to wait for others to curb his expansionist policies. The Cabinet must therefore consider the situation which was likely to arise if hostilities broke out between Israel and Egypt and must judge whether it would necessitate Anglo-French intervention in this area.

'The French Government were strongly of the view that intervention would be justified in order to limit the hostilities and that for this purpose it would be right to launch the military operation against Egypt which had already been mounted. Indeed, it was possible that if we declined to join them they would take military action alone or in conjunction with Israel. In these circumstances the Prime Minister suggested that, if Israel launched a full-scale military operation against Egypt, the Governments of the United Kingdom and France should at once call on both parties to stop hostilities and to withdraw their forces to a distance of ten miles from the Canal; and that it should at the same time be made clear that, if one or both Governments failed to undertake within twelve hours to comply with these requirements, British and French forces would intervene in order to enforce compliance. Israel might well undertake to comply with such a demand. If Egypt also complied, Colonel Nasser's prestige would be fatally undermined. If she failed to comply, there would be ample justification for Anglo-French military action against Egypt in order to safeguard the Canal.

'We must face the risk that we should be accused of collusion with Israel. But this charge was liable to be brought against us in any event; for it could now be assumed that, if an Anglo-French operation were undertaken against Egypt, we should be unable to prevent the Israelis from launching a parallel attack themselves; and it was preferable that we should be seen to be holding the balance between Israel and Egypt rather than appear to be accepting Israeli co-operation in an attack on Egypt alone'.

The Cabinet endorsed Eden's recommendation, for it 'agreed in principle that, in the event of an Israeli attack on Egypt, the Government should join with the French Government in calling on the two belligerents to stop hostilities and withdraw their forces to a distance of ten miles from the Canal; and should warn both belligerents that, if either of them failed to undertake within twelve hours to comply with these requirements, British and French forces would intervene in order to force compliance.'

The record of the Cabinet meeting on 25 October 1956 does not indicate unanimous support for Eden over military intervention in Suez, for an unattributed view was that 'our action would cause offence to the United States Government and might do lasting damage to Anglo-American relations. There was no prospect of securing the support or approval of the United States Government.'.[82]

Though ministers were interested in Suez and realised its implications in general, and some did not endorse Eden's policy with any enthusiasm or conviction, their lack of influence on 25 October reflected the fact that the most senior ministers, Eden, Macmillan, Lloyd, Kilmuir and Head, advocated military action, Butler did not oppose it, Monckton had serious reservations but refrained from outright condemnation, and Salisbury was not there. There were then no influential ministers around whom dissent could form. It does however seem that after the Cabinet meeting on 25 October Eden insisted upon making it clear to the French that no British military action would take place without a prior Israeli attack as a pretext and that the British position was that it would react to an Israeli attack on the Suez Canal zone if one were to take place. Such a position would seem to indicate that Eden had not abandoned all caution and that he was even at so late a juncture concerned regarding US opinion and seeking to be in a position to justify British military action to the US.

It does seem from the record of Cabinet meetings that Eden took care to apprise Cabinet of developments at each stage of the crisis and to secure Cabinet approval for the various diplomatic initiatives undertaken to appease the US, for military intervention in Suez in the event of their not achieving the objective of removing Nasser from Suez, and for actual military intervention on 25 October. Even so Cabinet was never informed by Macmillan of the warnings of US economic sanctions and their expected adverse effect on the economy before the invasion itself and was never informed by Eden that he had conspired with the French and the Israelis to contrive a pretext for military intervention, so Suez seems to have been a case of observance of the form of Cabinet government by Eden. Suez was, both in the withholding of information from Cabinet ministers and in the lack of any influence from dissenters, an instance of dominance of foreign policy by the Prime Minister and a small group of senior ministers. It was in the later stages of the conduct of the crisis an instance of liberal use of Prime Ministerial prerogatives in the form of unilateral diplomatic initiatives engaged in without prior consultation with Cabinet as a whole.

Lord Owen takes a different view of what the Cabinet knew of the secret talks with the French. He claims that 'there can no longer be any doubt that the Cabinet were fully told about this collusion on 23 October, arising from "secret conversations" in a confidential annex', and notes that a 'Cabinet of healthy men' were prepared to 'go along with the policy' on 23 October and 4 November before disowning it on 6 November.[83] The reference to what became known as the Protocol of Sèvres in a confidential annex does not though establish that Cabinet ministers knew of the plan to use the Israelis as a pretext for an invasion of the Suez Canal zone. Hennessy notes Shepherd's view that 'Eden, at the Cabinet meetings on 23, 24 and 25 October, sought to mislead the Cabinet. He kept the Sèvres Protocol secret and spoke as though the scheme that had in fact been agreed with the French and the Israelis was merely a contingency plan,' though Hennessy notes that there was no ministerial interrogation of Eden and a degree of deception of themselves by ministers.[84] Though there do seem to be two minutes of the Cabinet meetings on the 23 and 24

October 1956, with one in each case in the form of a confidential annex, and though there is reference to secret conversations with the French and the Israelis in these annexes, there is no actual admission of British collusion to devise a pretext for an Anglo-French invasion, despite Kyle's claim that the confidential annex on 23 October referred to the Cabinet's having been informed of 'direct contact with the Israelis about the casus belli'.[85] Having said that, Kyle notes that on 24 October the Cabinet was faced with the choice of being prepared to see the Egyptians running the Suez Canal following the UN's six principles or 'they could frame their demands in such a way as to make it impossible for the Egyptians to accept them – being resolved on an Egyptian refusal to take military action designed to overthrow Colonel Nasser's regime'. The sense was that the Egyptians would not in their running of the canal preserve British interests and the point was made that it left Nasser in power. Kyle's conclusion that 'the Cabinet was deceived about the extent of collusion with the Israelis or, at the least, not addressed with candour on the subject' seems accurate.[86]

Edward Heath's account of these later days of the crisis is revealing of Eden's demeanour at this time, and indicates the inner circle of those privileged to know of the plan for an Israeli invasion of the Suez Canal zone to legitimise British and French use of force, ostensibly to separate Egyptian and Israeli troops but really to secure the canal. As to ministerial reaction, Heath records a lack of enthusiasm for military action among some ministers but only one ministerial resignation from Cabinet over Suez—

'Secret discussions on the possibility of an invasion between the British, French and Israelis were carried out in Paris in the latter part of October. I was first told of these discussions after a meeting of the inner circle of Ministers and officials held at Chequers on 21 October. I was alarmed, but far from surprised, that a plan was being hatched to circumvent the negotiations in New York. Four days later, I went into the Cabinet Room as usual shortly before Cabinet was due to start, and I found the Prime Minister standing by his chair holding a piece of paper. He was bright-eyed and full of life. The tiredness seemed suddenly to have disappeared. "We've got an agreement!" he exclaimed. "Israel has agreed to invade Egypt. We shall then send in our own forces, backed up by the French, to separate the contestants and regain the Canal." The Americans would not be told about the plan. He concluded, somewhat unnervingly, that "this is the highest form of statesmanship". The Sèvres Protocol, as it became known, had been signed the day before, in a suburb of Paris. Sir Patrick Dean had signed on behalf of the Foreign Secretary, Selwyn Lloyd, and Christian Pineau and David Ben-Guiron had signed, respectively, on behalf of France and Israel. Only Lloyd, Macmillan, Butler and myself were to know about it. I did my utmost to change Eden's mind, warning him that it was unlikely that people would believe him – and that, even if the Protocol remained a secret and people accepted the official reason for going in, the very act of doing so was likely to split the country. Eden did not dispute any of this advice, but simply reiterated that he could not let Nasser get away with it.

'Before we could have a proper discussion, the door opened and the Cabinet began to file in. At the meeting which followed, Eden repeated what he had said to our conference about the need to use force only if necessary. Although several Ministers had doubts about military action, the only one who actually resigned was Walter Monckton, the Minister of Defence. He was replaced by Antony Head on 18 October and took a non-departmental post. On 30 October, the Prime Minister interrupted business in the House at 4.30 p.m. to make a statement announcing that Israel had attacked Egyptian territory and was moving towards the Canal. At the same time it had given an undertaking that it would not attack Jordan or other neighbouring countries whose independence we were concerned to maintain.'[87]

Earlier the same day, 30 October 1956, Eden had informed Cabinet of an Israeli invasion and threat to the Suez Canal. Notes were to be sent to the governments of Egypt and Israel to 'stop hostilities' and withdraw from the canal zone. If in twelve hours either government had not undertaken to comply, 'British and French forces should intervene in order to enforce compliance'. The Cabinet approved the notes. In an indication of an understanding of British economic dependence upon the US though not of an understanding that US economic sanctions had been threatened, the Cabinet minutes noted, apparently unattributed, 'we should do our utmost to reduce the offence to American public opinion which was likely to be caused by our notes to Egypt and Israel. Our reserves of gold and dollars were still falling at a dangerously rapid rate; and, in view of the extent to which we might have to rely on American economic assistance, we could not afford to alienate the United States Government more than was absolutely necessary.'[88]

Eden told Eisenhower of his impending statement to the House of Commons, confirming British preparedness to present the issue before the Security Council but confirming also the British decision to act in the event of Egyptian or Israeli failure to withdraw from the canal zone (Eisenhower had informed Eden of a US decision to ask for 'a United Nations examination and possible intervention' in relation to the Suez Crisis).[89] Eisenhower wrote back to Eden, in a letter issued to the press, in terms that must by this time have been familiar, expressing 'deep concern' at such military action when the matter was being considered by the Security Council, and expressing also his hope of a peaceful resolution.[90] There was no threat of US economic sanctions against Britain in this message. While Eisenhower may have been surprised by Eden's not consulting him beforehand (having learned, as he pointed out to Eden, from the press), it seems that both Eden and Macmillan believed that even if there was US disapproval there would be no US action against Britain (or Israel) given the historical associations between the US and Britain and the US and Israel and the Cold War context.

On 31 October Cabinet was told that the notes had been delivered and Eden said that he had authorised military intervention, and on 2 November Eden told Cabinet he intended to offer to transfer responsibility to a UN military force provided that the Egyptians and Israelis agreed that the UN force would remain until a settlement was reached over control of the canal. Butler said that a rapid transfer to a UN force could achieve objectives for the canal zone and 'restore our position within the Atlantic Alliance and the United Nations'. Lloyd referred to antipathy in the US, to the possibility of oil sanctions and to the alienation of Arab states. In an indication of the maintenance of the fiction of no collusion, there was reference to requiring an Israeli withdrawal to 'demonstrate to the world our impartiality'. And though Macmillan was not there, the Treasury was represented by Heath, the Parliamentary Secretary to the Treasury, and there is no reference to Britain's dire economic position or to the withholding of US support for sterling. When the Cabinet meeting resumed that evening, Eden told ministers that the French Foreign Minister had approved the transfer of responsibility in Suez to a UN force, though there had been objection to any indication that the Anglo-French military operation 'would be abandoned'. The Cabinet decided to offer to cease military action as soon as a UN force could replace British and French troops but not before.

On 4 November Eden told Cabinet that the UN had called for a ceasefire in Suez. Ministerial reaction was mixed, with as many as six ministers having serious reservations regarding 'continuing military action'. According to Gorst and Johnman, who refer to six ministers having reservations, even the hawkish Kilmuir and Salisbury defected, and Eden threatened to resign if military action was not continued. Even so, in an extraordinary instance of Prime Ministerial summing-up, Eden noted that 'the overwhelming balance of opinion in the Cabinet was in favour of allowing the initial phase of the military operation to go forward as planned'.[91] Though Macmillan was present there is no reference to Britain's economic situation or to the need for US economic support that could be withheld.

The same day, 4 November, Eden told Eisenhower, 'if you cannot approve, I would like you at least to understand the terrible decision that we had had to make', an indication of Eden's concern to maintain good relations between Britain and the US in general terms. Eden seems here to have had no sense of an impending US threat of economic sanctions, though the British Ambassador had been summoned by Dulles and when asked if Britain had known of the Israeli invasion had responded in a manner that Dulles found almost an admission of guilt, and Eisenhower had been outraged by the Israeli invasion and had said that he intended to invoke sanctions and go to the UN. He told Dulles, 'we should let the British know at once our position...that nothing justifies double-crossing us. If the British back the Israelis they may find us in the opposition.'[92]

For the purposes of this case study though what Eisenhower intended and for what reason is less relevant than what he communicated to Eden, in that what is of interest here is the causation of British foreign policy over the Suez Crisis, and what Eden believed was the US position is what matters to assessment of the causes of Eden's policy over Suez. As has been indicated above, Eisenhower did no more than indicate 'concern' over Eden's indicating taking military action over Suez on 30 October, and in fact his strategy despite his outrage was to support a UN ceasefire and a token UN force in Suez and to deny the UK any financial assistance or help with oil imports so long as British troops remained in Suez without making any announcement to that effect. The situation then deteriorated with alarming rapidity. On 5 November the Soviet Union threatened missile attacks on London, Paris and Tel Aviv and proposed joint action with the US over Suez, which Eisenhower refused, and on 6 November, as a result of a run on sterling and the Syrian oil pipeline having been severed, Macmillan requested US economic assistance, the US response to which was to make a ceasefire in Suez a precondition for US support for a loan to Britain from the IMF.[93] Lucas refers to Lloyd's account of Macmillan's having told him on 6 November 'that, in view of the financial and economic pressures, we must stop', and claims that Macmillan then informed ministers that without a ceasefire, 'he could not be responsible for Her Majesty's Exchequer.... If sanctions were imposed on us, the country was finished.'[94]

It is not known what the ultimate source of the latter quotation is, so it is difficult to assess its credibility, though the language does seem similar to Macmillan's in its apocalyptic tone. What is established is that at the Cabinet meeting on 6 November the only evidence, in a Cabinet discussion on Suez run by Lloyd rather than Eden, of the need for US assistance was oblique. The minutes note that policy should 'enlist the maximum sympathy and support from the United States Government', though Macmillan seems to have made no reference to Britain's economic situation or to US support that could be withheld in this Cabinet meeting either. The following day Eden told Cabinet that Eisenhower had said that implementation of the UN plan for an international force was imperative. That force would exclude the major powers. Cabinet agreed to attempt to apprise the US of the situation in the Middle East and to 'resume close relations with the United States Government'. On 8 November it was noted at Cabinet that the military intervention had not achieved its objective of securing the Suez Canal under international control, that Eisenhower was reluctant to discuss the longer term before British and French forces had been withdrawn from the canal, that a rapport with the US was needed and that 'an orderly transfer of responsibility' to the UN should occur.

On 20 November Cabinet was told that Eden was suffering from 'severe overstrain' and Macmillan at last told Cabinet of a sterling crisis and of the need to resolve the Suez Crisis to receive US financial assistance, though even then there was the hope that a convincing presentation of British policy over Suez would persuade the US government. On 21 November Cabinet approved withdrawal of troops, entry of a UN force and clearance of the canal being 'synchronised' as the basis for Lloyd in the Security Council debate on Suez. On 26 November Lloyd reported that a UN force would be prepared and that clearance of the canal would start when troops were withdrawn, with negotiations on the canal zone deferred to the time of withdrawal of troops. On 27 November there was a reiteration of the need for close relations with the US because of the drain on gold and dollar reserves, and because US support would be needed for sterling. The following day Lloyd, returned from the UN, noted that 'economic considerations are now more important than the political' and Macmillan, finally indicating urgency, referred to a need to announce the following week the 'losses of gold and dollars' during November 1956, to concern regarding the effect of such an announcement on confidence in sterling, to the need for an accompanying announcement of an IMF loan, and to a need for US support to that end that 'could not be obtained without an immediate and unconditional undertaking to withdraw the Anglo-French force from Port Said. He therefore favoured a prompt announcement of our intention to withdraw this force.'[95]

The context for this series of Cabinet meetings by which the British Government finally came to accept the inevitable was significant. On 24 November the UN had passed with an overwhelming majority a resolution censuring Britain and France for their use of force over Suez and demanding immediate British and French withdrawal. The US voted for this condemnatory resolution and then did not vote on a Belgian amendment that attempted to remove the censure and permit a gradual withdrawal of British and French troops. The US position was then all too apparent. Ministers at the Cabinet meeting on 28 November were apparently overwhelmed by Macmillan's advocacy, seniority and his position as Chancellor, which made pronouncements on what was needed for the British economy very much Macmillan's domain. Eden felt Macmillan had overstated the urgency of British obedience to US wishes and believed in the possibility of negotiation. In London however Macmillan and continued US demands exerted decisive influence in Cabinet. It is then apparent that Macmillan, initially the most hawkish of all British ministers and a likely influence on a then rather less certain Eden, became the foremost advocate of a humiliating withdrawal of British troops from Suez on the basis of the need for US support for Britain's economy (despite not having passed on to Cabinet a series of Treasury indications regarding the threat of US economic sanctions during the Suez Crisis, and though it is not known if he informed Eden there is no evidence that he did). Macmillan then told Cabinet that much needed US support for the economy could not be secured without immediate and unconditional withdrawal of British troops from Suez, becoming at the dismal end of the Suez Crisis a decisive influence on a Cabinet without Eden as PM.

After another series of Cabinet Meetings on Suez, on 3 December 1956 Cabinet approved a statement by Lloyd to the Commons indicating withdrawal of British troops from Egypt. Butler noted that the US government had committed itself to economic assistance to Britain once such an announcement had been made, and Eden, informed of the Cabinet's intention, indicated his approval. The Suez Crisis was over and much needed US economic assistance to Britain ensued.[96]

Eden's conduct of the Suez Crisis in its later stages, that of the secret talks with the French without informing Eisenhower, was a departure from his customary diplomatic caution and resulted in withdrawal from the Suez Canal zone without the objective of international control of the canal zone having been achieved, an indication of the impossibility of a British foreign policy that had not received the prior explicit approval of the US. In more personal terms Eden had misjudged Eisenhower in not informing him of his collusion with the French and in the conviction that Eisenhower would after the event offer tacit support for the UK. Eden then attempted to destroy all evidence of the Sèvres Protocol despite the number of sources of information on the secret talks, and he claimed in the Commons on 20 December 1956 that 'there was not foreknowledge that Israel would attack Egypt'. Owen notes that Eden had never misled the Commons before.

Eden's feelings regarding Suez were to remain understandably intense. His antipathy for Macmillan was long-standing. Referring to their wartime experience Rhodes James comments of Macmillan that 'Eden had never liked him',[97] though that would not of course have precluded

Macmillan's having been a decisive influence on an undecided Eden over Suez on 27 July 1956, or later on throughout the Suez Crisis, not least given Macmillan's certainty, seniority as a Cabinet minister and influence. The Suez affair unsurprisingly did nothing to diminish Eden's low regard for Macmillan, and despite Macmillan's almost imploring him Eden declined to endorse him as PM in the 1959 election.

Thorpe notes Macmillan's extraordinary overtures to the Americans while Eden was convalescing in Jamaica, claiming that Macmillan 'continued to tell Winthrop Aldrich that he was 'Eden's deputy', despite the fact that Butler was acting Prime Minister, and notes too that Macmillan understood that Eden's successor would be the one 'most acceptable to Washington'. Aldrich was the US Ambassador to the UK. Yet more amazingly, Macmillan then proceeded to offer withdrawal of British troops from Egypt and a change of government involving 'the replacement of Eden' in return for US economic support. While of course the US would have no direct vote on who should succeed a British PM in the event of that PM's resignation it does seem plausible that Macmillan would have felt that his credentials for PM would have been improved by his being accepted by the Americans. In Aldrich's account Macmillan also attempted to arrange a meeting between him as 'Deputy Prime Minister' and Eisenhower, and seems to have indicated to Aldrich that his appointment as Deputy Prime Minister was being considered to facilitate such a meeting after the withdrawal of British troops from Suez (which was quite untrue).

The alternative hypothesis, that Macmillan was merely trying to secure for Britain the economic support he believed was so desperately needed, is not supported by the evidence as that would have only required Macmillan's making the case for withdrawal of British troops from Suez in Cabinet, not attempting to meet Eisenhower as 'Deputy Prime Minister' or reference to the replacement of Eden as PM. It is worth noting too that Macmillan could not have known at the time that Eden would not return as PM, for Eden himself did not yet know that, which makes the disloyalty even more profound. It is unlikely that Eden knew of the extent of Macmillan's manoeuvrings while he was convalescing. Though throughout the Suez Crisis Macmillan was a decisive influence on British foreign policy and author of a remarkable *volte-face*, he seems to have succeeded in evading culpability for his part in it, and given what the Americans knew of Macmillan's taking advantage of Eden's being unwell, it is surprising that the US found Macmillan a congenial prospect as PM. It is even more surprising, given that it seems that Eisenhower was told of Macmillan's machinations and encouraged Aldrich to cultivate Macmillan, that he would prefer him as British PM because, in Eisenhower's phrase, Macmillan was 'a straight, fine man'. Thorpe notes the conclusion of an American academic to the effect that, 'to some observers it appeared that Eisenhower, and certainly Macmillan, were attempting to ease Eden from power'.[98] Macmillan's brazenness with the Americans was in fact quite extraordinary. The report by Dulles of his conversation with Macmillan, dated 12 December 1956, indicates that Macmillan referred to British 'deception' of the US over Suez and that Macmillan told Dulles that 'he, personally, was very unhappy with the way the matter was handled and the timing but…Eden had taken this entirely to himself and he, Macmillan, had had no real choice but to back Eden'. Dulles added that Macmillan had said that Eden could 'resign at once' because of his health or 'hold on for six months' though as no more than 'a constitutional Prime Minister'.[99]

Eden's personal bitterness regarding US policy is also clear in his memoir on Suez—

> 'If the United States Government had approached this issue in the spirit of an ally, they would have done everything in their power, short of the use of force, to support the nations whose economic security depended upon the freedom of passage through the Suez Canal. They would have closely planned their policies with their allies and held stoutly to the decisions arrived at. They would have insisted on restoring international authority in order to insulate

the canal from the politics of any one country. It is now clear that this was never the attitude of the United States Government. Rather did they try to gain time, coast along over difficulties as they arose and improvise policies, each following on the failure of its immediate predecessor. None of these was geared to the long-term purpose of serving a joint cause.'[100]

Eden's remarks here do not allude to his having received specific US indications that there would not be any US action against Britain for an invasion of Suez after exhaustive efforts to achieve a diplomatic rather than military resolution of the Suez Crisis. They are rather more general criticisms of US policy in its orientation and lack of support for Britain. In part Eden's remarks may reflect the fact that the diplomatic language used by Eisenhower and Dulles was such that Eden had never been apprised of the possibility of lack of US support for Britain over Suez, let alone the threat of US economic sanctions that ultimately resulted in the humiliating British withdrawal from Suez. In fact, as has been seen, Eden inferred from Eisenhower's letter of 31 July 1956 that use of force over Suez had not been ruled out. In this assessment of what Eden knew of the real US attitude one would have to add that Macmillan had a role in withholding from Eden specific information on the possibility of US economic sanctions for British military action over Suez and on their likely effects on the British economy, which Macmillan did not it seems pass on to Eden, the Egypt committee (suspended as it was between 17 October and 1 November) or the Cabinet until 6 November, after the invasion. There were also in the language used by Eisenhower and Dulles various expressions of understanding of and sympathy for the British difficulty with Nasser and over Suez and encouragement to exhaust all diplomatic means of resolving the crisis, which Britain did attempt, rather than a specific threat of repercussions should Britain use force under any circumstances.

There is also however a sense that Eden may have convinced himself of what he preferred to believe, that the US would never act against Britain in the way it did and that the US would in the end accept the British military action and its pretext when it succeeded in securing the Suez Canal. It does then seem that the diplomatic language used by both Eisenhower and Dulles with Eden and Eden's own desire to believe in US support or at least no disapproval combined to permit Eden to believe that Britain could take military action over Suez without any adverse reaction from Eisenhower. And there was Macmillan's not passing on Treasury warnings to Eden until after the invasion. Having said that Eden did have reason to believe that the US would not act against Britain following a British military intervention in Suez, because Eisenhower's and Dulles' communications had never threatened such action and because of Eisenhower's acknowledgement that force might have to be used in the end.

Eden's own view is indicated by Pierson Dixon's note of a conversation with Eden over his memoirs—

'A. E. admitted that he had miscalculated on the U.S. attitude. But who could have accepted that they would have actively opposed us? He had anticipated grumbles and irritation, but when they had got over that he reckoned on at least tepid neutrality. Even after the intervention started he had some reason to expect that attitude from telephone conversations with the President, who had been very understanding. He had certainly been assured by the President, after the cease-fire, that we should not be hurried out but allowed to stay on improving our bargaining position.'[101]

In terms of responsibility for the Suez debacle within the British political and official establishment Mackintosh argues that the Suez Crisis is an example of the power of the British PM over Cabinet and Commons especially in a time of (perceived) crisis. He points to the speed of movement of events, to the salience of international diplomacy over domestic political arrangements and to Eden's confining decision-making to a Cabinet committee that was informed while the rest of the Cabinet was so ignorant that some ministers did not realise Britain was actually at war, which would hardly seem an advertisement for the doctrine of collective responsibility. In fact the Egypt committee meetings were suspended between 17 October and 1 November.

Mackintosh also indicates that at critical junctures of 'delicate negotiation' in the Suez Crisis British diplomacy in the sense of 'the actual planning of action and taking of decisions was confined to one or two ministers or even to the Prime Minister alone'.[102] Though Mackintosh does not allude to it, such institutional Prime Ministerial power does not preclude influence from senior ministers of firm views and robust personalities on the PM. Certainly Eden knew of the PM's enormous powers and prerogatives in time of crisis from his experience under Chamberlain and Churchill (both of whom used Prime Ministerial power liberally and who were domineering in Cabinet and over foreign policy).

Examples of Eden acting with Selwyn Lloyd as Foreign Secretary, without any other Cabinet colleagues, do seem similar to the partnership of Chamberlain and Halifax. One view of Cabinet involvement over Suez is then that the Cabinet met to discuss the Suez Crisis with some frequency but that the level of ministerial incomprehension was such that no effective restraint on the PM could be conceived of, that the Cabinet as a whole exerted no influence at all on British foreign policy over the Suez Crisis, that uninformed Cabinet ministers were unlikely to proffer any serious opposition and that because a majority of ministers, including those most influential and senior, such as Macmillan, endorsed Eden's approach those who did dissent were marginalised by the dynamics of the Cabinet and the law of numbers.

Even so, ministers were informed by Eden and endorsed Eden's policy at the outset of the crisis, though at that time it was relatively uncontroversial in acquiescing in American wishes that all diplomatic possibilities be exhausted and be seen to be exhausted before any resort to military force. Thereafter Eden did not obtain ministerial approval for secret talks with the French. Nor, in telling the Cabinet of the ostensible outcome of such talks, did Eden inform ministers of Anglo-French collusion with the Israelis to contrive a pretext for invasion of Suez, for ministerial colleagues were told of a likelihood of Israeli action that could precipitate a crisis, not that Eden and his French counterparts had colluded to contrive a pretext for invasion of Suez. Though there was Prime Ministerial involvement of Cabinet in the early stages, when policy reflected US dictates, there seems to have been no influence from Cabinet outside the small group of senior ministers on Eden, and thereafter the record indicates Prime Ministerial evasion of and deception of Cabinet in the phase of secret talks with the French.

As to possible influence on Eden from the Egypt Committee, the Cabinet committee set up on 27 July 1956, the day after Nasser announced nationalisation of the Suez Canal, the Egypt committee was at that time 'overwhelmingly hawkish in its composition'.[103] Its members were to begin with Eden as PM, Macmillan as Chancellor of the Exchequer, Salisbury as Lord President of the Council and Leader of the House of Lords, and Home as Commonwealth Secretary, with Selwyn Lloyd as Foreign Secretary and Walter Monckton as Defence Minister joining later (it is worth noting that Mackintosh has the membership of this crucial Cabinet committee as being Eden, Macmillan, Lloyd, Butler, Head, Salisbury and Sandys, which may be indicative of the difficulties of reliance on personal accounts before the release of Cabinet papers under the thirty-year rule, for Mackintosh was writing in 1981 and the Suez papers were released in 1987, which means that he was at the mercy of those willing to disclose their accounts to him, sources which of course selected themselves, would not have been without motive, and would have been susceptible to inaccuracies of recall).

The exclusion of Selwyn Lloyd as Foreign Secretary and Monckton as Minister for Defence from the Egypt committee at the outset is astonishing, and Selwyn Lloyd's exclusion is indicative of Eden's view of him and of the extent of his influence on British policy over Suez. Members of this committee met very frequently and would have been informed as to each development in the Suez Crisis, with Macmillan an influential figure and an early advocate of military action over Suez, so it is possible that he exerted significant influence in the Egypt committee on Eden. Even so it does seem that even the Egypt committee was excluded as Eden proceeded with military discussions with the French with Selwyn Lloyd, and as has been seen the Committee did not meet between 17 October and 1 November. Such private discussions with the French do not of course preclude significant influence from Macmillan or other members on Eden prior to that time.

As to possible influence from officials in the Foreign Office and elsewhere in the Civil Service on Eden and British policy over Suez the evidence is that Eden did not disclose the decision-making of the Egypt committee to officials who could then offer alternative views or constrain Eden's freedom of decision and manoeuvre. Though Kirkpatrick as PUS at the FO was hawkish on Suez Gorst notes Logan's view that Eden knew what the Foreign Office view would be and avoided it, and Foreign Office dismay at their having been deliberately excluded from the decision-making process over Suez. He also notes that Eden used Dean of the Foreign Office as liaison to do what he, Eden, wanted done rather than obtaining Foreign Office advice. The conclusion drawn is that 'the identification of the Foreign Office's chief official with Prime Ministerial dogmatism, combined with the system of ad hoc committees, had the effect of marginalising the Foreign Office,' for Kirkpatrick's advocacy of the use of force extended even to involvement in devising a pretext for it and to being impervious to the counsel of Beeley as Assistant Under-Secretary, Ross as Under-Secretary responsible for the Middle East, and Fitzmaurice as the Foreign Office's chief legal adviser.[104]

To what should one attribute Eden's emerging decisiveness over the Suez Crisis, not least in the context of his wartime *Realpolitik* over the Baltics and continuing indecision and cultivation of diplomatic harmony over the future of Germany, and his initial indecision and uncertainty over Suez? It could not be Eden's conceptualisation of the powers and prerogatives of the role of PM as against those of Foreign Secretary, especially in time of crisis, and that having finally become premier he was resolved upon using the powers of the PM, for Eden had such powers in the initial phase of characteristic prudence and caution over Suez. The more plausible inference is that departure from the norm of open consultation with the US reflected an accumulation of the medicines Eden was taking and that Eden's judgment was affected by them as such medicine made him more confident and dictatorial and less susceptible to any restraining influence that did exist. For it seems that Eden had ten consultations with doctors between the beginning of the Suez Crisis and late October 1956. Set against the inference of an effect from his medicine on Eden is the evidence of Eden's irrationality on the telephone to Nutting even in March 1956, though that phone conversation does represent little more than an outburst (of the sort Eden had been given to throughout his long political career) rather than a policy decision like that to pursue secret talks with the French and the Israelis.

Even so there was the interaction of facilitative institutional factors such as the power of the PM over Cabinet and Commons, and the prerogatives of the PM in terms of unilateral diplomatic overtures, with circumstantial ones, as the powers of the PM in Cabinet and in the Commons are especially pronounced in a time of crisis given the orientation at such times to international diplomacy and because the need for speed of decision itself necessitates executive decision-making. The effect of Prime Ministerial dominance is enhanced in crises by a lack of information for ministers that precludes formation of a definite ministerial view in opposition to that of the PM, especially where the PM is supported or at least not opposed by other senior ministers. And there were more personal factors that exerted influence on the specific nature and direction of foreign policy, which reflected Eden's personality and personal experience.

There was his sense of his own anti-appeasement credentials and his place in history as PM, there was his experience of the Chamberlain and Churchill Cabinets and of both as PM in the role of Foreign Secretary and a possible desire to emulate their decisiveness as premiers in regard to British foreign policy, a sense that it was at last his turn to define British foreign policy. There was his sense of protocol and of the prerogatives and powers of positions in the British political establishment, which may have left him with a sense that he had a right to his own foreign policy as PM. There was his own personal experience of appeasement and sense that Nasser was just another Mussolini to be resisted by British resolve. And there were health and medicinal effects, which could have resulted in Eden's not noticing or being less susceptible to implications of US uncertainty over Suez (it was a recurrent British criticism of the US political system that it spoke with many voices and that it was difficult to know when a US foreign policy decision had been made), for it has recently become known that Eden had been taking a medicine called Drinamyl that was a combination of amphetamines and barbiturates and that has since been found to impair insight and judgement. Eden's decisiveness and confidence over Anglo-French talks held in secret without informing the US could be attributed to such medicinal use.

Set against such inferences of a medicinal effect on Eden's conduct of foreign policy over Suez there is a question of why in the early part of the Suez Crisis Eden was his usual self, uncertain, prudent, cautious and responsive to US demands for the exhaustion of diplomatic overtures to resolve the crisis, and then undertook the risk of not informing the US of British and French intentions to intervene militarily over Suez using an Israeli invasion of Sinai as a pretext. Owen claims that Eden's use of Drinamyl increased between July and October 1956, with an increase in August and another possible increase in October, and it is possible that the accumulation of such medicine resulted in increasingly erratic behaviour and a far less cautious approach to risk than had been characteristic of Eden before Suez and during the earlier part of the crisis, in his exchanges with Eisenhower. Owen notes that Drinamyl has been found to cause 'insomnia, restlessness, anxiety, over-stimulation and overconfidence', and refers to its adverse effect on judgement and decision-making.

Owen quotes Eden's notes prepared for his announcement to Cabinet on 9 January 1957 of his impending resignation as PM. These refer to increased use of drugs and of 'stimulants' to combat their effects over the course of the Suez Crisis and indicate that Drinamyl could have had an effect on Eden during the later stages of the crisis, when Eden undertook secret talks with the French. Owen contrasts the 'cautious' reaction of Eden at the start of the Suez Crisis on 26 July 1956, which was to 'prepare for but to postpone military action', with the decisions taken 'from 14 October', and notes that because the stimulant or the sedative effect of Drinamyl could be more influential Eden's behaviour could not be predicted. Owen refers to Dutton's observation that it is difficult to understand how Eden believed he would succeed in restoring international control to the Suez Canal by a policy of colluding with the French and the Israelis to contrive a pretext of military action that did not have the explicit approval of the US, without the explanation that Eden's judgement was diminished at the time, and that by the beginning of October Eden was close to a breakdown over Suez.[105] Owen's view is worth noting because of his combination of scrupulous attention to disconfirming evidence, his experience of the protocols of government and the FO given his time as Foreign Secretary, and his medical knowledge and meticulous reference to the literature. Having said that the Nutting recollection of Eden's ranting over Nasser in March 1956 indicates that Eden's erratic behaviour and alternation of moods were not confined to October 1956, though it does seem plausible that there was some effect from the increased dose of the amphetamine Eden was taking on his sudden departure from his normal cautious, prudent and indecisive approach to foreign policy, together with his state of poor health and natural volatility of personality that obtained earlier in the crisis. For periodic outbursts had been characteristic of Eden during the war and had no effect on his continuing caution, prudence and indecision regarding foreign policy and his tendency to exhaust all diplomatic possibilities.

Though Hamilton refers to Owen's research he claims that 'at no point did Eden ever consider the repercussions if Britain attacked Egypt' and that 'five minutes' reflection would surely have revealed to him that the use of force would immediately produce precisely the results he was trying to avoid', and he quotes Thorpe's recitation of the adverse consequences of British intervention over Suez. These claims do seem extraordinary given Eden's having explored various diplomatic means of resolving the Suez Crisis through conferences, the SCUA and reference to the UN to appease Eisenhower and Dulles, and given Eden's many messages to Eisenhower to explain the British position and his intentions over Suez. The claim that the briefest reflection would have made the consequences of military intervention in Suez obvious seems to be contradicted by the fact that they were not plain to the influential Macmillan, Salisbury, other Cabinet ministers or the majority of the Party in the Commons, and Hamilton takes no account of the Cold War context of recent Anglo-American resistance to the spread of communism in Berlin in 1948 and Korea between 1950 and 1953 or of the ambiguity in Eisenhower's and Dulles' communications with Eden, or in fact of Eisenhower's explicit acknowledgement of the possibility of an ultimate need to resort to force over Suez even as late as 8 September 1956. And to adduce Thorpe's reference to the adverse consequences of the Suez debacle as evidence of what Eden should have realised is to confuse hindsight with what was a rational inference at the time. One might with equal justification and on the same basis infer from Eisenhower's acknowledgment that his policy over Suez was the worst mistake of his presidency that he should have known that at the time too.

Hamilton's case is that British policy over Suez resulted from Eden's sensitivity to criticism, 'political inexperience', 'naivety in believing that Britain's collusion with France and Israel would remain a secret', failure to court the media and 'inability to keep his personal feelings separate from his political actions', though the latter is in fact just what Eden did do between the end of July and 14 October, when he was presented with the French plan at Chequers, though even Eden on that day indicated to Lloyd that he should continue negotiation with the Egyptians. Eden was without doubt sensitive to criticism, though that does not seem to have been a causal influence on his dealing with Suez, for though he did want not to be seen to 'dither' that did not preclude the extended period of diplomatic efforts to resolve the crisis. The claim that Eden lacked political experience does seem extraordinary. The change in Eden's approach to the Suez Crisis seems to have taken place between the middle of October and the end of that month and to have been in part a result of the increased Drinamyl Eden was taking by that time, as Owen argues, for before that time Eden's conduct of the Suez Crisis reflected the Eden of the wartime period in periodic outbursts of rage but continued preference for diplomatic overtures, prudence and caution or even indecision. Hamilton's claim that Eden's 'character' did not change between 26 July and 23 November seems to be intended to indicate that his behaviour and policy did not change, when in fact both do seem to have changed, with Eden more intense in expressive style and demeanour late on in the crisis and changing policy from continued diplomacy to military intervention arranged through secret talks. Hamilton's claim that Eden intended military intervention in Suez all along and only engaged in diplomacy during the period military preparations required is one for which he produces no evidence and that seems to be contradicted by Eden's instruction on 14 October 1956 to Lloyd to continue negotiations with the Egyptians, for the date for the invasion was originally 1 October and was deferred for political rather than military reasons, indicating military readiness at the beginning of October.[106]

Given his previous roles as Foreign Secretary under three PMs, Eden's relationship with his own Foreign Secretary, Selwyn Lloyd, is of interest in terms of its extent of influence from Foreign Secretary to PM and the extent to which Eden actually consulted Selwyn Lloyd over British foreign policy as opposed to emulating Chamberlain and Churchill as domineering PMs who regarded foreign policy as their own domain and would accept no dissent from their Foreign Secretaries. It is worth noting that prior to 1955 Selwyn Lloyd had served under Eden as a Minister for Foreign Affairs in the Conservative government of 1951–54, so he was very much a known quantity to Eden.

It seems from Kyle's account of Suez that Selwyn Lloyd replaced the influential and robust Macmillan as Foreign Secretary after a period in which Eden as PM sent Macmillan several notes a day on foreign policy and that Eden chose Selwyn Lloyd as Foreign Secretary to preclude any opposition to his foreign policy. According to Rothwell Selwyn Lloyd's appointment was 'greeted with extremes of derision in the Foreign Office' and represented Eden's wanting a 'diligent and obedient' Foreign Secretary. Lloyd seems to have understood his position and to have deferred to Eden constantly, which would have been exactly as Eden would have intended.[107] Though it has been claimed that Lloyd 'increasingly turned towards a negotiated solution to the crisis', there is no evidence that he exerted any influence on Eden at any time during the Suez Crisis.[108] Lloyd's doubts as to military intervention cannot then be said to have been a constraint on Eden or British policy over Suez, and the relationship between PM and Foreign Secretary was then one which almost replicated that between Churchill and Eden, with Selwyn Lloyd however having far less experience of foreign affairs than Eden did.

While Selwyn Lloyd as Foreign Secretary seems to have had no influence on Eden (and it seems that Eden chose him as Foreign Secretary because he felt he would be obedient) the general sense of Eden as the dominant influence in the British response to the Suez Crisis disregards the influence of the small group of senior ministers, not least Macmillan, and that of Cabinet after the British and French occupation of the Suez Canal zone and the threat of US economic sanctions that resulted in the British withdrawal from Suez. For the Suez Crisis is in fact indicative both of the powers and prerogatives of the PM when there is a group of senior ministers who endorse the PM's position and of the limitations of Prime Ministerial power in Cabinet when there is a preponderance of ministers, including senior and influential ones, against Prime Ministerial policy, and when Prime Ministerial policy has suffered a diplomatic reverse, though in the Suez case, as has been seen, Eden became so unwell he did not attend the final Cabinet meetings of the crisis.

A similar situation obtained with Chamberlain's Cabinet after Munich and Halifax's abandoning of appeasement, when the PM had to accept faster rearmament.[109] And there was the role of the influential and decisive Macmillan, who could in his initial confident advocacy of military action when Eden seems to have been less certain (in the early phase of the Suez Crisis) have been a decisive influence on Eden. Macmillan's concealing from Cabinet and it seems also from Eden the Treasury's warnings of adverse economic consequences of US economic sanctions for British military action until it was too late seems to have been another major influence on Eden's policy over Suez. For, as has been seen, despite compelling Treasury advice as to the possible monetary ramifications of British military action over Suez without the explicit approval of the US, Macmillan endorsed the military option in the early and middle stages of the crisis, and only abandoned his hawkish posture and began to stress the adverse economic implications of US disapproval when the invasion of Suez had been started. Such a radical *volte-face* by one of the architects of the disastrous British policy over Suez did not prevent Macmillan from succeeding the unfortunate Eden as PM.

Much has been made of Eden's loathing of Nasser as an individual. This loathing was without doubt genuine, and Eden argued to Eisenhower that Nasser could be seen as a new Mussolini. Even so, Eden's initial uncertainty and ensuing engagement in diplomatic overtures to resolve the crisis establish the influence of competing *Realpolitik* considerations that would have militated against influence on Eden from antipathy towards Nasser.

The extensive efforts of Britain to meet US wishes for diplomatic overtures to secure worldwide condemnation of Nasser and his approach to Suez are indicative of British understanding of the need to comply with US requests to maintain the relationship with the US, and even when the US was not told of the British and French secret talks Eden insisted that Britain would only undertake military action over Suez in the event of an Israeli attack on the Suez Canal zone, which would permit Eden to represent the British action as peace-making rather than invasion to the US (it is difficult to conceive of his being concerned regarding any other audience).[110]

While such a sequence of events over Suez returns the focus to the juncture at which it was decided that the US should be excluded from further British foreign policy over Suez, there was much less discontinuity between the more cautious and *Realpolitik* Eden of appeasement, the Baltic issue and German dismemberment and the Eden of the Suez Crisis than might be supposed. For over Suez Eden avoided risks that he perceived were risks, and though with hindsight it is apparent that Eden was running a risk in not obtaining prior and explicit approval from the US for a specific British policy of military intervention under certain circumstances over Suez it does seem that Eden believed he was running no risk with the US because of the lack of any specific ban on military intervention from Eisenhower (and the latter's general supportive and understanding tone and indication of understanding that force might prove necessary in the end over Suez), the fact that he had received no information from Macmillan as to the threat of US economic sanctions and their effect on the British economy, and because the medicine Eden was taking at the time could have resulted in a distorted perception of or attitude to risk and an adverse effect on judgement.

What this indicates is that foreign-policy decision-making takes place within the confines of the world as it is perceived by policymakers rather than the objective world. The perceptual lens and the attitudinal prisms of those who exert significant influence on foreign policy are then significant causal influences on the policy that emerges, as are the personalities of such individuals and their interactions. The institutional framework of prerogatives and powers, formally defined or defined by precedent, serves to indicate those with possible influence rather than to establish actual influence. In the case of the British political system the power of the PM may be no more than a channel for other more decisive influences on foreign policy in the event of a weak PM in terms of personality or position in Party and Cabinet or of a PM with little interest in foreign policy who is influenced by more decisive, influential and interested ministers.

In the case of the Suez Crisis, Macmillan seems to have exerted hawkish influence on Eden in the initial phase of the crisis and thereafter, and to have concealed US and Treasury warnings of adverse economic consequences of British military action over Suez from the Egypt committee until 6 November, after the invasion of Suez. It does seem that he concealed such warnings from Eden too, and that his concealment meant that Eden felt he was not undertaking any risk of US economic sanctions and an adverse effect on the British economy, not least given Eden's 'abysmal ignorance' of economic policy and of economics in general, which was known to the more economically astute Macmillan himself. Rothwell notes that 'Macmillan was convinced that Eden was genuinely tormented by knowledge of his incapacity in economic matters'.[111] If Macmillan did persuade Eden on 26 and 27 July of the necessity for threat of or use of force over Suez and then withheld information that would have apprised Eden of the adverse consequences for the British economy of invasion one would have to infer that Macmillan was a significant causal influence on British foreign policy over Suez. Macmillan told Eden from Washington as late as 26 September 1956 that 'Ike is really determined, somehow or another, to bring Nasser down. I explained to him our economic difficulties in playing the hand long, and he seemed to understand. I also made it clear that we *must* win, or the whole structure of our economy would collapse. He accepted this.'

Thorpe notes that in this letter from Macmillan to Eden 'Macmillan's interpretation of the President's attitude was, even then, seriously misleading, implying that in the end the Americans would stand by the British'. It is worth noting that Macmillan is stressing the adverse economic consequences of not succeeding over Suez, even though by the time of the letter to Eden Macmillan had received several Treasury warnings of adverse economic consequences following from British military action over Suez. One assumes from the language in the letter and from the fact that it reiterated the case Macmillan had made to Cabinet after receiving warnings from the Treasury regarding adverse economic consequences for Britain following US sanctions for a British military invasion of Suez that such Treasury warnings had not been passed on to Eden, as such warnings would have been dissonant with Macmillan's advocacy in Cabinet and with the letter of 26 September. Thorpe notes that on the day Eden received Macmillan's letter he flew to Paris with Lloyd to meet the French, and attributes this to Eden's impatience with Eisenhower's indication of 'serious misunderstanding between our two countries' in the event of British military action over Suez, and his desire to 'break free' of 'American caution'.[112]

It cannot however be the case that Eden was unaffected by Macmillan's reassurance that despite US preferences for a diplomatic resolution the US would in the end support Britain. Such an assurance would have been decisive in Eden's decision to intervene in military terms over Suez without explicit approval from Eisenhower. The role of Macmillan in misrepresentation of the US attitude and withholding of information is then a decisive influence on Eden over Suez, for even with Macmillan's reassurance from Washington Gorst and Kelly claim that Eden's 'concern about the overt belligerence of his French colleagues is clearly demonstrated in the record of his meetings on 26 September'.[113] That seems to indicate that Eden's characteristic caution and uncertainty and concern for diplomatic prudence obtained even in the context of Macmillan's assurances.

Thorpe claims that Eden continued to consider diplomatic means as late as 14 October, when the Soviets exercised their veto at the UN and Eden proposed to Lloyd an offer to the Egyptians of direct talks, and though it is possible to see Eden's proposal as an expedient by which to legitimise military action as the last resort, the documentary evidence presented above does indicate that even at late as 14 October Eden was genuinely uncertain regarding use of force over Suez without exhaustion of all diplomatic possibilities.[114] The French plan for military action in conjunction with the Israelis was presented to Eden that day. The French plan was for an Israeli attack on the Suez Canal zone with Britain and France intervening 'as peacemakers, to 'separate the combatants' and thus secure the canal as an international waterway'.[115]

As to Macmillan's involvement at this stage of the crisis, that is, since his reassuring letter to Eden on 26 September 1956 indicating Eisenhower's understanding attitude, Philip Murphy (not to be confused with Robert Murphy, the US Defence Secretary) notes Nutting's claim, in the unexpurgated copy of his memoir on Suez, that there was a meeting at 10 Downing Street on 16 October 1956 at which Eden told a group of ministers (including Nutting as representative of the Foreign Office in place of Lloyd, who was returning from the US) of conversations between Eden and Gazier, French Minister of Labour who was acting Foreign Secretary as Pineau was at the UN, and General Challe, of the French Prime Minister's 'personal staff', the previous Sunday. These, Eden said, referred to the possibility of Anglo-French intervention in Suez following an Israeli invasion as a pretext. Nutting claims that Macmillan was first to react, that he said that reference to the UN, the Menzies plan and the Canal Users' Association 'had got us nowhere', and that Macmillan concluded that 'we should support the French and the Israelis'. Nutting claims that he himself urged consultation with the American administration and that 'Eden exploded, 'I will not bring in the Americans ... Dulles has done enough damage as it is. This has nothing to do with the Americans. We and the French must decide what is to be done and we alone.' Nutting also claims that Kilmuir supported collusion and any ensuing military action.

In terms of possible influence on policy over Suez and the eventual collusion with the French and the Israelis to contrive a pretext for British and French intervention in Suez, it is worth noting that the meeting preceded the conclusion of what became known as the Sèvres Protocol on 24 October.

The credibility of Nutting's account, for which there is no documentary corroboration (though one would not expect documentary corroboration of a meeting of such secrecy), seems to be enhanced by its specificity of recall (including reference to its having been arranged by Eden's private secretary and naming of ministers present). And there is the fact Nutting deferred publication of his memoir on Suez, *No End of a Lesson*, for as long as eleven years after he resigned in November 1956 over Suez, and that he refrained from making a statement to the Commons at the time of his resignation because Macmillan persuaded him not to do so. And in 1967, after Nutting's having waited so as not to prejudice the interests of those involved in the Suez Crisis, there was an attempt by the Cabinet Office and the Foreign Office to remove the passage on the meeting on 16 October. Their argument was that Nutting's revelations violated the principle of collective responsibility and would not assist the credibility of British diplomacy. There was no attempt to dispute the veracity of Nutting's account, though Nutting's recollection of the meeting on 16 October 1956 did of course implicate Macmillan and Kilmuir in a most direct way with the collusion with the French and the Israelis and would have diminished Macmillan's and Kilmuir's political reputations.

Murphy notes that Macmillan's official biographer, Horne, does not even refer to the meeting on 16 October, though he does seem to have had an unexpurgated copy of Nutting's memoir. Instead Horne quotes Rhodes James' conclusion that though Macmillan supported 'virtually any means of bringing Nasser down', 'Eden did not confide in him any more than he did in Butler', and claims that Macmillan first knew of the planned collusion on 24 October, the day the Sèvres Protocol was signed, which would seem intended to indicate Macmillan was not an influence on it.

As to motive, it does not seem that Nutting had any personal animosity towards Macmillan. On the contrary, he seems to have been persuaded by Macmillan in November 1956 to refrain from any statement to the Commons regarding his resignation, presumably because Macmillan was concerned that any divulging of his endorsement of Eden's policy over Suez especially in its more controversial later stages would have diminished Macmillan's credibility with the US. Though Nutting does seem to have been a minister who counselled diplomatic caution and consultation with the US rather than unilateral military action over Suez there seems to be no evidence of an ulterior motive to discredit Macmillan. Further, if Nutting's account were fictitious the optimal Cabinet Office and Foreign Office reaction should have been to permit its publication and then to discredit it by refuting evidence from other claimed attendees, and as has been noted the veracity of Nutting's account was not challenged. It does then seem that Nutting's account is accurate.[116]

Verbeek, referring to Lloyd's account of the Suez Crisis, claims that at the meeting on 16 October 1956 Eden, Lloyd, Thorneycroft, Head, Monckton and Kilmuir were present but that Butler, Macmillan and Salisbury were not. He claims that there was an ensuing meeting on 21 October attended by Butler and Macmillan though not Salisbury and that Butler despite previous reservations accepted use of force and collusion with the French and Israelis, that on 23 October what Lloyd refers to as in effect the Egypt Committee met, so that Eden, Butler, Macmillan, Salisbury and Home must have been present, and that another meeting took place on 24 October between Eden, Butler, Lloyd, Macmillan and Head, at which it was agreed that a 'contingency plan' was to be presented to Cabinet. What is established by the accounts of Nutting and Lloyd is that Eden consulted with senior ministers before concluding the Sèvres Protocol on 24 October 1956.[117]

As to Lloyd's involvement and possible influence, Shlaim claims that Eden, having spoken with French representatives at Chequers on 14 October, summoned Lloyd from New York, that Lloyd had been negotiating with the Egyptian Foreign Minister, Fawzi, but arrived in time to join the ministerial meeting on 16 October, that Lloyd told Nutting that he had been right to reject the proposed collusion with the French but that Eden then persuaded Lloyd to his view and took him to Paris for a meeting with Mollet, the French PM, and Pineau, the French Foreign Minister, on 16

October. Shlaim claims that Lloyd was reluctant, that he felt he had no choice, and that he continued to prefer a diplomatic resolution to the Suez Crisis, an inference supported by reference to Lloyd's apparent antagonism towards the entire idea of collusion with the Israelis at an ensuing meeting with the Israelis.[118] Though much of Shlaim's work is predicated upon Nutting's recall long after the events themselves the Israeli evidence does seem to indicate Lloyd's preference for a diplomatic resolution and aversion for collusion with the Israelis over Suez. Gorst and Johnman have a similar account, claiming that Lloyd was summoned by Eden from New York following Eden's meeting with Gazier and Challe on 14 October, that Lloyd returned on 16 October with a proposal based on the UN Security Council's six principles, that Lloyd endorsed a paper by Nutting, Kirkpatrick and Ross of the Foreign Office arguing against acceptance of the Challe plan, and that Lloyd was then persuaded by Eden to go along with the French plan.[119] Regardless of Lloyd's disenchantment with collusion the evidence indicates that Lloyd exerted no influence on Eden then, for Patrick Dean was sent to France for the third Sèvres meeting, or at any time during the Suez Crisis.

Whether or not Macmillan's opposing Eden's colluding with the French and the Israelis to contrive a pretext for an Anglo-French intervention in Suez would have had a decisive effect on Eden in the middle of October 1956 is counterfactual and a matter for conjecture. Though it is possible that by this time Eden was so affected by his medicine that he was immune to restraining influence even from senior ministers such as the influential Macmillan and Kilmuir, and Heath's recollection of Eden on 25 October would support such an inference, Eden's characteristic uncertainty and need for reassurance seem to indicate that even with the effects of medication Eden called the meetings recalled by Nutting and Lloyd to obtain senior ministerial reassurance and support for what he intended to do. One inference is in fact that Nutting's and Lloyd's accounts are in general genuine because it seems so implausible that Eden would have acted without the reassurance he obtained from Macmillan and Kilmuir on 16 October or by 21 October 1956. It is also difficult to imagine why Eden would have called such meetings and have told ministers of the plan with the French and the Israelis, just before signing the Sèvres Protocol, other than to obtain the reassurance of the support of senior ministers such as Macmillan and Kilmuir. It seems that it was following the meeting on the morning of 16 October that Eden and Lloyd went to Paris for the talks that eventuated in the Sèvres Protocol.

Macmillan does then seem to have been influential in October 1956 as well as earlier in the Suez Crisis, in late July and September 1956, which indicates that the locus of decision-making power in regard to British policy over Suez would seem to be with him as much as with Eden. Despite Eden's intimate association with Suez as PM, then, and his powers as PM, one would in such an eventuality have to conclude that Eden's indecisiveness and uncertainty resulted in Suez's not being a classic case of Prime Ministerial power in time of crisis but rather an exemplification of the limitations of institutional power when the incumbent, despite having personal experience of historical precedents of liberal use of such institutional power, has a character that makes him susceptible to significant influence from another minister, even one institutionally not concerned with foreign affairs, whose personality and decisiveness (and ruthless exploitation of a Prime Ministerial weakness in regard to economic affairs) render him influential. It is in fact possible that Macmillan exploited not only Eden's uncertainty and susceptibility to influence but also his volatile personality (possibly exacerbated by medicine) to manipulate him into a policy that Macmillan felt would succeed, and then abandoned Eden, who continued to oppose withdrawal of troops from Jamaica, when it was obvious that a continued British military presence in Suez would mean no US assistance over sterling.[120] It would not be plausible to attribute to Macmillan a Machiavellian scheme to discredit Eden at the cost of a British diplomatic disaster throughout the crisis. It would however be plausible to ascribe to Macmillan a certain degree of responsibility for the Suez debacle because of his influence on Eden at a number of junctures in the crisis. There was Macmillan's advocacy of hawkishness with the Americans at the outset of the crisis to elicit from them diplomatic pressure on Nasser to restore international control to the Suez Canal, which was expected to result in Nasser's humiliation and fall from power. There was Macmillan's confidence that the US would support Britain once the invasion was complete given the context of the Anglo-American relationship and the Cold War. There was Macmillan's not passing on to Eden, the Egypt committee and the Cabinet the warnings he had received of US economic sanctions for British military action and their expected adverse effect on the British economy. There was Macmillan's support for Eden in defiance of Commons opposition to the use of force over Suez in September 1956. There was Macmillan's ensuing support for collusion with the French and the Israelis on 16 October. And, in an indication of Macmillan's motivation late on in the crisis, there was Macmillan's abandonment of Eden once the consequences of military intervention became apparent in the US response to British action in Suez. Rhodes James claims that it was Macmillan's 'role during the Suez Crisis in the summer and autumn of 1956 that gave him a reputation as a Machiavellian political operator of consummate ruthlessness that he never entirely lost', notes that Macmillan played 'a central role' in Eden's 'downfall', and claims that he had an 'eye on the main chance'.[121] Wilson noted that Macmillan was over Suez 'first in, first out', a derisive reference to Macmillan's vocal hawkishness over British military intervention at the start of and during most of the Suez Crisis and ensuing *volte-face* in the face of a very immediate US threat to the British economy and currency. Macmillan's motivation at the end of the Suez Crisis does then seem to be a causal influence on British policy under Eden as PM at that juncture.

Another factor in Eden's excluding the US must have been the very nature of the French plan, using an Israeli attack as a pretext to British troops being sent more as a peace-making force than an invading army, which he may have believed would, combined with military success and a Cold War context, have obtained US approval of the British use of force after the fact.

Eden's policy over Suez was then influenced by a number of factors, and the centrality of perception in foreign-policy decision-making indicates that the effect of each factor would have been through its influence on Eden's perceptions, which were themselves reflective of his attitudes. Though Eden's attitudes would have defined Eden's objectives over Suez, his personality would have influenced his use of Prime Ministerial power and his susceptibility to influence from ministers. The concentration on Eden reflects the powers and prerogatives of the PM in the British political system, both over ministers with much less information and in the sense of Prime Ministerial entitlement to engage in personal diplomatic overtures.

Another causal influence could have been Eden's desire not to be seen as an appeaser by history. Oliver Harvey notes that as early as late 1941 Eden was concerned that papers from the late 1930s that were due for early release would indicate that Eden was an appeaser – Harvey noted that 'everybody was an "appeaser" of Germany at one time or another'.[122] Eden regarded Nasser as another Mussolini and could have been concerned to avoid a reputation as an 'appeaser'. Eden's reference to the secret arrangement with French and the Israelis and not telling the US as 'the highest form of statesmanship' is indicative of his concern with his reputation as a world statesman and of his mistaken conviction that Suez would turn out well following such a plan.

The Suez affair had a tragic ending in the manner in which it diminished British international prestige, though in fact it was not so much a cause as a reflection of significantly diminished British military and economic power relative to the US and the Soviets, which had been apparent early on in the war (for even in 1940 Britain was bankrupt and needed US financial and materiel help to prosecute the war) and which became more so after the war, when Britain had to renegotiate a US loan on quite demanding terms to finance its domestic welfare programme and its problem of 'imperial overstretch', which was the result of maintaining and defending an empire that was beyond its means. And British diplomatic power and influence over the Americans had been much reduced since the early post-war interlude of genuine American diplomatic uncertainty over Europe and the threat of communism there and worldwide, an influence which culminated with and ended after Bevin's decisive influence on US policy over the Berlin Crisis in 1948.

Even without Suez Britain's economic and military decline was obvious and irreversible, as was the gradual loss of empire and of influence as a world power of the first rank. In that sense Suez seems more significant as a landmark and an exemplification of than a cause of British decline in the world. For Eden personally it meant the end of his political career. Eden's resignation was not so much because he could not have gone on, though his position was adversely affected by his conduct of the Suez affair and continuing to entertain hopes of salvaging something by negotiation when the US had made Britain's position hopeless, and by his sense of betrayal by the US, which was not conducive to the restoration of the special relationship on which the British economy so depended, as because of his poor health and medical advice.

Conclusion

One common theme seems to be Eden's sense that diplomacy had to be supported by military power or alliances, which was apparent in his insistence on faster British rearmament and his arguing for development of good relations with other major nations as a precondition to negotiation with Hitler under Chamberlain as PM (which was a logic of deterrence and a form of *Realpolitik*) and in his recommending not having a foreign-policy posture British military power could not enforce, as was so over appeasement of Germany and acceptance of the Soviet annexation of the Baltics in 1942 (he also deplored the fact that he had earlier been sent to meet Stalin with nothing to offer him despite the certainty of Soviet expectations that he would be arriving with good news).

Over post-war Germany Eden seems to have hoped for a federal Germany over which the West and the Soviet Union could collaborate or one that would face west if such collaboration proved impossible. That was unrealistic, as events in the east of Europe and the eastern zone of Germany were to prove, though Eden seems to have been wishing to exhaust all the diplomatic possibilities given the expected reality of Soviet power in post-war Europe and US isolationism. Some conflation of what was desirable or perceived to be necessary given the anticipated disposition of forces and power in post-war Europe with what was feasible or plausible seems to have been characteristic of Eden over German dismemberment. Even so it is worth noting that a policy of optimisation of the possibilities of collaboration with a nation of far greater economic and military power is consistent with a *Realpolitik* orientation to foreign policy in that both acknowledge the reality that any negotiating position must be supported by economic and military or diplomatic power through armaments or alliances, so that when there is no credible threat to the other party the remaining possibility is collaboration against a common threat, which in the case of Britain and the Soviet Union as the emerging major land power in Europe in 1943 and 1944 was Germany. There was then a consonance between what seem to have been different approaches in Eden's foreign policy.

Eden did not advocate standing up to Hitler in the appeasement period given Germany's relative power, or to Stalin in 1943 and 1944 given the power in Europe of the Soviet Union towards the end of the war, because he was convinced that diplomatic postures had to be supported by military and diplomatic power. Eden's view of Nasser, whom Eden compared to Mussolini and who was by British standards a minor dictator whose military power would not be able to resist Anglo-French military action, was quite different. Eden did however realise that the need for military and diplomatic power to support any foreign-policy posture even against Nasser meant in the Cold War world securing US support for British foreign policy.

While Eden seems, judging by outcome, not to have obtained such definite US support for British foreign policy in his handling of the Suez affair, it is also clear that Eden was not apprised of the threat of US economic sanctions and their likely effect on the British economy by Macmillan before the invasion of Suez by British troops, and that even so Eden had insisted that British military action over Suez would only take place if the Israelis invaded the Suez Canal zone, which would permit Eden to misrepresent the British action as a peacekeeping one to the US. It is also the case that by the time of the British invasion of Suez Eden had undertaken several diplomatic overtures to resolve the Suez Crisis, all of which seem to have been acquiesced in because of US insistence and to secure US pressure on Nasser or support for the use of troops.

Further, in addition to the fact that Macmillan had not warned Eden of the danger of economic sanctions imposed by the Americans for British military action over Suez until it was too late, there was Eden's warm personal relationship with Eisenhower, and the fact that both Eisenhower and Dulles indicated understanding that troops could be needed to resolve the crisis in the end. These combined to produce in Eden a sense that there was no risk of adverse US reaction over Suez, not least as Britain and the US shared a dislike of the Egyptian regime and a need for the Suez Canal to remain under international control. The sense seems to have been that the US would at very worst remain neutral. The theme of diplomatic caution, prudence and predicating foreign-policy postures on military and diplomatic power was then present in Eden over Suez even when he engaged in secret talks with the French to invade Suez on the pretext of separating the Israelis and the Egyptians. The inference that such traits were not present in him over Suez seems to be based on the consequences of Eden's Suez policy, which resulted more from his misjudgement of US support than from any sense of being free from the need for US support, which Eden seems to have understood was imperative for British post-war foreign policy even without the more explicit warnings of US sanctions and their effects on the British economy that Macmillan withheld from Eden until 6 November, by which time it was too late. That is not to say that Macmillan's withholding information was not influential, for had Eden been apprised of the explicit warnings of US economic sanctions and their expected effect on the UK economy his prudence would be expected to have resulted in his avoiding collusion with the French and the Israelis even with Eden's increased use of Drinamyl as the crisis wore on, which does seem to have affected his attitude to or appreciation of the risk being entertained in secret talks with the French and the Israelis and in military intervention in Suez.

From the point at which Eden decided to pursue secret talks with the French without telling the US Eden does seem to have had more confidence in US support than should have been inferred from the indications he had received from Washington, though there was a more general context that was conducive to rational belief in US understanding of and acquiescence in an Anglo-French military intervention that succeeded in restoring the Suez Canal to international control if not in actual US support. Even so Eden must have known that engaging in secret plans with the French for military intervention in Suez using an attack by the Israelis as a pretext represented a departure from the protocols of the relationship with the US, and it does seem plausible that Eden's medicine was conducive to a misplaced confidence.

The Eden of the Suez Crisis does then seem to be consistent with Eden's previous career in his initial uncertainty, caution, sensitivity to the diplomatic audience of the US, and preparedness to exhaust the diplomatic possibilities to resolve the conflict as recommended by Eisenhower, and indicative of a rather different, more decisive, confident Eden who seems to have had a distorted view of the risk of Anglo-French talks kept secret from the US and of military intervention without explicit US approval prior to actual troop commitment. In the latter Eden's judgement seems to have deserted him, though there were, as has been seen, mitigating circumstances in the form of the role of Macmillan, Eisenhower's lack of clarity over the US position on Suez, Eden's own poor health and the medicine he was taking for it.

Eden was as PM clearly one of the decisive influences on British foreign policy over the Suez Crisis and so at least partly responsible for a humiliating British foreign-policy failure that diminished Britain's international prestige. British policy over Suez was however not without reason, and there have since Suez been views that hold that the US failure to support the Anglo-French military action was a major US foreign policy mistake, a view which Eisenhower apparently shared later on in identifying Suez as his 'major foreign policy mistake'.[123] What does seem certain is that the Suez debacle indicated the extent of Western resolve to resist brinkmanship and the nature of the alliance between the UK and the US. While it is easy to say with the benefit of hindsight that Eden should have obtained specific assurances from Eisenhower as to US policy in the event of British military action over Suez there was at the time reason, in the tone and in fact the specific content of US communications over Suez, for Eden to have felt that no such assurances were necessary and that US support or at least understanding would be forthcoming.

Within the context of the wartime and post-war Anglo-American relationship there were of course minor strains, and Eden did not have especially harmonious relationships with Dean Acheson or his successor as Secretary of State, John Foster Dulles. Over Korea Eden endorsed British participation with the Americans in resisting communist North Korean and Chinese incursions into South Korea but did not agree that the war should be extended to China as an adversary, and would not endorse the US idea of a naval blockade of China. Further, Rhodes James notes that 'when the Americans bombed power stations on the Yalu river close to the Chinese border in June, although Eden defended the Americans publicly, his private reactions were censorious'. Rhodes James concludes, 'the Americans, who saw the communist peril everywhere, chafed at his caution and at his refusal to commit Britain further than was absolutely necessary.'[124] Even so Eden confined his serious reservations to the private sphere while publicly standing by a US policy with which he disagreed, unlike Eisenhower over Suez, and such disagreements were minor in relation to the reality that the only real support to the US over Korea came from the UK. The fact that the Anglo-American relationship was characterised by minor disagreements over foreign policy that did not adversely affect the endurance of the relationship itself may have made it impossible for Eden to conceive of the US not publicly supporting Britain even if it did not agree with the means pursued by Britain over Suez (on which there was however agreement on ends). After all that was precisely what Eden himself had done over Korea in a similarly adversarial Cold War context, and Britain had sustained significant casualties in and adverse economic effects from Korea, whereas Eden was not even asking for US troop commitment over Suez.

What Eden required from the US was a continuation of the special relationship Britain had with the US and no sanctions of any kind. It was then a minimal requirement of the US. Macmillan performed a *volte-face* over Suez because of US economic sanctions and then sought to cultivate the relationship with the US rather than draw the inference that too profound a dependence on US economic support left Britain void of autonomy in foreign policy. The alternative to the maintenance of the special relationship and dependence on the US would however have involved a withdrawal from empire and world-power status with its defence costs and a possible turning towards Europe. These were to come of course, with the wave of African independence of the 1960s and Macmillan's own 'wind of change' speech, and with Britain's joining the EU not that much later. Eden's approach to US support or at least understanding looks far less casual and far more comprehensible in such a context, not least given his desire to believe in it given his own objectives.

To address the issue of the relative causal influence on British foreign policy over Suez of the nature of the communications from Eisenhower and Dulles and Eden's and Macmillan's desire to believe that British military intervention would elicit no adverse US reaction, it could be argued that without a desire to believe in US acquiescence in any British military intervention British politicians, including Eden, would have sought very specific assurances from the Eisenhower administration as to the US attitude and reaction to British military intervention in Suez on any grounds, that is, to a *fait accompli* of British repossession of the Suez Canal through military means. Having said that, there was a context of an Anglo-American Cold War alliance that the UK had given effect to over Berlin and Korea, both of which could be regarded as recent instances of British support for the US policy of containment of communism, and of Eisenhower's and Dulles' diplomatic ambiguity in their communications over Suez, in which the prospect of a need for military intervention in the end was in fact acknowledged, so there was a rational basis for Eden's policy over Suez, regardless of any predisposition to believe that the US would support the UK in the event of British military action over Suez. Had Eisenhower or Dulles been less ambiguous and more definitive Eden and even Macmillan would certainly have been given reason to pause and reflect, and it is difficult to conceive of them proceeding with military intervention despite specific warnings of US economic sanctions for instance. It follows that Eisenhower and Dulles are in part responsible for British policy over Suez, though the radical departure by Eden to secret negotiations to devise a pretext for Anglo-French military intervention in Suez does seem to indicate a personal dimension of influence in the form of Eden's health and medicine on British policy over Suez.

What is more difficult to understand as being a rational response is Macmillan's disregard of Dulles' appeal to refrain from any intervention prior to the US Presidential election on 6 November, for that has to be attributed to an astonishing overconfidence or liberal attitude to risk on Macmillan's part.

The US vote to censure Britain and France at the UN and to force British and French withdrawal from Suez advertised to the Soviets and communists a split in the Western alliance and a lack of Western unity and resolve to defend the West's worldwide interests against communism and Soviet influence. It also had the character of an apparent abandonment of Britain, France and Israel in the light of Soviet and Warsaw Pact threats against Britain, France and Israel, which seemed a weak posture and hardly an example of the Truman Doctrine of containment. And US policy seemed also to indicate a lack of US preparedness to defend the flow of oil to the West from the Middle East, which was known to be a fundamental Western interest, and lack of readiness to support western countries against a Third World country that had looked for Soviet help under Nasser.

Even if Eisenhower preferred diplomatic means of resolving the crisis (and he did not rule out military action, just advocated exhaustion of all diplomatic possibilities), many diplomatic avenues had been explored and once military action had been undertaken by Britain, France and Israel the US could have been expected to have supported the western nations defending Western interests and confined any admonitions to private exchanges afterwards. The Hungarian rebellion and action of Soviet forces in crushing it was quite dissimilar to Western action to secure an international waterway and should not be presented as a pretext for US policy over Suez. It is not surprising given the US lack of resolve over Suez that Vietnam some years later came to be seen as the place for an exhibition of US resolve to resist the expansionism and opportunism of the Soviet Union and the spread of communism.

In terms of foreign-policy vision then Eden's stance on Suez may have been the right one in the longer term, with his having miscalculated over US support for an outcome of a process kept secret from them and with the US being mistaken in its policy of abandoning Britain, France and Israel. It was not that Eden was or became irrational in his emerging policy over Suez, that of collusion with the French and the Israelis to contrive a pretext for invasion of Suez, rather that he became more confident than he had been of US support for a *fait accompli* over Suez given the effect on Eden's confidence of the increased doses of Drinamyl in October 1956.

Eden does seem to have been influenced by the more certain Macmillan, for it is very unlikely that Macmillan would not have represented to Eden views he held so intensely and which he had expressed to the Americans on hearing the news of Nasser's action over Suez, and unlikely also that such views would have had no effect. It is also of course difficult to explain Eden's change from indecision on 26 July to robust certainty on 27 July without reference to some external influence, and the evidence indicates Macmillan's influence on Eden to pursue a policy of presenting a credible threat of British military intervention to optimise American diplomatic pressure on Nasser to achieve a restoration of international control of the Suez Canal and Nasser's downfall without actual resort to use of force. The other juncture that would seem to indicate the extent of Eden's autonomy and influence over British foreign policy would be that at which it was decided to no longer cultivate prior US approval but to present them with a *fait accompli* in the confidence that the US would then endorse it, and though it does seem that using the Israelis as a pretext for military action over Suez came from the French Eden did obtain the prior support of Macmillan and Kilmuir.

Eden favoured continued military action over Suez even after Macmillan no longer supported it because of the adverse US reaction, though Macmillan was an initial decisive influence in favour of presenting a credible threat of British military action to achieve British objectives in Suez. What Macmillan's *volte-face* could indicate is Macmillan's greater flexibility of response and the relative ease with which a Chancellor of the Exchequer could change his recommended policy compared to a PM whose reputation had become associated with the success of a foreign policy, or Macmillan's grasp of economic policy and Eden's known lack of grasp of economic policy, which may have left him less cognizant of the economic implications of US sanctions for the British economy than Macmillan. It is also possible that Eden was here manifesting a trait apparent over the future of Germany after the war, of finding it difficult to relinquish hope and possibility, in that case of Anglo-Soviet collaboration over a united Germany, in the Suez case of US support.

Eden had in his previous career avoided confrontation and the foreclosing of diplomatic options, for in the appeasement era Eden did not advocate confrontation with Hitler and in fact refrained from criticising Chamberlain even over Munich, instead confining himself to advocacy of faster rearmament and alliances to contain Hitler through deterrence (which could have taken place without confrontation), while over the Baltics he advocated acquiescence in Stalin's demands, which would have left diplomatic channels between Britain and the Soviet Union improved, and over German dismemberment he avoided taking a firm position and indicated being for and against German dismemberment to different diplomatic audiences before finally deciding in favour of a unitary Germany over which he hoped for collaboration with the Soviet Union after the war.

Over Suez Eden seems to have had some initial uncertainty and to have explained to Eisenhower the British position to elicit understanding from the US, and he did respond to US wishes for the public exhaustion of all diplomatic means of resolving the Suez Crisis. That seems to be consistent with the Eden of the appeasement and wartime period. What seems different is the Eden of the later Suez Crisis, in secret talks with the French to contrive a pretext for military force over Suez. Though it has been argued that Eden was just going through the motions with the UN and the London Conference in the conviction that such diplomatic means would come to nothing and necessitate military action in the end, there is evidence that even in the middle of October and after the failure of reference to the UN Eden was prepared to continue to negotiate with Nasser, indicating his preparedness to exhaust all diplomatic means of resolving the crisis even at the time he was entertaining the French plan. And it does seem that Eden's foreign policy over Suez was consistent with his approach to foreign policy prior to the Suez Crisis, in that even after the period of exhaustion of all diplomatic possibilities of resolving the dispute, that is, even during the period of secret talks with the French, Eden must have felt assured of the support of the US because of the Cold War context, Eisenhower's and Dulles' ambiguous indications over Suez, the lack of any reference to the threat of economic sanctions from Macmillan, the lengths to which Eden had gone to secure a diplomatic resolution to the crisis and the medicine Eden was taking. And there was of course Eden's desire to establish a reputation for rejection of appeasement as PM.

What is apparent is the interaction between the influence of the institutional context and the attributes of incumbents of positions of power, not least their interests, sense of their own aptitudes, their personalities, their sense of prerogatives and role, their relationships, attitudes and objectives. Eden exerted little influence on British foreign policy as Foreign Secretary and great influence as PM, an indication that incumbency of the premiership is a key attribute for influence on foreign-policy formulation and implementation in the British political system. Continuity of approach in one individual reflective of personal attributes is indicated in the case of Eden before and during the Suez Crisis, for Eden was over Suez characteristically undecided, cautious, prudent, sensitive to diplomatic necessities and *Realpolitik* considerations, susceptible to influence from more certain colleagues such as Macmillan, and given to outbursts of rage and desire for vengeance, at the outset and during the earlier phase of the crisis. Eden's ensuing apparent abandonment of such caution in not informing the US over secret talks with the French and the Israelis seems uncharacteristic of Eden and to be a consequence of the increased medicine he was taking, which seems to have had the effect of distorting Eden's perception of or attitude to risk though with the support of Macmillan and Kilmuir and insistence from the French.

There had by that time though been other influences on Eden's approach to the Suez Crisis. There was his volatile personality and immediate and continuing desire for some form of public retaliation against and humiliation of Nasser and to avoid being seen as an appeaser in the record of Suez. There was the ambiguity of Eisenhower's messages in their apparent exhortation to do no more than exhaust diplomatic possibilities of resolving the crisis for the audience of world opinion and their refraining from any reference to possible US economic sanctions should there be military intervention over Suez. There was the fact that Eden may have felt with some justification that he had obliged the US in having exhausted diplomatic means of resolving the crisis. There was the Cold War context that made US abandonment of the UK implausible over Suez. And there was the role of Macmillan in exhorting Eden to military action over Suez at the outset of the crisis and again in September, in not apprising Eden of the possible adverse economic consequences of not obtaining specific US approval for any action over Suez (not least given Eden's known lack of aptitude for economic matters), and in supporting Eden's intended collusion with the French and the Israelis on 16 October during Eden's meeting with a select group of ministers.

The extent of Prime Ministerial influence on foreign policy under Eden included the extent of Prime Ministerial interest in foreign policy and in the issue, which Eden had, intensity of attitude, also present in Eden, Prime Ministerial perceptions of the international context and consequences of various policies, which for Eden were influenced by Macmillan and Eisenhower, and Prime Ministerial personality and relationships with other ministers that dictated the extent of influence on Eden's decisions from ministers. In the case of Eden, his own indecision and uncertainty and Macmillan's certainty and personality meant that Macmillan's influence on policy over Suez was greater than it would have been with another PM of greater certainty or confidence, for instance Chamberlain. And had Macmillan been less certain and robust himself he would have exerted far less influence over Suez. Eden's pursuit of diplomatic means of resolving the crisis throughout August, September and the first part of October 1956 does not indicate diminished influence from Macmillan, for military preparations for an invasion of Suez took six to seven weeks to complete, so that diplomatic activity was not pursued as an alternative to the military intervention Macmillan advocated once it became apparent that the US administration was not going to exert diplomatic pressure on Nasser sufficient to restoring international control of the Suez Canal. Even so, on 14 October, by which time military preparedness was no longer a constraint, Eden instructed Lloyd to pursue negotiations with the Egyptians even after reference to the UN. The evidence indicates that Eden was, as he had been over the post-war future of Germany, indecisive, uncertain, cautious and with a preference for the exhaustion of diplomacy for most of the Suez Crisis.

Notes

[1]See for instance Kyle, Keith, *Suez: Britain's End of Empire in the Middle East*, I. B. Tauris, 2011, and Smith, Simon C. (ed.), *Reassessing Suez: New Perspectives on the Crisis and Its Aftermath*, Routledge, 2016. For the extensive historiography on the Suez Crisis see Lucas, Scott (ed.), *Britain and Suez: The Lion's Last Roar*, Manchester University Press, 1996, pages 1–4, which cover the period from the initial view of Thomas, Eden's attempt in his memoirs to justify himself by blaming the French and especially the US for not supporting the position he took over Suez, for the maintenance of an official line that there had been no secret agreement with the French and Israelis over Suez, a phase ended by Israeli publication of the Sèvres Protocol, through an ensuing phase that involved criticism of Eden's 'delusions of grandeur', lack of foresight or 'weakness of temperament' and defence of Eden by claiming the collusion was justified or explaining it by reference to Eden's poor health, to Carlton's biography with its claim that Eden was obsessed with defeating Nasser and Rhodes James' defence of Eden as PM, Neustadt's adding a dimension to the analysis in its partial attribution of policy and outcome over Suez to 'breakdown in communication, misperception and differences in objectives' between the UK and the US, and the emergence of works that referred to British official documents released in 1987 under the thirty-year rule. See also Pearson, J., *Sir Anthony Eden and the Suez Crisis: Reluctant Gamble*, Springer, 2002.

[2]See for instance Gorst, Anthony, and Johnman, Lewis, *The Suez Crisis*, Routledge, 2013, and Kyle, Suez, op. cit.

[3]See Boyle, Peter, *The Eden-Eisenhower Correspondence, 1955–1957*, University of North Carolina Press, 2006, pages 16–22 for the views of contemporaries and Eden's biographer on Eden's attributes but consensus on his volatile temperament and on his being more the astute, well-briefed diplomat with a grasp of detail and aptitude for cultivating compromise than strategist.

[4]See Daalder, Hans, *Cabinet Reform in Britain 1914–1963*, Stanford University Press, 1963, page 75, for reference to Baldwin's policy of non-interference in ministerial briefs. For reference to Baldwin's lack of interest in foreign policy see McKercher, B. J. C. (ed.), *Anglo-American Relations in the 1920s: The Struggle for Supremacy*, University of Alberta, 1990, page 210. Though the reference is to the 1920s the point regarding Baldwin's lack of interest in foreign policy is made.

[5]Even in relation to the permissive Baldwin administration Eden later complained of ministerial opposition and Baldwin's failure to support him. See Hughes, Michael, *British Foreign Secretaries in an Uncertain World 1919–1939*, Routledge, 2005, page 129. For Eden's astonishing row with Chamberlain over Mussolini, witnessed by Grandi, see McDonough, Frank, *Neville Chamberlain, Appeasement, and the British Road to War*, Manchester University Press, 1998, pages 53 and 54. Eden's continued resistance to Churchill over the Baltics is indicated in Louis, William Roger (ed.), *More Adventures in Britannia: Personalities, Politics and Culture in Britain*. I. B. Tauris, 1998, page 236. For the disagreement between Eden and Churchill at the Quebec Conference in 1944 see Rothwell, Victor, *Anthony Eden: A Political Biography, 1931–57*, Manchester University Press, 1992, page 44.

[6]Dilks, David, *The Diaries of Sir Alexander Cadogan, O.M., 1938–1945*, Putnam, 1972, entry for 8 January 1945, page 693.

[7]Jenkins. Roy, *Churchill*, Pan Macmillan, 2012, page 774, Colville diary entry for 9 January 1945.

[8]See Hamilton, Eamon, *Sir Anthony Eden and the Suez Crisis of 1956, Anatomy of a Flawed Personality*, MA Thesis, Birmingham University, 2005, and Sainsbury, *Churchill and Roosevelt*, op. cit., page 140.

[9]See Avon papers, 20/1/21, 22 and 23.

[10]Thorpe, D. R., *The Life and Times of Anthony Eden, First Earl of Avon, 1897–1977*, Random House, 2011, page 16.

[11]See Boyle, *The Eden-Eisenhower Correspondence*, op. cit., pages 15–16 and page 18.

[12]The Baghdad Pact was formed in 1955 to resist communist encroachment and to promote peace in the Middle East. Its members were Turkey and Iraq (from 24 February 1955), Britain (from 5 April 1955), Pakistan (from 23 September 1955), and Iran (from 31 November 1955).

[13]See Kyle, *Suez*, op. cit., pages 67 to 70. See Rothwell, *Eden*, op. cit., page 132 for evidence of Eden's poor health as Foreign Secretary between 1951 and 1954.

[14]See CAB 128/29, CM (55), 34th Conclusions, 4 October 1955.

[15]See Avon papers, 12/3/408C and 12/3/466H.

[16]See Smith, *Reassessing Suez*, op. cit., pages 62 and 63.

[17]See Gorst, Johnman, *The Suez Crisis*, op. cit., citing FO 371/121271, Eden to Eisenhower, 5 March 1956.

[18]See Nutting, Anthony, *No End of a Lesson: the story of Suez*, C. N. Potter, London, 1967, page 34. Nutting later claimed that Eden had used the word 'murdered', not 'destroyed'.

[19]See Smith, *Reassessing Suez*, op. cit., pages 2–3.

[20]See Kyle, *Suez*, op. cit., pages 136 and 137.

[21]See Pearson, *Sir Anthony Eden and the Suez Crisis*, op. cit., pages 2 and 22, and Scott Lucas, William, *Divided We Stand: The Suez Crisis of 1956 and the Anglo-American 'Alliance'*, DPhil Thesis, London School of Economics and Political Science.

[22]See Pearson, *Sir Anthony Eden and the Suez Crisis*, op. cit., pages 173 and 1, and Thorpe, D. R., *Supermac: The Life of Harold Macmillan*, Random House, 2011, pages 339 and 749, referring to Macmillan Diary, 1 August 1956, Macmillan dep. d. 27. See also Turner, Michael J., *British Power and International Relations in the 1950s: A Tenable Position?*, Rowman and Littlefield, 2009, page 266, and Bennett, Gill, *Six Moments of Crisis: Inside British Foreign Policy*, Oxford University Press, 2013, referring to Macmillan Diaries entries for 31 July–1 August 1956, pages 379–80.

[23]Wilby, Peter, *Eden*, Haus Publishing, 2006, page 98.

[24]See Pearson, *Eden and the Suez Crisis*, op. cit., page 3. See also Williamson's review of Pearson on H-net.

[25]PREM 11/1177, Eden to Eisenhower, 27 July 1956.

[26]Thorpe, *Eden*, op. cit., page 599.

[27]Wilson, Harold, *Memoirs: The Making of a Prime Minister, 1916–1964*, Weidenfeld and Nicolson, 1986.

[28]Gaitskell, Hugh, Williams, Philip Maynard, *The Diary of Hugh Gaitskell*, Cape, 1983, entry for 26 July 1956.

[29]Thorpe, D. R., *Supermac: The Life of Harold Macmillan*, Random House, 2011, page 334.

[30]See Verbeek, Bertian, *Decision-Making in Great Britain During the Suez Crisis – Small Groups and a Persistent Leader*, Ashgate, 2003, pages 43, 78–79, 84 and 157.

[31]See Verbeek, *Suez*, op. cit., pages 87, 88 and 97, citing PREM 11/1098, 31 July 1956 and 1 August 1956, CAB 128/30, CM (56) 56, 1 August 1956, and PREM 11/1099, Egypt Committee EC (56) 18, Confidential Annex, 20 August 1956.

[32]See Kyle, *Suez*, op. cit., page 135, and Smith, *Reassessing Suez*, op. cit., page 62, referring to Murphy's 'Diplomat among Warriors', London, 1964, pages 463 and 166.

[33]FRUS· 1988, Murphy to Dulles, 31 July 1956, document 33, pages 60–62, cited in Gorst, Johnman, *The Suez Crisis*, op. cit., pages 62–63.

[34]See Lucas, *Divided We Stand*, op. cit.

[35]CAB 128/30 (1), CM (56), 54th Conclusions, 27 July 1956.

[36]See Pearson, *Eden and the Suez Crisis*, op. cit., page 35.

[37]See Gorst, Johnman, *The Suez Crisis*, op. cit., page 62, citing PREM 11/1177 Eden to Eisenhower, 27 July 1956.

[38]See Foreign Relations of the United States (FRUS), 1990, 1955–1957, Suez Crisis, July 26–December 31, 1956, Volume XVI, document 35, Eisenhower to Eden, 31 July 1956, and Office of the Historian for Dulles' note.

[39]FRUS, 1988, memorandum of a conversation between Eden and Dulles, 1 August 1956, document 42, pages 98–99, cited in Gorst, Johnman, *The Suez Crisis*, op. cit., pages 66–67.

[40]See Rhodes James, *Anthony Eden*, Papermac, 1987, page 473.

[41]Kyle, *Suez*, op. cit., page 192.

[42]See Gorst, Johnman, *The Suez Crisis*, op. cit., page 67, and FRUS, 1955–1957, Suez Crisis, 26 July–31 December, 1956, Volume XVI, 1988, document 42, pages 98–99, Record of Conversation between Eden and Dulles, 1 August 1956.

[43]FRUS, 1955–1957, Suez Crisis, 26 July–31Deecmber, 1956, Volume XVI, document 41, Memorandum of Conversation, British Foreign Office, London, 1 August 1956.

[44]See Lucas, *Divided We Stand*, op. cit., citing FO 371/119081, Eden meeting with Lloyd and Pineau, 31 July 1956, and CAB 134/1216, EC (56) 4th meeting, 30 July 1956.

[45]Ibid.

[46]CAB 128/30 (1), CM (56) 56th Conclusions, 1 August 1956.

[47]CAB 128/30 (1), CM (56) 59th Conclusions, 14 August 1956, CM (56) 60th Conclusions, 21 August 1956, and CM (56), 61st Conclusions, 23 August 1956.

[48]CAB 128/30 (1), CM (56) 62nd Conclusions, 28 August 1956.

[49]Rothwell, *Eden*, op. cit., page 218.

[50]PREM 11/1100, Eisenhower to Eden, 3 September 1956.

[51]CAB 128/30 (1), CM (56) 63rd Conclusions, 6 September 1956.

[52]See PREM 11/1100, Eden to Eisenhower, 6 September 1956.

[53]See PREM 11/1100, Eisenhower to Eden, 8 September 1956, and Foreign Relations of the United States, 1955–1957, Suez Crisis, July 26–December 31, 1956, Volume XVI, document 190, for draft sent by Eisenhower to Dulles for comment. The draft argues against 'resort to military action when the world believes there are means available for resolving the dispute', indicates concern regarding reaction in the Arab world to military action not justified by Nasser's behaviour, argues for Nasser's isolation in the Arab world, and refers to what would happen 'if we are correct in our belief that the Egyptians cannot, and possibly even do not intend to, operate the canal for the benefit of all nations without prejudice to any', an indication of Eisenhower's agreeing with Eden over the need to resort to military action over time.

[54]See Horne, Alastair, *Macmillan: The Official Biography*, Pan Macmillan, 2012, and Turner, John, *Macmillan*, Routledge, 2014, page 119, citing T 236/4188, Bridges to Macmillan, 8 August 1956, and Macmillan's note of 12 August 1956.

[55]CAB 128/30 (1), CM (56) 62nd Conclusions, 28 August 1956.

[56]See Horne, *Macmillan*, op. cit., and Shaw, Tony, *Eden, Suez and the Mass Media: Propaganda and Persuasion During the Suez Crisis*, I. B. Tauris, 1996, page 246, citing T 236/4188, Bridges to Macmillan, 7 September 1956.

[57]Hennessy, Peter, *Having it so good: Britain in the Fifties*, Penguin UK, 2007.

[58]Kyle, *Suez*, op. cit., page 228.

[59]See CAB 128/30, CM (56) 64th Conclusions, 11 September 1956.

[60]Johnman, Lewis, 'Opportunity Knocks: Macmillan at the Treasury, 1955–7', in Aldous, R., and Lee, S., *Harold Macmillan: Aspects of a Political Life*, Springer, 1999, pages 44 and 45.

[61]Gorst, Johnman, *The Suez Crisis*, op. cit., page 130.

[62]See Warner, Geoffrey, 'Aspects of the Suez Crisis', in Di Nolfo, Ennio (ed.), *Great Britain, France, Germany and Italy and the Origins of the EEC, 1952–1957*, Walter de Gruyter, 1992, pages 56 and 57, referring to Macmillan's 'Riding The Storm', 1956–1959, *Macmillan*, 1971, page 149.

[63]See Rothwell, *Eden* op. cit., page 77.

[64]CAB 128/30, CM (56) 64th Conclusions, 11 September 1956. See also PREM 11/1100 for Lloyd's view on 6 September that the advantage of the SCUA would be that the US would be committed to the restoration of international control of the Suez canal under it.

[65]See Gorst, Johnman, *The Suez Crisis*, op. cit., page 84, and Kyle, *Suez*, op. cit., page 250.

[66]Ibid., page 202.

[67]See Di Nolfo, *Origins of the EEC*, op. cit., page 172 for reference to its having been 'Macmillan who

provoked Monckton into his "outburst" at the Egypt Committee on 24 August', according to a letter dated 25 August 1956 by Sir Norman Brook, the Cabinet Secretary, in PREM 11/1152.

[68]Kyle, *Suez*, op. cit., pages 207, 208 and 257.

[69]CAB 128/30, CM (56) 67th Conclusions, 26 September 1956.

[70]Kelly, Saul, and Gorst, Anthony (eds.), *Whitehall and the Suez Crisis*, Routledge, 2013, page 88.

[71]See Pearson, *Eden and the Suez Crisis*, op. cit., page 118.

[72]See Kyle, *Suez*, op. cit., page 273, and Pearson, *Eden and the Suez Crisis*, op. cit., page118.

[73]See Pearson, *Eden and the Suez Crisis*, op. cit., page 126, and Lucas, *Britain and Suez*, op. cit., page 73, citing PREM 11/1102, cable 854, Lloyd to Eden,14 October 1956, and PREM 11/1102, Cable 1198, Eden to Lloyd, 14 October 1956.

[74]See Shlaim, Avi, 'The Protocol of Sèvres, 1956: Anatomy of a War Plot', in *International Affairs*, 73:3 (1997), pages 509–530, for Shlaim's claims regarding Eden's enthusiasm for collusion with the French, his order to Lloyd to return from New York, and his concern to avoid being seen as responsible for an Israeli attack on Egypt. Shlaim's evidence of Eden's 'glee' is drawn from Nutting's 1967 memoir on Suez, and his claim that Eden ordered Lloyd to abandon talks in New York and return home is drawn from a conversation in 1997 with Shlaim, both well after the event. And of course Eden's being drawn emotionally to the French plan would not preclude his continuing to be rationally concerned as to diplomatic consequences. See also Gorst, Johnman, *The Suez Crisis*, op. cit., pages 90 and 91.

[75]See Louis, William Roger, *Ends of British Imperialism: The Scramble for Empire, Suez and Decolonisation*, I. B. Tauris, 2006, page 679 for reference to Macmillan's diary entries for the period between 10 and 13 September 1956 and Macmillan's sense that Eden 'wavered indecisively and stumbled in the midst of conflicting pressures of the Parliamentary debate'.

[76]See Boyle, *Eden-Eisenhower Correspondence*, op. cit., page 203, referring to Eisenhower's letter of 2 November 1956, which does seem to be self-exculpating and exonerating of his own responsibility for the British and French decision to intervene in Suez using military force.

[77]See CAB 128/30, CM (56) 62nd Conclusions, 28 August 1956, and CM (56) 68th Conclusions, 3 October 1956.

[78]See Thorpe, *Supermac*, op. cit., pages 348 and 349, and Horne, Alastair, *Macmillan: The Official Biography*, Pan Macmillan, 2012.

[79]Rothwell, *Eden*, op. cit., page 214.

[80]Thorpe, *Eden*, op. cit., pages 515–18.

[81]CAB 128/30, CM (56) 71st Conclusions, 18 October 1956, CM (56), 72nd Conclusions, 23 October 1956, CM (56) 73rd Conclusions, October 1956, and Verbeek, *Suez*, op. cit., page 116, citing FO 800/828, 18 October 1956.

[82]Hennessy, Peter, *The Prime Minister: The Office and Its Holders Since 1945*, Palgrave Macmillan, 2001, page 224. See also CAB 128/30, CM (56) 74th Conclusions, 25 October 1956.

[83]*QJM* Volume 98, Issue 6, June 2005, pages 387–402, Lord Owen, 'The Effect of Prime Minister Anthony Eden's illness on his decision-making during the Suez Crisis'.

[84]See Hennessy, *The Prime Minister*, op. cit., page 223.

[85]See CAB 128/30 CM 72 (56), 23 October 1956, Confidential Annex, cited in Gorst, Johnman, *The Suez Crisis*, op. cit., pages 95 and 96 for reference to 'secret conversations' in Paris 'with representatives of the Israeli Government', though without elaboration or reference to collusion.

[86]See Kyle, *Suez*, op. cit., pages 322, 327 and 334.

[87]See Heath, E., *The Course of My Life: My Autobiography*, A & C Black, 2011.

[88]CAB 128/30, CM (56) 75th Conclusions, 30 October 1956.

[89]See PREM 11/1105, Eisenhower to Eden, 30 October 1956.

[90]See Boyle, *The Eden-Eisenhower Correspondence*, op. cit., page 181.

[91]CAB 128/30, CMs (56) 75th, 76th, 77th and 79th Conclusions, 30 October, 31 October, 2 November, and 4 November 1956. See also Gorst, Johnman, *The Suez Crisis*, op. cit., page 118 for reference to ministerial reservations and Eden's threat of resignation, and *QJM* Volume 98, Issue 6, June

2005, pages 387–402, Lord Owen, 'The Effect of Prime Minister Anthony Eden's illness on his decision-making during the Suez Crisis', for Owen's observation that Macmillan had a 'wobble' at the Egypt Committee meeting on 4 November but endorsed a continuance of the military operation in Suez in Cabinet.

[92]See Alteras, Isaac, *Eisenhower and Israel: US-Israeli Relations, 1953–1960*, University Press of Florida, 1993, pages 223, 224 and 225, and Hahn, Peter L., *United States, Great Britain, And Egypt, 1945–1956: Strategy and Policy in the Early Cold War*, UNC Press, 2004, page 230.

[93]Bell, P. M. H., *France and Britain, 1940–1994: The Long Separation*, Routledge, 2014, page 148.

[94]See Lucas, *Divided We Stand*, op. cit.

[95]See CAB 128/30, CM (56), 80th, 81st, 82nd, 85th, 86th, 88th, 89th and 90th Conclusions, 6, 7, 8, 20, 21, 26, 27 and 28, November 1956, and Gorst, Johnman, *The Suez Crisis*, op. cit., page 126 for reference to Lloyd's having run the discussion on Suez on 6 November – there is in fact no reference to Eden's participation in the discussion in the minutes.

[96]CAB 128/30, CM (56), 96th Conclusions, 3 December 1956.

[97]Rhodes James, *Eden*, op. cit., page 286.

[98]See Thorpe, *Eden*, op. cit., pages 350, 352 and 353.

[99]See Lucas, *Britain and Suez*, op. cit., page 111.

[100]See Cooper, Chester L., *The Lion's Last Roar: Suez, 1956*, Harper and Row, 1978, page 238.

[101]Thorpe, *Eden*, op. cit., page 557, quoting from 'Notes on talk with Sir Anthony Eden, 17 April 1958 at Donnington Grove, Newbury Berks', from the private papers of Sir Pierson Dixon.

[102]Mackintosh, J. P., *The British Cabinet*, Stevens, 1981, page 25.

[103]See Gorst, Johnman, *The Suez Crisis*, page 61.

[104]See Kelly, Gorst, *Whitehall and the Suez Crisis*, op. cit., pages 121 and 151. See also page 62 for reference to Treasury and legal advice being ignored by Eden and the Cabinet. In fact the nature of Kirkpatrick's hawkishness mirrored that of Macmillan in his appreciation of what he regarded were the issues for Britain over Suez, referring on 10 September 1956 to Nasser's intention to 'wreck us', arguing that Middle Eastern oil was imperative to the maintenance of gold reserves that were in turn vital to the sterling area and so to affording the British military presence in Germany and defence of Britain, without which the country would be 'finished'.

[105]See *QJM* Volume 98, Issue 6, June 2005, pages 387–402, Lord Owen, 'The Effect of Prime Minister Anthony Eden's illness on his decision-making during the Suez Crisis'.

[106]See Hamilton, Eamon, *Sir Anthony Eden and the Suez Crisis of 1956*, Anatomy of a Flawed Personality, MA Thesis, Birmingham University, 2005.

[107]See Rothwell, *Eden*, op. cit., page 190.

[108]See Gorst and Kelly, *Whitehall and The Suez Crisis*, op. cit., page 121 for reference to Lloyd's preference for a negotiated settlement of the Suez Crisis, to Kirkpatrick's exclusion from the locus of decision-making over Suez and to Eden's using Dean to carry out a policy he had decided upon without FO advice sought or given.

[109]See Kelly, Gorst (eds.), *Whitehall and the Suez Crisis*, op. cit., page 150 for reference, in the context of an Israeli request for earlier RAF neutralisation of the Egyptian air force following an Israeli attack, to Eden as PM in the following way – 'Despite analyses that depict Suez as an example of Prime Ministerial autocracy, Eden invariably attempted to be constitutionally correct and referral to the Cabinet on a matter of such military significance would have been considered essential.' It is in fact difficult to imagine how the Cabinet could have been consulted regarding such a matter without the extent of British collusion in the Israeli attack's being disclosed, and anyway referral to Cabinet does not necessarily mean genuine consultation as it could be just observance of form, for instance with a distorted representation of the issues to Cabinet ministers and with Eden having assured himself of the support of the most senior, relevant and influential ministers beforehand. For the distribution of influence within the Cabinet one has to assess the perceived context and the views of ministers of varying seniority and role. In fact what seems to have been the case over Suez is that Eden and other senior

hawkish Cabinet ministers dominated other ministers in the earlier phases of the crisis and that when US adverse reaction became manifest and such senior ministers deserted Eden he had to accept he could no longer exert influence over Cabinet.

[110]Thorpe, *Eden*, op. cit., pages 515–18.

[111]Rothwell, *Eden*, op. cit., pages 77 and 189.

[112]Thorpe, *Eden*, op. cit., page 510.

[113]Kelly, Gorst, *Whitehall and the Suez Crisis*, op. cit., page 89.

[114]Thorpe, *Eden*, op. cit., page 512.

[115]Ibid., pages 513–15.

[116]See Smith, *Reassessing Suez*, op. cit., page 204, article by Murphy, Philip, 'Telling Tales out of School: Nutting, Eden and the Attempted Suppression of No End of a Lesson'.

[117]See Verbeek, *Suez*, op. cit., pages 115 and 116.

[118]See Shlaim, Avi, 'The Protocol of Sèvres: Anatomy of a War Plot', in Tal, David (ed.), *The 1956 War: Collusion and Rivalry in the Middle East*, Psychology Press, 2001, pages 122, 125, and 129.

[119]See Gorst, Johnman, *The Suez Crisis*, op. cit., page 91.

[120]See Lucas, *Britain and Suez*, op. cit., page 111.

[121]See Aldous, Richard, and Lee, Sabine (eds.), *Harold Macmillan and Britain's World Role*, Springer, 2016, pages 1–3.

[122]*The War Diaries of Oliver Harvey, 1941–1945*, Collins, 1978, page 61, entry for 8 November 1941.

[123]See Drachman, Edward R., and Shank, Alan, *Presidents and Foreign Policy: Countdown to Ten Controversial Decisions*, SUNY Press, 1997, page 75 for reference to what Richard Nixon claims Eisenhower told him and to Nixon's own observation that the effect was British and French withdrawal from east of Suez and the US being left to 'go it alone'.

[124]Rhodes James, *Eden*, op. cit., page 353.

Chapter Six

Decline and dependence or choices and consequences – the influences on British foreign policy in the Korean and Vietnam wars in the context of the special relationship between 1950 and 1968

Introduction and the post-war attitudinal, perceptual and actual context

ANGLO-AMERICAN RELATIONS in the context of the Cold War do have their own extensive historiography.[1] There is a much less extensive literature on British policy and Anglo-American relations during the Korean War, though rather more on British policy and Anglo-American relations during the more controversial Vietnam War.[2] There is however no comparison between different British foreign policies at different junctures in the Cold War to elucidate the reasons for very different decisions having been taken in relation to US preferences. The case being made here is that the evidence of the Korean and Vietnam wars indicates a combination of objective context and more individual attitudinal and perceptual influences on British foreign policy.

In terms of objective context there was the reality that the locus of power was increasingly in Washington, as is indicated by the diminution in autonomy for British foreign policy and in British influence on US foreign policy. At the beginning of the Berlin Crisis of 1948 and 1949 Bevin did exert significant influence on the Western response, though in the Korean War of 1950 to 1953 British representations regarding the risks attendant upon any escalation of the war and recommending avoidance of inflammatory rhetoric towards the Soviet Union and China and avoidance too of any resort to the use of an atomic weapon do not seem to have had more than minimal, if any, influence on US policy. And by the time of the Suez Crisis in 1956 and US involvement in Vietnam from 1964 there seems to have been no British influence on US foreign policy, and any autonomy in British foreign policy either attracted punitive US sanctions that reversed British foreign policy in a humiliating public indication of British dependence on the US, as was so over Suez, or reflected US Presidential perception of the propaganda constraint on the use of US power over Britain, as was so with Johnson and Wilson over British troops to Vietnam. Such British decline of foreign-policy autonomy and influence on US foreign policy reflected much diminished British economic, diplomatic and military power relative to the Soviet Union and the US, British economic, diplomatic and military dependence on the US in the Cold War, and increasing US confidence and autonomy in foreign policy, following an initial post-war interlude in which US inexperience of European policy meant that British diplomatic experience did exert some influence.[3]

One influence on British foreign policy in the Korean War and the Vietnam War was then the objective long-term relative economic, diplomatic and military decline of the UK and dependence on the US for continued world-power status and for security against Soviet hostility and expansionism. Other influences reflected the nature of foreign-policy decision-making in the British system and were more personal. These included the attitudes, foreign-policy objectives and perceptions of incumbent British Prime Ministers, Foreign Secretaries and Cabinet ministers, those within the locus of formal foreign-policy decision-making. And there was less direct influence from the views of MPs, the voting arithmetic in the Commons, the government's attitude to the Commons, governing Party dissent and the government attitude to such dissent and to the relationship between party and government. In other words, the British foreign policies that emerged were a function not just of the objective asymmetry of power between Britain and the US but also of the attitudinal orientation, perceptual lens, personalities, relationships and foreign policy and personal objectives of the major British decision-makers and those influencing them. Those decision-makers were Attlee and Bevin for the Korean War and Wilson for the Vietnam War, though on the US side there was the influence of the attributes of Truman and Acheson for the Korean War and of Johnson, Bundy and Rusk for the Vietnam War. I have excluded part of the duration of the Vietnam War, that between the end of the Johnson Presidency and the end of US involvement in Vietnam in 1975, from the discussion here, though reference shall be made to the ensuing relationship between Nixon and Wilson and then Heath over Vietnam at the end. The argument is that the British foreign policy that emerged over Korea and Vietnam did reflect the international context and the asymmetrical relationship between the US and Britain after the war, though only as seen through the perceptual lens of individual politicians and officials and set against foreign-policy objectives that reflected individual attitudes.

British foreign policy after the war was informed by the overriding attitudinal ethos of the British political, official and military establishment, which was that Britain was a world power of the first rank, should remain so regardless of its obviously much diminished economic and military power relative to that of the Soviet Union and the US in the post-war period, and should have as its foreign-policy objective the defence of traditional British European and imperial interests, including the maintenance of a balance of power in Europe as a means of safeguarding British security and defence of the British Empire. All British foreign policy during the 1940s, the 1950s and the 1960s was in a sense a means to this end of the retention of British world-power status and the protection of existing British interests regardless of much diminished economic and military power.

By the time of the Korean War the British political, official and military establishment had understood from the adverse experience of post-war British attempts at collaboration with the Soviet Union that Britain was faced in Europe with a Soviet Union not just of overwhelming military power but also of hostile intentions towards British social democracy and a general expansionism and opportunism in foreign policy, combined with a diplomatic style that included an escalation of demands, about-turns, insults and no attempt to create or maintain trust, in other words, a style that violated established diplomatic protocols.

In more specific terms, the immediate post-war period saw Soviet intransigence over any settlement of the future of Germany, Soviet subversion of the states of eastern Europe and Soviet attempts at influence on Turkey and Iran. Rapprochement with the Soviet Union consistent with the defence of traditional British interests in European and imperial terms was soon seen to be impossible (Britain would it seems have been prepared to accept some form of 'spheres of interest' agreement but not Soviet expansionism that threatened vital British interests in Europe or elsewhere, for instance, the Middle East).

British foreign policy under Attlee and Bevin, already reliant as it was upon the Americans given the necessity for a new US loan to fund Britain's maintenance of world-power status (and without which British foreign policy insistence on world-power status and the domestic programme of the Labour government could not have been undertaken together), then became to apprise the Americans of the real nature of Soviet intentions, of the nature of their diplomacy, and of the threat they posed to the security of western Europe, Britain and worldwide given Soviet expansionism and opportunism and their support for subversive communism. The objective was to elicit needed US diplomatic and military support to protect the UK against Soviet expansionism in Europe and its ideological hostility to social democracy.

Bevin's objective of ensuring American understanding of Soviet intentions seems to have been attained at the Paris Council in April and May of 1946, when the crude, ideologically hostile and unpredictable diplomacy of Molotov, who was, however, only reflecting Stalin's instructions, seems to have resulted in US appreciation of Soviet expansionism and its ideological hostility towards the West. What followed from US experience of Soviet diplomacy and Bevin's persuasiveness as to the need to resist Soviet and communist expansionism on a case-by-case basis was the emergence of the Truman Doctrine of 1947 and its containment of communism to eastern Europe. It also had links to what was to become known as Domino Theory, the idea that if the West permitted one state to fall to communism adjacent states would follow. Such falling of 'dominoes' could happen in the physical sense, in which a communist state would sponsor communist guerrilla activity over its border with a contiguous democratic state through supply of arms and ideological support, and when that state fell to communism the same thing would happen with the next democratic state, and also in the sense that if there were no exhibition of Western resolve to resist communism democratic forces elsewhere in the world would lose confidence in resistance to communist infiltration that would be encouraged by a lack of Western resolve to resist communism.

The result was that after the Paris Council in 1946 the Americans accepted Bevin's analysis of Soviet foreign policy as essentially opportunistic and expansionist, a danger to the security of western Europe and Britain, and a strategic concern for the security of the US. American commitment to the defence of Europe against communist encroachment in the form of the Truman Doctrine of containment in 1947, which surrendered eastern Europe to the Soviet Union (Soviet domination of eastern Europe was clear and complete by this time) but indicated US resolve to resist further communist encroachment, was accompanied by the Marshall Plan for the economic recovery of western Europe. There followed the division of Germany into a democratic west and a communist east after the Berlin Crisis of 1948–49, and the creation of the North Atlantic Treaty Organisation (NATO) that tied America to the defence of western Europe. Bevin's astute diplomacy had overcome the isolationism he feared could characterise US foreign policy after the war and had been an example of what the British hoped for with the US, of British diplomatic experience guiding the inexperienced Americans and so permitting Britain world-power status on the basis of British diplomatic experience and US economic and military power.

In a sense the emerging Cold War was prosecuted by a series of reactions to crises. The series of conferences over the future of Germany and Soviet attempts to exert influence in Greece, Turkey and Iran would seem to have been the means by which Western policy was formed after the war, with the Berlin Crisis the first exemplification of Western resolve to resist Soviet and communist expansionism in physical terms and the Korean War an exemplification of the lengths to which the West was prepared to go to defend and encourage anti-communist regimes by military means even outside the central theatre of the Cold War in Europe.

To what extent were there vital decisions in regard to the Cold War to be made at Cabinet level in Britain once the nature of the international situation became clear, including the antipathy of the Soviet Union to social democracy and Britain, the generally expansionist and opportunistic intentions of Soviet foreign policy, the threat posed by the Soviet Union and communism to the security of western Europe and so to traditional British security interests in Europe, and the British need for American support in economic, diplomatic and military terms that was met by a US loan and a US foreign policy that became dependably anti-communist? For given an ethos of Britain as a world and imperial power and an attitudinal context of anti-communism enhanced by Soviet opportunistic expansionism in eastern Europe and intransigence and chicanery in immediate post-war diplomatic exchanges, defence of traditional British imperial and European interests was seen to be incompatible with Soviet expansionism, opportunism and hostility to British social democracy and to require the cultivation of a 'special relationship' with the US for much needed economic, military and diplomatic support. The British need for US support not just for the British economy but also in any resistance to the Soviet Union and communism was made very clear in the Berlin Crisis of 1948–49.

Even with such obvious and understood dependence on the US, the British Cabinet did retain the power to approve or resist US requests for British diplomatic support and military intervention, though British Prime Ministers and Cabinet ministers would have understood the risk of adverse consequences for the British economy or even for British security of declining to support US foreign policy, and of course foreign-policy decisions are taken by individuals in positions of power or influence in relation to foreign policy, and are chosen from a number of perceived possible policies, each with their own perceived advantages and disadvantages relative to objectives informed by ethos and attitudes. Having said that, a government's attitudinal ethos is inherited and tends not to be questioned, so that some policies that are in fact genuine alternatives are not considered just because the attitudinal orientation of the government precludes consideration of radical policies. That would seem to have been so with both the Attlee and Wilson governments over the alternative to dependence on the US, withdrawal from world-power status, from empire and from the defence of western Europe in a foreign policy that could be afforded given Britain's much diminished economic and military power relative to the Soviet Union and the US. Such a policy would have permitted Britain to pursue a foreign policy independent of the US though with much diminished status and influence and was not considered because of the attachment to British world-power status of Labour politicians such as Attlee, Bevin and Wilson, though it does seem that there were other Labour politicians in the periods concerned who did advocate domestic social expenditure taking precedence over that on military commitment to support the US in foreign wars, as was apparent in the resignation of Bevan over Korea and the difficulties Wilson had with the Labour left wing over Vietnam.

If US resolve to resist Soviet opportunism in Europe was tested by the Berlin Crisis and responded to Bevin's dynamism and certainty that Western credibility had to be demonstrated through a policy that combined toughness and prudence over Berlin then Korea may be seen to have been the test of UK support for the US in resisting the spread of communism worldwide by means of controversial UK military commitment and so a test of the 'special relationship' that permitted Britain to remain a world power and to enjoy the security benefits of US support against the Soviets in Europe.

Korea

By 1950 the major American foreign-policy objective was resistance to communist and Soviet proxy expansionism around the world. The US was resolved upon the defence of capitalist democracy against communist encroachment supported by the Soviet Union and intended by such resistance to encourage democratic regimes to resist communist expansion. The British foreign-policy objective may have been just as ambitious given British economic and military decline relative to the Soviet Union and the US, that is, a continuing resolve to defend traditional British European and imperial interests against any form of encroachment, by which was meant, in the Cold War climate of the post-war world, Soviet and communist expansionism (though India, Ceylon and Burma were granted independence in 1948 Britain continued to have imperial interests to defend worldwide, including east of Suez). American and British foreign-policy objectives coincided in several instances but not in all, for example where the British had no European or imperial interests. Yet British dependence upon US support in diplomatic and military terms in any resistance to Soviet encroachment was very clear to British politicians and officials and had been since the latter half of 1945, when Soviet hostility became clear. Since that time, British reliance upon US military power had been especially evident on occasions such as the Berlin Crisis of 1948–49, despite the fact that Bevin's dynamism had been influential in personal terms on Western resolve to remain in Berlin rather than retreat to a more defensible frontier further west. A series of major understandings and decisions had then been reached by the US and Britain by 1950 on

Soviet aims and intentions and the need to resist them case by case. But there had also been a clear understanding that the British need for American support meant that the 'special relationship' was not an equal one. Such understandings did not however necessarily mean a British acceptance that British foreign policy would in future be a direct reflection of US foreign policy, though there was a British understanding of US power and of the possible consequences of declining to endorse and support US foreign policy.

To the extent that the first 'warm' exchange of the Cold War, which did establish Western resolve to defend western Europe against Soviet and communist encroachment, was the Berlin Crisis of 1948, the first 'hot' war was the Korean War, which began in 1950. The Labour government in 1950 does seem to have been convinced that US support against the Soviet Union in Europe was contingent upon British moral, diplomatic and military support for the US against communist encroachment elsewhere. Even so, the British position differed from US policy towards China after it became communist in 1949 – Britain recognised communist China in January 1950 and endorsed China's being admitted to the UN, for Bevin felt that China could emerge as more nationalist than communist, wanted to avoid alienating Nehru, and with Attlee felt that the Soviet Union and China could be separated. The US did not differentiate between the Soviet Union and China in its Cold War crusade, opposed communist China's admittance to the UN, and referred to 'centrally-directed communist imperialism', an inference of some concern to Attlee.

Such a combination of consonance over the need to resist the spread of Soviet and communist influence case by case and instances of dissonance over the means to be used reflects what seems to have been a pattern in post-war British diplomacy and foreign policy, of public exhibitions of ideological and political support for US foreign policy to maintain the 'special relationship' while attempting to restrain what were seen as the more extreme tendencies in US policy (in fact of course the Americans were correct as to China's ideological orientation), though doing what was necessary in terms of diplomatic and even military commitment to maintain the 'special relationship'. This was in part because of a different British view on some issues but also because of the natural British focus on British spheres of interest and the sense of a lack of British economic and military resources to maintain and defend even them. In the Korean War Britain supported the US to maintain the 'special relationship' that sustained Britain economically through the American loan and diplomatically and militarily through the support of US power against Soviet expansionism and opportunism.[4] The British did try to restrain the US in private, a stance that was to become customary for Britain in its relations with the US, one of public support and discreet restraint, with the argument that public support was the condition of any form of influence on the US. However the closeness that more or less unqualified British support brought did not facilitate British influence on US policy.

To set the Korean War in its ideological context, Western resistance to Soviet encroachment in Europe in the Berlin Crisis in 1948 and over Korea in 1950 reflected exactly what Bevin had told Vandenberg in January 1946 was essential in dealing with the Soviet Union, that is, demonstration of Western firmness on a case-by-case basis, by which Bevin meant resistance in every case of Soviet expansionism and opportunism (this stance of Bevin's is not be confused with the British Foreign Office tradition of a case-by-case approach, which involved treating every case on its merits in a pragmatic foreign policy, for Bevin was clear that there should be exemplary resistance to the Soviet Union in every case of Soviet expansionism). Bevin was however referring to Turkey and Iran, cases in which Soviet encroachment threatened British interests in the Middle East, in 1946.

The Korean case was different, in that there was no immediate or discernible threat to British interests, and in fact the British did not see Korea as within a British sphere of interest – as was clear from Churchill's dismissive remark to the effect that the only significance of the Korean War was enhanced American rearmament. This was unlike the situation further south, where the British felt that the fall of Indo-China would produce a domino effect that would threaten British Malaya, where there had been a communist insurgency since 1948. The British political and official establishment had had no involvement in the events in Korea that resulted in the initial partition of the peninsula, though it did regard the Korean War as a form of Soviet and communist expansionism rather than a local war between factions without any Cold War implications and saw it as a case in which there would have to be sufficient British support to maintain the 'special relationship'. The British did then have a sense that Korea was a test of Western resolve and that communism and Soviet influence should be resisted on principle and to deter any future expansionism rather than because of any strategic value (there was a consensus that Korea had no such value), but not with British troops already overstretched and a strain on the Exchequer. The clearest evidence of this sense that Korea had no relevance to what was conceived to be the sphere of British interests is that there had been no exchanges in the British Cabinet over Korea in the year and a half prior to the outbreak of the Korean War in June 1950.

The politicians and officials who influenced the British decision to commit British troops to Korea in such numbers were those who had negotiated British adjustment to the realities of British economic and military weakness, a Soviet and communist threat to British European and imperial interests derived from a combination of Soviet power, hostility to British social democracy and general expansionism and opportunism, and the need for US support in any resistance to Soviet and communist pressure. Attlee, Bevin and Dalton had understood that American economic support was vital to the maintenance of British world-power status as early as during the negotiations for a renewal of the US loan in late 1945. And by January 1946 the need for US support in any resistance to Soviet expansionism had been reinforced by experience of the nature of Soviet diplomacy at the London conference.

During 1946 continued exhibitions of Soviet intransigence and expansionism assisted these understandings, and the need for US air power in Berlin in 1948–49 made Britain's military dependence upon the US yet clearer. Bevin as Foreign Secretary had advocated resistance to Soviet and communist expansionism wherever it was encountered, and had been the means of persuading the Americans of the need for such resistance. As PM Attlee endorsed Bevin's foreign policy in general orientation and especially his dealing with the Americans and the Soviet Union. There was also support from the opposition for Britain's foreign policy, and by 1950 the left-wing unrest regarding the orientation of British foreign policy within the Labour Party was over, with Soviet diplomacy and foreign policy, not least Soviet action in support of a communist coup in Czechoslovakia in 1948 and over the Berlin Crisis of 1948–49, and the Marshall Plan of 1947 that facilitated the economic recovery of western Europe with American money combining to persuade those on the left that the interests of communism and social democracy did not coincide and that US support was imperative to defend western Europe. NATO followed the Berlin Crisis's end in 1949. This continuity of experience of Soviet diplomacy and intentions may have been vital in the understanding throughout the British political class of the need for US commitment to the defence of western Europe and so the need for British support for the US over Korea.

The Foreign Office view was that Britain shared 'to a slight extent the American interest in the retention of a non-communist foothold in the N.E. Asian mainland opposite to Japan, now that China has fallen to the Communists',[5] an indication of a sense of Korea's strategic insignificance, of its being beyond the major theatre of British Cold War concerns, which was Europe, and of its being outside any British sphere of interest. And in another indication of primary concern with theatres relevant to British interests (in this case in the Middle East), the Foreign Office advocated that 'all possible action should...be taken to prevent the aggressors from attaining their objective, both in order to safeguard the future of the United Nations Organisation, and to deter the Soviet Union from attempting aggression elsewhere (e.g. in Persia)'.[6] The FO did then endorse Bevin's conviction that communist expansionism had to be resisted case by case to provide a deterrent to further acts of encroachment on the non-communist world, a form of reasoning that had been apparent in the Truman Doctrine of 1947 and in practice in Bevin's resolve to remain in Berlin despite a Soviet blockade in 1948 and 1949. The Berlin Crisis had of course been an exemplification of the need for US power in any resistance to Soviet expansionism.

The first Cabinet meeting to discuss the Korean situation following the northern invasion of the south over the 38th parallel on 25 June took place on 27 June. The general sense among ministers was that it was by no means clear that the North Korean action had been instigated by the Soviet Union and that it might be diplomatic to assume that the North Koreans had acted on their own so as to give the Soviet Union a diplomatic interval in which it could dissociate itself from the North Korean invasion without any public *volte-face*, which was very similar to Bevin's policy of avoidance of any provocation that would preclude a Soviet withdrawal of the blockade of the western sectors of Berlin the previous year, a policy of resistance accompanied by diplomatic prudence. Such caution reflected a British desire to avoid any unnecessary Cold War confrontation or escalation of the Korean War, to avoid alienating China, in which Britain had economic interests, and to secure the status of Hong Kong. Britain had accorded communist China diplomatic recognition and had advocated such a policy, and Chinese membership of the UN in place of Taiwan, the status of which the British argued should be resolved by China, to the US. The US disagreed.

Attlee presented to the Cabinet meeting on 27 June 1950 the draft of an intended US statement that associated the North Korean invasion with the 'communist threat in other parts of Asia', which, it was felt, would be unnecessarily confrontational to the Soviet Union and would 'embarrass the United Kingdom government in their relations with the Communist government of China, and might even provoke that government to attack Hong Kong or to foment disorder there'.[7] This British inclination to pursue diplomatic possibilities with both the Soviet Union and China, and to perceive the possibility that the two communist powers could be divided from each other (and that their interests were not identical), separated the British from the Americans over Korea. There was however an understanding that it was in British interests to have the Soviet threat by proxy in Korea resisted, as was indicated by Attlee in his address to the Commons on 27 June.

Despite ministerial reservations regarding the risk of the escalation of any war in Korea and over there having been no exhaustion of diplomatic possibilities with the Soviet Union and China the Cabinet seems to have decided that the necessity to maintain the 'special relationship' was the overriding factor, for ministers agreed 'in principle' to UK support for US resistance to 'Communist aggression in Asia' and to UK support in the UN Security Council for a resolution calling for member states to provide support for South Korea against North Korea, though it seems to have been against a proposed US reference in its announcement to 'centrally-directed Communist imperialism'. And in a more practical indication of support for the US the Cabinet agreed that 'the Minister of Defence should arrange with the Chiefs of Staff to report to the Defence Committee what practical steps the United Kingdom could take to assist the Republic of Korea, in pursuance of the resolution which was being brought before the Security Council'.[8] As happened so often with Cabinet minutes in Attlee's administration, views do not seem to be ascribed to individual ministers, so it is not possible to assess the nature of the Cabinet discussion (Attlee also exhorted ministers not to insist that their dissent be recorded in Cabinet minutes, which may explain a protocol that used terms such as 'it was noted that'). There does however seem to have been some difference of view within Cabinet as to the involvement of the Soviet Union or the advisability of claiming such involvement rather than permitting the latter time to withdraw support for the North Koreans. Bevin, who was not present, had advised ministers not to isolate the Korean instance from other Communist 'encroachments' because such isolation could preclude US assistance to British Malaya and to French Indo-China, both seen to be threatened by communism, though his advice could be interpreted as an indication of his sense that the UK would have to support the US in whatever response it chose.

Following the Cabinet meeting on the morning of 27 June Attlee told the Commons that the North Korean invasion represented 'naked aggression' that 'must be checked'.[9] He also observed, referring to recent experience, that 'the salvation of all is dependent on prompt and effective measures to arrest aggression wherever it occurs', and told the Commons that the UK representative at the UN had been instructed to endorse the US proposed resolution recommending that UN states should provide assistance to South Korea to repel the North Korean attack. Attlee read the draft of the proposed US government statement to the Commons and received the endorsement of Churchill from the Conservative benches.

The CoS view was that there should be no dispatch of British forces to Korea unless the US position required it on military grounds because of existing British troop commitments to the defence of western Europe (regarding which the Joint Planners' concern was such that they recommended no air or ground support to Korea) and to the Malayan insurgency.[10] Attlee conveyed the CoS view to Cabinet on 6 July 1950 and the meeting noted there had been no adverse Commons reaction on Korea on 5 July.[11] At the rhetorical level Attlee reflected the British perspective and focused on the fact that the UN had endorsed action to repel the North Korean invasion. Attlee claimed, avoiding reference to the Soviet Union or to communism and with explicit reference to the UN, that failure to resist the northern invasion of South Korea could encourage further acts of similar aggression all over the world, a statement that was consistent with the lessons of appeasement in the 1930s, with the Truman Doctrine of containment and with Domino Theory. It was, he warned, therefore in the interest of the British electorate that Britain should resist over Korea.

Attlee's early reaction indicated moral and some material support for US resistance to communist expansionism in Korea, though there was a British sense that the Soviet Union should be permitted time in which to withdraw support from the North Koreans, accompanied by disapproval of the US association of the Korean invasion by the north with the Taiwan situation. It was not long before any idea that the Soviet Union might not be behind the North Korean action was dismissed by the British ambassador to the Soviet Union, Sir David Kelly. On 30 June 1950, he addressed the issue of Soviet involvement and policy directly. The Soviet Union knew of the North Korean action, which was 'almost certainly at Soviet instigation'. It had not anticipated such speed and decisiveness from the West over Korea. Kelly saw it as a case of Soviet opportunism that had not addressed the possibility of US intervention and felt that the Soviet Union would not wish to risk war with the US over Korea. There might be an abandonment by the Soviet Union of the North Koreans, or the Soviet Union might offer it in exchange for communist China's admittance to the UN, or the Soviet Union and China might start another crisis elsewhere. In fact Soviet records recently accessible indicate that Stalin's endorsement of the North Korean invasion of the south was reluctant rather than its being at Soviet instigation.

British desire to pursue diplomatic channels had no effect whatever on Truman or Acheson, and the US reaction was an indication of the lack of British influence on US policy, and the extent to which British foreign policy could be made without reference to American demands, to come. On 11 July Douglas, the US Ambassador to Britain, told Bevin that Acheson had directed him to indicate that the US would not endorse any negotiations with the Soviet Union or the idea that there could be some Western concessions in regard to China's being accepted as a member of the UN or over Taiwan, though it has been argued that it was Acheson's own speech to the Press Club that had resulted in the North Korean invasion, because he had then indicated that South Korea was outside the perimeter of US security concerns. The North Korean invasion followed almost at once.

When Sir Oliver Franks, the British Ambassador to Washington, had reported that he was being asked for some indication of genuine British support, the first response had been to send the British

Far East fleet to Korea to assist US naval forces against the North Koreans. At this stage, 28 June 1950, there had been no decision to commit British ground troops to Korea, though apparently 'the state department was imploring allies for help' and 'Acheson hoped at least Britain would help'.[12] On 20 July 1950, in part of a series of meetings between Bradley and Jessup from the US and Franks and Tedder from the UK, Bradley alluded to the need for UN land forces in Korea. The first US troops had arrived there on 1 July. Tedder reported that there had been an indication that even a minimal British troop presence would do, and that their deployment to Korea did not have to be imminent. Franks told Bevin to expect a request for at least a token force.

Franks was 'sure that the United States Administration attaches great importance to a British offer of troops for Korea' and said that the US felt a need for UK support to sustain the UN character of the intervention in Korea and expected other nations to follow the UK in providing troops. Franks went on to note that the US electorate regarded the UK as a natural ally and expected the UK to support the US. He claimed that if the Attlee administration did not commit troops to Korea it would be seen as an indication of disapproval of the US intervention there, and alluded to a possible adverse effect on 'additional appropriations for European defence', though he concentrated on the more general adverse longer term effect on the relationship between the UK and the US. There was a sense that the US would very much prefer an offer of troop commitment to having to present a formal request for troops. The response of the Attlee government was more or less immediate. The Defence Committee approved the sending of troops to Korea on 24 July, and Attlee told the Cabinet on 25 July that the 'political advantages' of sending troops to Korea mattered more than the military argument against sending them, because of their being an expression of 'Anglo-American solidarity', a reference to a sense of a need to show support for the US.[13] The Attlee government's commitment of troops to Korea in July 1950 reflected Attlee's and Bevin's sense of the need to maintain the 'special relationship' with the Americans to secure the continued support of US power in economic, diplomatic and military terms, and Franks' advocacy of what was needed to secure a continuance of the relationship with the US.

It had the desired effect. On 26 July Australian and New Zealand troops were committed, on 20 August France agreed to send a contingent, and the following day Canada did likewise. And though the British troops were not to come from Hong Kong, when the American position became desperate in the Pusan perimeter and Attlee was asked, on 16 August, for infantry to defend their final position in Korea, he responded at once, with Cabinet on 17 August authorising troops to be sent from Hong Kong to Pusan.[14] The troops arrived in Korea on 29 August. On 15 September MacArthur relieved the pressure on the Pusan perimeter by landing at Inchon, and by 9 October US forces were over the 38th parallel. By 19 October the 8th US army was in Pyongyang.

Within the Cabinet there was concern that any increase in defence spending would have an adverse effect on welfare spending in the UK. At the Cabinet meeting on 25 July 1950 Shinwell as Defence Minister asked for an additional £100 million, with a projected rise in defence spending for 1951–52 to £980 million. Though there were ministerial misgivings over the latter sum, which was perceived to result in a choice between a 'lower standard of living or longer dependence on US aid', the additional £100 million was approved. And at an ensuing Cabinet meeting on 11 August the period of National Service was extended from eighteen months to two years in a context of CoS difficulties in finding enough manpower for the Korean commitment.[15]

Both sides of the Commons were of the view that appeasement had to be avoided, and there was in fact little left-wing opposition within the Labour Party as a whole to commitment of British troops to Korea. At the Labour Party Conference in October 1950, assisted by a speech by Bevin on 2 October in which he told delegates that there was no alternative to committing the massive defence expenditure the Korean war required, that Britain's security depended on it and that appeasement had to be avoided, the Labour government's foreign policy was endorsed.

The possible reasons for this are interesting. Apart from the changed international context and altered view of the Soviet Union and the US which extended even to the Labour left wing, there had been a UN Security Council resolution that authorised intervention in Korea in response to what was clearly a North Korean invasion of the south (although this UN Security Council resolution had been taken without the Soviet Union being there). This of itself lent the Western action in Korea legitimacy it might otherwise not have had for the left wing, for their history of belief in world government would have necessitated endorsement of UN sanctions. And the perceived precedent might have been the Soviet and communist encroachment that precipitated the Berlin Crisis. The result was initial approval for Attlee's policy of support for US policy over Korea, to maintain the needed support of the US in Europe, to demonstrate Western firmness in the face of Soviet and communist expansionism, to indicate commitment to collective security under UN command, and to avert another war by avoiding appeasement.[16]

This attachment to US policy over Korea was to continue despite reservations. Bevin and Attlee were allured by the possibility of a final victory when North Korean forces began to be pushed back over the 38th parallel. Such a policy was informed by a belief that the North Koreans and the Soviet Union should be made to pay for the invasion of the south, and that the North Koreans should be nullified as a threat. Bevin drew a parallel with the Berlin Crisis. It was also believed that the Soviet Union would not react to a push north by UN forces and that the Chinese would not intervene. In the face of Chinese warnings and misgivings from the CoS, especially Air Chief Marshall Slessor, Attlee chose to listen to Bevin, who was concerned that the US was committed to advance north and worried that there would be a fall in US commitment to Europe should it seem to the Americans that Britain was in favour of appeasement over Korea. There was a sense anyway that the US was doing most of the fighting.

The difference between the British and American views of the relationship between the Soviet Union and China was that the US regarded China and North Korea as satellites of the Soviet Union, while Britain saw the two major communist powers as different and not necessarily allied over all issues. While CoS misgivings regarding Chinese intervention were disregarded, Bevin was concerned to limit the war to Korea.

Chinese forces invaded Korea on 19 October 1950, by way of reaction to the American advance so far north, and on 25 October engaged with US and UN troops. On 13 November 1950 Bevin told ministers that despite his own efforts to avert Chinese intervention in Korea the fact that the Chinese had intervened meant that there was 'a grave risk of general war in the Far East'. Bevin proposed a demilitarised zone in North Korea south of the Manchurian border, though it was noted that the proposal would have to be endorsed by the US. In an indication of Bevin's continuing concern regarding an escalation of the war, on 20 November Bevin recommended to ministers that a 'direct approach' to the Chinese government should be made to reassure China and remove any 'misapprehensions' as to Britain's objectives in Korea and the Far East, and indicated that he would tell MPs that the intention was to 'confine the area of hostilities', an enduring concern for Bevin and for Attlee.[17] Such British attempts to preclude war with the Chinese were overtaken by events, as Chinese attacks along the front in November 1950 resulted in an American withdrawal that represented the start of what was to become the longest retreat in American military history. By 27 November 1950 US forces were surrounded by Chinese troops at the Chosin Reservoir and forced to withdraw from North Korea.

On 30 November, in a White House press conference, Truman did not rule out American use of the atomic bomb on China, an alarming development for the more cautious British, concerned to avoid any escalation or widening of the Korean War in a context of an enduring British concern, not least among the CoS, regarding MacArthur's freedom of decision in Korea. For the American military the situation was dire, with US forces pushed south of the 38th parallel before a Chinese offensive by 31 December 1950 and with Seoul reoccupied by the communists on 4 January 1951, so that by early 1951 there was in the US administration a sense that Korea could have to be abandoned and the war pursued against China by economic and military means, which in turn could have meant the widening of the conflict through the bombing of China. There was considerable unrest in the Commons on 30 November, when Bevin said he had no real idea of what US policy towards China was and both Labour and the Conservatives wanted to avoid a widening of the conflict and any risk of war with China (Churchill made it clear that war with China should be avoided and that Europe was the major theatre in the Cold War).

The government position was precarious, for by this time its majority in the Commons was slender. Having secured power in a massive landslide with a majority of 145 seats in 1945 Labour had won the general election on 23 February 1950 with a majority of only 5 seats in the Commons. Given the condition of the economy Britain needed China as an export market, and needed also to limit international adversaries to those that actually threatened vital British interests. The general approval of British participation in the Korean War had disappeared, with the CoS concerned as to the position of UN forces on the Yalu River (before the Chinese invasion in October), the FO worried that Chinese reaction might be one that would be driven by a desire not to lose face, some ministers averse to the domestic consequences of war expenditure, and the threat that the US might use the bomb. Bevin indicated British concern to Washington.

Attlee then undertook to go and see Truman in Washington. There, in early December 1950, he received a reassurance that Europe remained the central theatre of the Cold War, that the bomb would not be used without prior consultation with Britain (Truman had not intended to indicate imminent resort to the bomb) and an understanding that the 38th parallel might be the final divide between North and South Korea. The promise of prior consultation over the use of the bomb does in fact seem to be controversial, with British accounts claiming that there was a promise of consultation and American accounts challenging that and claiming that the undertaking was to inform rather than to consult over the use of the bomb. In any case even consultation would not indicate that there would be any influence for the Attlee government on US policy over use of the bomb, for consultation concerns the form rather than the content of diplomacy, and it would have been entirely possible for the Americans to have consulted the British over use of the bomb and then to have disregarded the British view that it should not be used. And though the abandonment of the idea of Korean unification under Western auspices was a change of policy for the US administration it seems to have been a reflection of the realities on the ground in Korea rather than from any British influence. Attlee was also assured by Truman that Korea would not be abandoned for political reasons associated with a redirection of US policy towards confrontation with China – any US withdrawal would result from military considerations alone, though that too does not indicate influence from Attlee on Truman, for Truman indicated to Attlee that there would be no withdrawal from Korea because that would be an 'abdication of responsibility' and a betrayal of the anti-communist South Koreans.[18] The Americans did not endorse Attlee's idea that the Chinese could be divided from the Soviet Union and rejected the idea that there should be any concessions to China over Taiwan or UN membership – it was in fact an odd proposal coming from the British, who through Bevin had explicitly rejected any similar linkage of the Berlin Crisis to the wider issue of Germany in 1948–49 and had in that crisis opposed on principle any concessions that would be seen as rewarding Soviet brinkmanship, which was the American position over Korea. In more general terms there was a British preference for negotiation and compromise with the Chinese over Korea associated with a fear of an escalation of the Korean War into a more general ideological conflict with the Chinese in the Far East that would present the Soviet Union with an opportunity in western Europe. The US wanted threats of sanctions against China for its military intervention in Korea rather than negotiations that may have seemed like appeasement to them.

The extent of British influence on US policy over China and in general was in fact such that the British delegation was concerned 'not to have convinced the Americans of the need to make a serious effort to reach a political settlement with the Chinese, and not to have shaken them in their intention to undertake some form of "limited war" against China'.[19]

Despite Attlee's and Bevin's misgivings regarding US policy over Korea, there had been a continuing understanding of the need to preserve the relationship with the US. For prior to his visit to Washington, in a context of appreciation that the 'Chinese had mounted a major offensive' 'with the aim of destroying the UN forces in Korea' and advice from Franks that the State Department wanted to charge communist China with aggression at the UN, Attlee told Cabinet on 29 November 1950, 'if we were to withdraw our support for United States strategy in the Far East, the United States government would be less willing to continue their policy of supporting the defence of western Europe.' As is so with many of Attlee's Cabinet meetings, some of the views expressed are not attributed to individual ministers, though the record does refer to the view that 'the ultimate threat to our security came from Russia, and we could not afford to break our united front with the United States against our main potential enemy', that 'we could not afford to lose America's support in Europe', and that because of that there would have to be acceptance of American dictates over the Far East. These statements, though unattributed, must have come from Attlee or Bevin or have been made with their approval. In what seems to have been an extensive discussion, Bevin said he had feared that MacArthur would pursue attacks beyond the Manchurian frontier but had been reassured by Acheson that the US intended to deal with the situation at the UN rather than by force on the ground, and that the US objective was 'resist aggression' and 'localise the area of hostilities', and Attlee counselled avoidance 'of any precipitate action at the present stage'. Though Cabinet found it 'disquieting' that the US was considering charging China with open aggression at the UN, with the possibility of war with China and defence commitment to the Far East that would expose Europe and the Middle East, the theatres of most concern to the UK,[20] the need for US support in Europe, a compelling British sphere of interest, does seem to have dictated British support for the US over Korea in November 1950.

Yet if Attlee's proposal that there should be concessions to the Chinese over UN membership and Taiwan was odd given a long history of British opposition to concessions on principle, so was the American sense that the British were going soft on communism, which seemed entirely to disregard the fact that it had been Bevin who had been the advocate of the policy of resisting Soviet and communist expansionism and opportunism on every occasion with firmness to demonstrate Western resolve and avoid giving the Soviet Union the sense that brinkmanship would succeed. In January 1946 this was exactly his exposition to Republican senators Dulles and Vandenberg over Soviet advances on Turkey and Iran, and it had been Bevin's dynamism over Berlin, when he had been the first to make public a resolve to remain in Berlin (when the American military were dubious as to whether Berlin could be held and were considering a more defensible frontier), that set the standard for the Western response.

There was in fact no question of Attlee's going soft on communism, just a serious question of how to optimise limited British defence expenditure to meet the most vital British foreign-policy objectives. For the differences in approach over Korea may be attributed to the fact that the British did not conceive of Korea as being within their sphere of interest and felt it had no strategic significance – had there been a similar crisis in Europe British foreign policy would have been, as it had been during the Berlin Crisis, one of no concessions or compromise, with diplomacy being pursued on the ground, as Bevin had done over Berlin. While it was not stated in any direct way (and one would not expect it to be so stated), British policy remained governed by its fundamentals, the maintenance of Britain as a world power and defence of existing, traditional British interests in Europe and worldwide, which included precluding the domination of Europe by any one great power (and especially western Europe and the Low Countries) and the protection of British imperial possessions and the sea routes to them (though the latter was challenged in an age of air power).

What this and the reality of British decline in economic and military power meant was that Britain wished to maintain US commitment to NATO and the defence of western Europe using US troops and armaments and US diplomatic and military support for Britain in the war against communism within the British sphere of interest. Elsewhere it was necessary to prevent communist advances to discourage other communist insurgencies within the British sphere, but the British ideal was that this should be done by US troops given the limited British defence budget and the domestic difficulties that high defence spending caused not just in Parliament but also in the Cabinet itself. Even so the advocacy of compromise and concessions was inconsistent with the policy of Attlee and Bevin over the Baltics during the war and their general aversion to rewarding communist brinkmanship and expansionism or opportunism that had been apparent over Germany, Turkey and Iran, and of course Berlin in 1948, and reflected the contingency of what seemed to be a principle.

From the American perspective, unless British troops were committed to Korea, Britain's commitment to containing communism would have seemed to be with American troops. The British wanted to avoid such troop commitment and saw Korea as being of no strategic value whatever but did what was necessary to maintain the Atlantic relationship and US support in Europe and NATO. For the US, while Korea may have had no strategic significance, it did have great symbolic value, in that it was the first case of communist military aggression (and it could be seen as being within the US sphere of interest in being so near to Japan). The US agenda was to show not just to the Soviet Union and China but also the rest of the world that communism would be resisted by the US. Korea was the first instance in which the Truman Doctrine of containment was challenged by direct communist military force. The US wanted British moral and military support for international and domestic audiences, in that British troop commitments (and those from other nations that the British commitment elicited) lent the US endeavour in Korea an international legitimacy it would not have had had the US been alone. The US domestic political arena had significant isolationist tendencies and a significant right wing advocating a tougher line against communism, a focus on Asia at the expense of Europe, and vigorous action against communist China, and Acheson was not averse to references to such Republican pressures in his demands for British support of the US position in Korea. In what seems a rather blunt indication for a diplomatic encounter Acheson noted that if the UK did not support the US in Korea the US electorate (rather than just the extreme right wing of US politics) could reject plans to enhance the power of NATO.[21]

As has been indicated, the situation in Korea deteriorated after Attlee's visit to Truman in December 1950, with the retreat and falling morale of United Nations Command in Korea (UNC). Slessor believed that MacArthur might withdraw before the Chinese to Pusan and thereafter from Korea, and continue the war against China by other means. Slessor felt this could result in a world war for which the West was unprepared. The CoS warned that war with China would benefit the Soviet Union, not least as troops would be diverted from Europe to Asia, and could result in China's appealing to revolutionary movements in southeast Asia. Cabinet and CoS concern was such that Slessor was sent to Washington to argue against Korea's being abandoned and against war with China and to establish US objectives and intentions in Korea.[22] Bradley confirmed Truman's indication to Attlee that Korea would only be abandoned if it could not be defended militarily and that Europe was regarded by the US as primary to the Cold War (and that the Truman administration did not intend to transfer US troops from Europe to Asia, which was a major British concern). He did however say that he regarded UNC withdrawal to Pusan and thence from Korea as likely. He also alluded to an adverse view of the UN and increasing isolationism in US public opinion, while Rusk said the US defence chiefs wanted UN condemnation of China as an aggressor state.

By this time the Korean War, funding for which had initially attracted little controversy, was causing friction within the British political establishment. There was the matter of limiting American actions and confining the crisis to Korea, which exercised British politicians throughout the Korean War. But defence expenditure had been a controversial issue since the beginning of the Cold War and remained so in 1951. Since the beginning of the Labour administration Attlee and Dalton had attempted to rein in defence expenditure, while Bevin fought something of a rear-guard action to ensure that his diplomacy with the Soviet Union and the US had sufficient support in terms of military power to make British world-power status credible. Though everyone in the Labour leadership, with the possible exception of Bevan, were agreed that it was imperative that Britain should retain its world-power status (Dalton may however have had a slightly different view as to what that implied than Attlee and Bevin, not least in relation to Soviet power in Europe), the level of defence expenditure resulting from continued commitment to the Korean War meant rising taxes and threat to the welfare budget. Questions were raised as to the necessity of such radical rearmament and the possibility of Britain's drifting into a wider war because of the manner in which British policy seemed to be controlled by Washington.

Over the US demand for a UN condemnation of communist China as an aggressor state, the Foreign Office worried that any such resolution would be a prelude to, and lend legitimacy to, an attack on China using US air power. Such was the concern that, on 28 November 1950, the Foreign Office view was that Britain had 'a choice between a serious split in Anglo-American relations, or joining reluctantly in a war which would divide the Commonwealth, dissipate Western resources and weaken our defences without any corresponding gains'.[23] In Cabinet Bevan and Dalton felt Britain should demonstrate some independence from US policy over Korea. Bevin advocated acceptance of US demands, and as has been seen Attlee indicated to Cabinet on 29 November 1950 that failure to support the US over Korea could imperil NATO funding.

Bevin was ambivalent regarding US policy and reluctant in his endorsement of its demand for a UN condemnation of communist China, for he foresaw its possible corollaries, including bombing of China, with all the implications of escalation and possible Soviet attack on an unprepared western Europe that would bring. Bevin's acceptance of US policy despite such serious misgivings is indicative of the power of a credible threat from US policy over British foreign policy in the context of British weakness and need for US support in the defence of Europe. For on 8 January 1951 Acheson reiterated what he had said when Attlee met Truman in December 1950, that British support for the US in the Far East was linked to US support for resistance to communism in Europe, telling Bevin of isolationist tendencies in the US and the risk of diminished US support for NATO if Britain was not seen to be supporting the US over Chinese intervention in Korea.[24] At the FO Strang and Dixon advocated acceptance of US demands to maintain the Anglo-American alliance despite the risks of provocation of the Chinese through condemnation at the UN.[25] Gaitskell, whose job as Chancellor of the Exchequer made clear the extent of British economic reliance on US policy, supported Bevin's advocacy of acceptance of US policy. But with Bevin away unwell the Cabinet on 25 January 1951 agreed that it should contemplate resisting the US resolution condemning China unless there was some change to the wording. The incipient resistance to the Americans did not last long, for, with some assistance from Acheson's changes, Attlee persuaded his ministers to support the US resolution. The changes to the UN resolution referred to negotiation prior to the imposition of sanctions and could not be described as a victory for British influence within the special relationship, for the threat of sanctions remained. On 1 February 1951 there was a UN censure of China for 'aggression'.

The danger of US action against China receded in 1951, though not because of British pressure, for it was Ridgway's demonstrating on 25 January in a combined US, UN and South Korean offensive that Korea could be held using conventional weapons, culminating in his retaking of Seoul on 18 March. Other changes in US policy, such as the understanding that the 38th parallel should be the foundation of armistice negotiations, which was a major abandonment of an earlier US policy of a unified Korea opposed to communism, were also not due to British persuasiveness but to Chinese military successes on the ground in Korea that made uniting Korea under anti-communist auspices seem impossible.

Then, on 24 March, MacArthur issued, without authorisation from Truman, a demand that China negotiate with the UN or face bombing. The British were appalled, and alarmed also by indications that the US wanted to give the UN commander power to authorise bombing Chinese air bases if UN troops were attacked. In the event MacArthur was sacked by Truman on 5 April, not as a result of British concern but because of his own overt insubordination and statements that denigrated Truman's policy.

What remained for British politicians and officials was then the issue of expenditure on defence. On 25 January 1951 the British Cabinet, to demonstrate British commitment to the defence of Korea and the Cold War, approved massive rearmament. It meant that British tax revenue was being spent on arms rather than social spending. In the ensuing Commons debate on defence policy on 14 and 15 February 1951 Shinwell stressed British membership of NATO but Churchill, having previously indicated a continuation of the traditional bipartisan approach to British foreign policy, claimed the government was divided because the Labour Party included many with communist sympathies. The censure motion proposed by Churchill failed when the Liberals voted with Labour, but the government was exhausted and continuing to face the problems associated with a policy of maintaining world-power status and commitment to the Welfare State. Strikes in the docks and coal mines amidst further rationing provided the domestic context for decisions regarding Korea, and there was the government's small majority and its own divisions.

The issue of British defence expenditure had in the interim continued to exercise ministers. Vickers points to the extent of the escalation in defence expenditure consequent on the Korean War commitment, noting that on 29 January 1951 Attlee told the Commons that defence expenditure, originally estimated at £780 million, was to be increased from £3.4 billion to £4.7 billion, an increase from eight per cent of GNP before the war to fourteen per cent of GNP.[26] Such a magnitude of increase was bound to have adverse effects on expenditure elsewhere, and on 22 April 1951 Bevan and Wilson resigned, ostensibly over increased health charges, though the issue was linked to taxes and war expenditure. The 'Bevanite revolt' split the Cabinet and the Party but Attlee confirmed the government's policy of high defence expenditure to retain the Atlantic relationship. The position of Attlee as PM had been made more difficult by the departure of the loyal and experienced Bevin, whose poor health had finally meant he could no longer continue as Foreign Secretary in March 1951, though for much of the Korean War Bevin had been unwell and the conduct of British foreign policy had fallen to Attlee.[27]

Bevin's final loss meant an end to the way in which Attlee had arranged government business by assigning broad swathes of policy to senior ministers, for it had been Attlee's custom to discuss and agree foreign policy with Bevin in private before Cabinet meetings, so reducing Cabinet scrutiny of foreign policy both by not involving other ministers throughout and because the decisions would have been made before the Cabinet met. Attlee's way of conducting government business avoided extensive Cabinet discussion between ministers (and dissent from ministers), not least because another effect was that grasp of issues related to a specific minister's brief was limited to that minister and the PM. It is difficult to know if Attlee had intended these effects, and one should not infer intent from consequence, but it was known that Attlee disliked extensive expatiation over issues and had asked that ministers should not insist that their dissent be recorded in the minutes.

The system had permitted the government to get through an astonishing amount of business in the Attlee administration.

Bevin's successor, Morrison, did not have Bevin's grasp of foreign policy, with the result that foreign policy became more Attlee's province than when he had had Bevin as Foreign Secretary. And earlier, in October 1950, another Labour big gun had become too unwell to continue, the Chancellor of the Exchequer, Cripps, although his replacement, Gaitskell, proved an ally to Attlee in the latter's insistence that British troops had to be retained in Korea and in his belief that US foreign policy there had to be supported to ensure that the British economy would receive US support (given his wider brief, Attlee also worried over US support for NATO and the defence of western Europe). It was in this adverse context that Bevan and Wilson resigned.

The Cabinet meeting at which Bevan indicated his intention to go is instructive in its revealing Attlee's own understanding, and that of ministers, of the gravity of the situation for the government and the Labour Party. The record of the Cabinet meeting on 9 April 1951, held without Attlee himself, as he was in hospital, indicates clear ministerial appreciation of the link between high defence expenditure caused by British troop commitment to support the US in Korea and NHS charges through the need to control the budget. Bevan warned of the possible grave consequences of imposing NHS charges for the government majority in the Commons and the possibility of a serious government defeat resulting in an election in which the Conservatives could claim to support a free NHS. Several ministers expressed the view that if Bevan were to resign 'an acute political crisis would develop. With their present Parliamentary majority the Government could not afford any diminution in their voting strength in the House of Commons. And, if the Government fell, as a result of divided counsels within the Cabinet, the Labour Party's prospects at the following General Election would be very gravely prejudiced' (as has been noted above, the Labour government had had, since the general election on 23 February 1950, a majority in the Commons of a mere five seats).

The issue was regarded as so serious that the Foreign Secretary, Morrison, said he would consult Attlee in hospital. Attlee's response was one of astonishing robustness and sense of ministerial duty to the future of the government and the Labour Party. It is worth quoting at some length for the insight it gives into Attlee's attitude as PM to ministerial dissent and threats of resignation from Cabinet. Morrison reported to a resumed meeting as follows—

'The Prime Minister had asked him to convey to the Cabinet the following expression of his views. First, he had pointed out that in all Cabinet discussions of Budget proposals there must be a substantial measure of give and take between Ministers. The Chancellor of the Exchequer had particular responsibility for the national finances; and no other Minister ought to claim that any particular estimate should be treated as sacrosanct. It would be a most unusual thing for a Minister to resign on a Budget issue: so far as he was aware, the only Minister who had ever taken this step was Lord Randolph Churchill, whose political fortunes had never recovered thereafter. Secondly, a Minister who found himself in disagreement with a particular part of the present Budget proposals should consider, not only his personal position, but the effect which his resignation would have on the present and future fortunes of the Labour Party. Thirdly, the Prime Minister had said that it would be folly for any Minister to provoke a political crisis at the present time, for there could hardly be a worse moment for a General Election. As the summer went on, the conditions might become more favourable – the meat ration might be increased, the weather might improve and there might be some change in the international situation. But a General Election at the present time with a Labour Party torn by divided counsels, would prejudice the fortunes of the Labour movement for years to come. Fourthly, if the Government were forced to face the electors in these circumstances, they could hardly hope to win the election; and, after such a debacle, the Conservatives might remain in office for a long period. If the situation arose, the responsibility for bringing it about would rest with any Ministers who resigned from the Government at the present juncture. For all these reasons the Prime Minister urged his Cabinet colleagues to give solid support to the Budget proposals put forward by the Chancellor of the Exchequer; and, in particular, to adhere to the decisions which they had taken, as a Cabinet, on 22nd March regarding the future level of expenditure on the National Health Service.'[28]

Apart from being appalled that a minister should be considering putting himself before the government and party, Attlee's message was that no minister was going to alter government policy under him as PM. Though it is possible that reference to the threat to the Labour government formed part of ministerial and Prime Ministerial argument intended to secure support for increased defence expenditure from dissenting ministers, or at least their remaining in the Cabinet, the more plausible inference is that ministers at the Cabinet meeting on 9 April 1951 and Attlee himself genuinely believed that ministerial resignations threatened the survival of the government, not least given its slender majority in the Commons. The Cabinet minutes also reveal that Bevan offered compromises that did not involve reduced defence expenditure, though they were inflationary. But Attlee supported Gaitskell in rejecting them.

These minutes are the most eloquent indication of Attlee's attitude towards dissent, pressure and what he seems to have regarded as blackmail. In fact Bevin and Attlee had a sense of a clear separation between domestic and foreign policy, and Attlee's view that the 'hard and inescapable facts of international life' were 'impervious to ideological treatment'[29] had been endorsed by Bevin at the Labour Party Conference in 1945.[30] Attlee's indifference to threats to his premiership was part of his personality, for Bevan's own assessment of Attlee was that 'in defeat and victory, he was unperturbed'. Bevan also noted Attlee's extraordinary robustness under fire, as 'with crisis piled on crisis' it was 'a constant source of wonder how he was able to bear the strain'.[31] Foot notes that Attlee remained an 'enigma' to Bevan, Cripps and Dalton, for while they showed the strains of office 'Attlee seemed immune, almost disinterested'. And Francis Williams, who knew Attlee as well as it was possible to know him as his public relations adviser and co-author of his autobiography, remarked that Attlee appeared to be 'a true solitary who required less than most men the support (or, one might add, the friendship) of others'.[32] Of Attlee's singular lack of ambition, Burridge notes 'one could be certain that his actions could not gratify any personal ego',[33] while Attlee himself had been by his own laconic standards almost eloquent on the subject. In a telling commentary on his indifference to loss of power and so immunity to threat or dissent he noted, 'men who lobby their way forward are likely to be lobbied back out of it. The man who has control over his followers is the man who shows no fear. And a man cannot be leader if he is afraid of losing his job.'[34] The passage from these extraordinary Cabinet minutes is also typical in its conveying Attlee's succinct and decisive style of premiership in Cabinet in its summation of the argument and indication of a decision. Attlee's reaction to influence from outside the Parliamentary Labour Party was equally robust. Burridge notes that 'between 1946 and 1948 the Government's position at the annual conference suffered eight defeats (on minor matters). They made no difference to the Government's policy,'[35] while Attlee himself commented, 'if you begin to consider yourself solely responsible to a political party you're half way to a dictatorship.'[36]

Attlee's sense of public duty in government and of allegiance to the British political system was profound. A conviction politician whose formative political experience had been in London's deprived East End, he was of a generation that had World War I experience, having served throughout in the army, and had been witness to the destructive rift in the Labour Party in the

1930s. Such experiences had left him with a sense of responsibility to the electorate and to government, part of which meant a resolute approach to attempts at influence from quarters he did not believe had a constitutional right to such influence. The other obvious and compelling influence was his essential nature, his lack of ambition in personal terms and his preparedness to serve or not to serve, and his proclivity for 'getting on with the job'. Attlee's attitude to pressure from the Party was to remain firm and to regard it as irresponsible, not to compromise to remain popular or in power.

The other matter that caused some controversy between Britain and the US was that of economic sanctions to be applied to China. The US position was that there should be no trade with a country that was an enemy combatant against UNC forces in Korea. Yet Britain had continued to trade with communist China while the war was being fought in Korea and felt that economic sanctions would enhance Chinese relations with the Soviet Union. And while the period between March and June 1951 saw increasing British compliance with US demands the British attitude was abhorred by a Republican right wing that felt Britain was a country that had gone soft on communism, was doing less of the actual fighting in Korea than it should, had been reluctant to condemn China as an aggressor state and had actually advocated communist China's admission to the UN and control over Taiwan.

The extent to which the Truman administration used such concerns regarding right-wing opinion and references to American tendencies towards isolationism to persuade the British to conform to US demands is unclear. Another issue between the US and Britain was over possible US attacks against Chinese bases used to attack UNC forces in Korea. Acheson told Morrison that the US intended to retaliate, and the Attlee Cabinet agreed privately provided there was prior consultation in what was another example of the lack of British resistance to US policy in Korea.

The split in the Labour Cabinet that ended in Bevan's, Wilson's and Freeman's resignations weakened an exhausted Cabinet divided by factionalism and which wanted to see an end to the war. In fact the Korean situation had reached an obvious stalemate, with further Chinese offensives on 27 April and 15 May 1951 resisted by the Americans and the British in the UNC. There was this time no UNC offensive in the north. On 2 July there was agreement between China and the US on talks for an armistice. They began on 10 July but became stalled over the question of repatriation of enemy prisoners of war. The Geneva conventions required automatic repatriation of POWs, but the US did not want it to be compulsory, and favoured a scheme of voluntary repatriation which the Chinese and North Koreans rejected. While the US motive seemed humanitarian it was a part of Cold War rhetoric.

Meanwhile in Britain the debate over British foreign policy within the governing party went on in public, with Bevan and Wilson being party to a pamphlet published by Tribune on 11 July 1951 claiming that Britain could not afford the rearmament to which the government was committed and that the optimal means of containing communism was aid to the Third World in conjunction with a rapprochement with the Soviet Union. For them the entire orientation of government foreign policy was mistaken. Even so the exhausted government did not change course or its commitment to the Korean War.

A balance-of-payments crisis followed in September 1951, an indication of endemic economic problems of competitiveness exacerbated by the demands of war expenditure. To resolve the problems attendant upon governing with so small a majority (and oddly at the King's instigation) Attlee called a general election on 25 October 1951. Churchill won with a majority of seventeen seats, despite Labour's winning the popular vote and in fact more votes than they had at the 1945 election. It was a good result for a party in which factionalism was rife. There was as a result no dramatic change in British policy over Korea.

The new government faced the same problems of insufficient resources to finance the Korean

War commitment (and others overseas, not least Malaya) and the Welfare State. In fact, the economic situation had worsened and the Conservative defence review of Labour's defence plans decided the timescales had to be extended. Meanwhile the new PM had been treated to an indication of Britain's reduced status in his visit to Truman in December 1951, and there was little reference to Korea. Churchill made clear his view that Korea was outside Britain's sphere of interest in his reference to the war's only worth being the enhancing of US defence and military spending. Korea to him was itself an irrelevance, and, as has been seen, it was in fact of no strategic value whatever – it did however possess enormous symbolic value. British policy continued to be one of support for US policy over Korea, and in fact the new PM was rather more cavalier regarding a possible US attack on communist China than Labour politicians had been. Yet Churchill wanted to end the war to reduce British expenditure on arms which exacerbated British economic dependence on the US.

In fact Churchill had identified the dilemma that was to face all post-war British premiers in one form or another. Given that the British ethos of maintaining world-power status and defending existing interests in a context of British economic and military decline meant dependence upon the US, Britain was obliged to respond to US insistence upon military commitment in support of US policy. This was too expensive for the failing British economy, caused balance of payments deficits and threatened the value of sterling. The result was need for more US help to support sterling. As Foreign Secretary Eden demonstrated the commonality of view he had had with Bevin over British foreign policy in general in wanting to preserve the relationship with the US but also restrain US policy from any widening of the conflict. In specific terms Eden feared an attack on Hong Kong and in more general terms the risk of war with China or the Soviet Union. The adverse effect on the British economy was another case against risking a widening of the war and in favour of an armistice, as was the slender Conservative majority, which needed safeguarding. British policy then exhibited genuine continuity, with support for, and attempts at influence over, US policy in what was seen to be a US sphere of interest (as the entire Pacific had been before and during the war, a situation which had only been reinforced by there being a US Military Governor of Japan after the war).

The continuity of British policy over the Korean War between the Attlee and the Churchill administrations was apparent almost at once, for on 4 December 1951 the new Foreign Secretary, Eden, told Cabinet that it was possible that the communists were using armistice talks to prepare for another attack on UN forces in the south. Eden reported that after consultation with Churchill as PM and the CoS, he had told the US government that any warning to the communists should be general and be by the US, the UK and as many UN member states who contributed to the UN Korean War effort as possible, and should refer to the difficulty of localising the war to Korea if the communists attacked UN forces. He told Cabinet that he had said in his note to the US government that the UK government 'could not support proposals for a naval blockade of China' but would endorse bombing of Chinese airfields north of the Yalu River as a threat of retaliation for any communist aggression. The Cabinet approved of what Eden had done, though it had not been consulted before the statement of UK government policy to the US government. A week later the same sense of UK policy being generally supportive of US policy over Korea though attempting to exert influence to moderate US policy was apparent, for Eden told Cabinet that he proposed to advise the US government that the indication in the draft warning that communist aggression after the armistice had been concluded would 'result in hostilities outside Korea' was 'too threatening' and should be replaced by reference to 'united and prompt' reaction and to 'consequences so grave that it might be impossible to confine hostilities to Korea'.[37]

The difference between the two Cabinet meetings was not the nature of British foreign policy but in the fact that whereas on 4 December Eden had simply told ministers what he had told the

Americans, on 11 December he was requesting Cabinet approval, which was granted. The dominant influence of Churchill as PM and Eden as Foreign Secretary on British foreign policy over the Korean War, and of little influence from other Cabinet ministers, seems very similar to that of Attlee as PM and Bevin as Foreign Secretary and Attlee alone after Bevin's departure, though in the case of the Attlee administration there were ministerial resignations by Bevan, Wilson and Freeman, even if they were more over the effect of the high defence expenditure caused by commitment to the Korean War on the welfare budget than outright opposition to the war on principle.

Over US insistence upon voluntary (as opposed to forced) repatriation of POWs, which prevented an end to the war, Churchill supported the US position for moral and political reasons. Eden and the Foreign Office were concerned as to the nature of the camps, a concern reinforced by riots there in May 1952, but Eden endorsed the PM's support for the US position. The US also intended to indicate to the Chinese that any violations of the armistice would be met with US air strikes against China and a naval blockade of its coast, which Eden felt could provoke the Chinese to attack Hong Kong but supported on the basis that the US would pursue the policy regardless of British dissent. There followed intensified British efforts to effect peace, but these did not succeed, and it was the death of Stalin in 1953 that brought the war to an end.

The Korean War made the extent of British post-war dependence upon the US all too clear, for it was manifest that British politicians felt they could not follow a foreign policy not approved by the US, and that maintenance of the Atlantic relationship by British support for US foreign policy did not mean that there was any genuine British influence on US foreign policy. British economic and military weakness (with the latter predicated upon the former) was such that the Attlee government felt that to demonstrate to the US that Britain was an ally worth supporting in Europe (by British troop commitments elsewhere in the world in support of the Western policy of containment of Soviet communism, as in Korea), Britain had to endure the adverse effects of increased military expenditure on taxation, social spending and British exports. One effect was that production was diverted from commodities that could be exported to obtain foreign currency into armaments, with resulting adverse effects on the balance of payments and on the British currency, which was left even more susceptible to US pressure, as Churchill found. While British support for the recognition of communist China and its admittance to the UN was tolerated by the US, which took a very different view, the British posture made no difference to the reality of China's exclusion and it remained clear that when the US demanded British support, as over British troop commitment to Korea, British support was forthcoming because the most influential British politicians felt there was no alternative given British economic and military dependence on the US.

There were differences not just of style but of policy between Attlee's premiership and that of Churchill in his second term as premier. Churchill approved of Attlee's handling of the Korean War and of the commitment of British troops there but continued to believe in personal diplomacy and summits, and rather than merely continuing to support the US as Attlee had done (despite Attlee's voiced misgivings regarding US policy on many occasions). He attempted to end the war by approaching the Soviet Union for help in persuading the North Koreans that the war should end. By this time of course all the parties to it had achieved what was there to be achieved in the war, which had degenerated into a stalemate, though the two Koreas would have wished to retain the support of major powers for their sides. The West had been seen to have resisted communist forces in the first hot war of the Cold War, and the communist powers backing the North Koreans knew there was nothing further to gain from prolonging the war. As has been seen above, Churchill had a clear motive in ending the war, for British influence was diminished by the fact that British expenditure on the war weakened the British economy to a serious extent and that the result of that was reduced British influence. Even in the same international and attitudinal context (for both PMs believed the Atlantic relationship to be vital to the ethos they advocated, that Britain should remain a world power) there were policy options and decisions to be made in British foreign policy, and British foreign policy reflected Prime Ministerial personalities and attitudes.

There were further indications of the extent to which the British were prepared to follow US policy or give in to US demands as the armistice talks began and the war dragged on, and of US immunity to British influence. On 23 June 1952 the UNC bombed power stations on the Yalu River without any prior consultation with the British, which caused genuine difficulty for the government in the Commons. Then, with the change of regime in the Soviet Union following Stalin's death, Churchill made overtures to secure détente and an end to the Korean War with Molotov. The British Cabinet and Eden were not enthusiastic and the overture was against Eisenhower's better judgement. The Soviet reaction was positive over Korea, and American threats to Rhee secured the armistice that ended the war. It is impossible to know if this final British initiative was decisive, but the sense is that Soviet policy over Korea had changed, and that Eisenhower was also looking for a way to end the conflict.

Though, as has been seen, there were British attempts to restrain the Americans during the Korean War, over the risk of escalation of the war, use of the atomic bomb and US policy towards communist China, British influence on US policy over Korea seems to have been negligible, and the Korean War indicated the supportive role to which Britain had been reduced, the degree of British dependence on the US and the understanding of the nature and extent of that dependence by Attlee, Bevin and most of the Cabinet. Though Hennessey argues that Britain 'did have – albeit a limited – influence over American decision-making during the Korean War', he acknowledges a historiography that argues that Britain exerted minimal influence on US foreign policy over Korea, and notes that contextual issues may on occasion have made the US administration more susceptible to British advice, which of course makes it impossible to isolate the extent of British influence on US policy from the influence of context. The evidence Hennessey produces seems to be of minimal British influence on US policy over Korea, as over condemnation of China as an aggressor at the UN, where British influence was confined to minor changes in the wording to a proposed US resolution that did not alter the nature of US policy. Over Attlee's decision to commit British troops to Korea, Hennessey refers to 'how much influence HMG might lose by not committing its forces', hardly an indication of any British influence on US policy, and the decision was in fact dictated by Attlee's sense of a threat to US support for NATO should British troops not be committed to Korea in support of the US rather than by some conviction that Britain could by providing troops influence US policy in Korea. Hennessey concludes by claiming that the closeness of the Atlantic relationship permitted Eden to understand that Eisenhower and Dulles were prepared to resort to nuclear weapons and to negotiate the Geneva Accords in 1954 over Indo-China and so preclude US use of such weapons there, though that does not indicate any British influence on US policy, just an appreciation of its nature and adjusting to it.[38]

The first 'hot war' confrontation of the Cold War had ended in stalemate. The US and the West under the auspices of the UN had shown resolve in preventing the takeover by the communist North of South Korea and had been seen to have given effect to the Truman Doctrine of containment. Western preparedness to fight over Korea emulated Western defiance over Berlin in 1948 and predicted similar resistance over Vietnam in the early 1960s, on the basis of an identical logic, of resisting communist encroachment case by case and in so doing setting an example to, and encouraging, other anti-communist forces worldwide to resist communism. From the Soviet perspective a different form of brinkmanship, of expansionism by proxy (through the Chinese and the North Koreans) had failed. There was little advantage left in Korea for either the Soviet Union or the US once it became apparent that neither could win in Korea – the US would not permit the loss of the peninsula, and the Soviet Union would not countenance the loss of the communist North of Korea. On 27 June 1953 the Korean War ended and the states of North and South Korea remained divided by the 38th parallel.

Vietnam

By the time of the Vietnam War the British government was very different in outlook. Unlike the situation that obtained in the Korean War, ministers were no longer individuals who had had direct experience of Soviet foreign policy and diplomacy immediately after the war, when British weakness and Soviet power and expansionism threatened vital British interests in Europe and British world-power status (in fact Attlee and Bevin had also had experience of the effects of appeasement before the war and of dealing with Soviet demands, as over the Baltics, during it). Though by the 1960s the Cold War was established as the dividing line between east and west and formed the basis of US and UK foreign policy, Wilson as PM was faced with pressures from not just the left wing of, but also from moderates within, the Labour Party to offer no military or moral support to the US in Vietnam. Some time, in the interval between the left's understanding of Soviet and communist intentions and of the need for the US to resist them in Europe and elsewhere (which took place in the late 1940s) and the time of the Vietnam War after Labour's election in 1964, the left had recovered its earlier fervour for opposing US influence on British foreign policy. There is some sense here that the humanitarian left was opposed to war in principle and appalled by its nature but also that there was some idealisation of the Vietnamese communists and characterisation of the war as one of 'national liberation'.

The context for the relationship between the US and the UK had also changed. For the prestige that British diplomacy had had for US politicians and officials immediately after the war, when US diplomatic experience of European politics had been scarce, had been replaced by an American attitude that was inclined to accord Britain a role and extent of influence that reflected the dramatic decline of British economic and military power in relative terms since the war. It was also significant that those who had had experience of British politicians and officials during the war were, like their British counterparts, no longer in office. What this meant was that the respect for British wartime resolve and sacrifice that had been prevalent among a previous generation of American politicians and officials was no longer a salient feature of the Anglo-American relationship by the early 1960s, and the close personal relationships that had characterised the war period and that immediately after it were no longer a factor. Lord Harlech, the departing UK Ambassador to the US in March 1965, commented that the 'myriad of close personal friendships built up at all levels during the war and the immediate post-war years are a diminishing asset', an indication that the relationship would in future reflect the extent of British utility to the US.[39] It does in fact seem that the interlude of US diplomatic inexperience and reliance on British diplomacy had been confined to the years immediately after the war and to a European context, ending with Bevin's influence on US policy over the Berlin Crisis of 1948–49, for it has been seen that British foreign policy over Korea was dictated by British concern that the US could diminish its commitment to NATO and the defence of Europe if US requests for military commitment to Korea were not met, an indication of the effect of British economic and military weakness and dependence on the US for security in the post-war world and of the lack of influence of personal relationships between Britain and the US. Though Johnson felt no special affinity for Britain and had no history of the ties that Truman and Acheson had, and no affinity for Wilson either that could be compared to the regard that Truman and Acheson had for Attlee and Bevin, the decisive influence on the relationship between Britain and the US over Vietnam was no different to that over the Korean War, that is, British and American optimisation of support from each other. Both Wilson and Johnson were then pragmatic in their approach to the Atlantic relationship, though with very different objectives and with Wilson's displaying an affinity for association with Johnson and US power that Johnson did not reciprocate, his purpose remaining throughout to optimise support for the US in Vietnam.

Though some historiographical interpretations of the 'special relationship' have idealised it as a relationship of genuine interdependence with a significant British contribution and influence, others have seen it as far more asymmetrical and reflective of the imbalance of power between the US and Britain.[40] What is apparent is that while Britain needed economic, diplomatic, military and strategic support from the US, the US found British endorsement of US foreign policy an expedient means by which to forestall the criticism both in the international and US domestic context that US foreign policy was not approved of even in the Western, democratic world. That did of course represent an asymmetry of need as well as of power and was reflected in the extent of British influence on US policy and that of the US on British foreign policy.

The Atlantic relationship has also been seen to be predicated upon similarities of ideological, political and cultural identity born of historical ties, resulting in a common desire to resist Soviet influence and communism on the part of British and US governments since the war that has reflected a common commitment to democratic values and an ethos of containment of communism to defend democratic principles and regimes against communist expansionism. In addition to historical ties stretching back over centuries, from which British and US political culture derived similarities of political system, there was a series of institutional and administrative links between Britain and the US concerning strategic and defence matters, and links of an economic nature consequent upon the US loan. There was also however a trend of increasing US diplomatic confidence and of waning British influence reflective of British economic and military dependence that meant that when Britain differed over foreign policy with the US there was an imperative to ensure that any difference was explained to the US and within parameters defined by the US as permissible. That was apparent, as has been seen above, in British compliance with the US desire for a commitment of British troops to Korea and in the minimal influence exerted on US foreign policy during the Korean War by British politicians. It was yet more apparent in the debacle of Suez, where the US imposed on the UK a humiliating and public withdrawal that confirmed that there could be no independence for British foreign policy from US preferences because of the ruinous consequences of no US support for sterling.

Here I shall argue that this trend continued during the Vietnam War, with US influence on British foreign policy profound and limited only by the nature of US purposes. And yet such a crude picture of US domination of British foreign policy is a partial picture of a more complex reality, for British economic and military dependence on the US was a reflection of the British ethos of remaining a power of the first rank while not having the economic and military means to support world-power status, a truth that has been a constraint on all British PMs and Cabinets since the war. Yet it remained within the domain of an elected British government to dispense with such an ethos and effect a retrenchment to a foreign policy more consistent with what Britain could afford without such dependence on the US. Further, while such objective factors as British economic and military weakness constrained Britain's foreign policy choices, there remained room for manoeuvre in British foreign policy, as I argue here in relation to the very different styles and personalities of Attlee and Wilson as premier. I shall elaborate upon the comparison between their premiership styles and personalities below, but shall now return to the context of the British response to US demands for British troops in Vietnam.

Since the end of the Korean War the Cold War had proceeded following a US policy of resisting communist encroachment. While the US continued support of NATO, the lack of a decisive Western reaction to the workers' revolt in East Germany in 1953 and to the Hungarian Uprising in 1956 were indicative of the other side of the Truman Doctrine of containment, an acknowledgement that eastern Europe was in the Soviet sphere. The Suez Canal Crisis of 1956 indicated the extent of British dependence upon the US in any foreign-policy initiative and was a demonstration of US economic power over Britain, as Eisenhower's declining to support sterling against devaluation (there was a run on sterling in New York on the day of the first British action) resulted in a British withdrawal from Suez.

Eden's premiership over the Suez Crisis is a perfect example of the powers and prerogatives of the British PM and of the influence of attributes personal to the PM on British foreign policy (in Eden's case the nervous nature with which he was afflicted and the poor state of his health at the time, combined with medicines he was taking). It is also indicative of the limits on Prime Ministerial power imposed by US economic power, in this case a specific and credible threat to sterling. As a context for Wilson's foreign policy and diplomacy over Vietnam it is worth noting for its commentary on the essential asymmetry of the Atlantic relationship. The ensuing Macmillan premiership faced the enduring problem of British uncompetitiveness, low investment, poor productivity and consequent threat to the value of sterling, for which US support was needed, and in fact Macmillan's first act as premier was to mend and cultivate the relationship with Eisenhower to secure US support for the British economy and for sterling. Though there was some limited adjustment to the realities of British economic weakness in Macmillan's 'Wind of Change' speech in 1960 and ensuing decolonisation of Africa and in the British attempt to join the EEC in 1963, the maintenance of British forces east of Suez, a priority for the US, and associated defence costs remained. The strain on sterling was of course exacerbated by such commitments.

As to the Vietnam War, while Wilson's providing moral though not material support for the US in Vietnam would seem to be an instance indicative of the extent of room for manoeuvre for British policy within certain parameters required to maintain the 'special relationship', these parameters were defined by the US and in this case Johnson's own sense of the need to be circumspect in the use of US power given the nature of US objectives for the presence of British troops in Vietnam. These shall be elaborated upon below. Korea and Vietnam (and Suez) are instances of Western containment of communist expansionism (for Nasser was seen to be susceptible to Soviet influence), while also being part of the development of Anglo-American relations after the war. Yet each crisis was both indicative of the state of relations between Britain and the US in the context of the Cold War and formative in the sense that each crisis affected attitudes and perceptions, and so policy formation, in a continuous process, albeit one in which some interludes exerted more influence than others.

While Wilson ostensibly had to concern himself with maintaining the government's position in the Commons with a very small majority, in late 1964 and 1965 the Foreign Office, unconcerned with such party-political matters, formed its own initial view as to the optimal British policy over Vietnam. In an indication of the British tendency to see international threats in terms of spheres of interest, with East Asia outside the British sphere, the Foreign Office view in June 1965 mirrored that of the CoS over Korea, that Vietnam was of itself of little relevance for British foreign policy apart from in two critical respects. There was concern that Vietnam might 'escalate into a global or regional war in which we might be involved' and yet also that Britain's 'interests as a non-communist power would be impaired if the United States government were defeated in the field, or defaulted on its commitments'.[41] As Ellis notes, there had been an earlier sense, in late 1963, when J. E. Cable became head of the South-East Asia department in the FO, of the pursuit of a military solution in Vietnam 'risking a confrontation with either the Soviets or the Chinese, and that the United States would ultimately face ignominious defeat'.[42] In an indication that the Foreign Office felt that it was imperative that any war into which the US entered in Vietnam should not be lost but that it was for US troops to fight it, and that alienation of the Americans would be unwise as it could imperil other areas of collaboration with the US that were vital to Britain, the Foreign Office recommended that Britain's best interests would be served by a policy of moral (but not material) support for the US in Vietnam. It was a policy that Britain should 'hope for the best' in Vietnam. Though the general orientation of British foreign policy over Vietnam may then be seen to have been very similar to that over Korea over a decade earlier, in the form of concern as to the risk of escalation to a confrontation with the Soviet Union and China but also a feeling that communism had to be resisted case by case for reasons of deterrence, a series of factors complicated the context for the British decision.

There was to begin with some domestic Labour Party antagonism to any association with the US military commitment to Vietnam, that is, antipathy to any support whatever, military or moral. Vickers observes that 'whereas Wilson and other Labour leaders saw Vietnam within the context of the Cold War, many rank-and-file members saw Vietnam largely as a war of national liberation', and the Labour 1964 election manifesto was an idealistic left-wing tract that referred to an 'end to colonialism', diminished Cold War confrontation, disarmament, and the replacing of power politics with 'a genuine world community and the rule of law'.[43] Just how the Labour left wing could have genuinely believed in such policies in a Cold War context is difficult to imagine, and it is worth noting that the ensuing decade of détente under Nixon was predicated upon US power and defence spending combined with exploitation of the split between the Soviet Union and the communist Chinese rather than upon idealism and conviction that communism should not be resisted if it seemed to be wanted by the people.

The other context of Wilson as he became PM in 1964 was the very adverse experience of the Korean War in terms of the strain on the budget of the weak economy of the UK, and the opportunity cost in terms of welfare expenditure that had resulted in ministerial resignations from the Attlee Cabinet. Having said that Britain's membership of the South East Asia Treaty Organisation (SEATO), and the commitment of British troops to fight communists in Malaysia from Sukarno's Indonesia, meant that criticism of US defence of South Vietnam would have caused difficulties for British foreign policy. There was also the weakness of sterling and the prospect of needed US help to resist devaluation, of which Wilson had had experience in 1949 under the previous Labour administration.

The result was that Wilson, wanting good relations with the US to maintain British influence on the world stage, to protect the British currency and to enhance his own image as a world statesman though being concerned not to alienate the left wing of the Labour Party at home, endorsed the FO recommendation that Britain should provide moral but not material support to the US over Vietnam. It is worth noting however that the issue of sterling and its defence at a certain value was not only a British interest, for the US at the time perceived it to be in its economic interests to maintain sterling at a certain rate against the dollar. A devalued sterling would make British exports more competitive in world markets and would reduce British imports of US goods as US imports became more expensive – the US was also concerned that Britain should not take the step of protecting sterling by raising interest rates in London because of the deleterious effect such action would have on the value of the dollar as the concern was that international money would chase the highest rate and desert New York for London. It is also true that there was a degree of interdependence in the relationship in the US interest in Britain's maintaining a presence east of Suez, not just for its strategic value but also for its effect on the way the role of the US in Vietnam was seen in the US and worldwide, in that it reduced the sense of American isolation over Vietnam.

Wilson has been seen in very different ways by various biographers, historians and observers, as an opportunistic 'careerist'[44] or as a PM beset by serious endemic difficulties who showed great guile and diplomatic acumen in balancing the competing demands of the US and the Labour Party in a context of sterling weakness and 'imperial overstretch' while remaining principled.[45] A state department assessment of Wilson in 1964 noted that Wilson had resigned with Bevan in 1951 over NHS charges but had then taken Bevan's place in the shadow cabinet when the latter resigned in 1954 over defence and foreign policy. It noted too that though Wilson, switching allegiance from the left to the right wing of the Labour Party, had supported Gaitskell as candidate for Labour Party leader, he did nothing to help Gaitskell against attacks from the left and then stood against him in 1960. Manoeuvrings of that sort of magnitude lend credibility to the inference that Wilson was opportunistic and careerist and had no political principles that withstood time and circumstance. Bundy told Johnson that Wilson was 'widely accused of opportunistic insincerity', while a CIA appraisal referred to him as a 'pragmatist'.[46] Colman claims that the US feeling was that Wilson would be 'more British than Labour',[47] though that does not follow from the other characterisations of Wilson referred to here, in that careerism and pragmatism would seem to indicate that Wilson would have pursued a policy of compromise with the left wing of the Labour Party to secure his domestic political position in the government and Labour Party and a similar policy of minimal compliance with the wishes of Johnson as US President.

Such compromise is in fact just what Wilson's policy over US involvement in Vietnam represented, in Wilson's providing moral but no military support for the US in Vietnam. Wilson took great care to explain to Johnson on a number of occasions that he could not offer British military support even in small numbers and to reassure Johnson of his own personal support for the American purpose in Vietnam. Though there seems to have been no direct threat to sterling from Johnson to secure British troop commitment to Vietnam, the endemic weakness of sterling and the periodic need for US support for it was an enduring concern for Wilson, added to which was his own idealisation and misrepresentation of his relationship with Johnson and desire to enhance his reputation at home and as a world statesman by the connection and by his various peace initiatives.[48] As to the vocal opposition of the Labour left wing to a policy of even moral support for the purpose of US intervention in Vietnam, Wilson defended the policy of moral support to the Labour Party, and his refraining from actual troop commitment despite requests from the US administration seems to have been enough to limit direct opposition to his policy on Vietnam to the extreme left wing and to have facilitated the survival of his premiership and leadership of the Labour Party. In Washington, though there seems to have been understanding of what Wilson needed to do for domestic political reasons, it was felt that he derived status from association with Johnson, though it seems that Wilson's repeated requests for meetings with Johnson in Washington reflected both a desire to enhance his prestige internationally and at home and Wilson's idealisation of the Atlantic relationship as being one of closeness that Johnson felt neither for Britain nor for Wilson.

The history of Wilson's more specific views on Western involvement in Indo-China indicates the lack of enduring principle and the dominance of political expediency and compromise in Wilson's politics. In May 1954, not long after his resignation with Bevan over the domestic consequences of expenditure on the Korean War to support US policy there, when Wilson was on the left of the Labour Party, he had said that there should be no support for 'French colonisation' or for an 'anti-Communist crusade' in Indo-China dictated by the US. When he assumed office as PM in 1964 Wilson continued to oppose any commitment of British troops to Vietnam and to resist Johnson's requests for British troops even in small numbers. Having said that, Wilson did provide continued moral support for Johnson and the US objective in Vietnam, a direct contradiction of his previous policy, pursuing a compromise between the wishes of the US administration and those of the left wing of the Labour Party in what seems an indication of his pragmatism and tendency to compromise to obtain his objectives of continued premiership, popularity in the Labour Party if not with the left wing, and status as a world statesman from being seen to have influence with Johnson and from Wilson's various peace initiatives, which were countenanced if not welcomed by Johnson.

I now turn to the detail of the sequence of events regarding British policy over Vietnam following Wilson's becoming PM. Wilson was asked for a commitment of British troops to Vietnam by Johnson at the first Washington summit meeting in December 1964, just months after the Labour election victory in October. Though it seems from Johnson's account to Bundy of his first meeting with Wilson that Wilson had been the recipient of a 'bullying tirade' from Johnson on 7 December 1964, Johnson, having been briefed extensively by Bundy regarding Wilson's domestic difficulties, seems to have been as tentative and limited in his request for British troops in Vietnam as he could have been. He told Wilson on 7 December that 'a United Kingdom military presence, on however limited a scale, might have a significant effect. A few soldiers in British uniforms in South Vietnam, for example, would have a great psychological and political difference.'[49] It is worth noting that the context to the visit to Washington was a sterling crisis following the budget on 11 November 1964 and US Federal Reserve Bank support, an indication of the extent of need for US economic support to maintain sterling at the existing rate.

Wilson's response was characteristically emollient. He evaded committing British troops to Vietnam by reference to Britain's role over the Geneva Accords that ended the first Indo-China War in 1954 and by reference to the commitment of British troops in Malaysia against a communist insurgency from Indonesia there (of which Johnson seemed to have been ignorant), but offered assistance 'by maintaining the Thompson advisory commission', 'providing police in Saigon' and training Vietnamese troops in jungle warfare in Malaysia.[50] These evasions were pretexts rather than reasons, for the US request had been for British troops in very small numbers to show support for the US presence, and while the commitment of British troops to Malaysia was considerable the warfare there was low-intensity and with low casualties (unlike Vietnam).

Wilson's awareness of the sensitivity of the issue of supporting the US over Vietnam and especially over the commitment of ground troops to support US forces there was apparent in his indication to his colleagues in London that 'we have not accepted any new commitments as regards South Viet Nam', and on his return to London he told the Cabinet on 11 December that he had resisted US 'pressure for a United Kingdom military presence in Vietnam'.[51] Wilson had agreed however to the maintenance of a British presence east of Suez. What is remarkable in what followed was the discretion with which Johnson and the American administration pursued their objective of obtaining the maximum British support possible for US involvement in Vietnam. For there were a series of rather ambiguous diplomatic encounters in 1964 and 1965 that made the acrimonious telephone call of 11 February 1965, in which Johnson told Wilson that if he wanted to help he should 'send us some men', stand out. That telephone call by Wilson was on the occasion of a Vietcong attack and fears of US retaliation, to which Wilson's initial reaction was to propose to visit Washington again. Advised by Lord Harlech, the UK ambassador to Washington (Patrick Dean's predecessor), not to consider such a visit without a prior conversation with Johnson, Wilson called to propose the visit. Johnson was belligerent, and even went so far as to indicate he was not going to be used to assist Wilson with his domestic difficulties (this was an enduring suspicion, that Wilson was using a claimed close and warm relationship with, and influence on, Johnson to bolster his prestige and standing in UK domestic politics, which Johnson resented). Johnson told Wilson such a visit would look like panic and said, 'why don't you run Malaysia and let me run Vietnam?'[52] In what was to become a characteristic pattern of presumed familiarity and attempts at influence, Wilson relented and promised Johnson his support. Such a sequence was usually followed by Wilson's misrepresenting the nature of the interaction to some extent, exaggerating its warmth and closeness, to Cabinet and the Commons.[53]

The general view of contemporaries seems to have been that Johnson had a combination of contempt and dislike for Wilson, and even if the more lurid accounts of Johnson's language in describing their relationship and Wilson himself are discounted the view of Bruce, US Ambassador to the UK, confided to his diary on 22 March 1965, was that 'the President has an antipathy for the Prime Minister', and that, 'he believes Wilson, for his own domestic political purposes, wishes to capitalise on a supposed close relationship with Johnson which is non-existent.' Though some interpretations of the Wilson-Johnson relationship claim that there was a preservation of the 'special relationship' and personal liking between Wilson and Johnson, most seem to stress one or more of a number of negative characteristics of their relationship. These include Johnson's personal dislike and suspicion of Wilson, their temperamental incompatibility, the American belief that Wilson had no political convictions and Wilson's 'Walter Mitty' characteristic and misrepresentation to ministerial colleagues of the closeness of his relationship with Johnson. Though Johnson does seem to have been alienated by Wilson's ingratiation and apparent desire to enhance his status at home by association with Johnson, their relationship was decisively influenced by Wilson's political difficulties over support for the US in Vietnam and policy of compromise, which exasperated and alienated the increasingly beleaguered Johnson, whose agenda was to optimise British support for the US over a war in Vietnam that became the major preoccupation of his Presidency especially as the American involvement in Vietnam escalated. In that context the personal relationship between Wilson and Johnson does not seem to have exerted any influence on British foreign policy over the Vietnam War. On the contrary, British foreign policy over the Vietnam War was influenced by a combination of Wilson's fundamental aspiration to remain in power, his tendency to compromise to do so, his desire to enhance his credibility in domestic terms and as a world statesman through association with Johnson, his desire to avoid a devaluation of sterling, his lack of political principle and of any genuine opposition to the US objective in Vietnam, and Johnson's objective of securing as much British support for the US over the Vietnam War as was likely to be forthcoming to preclude an impression of the US acting alone over Vietnam without the support or approval of the rest of the free world.[54]

If the first summit, in December 1964, had been one in which the basic positions had been established, the second summit, on 15 April 1965, imposed by Wilson on a reluctant Johnson concerned that it should seem as if he were being advised by Wilson, added little. There was no new request for British troops, and Johnson endorsed Wilson's tentative peace mission. There seems to have been an understanding that Wilson would endorse US policy in Vietnam in public (without sending troops) and that Johnson would in return approve of any peace mission that seemed feasible. In May 1965 there was a US attempt to obtain Commonwealth military support through SEATO that was resisted.

Meanwhile the British government continued to grapple with the endemic problem of how to remain a world power and defend existing worldwide commitments without the economic and military power to do so. The resulting reliance on the US for the value of sterling and to defend British interests in a Cold War context meant that Britain had to secure approval for its foreign policy from the US, which demanded British support for US policy in military terms, or in the case of Vietnam at least moral support and support through the maintenance of a British presence east of Suez. This latter requirement for US support placed great strain on the British economy and on the value of sterling as resources that could have resulted in export earnings were diverted to arms, with balance-of-payments deficits becoming endemic (other factors included poor working practices).

The Americans were unsympathetic, feeling that they had supported sterling repeatedly while the British had failed to take the needed deflationary measures to defend sterling. The Labour left felt the opposite, that too much was being spent on defence and foreign commitments while welfare spending suffered. There were then very different attributions as far as the cause of the British economic malaise was concerned, not least the threat to the value of sterling. A Defence Review started by Labour upon becoming the government in October 1964 was tasked with reducing the contribution of defence spending to the balance of payments deficits.

Wilson himself wanted both reduced defence expenditure and yet to maintain a presence east of Suez. This was amid fears of American isolationism should Britain abandon its world role. Wilson's sense of a need to maintain a British presence east of Suez as an essential component of Britain's relationship with the US was supported by Gore-Booth, the PUS at the Foreign Office, who described the British presence east of Suez as 'essential' to 'our association with America' and worried over the possibility, should Britain withdraw from its world role, over 'a gradual return to isolationism within the United States'.[55] Wilson's attachment to a commitment east of Suez was however attacked within the British Cabinet and by ministers with some standing in the Labour Party. Moral support and sycophancy was one thing, but maintaining a commitment east of Suez at great expense and with not insignificant adverse effects on the balance of payments and so on the value of sterling for no good strategic reason was another. On 19 May 1965 George Brown objected that the east of Suez policy had an adverse effect on the balance of payments, that the money would be better spent on welfare in Britain, and that it resulted from Wilson's attempts to please Johnson. Healey, whose position as Minister of Defence might have left one expecting him to argue for maintenance of British troops east of Suez, wanted to save money in an area in which there was no real role for Britain.[56] Both were senior ministers in Wilson's government but seem to have exerted little effect on the policy pursued in their dissent.

Foreign Secretary Gordon Walker's report of a trip to South East Asia advocated support of the US objective in Vietnam (Gordon Walker was generally understanding and supportive of the US purpose in Vietnam – see below) but also a more frank exposition of British differences of view as to ultimate outcome and over the unity of the communist bloc (an echo of previous differences at the time of the Korean War). He also said that any US bombing of Hanoi would have to be condemned (he foresaw the possibility of such bombing in the event of the then current bombing campaign's failing).[57] Wilson welcomed the report but did not act on its more risky recommendation that he should be open regarding British differences of view with Johnson. The same month, May 1965, saw a combination of an IMF loan and austerity measures to bolster sterling.

During the summer of 1965, in the context of an Americanisation of the Vietnam War, members of the Johnson administration indicated an explicit linkage between US support for sterling and commitment of British troops to western Germany and east of Suez, which assisted the US strategic position in Asia and rendered the US position in Vietnam less isolated. Then, on 28 July 1965, National Security Adviser McGeorge Bundy proposed that British troop commitment to Vietnam could be a condition of continued US support for sterling.[58] Johnson did not pursue the proposal because he felt that British troop commitment to Vietnam would not be a propaganda victory if it became known that it had only been forthcoming because of US threats to withdraw support for sterling, a clear case of presidential influence on US foreign policy.

To set the advice in context and to indicate the effect of Wilson's policy of moral support for the US in Vietnam on those advising Johnson (if not on Johnson himself directly), Bundy had the previous month, June 1965, told Johnson that every 'experienced observer from David Bruce on down has been astonished by the overall strength and skill of Wilson's defence of our policy in Vietnam and his mastery of his own left wing in the process' and that British support 'has been of real value internationally – and perhaps of even more value in limiting the howls of our own liberals'.[59] He noted that Johnson had been sceptical of the genuineness of Wilson's support. It might then seem odd that it was Johnson who resisted Bundy's recommendation that US support for sterling should be associated with British troops being committed to Vietnam.

The inference is that Bundy believed that pressure on sterling would force Wilson to decide on British military support to the US in Vietnam, while Johnson feared Wilson would evade it and make it public in some way, thereby reversing any possible propaganda value (a view that reflected Johnson's mistrust of Wilson). Yet Bundy's advice looks all the odder when considered in the context of his previous assessment of Wilson, in which he inferred that Wilson's support for the

US was contingent, and that 'Wilson prefers his own survival to solidarity with us.'[60] In the event in the summer of 1965 sterling received needed US support to avoid devaluation, though there is some controversy as to the conditions associated with the support, for though some have claimed that Wilson had to commit to maintain worldwide defence commitments and to introduce a prices and incomes policy to obtain it, Wilson's own agenda was avoidance of devaluation, maintenance of a presence east of Suez and control over prices and incomes, so the extent of US imposition of policy seems minimal. Even so Wilson did know that any withdrawal from east of Suez would result in a threat to sterling from withdrawn US support and an altered relationship with Johnson and the US.[61]

It is worth assessing the influence on British and US perceptions and attitudes of the two ambassadors. Bruce was the US Ambassador to Britain. While not perhaps emulating the closeness to the British that Douglas, who virtually became an apologist for the British point of view, had had with Bevin, Bruce went to some lengths to explain to Washington the criticism and obloquy that Wilson was sustaining because of his position of moral support for the US in Vietnam, the implication of which was that he could not be expected to do more.

Bruce was admired and influential in Washington and a vital part of the way in which Wilson and British foreign policy were perceived there. Wilson himself described Bruce as 'a giant among diplomats, with more experience and wise judgement than possibly anyone in the diplomatic profession in any country'.[62] Dean had less influence in Washington but was part of a general Foreign Office orientation attached to Britain's world-power status and keen to inform Wilson of the adverse effects a British withdrawal from overseas commitments would have on relations with the US (of course the FO brief was limited and did not include political consequences in the domestic sphere or political matters in the Commons). Ellis claims that both ambassadors, Bruce in London and Patrick Dean in Washington, played a 'decisive role' in maintaining the understandings that were reached.[63] And yet one does wonder. The possible influence of ambassadorial staff on a nation's perceptions of another nation and its intentions is clear in the case of Roberts, whose despatches have been seen by some historians to have informed the British view of Soviet intentions in 1945 and 1946, yet even his influence was contingent upon its being congruent with the understanding of the Foreign Office and Bevin as Foreign Secretary and in a situation in which ambiguity was high and genuine diplomatic contact in which there was a degree of openness was minimal, conditions in which the influence of ambassadorial staff would be at its greatest. Between Wilson and Johnson contact was regular and frank if couched in diplomatic language. Even so the explanations of Wilson's predicament by Bruce would have set the parameters of Johnson's expectations of Wilson and would have provided confirmation that Wilson's account of his problems with the Labour Party and efforts to represent the US position over Vietnam was true.

To set the expectations of ambassadorial influence as a context, the expectation would not be that Dean would have influenced Wilson's foreign-policy objectives of no devaluation, obtaining US support for sterling and for Britain's world-power status, or meeting a personal desire to be a world statesman and to that end being on good terms with Johnson. Such influences on British foreign policy would have to be attributed to Wilson himself, and Dean as British Ambassador to the US would have had a role that required him to warn Wilson of US sensitivities and advise on issues of timing and presentation. The inference is that ambassadors exerted a facilitative influence in the domain of perceptions rather than having any influence on the attitudes or objectives of those making or influencing foreign policy in the US and the UK.

In September 1965 there was another instance of US support for sterling to preclude devaluation, though as Wilson himself observed there was no attempt by Johnson to link such support to Wilson's providing troops to Vietnam. There was a sense that the relationship between Britain and the US had to be considered as a totality, and that British support for the US in Vietnam by maintaining a presence east of Suez and providing moral support, and US support for sterling were critical parts of that totality. The US administration felt it had secured an understanding that they would be consulted before any decision was made to withdraw the British presence east of Suez and that no decision would be taken that would adversely affect the US position in Vietnam. The British felt that no such specific commitment had been made.

Such diplomatic ambiguity was one aspect of the relationship between the Wilson and Johnson administrations over Vietnam. The other was the nature of the moral support that Wilson provided the US government over Vietnam to maintain the special relationship and US support for sterling. For Wilson was in diplomatic terms very effusive, almost sycophantic, and his visits to Johnson continued regardless of the obloquy they occasioned from the left wing of the Labour Party (and, as the war went on and American tactics became more draconian, in the bombing of North Vietnam, from moderates within the Labour Party). This was it seems part of Wilson's odd idealisation of the nature of the relationship both between Britain and the US and between him and Johnson.

Colman quotes with obvious approval Crossman's assessment that British foreign policy had a 'peculiarly Wilsonian touch', and notes that Wilson's Foreign Secretaries, Walker, Stewart and Brown, were 'overshadowed by Wilson', though all of them supported cultivation of the relationship with the US.[64] His inference is clear, though no direct evidence is presented – British foreign policy over the Vietnam War was a Wilson invention. Colman claims that given the voting arithmetic in the Commons Wilson could not have done more to assist the US over Vietnam without putting his government at risk both in the first Wilson administration, which had a very slender majority of just four seats in the Commons following the general election on 15 October 1964, and in the ensuing one, which after the election in 1966 had a majority of ninety-six seats, for in the latter case the election had brought to the Commons a number of left wingers whose views had to be taken into account. And though an inference that contextual factors alone were decisive is not correct, for they interacted with Wilson's own personal and political objectives, it is interesting that Wilson's foreign policy was seen by David Bruce, the US Ambassador to London, and others within the Johnson administration as the best that could be expected from a British PM in Wilson's position.

Wilson's idealisation of the relationship with Johnson and the US continued even in a context of some American bluntness on occasion regarding British policy over Vietnam, not least as a result of Wilson's finding it necessary not just to differentiate moral from material support but also support for American intentions from the means they employed to achieve them, which he criticised and attempted to influence, a futile endeavour, as the war went on. This was Wilson's stratagem of dissociation from US bombings of North Vietnamese cities given the storm of protest it elicited within the Labour Party. In fact, Wilson's preparedness to endure 'poor treatment from Washington' was part of the relationship that Wilson developed.[65] Wilson's 'emotional' attachment to the Americans was also manifest in Wilson's repeated requests for summits in Washington, though these were seen by Johnson in Washington as attempts to bolster his credibility at home.

The result of all these characteristics in Wilson was that it was difficult for the US administration to identify the optimal foreign policy towards the British over Vietnam. Wilson's public moral support was of immense value, not least given its being alone among the Western democracies apart from West Germany and its being continued despite the public and political obloquy Wilson experienced as a result. There were then serious risks for the US in associating US support for sterling with British troops in Vietnam. There was the possibility that the British would reject such association, devalue, which in itself would have had adverse consequences for the US economy, or raise rates of interest to protect sterling, which would threaten the value of the dollar, and pursue a foreign policy which involved public criticism of the US stance in Vietnam. The other possibility is that a minimal number of British troops would be provided to Vietnam though with adverse publicity indicating the US tactics used to secure them, which would have negated their propaganda value. Johnson's decision not to link US support for sterling to British troops in Vietnam is then more comprehensible than it appears at first sight. It was also an indication that power is mitigated by the purposes it is used for and when use of power is perceived by the party wielding the power to be likely to have adverse effects on its foreign policy or on its electorate. Perception is central to foreign-policy decisions and over Vietnam it seems that Johnson did not believe that the British would comply with the US request for British troops in Vietnam under threat of withdrawal of US support for sterling without adverse publicity that would negate the propaganda value of having British troops in Vietnam.

Wilson continued to cultivate Johnson and idealise the Atlantic relationship despite Johnson's treatment of him fluctuating between aversion and encouragement. The Commonwealth Peace Mission approved by Johnson in April 1965 was very much on US terms. It failed due to lack of desire on the part of any of the participants and because Wilson's positioning of British foreign policy and the terms offered made it seem that he was running errands for the White House. Pimlott claims that Wilson's peace efforts were an attempt to assist the US given his reluctance to commit British troops to Vietnam to support the US militarily, though there is no evidence for that inference (and Pimlott does not adduce any). Johnson wanted British moral, diplomatic and military support, not advice or interference, and had made his position brutally clear to Wilson on a number of occasions.

The US evidence is that Wilson was permitted to pursue such negotiations as a concession. The far more likely motive was Wilson's widely acknowledged desire to be a world statesman and bizarre conviction that he could broker a deal between the US, South Vietnam, the Soviet Union, China and North Vietnam. Though this could be seen as reflective of Wilson's 'Walter Mitty' characteristic, there was also the compelling advantage of being seen by his Labour Party left wing and by moderates opposed to the Vietnam War to be doing all he could to bring the war to an end and so gaining their approval, which would secure the position of his government and his own personal power.[66] As Pimlott himself notes, Wilson's 'inclination was to compromise.'[67] Then, in December 1965, again at Wilson's instigation, another summit took place, again in Washington. There Wilson explained the outcome of the Defence Review but assured Johnson of a continued British presence east of Suez. In his turn Johnson offered support to British peace efforts over Vietnam. There seemed to have been some mutual understanding of what Britain could afford and of the political circumstances Wilson was facing in Britain.[68] The 'Walter Mitty' characteristic of Wilson seems the most plausible explanation for Wilson's continued desire to visit Johnson, even after the rough treatment he received from Johnson at their first meeting on 7 December 1964 and the aggression shown by Johnson towards Wilson on the telephone on 11 February 1965, for there was even after such treatment a request from Wilson to visit Washington in April 1965, which Johnson granted only on the basis that Wilson would be supportive of the US over Vietnam. The inference is that Wilson misrepresented the nature of such meetings and the relationship with Johnson both to Cabinet ministers and to himself.

Though Wilson had warned Johnson that he would have to dissociate himself from the resumed US bombing of North Vietnam in February 1966, Wilson's own Foreign Secretary Stewart had publicly supported such resumption, and at a meeting of the Parliamentary Labour Party on 2 February 1966 Wilson despite private anger at Stewart's statement felt obliged to endorse it and gave a robust defence of his government's support for the US over Vietnam. What is significant is that this did not stop Wilson from pursuing a middle path of compromise between the competing demands of the Labour Party and the US, and that Wilson's dramatic account of the meeting to Johnson was aimed at US understanding of Wilson's domestic political difficulties but also indicative of a wish to please Johnson and be approved of by him.

Referring to his own resolve to meet 'the challenge' 'whatever the risk', he claimed the meeting and 'the rout' of opposition in Parliament on 8 February 1966 to have been a 'total success'.[69] What was true was that Wilson had defended his support for the US purpose in Vietnam in the House of Commons on 8 February 1966 in reiterating what he had said on 19 July 1965, that 'unilateral withdrawal' by the United States from Vietnam would make the world wonder if the US would abandon other regimes resisting communism 'when the going got rough', an endorsement of the Truman Doctrine of containment, of Domino Theory, deterrence and US policy in Vietnam. The issue was though also indicative of a tendency to misrepresent the nature of things for audiences. For on 3 February the resumption of US bombing was the occasion of 'the most spirited wrangle yet on Vietnam'. According to Castle she, Crossman, Cousins, Lee and the Labour Chief Whip Short protested over Stewart's statement.[70] While the Cabinet minutes are more opaque than they might be, referring to 'considerable disquiet' among ministers, there were it seems many who felt that there could have been some British dissociation from the resumption of US bombing while maintaining overall approval of the US purpose in Vietnam. Wilson and Stewart produced an argument that was to become generic, that avoidance of criticism of the US was needed were Britain to affect its foreign policy over Vietnam.[71] Ministers were not to know that Wilson's influence on Johnson was far less than he represented it as being. When Wilson claimed that the bombing halt had been extended due to his own and Stewart's influence, they had no means of knowing otherwise, when in fact Johnson was responding to domestic concerns that the possibilities of peace should be exhausted.[72]

The Labour election victory on 31 March 1966 increased Wilson's majority but resulted in more Labour dissidents over Vietnam than before. Forewarned of further impending bombing of North Vietnam Wilson explained the British government position again to Johnson and reassured him of continued support for the US purpose in Vietnam. Johnson, apparently mystified by Wilson's experiencing more rather than less difficulty with an increased majority, was persuaded by his aides and by Bruce that the decision by Wilson to dissociate himself from US bombing of military targets in Hanoi and Haiphong on 28 June 1966 was necessary to Wilson's political position in Parliament. Wilson's actual statement in the Commons on the day of the US bombing reflected the US dictated contextual detail Johnson had asked Wilson to include in any such statement, a clear indication that Wilson was doing what he could to defend the US position on the bombings by contextualising them.

Bruce's remarks as to Wilson's nature and degree of influence on British foreign policy in the context of this latest issue are interesting, not least given Bruce's positioning and reputation in London. He told Johnson on 11 July that Wilson was 'a political animal, highly skilled, intelligent, a master at infighting' who was 'adept at making ambiguous public statements to serve his political aims' but that he was facing a political threat over Vietnam not just from known left wingers but from MPs in the centre of the Party and even from the right wing, which meant 'the problem of party management threatened to get out of hand'.[73] He added that there was a significant risk to Wilson's leadership of the country and of an election. He advised that Johnson should point to the support of US involvement in Vietnam of Heath, who had in the Commons criticised Wilson's support for US ends while deploring necessary means in Vietnam. In Washington on 29 July 1966 Wilson reaffirmed his support for US policy over Vietnam (regardless of reservations regarding specific incidents) and commitment to a British presence east of Suez and to maintain sterling at the present value.[74]

Johnson seemed reassured and pleased with Wilson's affirmations of support. The visit had in fact only been approved by Johnson on the understanding that Wilson would support and assist the US effort in Vietnam by his visit to Washington and as a result of specific assurances to the US Ambassador that such support would be given. Even so, in an indication of the continued importance Johnson attached to British military support, he did tell Wilson that 'a platoon of bagpipers would be sufficient, it was the British flag that was needed'. As Franks had indicated to Attlee in his assessment that the US administration and public did not like going it alone over Korea, the Johnson administration seems to have continued to hope for even a militarily insignificant UK troop presence in Vietnam.[75] In an indication of the US attitude at the time Dean, the British Ambassador to Washington, told the Foreign Office that the US regarded it as being in its interests to avoid 'the political and economic demise of the only other Western country which exercises some worldwide responsibility'.[76] Ellis takes a very different view of the effect of British policy over the US bombing of Haiphong and Hanoi in 1966, claiming that Wilson's 'public act of dissociation' from the US bombings was a break point in the relationship between Wilson and Johnson. It does seem true that Wilson's public dissociation represented a departure from his previous posture of moral support for Johnson over Vietnam, and that it came at a time at which Johnson was beleaguered by increasing opposition at home and uncertain as to the prospects of a military victory in Vietnam given the continued resistance and progress of the North Vietnamese and Viet Cong despite the commitment of increasing numbers of US combat troops to Vietnam.[77]

Wilson's very genuine difficulties were exemplified by ministerial reactions to the commitment east of Suez that eventuated from the Defence Review. The earlier objections of Brown and Healey (see above) were now reinforced by Crossman's and Benn's own criticisms of the commitment on the basis of reliance on the US and difficulties over maintaining the value of sterling. In fact pressure on sterling was such that the budget of 20 July 1966 contained severe deflationary measures that would adversely affect the standard of living at home and which drove a wedge between Wilson and ministers in his own Cabinet, with Frank Cousins the first ministerial resignation. Despite its cost, as has been seen, Wilson assured Johnson of the British commitment east of Suez. And yet US perceptions were now wavering, with some of Johnson's advisers feeling that the British commitment east of Suez was worth something in terms of support for the US presence in Vietnam while others wondered as to Britain's future as a world power given its chronic economic difficulties.

By the summer of 1966 Fowler, the US Secretary to the Treasury, and Ball, the US Under-Secretary of State, were less prepared than they had been in November 1964 and August 1965 to intervene to support sterling, with a sense at the British Embassy that the US felt the dollar would not be that adversely affected by a sterling devaluation. Fowler told Johnson that sterling's weakness was being exacerbated by US demands for British world-power maintenance and that the British economic problem was endemic, and Ball even proposed that US policy should be to encourage Britain to relinquish such world-power status, abandon its presence east of Suez, and turn to Europe. These were significant changes in US perceptions of the need for and utility of British support east of Suez, and of the advantage to the US of supporting sterling. As has been seen above, however, these views had little effect on Johnson on 29 July, when he met Wilson in Washington.

And yet the fundamental realities of the link between the cost of Britain's world role (not least its commitment east of Suez) and the precariousness of sterling's value would not go away. British economic weakness made an end to its role east of Suez a compelling foreign-policy alternative, and a British withdrawal from east of Suez by the mid-1970s was announced on 18 July 1967 despite Johnson's opposition and following severe domestic pressure on Wilson to enact the policy. In fact it only reaffirmed and made public a Cabinet decision earlier in 1967 to cut by half British troops in Malaysia and Singapore and to withdraw from east of Suez by the mid-1970s.[78] While the British decision to withdraw from commitments east of Suez might have been one that could not over time have been avoided, there was genuine concern as to the timing of the announcement in the context of British support for the US over Vietnam and as to its presentation to the US administration and to Johnson himself. Wilson had after all given several previous commitments of a British presence east of Suez. Johnson's own concern was such that Wilson was for the first time invited to Washington. Wilson had been advised by Bruce to defer any decision on British policy east of Suez and to meet Johnson first, and Johnson had been advised of the significant domestic pressure Wilson was under, including an accusation that British people were suffering from the imposition of severe economic policies to please Johnson.

In fact, transatlantic relations had been strained by an earlier American *volte-face* in February 1967, over Wilson's attempt to effect a negotiated settlement of the Vietnam War. Hoping to use Kosygin's visit to promote the talks, Wilson was humiliated by the US administration's insistence on assurance that North Vietnamese infiltration into South Vietnam had stopped before any cessation to the US bombing of North Vietnam, an alteration to terms originally agreed that stipulated US assurance that there would be a stop to such infiltration, with the result that Wilson's diplomacy was discredited. The US fear was that the North Vietnamese might exploit any cessation in US bombing militarily. Wilson was stranded by the US and his credibility as a mediator was seriously affected. Wilson had been under serious pressure in the Commons over Vietnam due to the US bombing of the north and had argued in his defence of approval of US purposes in Vietnam that the US was prepared for peace talks while the North Vietnamese were not. In fact Johnson had little conviction in talks that were not direct and bilateral with the North Vietnamese, who had shown no interest in Wilson's proposed talks, and there was a sense within the administration that Wilson's purpose in pursuing the talks was to enhance his prestige for domestic political purposes, a motive to which Johnson was sensitive. The affair was glossed over in diplomatic terms, but its effect was to diminish Wilson's enthusiasm for the 'special relationship'. Wilson also during this critical period in relations with the US chose to join the EEC, reassuring Johnson of the sanctity of the Atlantic relationship to Britain and expressing the hope that Europe would look outwards as a result. Johnson seemed enthusiastic. In the event of course entry to the EEC was blocked by de Gaulle and took place under Heath after de Gaulle had passed on.

At the summit on 2 June 1967 Johnson was preoccupied with the apparent British need to announce the withdrawal from east of Suez nearly a decade in advance of the planned withdrawal date and in circumstances in which the US was at war in Vietnam. Wilson told Johnson of Cabinet insistence that no significant numbers of troops be kept east of Suez, at Singapore or elsewhere. Johnson alluded to the possibility of US troops' being withdrawn from Germany, but Wilson was unmoved. Yet could the British not at least defer the public announcement of their decision? Johnson told Wilson that the timing was unpropitious for an announcement while US forces were committed to Vietnam. Wilson made no commitment. Yet Johnson seems to have entertained the hope that the announcement would be deferred. It was not. Wilson had bowed to domestic pressure. On 18 July the 'Supplementary Statement on Defence Policy' referred to reducing by 'half the forces deployed in Singapore and Malaysia during 1970–1971', a reaffirmation of the Cabinet decision taken earlier that year. US reaction was muted, for any publicity would have had an adverse effect on the perception of the US presence in Vietnam.

The east of Suez decision nevertheless constituted a decisive break between Britain and the US. When sterling again encountered difficulties in October 1967 Wilson attempted to obtain US assistance to support it by reference to possible further cuts in defence expenditure. In another example of Wilson's misplaced confidence in his bargaining power, the Atlantic relationship and his own personal brinkmanship, Wilson told his Chancellor, Callaghan, that Johnson should be warned 'that we would be forced to take all, or most, of our troops out of Germany and withdrawal from the far east, Singapore, etc, not in 1975, but immediately'.[79] Wilson requested permission for yet another visit to Washington to see Johnson, despite Bruce's attempts to dissuade him. Wilson's request was denied, and the threat to withdraw at once from east of Suez should no US assistance for sterling be forthcoming was communicated to Johnson in correspondence.

Even so, continuing to believe in the efficacy of the threat, Wilson sent Denis Rickett, a senior Treasury minister, to Washington to make the case forcibly. Yet there was little US interest given Britain's already having announced, in July 1967, a British withdrawal from east of Suez by the mid-1970s, and an altered US perception of the effect of British devaluation on the dollar and US trade. Johnson was in fact by this time more focused on measures to reduce the effect of a sterling devaluation than to prevent it. As Callaghan as Chancellor of the Exchequer told ministers at a Cabinet meeting on 16 November, there was a need for 'unprecedented' 'international support' to maintain sterling at its present value and there was 'no prospect that such support would be provided'. The US was, he said, 'motivated primarily by concern about the United States dollar', and there was no prospect of enough US support for long enough to avoid devaluation. There was some dissent at the meeting, with Crossman and Jenkins objecting to the presentation of a devaluation package that recommended both devaluing the currency and measures to protect the devalued currency in the form of public expenditure cuts without any prior circulation of a Cabinet paper to ministers.[80] Callaghan told Cabinet that the major cuts would come from civil expenditure though that would necessitate 'further economies in defence expenditure' to facilitate their political acceptance. To that end he had agreed with Healey as Defence Secretary defence savings that were to be found without effect on the commitment east of Suez. Crossman advocated major cuts to the defence budget, including a quick withdrawal from east of Suez and the Middle East and the abandonment of the F-111 programme and the nuclear deterrent.[81] Despite the reservations of senior figures in the government then the Cabinet approved the proposed devaluation and cuts to defence.

Sterling was consequently devalued on 18 November. Though Wilson sought to mitigate what he feared would be devaluation's effect on his relations with Johnson, he need not have worried. Johnson was sympathetic to the efforts made by Wilson to avert devaluation and the lengths Wilson had gone to explain the rationale to him. And, having brazenly attempted to blackmail Johnson into bailing out sterling by threats of immediate withdrawal from east of Suez, Wilson now told him that, despite 'some reductions in defence expenditure', he would 'maintain, both in Europe and East of Suez, the policies set out in the Defence White Paper, as I explained them to you at our last meeting'.[82]

The devaluation was a failure, and pressure on sterling continued. In an indication of the extent of the interrelationship between the value of sterling and defence costs (it has been clear from the above that high defence spending reduced export earnings and so left sterling under pressure) the devaluation in November 1967 resulted in a significant hike in the costs of defence. The reaction to the continued weakness of sterling of Roy Jenkins, Wilson's new appointee as Chancellor of the Exchequer, was to advocate greater financial stringency in the form of major cuts to public expenditure.[83] Wilson endorsed the necessity for such financial stringency, possibly because without US support for sterling something radical had to be done to stabilise and protect the currency given that the devaluation and proposed austerity measures under Callaghan had not done so. One of Jenkins' proposals was to withdraw from east of Suez earlier than planned. The Labour left naturally opposed the alternative of welfare cuts to save money that would then be spent on supporting British imperialism and a US policy in Asia with which they radically disagreed. Though Wilson was at the time unpopular, having been weakened by the devaluation, and so could have felt himself in need of the support of Jenkins as the latter was seen as an alternative PM, Crossman notes that Wilson became from June 1966 more Prime Ministerial in style with Cabinet and followed a 'strictly Presidential line'. Crossman refers to Wilson's 'fixing decisions with individual ministers, making more decisions, and being at the very centre of his government', and it is worth noting that there had been what Wilson referred to as a 'preliminary meeting' prior to the Cabinet meeting on 4 January 1968 at which the decision to withdraw earlier from east of Suez was taken.[84]

As Minister of Defence Healey told Wilson that he would have to tell Johnson that 'if there were to be large defence cuts arising out of the Government's present review, these were bound to affect the speed of our withdrawal from present positions and commitments outside Europe.' Wilson agreed.[85] From Washington Dean warned of a strain of isolationism in the US that reasoned that if no one else was making any effort why should the US?[86] Dean indicated that there would be 'much upset' in the US administration if withdrawal from east of Suez were brought forward and that there was a sense in the US that the welfare state in the UK was being paid for by means of passing the burden of defence costs to the US.[87]

The Cabinet meeting on 4 January 1968 discussed several memoranda on 'post-devaluation measures to restrain public expenditure'. Jenkins told ministers of a proposed statement to the Commons to the effect that 'the Government had decided that the United Kingdom should now withdraw from its political and defence responsibilities in the area East of Suez by the end of the financial year 1970–71, instead of by the mid-1970s as provided for by previous policy decisions in this field,' though he noted that 'he differed from the Ministers responsible for external policy and defence, who accepted the proposed withdrawal in principle but felt it should not be completed until the end of the financial year 1971–72.' Jenkins had in fact been given a rough time by Brown, Thomson and Healey on 20 December 1967 regarding withdrawal from east of Suez.

Brown, who had been appointed Foreign Secretary on 11 August 1966, noted that the decision to withdraw from east of Suez had been made as long ago as in the Defence Review of July 1967 and that the UK's allies had endorsed that decision on the basis of there being no precise date for the withdrawal from the Far East through reference to its being in the 'middle 1970s'. He told ministers, 'we could not afford to flout international opinion in the way the French did,' a reference it seems to the views of the US and the Commonwealth. Despite ministerial representations to the effect that UK interests in the Far East could be adversely affected by withdrawal before 1972 and to the risk of communism there, with Callaghan and Stewart joining Brown in advocating no withdrawal from east of Suez before 1972, Wilson, summing up what seems to have been a genuine diversity of ministerial view, noted 'the decision of the Cabinet was that withdrawal from the Far East should be completed by the end of the financial year 1970–71 and that we should withdraw from the Persian Gulf by the same time.' Wilson chose not to ask for another audience with Johnson in Washington to tell him directly of the Cabinet decision. Brown was to inform Rusk, the US Secretary of State, of the decision to withdraw from east of Suez earlier than planned. Cabinet agreement is recorded, though any adverse reaction to the decision by governments in the Far East and the US would be considered.[88]

Brown's approach differed profoundly from Wilson's diplomatic discretion. He told Rusk on 11 January 1968 in the plainest terms that 'Britain had lost the battle to avoid devaluation' because of domestic and international commitments without adequate resources. 'To avoid further devaluation' the government had to save money and balance domestic cuts in 'cherished social programmes, such as health and education' with savings in overseas commitments. The withdrawal from east of Suez would be complete 'by March 31 1971, instead of by the mid-70s'.[89] Rusk was appalled and must have reported the change to Johnson almost at once, for that same day Johnson told Wilson that he regarded it as a 'British withdrawal from world affairs' and asked Wilson to defer Britain's departure from east of Suez. On 15 January Johnson pursued his earlier communication by more specific references to the difficulties the British withdrawal would cause the US, to the reported cancellation of British orders for the F-111 and to an end to collaboration over defence between Britain and the US.

The same day a Cabinet meeting took place at which, according to Dockrill, the 'Old Guard' of Brown, Callaghan, Healey, Stewart and Wilson challenged Jenkins' insistence on withdrawal from east of Suez by the end of March 1971. As Commonwealth Secretary Thomson reported adverse reaction from Singapore, Malaysia, New Zealand and Australia, and Wilson told ministers that in conversation Singapore Prime Minister Lee had resisted anything earlier than 1973 on security grounds. Wilson then told Cabinet of Johnson's reaction, that 'an earlier withdrawal from the Far East and from the Persian Gulf would create serious problems for the United States Government and for the security of the free world' and that Johnson had reproved cancellation of the F-111 programme. The Cabinet Conclusions record without attribution to individual ministers the case for deferring withdrawal to 31 March 1972 because of the UK's dependence upon US 'goodwill', the argument against, that the US would not engage in any retaliatory action and the argument for a date of 31 December 1971 for 'presentational' reasons. Wilson summed up that the Cabinet was agreed on deferring withdrawal from east of Suez to the end of 1971.[90] Though the Cabinet Conclusions do not attribute relative influence the meeting does seem to be an indication of Wilson's aptitude for compromise to please different audiences, in this case Johnson and the spending ministers through the deferral of withdrawal from east of Suez, and Jenkins (who advocated greater financial stringency) and the Labour left (with its abhorrence for what it regarded as sacrifice of welfare at home for imperial pretensions and acquiescence with American wishes abroad) through continuance of the policy of earlier withdrawal from east of Suez than had been originally planned. Despite a proposal from Healey that the F-111 programme should be minimised rather than cancelled Cabinet approved cancellation of the programme.

Wilson's response to Johnson over the east of Suez issue claimed that the British decision to withdraw from east of Suez did not reflect an attempt to appease the left wing of the Labour Party by making it clear that British foreign policy was shouldering its part of the reduction in government expenditure. Wilson claimed it was not just to make the case that it was not just welfare benefits that were to be affected. Rather, he claimed, the change was part of a more general reorientation of British foreign policy to align it with what could be afforded without deleterious economic effects.

He then told Johnson that US concerns had resulted in a British decision 'to defer our withdrawal for a further nine months, i.e. to the end of 1971'. There was no movement on the F-111 orders, which were cancelled.[91] The tone of Wilson's message is worth noting for its explaining to Johnson the reasons for the change of policy over withdrawal from east of Suez and assuring him that there would be a continuing UK world role, the implication being that it would be in support of US foreign policy, not least in the case of Vietnam.[92] In fact of course the Labour left was an influence on the decision to withdraw earlier from east of Suez than had been planned in 1967, especially in the context of the major public-expenditure cuts felt to be necessary as a consequence of the continued weakness of sterling after the devaluation of November 1967, and Wilson's reference to the UK's continuing to play a world role made little sense when the plan was to remove the means of continuing UK influence, the presence of troops east of Suez.

In an interesting indication of relative influence within the Cabinet, Jenkins, whose advocacy of financial stringency had been seemingly so influential with Wilson late in 1967, seems not to have spoken in the debate, for had so senior a minister contributed the expectation would be that his contribution would have been recorded and attributed to him. It is of course possible that Wilson and Jenkins had discussed the matter prior to the meeting and resolved upon the necessity for some form of compromise, though there is no evidence to that effect.

In an appreciation of the dynamics within the political and official establishment over the east of Suez issue, Pham claims that following the devaluation and its failure Wilson was weakened and Jenkins became more influential as Chancellor of the Exchequer, with the previous alignment of

Wilson as PM and the defence and overseas ministers being replaced by Wilson's support for Jenkins' insistence that withdrawal from east of Suez was necessary as a prelude to welfare cuts that could not be avoided but that were so unpopular with Labour ministers, MPs and the Party. Pham claims that with 'the defence and overseas ministers almost sidelined' without Wilson's Prime Ministerial support, 'Cabinet became the central decision-making body,' with 'Whitehall departments and officials almost irrelevant' and Wilson no longer engaging in creative summing-up of Cabinet discussion 'against the wishes of the strict majority'. Pham's claim that Wilson's Prime Ministerial behaviour in Cabinet became less manipulative and influential over the east of Suez issue in early 1968 does seem at variance with Crossman's claim that Wilson followed a 'Presidential line' after 1966 and with evidence from the Cabinet meeting on 4 January 1968 of Wilson's creative summing-up in favour of withdrawal from east of Suez despite genuine diversity of ministerial view on the issue. In the context of Wilson's tendency to compromise for political survival the evidence seems to indicate that Wilson adjusted to his weakened position following the devaluation of sterling and its failure and to the need to be seen to be cutting foreign expenditure before cuts in the welfare budget by withdrawing from east of Suez far earlier than had been planned. The FO, the CoS and other Whitehall departments do seem to have exerted no influence on the decision to withdraw from east of Suez.[93]

Despite Wilson's concession over the date of earlier withdrawal from east of Suez and his ending with a personal plea for understanding, the effect of the policy, announced on 16 January 1968, was clear. The US was on its own. There was significant US resentment not just over the British decision, which was seen as a reneging on undertakings given Johnson by Wilson, but over the manner of their having been informed of it rather than consulted over it. Dean regarded the policy change as a 'watershed' that ended all British influence over US foreign policy.[94] The following summit in Washington on 8 February was cordial but achieved nothing apart from a continuation of a relationship impaired by the reality of necessity for retrenchment on financial and political grounds in the UK and the US reaction to it. Though Wilson continued to support the US in Vietnam in moral terms Johnson remained disenchanted, and on 31 March 1968 announced he would not stand for President in the coming elections. The Democrats lost. Wilson's attempts to cultivate good relations with Nixon are beyond the domain of this work.

Historians differ in their judgement of Wilson's policy on Vietnam in terms of its consequences for Anglo-American relations. Smith disputes Vickers' claim that Wilson 'kept Britain out of the fighting but retained the "special relationship" with the United States'. He points to Wilson's own admission of there having been 'terrible rows' with Johnson and endorses Logevall's conclusion that what was seen as British 'interference' was resented by Johnson. The evidence of Wilson's ingratiating himself with Johnson between 1964 and 1968 tends to challenge Wilson's claim of open antagonism between him and Johnson and to suggest that such a claim was intended to enhance Wilson's standing with Johnson as seen by Wilson's domestic audience. And in more general terms the evidence seems to indicate that the special relationship was diminished by American realisation that Britain's limited economic capacity meant withdrawal from its previous world role in the form of the withdrawal from east of Suez, rather than by American displeasure at Wilson's unwelcome attempts to interfere with US foreign policy. For ensuing American alienation and detachment from support for sterling were indicative of the diminished power and abandoned world role of the UK.[95] The irritation Wilson caused by his ingratiation with Johnson and repeated pleas to be admitted to Washington for talks that seemed to Johnson to be aimed at enhancing Wilson's prestige at home seems to have been a fleeting episode that had little lasting effect when set in the context of the preceding harmonious Kennedy-Macmillan relationship and the cordial Wilson-Nixon relationship. Wilson's attempts to enhance his domestic and international world status by association with Johnson and his unwanted and futile peace initiatives made little difference in the long run. What did make a difference was the diminution in British economic power and capacity for a world role in support of the US, for that reduced US expectations of the UK to diplomatic support rather than any material assistance. An understanding seems to have been reached between Britain and the US during the Vietnam War that reflected British weakness and decline in terms of economic, military and diplomatic power and world role. That understanding of the special relationship was to endure until the Balkan Crisis, when Blair elicited Clinton's support in what seems a quite astonishing case of British influence on US policy despite British weakness. Over the first Iraq War there was a return to British military involvement to support the US after a period of four decades without any such British military intervention in support of US foreign policy. There followed further British military intervention to support the US in Iraq and Afghanistan, both of which resulted in adverse military outcomes as British military forces were interned in Basra and had to be supported by the US in Helmand Province. Whatever the diplomatic value to the US of British support in the form of troops in Iraq and Afghanistan it does seem that the Americans have been drawn to the conclusion that British troop involvement is no longer a military asset.

Korea and Vietnam compared – individuals and contexts, commonalities and differences, and attribution of influence on British foreign policy under Attlee and Wilson

I now turn to the commonalities and differences between the contexts faced by the Attlee and Wilson administrations over the Korean and Vietnam wars respectively and to the influence of the attitudes, perceptions and personalities of those involved.

One commonality of external context was continuing post-war British economic and military weakness set in a context of the threat of Soviet expansionism and opportunism and Soviet ideological hostility to Western social democracy worldwide and not least in the central theatre of the Cold War, Europe. The other was economic, diplomatic and military dependence on the US for economic support and for security against the Soviet threat.

Another commonality was a continuing ethos of Britain as a world power, which resulted in greater economic dependence on the US than would otherwise have been necessary, especially during the Attlee administration in the time of the Korean War as there was then a commitment to defend an empire that by that time had only relinquished India, Ceylon and Burma and a commitment too to support the US militarily in Korea.

By contrast by the time of the Wilson governments from 1964 onwards most of the African colonies had been granted independence and there had been withdrawal from Malaya in 1957. Under Wilson's premiership even the commitment to a presence east of Suez was in the end withdrawn, an indication that unlike economic and military weakness and the Soviet threat 'imperial overstretch' was not a characteristic of the context that could not be changed. On the contrary, it was a consequence of an ethos of world and imperial power status that committed expenditure to the defence of empire that was attitudinal and could be changed (and was by Wilson in the end with the decision to withdraw from east of Suez because the economy could not afford the expense). The Wilson decision to withdraw from east of Suez in spite of US expectations and requests to remain there is indicative too of the contingency of the dependence on the US, for the alternative of withdrawal from empire and from world-power status existed for both administrations throughout and was not pursued before for reasons of attachment to world, European and imperial power status and the security provided by US support for NATO under Attlee and for reasons it seems of more personal aggrandisement under Wilson, whose desire to establish himself as a world statesman seems to have been influential in his desire for a world role for Britain under him as PM.

One difference of context was that the Korean War had the international legitimacy of a UN Security Council resolution, though only because the Soviet Union was not present, whereas the US involvement in Vietnam had no such UN sanction and attracted worldwide condemnation in certain quarters, and in the US especially after the introduction of conscription. The effect was that whereas Attlee had Cabinet and Commons support initially, though that was not to last as the opportunity cost for welfare of the defence expenditure necessitated by support for the US over Korea resulted in rifts in the Labour Cabinet and Party in 1951, the Wilson governments of the 1960s had to defend the stance of moral support of the US purpose in Vietnam against a left wing in the Labour Party throughout.

Beyond these contextual commonalities and differences were attitudinal, perceptual and personality differences between the major foreign-policy decision-makers in the British political establishment. Attlee and Bevin were convinced of the need for US power to protect western Europe and so Britain against Soviet communism and for US support for the economy and Britain's world-power status. There were differences with the US, over the relationship between the Soviet Union and China, recognition of China and Chinese inclusion in the UN, the risk of escalation of the Korean War into a more general conflict, and concessions to the Chinese following the Chinese invasion of Korea. The Attlee administration advocated containment of the war to Korea, avoidance of provocation of the communist powers and of escalation of the war, and some concessions to the Chinese, whereas the US believed that what it regarded as 'centrally-directed Communist imperialism' should be resisted. Even so there was a common conviction that communist encroachment should be resisted case by case to deter communist movements and encourage democratic resistance to communism. And though such differences were not hidden in exchanges between Attlee and Bevin and the Americans with whom Attlee and Bevin dealt, not least Truman and Acheson, the outcome was British acceptance of US requests for troops and defence expenditure, and acceptance of US policy over Korea in regard to which the British government had minimal, if any, influence, because of the perceived need to secure US commitment to NATO in Europe.

By the time of the Vietnam War there seems to have been no threat of US withdrawal of support of NATO either from the US side or perceived by Wilson and his Cabinet. That may have been because the US commitment to resist communist expansionism by proxy in Vietnam indicated that Europe, the central theatre of the Cold War, would never be abandoned by the US. Wilson's success in pursuing a policy of moral support without troop commitment despite US requests seems to be a consequence of US appreciation of Wilson's predicament with his own left wing and resistance to demands for moral condemnation of the US in Vietnam, the propaganda value of Wilson's moral support in a context of very little elsewhere, and Johnson's sense that demanding troops from Wilson could remove the propaganda value of their commitment should the extent of US insistence be known. There was too for a time a US sense that permitting sterling to devalue would diminish the prospects of the US economy, though avoidance of a sterling devaluation was replaced over time by a policy of preparation for a sterling devaluation. Wilson's personal ingratiation with Johnson and attempts to influence US policy seem to have been an irritant to the US administration and to Johnson, though Acheson had been irritated with Bevin's representations and advice and there seems to have been a general sense in both wars that compliance and silence from Britain would have been preferred given the intensity and conviction of US anti-communism by the time of the Korean War and throughout the Vietnam War.

There were personal differences between Attlee and Wilson. One major difference was in the conceptualisation of the role of PM. Attlee conceived of it as being a duty and a responsibility to the country and put government and the country before party and certainly before any personal interest, though it seems that Attlee had no desire to hold on to the premiership just to remain in power or to be seen as a world statesman. In fact Attlee seems to have been devoid of any personal desires and to have been indifferent to consequences for his own political career. The result was that Attlee was immune to dissent in the Commons and the Party and foreign policy under him and Bevin, who shared Attlee's attributes of indifference to consequence and immunity to Party demands, reflected what Attlee and Bevin conceived to be the best interests of the country. When in April 1951 there were the threatened resignations of Bevan, Wilson and Freeman, Attlee declined to alter policy even given the government's slender majority in the Commons and the threat of loss of power.

By contrast Wilson tended to compromise to ensure his own political survival and to establish himself as a world statesman and was as a consequence attentive to the demands of the left wing of the Labour Party and obsequious with Johnson. When Wilson found himself in a similar position to Attlee, with a small majority in the Commons, he chose to compromise with the Labour left wing and refrained from sending even a small force of troops to support the US in Vietnam, and even when his majority was far greater, after the 1966 election, he continued his policy of moral though no military support for the US in Vietnam. Though the 1966 election did bring into the Commons a number on the Labour left, the revolt in the Commons in July 1966 over Vietnam, after the bombing of Hanoi, took the form of 32 Labour MPs abstaining from support for Labour Party policy on Vietnam, and though 100 Labour MPs signed a motion against the war a no-confidence motion in July 1966 only succeeded in dividing the left of the Labour Party, so there does not seem to have been any imminence of a vote of no confidence that would have removed the Wilson government from power. And though late the following year, 1967, the Chief Whip claimed that 'opposition on Vietnam was no longer the prerogative of the left, but now spread across the centre and right' there is a difference between dissent and government backbench MPs being prepared to vote against the government.

Such evidence does though refer to the reaction of the Labour left to Wilson's policy of moral though no military commitment to support the US in Vietnam, and the nature of Labour left-wing reaction to military commitment of troops would of course have been much more adverse. The most plausible inference is that Wilson compromised with the demands of the Labour left in part because of his compromising nature, though there seems little doubt that he did receive very vocal and intense criticism from the Labour Party in the Commons and from the Labour movement too, and in part because he perceived that military commitment of troops would have resulted in a more major revolt of Labour MPs.[96]

Though the influence of the Labour Party on Wilson's policy over Vietnam is apparent, there seems to have been very limited influence from Cabinet ministers on decisions regarding British policy over the Vietnam War. Part of the reason for that may have been that there was a lack of ministerial dissent over policy confined to moral support of the US purpose in Vietnam. The issue of withdrawal from east of Suez is different, an instance of extensive Cabinet discussion and diversity of expressed preference, where the decision taken seems to have reflected both Wilson's ingenuity in compromise and his authority as PM over ministers. That indicates the extent of Wilson's Prime Ministerial influence over Cabinet and so the influence on policy of Wilson's personal objectives to remain Labour leader and Prime Minister and to be seen to be close to and influential with the President of the United States as part of establishing world-statesman status. The inference from the evidence of Cabinet decisions and from Crossman is that despite ministerial reservations over withdrawal from east of Suez, Wilson did introduce policies that were consonant with his own objectives in his first term as PM. Of course part of the reason for the extent of Wilson's influence over policy on Vietnam is to be found in certain attributes in Wilson as PM, not least the sense of entitlement as Prime Minister to run the government in what was seen to be a 'presidential' manner, including the departmentalism that Crossman so deplored and that permitted Wilson to form policy with individual ministers, the liberal use of the Prime Ministerial prerogative of summing up, and the aptitude for compromise consonant with personal ends, though the inexperience of his ministers in the government of 1964 following thirteen years out of office for Labour conferred on Wilson a genuine advantage, as he had been a minister in the post-war Labour government.

It is worth noting that over the withdrawal from east of Suez Wilson disregarded the adverse Foreign Office view, indicating that the Treasury need for control over public expenditure and the Labour Party demand that foreign expenditure should be cut to limit the cuts in welfare expenditure were more influential considerations for Wilson at the time. It also indicates that the earlier consonance between Wilson and the FO over moral without military support for the US in Vietnam was pursued by Wilson because of the need to limit Labour dissent and to maintain the relationship with the US, not because of FO influence on Wilson.[97]

Wilson did in fact have no personal objections to the US purpose or to US tactics over Vietnam, and seems to have had, over and above the need for US economic and diplomatic support to permit Britain to remain a world power, to assist his being a world statesman, and to support him in the domestic sphere, a genuine personal emotional attachment to the US and to Johnson as its president. This was apparent in his continuing idealisation of the relationship and general effusiveness and desire for close association with Johnson despite some rough treatment from him, and in his liking for the ceremonial aspects of the relationship. His pleas for permission to visit Johnson continued throughout the period under consideration here. Crossman noted the 'peculiarly Wilsonian touch' of Britain's relations with the US under Wilson's premiership, one in which, he claimed, there was a 'personal reliance on LBJ'.[98] And Neustadt, an adviser to the White House in 1965, noted that Wilson had 'an emotional commitment to the US' 'personified…in LBJ'.[99] It seems that Wilson very much wished to emulate the warm relationship that had existed between Macmillan and Kennedy.

What one infers from this profound attachment is that had Wilson not had the pressure to resist US demands from the Labour left he would most likely have assented to the commitment of British troops to Vietnam in the small numbers that were initially requested by Johnson. Vickers refers to the claim by Jack Jones, the Transport and General Workers Union leader, that Wilson had told him that 'he would have much more influence with President Johnson if we could send in a token force', an indication that Wilson had no 'ethical concerns' regarding British troop commitment to Vietnam and that Wilson's refraining from troop commitment represented political pragmatism and what he perceived he needed to do to remain in power given the opposition of the Labour left to any support for US policy in Vietnam.[100]

By contrast Attlee's and Bevin's relationships with Truman and Acheson were not characterised by such a desire on the part of the British politicians for the good regard of their American counterparts in personal terms. For Attlee and Bevin it was the support of the US government for Britain's world-power status and for protection against Soviet expansionism in Europe and in other theatres of British interest that mattered, not personal aggrandisement by association or through ingratiation, and there seems to have been no personal agenda in either Attlee or Bevin.

Wilson's tendency towards compromise rather than confrontation and putting personal political survival above any informing principle are apparent in the fact that, even with such profound personal leanings towards the US, he was more responsive to the demands of the Labour Party, for though he did resist left-wing demands to condemn US intentions in Vietnam he did in the end withdraw from east of Suez despite Johnson's displeasure. Though Johnson did not explicitly threaten sterling, Wilson's withdrawal from east of Suez under political pressure from the Labour Party seems to indicate that he would have resisted sending troops to Vietnam and withdrawn from east of Suez even if threatened with devaluation because responsiveness to Party demands to remain in power exerted more influence on Wilson.

Even when Bundy advocated linking support for sterling to British troops in Vietnam, Johnson declined to take his advice, at least for a time. As to the effect of individual difference, one does not know what an individual like Acheson would have done in Johnson's circumstances. The indulgence of Wilson by Johnson seems more odd in the earlier period, for though there was at its height massive disapproval of the Johnson administration's policy over Vietnam, so that then the propaganda effect was vital, when Johnson first requested the commitment of British troops to Vietnam, in December 1964, there was far less adverse political and public opinion towards the Vietnam War in the US and worldwide – a march on Washington in December 1964 demonstrated this as it attracted so few people (conscription in the US, introduced in 1965, triggered more anti-war protests, in the way that war seems most morally repugnant when one is being asked to risk one's own life for it).

It does seem that Johnson felt that Wilson was doing his best in difficult domestic circumstances and that, as British troops were wanted in Vietnam not for their military contribution but for the international legitimacy their presence would lend to the US presence there, risking adverse publicity over US demands for British troops in Vietnam being linked to US support for sterling and risking also an end to Britain's position of moral support for US intentions in Vietnam, which Wilson took care to make very clear on a number of occasions, would not achieve the US objective of having public international support over Vietnam.

The above references to Bundy's appreciation of Wilson's efforts and the value of his support indicate that there was such an appreciation of the position in the US administration before the war became very unpopular. Of course the context of the Vietnam War could have been different from that of the Korean War as far as British confidence in continued US support for NATO was concerned, for though in the Korean War the US did demonstrate resolve to defend even a peripheral theatre against Soviet and communist incursion (and had shown the same resolve in Europe in the Berlin Crisis), there was the perceived possibility of diminished US support for NATO, whereas by the early 1960s the Cold War and American anti-communism dominated US politics and culture and US resolve to resist the spread of Soviet influence and communism was the primary objective of US foreign policy, indicating no possible diminished US commitment to the defence of western Europe.

The effect of US power on British foreign policy over Vietnam was then constrained by the nature of the Cold War context and the purpose the US under Johnson had for British troops in Vietnam. There was also the fact that the US had its own interest in support for sterling, for any British devaluation was seen to have been likely to have a deleterious effect on US trade as British exports would become more competitive and UK imports of US goods would reduce, and there was also the effect on the value of the dollar of any British hike in interest rates to defend sterling, though as has been seen by 1966 the Johnson administration had moved from a policy of avoidance of British devaluation to measures to cope with its effects, and sterling was in the end devalued.

In terms of attribution of causal influence then one should conclude that it was at least in part Johnson's own purpose for British troops in Vietnam that constrained him, and it was his judgement that resulted in continued US support for sterling for a time during the war, and so facilitated a British policy that confined itself only to moral support for the US in Vietnam (it is also clear that Johnson understood the relationship between British devaluation or attempts to avert it and the effects of such British policies on US trade and currency). It would then seem that the success of Wilson's policy was predicated upon Johnson's restraint and sense of context, for had Johnson told Wilson that support for sterling would be withdrawn if Wilson did not commit British troops to Vietnam Wilson would have had to make a choice. He could have chosen to defy Johnson to mollify the left wing of the Labour Party, but this would have meant countenancing devaluation of sterling which could well have been perceived to have meant a diminution in Britain's world role. Or he could have opted for assenting to British troops in Vietnam, thus causing outrage on the Labour backbenches and among ministerial colleagues but protecting sterling and Britain's world-power status possibly at the cost of his own premiership and government.

Wilson's tendency to compromise with rather than defy the Labour Party and Johnson was characteristic of a political survivor who aspired to world statesmanship status, though his withdrawal from east of Suez indicates that he chose political survival over cultivation of Johnson to appear to be a world statesman. Wilson's policy of moral but no material support, of dissociation from specific US actions in Vietnam accompanied by indications of support for US intentions there and pleas for American understanding of his position (supported by reports from the US Ambassador to the UK confirming Wilson's unpopularity over Vietnam), succeeded in pleasing no one but placated both the US and the Labour left wing, though as has been seen in the end the Johnson administration did countenance a devaluation in sterling.

Wilson then tested the limits of US indulgence of a British policy that was other than the US would have wished for in a foreign policy which sustained the Atlantic relationship (though the US did permit sterling to devalue in the end), while taking account of the demands of the Labour left wing. Despite several visits to Washington, however, Wilson exerted no influence whatever on US policy in Vietnam and no influence either on the outcome of the war through peace efforts which succeeded only in appeasing Labour left wingers (and may have been devised primarily to that end). Johnson wanted British support, not advice, and as has been seen told Wilson to take care of Malaysia and let him take care of Vietnam. Some commentators have alluded to Wilson's courage and bravery in resisting Johnson over the commitment of British troops to Vietnam.[101] These are odd terms to use in the context of a policy that was essentially one of compromise, of achieving the minimum necessary to placate Johnson, with whom Wilson attempted to ingratiate himself, and the left wing and moderate dissidents over Wilson's Vietnam policy in the Labour Party. One could say he was slightly less than brave with the Labour Party, less so than Attlee might have been, for instance. In fact Pimlott seems to conclude that Wilson was a compromiser and courageous, which would seem to be inconsistent.[102] In the end Wilson responded to what was politically necessary to remain in power in the withdrawal from east of Suez despite disapproval from Johnson, an indication of his careerist and compromising nature. As has been seen, the view of Wilson has varied, with Pimlott claiming Wilson acted on principle in a very difficult context of competing demands from Johnson in the US and the Labour Party, and others seeing Wilson as unprincipled and careerist. Noting a decline in Wilson's political reputation over time from meritocratic moderniser to efficient 'party manager' and 'communicator', Donoughue, who created the Downing Street Policy Unit for Wilson in his 1974–76 administration, found Wilson to be 'much shallower' than Callaghan, and claims there was a 'tricky Harold, the clever and devious political manipulator', and beneath that 'a kindly, weak and indecisive man'. Hughes claims that Wilson came to be seen by both right and left as a 'charlatan' who concentrated more on style than policy and who exaggerated 'his attributes as an international statesman', with an enduring image as a 'shallow opportunist with a penchant for deceit and self-delusion'.[103] Wilson's careerism, delusions as to his relationship with Johnson, aspirations to world-statesman status and belief in the possibility of facilitating peace between the US and the North Vietnamese, combined with compromising to secure his own political survival and apparent lack of informing political principle do seem to reflect the personality traits ascribed to Wilson here, not least the combination of aspiration, weakness, indecision and insecurity that seems to explain Wilson's deviousness and tendency to compromise to survive and to achieve world-statesman status. In these characteristics Wilson was altogether different from the more direct, terse, austere, business-like and efficient Attlee, who saw the premiership as a great responsibility and who was indifferent to his image, popularity or tenure in the job and so impervious to threats to his position as premier.

Apart from the differences of view between the Labour governments and the Party rank and file over both Korea after 1950 and Vietnam, there are other clear commonalities between the British experience of the Korean War and Vietnam. In both cases British policy was to maintain the 'special relationship' with the Americans for the world-power status it permitted Britain to maintain, though also in the case of the Korean War to maintain US participation in the defence of Europe and in NATO and in the case of the Vietnam War to protect sterling and to enhance Wilson's reputation as a world statesman, but to do the minimum necessary to that end (as has been seen, Attlee committed British troops to Korea only once Franks had indicated that British troops to Korea were needed to maintain the relationship with the US) and to use the 'special relationship' to restrain American extremism in dealing with world communism (as was seen in Attlee's mission to Washington over Truman's threat to use the atomic bomb and Wilson's repeated attempts to effect a ceasefire in Vietnam) – this theme of needing to be close to the Americans in order to exert influence on American policy is one that endures today, though over Korea and Vietnam the extent of actual British influence on US policy seems to have been minimal if it existed at all. It is in fact odd that the British political and official elite should have continued to believe in the possibility of British diplomatic influence on US policy when the very need for US diplomatic and military support for British foreign policy was predicated upon the British belief that diplomacy had to be supported by power.

The British experience with the US over Korea confirmed that influence did depend upon power, and Britain's diminished power was matched by negligible influence on US policy. Over the Vietnamese war Johnson made it very clear to Wilson that any attempt to counsel or offer advice was unwelcome and that what was required of the British was moral and material support. The instances of Korea and Vietnam indicated that the very brief interlude of the Americans' being influenced not just by their own direct experience of events (as seen through the prism of their attitudes) but also by British diplomatic experience in Europe was over. The effect of US policy on British policy was a different matter, with British conformance to US demands to avoid perceived adverse consequences, though the fact that Wilson withdrew from east of Suez despite US requests does indicate that the final decision rested with the PM and Cabinet.

The influence on policy of the moderate and left-wing factions within the Labour Party opposed to support for US involvement in Vietnam has to be juxtaposed against the influence of the international context. For, given the Labour Party's history of being a workers' movement, its diversity of view and lack of discipline, the PM may be constrained not just by Cabinet or by MPs in the Commons but also by the Labour Party Conference with its constituency parties and left-wing activists, for it is the Labour Party Conference that decides upon policy, though its views are not binding on a Labour government. At the Labour Party conferences in 1966 and 1967 the policy of the Wilson government over Vietnam, of moral though no military support for the US there, was reproved, though without any effect on government policy. With resistance from Cabinet ministers, a Labour PM may, just like any other PM, sack and replace them, but would find his credibility eroded by resignations or defections from support for Prime Ministerial policy from senior ministers with some following in Parliament, the Labour Party or the Labour movement. As a case indicative of ministerial constraint, even the dominant and stubborn Chamberlain found his control of Cabinet eroded by policy failure and the defection of Halifax, a Foreign Secretary who commanded significant respect in the Conservative Party of the late 1930s.

The power of the Commons depends on the extent of the government majority, feeling on the issue on the government backbenches, and the attitude of the opposition towards government policy. Given the voting arithmetic in the Commons it would be possible for a government to pursue a policy with opposition support to overcome dissent from its own backbenches, though this would have adverse implications for party unity and electoral prospects in the future, as the electorate tends not to vote for political parties that are not united.

The reaction of Attlee to ministerial dissent and threats to resign has been discussed above, even when the general election of 24 February 1950 had reduced the Labour majority in the Commons to just five seats. Attlee's continuing disdain for ministerial dissent and resolve to support the Atlantic relationship seems when put into so adverse a context remarkable, not least given his understanding of the consequential nature for the future of the government of the threatened resignation of two Cabinet ministers, one of whom had massive influence within the Party. It is impossible to avoid the conclusion that Prime Ministerial personal characteristics made an enormous difference to British foreign policy in the case of Attlee in 1951. It is worth noting too that Attlee's situation in 1951 was worse than Wilson's in political terms, in that there was a direct threat to the future of the government, and Attlee perceived the threat. With Wilson, while there was a great deal of public and political disapproval of his Vietnam policy, there seems to have been no direct imminent threat to either administration, at least not from within the Cabinet, though there is the question of Wilson's perception of his own position and its political precariousness. One should add that Cabinet minutes might be of limited use here, in that, as was clear from the comparison between the rationales presented by Chamberlain to his Cabinet and in his letters to his sisters, the reasons presented to Cabinet may not be the real motive for the policy being proposed. And as has been noted Wilson misrepresented the nature of his relationship with Johnson to Cabinet.

In another indication of the effect of individual attitude and perception on government reaction to possible influence, as premier Wilson lectured the Labour Party Conference on the difference between politics and government but then pursued a foreign policy that took account of views expressed at the Labour conference, while Attlee and Bevin disregarded Conference and dissent. Wilson's reaction was to compromise, to do enough to maintain the special relationship but to go some way to take account of adverse opinion within his own party, through a policy of moral but not material support for the US in Vietnam and one of dissociation from specific US acts in Vietnam but approval of US intentions in Vietnam. Such a balancing act secured Wilson's premiership and role as a world statesman. Attlee by contrast does, as has been seen, seem to have been without aspiration to remain premier or to be recognised as a world statesman. The consequence was that he was impervious to left-wing dissent from within or outside the Cabinet and immune to threats to his position as PM, and the policy he pursued represented what he felt was optimal for the country rather than a compromise to secure his political future.

The positions of Attlee and Wilson as leaders of the Labour Party and as premiers were different. In the Attlee government there were a number of the really big guns of the Labour Party and movement. There was Aneurin Bevan, who commanded great loyalty on the Labour left, Ernest Bevin, who had massive personal stature in the Trades Union movement and the rank and file of the Party, the austere Stafford Cripps, the intellectual Hugh Dalton and the devious and scheming Herbert Morrison. And though many commentators have claimed that Attlee was the only one who could draw the various factions in the Party together and form a government, the record shows that there were a number of challenges to his premiership, not least from Morrison, who tried to replace Attlee even before he was made premier. The decisive feature in all of this was Attlee's indifference to such threats and even to the possibility of their success. There was no sense that policy changed to maintain Attlee as premier.

Wilson's position was quite different. There seems to have been no clear alternative to him as PM in Cabinet or the Labour Party, despite there being a number of undisciplined ministers, not least the erratic George Brown, the treacherous Richard Crossman and of course Tony Benn. From this one would expect that Wilson would have felt more assured of his position as premier than Attlee and have been more robust in dismissal of criticism from the Labour Party and the Commons. This was not the case. For the critical feature in terms of actual effect on policy was the premiers' reaction to criticism of their foreign policies.

It is then apparent that British foreign policy over Korea and Vietnam reflected the interaction of a number of different factors. There were contextual factors such as relative British economic and military decline and the threat of Soviet ideological hostility, expansionism and communism, and the need for US economic and diplomatic support to permit Britain to remain a world power and defend existing British interests worldwide. The ethos of Britain as a world power was not challenged by either Attlee or Wilson, both of whom inherited and accepted a primary objective to maintain a status that was anachronistic because of the country's economic and military decline. There was the alternative of abandonment of world-power status and imperial pretensions, and of cultivation of collaboration with the Soviet Union over Europe, which would have permitted Britain to pursue a foreign policy rather more independent of the foreign policy of the US, though the possibility of a rapprochement with the Soviet Union over Europe does seem to have been delusional given the Soviet ideological hostility to British social democracy and the expansionist nature of Soviet communism.

The acceptance of that ethos of British world-power status as a foreign-policy objective reflected Attlee's sense of its being imperative to secure US support for the defence of western Europe and Wilson's desire to be seen as a world statesman and to avoid a devaluation of sterling. There were then individual influences in attitudes that were reflected in foreign-policy objectives and perceptions of intentions of other countries, and these combined with the personalities of the incumbents of positions from which influence on British foreign policy was possible or certain, for there is an irreducible perceptual and individual quality to foreign-policy decision-making, in that decisions are made on the basis of perceptions rather than reality itself, and perceptions reflect personal preconceptions and individual attitudes. Such attitudes also influence foreign-policy objectives. Added to this is the influence of the personalities of ministers of varying seniority and position in relation to foreign policy and the influence of the nature of ministerial relationships. Those of the PM, given the enormous powers of the PM in the British political system, and the Foreign Secretary by virtue of his appointment and brief, are especially of concern here.

There would seem to have been little difference between Attlee, Bevin and Wilson in terms of their basic attitudinal orientation, for Wilson shared Attlee's and Bevin's resolve that Britain should remain a world power and Cold War concerns regarding communist and Soviet expansionism. There was also a clear common understanding of the need for the Americans in the maintenance of British world-power status and in resistance to Soviet and communist pressure anywhere in the world and of British economic dependence on the US for world-power status.

The dissimilarity between the Labour administrations arises not in attitudes, priorities or understandings but rather in personalities and relationships. Attlee and Bevin were, though temperamentally dissimilar, both essentially authoritarian in outlook as far as responsiveness to Labour Party or ministerial criticism was concerned. Attlee treated dissent with complete indifference, while Bevin regarded it as a form of treachery that weakened the country's diplomatic bargaining position. Both made it clear that they were not going to be dictated to by the Party and Bevin indicated that the Party would have to find another Foreign Secretary if it wanted a different foreign policy. Attlee made it clear in April 1951 that even threatened senior and consequential ministerial resignations would not dissuade him from his chosen policy. Wilson was a different character, a compromiser who exhibited great guile and creativity in devising a foreign-policy stance that mollified the left wing of his own party enough to permit him to remain in power while maintaining the 'special relationship' vital to British world-power status and to the stability of the British economy.[104]

Given the centrality of the PM to decision-making in the British political system and Prime Ministerial powers in Cabinet (including those of appointment and dismissal of ministers, control of the Cabinet agenda and summing up and prerogatives regarding unilateral diplomatic overtures), it is axiomatic that the PM is a major factor in British foreign-policy decision-making. It follows that the attributes, attitudes, personalities and relationships of British PMs have a profound effect on the foreign policy that is pursued by any British government.

Wilson's policy of moral but no material support for American policy in Vietnam combined with his peace initiatives (which had no effect whatever because of lack of interest in the warring parties and a belief that Wilson represented Johnson but placated the left wing of the Labour Party – it seems that some of these were intended to do just that) and policy of dissociation of reproved specific incidents in US policy from a general approval of US intentions over Vietnam to facilitate his government's holding the Labour Party together though not responding to demands for outright condemnation of US policy in Vietnam from within the Labour Party. It also maintained, albeit under some strain and with some diminution in US confidence, the 'special relationship' with the Americans.

One would have to conclude that, while Wilson did warn the Labour Party of the difference between politics and government, he pursued a policy that reflected not just the government's international priorities but also Labour Party demands. It is worth noting that Wilson's policy of moral support for US policy in Vietnam but no actual British troop commitment (and of criticism of specific American actions but general approval of US overall objectives in Vietnam) was supported by his Foreign Secretaries Patrick Gordon Walker and Michael Stewart, so that the relationship between PM and Foreign Secretary, while not necessarily similar to that which obtained between Attlee and Bevin, was one in which Wilson received support for his foreign policy – one should add that Wilson relied also on informal advisers to an unusual extent, so that the locus of foreign-policy decision-making in the Wilson administration is more complex than the relations between PM and Foreign Secretary.[105] Given Wilson's domination of foreign policy (and Gordon Walker's notorious right-wing sympathies and Stewart's affinity for the US and foreign-policy inexperience) it is likely that Wilson's Foreign Secretaries would have supported policies of military as well as moral support for the US in Vietnam had Wilson chosen to send a token presence to Vietnam. In other words, it does seem that the compromise came from Wilson alone, not least given his powers and prerogatives as PM and his control over information regarding the relationship with the US presented to Cabinet.

The example of Attlee in 1951 is indicative of the difference the attributes of the PM make in dealing with dissent from within the governing party and the extent to which foreign policy reflects not only the PM's attitudes but also personality, tendency to compromise and desire to hold on to power. The conclusion is that British foreign policy over Korea and Vietnam reflected the attitudes, priorities and personalities of the PMs – Attlee disdained ministerial and Party dissent and remained beyond its influence, in part because of his sense of responsibility as PM and in part because of his relative indifference to remaining PM, while Wilson was acutely political and tended to compromise to retain the premiership, to secure his position in the Labour Party and to maintain a good relationship with Johnson for the possibility it offered of world statesmanship. As has been noted above, Attlee seems to have had no such motives or pretensions.

Wilson seems to have exerted no influence on US policy over Vietnam because of the fundamental asymmetry of power and need between Britain and the US and because of Wilson's policy of moral without material support for the US in Vietnam. For it was apparent to those involved at the time that British influence in the generation in power in 1964 would depend upon British utility to US purposes rather than reflecting long-term friendships formed in the war or the early and formative Cold War period. And it became very apparent, when early in 1965 Wilson did attempt to influence Johnson, that such intervention was radically deplored and disregarded, an expected outcome given that the UK had no credible threat that would ensure influence.

It does not seem that Attlee and Bevin would in Wilson's position have chosen a similar policy of responsiveness to left-wing or even moderate Labour Party criticism. Given their attitudes towards ministerial and governmental responsibility, towards the Labour movement as a whole and towards left-wing criticism from within the Parliamentary Labour Party it does not seem plausible that they would have been as responsive as Wilson was. Attlee's and Bevin's idea of Labour unity was a movement behind the government and supportive of its policies. Furthermore, neither Attlee nor Bevin was in terms of personality likely to be coerced by the Labour Party, and in fact both made references to being prepared to go under certain circumstances. Attlee's attitude towards the premiership was not one in which there was a sense of personal career or status, and he was not prepared, as is apparent from his robust reaction to Bevan's threat in 1951, to compromise to remain in office.

It is not that contextual factors do not have an effect, just that they do so through the perceptual lens, attitudinal prism and personalities of those making and influencing foreign-policy decisions. While all policy options have consequences it is the perceiving and valuing of those consequences that is the individual domain. In the case of Vietnam, there is clear evidence of agency both in Britain and the US. And, while it may seem as if contextual factors were overwhelming for British policymakers, the distinction between context and agency is in fact difficult to sustain. For Johnson's 'definition of the situation' as far as British involvement over Vietnam was concerned, his objective of having British troops in Vietnam to preclude the accusation that the war was a US crusade against communism, and his not being prepared for that reason to link US support for sterling to British troops in Vietnam, provided the context for Wilson's foreign policy. And it was Wilson's testing of the limits to which he could go in resisting US demands for troops in Vietnam that took advantage of Johnson's restraint. There was also his astute positioning of British polices in the sense of moral but not actual support that resulted in Johnson's receiving mixed advice, though in the end he resisted advice to link US support for sterling to British troop commitment to Vietnam. Context and agency are then linked in that the behaviour of one political actor provides the context for another and in the sense that context exerts influence on decisions through the lens of individual perception and the prisms of individual attitudes and personalities.

I have demonstrated the effect of individual attitudes and perceptions of alternatives and their outcomes on British foreign policy. I have also stressed the centrality of individual personalities, not least in terms of reaction to criticism, aspiration to world-statesman status and desire to hold on to office, and objectives for relationships. These relate to individuals whose positions made influence on the foreign policies of their country possible or certain. I have also alluded to the effect of relationships on foreign policy, such as that of Attlee and Bevin, for instance. Yet what should one conclude as to the effect of transatlantic relationships on British foreign policy and US influence upon it? Here the evidence of the Korean and Vietnam wars is clear. Though Truman and Attlee were never close Truman respected Attlee, and Acheson admired and was even fond of Bevin, but American policy was to insist upon a level of UK defence expenditure that the country could not afford and to allude to US isolationist disapproval of enhanced US support for NATO if there was a lack of British support for US policy in Korea. Further, after a period in which American inexperience of European diplomacy lent Britain a diplomatic value, British diplomacy over Korea seems to have had minimal if any effect on US foreign policy.[106] By contrast, Wilson was disliked by Johnson, who questioned his motives in cultivating the Atlantic relationship, though his not being prepared to listen to advice on US policy in Vietnam from Wilson was because no British troops were being committed to Vietnam to support the US effort there.

The conclusion is that relations between Britain and the US reflected their perceived interests (which in turn reflected their attitudes and perceived outcomes of alternative policies) rather than the personal relationships between PMs and Presidents over Korea and Vietnam. That does not of course mean that the personalities of Attlee and Wilson, and of Truman and Johnson, were not influential in terms of British foreign policy over Vietnam, for their personalities affected the extent to which their attitudes and perceptions were reflected in policy, as was so with Prime Ministerial reaction to Labour left dissent, and the extent to which Truman's and Johnson's personal preferences (rather than those of advisers to the Presidents from various sources) were reflected in US foreign policy towards the UK over Korea and Vietnam.

These conclusions regarding the locus of foreign-policy decision-making power in the British political and official establishment in the Korean War and the Vietnam War a decade later do elicit certain questions. To begin with, is it no more than an obvious truth to say that the PM was a decisive influence on British foreign policy? One might argue that this is not necessarily so in actuality, because the case of Baldwin establishes that a PM who was a compromiser and whose interest was in social rather than foreign policy had little effect on British foreign policy, which would indicate that the attributes of the PM affect the extent and nature of an individual PM's influence. Yet Baldwin had an effect simply by being less interested in foreign policy, for it meant that other parts of the political and official establishment exerted greater influence than would otherwise have been the case. What does seem true is that the PM is a possible decisive influence on British foreign policy because of the enormous powers and prerogatives of the PM in the British political system and is not a decisive influence only if Prime Ministerial attitudes and priorities, interests, personality and interactions are such that Prime Ministerial influence on foreign policy is diminished or nullified. While the British PM is then central by virtue of powers in an informal constitution in which precedent is a profound influence an investigation into the causes of British foreign policy requires consideration of those attributes of the PM that enhance or diminish Prime Ministerial influence on British foreign policy.

Chamberlain was a PM with all the attributes that would indicate dominance over foreign policy in Cabinet. These included a sense of Prime Ministerial entitlement, attitudes relevant to foreign policy that were held with some intensity and conviction, a personality immune to influence and possessed of personal assurance regardless of the extent and nature of opposition, which he derogated, and a guile and adeptness in the use of the powers of the PM to evade Cabinet scrutiny and control. Yet even Chamberlain found, after a period of genuine dominance of Cabinet predicated in part on a lack of talent and confidence in the Conservative Party at the time, that his dominance of Cabinet was challenged, in his case by the defection of his Foreign Secretary in a context in which Chamberlain's policy had clearly failed. Prime Ministerial dominance may then be mitigated by policy failure and ministerial defections that produce a Cabinet majority against the PM.

As a corollary, though I have argued for individual (as well as contextual) influence on British foreign policy by claiming that the British PM could have disregarded contextual factors and decided in Attlee's case not to commit British troops to Korea (that is, to reject US demands despite implicit US threats) and in Wilson's case to commit British troops to Vietnam (that is, not to give in to the Labour left wing), it remains true that, as the case of Chamberlain proves, Cabinet ministers would have had to approve or at least not resign in such numbers as to make the PM's position impossible – some form of consensus is implicit in the British system, though of course it may be contrived and reflect asymmetries of power that work behind the scenes. And even where the PM does have ultimate freedom of decision contextual factors that affect the domestic and international consequences of alternative policies could be more compelling in one case than in another when set against British foreign policy objectives that reflect not just a general British attitudinal orientation but also the personal attitudes of those involved in British foreign policy and the power they exert over it – Wilson's sense of the need for US power to sustain Britain as a world power and to avoid a devaluation of sterling (both generally shared by ministers), and his attachment to the premiership and world-statesman status, would be an example of the way in which perceived policy outcomes are evaluated against general and personal attitudes and objectives.

It would also seem that the statement that foreign policy results from the perception of the domestic and international context of the PM and others involved in foreign-policy decisions (and from their attitudes, personalities and relationships) is true, in the sense that it is the perceived rather than the actual world that affects decisions, and in the sense that such perceptions are influenced by attitudes, and their influence by personality attributes and interactions. Having said that it is the detail of individual attributes that affects the prism through which external contexts are seen, and the nature of interacting personalities that affects the nature and extent of individual influence.

If foreign-policy decision-making is a matter of individual attitudes, perceptions, personalities and interrelationships, it seems natural to ask if policy was, though possibly for different reasons and as a result of different processes, exactly what it would have been under an alternative PM in the Korean and Vietnam War. For while it is true to say that Wilson's policy reflected his tendency to compromise and his deftness in achieving a balance between the demands of his own left wing and the US to sustain his own position as PM and world statesman, it may be that a Conservative PM would not have pursued a different policy.

There was after all bipartisan support for restraint on the US over Vietnam and a sense of the British position's being constrained by being co-chairman of the Geneva Conference in 1954 that ended the French Indo-China War and the French imperial presence, and that drew the 17th parallel as the dividing line between the communist north and the democratic south. Both parties also shared a serious concern regarding the possibility of escalation of the Vietnam War into a major Cold War confrontation if the Soviet Union and China felt the need to intervene to support the North Vietnamese. Set against such shared concerns the previous Conservative British government had supported Kennedy's initial commitment to defend South Vietnam, and the relationship between Macmillan and Kennedy had been warm. While opposition policy may remain dubious, even if one concludes that Conservative policy would have been no different to that actually pursued by Wilson it does not follow that British policy as it materialised should not be attributed to Wilson's personality and preference for compromise and political survival. There is of course also the plausible possibility of a Conservative government's endorsing Johnson's request for a token British troop commitment to Vietnam, not least in the conviction that such British troop commitment could enhance the possibility of British restraint on US extremism against communism in the Far East and preclude an escalation of the Vietnam War.

It is also true that another Labour PM might have given in to the Labour left wing and condemned the US presence in Vietnam or, on the contrary, have disregarded the Labour left wing and offered British troops to support the US over Vietnam. Given the realities of the domestic and international contexts, the way in which they are perceived and compared against foreign-policy objectives informed by personal attitudes, and the way in which the various policy options are considered and assessed (with their consequences), are very much individual matters. There were choices and Wilson made them, as did Johnson for the US foreign policy that was part of the context for Wilson's foreign policy deliberations.

There was a choice too for Attlee, between the policy he chose, of a foreign policy over Korea that preserved US support, and one of withdrawal from world-power status, empire and Europe, which would have meant no dependence on American economic, diplomatic and military support, though it would have carried the perceived risk (so soon after the Berlin Crisis's exemplification of the Soviet threat to Europe and the need for the US to resist it) of Soviet expansionism and opportunism in western Europe and a threat to the security of Britain should US support for NATO be withdrawn or be insufficient to deter Soviet expansionism or to contain it in actual crises, as over Berlin.

In the choice he made Attlee's personal attributes, which combined control, calmness and authority with resistance to ministerial and Party influence on a decided policy in which he believed, and a profound sense of responsibility he expected to be mirrored in other ministers, were decisive. When there was a genuine threat to his government Attlee held fast to his declared policy on Korea and defence expenditure and delivered a lecture on ministerial responsibility to his ministers. The only other individual with similar views regarding ministerial and Party dissent and with similar resolve was Bevin, who was no longer living. It is possible that another PM, for instance Morrison, despite previous support for Attlee and his foreign policy, would have taken a different approach to ministerial threats to the government and attempted some form of compromise.

Of course Bevan himself would have changed policy at once. It is worth noting that though Attlee and Wilson both endorsed the ethos of Britain as a major power on the world stage and agreed on the threat posed by Soviet communism to British security and worldwide interests that had to be protected, and on the necessity of the Atlantic relationship to Britain's economic welfare and international influence, there were differences associated with Wilson's desire to be seen as a world statesman and to be accepted by the US President, and Wilson's tendency to compromise with resistance in the Party to remain premier, none of which motivated Attlee. Wilson compromised and minimised British support for the US over Vietnam. Attlee worried that the US could leave NATO with insufficient power to resist the Soviet Union in Europe and did not evade US requests for British troops in Korea.

Conclusion

The context for the Korean and Vietnam wars was one of British decline in economic and military terms relative to the emerging superpowers of the Soviet Union and the US and an attitudinal ethos among the British political and official establishment that assumed that Britain would, and demanded that Britain should, remain a world power of the first rank. Given the undisguised hostility and threatening intentions of the Soviet Union towards British social democracy and British interests in Europe and elsewhere, Britain turned to the US not just for economic support to sustain both the Welfare State and world-power status but also for military and diplomatic support to defend British interests against Soviet and communist encroachment. At first British diplomatic experience and an American sense of their own inexperience in the European context made continuing British influence possible. That ended with the Berlin Crisis, after which US diplomatic confidence rendered British foreign policy bereft of influence in US circles. Alongside this diminished British diplomatic influence there was increased US influence on British policy. Though Bevin had realised as early as 1946 that British policy would need US support and approval, the trend was one of increasing US influence on British foreign policy and one in which any degree of apparent British autonomy was in fact a reflection of constraint imposed by the nature of US purposes and in which British independence had adverse consequences for the economy.

Within this overall context that established the basic orientation of British foreign policy (which was itself the choice of the British political elite, and opposed by a Labour left wing that challenged the idea that Britain should remain a world power and believed in the UN, an echo of an idealism associated with ideas of world government) the attributes of individual ministers and participants on both sides of the Atlantic made a difference to the actuality of British policy in the Korean and Vietnam wars, for it was through the attitudinal prism and perceptual lens of the major participants in foreign-policy decisions that the international context and alternative policy outcomes became influences on policy.

The effect on foreign policy of the personal objectives and strategies of such individuals is plain in the cases of Wilson, who even after the object lesson of American economic power in the Suez

Crisis tested the limits of latitude possible with the US, and Johnson, who did not attempt to exercise the economic power the US had over sterling to force Wilson to commit British troops to Vietnam. For it was the interaction between them, their personalities, purposes and strategies that made British policy what it was over Vietnam. Over Korea Attlee's immunity to criticism from the Labour Party and indifference to his own political career were decisive in his response and in British policy. It was then individuals who made the vital foreign-policy decisions and addressed the issues in their context, and their attitudes, perceptions, personalities and interactions were vital to the foreign policy that emerged.

The result was that, if maintenance of the 'special relationship' with its inherent asymmetry of power was a theme, it was one chosen by British politicians, and there were variations on that theme as a result of the influence of individual attributes, for even given an enduring British ethos of world-power status and sense of a need for US support for the defence of western Europe as a means of guaranteeing the security of Britain itself, there was nothing automatic to Attlee's sending British troops to Korea. For another Prime Minister could have reasoned that the US would never diminish its support for NATO in the central theatre of the Cold War, Europe, to compel a British Prime Minister to send troops to a peripheral theatre, Korea, and could have continued to plead the case of imperial overstretch and sterling difficulties that would be seriously exacerbated by commitment of British troops to Korea.

The same centrality of perception had been apparent over the Berlin Crisis of 1948, when Bevin's resolution to remain in Berlin was not an automatic consequence of his anti-communism and anti-Sovietism, for the US Joint Chiefs of Staff shared such attitudes but advocated withdrawing to a more militarily defensible position further west, whereas Bevin believed that the future of western Europe would be endangered if the West made any concessions to Soviet brinkmanship over Berlin and that the Soviet Union did not intend to go to war over Berlin. Over Suez another Prime Minister could have interpreted Eisenhower's communiqués as genuine warnings and could have avoided any secrecy that excluded the US. And over Vietnam Wilson could either have accepted the risk of sterling's devaluation before he did in the end (it was Wilson himself who was adamant that sterling should not be devalued) and condemned US involvement in Vietnam or sent ground troops and challenged the Labour left wing to get rid of him as PM. There is then an irreducible individual quality to foreign-policy decision-making and policies that seem natural and that are in fact choices.

One way to characterise the difference in British foreign policy and the 'special relationship' between the Korean and Vietnam wars is to introduce the notion of credible threat to something of ultimate value to the recipient of such threat. For in the Korean case the perceived risk of insufficient US commitment to the defence of Europe through NATO seems to have been a credible threat to the defence of Europe against Soviet and communist incursion to the Attlee government. That and the appreciated dependence on the US loan were enough for Attlee and Bevin, to both of whom anti-communism and the containment of Soviet expansionism and maintenance of Britain's world-power status were imperative, to provide troops to the war in Korea despite the resulting defence expense that the country could not afford. The reaction of Attlee and Bevin to US demands was facilitated by their authoritarian approach to dissent from within the Labour Party, the Commons, the CoS and even the Cabinet itself, and their apparent indifference to losing their jobs in government. The presumption is that the Americans did not care if their demands and threats to the British government were made public because of the influence of the right-wing Republicans in US politics at the time, for such Republicans would have approved such use of US power to obligate the British to compliance with US demands. The other explanation is that the US felt assured that Attlee would not make public any US threat as to support for NATO given his discretion.

The Vietnam War case was entirely different, in that Johnson seems to have avoided the introduction of a credible threat to sterling to make Wilson comply with his request for British ground troops in Vietnam. It seems that part of the reason is that the domestic and international contexts were different in the 1960s, with more anti-war sentiment than right-wing influence on the US government in favour of the war. Other factors seem to have been the enhanced importance of the propaganda war in the 1960s compared to the early 1950s, for adverse publicity indicating that the US had coerced Britain into providing troops to Vietnam would have negated the entire purpose of having them in Vietnam, the cultivation of the impression that the Vietnam War was not part of an entirely American crusade against communism.

It also seems that the US administration and Johnson were reluctant to threaten to abandon sterling if British troops in a token presence were not provided to Vietnam because of the propaganda value of Wilson's moral and diplomatic defence of US intentions in Vietnam, and because of the possible adverse effects of British devaluation, the consequence of the withdrawal of US support for sterling, on the US economy through diminished US competitiveness, lower exports to the UK and possible loss of capital from New York to London should the Wilson government react with hikes in interest rates, though Johnson's administration had by 1966 changed its view on the adverse effects of UK devaluation and prepared for them rather than attempting to preclude such UK devaluation, and sterling was in the end devalued. Wilson's probable reaction to any direct threat to sterling that was linked to the sending of British troops to Vietnam is counterfactual and cannot be known, though the Wilson approach to government and dissent was entirely different to that of Attlee, as has been seen, being more inclined to compromise with the Labour left wing to remain in power, though he also wanted to cultivate the US and Johnson for the prestige such association offered him. An indication is that in the end Wilson did despite Johnson's displeasure withdraw from east of Suez for domestic political reasons.

Over the Korean War the nature of the diplomatic contact between Attlee and Bevin and Truman and Acheson was such that the UK government perceived that there was a threat to enhanced US support for NATO should Britain decline to commit troops to Korea and to sustain the high levels of defence expenditure that the war necessitated, and so complied with US requests for British troops to Korea even when the opportunity cost in terms of budget deficits and welfare spending was significant and when the domestic political consequences for the Attlee government were adverse. If Attlee had publicly declined to send British troops to Korea and publicised US insistence and the perceived threat to the security of western Europe the intended positive effect on US diplomacy and standing as guardian of the free world that was the objective of the US demand would have been replaced by a negative propaganda effect as the Korean War would have been seen to be an American anti-communist war rather than one of free nations protecting another free nation against communism under a United Nations mandate. Any British moral, diplomatic and political support would also have been discredited. And of course if there had not been sufficient US commitment to NATO and the defence of Europe the US would have found itself in the rather odd position of having abandoned what it accepted was the critical theatre of the war against Soviet expansionism and communism (that the US had defended at great expense in the very recent Berlin Crisis) to punish the one Western country upon which it could depend for diplomatic support because that country had declined to provide ground troops in what was conceived to be a theatre so peripheral to US interests that Acheson had given the press the impression just before the start of the Korean War that it was not within the domain of US security concerns in the Far East.

If the US had punished the UK government for not providing troops to Korea or for not continuing to commit itself to the high defence spending necessary because of the Korean War, by withholding an enhancement of the US commitment to NATO, such US action would not have helped the American military position in Korea at all, and no other nations would have joined US forces in Korea. The logical credibility of a threat of no enhancement to the US commitment to NATO does then have to be questioned. In terms of what was perceived by British politicians at the time of the Korean War the recent experience of US commitment to the western sectors of Berlin in 1948 and 1949 would have indicated both the extent of US resolve to resist Soviet expansionism and opportunism in Europe, which would have made the likelihood of diminished US commitment to NATO less credible, and the UK need for the US commitment to NATO for the defence of Europe.[107] Of course a rational reaction to what was seen to be a very adverse consequence would be avoidance even if its likelihood is low, and sometimes the perception of adverse consequences precludes rational consideration of their likelihood, so the reaction of the UK government to send troops to Korea under such a threat from the US seems comprehensible. The ensuing record is of reluctant compliance with US demands over Korea because of such a perception at the time on the part of British ministers and the British PM.

Over Vietnam Johnson seems to have taken the opposite view to that taken in the Truman administration, that is, he seems to have felt that the propaganda value of British moral and political support and refraining from criticism was worth maintaining and that any demand for British ground troops in Vietnam explicitly associated with US threats of withdrawal of support for sterling could have resulted in the British declining to send ground troops to Vietnam given Wilson's known problems with the left wing of the Labour Party and his known tendency to compromise to secure his position as PM, and the loss of the propaganda value of British moral and political endorsement of the US stance over Vietnam. It does seem that though for a time the Johnson administration believed that any action against sterling would result in adverse economic effects for the US, that belief was replaced by 1966 by one that prepared for the effects of a sterling devaluation rather than avoidance of such British devaluation. There does not then seem to have been US concern for the economy of the one country that could be depended upon for diplomatic support in the Cold War against communism even in Indo-China. In the event of course Johnson and the US administration did countenance a sterling devaluation that was in fact consequent upon the very maintenance of a strategic presence east of Suez upon which the US had insisted and which resulted in a decision to withdraw from east of Suez despite Johnson's protests. The 'special relationship' in Wilson's premiership permitted Wilson more latitude as there seems to have been acceptance that Wilson was doing all he could to support the US in Vietnam through his moral and diplomatic support and presentation of the US case to his own left wing.

The context was of course different, in that whereas the Korean intervention was endorsed by a UN Security Council resolution and did not attract popular resistance the US stance in Vietnam had no such UN legitimisation and did attract colossal opprobrium in the US and the Western world. And whereas in 1950, at the start of the Korean War, NATO had just been established, in the period of the escalation of US involvement in Vietnam NATO was the form of deterrence to Soviet expansionism in Europe and not one that could be abandoned in the Cold War context of the time if US credibility was to be maintained, the very reason for the US involvement in Vietnam.

Though perceptual and attitudinal factors were decisive in the decisions made by Attlee and Bevin over Korea and Wilson over Vietnam, the influence of the objective context of British economic and military weakness on its eventual foreign policy in the post-war period may be seen by taking a rather longer term perspective. For in the end there was an abandonment of empire in the East and in Africa, and even of a presence east of Suez despite US requests for the maintenance of such a presence. And in the economic sphere, despite US support in the form of a renegotiated loan and in support for the value of sterling, sterling was in the end devalued. Though it has been seen that Johnson did in fact in the end take the view that a sterling devaluation would not be that adverse in its effects on the US economy, and permitted sterling to devalue, even with US economic support for sterling and the ethos of Britain as a world, European and imperial power, it does seem that the costs of a Welfare State, an interventionist mixed economy, defence of the empire and maintenance of a presence east of Suez were in the end going to be impossible to sustain, not least in a context of low productivity, union power, outdated working practices and poor management.

In other words something had to give, and given the electoral salience of domestic policy and the commitment to the mixed economy and the Welfare State by both major political parties on ideological and electoral grounds it was bound to be Britain's overseas commitments. In the long run then, objective factors in the form of economic and military weakness and public expectations of government do seem to have become influences on those within the locus of foreign-policy decision-making power in the UK through experience of the adverse economic consequences of the ethos of commitment to empire and a presence east of Suez.

The indication is that though attitudinal and perceptual factors do intervene between objective context and decisions regarding foreign policy, over the longer term objective factors dictate a certain foreign policy through indications to those involved in foreign-policy decision-making of the consequences of disregarding the imperatives of the objective context. In the case of the British Empire and a British presence east of Suez it became clear that neither could be afforded even with US economic support in the form of the US loan, and withdrawal became imperative on economic grounds given the strain of defence expenditure on the budget and its opportunity cost in terms of domestic spending that was regarded as imperative for electoral reasons.

The adjustment of British foreign policy to the reality of economic weakness and 'imperial overstretch' through withdrawal from empire and from east of Suez, and a consequent turning towards Europe to compensate for economic weakness and to optimise diplomatic influence, does seem to have been reflective of an increasing realism that became more influential than attitudinal factors such as an ethos of world, European and imperial power status for the UK.

Even so there has been a lingering attachment on the part of politicians and PMs of both the major parties to the preservation of the Atlantic relationship even given its asymmetry, cost and the fact that the US loan has been repaid. That has resulted in involvement with the US in Iraq and Afghanistan at great human and economic cost and in military humiliation so difficult to disregard that it now seems that the US would prefer no commitment of ground troops from the UK, for in Basra and Helmand such troops could not cope, were not an advertisement of Western power, and did not enhance Western credibility. In the process of adjustment to economic and military decline that continues even now the Korean and Vietnam wars were instances of very different foreign policies, and the policy of Wilson in not sending troops to Vietnam has been vindicated by the adverse experience of ensuing troop commitments to support the US. For just what the UK has received in recent times in return for the high levels of defence expenditure and the foreign interventionism associated with the preservation of the 'special relationship' is difficult to identify. After all, other member nations of NATO receive just as much US protection and support as the UK does without the opportunity cost of such defence commitments.

The argument seems to have been that the UK exerts greater influence in world politics and on the US government as a consequence of the relationship with the US, though that rationale is impossible to verify by reference to specific instances that have conferred an identified advantage on the UK and seems to reflect the desire of PMs to be seen to be world statesmen or aversion to some perceived political risk associated with ending the special relationship with the US.

The above has been limited to a comparison of British foreign policy in relation to the Korean and Vietnam wars under the Attlee and Wilson premierships respectively (the latter until the end of the Johnson Presidency). It is though worth noting that the ensuing relationship between Wilson and Nixon was characterised by a similar ingratiation on Wilson's part and a similar desire to be the world statesman, including another offer of mediation. Nixon though does seem to have been entirely different to his predecessor, Johnson. In diplomatic style he was more urbane and circumspect than the often abrasive Johnson, and he had a grasp of foreign policy that was global rather than entirely concentrated on the crisis in Vietnam. Nixon noted the enhanced power of western Europe as a deterrent to the Soviet Union in Europe and wanted to cultivate relations with free western European countries while at the same time improving relations with the communist Chinese to exacerbate the split in the communist camp and to cultivate détente with China and then with the Soviet Union under threat of an alliance with the Chinese.

In that context Vietnam seems to have been less central to Nixon's foreign policy than it had been to that of Johnson, and by the time of the Nixon Presidency in early 1969 Britain's policy of withdrawal from east of Suez was known to be a settled policy. In fact Nixon's policy in Vietnam was to extricate the US from a conflict that the US was not winning on the ground and to do so without too much loss of credibility for US power through a policy of Vietnamisation of the war and by bringing the North Vietnamese to peace talks through bombing of North Vietnam. Nixon's diplomatic style and objectives in Vietnam and in terms of US foreign policy worldwide and Wilson's policy of withdrawal from east of Suez though remaining a moral supporter of the US purpose in Vietnam then combined to produce a more harmonious relationship between Wilson and Nixon and a situation in which the UK exerted no influence whatever on US foreign policy and in which British policy was not dissonant with US foreign-policy objectives. What had changed of course was the nature of the purposes of the US President and their becoming more conducive to acceptance of the British position on Vietnam.

Heath's government took a position on Vietnam that was not dissimilar to that of Wilson. In July 1970 Heath told Nixon of the support of the UK government for his foreign policy over Vietnam and even when there was very controversial US bombing of Hanoi and Haiphong Douglas-Home, the Foreign Secretary in the Heath government, defended the US bombing in the Commons. Of course Heath's position differed from that of Wilson in that he did not have to placate or endure the obloquy of left wingers in his own party. By the time Ford became President upon Nixon's resignation in 1974 the Paris Peace Accords had been agreed and by 15 August 1973 ninety-five per cent of US troops had left Vietnam. British approval of US foreign policy over Vietnam was no longer needed.

Notes

[1]See for example, Dumbrell, John, *A Special Relationship: Anglo-American Relations in the Cold War and After*, Macmillan, 2001, Baylis, John (ed.), *Anglo-American Relations Since 1939: The Enduring Alliance*, Manchester University Press, 1997, and Ellis, Sylvia, *Historical Dictionary of Anglo-American Relations*, Scarecrow Press, 2009, and Dobson, Alan, *Anglo-American Relations in the Twentieth Century: Of Friendship, Conflict and the Rise and Decline of the Superpowers*, Psychology Press, 1995, which take a longer perspective on Anglo-American Relations but include the Cold War period.

[2]For British policy and Anglo-American relations during the Korean War see Hennessey, Thomas, *Britain's Korean War: Cold War Diplomacy, Strategy and Security 1950–1953*, Manchester University Press, 2013, which is especially good on the documentation, and McLaine, Ian (ed.), *A Korean Conflict: The Tensions between Britain and America*, I.\B. Tauris, 2015. For the Vietnam War see Vickers, Rhiannon, *Harold Wilson, the British Labour Party, and the War in Vietnam, Journal of Cold War Studies*, Volume 10, No. 2, Spring 2008, Ellis, S., *Britain, America and the Vietnam War*, Praeger, London, 2004, Colman, Jonathan, *A 'special relationship'? Harold Wilson, Lyndon B. Johnson and Anglo-American relations 'at the summit'*, 1964–68, Manchester University Press, 2004, Dobson, Alan, 'The Years of Transition: Anglo-American relations, 1961–1967', *Review of International Studies*, Volume 16, No. 3, July 1990, pages 239–358, and Dumbrell, John, 'The Johnson administration and the British Labour Government: Vietnam, the Pound and East of Suez', *Journal of American Studies*, Volume 30, No. 2, 1996, pages. 211–37.

[3]See Dumbrell, *A Special Relationship*, op. cit., page 51, citing FO 371/76385, PUSC (51), 'Anglo-

American Relations: Present and Future', 24 August 1949, for the Foreign Office view that Britain should attempt to remain the 'principal ally' of the US to secure a worldwide role for the US and to optimise British influence on US policy and for FO concerns regarding the effect of diminished British power on the prospects for the maintenance of such a relationship.

[4]The US loan, renegotiated in late 1945 after Truman had summarily withdrawn the wartime loan, required free convertibility of sterling, and its adverse terms, which caused some limited controversy within the British Cabinet, exemplified the need for the loan if Britain were to maintain world-power status and overseas commitments, as Keynes made clear at the time. Further, in 1949 sterling was devalued, another indication of the extent of British need for US support for sterling.

[5]FO 371/ 84059, Foreign Office minute, 25 June 1950.

[6]FO 371/ 84058, Foreign Office minute, 26 June 1950.

[7]CAB 128/17, CM (50) 39, 27 June 1950.

[8]CAB 128/17, CM (50) 39, 27 June 1950.

[9]Gordon, Michael R., *Conflict and Consensus in Labour's Foreign Policy, 1914–1965*, Stanford University Press, 1969, page 226.

[10]See French, David, *Army, Empire and the Cold War: The British Army and Military Policy, 1945–1971*, OUP, 2012, pages 133 and 134, for reference to extensive documentary evidence of the CoS view that troops should not be committed to Korea because they were already committed elsewhere, of the CoS recommendation that the US should be supported over Korea by no more than a naval presence and of CoS concern that any diverting of troops to Korea would make it less possible to resist Soviet expansionism and opportunism in other theatres.

[11]See CAB 128/18, CM 43 (50), 6 July 1950.

[12]Beismer, Robert, *Dean Acheson: A Life in the Cold War*, OUP USA, 2009, page 345.

[13]See Hopkins, Michael F., *Oliver Franks and the Truman Administration: Anglo-American Relations, 1948–1952*, Routledge, 2004, pages 168 and 169 for the influence of Franks, and see CAB 128/18, CM 50 (50), 25 July 1950 for Attlee's representation to Cabinet. See also Hennessey, *Britain's Korean War*, op. cit., pages 48–52.

[14]See McLaine, *A Korean Conflict*, op. cit., for reference to Acheson's instruction to Douglas to see Attlee to get him to expedite the sending of British troops to Korea 'at once'. By 10 August the CoS advice had changed, and endorsed sending British troops from Hong Kong to Korea to support the US there.

[15]See CAB 128/18, CM (50) 50, Cabinet Conclusions, 25 July 1950, and CM (53) 50, Cabinet Conclusions, 11 August 1950.

[16]See Garner, Robert, and Kelly, Richard N., *British Political Parties Today*, MUP, 1993, page 143, for the view that 'during the 1945–51 Labour Governments, the Left's voice was muted' and that the main conflict came over Korean War expenditure and its concomitant of introduction of NHS charges.

[17]See CAB 128/18, CM (73) 50, and CM (76) 50, Cabinet Conclusions, 13 November and 20 November 1950.

[18]See Cotton, James, and Neary, Ian (eds.), *The Korean War in History*, Manchester University Press, 1989, page 88.

[19]FO 371/83018, Foreign Office minute, 8 December 1950.

[20]CAB 128/18, 78 (50), 29 November 1950.

[21]See Beisner, Robert, *Dean Acheson: A Life in the Cold War*, OUP USA, 2009, page 420. See page 354 for evidence of Acheson's irritation with Bevin's recommendation that there should be some compromise or concessions to communist China over Korea, and page 418 for his having to control Truman's desire to punish the Chinese, and his pursuing a policy that would avoid escalation without concessions to the Soviet Union or the communist Chinese, very much the Truman Doctrine policy of containment as a form of deterrence.

[22]See Cotton, James, and Neary, Ian (eds.), *The Korean War in History*, Manchester University Press, 1989, pages 81 and 82 for reference to Slessor's adverse view of US action north of the 38th parallel, of the dangers of Chinese intervention in Korea, and of the freedom MacArthur seemed to enjoy over Korea.

[23]FO 371/84121, Foreign Office minute, 28 November 1950.

[24]See Cotton, Neary, *The Korean War*, op. cit., page 88, for Acheson's linking US support for Europe to British support in Korea, and to a need for enhanced British commitment to defence and with the US to NATO, and PREM 8/1438, Acheson to Bevin, 8 January 1951.

[25]See Hennessey, *Britain's Korean War*, op. cit., page 139, for the FO recommendation.

[26]Vickers, Rhiannan, *The Labour Party and the World Volume 2: Labour's Foreign Policy Since 1951*, OUP, 2011, page 30.

[27]See Younger, Sir Kenneth Gilmour, and Geoffrey Warner, *In the Midst of Greats: The Foreign Office Diaries and Papers of Kenneth Younger, February 1950–October 1951*, Psychology Press, 2005, page 12, for reference in Younger's diary entry as early as 8 April 1950 to Bevin's being 'unwell' and to concern as to how long Bevin could or should continue as Foreign Secretary, despite his 'grip on the realities in most respects'. Younger was Minister of State at the Foreign Office and deputised for Bevin when he was unwell. See also Radice, Giles, *Odd Couples: The Great Political Pairings of Modern Britain*, I. B. Tauris, 2015, page 79, for reference to Bevin's having been unwell for months before his resignation on 9 March 1951 and to Attlee's having had 'often to stand in as an unofficial foreign secretary', and page 78 for Acheson's seeing Bevin in London in the spring of 1950. Acheson was shocked by Bevin's condition, and noted that he was in 'distressing shape' and would 'doze off quite soundly during the discussion'.

[28]CAB 128/19, CM (51) 25th meeting, 9 April 1951.

[29]Gordon, *Conflict and Consensus*, page 138.

[30]Ibid., page 97.

[31]Bevan, A., 'Clem Attlee', *Tribune*, 16 December 1955.

[32]Burridge, T, *Clement Attlee, A Political Biography*, Jonathan Cape, London, 1985, page 3.

[33]Ibid., page 316. See also Thomas-Symonds, Niklaus, *Attlee: A Life in Politics*, I. B. Tauris, 2012, for reference to the view of Arthur Moyle, who was to become Attlee's PPS, that Attlee was 'without affectation of any kind' and had an 'unassuming integrity' and to the reference in *The Times* on 28 July 1945, as Attlee assumed power, to Attlee's 'disinterested service to his party' and 'high conception of public duty'. And see Jago, Michael, *Clement Attlee: The Inevitable Prime Minister*, Biteback Publishing, 2014, for reference to Attlee's 'retiring manner and the more charismatic style of his senior colleagues', referring it seems to Bevin, Cripps, Dalton and Morrison.

[34]Attlee, C., 'What sort of man gets to the top?' This source on its own lacks credibility, as it may well be one that is not contemporaneous with Attlee's own premiership and so be rhetorical in nature. But taken with evidence of Attlee's nonchalant reaction to Morrison's claim that Bevin wanted Attlee's job when he was premier (which took place while Morrison was in the room with Attlee) and Attlee's reaction to Bevan's threat of resignation outlined above, it does seem clear that Attlee was truly indifferent to the loss of the job of premier if a better candidate could be found. And it is clear that he was not prepared to be swayed on British foreign policy by influence from ministers.

[35]Burridge, op. cit., page 191.

[36]Williams, Francis, *A Prime Minister remembers*, Heinemann, 1961, pages 90 and 91.

[37]See CAB 128/23, Cabinet Conclusions 14 (51), 4 December 1951, and CAB 128/23, Cabinet Conclusions 16 (51), 11 December 1951.

[38]See Hennessey, *Britain's Korean War*, op. cit., pages 3 and 280–83. In any event the purpose here has been to address the influences on British foreign policy over the Korean War rather than to assess the influence of British policy on US policy.

[39]FO 371/179558, AU 1015/18, Lord Harlech's Valedictory Despatch, 15 March 1965.

[40]See Hennessey, *Britain's Korean War*, op. cit., pages 280 and 281 for attribution of some influence on US policy over Korea to the British government, though the evidence produced does not seem to indicate any significant British influence on US policy, and for reference to a historiography that attributes very little influence on US policy over Korea to Britain.

[41]Colman, *A 'special relationship'?*, op. cit., page 87.

[42]Ellis, Britain, *America and the Vietnam War*, op. cit., page 267.

[43]See Vickers, *Harold Wilson*, op. cit., page 41.

[44]Morgan, Austen, *Harold Wilson*, Pluto, London, 1992, page ix.

[45]Pimlott, B., *Harold Wilson*, Harper Collins, London, 1992, pages 562–63. There does not seem to be any persuasive evidence of attachment to political principle in Wilson. See Ellis, *Britain, America and the Vietnam War*, op. cit., page 10 for reference to 'most recent scholarship' 'ascribing no particular political philosophy' to Wilson and reference to Wilson as 'pragmatic' though with 'delusions of grandeur when it came to his international role'.

[46]Ellis, *Britain, America and the Vietnam War*, op. cit., page 10.

[47]Colman, *A 'special relationship'?*, op. cit., page 11.

[48]See Colman, *A 'special relationship'?*, op. cit., page 178 for reference to US support for sterling in November 1964, September 1965 and July 1966.

[49]Colman, *A 'special relationship'?*, op. cit., pages 38 and 41.

[50]CAB 133/266, 'Meeting held at the British Embassy…And later at the White House, on 7 December at 3.30 p.m.'

[51]See Dorey, Peter (ed.), *The Labour Governments 1964–1970*, Routledge, 2006, page 132, citing PREM 13/104, The Prime Minister to the First Secretary of State, 9 December 1964, and CAB 128/39, CM (64) 14th Conclusions, 11 December 1964.

[52]Foreign Relations of the United States 1964–1968, Volume II, *Vietnam: January–June 1965*, pages 229–32.

[53]See CAB 128/39, CM (65) 9th Conclusions, 11 February 1965 for Wilson's misrepresentation of the nature of the telephone call with Johnson.

[54]See Smith, Simon C. (ed.), *The Wilson-Johnson Correspondence, 1964–69*, Routledge, 2015, pages 1–8.

[55]FO 371/179574, AU 1051/35/G, 'The present United States-United Kingdom relationship', 12 August 1965.

[56]Colman, *A 'special relationship'?*, op. cit., page 77.

[57]PREM 13/304, Gordon Walker's report of tour of SE Asia, 14 April–4 May 1965.

[58]See Colman, *A 'special relationship'?*, op. cit., page 167, for reference to a 'secret deal' between the US and Britain, involving an exchange of US support for sterling for British maintenance of an 'international role'. See Ellis, *Britain, America and the Vietnam War*, op. cit., page 270, for reference to Bundy, McNamara and Rusk all being 'tempted' to relate US support for sterling to British troops being sent to Vietnam. The result was exhaustive discussions as to the relationship between sterling and defence, which US representatives felt were intimately linked and which British politicians and officials resisted. There was also a sense that the US had some interest in ensuring that sterling should not be devalued.

[59]Bundy to Johnson, 3 June 1965, Foreign Relations of the United States 1964–1968, Volume II, *Vietnam, January–June 1965*, pages 716–17.

[60]Bundy to Johnson, 22 March 1965, FRUS 1964–1968, Vol. II, pages 468–69.

[61]See Dockrill, S., *Britain's retreat From East of Suez: The Choice between Europe and the World?*, Springer, 2002, pages 115 to 117 for a detailed exposition of the extent of sterling's dependence on US economic support and of British understanding of the link with maintenance of British commitments to troops in Germany and to a presence east of Suez.

[62]Colman, *A 'special relationship'?*, op. cit., page 174.

[63]See Ellis, *Britain, America and the Vietnam War*, op. cit., page 276.

[64]Colman, *A 'special relationship'?*, op. cit., page 171.

[65]Colman, *A 'special relationship'?*, op. cit., page 53.

[66]See Hughes, Geraint, *Harold Wilson's Cold War: The Labour Government and East-West Politics, 1964–1970*, Boydell & Brewer Ltd., 2015, page 2 for this characteristic of Wilson as popularly conceived and for reference to Wilson's belief that he could act as intermediary between the Soviet Union and Johnson as US President.

[67]Pimlott, *Wilson*, page 389. See also Hughes, *Harold Wilson*, op. cit., page 2 for reference to the view that Wilson was a 'shallow opportunist'.

[68]See Ellis, *Britain, America and the Vietnam War*, op. cit., page 272 for reference to her claim that two understandings emerged between Britain and the US, that Britain would provide public support for the US in Vietnam in return for US support for British peace initiatives over Vietnam, and that Britain would maintain a presence east of Suez in return for US support for sterling.

[69]PREM 13/1196, Prime Minister to President, 9 February, 1966.

[70]Castle, Barbara, *The Barbara Castle Diaries 1964–76*, Papermac, London, 1990, page 52, entry for 3 February 1966.

[71]CAB 128/41, CM (66) 5th Conclusions, 3 February 1966.

[72]Such ignorance of foreign policy and its imperatives seems characteristic of the British system, with the PM and Foreign Secretary deriving power in Cabinet from it. The case of Attlee and Bevin makes this clear, as does the earlier case of Chamberlain and Halifax.

[73]Bruce to State, 11 July 1966, in Colman, *A 'special relationship'?*, op. cit., page 108.

[74]Pham, P. L., *Ending 'East of Suez': The British Decision to Withdraw from Malaysia and Singapore 1964–1968*. OUP, 2010, page xxxi.

[75]See Petersen, Tore T. (ed.), *Challenging Retrenchment: The United States, Great Britain and the Middle East 1950–1980*, Tapir Academic Press, 2010, page 28.

[76]See Dorey, *The Labour Governments*, op. cit., page 133, citing PREM 13/1262, Patrick Dean to C. M. MacLehose, Foreign Office, 6 August 1966.

[77]See Ellis, *Britain, America and the Vietnam War*, op. cit., page 275.

[78]See CAB 128/42, CC (67) 16th Conclusions, 4 April 1967, for reference to defence studies that assumed cutting by half British forces in Singapore and Malaysia by 1970–71, and for Healey's indication to Cabinet of a need for a greater withdrawal from overseas commitments to achieve needed defence cuts, with reference to more savings if there were a 'firm plan to withdraw our forces from Singapore and Malaysia no later than 1975–76', which would have meant withdrawal from east of Suez by that date and have left a minimal military presence in Australia. Healey did counsel a need to consult the US, New Zealand, Australia, Singapore and Malaysia before proceeding with such a withdrawal from east of Suez.

[79]Pimlott, *Wilson*, page 476.

[80]CAB 128/42, CC (67) 66th Conclusions, 16 November 1967.

[81]See Pham, *East of Suez*, op. cit., pages 204 and 205.

[82]PREM 13/1447, Wilson to Johnson, 17 November 1967. Healey confirmed to McNamara that there would be no change to British policy East of Suez.

[83]Though public expenditure cuts did not address the root causes of the UK's recurring balance of payments deficits and sterling crises, the endemic uncompetitiveness of British business that reflected poor management, long-term underinvestment and Trade Union power that resisted necessary changes in working practices and demanded wage settlements in excess of productivity increases and were as a consequence inflationary, Jenkins's deflationary fiscal policy did indicate government resolve to control inflation to preclude balance of payments and sterling crises, though of course devaluation was itself inflationary in that it raised the cost of necessary imports to the UK and so exacerbated the cost-push inflation of Trade Union power and inflationary wage settlements. The UK's endemic inflation and uncompetitiveness were not to be resolved until the Thatcher premiership with its resort to the blunter instrument of monetary policy to deflate the economy, legal controls on Trade Union power and perseverance to break its basis in strike action, tolerance of high unemployment, and letting the free market decide what businesses survived as the public sector was reduced by privatisation and government support was withdrawn.

[84]See Honeyman, Victoria, *Richard Crossman: Pioneer of Welfare Provision and Labour Politics in Post-War Britain*, I. B. Tauris, 2007, page 119, referring to Crossman's diary entry for 1 April 1965. Though Crossman might be seen to be just one source, and one whose impartiality could be challenged, on the nature and dynamics of the Wilson administration of 1964, there is evidence that Wilson himself later understood that his first term as PM had been rather more Prime Ministerial in style than it might have

been. See Donoughue, Bernard, *Prime Minister: the Conduct of Policy under Harold Wilson and James Callaghan*, Cape, 1987, page 15 for Donoghue's view that Wilson was 'anxious not to repeat the 'presidential' experience of 1964'.

[85]PREM 13/1446, Palliser to Broadbent, 20 December 1967.

[86]PREM 13/ 3551, Dean to Foreign Office, telegram No. 3, 1 January 1968.

[87]Pham, *East of Suez*, op. cit., page xxi.

[88]CAB 128/43, CC (68) 1st Conclusions, 4 January 1968.

[89]Brown-Rusk conversation, 11 January 1968, FRUS1964–1968, Volume XII, pages 603–5.

[90]See Dockrill, *Britain's retreat From East of Suez*, op. cit., page 207, and CAB 128/43, CC (68) 7th Conclusions, 15 January 1968.

[91]See Johnson to Wilson, 11 and 15 January 1968, FRUS 1964–1968, Volume XII, pages 608–9 and 609–11. See also Wilson to Johnson, 15 January 1968, FRUS 1964–68, Volume XII, pages 611–14.

[92]See Dockrill, *East of Suez*, page 207.

[93]See Pham, *Ending 'East of Suez'*, op. cit., pages 519–21.

[94]FCO 7/741, AU1/4, Dean to Gore-Booth, 2 February 1968. See also Smith, *The Wilson-Johnson Correspondence*, op. cit., pages 7 and 8, for reference to the view of Clark Clifford, the US Defense Secretary, following the British decision to withdraw from east of Suez, that Britain was no longer of any use to the US in 'any big world problem' as 'they cannot afford the cost of an adequate defense effort', and for reference to the feeling in the FO that the east of Suez decision alienated many Americans and elicited resentment at British failure to support US efforts to contain communism especially over China and Vietnam and that the US administration felt only contempt for British economic difficulties. And see Colman, *A 'special relationship'?*, op. cit., page 168 for Colman's reference to a fundamental change in the relationship between the US and Britain between 1964 and 1968 predicated upon altered US administration assessments of British utility to US purposes, which Colman attributes to Britain's endemic economic weakness, overvaluation of sterling and need for retrenchment from its world role resulting in a British withdrawal from such a role, not least from east of Suez, and a consequent diminution of the Atlantic relationship – he attributes less influence on the change to Wilson's policy of moral without military support for the US in Vietnam and to Wilson's dissociation from US bombing of North Vietnam.

[95]See Smith, Simon C., 'Anglo-American Relations and the end of empire in the Far East and the Persian Gulf, 1948–1971', in Petersen, *Challenging Retrenchment*, op. cit., page 27.

[96]For reference to the circumstances of 1966 and 1967 see *The Campaign Guide: The Unique Political Reference Book*, Conservative and Unionist Central Office, 1970, page 688, and Young, John W., *The Labour Government's 1964–1970 International Policy*, MUP, 2003, page 79.

[97]See Colman, *A 'special 'relationship'?*, op. cit., page 171 for reference to FO support for Wilson's cultivation of the relationship with the US and for the commitment east of Suez.

[98]Crossman, Richard, *The Diaries of a Cabinet Minister, Volume II, Lord President of the Council and Leader of the House of Commons, 1966–68*. Hamish Hamilton, London, 1976, page 181, entry for 1 January 1967.

[99]Colman, *A 'special relationship'?*, op. cit., page 172.

[100]See Vickers, *Harold Wilson*, op. cit., page 47. Vickers also notes that the Wilson government did provide napalm and bombs to the US in Vietnam despite Wilson's denials in the Commons, and that other British aid to the US in Vietnam included military training of South Vietnamese in Malaysia, signals information from Hong Kong, medical aid and advisers.

[101]See for instance Pimlott, *Wilson*, page 388.

[102]Ibid., pages 388 and 389.

[103]See Pearce, Robert, and Goodlad, Graham, *British Prime Ministers From Balfour to Brown*, Routledge, 2013, pages 190 and 191 for Donoghue's views, and Hughes, *Harold Wilson's Cold War*, op. cit., page 2.

[104]When personal inclination and contextual influences tend in the direction of the same policy it is impossible to assess the influence of either on policy. In June 1950 for instance Attlee experienced no

Labour dissent over committing British troops to Korea, and the decision to do so despite reservations as to cost and imperial overstretch in the context of the Malayan emergency (and a sense that Korea was in the US sphere of interest) reflected Attlee's own commitment to the US and the 'special relationship'. In 1951 the threatened resignation of Bevan and Wilson over war expenditure and its effect on that for the NHS provided a clearer case of the influence of Attlee's own attributes on British foreign policy over Korea. In the case of Wilson the shifting nature of his compromises between the demands of the Labour Party and the US reflected his compromising nature and desire to remain in power and a world statesman. Attlee then seems the conviction politician, Wilson the careerist.

[105]Stewart later recalled that 'human liberty' was a major issue for him over the Vietnam War, which would indicate that he and Wilson shared a genuine commonality of attitude and policy over British policy over Vietnam, that is, approval of the endeavour while entertaining reservations regarding the means and not committing British troops. Stewart does however seem to have followed Wilson's direction while in the US to protest against US use of napalm. It is possible Stewart's memoir reflects a desire to justify his position after the fact, that is, after compliance with but no belief in Wilson's policy of moral but no material support and approval of the ends but not necessarily the means of US involvement in Vietnam. See also Embassy to State, 16 October 1964, *Foreign Relations of the United States 1964–1968, Volume XII, Western Europe*, pages 464–67 for Bruce's view that Wilson would dominate both domestic and foreign policy in the new government, though this represents the US Ambassador's anticipation and view of Wilson's ministers rather than evidencing the actuality of the Wilson Cabinet.

[106]See Hennessey, *Britain's Korean War*, op. cit., pages 281 and 282 for reference to Eisenhower's being more averse to concessions to the British point of view than Truman, pages 137 to 140 and 280 for Younger's having argued for a British foreign policy more independent of that of the US over condemnation of China as an aggressor at the UN and in more general terms, and page 282 for Morrison's having been more accepting of US bombing when he replaced Bevin as Foreign Secretary, though as has been indicated Attlee's influence on Truman in terms of actual US policy was minimal, and Younger, though as Minister of State at the Foreign Office who deputised for Bevin when the latter was unwell and so part of the debate over British policy over Korea, not least in regard to condemnation of China at the UN, was far less influential on British policy over Korea than Attlee, who took over the running of policy on Korea from Bevin when Bevin was unwell and after he had to leave office due to poor health. In an indication of that Younger's preference for more independence from the US was not the policy pursued. Though Hennessey claims that Younger's influence following Bevin's departure resulted in Britain's coming nearer to a 'break' with the US over condemnation of China as an aggressor at the UN and that US concessions averted an open breach between Britain and the US, the evidence of November 1950 indicates that Attlee understood that there could be no break with the US because of the need for US support for Europe (see Hennessey, pages 280 and 281). Though the influence of individuals and their perceptions is then established, the influence of individual relationships between Britain and the US can then be overstated, as the asymmetry of power seems to have been the fundamental influence on the direction and extent of influence between Britain and the US over Korea. See page 281 for Hennessey's acknowledgement that 'Anglo-American interdependence' 'ultimately' 'depended on American sufferance of British views'.

[107]In the event Congress approved the enhanced military commitment to NATO on 4 April 1951, in the form of US troops in Europe, though even after that time the policy of the Attlee government remained unaltered, conforming to the dictates of the Truman administration while attempting to moderate what were perceived to be the more extreme and risky aspects of US policy towards Korea, not least the dangers of escalation through provocation of the Chinese. Such evidence indicates that the Attlee government was concerned to preserve the relationship with the US in more general terms than those confined to the defence of Europe, though it could be argued that the Attlee government believed that US commitment to the defence of Europe could be withdrawn in the event of lack of UK support for the US over Korea.

Chapter Seven
Conclusion

THOUGH I SHALL not reiterate the detailed conclusions of each case study some general inferences may be drawn regarding the influences on foreign-policy decision-making in the British system. The indication from the case studies is that the locus of foreign-policy decision-making power and the nature of influence reflect different combinations of attitudinal, perceptual and objective causal factors in the different cases.

Chamberlain's dominance of Cabinet and of foreign policy prior to the issue of negotiations for an alliance with the Soviet Union in 1939 reflected his liberal use of the powers and prerogatives of the PM, his personal conceit and deviousness in dealing with Cabinet, and the lack of a senior minister with significant standing in the Conservative Party around whom dissent could gather because Halifax, who had such attributes, was not prepared to defy Chamberlain. Even so, over the issue of entering into negotiations with the Soviet Union for an alliance there emerged within Cabinet an ultimately irresistible insistence that talks should start, despite Chamberlain's opposition, a reflection of the influence of senior ministers who together seem to have persuaded ministerial colleagues to their view over a period of time even with so dominant a PM, albeit one diminished in credibility by the public failure of his policy of appeasement of Germany and his reluctant acceptance of deterrence in the guarantee to Poland.

When Halifax as Foreign Secretary became convinced as to the need to enter into negotiations for an alliance with the Soviet Union Chamberlain was left with no choice but to acquiesce given his isolation in Cabinet. Had Halifax been less susceptible to endorsing what he conceived to be the majority view Chamberlain might have prevailed given his standing as PM even with a dissenting majority in Cabinet, an indication of the influence of the attributes of individuals in certain roles. The FO seems to have had no influence on the course of British policy over the negotiations with the Soviet Union in 1939, not least because of Chamberlain's contempt for the FO, though it does seem possible that Halifax was influenced by Cadogan in his ultimate abandonment of belief in the worth of any Anglo-Soviet alliance on 4 July 1939, and Halifax does seem to have been influenced by the CoS warning of the possibility of a pact between the Soviet Union and Germany when he joined other ministers in insisting that talks should start on 24 May 1939. The argument here has been that the end of the talks reflected British experience of the form and content of Soviet diplomacy and the mistrust it elicited rather than the influence of changing dynamics within Cabinet, of Chamberlain's continuing influence in Cabinet or of pre-existing British political and official elite aversion for the Soviet Union as a state and for communism. What emerged was a commonality within the British political and official elite that represented a rational response to very adverse diplomatic experience, an example of a change in foreign policy directly attributable to external influence in the form of Soviet diplomacy, in that it has been argued that any government, regardless of its attitudes to the Soviet Union and to communism, would have come to believe as the British government did that any alliance with the Soviet Union would be worthless because the Soviet Union could not be trusted.

The wartime case studies indicate the power of the PM in time of war when there is no credible alternative to him as wartime PM even when he is unpopular with some of his party, as was so with Churchill for some of the war. Churchill's dominance was aided by his acquiescent Foreign Secretary Eden's indecisive personality and sense of Prime Ministerial prerogatives in regard to foreign policy, by Eden's uncertainty over the future of Germany and by the lack of a senior minister around whom dissent could form, by Churchill's own sense of Prime Ministerial powers and prerogatives and right to use them, and by Churchill's confidence as war premier. Neither Churchill nor Eden seems to have been influenced by the extraordinary effort to devise an optimal policy over the Baltics or the future of Germany on the part of the FO, or by the extended debate between the FO and the CoS over the future of Germany, over which CoS views advocating the dismemberment of Germany were disregarded, and British foreign policy was under Churchill oriented to optimising the war effort through maintaining the wartime alliance. The role of external influences is indicated in Churchill's sense of the need to maintain the wartime alliance at all costs and to acquiesce in or to defer controversial foreign policy decisions to that end, though while Churchill's concern that the Soviet Union or the US could be alienated and proffer less support for the wartime alliance was predicated upon a realistic appreciation of British relative weakness in economic and military terms and of the need for the Soviet Union and the US to win the war, his perception of the risk of either country abandoning the alliance and his policy of unconditional surrender may not have been shared by another PM.

The Berlin Crisis indicates the power of a Foreign Secretary of extraordinary personal qualities with a PM who is not domineering and with whom there is a commonality of attitude and objective. There was also a commonality of objective with the rest of the Labour Party and the FO over policy in Berlin and Bevin's early dynamism in indicating intention to stay in Berlin was, with his stature with the Americans, influential in the US decision to support the western sectors of Berlin and break the blockade. The influence of the Soviet Union on British policy is obvious in their brinkmanship over Berlin, and that of the US is apparent in the economic and military dependence of the UK on the US that resulted in Bevin's understanding of the need to negotiate a balance between attempts at influence on US policy and the need to accept parts of it regardless of his own policy preferences.

The Suez Crisis is another indication of the influence of the PM's personal attributes on foreign policy. Though Eden came to the premiership after long experience of its powers and prerogatives under Churchill as PM, not least over foreign policy, and had a desire to be seen to be decisive as PM, he seems to have been as uncertain and indecisive in the early phase of the crisis as he had been as Foreign Secretary during and after the war, though he does seem to have had a clear understanding of the *Realpolitik* need for US support over Suez and undertook a series of diplomatic attempts to resolve the crisis without resort to force to comply with US wishes. Eden's indecisive and uncertain personality does though seem to have rendered him susceptible to the hawkish advocacy of the more certain and confident Macmillan, who though a senior minister with influence in the Conservative Party was Chancellor of the Exchequer and so had a brief only tangentially connected to foreign policy through expenditure, and the medicine Eden was taking because of his poor health seems to have been an influence on his abandoning his customary caution and preference for the exhaustion of diplomatic possibilities in favour of secret talks with the French and Israelis to derive a pretext for a military intervention in Suez, in that the medicine seemed to alter fundamentally Eden's perception of or attitude to risk. The FO and the Foreign Secretary seem to have exerted no influence on policy over Suez, despite Eden's own experience at the Foreign Office, the inference being that Eden believed in the powers and prerogatives of the PM over foreign policy. And the CoS were disregarded in the initial decision to prepare for the use of force over Suez, though the time taken to prepare a military intervention does seem to have been an influence in giving time for diplomatic attempts to resolve the crisis. What would have happened had the CoS indicated preparedness to engage in a military invasion of Suez when the crisis started is counterfactual and so cannot be known, though Eden's indecision and diplomatic caution would be expected to have been an influence, as would Macmillan's hawkishness. The influence of Eden's understanding of the need for US moral support and understanding at least is apparent in the earlier stages of the crisis, in the many diplomatic attempts to resolve it, and of the effects of misunderstanding US policy and the will to use US power in the denouement.

The comparison between the policies of the Attlee and Wilson administrations over Korea and Vietnam is another indication of the centrality of the attributes of the PM in British foreign-policy decision-making. For whereas Attlee was immune to threats of resignations by Cabinet ministers, even influential ones with standing in the Party such as Bevan, and indifferent to being replaced as Labour leader and PM, Wilson was concerned to remain in power and to enhance his standing as a world statesman by cultivating Johnson though at the same time providing only moral and no materiel support for the US in Vietnam to placate the Labour left wing. For Attlee his perception that to optimise US support for NATO Britain had to send troops to Korea to support the US there was decisive, in that his primary concern was to maintain the Atlantic relationship to optimise US defence of western Europe and Britain itself. For Wilson there seems to have been no threat, perceived or actual, to US commitment to NATO, and for some time no threat to sterling either, it seems because Johnson did not want to be seen to be coercing Britain into sending troops to Vietnam as the propaganda effect would then have been negated. Even so, when Johnson did protest over Britain's withdrawal from east of Suez far earlier than expected, Wilson enacted the changed policy to ensure his own political survival despite Johnson's displeasure. Wilson's tendency to compromise was then an enduring characteristic, and the nature of the compromise reflected the competing pressures he was under and his view of the optimal policy for his own political survival.

Over Korea the FO, though primarily concerned with the defence of British interests, shared Bevin's concern to resist Soviet expansionism on a case-by-case basis, to retain the relationship with the US for reasons of defence and to confine the war to Korea without escalation or provocation of communist China and without any US resort to the bomb. The consonance of view between Bevin and the FO of the Berlin Crisis seems to have continued through the period of Bevin's tenure during the Korean War, including reluctant acceptance of US demands over condemnation at the UN of communist China as an aggressor. CoS advice against commitment of ground troops to Korea on the basis that British forces were already committed to the defence of Europe and in Malaya was disregarded by Attlee and Bevin in July 1950, when Attlee told Cabinet of the political need to commit troops despite the military case against such commitment. Having said that CoS concerns regarding the escalation of the war, US use of the bomb, US provocation of the Chinese, Chinese intervention in Korea and MacArthur's freedom of decision in Korea were all areas of broad commonality with the rest of the political and official establishment. The FO seems to have exerted no influence on Wilson over Vietnam, for though the FO and Wilson concurred over a policy of moral without military support for the US over Vietnam Wilson disregarded the FO view in his decision to withdraw from east of Suez, indicating that the earlier concurrence reflected Wilson's desire to mollify the Labour Party rather than FO influence. The CoS endorsed Wilson's proposal to withdraw from east of Suez, though Wilson's decision seems to have been the consequence of Treasury, ministerial and Party influence rather than the CoS view. The influence of the US seems to have been more direct and compelling in the Korean case because of the perceptions and lack of aspiration to remain in post at all costs of Attlee as PM and Bevin as Foreign Secretary. In the Vietnam case Wilson balanced the demands of Johnson and the Labour Party to optimise his chances of political survival and was aided by Johnson's refraining from any threat to sterling for some time.

The case studies indicate a number of characteristics of foreign-policy decision-making in the British political system. To begin with there are the powers of the Prime Minister, of appointment and dismissal of ministers, control of the Cabinet agenda and presentation to Cabinet of the issue to be decided upon, possession of information not accessible to many ministers (though the Foreign Secretary would be privy to most information the PM has), the chairing of or appointment of chairs to influential Cabinet committees, the power of summing up Cabinet discussions and the right to engage in unilateral foreign-policy diplomatic overtures. The Prime Minister's extent of interest in foreign policy and attitudes towards foreign policy issues, the Prime Minister's attitudes to the premiership and its powers and preparedness to use them, the Prime Ministerial sense of self, of personal competence in regard to foreign policy and attitude to Cabinet government and to the views of dissenting ministers, are all then influences on the locus of foreign-policy decision-making in the British system, as is the influence of the PM's personality on his relationships in terms of susceptibility to influence and preparedness to consider dissenting ministerial contributions and assess all possible policies before deciding upon a policy. The contrast between Baldwin, ageing, compromising and interested primarily in domestic policy, and Chamberlain, whose interest in foreign policy was profound and whose conceit resulted in his conviction in his own diplomatic prowess and understanding of foreign policy and in disregard and derogation of dissent, is indicative of the influence of the attributes of the Prime Minister on the locus of foreign-policy decision-making in the British system. The case of Eden with his poor health, volatile personality and medicinal use is indicative of the effect of other Prime Ministerial attributes on foreign policy.

The Foreign Secretary and the PM are privy to information other ministers do not have and may form an axis that dominates foreign-policy decision-making through control of presentation of the issue, though other Cabinet ministers may exert influence on foreign policy by virtue of their seniority, popularity in the Party, personality and relationships. That seems to have been so with Macmillan and his influence on Eden and Cabinet during the Suez Crisis. Though such influence from individual ministers on the PM would depend upon the PM's personality and susceptibility to influence, where there is time for senior ministers to form a dissenting view on an issue and persuade other ministers to their view through a period of discussion it does seem possible for a Prime Minister's wishes to be defied by Cabinet and for a PM to have to choose between resignation and surrender to ministerial wishes, as was so for Chamberlain over entering into negotiations for an Anglo-Soviet alliance in 1939.

The Foreign Office and the CoS may exert influence on the Foreign Secretary or the PM if there is preparedness to listen to their expertise rather than devise foreign policy on the basis of personal confidence and sense of political prerogatives. That seems to depend upon circumstance, the personalities of the PM and the Foreign Secretary, and the extent of consonance of view between the PM or Foreign Secretary and the FO or CoS. Halifax for instance does seem to have been influenced in 1939 by Cadogan at the FO and by the CoS, whereas Attlee and Bevin disregarded CoS advice in committing troops to Korea in 1950. The Commons in a first-past-the-post system with discipline imposed by government whips would be expected to exert little influence on foreign policy, though over the Vietnam War Wilson found it necessary to find a compromise between the demands of an undisciplined Labour Party and those of Johnson to optimise his outcomes. In the other cases studied there seems to have been little influence from the Commons.

The preceding paragraphs have addressed the locus of foreign-policy decision-making in each of the case studies and have indicated the reasons for the locus of foreign-policy decision-making power found in each study by reference to the nature of the British political system and the specific circumstances of, and the characteristics of individuals involved in, each case study. That has identified the individuals in the British political and official establishment whose personalities, relationships, perceptions, attitudes and foreign-policy objectives influenced British foreign policy in each case study. I now turn to the influence of the attitudes and perceptions of such individuals on the nature of the foreign policy that emerged from the decision-making process, and the relationship between their attitudes and perceptions and the external environment of international politics, asymmetries of power and actual and perceived threats. In what follows the centrality of attitudinal orientation and perception to decision-making shall be indicated, in that the external environment only becomes an influence on foreign-policy decision-making through the attitudinal prism that informs objectives and the lens of perception that so influences understanding of the various policy options and their consequences.

The experience of 1939 seems to have been in a world in which the Cabinet accepted Chamberlain's view that the US could not be trusted in an alliance against Germany and that it was not needed to contain Hitler, despite Eden's advocacy of the cultivation of alliances and of good relations with Roosevelt. And at the end of the negotiations for an alliance with the Soviet Union in 1939 there seems to have been an indifference towards the Soviet Union as a country seen to be of little if any use as an ally and no compelling threat as a potential adversary, a view that seems odd given that just months earlier anti-communist and anti-Soviet ministers had become so convinced of the necessity of an Anglo-Soviet alliance to contain Hitler, not least to preclude the possibility of a pact between the Soviet Union and Germany, that they had been prepared to negotiate with the Soviet Union despite personal aversion and to make a series of significant concessions to the Soviet Union to achieve an alliance. The inference is that by the late summer of 1939 the British view was that any Anglo-Soviet alliance would be worth very little because the Soviets could not be trusted to meet any of the obligations in an alliance, and that British policy could not cede to the Soviet Union the decision as to when and for what purpose Britain should go to war. Though that seems to have been a rational response to the experience of the negotiations, it did mean that there were then no means of deterring Hitler from further European expansionism, not least given Chamberlain's record of appeasement and its indication of his desire to avoid war at all costs, and no realistic adjustment of British foreign policy to diminished British power relative to Germany in the form of the cultivation of alliances.

Chamberlain's loathing of war, fear of responsibility for taking the country to war and desire to avoid it could have dictated a resolve to deter Hitler from expansionism by the formation of alliances, and it was Chamberlain's perception that encircling alliances would provoke rather than deter Hitler that resulted in Chamberlain's avoidance of cultivation of alliances until Hitler's disregard for undertakings he had made to Chamberlain at Munich made it plain that appeasement had failed and that a policy of deterrence was politically necessary, though even then Chamberlain contrived to limit the Anglo-French guarantee of Poland to Poland's independence, not its territorial integrity, and opposed an Anglo-Soviet alliance before and throughout the Anglo-Soviet negotiations for an alliance in 1939. Another crucial perception that exerted decisive influence on Chamberlain's policy of appeasement was his delusional conviction that Hitler's objectives in Europe were limited and could be countenanced without risking the domination of Europe by one great power that was in the conventional wisdom of the time antithetical to British interests and security, and that he could by his own diplomatic prowess and through the respect he had elicited in Hitler exert a moderating influence on Hitler and maintain European peace without prejudice to British interests, despite the fact that he, Chamberlain, had diminished any credible threat from Britain through his advocacy of limited and defensive rearmament and his open aversion to war and desire to avoid it. The external environment and generational and individual attitudes and objectives did not then dictate any specific policy and were influential on policy only through the lens of perception of Chamberlain as the dominant influence on British foreign policy during the appeasement era that ended just before the negotiations for an alliance with the Soviet Union in 1939. Thereafter, as has been seen, the dynamics of Cabinet discussion changed radically as under the influence of a number of senior ministers the majority of the Cabinet gravitated to the view that an alliance with the Soviet Union was necessary to contain German expansionism in Europe and Chamberlain was compelled to acquiesce in the opening of negotiations with the Soviet Union for an alliance in May 1939. The failure of Chamberlain's policy of appeasement was an influential objective context in both the emerging ministerial sense of an Anglo-Soviet alliance's necessity to contain German expansionism in Europe and ministerial defiance of Chamberlain's previous domination and manipulation of his Cabinet. As to attribution of responsibility for the final breakdown of talks and the failure to conclude an Anglo-Soviet alliance in 1939, it has been argued that though the attitudinal context of anti-communism and anti-Sovietism would have continued to inform the lens of perception and attitudinal prism of British Cabinet ministers and their experience of Soviet diplomacy, the form and content of the latter was such that any party to such talks with the Soviet Union would have doubted the Soviet Union's reliability as an ally, regardless of attitudes towards communism and the Soviet state. It follows that Soviet diplomacy in form and context was on its own a sufficient condition for the breakdown of the talks, and that British-establishment anti-communism and loathing of the Soviet Union as a state was not a necessary condition to such breakdown of talks.

By early 1942 the value of Soviet resistance to the German advance in the east was seen to be worth surrendering the Baltics for, indicating an appreciation of British relative weakness and of the need to preserve the wartime alliance with the Soviet Union and the US, in that before the decision was made Roosevelt was consulted and his approval of an exception to the Atlantic Charter obtained. Over deliberation as to the future of Germany in 1943, 1944 and early 1945, there was consideration of possible collaboration with the Soviet Union to hold Germany in check after the war and an appreciation of the likelihood of far greater Soviet power in Europe after the war, and the intention was to cultivate a collaborative relationship with the Soviet Union over the future of Europe given the prospect of US isolationism when the war ended. Here too perception seems to have influenced the extent of effect the external context had on British foreign policy, in Churchill's concern in early 1942 that should Stalin's demand over the Baltics not be conceded there was a genuine risk of Stalin's negotiating a separate peace with Hitler, for Churchill had in late 1941 opposed acceptance of Stalin's demand. And there was a similar influence of perception on foreign policy in Churchill's deferring the issue of the future of Germany to preserve the wartime alliance and seeming to compromise to some extent though with reservations to Roosevelt's and Stalin's changing preferences over the issue. Though British perception of the possibility of collaboration with the Soviet Union over a united Germany after the war diminished when undertakings regarding free and fair elections in eastern Europe were not met, the issue of the future of Germany was resolved by a Soviet *volte-face* against dismemberment. That of course reflected Churchill's exclusive orientation to maintaining the wartime alliance and preference for leaving the future of Germany to be decided after the war was won.

By the time of the Berlin Crisis there was a shared Western understanding of the ideological and expansionist nature of Soviet foreign policy between the British and the US, and an appreciation on the part of British politicians and officials of the need for US support in any resistance to Soviet opportunism in Europe or elsewhere given post-war British economic and military weakness relative to the Soviet Union and the US. Even so there was a conviction that British diplomatic experience and American inexperience regarding Europe could permit British influence on US policy towards post-war Europe.

The Berlin Crisis indicates the centrality of perception in foreign-policy decision-making in that Bevin's conviction that the Americans would be resolved upon resisting Soviet opportunism and expansionism in Europe and that the Soviet Union would not risk war in Europe over Berlin seem to have been decisive influences on his policy of remaining in Berlin, for had he been unsure whether or not the US would support remaining in Berlin following his announcement of British intention to stay there he would have deferred making the public statement of British policy, and had he not been convinced that the Soviet Union would not risk war over Berlin he would have been far more circumspect in his deliberations over the Berlin Crisis at its outset. The external context of Soviet and American diplomacy was susceptible to various interpretations and did not dictate in any obvious way a specific foreign policy over Berlin to Attlee or Bevin, whose perceptions were the decisive influences on the policy that emerged. The interrelationship between foreign-policy objectives and perceptions is demonstrated by the Berlin Crisis, in that Bevin saw his objective of western union as threatened by any retreat from Berlin and was resolved upon avoidance of any negotiation that would have countenanced a reopening of discussions over the future of Germany in return for Soviet endorsement of the Western right to be in Berlin. In that resolution there was a link between earlier decision-making and ensuing decisions, for decisions earlier on in 1948 influenced the decision to remain in Berlin and to refuse to negotiate over Western right to be there, not least Bevin's abandonment of four-power control over Germany in fact if not in rhetoric and turning to efforts to optimise the power and security of western Europe to combat Soviet expansionism and opportunism through western union in 1948. In another indication of the centrality of perception and attitude, Bevin was by 1948 convinced that any surrender to Soviet opportunism would invite more expansionism and diminish Western confidence in resisting communism and its spread, a factor that would have been relevant to Bevin's insistence upon remaining in Berlin to preserve western European confidence in western union.

The Suez Crisis was the most obvious exemplification of the significance of British economic dependence on the US for British foreign policy, for though no US military help was called for Britain had to effect a humiliating public withdrawal because of the US threat to the British economy. Here too the centrality of attitude and perception is indicated, in that both Eden and Macmillan wanted to assert British prestige in the Middle East at Nasser's expense, and neither could conceive of US abandonment of Britain in the event of British military intervention in Suez so soon after British support for the US in the Korean War and in the context of the Cold War.

The comparison of Korea and Vietnam indicates the room for manoeuvre for British foreign policy in relation to US demands in certain circumstances, and represents another indication of the centrality of perception in foreign-policy decision-making. For British troop commitment in Korea ensued from Attlee's and Bevin's perception that British troops' being sent to Korea was necessary to secure optimal US support for NATO in Europe, whereas Wilson's declining to commit even a token force to support the US in Vietnam reflected Wilson's understanding that Johnson would accept Wilson's position of moral though no materiel support for the US in Vietnam as being the best he could do given his difficulties with the Labour Party.

The independent contributions of attitudes and perceptions to foreign policy are indicated above, in that Attlee and Bevin, Eden and Wilson all shared the ethos of Britain as a world power of the first rank and had as the primary objective of foreign policy the maintenance of that status. And they shared too a sense of the Soviet threat to British social democracy and to western Europe that was seen to be a threat to the security of the UK and appreciated the need, given British economic and military weakness, to cultivate the relationship with the US to maintain British world-power status and security. Even so the premiers pursued very different policies in relation to the policies of the US as a consequence of different perceptions of how the US would react.

To elaborate upon the centrality of perception to foreign-policy decision-making, Attlee could have had the very rational alternative perception that the US would not endanger the security of Europe, the central theatre of the Cold War, to punish the UK for not providing troops to the more peripheral theatre of Korea, as that would have been irrational in the context of the anti-Soviet and anti-communist foreign policy of the US. In a similar way Wilson could have believed that US economic support had to be secured by providing a token UK force to Vietnam, and Eden could have interpreted Eisenhower's and Dulles' messages as indicating threat of sanctions and could have continued diplomatic efforts to isolate and punish Nasser to restore international control of the Suez Canal and to maintain British prestige in the Middle East.

Despite the influence of attitudes and perceptions in foreign-policy decision-making, over time the nature of the external environment did make itself felt. In the case of the negotiations for an Anglo-Soviet alliance in 1939 the declining influence of a discredited Chamberlain who had to concede to ministerial insistence upon negotiations reflected a changed situation in Europe given Hitler's violation of his promises to Chamberlain at Munich and the humiliation of Chamberlain's policy of appeasement, and the influence of the international context was decisive in the refusal of the British to accept the Soviet definition of 'indirect aggression' in the Baltics because it ceded to the Soviets the circumstances under which Britain would go to war in a context of experience of Soviet diplomacy that engendered such mistrust in the Soviet Union that an Anglo-Soviet alliance was seen as virtually worthless.

The delusional conviction that Britain needed neither the Soviet Union nor the US against Hitler did not last long, invalidated as it was by German successes in the west and the east and a succession of British defeats in the earlier part of the war, and Britain's economic and military dependence on the US was understood by Churchill as wartime premier and by him, Attlee, Eden and Wilson as post-war premiers in the context of the Cold War. Deference to US wishes became part of the Atlantic relationship given the asymmetry of power between the two countries, and though Bevin did exert influence on the Americans over Berlin in the initial stage of the crisis in 1948 in his declaration of intent to remain in Berlin he did thereafter have to acquiesce in US wishes to a significant extent. Over Korea British deference to US wishes was obvious despite the unaffordable economic and significant political cost to the Attlee administration even though British influence on US policy seems to have been negligible, for though there were attempts to constrain US tendencies to belligerence towards communist China and widening the war, there is no evidence that such overtures had any effect on US policy over Korea and China. Over Suez Eden's pleas for Eisenhower's understanding made no difference in the end to Eisenhower's abandonment of Eden and imposing a humiliating public display of weakness and dependence on a Cold War ally and by the time of Vietnam British advice was neither welcomed nor heeded. That seems to be in part a reflection of enhanced US diplomatic confidence and sense of world-power status as the representative and defender of the free world and in part a reflection of Britain's dependence on the US and diminished contribution to US foreign-policy objectives. As to the influence on possible British foreign policy from the relationships formed by successive Prime Ministers and Foreign Secretaries with their transatlantic counterparts, there seems to be little evidence of any such influence, with the cases of Attlee, Eden and Wilson over Korea, Suez and Vietnam respectively indicating that the nature of the relationships with US Presidents and members of US administrations mattered far less in terms of influence on British foreign policy than British attachment to a world-power ethos and British and US appreciation of the asymmetry of need and power in the Atlantic relationship. What does seem to have made a difference is the extent of US diplomatic confidence, for there is the anomalous instance of the autonomous influence of Bevin as Foreign Secretary on US policy over the Berlin Crisis of 1948–49 in that brief interval of US uncertainty as to the politics of post-war Europe and as to Soviet intentions in Europe and elsewhere after the war. In more general terms, the relationships which were influential on British foreign policy in the period between 1939 and 1968 seem to have been those of personalities within the locus of foreign-policy decision-making within the British political system rather than those with members of foreign governments, whose policies and influence seem to have been dictated by their perception of the optimal foreign policy for their interests rather than their personal relationships with British politicians.

In some instances there seems to have been a two-way interaction between foreign policy and the international context. For though the external environment obviously provided the context for the influence of the perceptions and attitudes of those in the British political and official establishment whose positions were such that influence on foreign policy was possible, in the cases of Chamberlain and Eden their policies affected the nature of the external environment they then had to face, their personal standing in Cabinet, Commons and country, and the policies forced upon them as Prime Ministers. For Chamberlain the public discrediting of his personal diplomacy with Hitler and the failure of his policy of appeasement seem to have diminished his personal authority in regard to foreign policy in Cabinet to such an extent that he was compelled to accept the Anglo-Soviet negotiations to which he was so opposed. For Eden the correctives to the powers and prerogatives of the PM were not just his own indecision, caution and susceptibility to influence but also the very adverse US reaction to his policy of devising a pretext for a military invasion of Suez in secret. In both cases the effect was to present the PM with a changed external environment, and to diminish Prime Ministerial authority and the legitimacy of Prime Ministerial dominance over foreign policy in Cabinet. Though both cases do also of course reflect Britain's weakness relative to other powers, in the Chamberlain case to Germany, and in the Eden case to the US in a context of Britain's economic dependence on the US, in the Chamberlain case greater military power would not have helped given Chamberlain's advertised reluctance to go to war for any cause.

Though the cases have been drawn at random or in fact because they represent break points in British foreign policy in a period of declining economic, military and diplomatic power, that is, without any bias that could distort the findings regarding the locus of foreign-policy decision-making power in the UK, it does remain possible though not plausible that a different selection of cases would produce a different set of inferences. That is of course inherent in any case-study approach. The argument presented here is counter-revisionist in nature, in its indicating that individuals' perceptions and attitudes, and personalities and relationships, are central to the foreign policy that emerges, for such attributes provide the lens through which the external environment is perceived by those who make foreign-policy decisions.

Bibliography

BIBLIOGRAPHY FOR CONSEQUENTIAL DIPLOMATIC EXCHANGES

'Cato', *Guilty Men*, Purnell, London, 1940.

Arad, Yitzhak, *The Holocaust in the Soviet Union*, University of Nebraska, 2009.

Aster, S., '"Guilty Men": The Case of Neville Chamberlain', in Boyce, R., and Robertson, E. M., *Paths to War. New Essays on the Origins of the Second World War*, London, 1989.

Bond, Brian (ed.), *Chief of Staff. The Diaries of Lieutenant General Sir Henry Pownall*, Volume I, 1933–40, Leo Cooper, London, 1972.

Carley, Michael Jabara, *1939: The Alliance That Never Was And The Coming Of World War II*, Ivan R. Dee, Chicago, 1999.

Charmley, John, *Chamberlain and the Lost Peace*, Macmillan, London, 1989.

Dilks, D. (ed.), *Retreat From Power: Studies In Britain's Foreign Policy In The Twentieth Century*, Volume 1, Macmillan, London, 1981.

Dilks, David (ed.), *The Diaries of Sir Alexander Cadogan, OM, 1938–1945*, Putnam, 1972.

Documents on British Foreign Policy Series 2, Volume 12 and Series 3, Volumes 5, 6 and 7.

Doerr, Paul W., *British Foreign Policy 1919–1939*, Manchester University Press, Manchester, 1998.

Dutton, D., *A Political Biography of Sir John Simon*, Aurum, London, 1992.

—, *Chamberlain*, Bloomsbury Academic, 2001.

Fitzsimmons, M. A., *The Foreign Policy of the British Labour Government 1945–1951*, University of Notre Dame Press, Notre Dame, Indiana, 1953.

Gilbert, M., *The Roots of Appeasement*, Weidenfeld and Nicolson, 1966.

Harvey, John (ed.), *The Diplomatic Diaries of Oliver Harvey 1937–1940*, Collins, London, 1970.

Hill, Christopher, *Cabinet Decisions on Foreign Policy: the British experience October 1938–1941*, Cambridge University Press, 1991.

Keeble, Curtis, *Britain and the Soviet Union, 1917–89*, Macmillan, London, 1990.

Kennedy, P., *The Realities Behind Diplomacy. Background Influences on British External Policy, 1865–1980*, London, 1981.

Middlemas, Keith, *Diplomacy of Illusion: The British Government and Germany, 1937–1939*, Weidenfeld and Nicolson, London, 1972.

Namier, Lewis B., *Diplomatic Prelude, 1938–1939*, Macmillan, London, 1948.

Neilson, Keith, *Britain, Soviet Russia and the Collapse of the Versailles Order, 1919–1939*, Cambridge University Press, 2006.

Northedge, F. S., *The Troubled Giant. Britain among the Great Powers, 1916–1939*, London, 1966.

Overy, R., and Wheatcroft, A., *The Road to War*, London, 1989.

Parker, R. A. C., *Chamberlain and Appeasement. British Policy and the Coming of the Second World War*, St. Martin's Press, London, 1993.

Rees, Laurence, *World War Two Behind Closed Doors. Stalin, the Nazis and the West*, BBC Books, 2008.

Robbins, K., *Munich 1938*, London, 1968.

Roberts, Andrew, *The Holy Fox*, Weidenfeld and Nicolson, London, 1991.

Shaw, Louise Grace, 'Attitudes of the British Political Elite towards the Soviet Union', in *Diplomacy and Statecraft*, volume 13, no. 1 (March 2002), pages 55–74.

—, *The British Political Elite and the Soviet Union 1937–1939*, Frank Cass, London, 2013.

Uldricks, Teddy J., 'Soviet Security Policy in the 1930s', in Gorodetsky, Gabriel (ed.), *Soviet Foreign Policy, 1917–1991: A Retrospective*, Routledge, 2014.

Watt, D. C., 'Appeasement. The Rise of a Revisionist School?', *The Political Quarterly*, 36 (1965).

—, *How War Came. The Immediate Origins of the Second World War, 1938–1939*, London, 1989.

Weinberg, Gerhard L., *Germany and the Soviet Union*, Brill Archive, 1972.

BIBLIOGRAPHY FOR BRITISH FOREIGN-POLICY DECISION-MAKING TOWARDS THE SOVIET UNION DURING THE WAR

Addison, Paul, *Churchill: The Unexpected Hero*, OUP, 2005.

Alanbrooke, Lord Field Marshall, *War Diaries*, University of California Press, 2003.

Barker, E., *Churchill and Eden at War*, Macmillan, London, 1978.

Barnett, Corelli, *The Collapse of British Power*, Alan Sutton, Stroud, 1972.

Best, Geoffrey, *Churchill: A Study in Greatness*, A & C Black, 2001.

Charmley, John, *Churchill: The End of Glory*, Hodder and Stoughton, 1993.

—, *Churchill's Grand Alliance, The Anglo-American Special Relationship 1940–57*, Hodder and Stoughton, London,1995.

Dewey, Peter, *War and Progress: Britain 1914–1945*, Routledge, 2014.

Dilks, D. (ed.), *The Diaries of Sir Alexander Cadogan, OM, 1938–1945*, Putnam, 1972.

Dockrill, Michael and McKercher, Brian J. C., *Diplomacy and World Power: Studies in British Foreign Policy, 1890–1951*, CUP, 2002.

Dutton, David, *Anthony Eden, A Life and Reputation*, Arnold, London, 1997.

Eden, Anthony, and Eisenhower, Dwight D., *Eden-Eisenhower Correspondence, 1955–1957*, University of North Carolina Press, 2006.

Folly, M. H., *Churchill, Whitehall and the Soviet Union, 1940–45*, London: Macmillan, 2000.

Foschepoth, Josef, 'British Interest in the Division of Germany after the Second World War', *Journal of Contemporary History*, Volume 21 (1986).

Gilbert, M., *Winston S. Churchill, Volume VII, Road to Victory 1941–1945*, Heinemann, London, 1986.

Gilbert, Martin, *Churchill: A Life, Heinemann*, London, 1991.

—, *Second World War*, Phoenix Press, London, 2000.

Harrod, R. F., *The Prof, A Personal Memoir of Lord Cherwell*, Macmillan, London, 1959.

Heyward, Samantha, *Churchill*, Routledge, 2003.

Jefferys, Kevin, *The Churchill coalition and wartime politics, 1940–1945*, Manchester University Press, Manchester, 1991.

Jenkins, Roy, *Churchill*, Pan Macmillan, 2012.

Keeble, Curtis, *Britain and the Soviet Union, 1917–89*, Macmillan, 1990.

Kennedy, P., *The Realities behind Diplomacy: Background Influences on British External Policy, 1865–1980*, Allen and Unwin, London, 1981.

Kimball, W. F., *Forged in War, Churchill, Roosevelt and the Second World War*, HarperCollins, London, 1997.

Kitchen, M., *British Policy Towards the Soviet Union During the Second World War*, London, Macmillan, 1986.

—, 'Winston Churchill and the Soviet Union During the Second World War', *Historical Journal* XXX-2 (1987).

Lord Avon, *The Reckoning*, Cassell, London, 1965.

Harvey, J. (ed.), *The War Diaries of Oliver Harvey*, Collins, London, 1978.

James, Robert Rhodes, *Anthony Eden*, Papermac, 1987.

Mawdsley, Evan, *December 1941: Twelve Days that Began a World War*, Yale University Press, 2011.

Moran, Lord, *Winston Churchill, The struggle for survival, 1940–1965*, Constable, London, 1966.

Rose, N., *Churchill, An Unruly Life*, Simon and Schuster, London, 1994.

Ross, G. (ed.), *The Foreign Office and the Kremlin, British Documents on Anglo-Soviet Relations 1941–45*, Cambridge University Press, Cambridge, 1984.

Rothwell, V., *Britain and the Cold War 1941–1947*, Jonathan Cape, London,

Rothwell, Victor, *Anthony Eden: A Political Biography, 1931–1957*, Manchester University Press, 1992.

Sainsbury, Keith, 'British policy and German unity at the end of the Second World War', in *English Historical Review* (Great Britain) 94 (373), October 1979.

—, *Churchill and Roosevelt at War*, Macmillan, London, 1994.

Mackintosh, J. P., *British Prime Ministers In The Twentieth Century, Volume II – Churchill to Callaghan*, Weidenfeld and Nicolson, London, 1978.

Rothwell, V., 'Review of M. Kitchen, British Policy towards the Soviet Union during the Second World War', in *Soviet Studies* 39 (1987).

Smyser W. R., *From Yalta to Berlin*, Macmillan, London, 1999.

Woodward, Llewellyn, *British Foreign Policy In The Second World War*, Volume II and Volume V, HMSO, London, 1971.

BIBLIOGRAPHY FOR THE BERLIN CRISIS

Barker, Elisabeth, *The British Between The Superpowers, 1945–50*, Macmillan, London, 1983.

Becker, Josef, and Knipping, Franz, *Great Britain, France, Italy and Germany in a Postwar World, 1945–50*, Walter de Gruyter, 1986.

Blackwell, Michael, *Clinging to Grandeur*, Westport: Greenwood Press, 1993.

Boettcher, William A., *Presidential Risk Behavior In Foreign Policy. Prudence Or Peril*, Palgrave Macmillan, 2005.

Bullock, Alan, *Ernest Bevin, Foreign Secretary, 1945–1951*, Heinemann, 1983.

Burridge, Trevor, *Clement Attlee: A Political Biography*, London: Jonathan Cape, 1985.

Cornish, Paul, *British Military Planning for the Defence of Germany, 1945–1950*, Springer, 1995.

Davison, W. Phillips, *The Berlin Blockade, A Study in Cold War Politics*, Princeton University Press, Princeton, 1958.

Deighton, Anne, *The Impossible Peace: Britain, the Division of Germany and the Origins of the Cold War*, Clarendon Press, 1990.

Field, Frank (ed.), *Attlee's Great Contemporaries: The Politics of Character*, Bloomsbury Publishing, 2009.

Foreign Relations of the United States, 1948, Volume IV, *Eastern Europe, The Soviet Union*, and Volume VII, *Germany and Austria*.

Gladwyn, Lord, *The Memoirs of Lord Gladwyn*, London: Weidenfeld and Nicolson, 1972.

Gordon, Michael R., *Conflict and Consensus in Labour's Foreign Policy, 1914–1965*, Stanford University Press, 1969.

Greenwood, S., *Britain and the Cold War, 1945–91*, Palgrave Macmillan, 1999.

Grob-Fitzgibbon, Benjamin, *Continental Drift*, Cambridge University Press, 2016.

Grogin, Robert R., *Natural Enemies: The United States and the Soviet Union in the Cold War*, Lexington Books, 2001.

Harrington, Daniel F., *Berlin on the Brink: The Blockade, the Airlift, and the Early Cold War*, University Press of Kentucky, 2012.

Harris, Kenneth, *Attlee*, London, Weidenfeld and Nicolson, 1982.

Hennessy, Peter, *Never Again: Britain, 1945–1950*, Penguin UK, 2006.

—, *The Prime Minister: The Office and Its Holders Since 1945*, Palgrave Macmillan, 2001.

Kolko, J. and G., *The Limits of Power, The World and United States Foreign Policy, 1945–1954*, Harper and Row, New York, 1972.

Marshall, George Catlett, and Stevens, Sharon Ritenour, *The Papers of George Catlett Marshall: The Whole World Hangs in the Balance*, JHU Press, 1981.

Morris, E., *Blockade, Berlin and the Cold War*, Hamish Hamilton, London, 1973

Northedge, F. S., *Descent From Power, British Foreign Policy, 1945–1973*, Allen and Unwin, 1974.

Ovendale, Ritchie, *The Foreign Policy of the British Labour Governments, 1945–1951*, Leicester University Press, 1984.

Phythian, Mark, *The Labour Party, War and International Relations, 1945–2006*, Routledge, 2007.

Powaski, Ronald E., *The Cold War: The United States and the Soviet Union, 1917–1991*, OUP, 1997.

Saville, John, *The Politics of Continuity*, Verso, 1993.

Shlaim, A., *The United States and the Berlin Blockade, 1948–1949: A Study in Crisis Decision-making*, University of California Press, London, 1983.

Sirimarco, Elizabeth, *The Cold War*, Marshall Cavendish, 2005.

Strang, Baron William, *Home and Abroad*, Deutsch, 1956.

Tusa, J. and Tusa, A., *The Berlin Airlift*, Atheneum, 1988.

Yergin, D., *Shattered Peace, The Origins of the Cold War and the National Security State*, André Deutsch, London, 1977.

BIBLIOGRAPHY FOR EDEN AND SUEZ

Aldous, R., and Lee, S., *Harold Macmillan: Aspects of a Political Life*, Springer, 1999.

Aldous, Richard, and Lee, Sabine (eds.), *Harold Macmillan and Britain's World Role*, Springer, 2016.

Alteras, Isaac, *Eisenhower and Israel: US-Israeli Relations, 1953–1960*, University Press of Florida, 1993.

Bell, P. M. H., *France and Britain, 1940–1994: The Long Separation*, Routledge, 2014.

Bennett, Gill, *Six Moments of Crisis: Inside British Foreign Policy*, Oxford University Press, 2013.

Boyle, Peter, *The Eden-Eisenhower Correspondence, 1955–1957*, University of North Carolina Press, 2006.

Cooper, Chester L., *The Lion's Last Roar: Suez, 1956*, Harper and Row, 1978.

Daalder, Hans, *Cabinet Reform in Britain 1914–1963*, Stanford University Press, 1963.

Di Nolfo, Ennio (ed.), *Great Britain, France, Germany and Italy and the Origins of the EEC, 1952–1957*, Walter de Gruyter, 1992.

Dilks, David, *The Diaries of Sir Alexander Cadogan, OM, 1938–1945*, Putnam, 1972.

Drachman, Edward R., and Shank, Alan, *Presidents and Foreign Policy: Countdown to Ten Controversial Decisions*, SUNY Press, 1997.

'Suez Crisis, July 26–December 31, 1956', in *Foreign Relations of the United States, 1955–1957*, Volume XVI.

Gaitskell, Hugh, Williams, Philip Maynard, *The Diary of Hugh Gaitskell*, Cape, 1983.

Gorst, Anthony, and Johnman, Lewis, *The Suez Crisis*, Routledge, 2013.

Hahn, Peter L., *United States, Great Britain, And Egypt, 1945–1956: Strategy and Policy in the Early Cold War*, UNC Press, 2004.

Hamilton, Eamon, 'Sir Anthony Eden and the Suez Crisis of 1956, Anatomy of a Flawed Personality', MA Thesis, Birmingham University, 2005.

Harvey, Oliver, *The War Diaries of Oliver Harvey (1941–1945)*, Collins, 1978.

Heath, E. *The Course of My Life: My Autobiography*, A & C Black, 2011.

Hennessy, Peter, *The Prime Minister: The Office and Its Holders Since 1945*, Palgrave Macmillan, 2001.

Horne, Alastair, *Macmillan: The Official Biography*, Pan Macmillan, 2012.

Hughes, Michael, *British Foreign Secretaries in an Uncertain World 1919–1939*, Routledge, 2005.

James, Robert Rhodes, *Anthony Eden*, Papermac, 1987.

Jenkins, Roy, *Churchill*, Pan Macmillan, 2012.

Kelly, Saul, and Gorst, Anthony (eds.), *Whitehall and the Suez Crisis*, Routledge, 2013.

Kyle, Keith, *Suez: Britain's End of Empire in the Middle East*, I. B. Tauris, 2011.

Louis, William Roger (ed.), *More Adventures in Britannia: Personalities, Politics and Culture in Britain*, I. B. Tauris, 1998.

Louis, William Roger, *Ends of British Imperialism: The Scramble for Empire, Suez and Decolonisation*, I. B. Tauris, 2006.

Lucas, Scott (ed.), *Britain and Suez: The Lion's Last Roar*, Manchester University Press, 1996.

Lucas, Scott William, 'Divided We Stand: The Suez Crisis of 1956 and the Anglo-American "Alliance"', DPhil Thesis, London School of Economics and Political Science.

Mackintosh, J. P., *The British Cabinet*, Stevens, 1981, page 25.

McDonough, Frank, *Neville Chamberlain, Appeasement, and the British Road to War*, Manchester University Press, 1998.

McKercher, B. J. C. (ed.), *Anglo-American Relations in the 1920s: The Struggle for Supremacy*, University of Alberta, 1990.

Nutting, Anthony, *No End of a Lesson: The Story of Suez*, C. N. Potter, London, 1967.

Owen, Lord David, 'The Effect of Prime Minister Anthony Eden's illness on his decision-making during the Suez Crisis', in *QJM* Volume 98, Issue 6, June 2005.

Pearson, J., *Sir Anthony Eden and the Suez Crisis: Reluctant Gamble*, Springer, 2002.

Rothwell, Victor, *Anthony Eden: A Political Biography, 1931–57*, Manchester University Press, 1992.

Sainsbury, Keith, *Churchill and Roosevelt at War*, Macmillan, London, 1994.

Shlaim, Avi, 'The Protocol of Sèvres, 1956: Anatomy of a War Plot', in *International Affairs*, 73:3 (1997).

Smith, Simon C. (ed.), *Reassessing Suez: New Perspectives on the Crisis and Its Aftermath*, Routledge, 2016.

Tal, David (ed.), *The 1956 War: Collusion and Rivalry in the Middle East*, Routledge, 2014.

Thorpe, D. R., *Supermac: The Life of Harold Macmillan*, Random House, 2011.

—, *The Life and Times of Anthony Eden, First Earl of Avon, 1897–1977*, Random House, 2011.

Turner, John, *Macmillan*, Routledge, 2014.

Turner, Michael J., *British Power and International Relations in the 1950s: A Tenable Position?*, Rowman and Littlefield, 2009.

Verbeek, Bertian, *Decision-Making in Great Britain During the Suez Crisis – Small Groups and a Persistent Leader*, Ashgate, 2003.

Wilby, Peter, *Eden*, Haus Publishing, 2006.

Wilson, Harold, *Memoirs: The Making of a Prime Minister, 1916–1964*, Weidenfeld and Nicolson, 1986.

BIBLIOGRAPHY FOR DECLINE AND DEPENDENCE

Baylis, John (ed.), *Anglo-American Relations Since 1939: The Enduring Alliance*, Manchester University Press, 1997.

Beismer, Robert, *Dean Acheson: A Life in the Cold War*, OUP USA, 2009.

Bevan, A., 'Clem Attlee', *Tribune*, 16 December 1955.

Burridge, T, *Clement Attlee, A Political Biography*, Jonathan Cape, London, 1985.

Castle, Barbara, *The Barbara Castle Diaries 1964–76*, Papermac, London, 1990.

Colman, Jonathan, *A 'special relationship'? Harold Wilson, Lyndon B. Johnson and Anglo-American relations 'at the summit', 1964–68*, Manchester University Press, 2004.

Cotton, James, and Neary, Ian (eds.), *The Korean War in History*, Manchester University Press, 1989.

Crossman, Richard, *The Diaries of a Cabinet Minister, Vol. II, Lord President of the Council and Leader of the House of Commons, 1966–68*, Hamish Hamilton, London, 1976.

Dobson, Alan, *Anglo-American Relations in the Twentieth Century: Of Friendship, Conflict and the Rise and Decline of the Superpowers*, Psychology Press, 1995.

—, 'The Years of Transition: Anglo-American relations, 1961–1967', *Review of International Studies*, Volume 16, No. 3, July 1990.

Dockrill, S., *Britain's retreat From East of Suez: The Choice between Europe and the World?*, Springer, 2002.

Dorey, Peter (ed.), *The Labour Governments 1964–1970*, Routledge, 2006.

Dumbrell, John, *A Special Relationship: Anglo-American Relations in the Cold War and After*, Macmillan, 2001.

—, 'The Johnson administration and the British Labour Government: Vietnam, the Pound and East of Suez', *Journal of American Studies*, Volume 30, No. 2, 1996.

Ellis, S., *Britain, America and the Vietnam War*, Praeger, London, 2004.

Ellis, Sylvia, *Historical Dictionary of Anglo-American Relations*, Scarecrow Press, 2009.

Foreign relations of the United States 1964–1968, Volume II, *Vietnam: January–June 1965*, and Volume XII.

Garner, Robert, and Kelly, Richard N., *British Political Parties Today*, MUP, 1993.

Gordon, Michael R., *Conflict and Consensus in Labour's Foreign Policy, 1914–1965*, Stanford University Press, 1969.

Hennessey, Thomas, *Britain's Korean War: Cold War Diplomacy, Strategy and Security 1950–1953*, Manchester University Press, 2013.

Honeyman, Victoria, *Richard Crossman: Pioneer of Welfare Provision and Labour Politics in Post-War Britain*, I. B. Tauris, 2007.

Hopkins, Michael F., *Oliver Franks and the Truman Administration: Anglo-American Relations, 1948–1952*, Routledge, 2004.

Hughes, Geraint, *Harold Wilson's Cold War: The Labour Government and East-West Politics, 1964–1970*, Boydell & Brewer Ltd., 2015.

Jago, Michael, *Clement Attlee: The Inevitable Prime Minister*, Biteback Publishing, 2014.

Lowe, Peter, *Continuing the Cold War in East Asia: British Policy Towards Japan, China and Korea, 1948–1953*, Manchester University Press, 1997.

McLaine, Ian (ed.), *A Korean Conflict: The Tensions Between Britain and America*, I. B. Tauris, 2015.

Morgan, Austen, *Harold Wilson*, Pluto, London, 1992.

Petersen, Tore T. (ed.), *Challenging Retrenchment: The United States, Great Britain and the Middle East 1950–1980*, Tapir Academic Press, 2010.

Pham, P. L., *Ending 'East of Suez': The British Decision to Withdraw from Malaysia and Singapore 1964–1968*, OUP, 2010.

Pimlott, B., *Harold Wilson*, Harper Collins, London, 1992.

Radice, Giles, *Odd Couples: The Great Political Pairings of Modern Britain*, I. B. Tauris, 2015.

Smith, Simon C. (ed.), *The Wilson-Johnson Correspondence, 1964–69*, Routledge, 2016.

The Campaign Guide: The Unique Political Reference Book, Conservative and Unionist Central Office, 1970.

Thomas-Symonds, Niklaus, *Attlee: A Life in Politics*, I. B. Tauris, 2012.

Vickers, Rhiannon, *The Labour Party and the World, Volume 2: Labour's Foreign Policy Since 1951*, OUP, 2011.

—, 'Harold Wilson, the British Labour Party, and the War in Vietnam', *Journal of Cold War Studies*, Volume 10, No. 2, Spring 2008.

Williams, Francis, *A Prime Minister Remembers*, Heinemann, 1961.

Young, John W., *The Labour Governments 1964–1970: International Policy*, MUP, 2003.

Younger, Sir Kenneth Gilmour, and Geoffrey Warner, *In the Midst of Greats: The Foreign Office Diaries and Papers of Kenneth Younger, February 1950–October 1951*, Psychology Press, 2005.

Index

Other CentreHouse Press
Authors and Titles

Andrew Elsby

The Burghers of Ceylon. *The Burghers of Ceylon* traces the origins and history of the mixed-race populations of imperial Ceylon. It explains how, and why, those populations emerged, how they developed, how they were distinguished – and how they distinguished themselves – from the Europeans and from the native populations. It explores the components of burgher identity. The author also provides answers to the following questions. How reliable is the evidence of the Dutch Burgher Union's genealogies? How prevalent is racial misrepresentation, and what were the motives behind it? How were the mixed-race populations treated by the European colonial powers? What happened to those mixed-race populations when colonial rule ended in 1948?

  The author's interest in the burghers of Ceylon came about after his mother's death, when he discovered she was from a Dutch burgher family in Ceylon. Her mother was half English and half native, and her father, Raoul Frank, was a Dutch burgher descended from a long line of German, French, Dutch, Belgian and British European male ancestors, with native or mixed-race female ancestors from the Dutch and British periods in Ceylon.

Chamberlain and Appeasement. Neville Chamberlain was Prime Minister of the United Kingdom from May 1937 to May 1940, and is identified with the policy of 'appeasement' towards Adolf Hitler's Germany in the period preceding World War II. In this new study Dr Andrew Elsby assesses the different explanations of appeasement, taking into account evidence as to its causes. He rejects the revisionist case, and develops a counter-revisionism, establishing a more comprehensive assessment of the causes of British foreign policy during the period, using minutes of Foreign Policy Committee and Cabinet meetings, Chamberlain's personal papers, and in addition literature on the theory of foreign-policy decision-making apropos of the British political system. Stress is laid on the effect of attitudinal and motivational factors and individual influence, not least that of the Prime Minister himself. Conclusions reached by this new study are timely, and are of relevance now, vis-à-vis the UK and its relationship with Europe.

Garry O'Connor

The Vagabond Lover. Cavan O'Connor was born into near destitution in Nottingham in 1899, but quickly rose to become the legendary 'Vagabond of Song'. He was one of the most famous singing legends of his era. He topped Variety bills. He was an adventurer, who cut a swashbuckling figure. In the golden age of radio, his broadcasts reached listening figures of over thirteen million. With his flawless tenor voice his status was as latter-day troubadour, a star of stage imitated by romantics young and old all over the civilised world. But what lay behind the idealised celebrity? Was he a gift from God, or a flawed, vulnerable being like the rest of us? Enter the writer son Garry O'Connor, who answers that question emphatically. In his memoir *The Vagabond Lover*, the father-son dispute unveils without sentimentality the general mess of domestic and family life, of which Cavan was the head. Revealed – in this searing, honest, dark revelation – are the miserable depths the sweet singer of lyrical song plumbed, and remorselessly so. O'Connor *fils* does not spare the reader, refusing to gloss over the traumas and crises of family conflict, as they run in parallel to his own fortunes and vicissitudes. He is dispassionate with the biographical detail, yet impassioned enough to recall one of his own plays, penned in his Cambridge youth, where the father Cavan is reimagined. In fiction as in life he is cast as the pivotal character in a family drama painful in its climaxes. Overarching is a first ever account of those Cambridge years, peopled with familiar icons of twenty-first-century culture. It's a fast-moving, two-pronged probe into the nature of celebrity, arriving at a profound resolution as the author shrugs off the flaws and setbacks packaged as part of the celebrity deal.

'An enthralling family biography, full of gossip, wise insights and fascinating revelations.' **Sir Ian McKellen**

G. K. Chesterton

Orthodoxy. G. K. Chesterton wrote of *Orthodoxy* that it represented an attempt 'to state the philosophy in which I have come to believe' and to do so 'in a vague and personal way, in a set of mental pictures rather than in a series of deductions'. For most of its readers, it is the wittiest and most rollicking defence of the Christian faith ever written. Anticipating much modern theology, Catholic and Protestant, Chesterton's apologia is more personalistic than propositional. He understands that, in order to be credible, a belief system must appeal to the heart as well as to the mind. No one has set out more engagingly the reasons for believing in Christianity as the timeless truth about who we are, and rejecting the alternatives as fads and fashions. Jon Elsby, author of *Light in the Darkness* and *Wrestling With the Angel*, has written extensively on Christian apologists and apologetics, and has penned an illuminating introduction for this edition of *Orthodoxy*, which also contains brief notes and an index.

Jon Elsby

Coming Home. *Coming Home* looks, in the broadest sense, at the Catholic Church and the phenomenon of conversion. It considers, among other things, the varied components of Catholic identity; the complex, multifaceted relations between Catholicism and postmodernism, and between Church doctrine and pastoral praxis; and the controversies between so-called conservatives and liberals over the direction the Church should take in the future.

The Catholic Church, with its 2,000 years of accumulated doctrine and definition, claims to be the one and only divinely appointed repository of religious truth and wisdom, authoritatively taught and preserved for transmission to posterity. No other institution makes such a claim. It would be unwise to dismiss that claim in accordance with some dogmatic presupposition rather than weighing it impartially according to the evidence.

Coming Home invites the reader to consider all the evidence before making up his or her own mind.

Light In the Darkness: Four Christian Apologists. Christian apologetics is an important area of intellectual endeavour and achievement, standing at the boundaries between theology, philosophy and literature. Yet it has been largely neglected by historians of literature and ideas.

In these essays, the author attempts to establish apologetics as a subject deserving of respect in its own right. He analyses the apologetic arguments and strategies of four of the greatest Christian apologists of the twentieth century – Hilaire Belloc, G. K. Chesterton, Dorothy L. Sayers, and C. S. Lewis. He shows how different lines of argument support each other and converge on the same conclusion: that what Chesterton called 'orthodoxy' and Lewis 'mere Christianity' represents the fundamental truth about the relations between human beings, the universe, and God.

Wrestling With the Angel: A Convert's Tale. Who am I? Am I an autonomous being, able to define myself by my own free choices, or a created being with a given human nature, living in a world which, in significant respects, does not depend on me? Are these two views necessarily opposed?

Wrestling With the Angel is one man's attempt to answer those questions. Raised as a Protestant, the author lost his faith in his teenage years, and then gradually regained it – but in an unexpected form. This is the story of a spiritual and intellectual journey from Protestantism to atheism, and beyond: a journey which finally, and much to the author's surprise, reached its terminus in the Catholic Church.

Wresting With the Angel has the form of an intellectual autobiography, along the lines of Newman's *Apologia pro Vita Sua* but, like that older work, has much wider implications than that of a merely personal story. Elsby's style is engaging and the meaning of his prose – unlike much modern theology – clear.' **Stephen Lovatt**

Heroes and Lovers. What is a tenor? What makes some tenors great? Why are tenors so rare? *Heroes and Lovers* suggests answers to these questions and offers critical essays on twenty-six tenors and shorter assessments of thirty-four others. The tenors covered range from Francesco Tamagno, the first Otello, and Fernando de Lucia, both of whom recorded in the early years of the twentieth century, to Joseph Calleja and Rolando Villazón today. The book also comprises an introductory essay and separate essays on the early tenors of the recorded era, the popular tenors, the British tenors, and the specialist categories of Mozart tenors and Heldentenors.

This is a personal selection and it will please, stimulate, provoke, and infuriate in equal measure.

'This truly is a book for lovers of the Art of Singing and the tenor voice.' **Alan Bilgora in *The Record Collector***

Peter Cowlam

Who's Afraid of the Booker Prize? Winner of the 2015 Quagga Prize for Literary Fiction. For Alistair Wye, assistant to 'top' novelist Marshall Zob, Zob makes just two mistakes. First, he plans a commemorative book celebrating the life and work of his dead mentor, John Andrew Glaze, whose theory of 'literary time' is of dubious philosophical pedigree. Second, Zob turns the whole literary world on its head through the size of advance he instructs his agent to negotiate for his latest, and most mediocre novel to date.

Secretly Wye keeps a diary of Zob's professional and private life. Comic, resolute, Wye stalks through its every page, scattering his pearls with an imperious hand, while an unsuspecting Zob ensures perfect conditions for the chronicler of his downfall.

Set in the relatively safe remove of London's beau monde in the early 1990s, *Who's Afraid of the Booker Prize?* unremittingly debunks the phenomenon of literary celebrity. The plot revolves round a researcher working through an archive of computer discs, emails and faxes, and his own diary entries recording his reactions to life in proximity of bookish heavyweight Marshall Zob. It's a roaring satire, with a serious message, and remarkably funny, in the best English comedic tradition.

'Altogether, a wicked glance at the farce of prizes and the hype that precedes them.' **David James**

'Deliciously wicked and extraordinarily funny, *Who's Afraid of the Booker Prize?* is satirical eloquence at its best....' **Book Viral**

Across the Rebel Network. Anno centres a federated Europe in an uncertain, and not-too-distant digital future, when politics, the media and mass communications have fused into one amorphous whole. He works for the Bureau of Data Protection (BDP), a federal government department responsible for monitoring the full range of material, in all media, posted into cyberspace. The BDP is forced to do this when rebel states are seceding, small satellites once of the federation but now at a remove from it, economically and socially. A handful of organised outsiders threatens to undermine the central state through a concerted propaganda war, using the federation's own digital infrastructure. It is this climate of mutual suspicion that to Anno makes inevitable decades of digital guerrilla warfare. While his department takes steps to prevent this, he doesn't reckon on the intervention of his old college sparring partner, Craig Diamond, who is now a powerful media mogul. The two engage in combat conducted through cyberspace, in a rare concoction of literary sci-fi.

'Peppered throughout with references to Nabokov's *Bend Sinister*, *Across the Rebel Network* shares something of the purpose and aesthetic of that predecessor. It's a good night now, but not for mothing.' **Jack d'Argus**

New King Palmers. Winner of the 2018 Quagga Prize for Literary Fiction. Set in the late 1990s, in the months up to and after the death of Princess Diana, *New King Palmers* is narrated by its principal character Humfrey Joel, a close friend of Earl Eliot d'Oc. The earl's ancestry is bound up with the Habsburgs and the Austro-Hungarian Empire. D'Oc is a member of the British Privy Council and a close friend of Prince Charles and Princess Diana. In the months preceding Diana's death, he commissions a young theatre professional to develop a play. The play's theme is constitutional issues surrounding Prince Charles, with the heir's interests served by UK withdrawal from the EU, before it becomes a federal superstate. The commissioned play is called *New King Palmers*, and d'Oc maintains rigorous editorial control over it. When d'Oc's death shortly follows Diana's, Joel is named as d'Oc's literary executor, with the task of bringing the play to the English stage. Supposedly written into the text is an encoded message from the British Privy Council on behalf of the House of Windsor, addressed to the stewards of the EU. When news of this leaks out no one in the British literary and theatrical worlds believes it. In fact most come to see Earl d'Oc as an invented character behind which Joel shields himself, when his own motives are themselves sinister. So sinister, an MI5 spook is put on the case.

Utopia. Mystery surrounds the source of Zora Murillo's unfathomable wealth. But that's not all the locals want to know about. Intrigue surrounds her arrival in a quaint old English market town, when the hotel she buys, the Pleiades, is transformed into a living cabaret act and the scene of political reprisal. What also of the shadowy M, or Em, or Emoticon, as he styles himself, who claims only to be the writer of a gossip column? His rapport with Zora suggests he knows what it is that has brought her to the town of Hoe. Moreover, M has played his part in aiding her father, an acknowledged leader in AI and robotics, in resisting the changes brought to his country, with its so-called F regime. The coup led by General Forsiss, who in no sense of irony refers to his brave new state as Utopia, might be an ocean away, but the scars it has left are deep and permanent. But exactly what grief is it that the Forsiss regime has inflicted on the Murillo family, drawing its net ever tighter? Dr Murillo has lain awake at night fearing the midnight knock, and the black van waiting outside, knowing little of Zora's ingenious attempts to rid them both of the clutches of Forsiss and his cronies.

Eliza Granville

Once Upon a Time in Paris. Like her last novel, *Gretel and the Dark*, *Once Upon a Time in Paris* cleverly combines a fairy-tale element with magic realism: in this case, an account of events in the life of Charles Perrault. Set in Paris in 1695, intertwining historical fact with multiple layers of fiction, *Once Upon a Time in Paris* invites readers to consider the possibility that the *Tales of Mother Goose* were not written by Charles Perrault (nor by his son, Pierre Darmancourt, as originally claimed), but by a reclusive figure almost entirely overlooked by history. The novel is set at that point where the tradition of oral story-telling is fast being absorbed by the written tale, and our mysterious recluse is caught between the two practices. *Once Upon a Time in Paris* offers a dazzling new insight into the connection between the ogre of folklore and fairy-tale and the post-Enlightenment feminist struggle.

'Twists, turns, knots and kinks…' No shortage of those in this deliciously smart, mischievous and engrossing novel. Not a goose feather in sight – like Perrault's own fairy tales, Granville's novel has been written with a swan's quill. I read it in a sitting.' **Professor Richard Marggraf Turley**

'Real world and fairy-tale blend and interpenetrate until the boundaries between fantasy and reality blur and meld. The relations between fact and fiction, actual and imaginary realities, are continually brought into question in this subtle and always engaging narrative.' **Jon Elsby**

Milton Keynes UK
Ingram Content Group UK Ltd.
UKHW010841140924
448309UK00009B/334